THE ETERNAL PLAN OF HAPPINESS

GARTH L. ALLRED

PUBLISHING & DISTRIBUTION

Published and Distributed by:
Granite Publishing and Distribution, L.L.C.
270 S. Mountainlands Dr Suite 7 • Orem, UT 84058
(801) 229-9023 • Toll Free (800) 574-5779 • FAX (801) 229-1924

ISBN: 1-890558-47-8
Library of Congress Catalog Card Number: 98-75810
Production by: *SunRise Publishing, Orem, Utah*

PREFACE

Dear Reader,

Welcome to the wonderful world of learning more about your Father's eternal plan for your happiness. In this book I hope to share with you some of the exciting and hope engendering principles that have brought light, life, and beauty into my life.

Over the past three decades I have had the exceptional opportunity of working in The Church Educational System (The Church of Jesus Christ of Latter-day Saints) as a seminary teacher, a curriculum writer, an Institute Director and teacher, and as a Professor at the Brigham Young University—Hawaii Campus and the Jerusalem Center for Near Eastern Studies. These have been choice wonderful years as I have been able to teach the gospel of Jesus Christ to my brothers and sisters from around the world. I hold these experiences and relationships dear to my heart, even sacred to me.

Some of you who read this book will be my students. Others will be old and dear friends. Still others will be brothers and sisters I have not met yet. This book is my gift to you. My gift is an attempt to share with you the precious ideas, doctrines, principles, laws and ordinances of the Gospel of Jesus Christ as they have been given to us through the Prophet Joseph Smith.

Studying the gospel through the teachings and contributions of the Prophet Joseph Smith is important because the Lord said of him, "This generation shall have my word through you" (D&C 5:10). Understanding and living the principles of the gospel that have been given to us through Joseph Smith, the latter-day Seer, is critical to our eternal happiness and salvation.

In an earlier book entitled, *Unlocking the Powers of Faith,* I stressed the idea that before we can have faith in Christ we must have a *knowledge* of him and his teachings as the Son of God. Additionally, before we can have faith in ourselves to make right decisions and come unto Christ, we must have a *knowledge* of our own divine nature as sons and daughters of God. As such, we have the ability to learn and cling to healing principles of truth when we encounter them.

In this work you will find gospel knowledge that will instruct, edify, and help you form a more firm foundation for your growing faith. Your readings will help you understand more fully the Divine Sonship of Jesus Christ, your own place in the family of God, and the great plan of happiness that can lead you to eternal life, the greatest of God's gifts.

In stressing the importance of studying the plan of salvation, Elder M. Russell Ballard, of the Quorum of Twelve Apostles, said the following in April, 1986, General Conference:

It seems clear to me, as this great work continues to roll forth, that the leaders of the Church at every level...*need to understand God's plan for his children* and then to teach these principles to their people.

The building up of the Church will surely be enhanced if all Church leaders will teach the pure, simple, doctrinal truths that bring the children of God to a spiritual understanding. The Lord said, "And I give unto you a *commandment* that you shall teach one another the doctrine of the kingdom. Teach ye diligently and my grace shall attend you" (D&C 88:77-78; emphasis added).

In my judgment, the greatest motivator that we have in the Church is to have Church members understand the plan of salvation. Stake presidents and bishops, you are the key to having your members come to this understanding.

Every leader should strive to motivate the people to good works by teaching the doctrines of the kingdom. The scriptures are our text, for "in them ye think ye have eternal life" (John 5:39). From them we glean truths that will open to us a clear understanding of man's eternal possibilities (*Conference Reports*, P. 16; emphasis added).

This book, then, will provide you with an in-depth view of the whole plan of salvation—building on the same principles presented in the missionary discussions and in the Gospel Essentials classes. These readings will help you who are searching souls, understand that there is great depth to our Lord's plan of happiness—wonderful love, abundant mercy, and marvelous healing. This book will present specific truths on which you can focus your faith and chart your course through this world of oft times sorrow and sin.

In addition, this work will open doors to possibilities that even experienced readers may not have encountered before. Herein are presented cups full of gospel-milk and generous portions of gospel-meat. Some of you will recognize familiar themes as well as much that is new and refreshing. Hopefully these truths will motivate you to good works and will open to you a clearer understanding of your grand and eternal possibilities.

The conclusions I have reached and stated throughout the book, after considering the words of the prophets, are my own. I make no claims that my conclusions represent official positions of the Church, but I believe them to be true, recognizing that the Lord has much yet to reveal to us regarding his great and eternal plan of happiness.

I share these principles and truths with you with great love and affection, trusting that as you read, ponder, and pray, you will find great joy, satisfaction, and hopein your Father's great and eternal plan for your happiness.

—Aloha nui loa
Garth L. Allred

ABOUT THE AUTHOR

Garth L. Allred was born in Cardston, Alberta, Canada and reared until the age of nine in the small Latter-day Saint community of Hillspring, about 20 miles northeast of Cardston. He is the fifth of six children. In 1948 his parents moved their family from Hillspring to Provo, Utah, so that the children could attend BYU. In Provo he received most of his early formal education. During his impressionable teenage years he had a variety of jobs including working during the summer months for his sister and brother-in-law who still lived in Canada—events and circumstances to which he often refers in this book.

After completing a two-year mission in the Eastern States, Garth returned to Provo and continued his education at Brigham Young University where in 1965 he received his bachelor's degree in psychology and English. At this time he also became reacquainted with Mary Best from Springville, Utah, and they were married in 1963. They have eight children of their own ranging in ages 34 to 18 and have enjoyed having two Native American children live with them as part of the Church's Placement Program.

Before receiving his BS degree Garth was employed by the Church Educational System to teach seminary in Richfield and Monroe Utah. Concurrently he was assigned to be coordinator of Indian Seminaries in Richfield, Utah. Subsequently he was assigned to be the principal of Monroe and Gunnison seminaries. After teaching in Gunnison for three years, he and his family returned to Provo where he was asked to write LDS curriculum materials for the Seminaries and Institutes of Religion and serve on a Priesthood Correlation task Committee. For a little over a year Garth also sang with his brother (Hugh) and sister (Orvilla) in the Mormon Tabernacle Choir.

After completing a Master's Degree at BYU in Marriage and Family Relationships with a minor in Religious Education, Garth moved his family to Tallahassee, Florida, where he served as Director of the Tallahassee Institute of Religion adjacent to Florida State University. He also was the coordinator of Early Morning and Home Study Seminaries in parts of three southern states: Florida, Georgia, and Alabama. While in Tallahassee Garth received his Ph.D. in Marriage and Family Relationships with an emphasis on therapy. During this time in Tallahassee he was called by President Spencer W. Kimball to serve as the first bishop of the newly formed Tallahassee Ward. He subsequently served as a member of the Tallahassee Florida Stake Presidency.

After receiving his doctorate degree in 1977, Garth and his family moved to St. George, Utah, where he taught at the Institute of Religion and maintained a thriving marriage and family therapy practice in the community until 1986. In 1986, he joined the Religion faculty at BYU at Laie, Hawaii. Since then—except for the school year 1992-93 when he was invited to be a Religion Professor at the BYU Jerusalem Center for Near Eastern Studies—Garth has taught at BYU-Hawaii. In 1992 Garth was appointed Chair (Associate Dean) of the Division of Religious Instruction and Family Studies, a position which he currently holds.

Though he spends considerable time in his administrative role, Brother Allred loves teaching and working with the multinational student body attending BYU-Hawaii. In his role as a teacher, he teaches honors classes in the Book of Mormon, the Doctrine & Covenants, Gospel Principles and Practice, and Achieving an Eternal Marriage and Building an Eternal Family.

Brother Allred has served many years as a temple officiator in both the St. George and Hawaii Temples. In March 1997, he was called to serve as the Stake President of the BYU-Hawaii 2nd Stake (married students), a calling which he truly enjoys since it gives him the opportunity to work with and serve in an even closer manner the students he so deeply loves. And the students love him.

In 1988 he was named "Teacher of the Year" on the BYU-Hawaii campus. He is a much sought after speaker for campus forums and firesides. He frequently is asked to conduct workshops on gospel doctrines and family relationships throughout the stakes of the Church in the Hawaiian Islands. He also is a popular presenter at Know Your Religion and Education Weeks.

Brother Allred has published several books and articles. A consistently popular book of his is entitled *Unlocking the Powers of Faith* in which Garth effectively connects eternal gospel principles with established principles of professional therapy.

Brother Allred loves teaching students, visiting with clients, reading books, and gardening—whether it be people or plants he loves to help things grow. He also loves to walk along the beach across the street from their home in Laie—especially when the moon is full and the palm trees are silhouetted against the sky. He enjoys riding the family motorcycles or scooters along the beach-front road to the North Shore or south toward Kaneohe.

Garth also loves the cultural diversity of the Islands. The ward he lives in has few Caucasians. His wife says the reason he loves the Aloha Spirit of the Islands so much is because he is naturally outgoing, loving, and concerned with others. Though he has many loves, most importantly, Brother Allred loves the Lord, his family, his friends, and the gospel—he believes they are all interconnected.

Even as a child, Garth yearned to know and understand the things of the Spirit—not only for his own satisfaction, but also so that he could bring others into the light of truth as well. That quest is still with him.

This comprehensive and sensitively written book on the Lord's great plan of happiness, reflects Garth's love for the truth and carries an outreaching spirit inviting others to come unto Christ and to partake of his eternal gifts.

—*The Publishers*

TABLE OF CONTENTS

LIST OF FIGURES

This book is lovingly dedicated to my wife, Mary,
and my children: Scott, Darron, Angela, David,
JoEll, Michael, Amber and Marc.

Deep gratitude is also expressed to Marguerite Delong
whose encouragement and sensitive suggestions regarding
organization, transition, and detail
have proven to be invaluable.

CHAPTER ONE

OUR HEAVENLY FAMILY

Knowest thou not that eternities ago thy spirit, pure and holy, dwelt in thy Heavenly Father's bosom, and in His presence, and with thy mother, one of the queens of heaven, surrounded by thy brother and sister spirits in the spirit world, among the Gods?

—John Taylor

From my birth till I was about nine years old, the places and the people of southern Alberta had an enduring effect on my impressionable young mind. The rolling prairies around Cardston are a great place to raise cattle, horses, sheep, grain—and children. Blessings available in those western Canadian communities include strong Church leadership and gospel-centered activities that influence the thoughts and feelings of children during their formative years.

I clearly remember, as a five-year-old boy, sitting in a sacrament meeting in the Hillspring Ward and seeing our family's dear friend, Patriarch Fisher, sitting with the priests as they blessed the sacrament. While the sacrament was being passed, I could hear the glass water cups clink in their trays—this was before paper cups were used. When the passing of the sacrament was completed, the priests and the patriarch left the sacrament table and sat with their families in the congregation. Then Brother Fisher would often beckon to me and my parents would let me sit by him during the rest of the meeting. He was, my parents explained, a very spiritual man who gave special blessings to people—patriarchal blessings. I couldn't say the word right.

Invariably Brother Fisher had a cellophane-wrapped caramel candy in his coat pocket that he discreetly slipped to me. I still remember the feelings of peace and warmth that surrounded this man of faith. I loved him for his kindness with the candy; but more than that, I loved how I felt as I sat by him. I sometimes wondered what it would be like to receive a blessing from him—his hands were very soft. Later, I did receive my Patriarchal blessing from him, and each time I read it I remember the warm feelings I had with Patriarch Fisher.

Many other instances in my early life in Canada influenced me spiritually. Rarely was a meal served on our wooden family dinner table without a gospel topic being discussed. Stories of faith were abundant. My parents often spoke of experiences from the life of President Edward J. Wood, who for many years served both as Temple and Stake President in Alberta. This spiritually gifted man, while a missionary in the South Pacific, actually raised the dead and calmed enraged seas. In the temple he shared some of his sacred experiences with my parents, and they in turn passed them on to me and my brothers and sisters— around that old wooden dinner table.

I grew to love these spiritual stories, and my understanding and appreciation for sacred things increased. There was a spiritual fulness, a completeness, in those early days that I still use as a kind of touchstone for measuring the truth of things in the present. As I reflect on these and other childhood events, I can still see in my mind's eye the full-time missionaries leaning on the towel rack (something that was forbidden for us) that was on the inside of our front door. They were talking about Joseph Smith's First Vision. They had just come from a cottage meeting and were excited about the people they were teaching. As they bore their testimonies to us, I felt the whispering of the Spirit and the first glow of testimony.

Another memory I have is of a non-member family who moved into our little community of Hillspring. They had a son near my older brother's age. He told me that his church was true and that ours was wrong. He told me things about Joseph Smith and our Church leaders that I knew were not true, but at the time I did not know how to respond to him. After I explained my frustration to my mother, she said, "Well, be kind to him, but tell him that Jesus' true Church has been brought back to the earth by angels." That simple statement of truth and other such straightforward answers from family and friends stimulated within my boyish mind a keen interest in gospel doctrine and a firm commitment to things of the Spirit.

I was blessed by having gospel truths taught to me in my youth. Many have not had this chance, but each has had experiences according to the wisdom, foreknowledge, and love of a kind Heavenly Father. Even difficult experiences are provided for our growth. I am grateful for both my stressful and my spiritual experiences.

I deeply love and appreciate my earthly family, my father and mother, brothers and sisters, wife and children. I sense the feelings and meanings of fatherhood as I hold my own children in my arms. During these sweet moments I think I feel, to some extent, what our Heavenly Father feels for each of us, and I offer a silent prayer of gratitude for the chance to be a father. I know that earthly families can provide a taste of heaven.

EARTHLY FAMILIES: A GLIMPSE OF HEAVEN

What are your childhood memories, your family reflections that give you a sense of belonging, security, love, or even a glimpse of heaven?

Some of you who read this book may not have had good experiences while you were growing up. Some of you may have been abused in various ways. Today there are homes that are ravaged by horrible abuse and wrenching divorce that affects family members in harsh and hurting ways, inflicting pain and suffering. Problem families will continue to exist, I suppose, until the Lord comes, but be assured that these conditions will not last forever. Through the Atonement of our Savior Jesus Christ the time will come when such pain will cease and broken hearts will be healed. Even now, if you are one of these suffering souls, you can be wrapped in the arms of his safety (Alma 34:16). Your heavenly petitions for a loving family will not be ignored nor forgotten—the Lord has promised his faithful children peace in spite of adversity (D&C 59:23).

At a BYU Devotional Elder Vaughn J. Featherstone, a member of the First Quorum of the Seventy, echoed this promise as he reminded his audience of the healing powers of the Savior by citing the nursery rhyme "Humpty Dumpty". With a voice cracking with emotion, he said, "And all the king's horses and all the king's men couldn't put Humpty Dumpty back together again—but the King could, and the King can, and the King will if we come unto Him."[1] Through Christ's love and infinite sacrifice all things that have been broken eventually will be made whole again.

Recognizing that problem families exist does not mean that we should lose sight of the kind of family relationships the Lord *wants* us to have. President Gordon B. Hinckley, at the September, 1995, Women's Conference said, "I believe that it should be the blessing of every child to be born into a home in which that child is welcomed, nurtured, loved and blessed—with parents, a father and a mother, who live with loyalty to one another and to their children."

I believe this, too, and I frequently remind my students that even though they may not have chosen the family environment into which they were born, they can choose the kind of family in which *their* children will grow—and so can you.

This book can help you teach your children the principles of the gospel that bring peace in this world and eternal life in the world to come (D&C 59:23). When parents and children build their family relationships upon the solid foundations of the gospel they will enjoy a taste of heaven and will glimpse the happiness of eternal family relationships. I know this to be true, for I have experienced this in my father's family and in my own. Earthly homes can indeed help us remember some of the joys we must have felt in our heavenly home, especially when the great plan of happiness, the Plan of Salvation, was presented to us by our Heavenly Father—which will be the topic of the following sections.

OUR INTELLIGENCE IS ETERNAL[2]

Before we can discuss in detail our heavenly home—where we existed as spirit children of God—it will be helpful to discuss a condition. Before our spirit birth the scriptures explain that we existed as *intelligence*.

We do not know very much about the nature of intelligence, for example we don't know if we existed there as male and female; we do not know if we had form or features. We do know, however, that our individual intelligence is eternal! The Lord has explained that, "Man was also in the beginning with God. Intelligence, or the *light of truth*, was not created or made, neither indeed can be" (D&C 93:29; emphasis added).

This is a remarkable concept! Did you know before that you are an eternal being? Do you realize that "nothing" is something you never have been nor ever can be? You have always existed—you can never *not* exist. You can only grow in your intelligence—in light and truth—or slide backwards and diminish.

The Prophet Joseph Smith clearly taught that we are eternal in our basic natures. He explained, "We say that God himself is a self-existent [eternal] being. Who told you so? It is correct enough; but how did it get into your heads? Who told you that man did not exist in like manner upon the same principles? *Man does exist upon the same principles.*"[3]

In other words, our intelligence, our minds, are as eternal and everlasting as God. The major difference between us and our Heavenly Father is that he has advanced much further than we; he has increased in his intelligence, light and truth to a fulness. He, according to Abraham's record, is "more intelligent" than all of us (Abraham 3:19). As has been mentioned, intelligence can increase in light and truth. In scriptural language, we can be "added upon" (Abraham 3:26).

This process is a very important concept in relationship to the great plan of happiness. It seems that we experience joy as we are "added upon" the following ways: by receiving more light and truth, by gaining physical bodies, by getting married and by having and rearing children. God promotes cooperative unions that bring us life and joy—Satan promotes competitive unions that bring death and misery. Happiness is connected with being added upon, with creation, life, light, and beauty. Misery is connected with being subtracted from, with chaos, destruction, death, and disease.

Sometimes in my lighter moods I present to my students an "added upon" lesson called "Let's Get Together, We Will Have More Fun"! and I review the steps in the Plan of Salvation. Abraham was taught that those who keep their first and second estates (who are faithful in their premortal and mortal lives) will be "added upon...forever and ever" (Abraham 3:26). This idea of being added upon will be a continuous thread that will run through the remainder of this book.

Joseph Smith taught that it was a wonderful and benevolent plan that our Heavenly Father initiated so that weaker intelligences could advance and become exalted beings like unto himself. The Prophet explained:

> God himself, finding he was in the midst of spirits and glory, because he was more intelligent, saw proper to institute laws whereby the rest could have a privilege to advance like himself. The relationship we have with God places us in a situation to advance in knowledge. He has power to institute laws to instruct the weaker intelligences, that they may be exalted with himself, so that they might have one glory upon another, and all that knowledge, power, glory, and intelligence, which is requisite in order to save them in the world of spirits.
>
> This is good doctrine. It tastes good. I can taste the principles of eternal life, *and so can you*.[4]

Jesus, our eldest brother, the premortal Jehovah, was the first to pass from primal intelligence to become a spirit child of God. Since that time, Jesus has been called the *Firstborn*. He and all of us who came later, grew up before the Father, increasing in light and truth, understanding and devotion. As children of Heavenly Father we were—and still are—known and deeply loved by him.

Solomon expressed an understanding of the great love Heavenly Father had for him before his mortal birth, before the foundations of the earth were even laid. He wrote:

> The Lord possessed me in the beginning of his way, before his works of old. I was set up from everlasting, from the beginning, or ever the earth was.
>
> When there were no depths, I was brought forth; when there were no fountains abounding with water.
>
> Before the mountains were settled, before the hills was I brought forth... Then I was by him, as one brought up with him: and *I was daily his delight, rejoicing always before him* (Proverbs 8:22-30; emphasis added. Also note the reference to pre-existence in the above chapter heading).

Solomon's description should remind you and me that we too were loved by our Heavenly Father, and we were daily his delight.

Sometimes I have tried to imagine the vast number of children our Father has begotten since the spirit birth of Jehovah in that heavenly realm. We are all so numerous, and yet, he has given us the assurance that he knows each of us intimately and personally (see Matthew 10:30-31).

WE ARE LITERALLY THE CHILDREN OF GOD

From intelligences we were organized and our premortal life began as we became spirit children of our Heavenly Father. Our spirit bodies were brought forth in his divine image.[5] This involved a process of spirit birth. In explaining how our intelligences became spirit children of God, President Heber C. Kimball said, "Now, . . . you have got a spirit in you, and that spirit was created and organized [from intelligence]—was *born* and *begotten* by our Father and our God before we ever took these [mortal] bodies."[6] As spirit children we are *literally* the offspring of God.

This is one of the greatest truths brought forth through the Prophet Joseph Smith (see Doctrine and Covenants 76:24). We are of the same kind, species, and form as God; we are his family; we were born and begotten in his own image and likeness—and this is to be understood in the most literal way.

We are in actual fact the race and family of God. We lived with him before we ever came to this earth. To my knowledge we are the only Christians that believe this—that we had a life before this one. Other Christians believe that our beginning occurred *here* with our conception in our mother's womb. But we take literally the concept that we are the "children of God".

Others take the "children of God" notion as simply a figure of speech—sort of like George Washington was the "father of the United States of America".

Elder Boyd K. Packer has observed, "There is no way to make sense out of life without a knowledge of the doctrine of premortal life. The idea that mortal birth is the beginning is preposterous. There is no way to explain life if you believe that. . . . When we understand the doctrine of premortal life, then things fit together and make sense".[7]

So, as Latter-day Saints, we believe that we are literally, truly, honestly, actually and without equivocation the children of our Heavenly Father. This is one of the most meaningful doctrines ever revealed to the inhabitants of the world! When you grasp this idea, you will begin to understand who you really are and what your divine potential entails. You will begin to understand why there is a great plan of happiness—a father's plan for the happiness of his children.

In my own life the idea that we are literally the children of God has been affirmed and reaffirmed many times. Not only was I taught this doctrine as a child, but as an adult the spirit has whispered to me over and over again the reality of this sacred truth. As a bishop in Lale, Hawaii, I witnessed many baptismal services at the beautiful Kekela Beach Park across the highway from my home. Almost always, at some time during the service, those wonderful Polynesian Saints would sing Naomi Randall's hymn, "I Am a Child of God". These brothers and sisters would weep tears of happiness as they would sing these poignant words:

I am a child of God,
And he has sent me here,
Has given me an earthly home
With parents kind and dear.
Lead me, guide me, walk beside me,
Help me find the way.
Teach me all that I must do
To live with him some day.[8]

THE SCRIPTURES DECLARE OUR PREMORTAL LIFE

That we are literally the children of God and that we had a former life in his presence is taught in various passages throughout the scriptures.

In modern day revelation we have affirmed the idea that the Lord. created all things spiritually before he created them physically. The Lord explained to Moses: "For I, the Lord God, created all things, of which I have spoken, spiritually before they were naturally upon the face of the earth... and I, the Lord God, had created all the children of men; and not yet a man to till the ground; *for in heaven created I them*" (Moses 3:5; emphasis added).

The prophet Jeremiah wrote; "Then the word of the Lord came unto me, saying, Before I formed thee in the belly I knew thee; and before thou camest forth out of the womb I sanctified thee, and I ordained thee a prophet unto the nations" (Jeremiah 1:4-5). In other words, the Lord knew Jeremiah as his spirit child and called him, because of his faithfulness, to be a prophet here in mortality. Jeremiah and all of us were known and deeply loved by our Heavenly Father.

Another scriptural example can be found in the Old Testament when the Lord asked Job the question about where he was when "the foundations of the earth" were laid, "when the morning stars sang together, and all the sons of God shouted for joy" (Job 38:4-7). Of course Job, like we, could not remember his premortal life.[9] But, Job's condition was like Jeremiah's and our own—we all lived with our Heavenly Father before the creation of the world, and we shouted for joy, taking great delight at the prospects of coming to this earth. In the book of Ecclesiastes we read that at death, "The spirit shall return unto God who gave it" (12:7). We could not *return* to God unless we had once lived with him.

The New Testament, too, provides important evidence of a pre-earth life. For example, the disciples of Jesus observing a man who had been born blind, put the following question to their Master: "Who did sin, this man, or his parents, that he was born blind?" (John 9:2). From the nature of the question it is evident that the disciples considered it possible for a man to sin before he was born and in consequence of such sin, he might be "born blind."

In his famous speech on Mars Hill, Paul used specific language to declare to the Athenians that "we are the *offspring* of God" (Acts 17:28-29). Again, to the Hebrews, Paul wrote, "Furthermore we have had *fathers of our flesh* which corrected us, and we gave them reverence: shall we not much rather be in subjection unto *the Father of spirits*, and live?" (Hebrews 12:9; emphasis added).

In a very clear statement, Jesus said, "I was in the beginning with the Father, and am the Firstborn. . . . Ye were also in the beginning with the Father" (D&C 93:21-23).

To Moses the Lord said, "I made the world, and men *before they were in the flesh*" (Moses 6:51; emphasis added). This same doctrine is found in Numbers 16:22 which states that God is the Father of us all, and hence he is "the God of the spirits of all flesh".

As an aside, it is interesting to reflect upon a uniquely Latter-day Saint doctrine that states that our Heavenly Father has children on other worlds besides this one—that we have brothers and sisters on other worlds. They too are "begotten sons and daughters unto God" (D&C 76:24). This startling information should prepare our minds so that we will not be too surprised if and when contact is ever made with them, and we are able to compare gospel notes with these kindred souls from another sheepfold—they who are also redeemed by and through our same Savior, Jesus Christ.[10]

As I read and reflect upon these wonderful passages about our heavenly family, my mind is illuminated and my heart swells with the light they impart. I rejoice that we have been permitted to have this peek into eternities past—to learn that we have come to this earth leaving behind an extensive history of endearing relationships involving our kind and loving Heavenly Father, our brothers and sisters and many, many other relatives and friends—many of whom live on other worlds.

MAN OF HOLINESS IS HIS NAME

No person on the earth in modern times knew that the God of heaven was truly our Father until it was revealed to the Prophet Joseph Smith. From him we learn that our Heavenly Father is a man—a celestial, resurrected, exalted, and glorified Man of Holiness.

In latter-day scripture we witness God declaring to Enoch: "Behold, I am God; Man of Holiness is my name" (Moses 7:35). This name-title reinforces the wondrous truth that God the Father is an exalted man "of flesh and bones" (D&C 130:22), and that every aspect of his character is holy.[11] In Enoch's record we read, "In the language of Adam, *Man of Holiness* is his name, and the name of his Only Begotten is the Son of Man, even Jesus Christ" (Moses 6:57; emphasis added). The expression "Man of Holiness" is the basis for the New Testament expressions referring to Jesus as the "Son of man" (for example, see Matthew 8:20). These fragmentary expressions are referring to Jesus as "Son of Man of Holiness"!

All human males have been created in the physical image and likeness of their Heavenly Father—and all females have been created in the physical image and likeness of their Heavenly Mother (see Genesis 1:27)—for our premortal family does indeed include a celestial, exalted, glorified, and loving Mother in Heaven.

WE HAVE A MOTHER THERE

As members of the Church, we are taught that we have a Mother in Heaven, and that we were born and begotten by *Heavenly Parents* even as we were born into this world through mortal men and women. Both male and female are necessary in order to bring forth spirit children.

The scriptures are silent about our having a Heavenly Mother, but this doctrine was taught by the Prophet Joseph Smith during his life time, and has been taught by all his successors. In our popular Mormon hymn, "O My Father", written by Eliza R. Snow in the year 1843—during the lifetime of the Prophet Joseph Smith—reference is made to our Mother in Heaven.

I had learned to call thee Father,
Through thy Spirit from on high;
But until the key of knowledge
Was restored, I knew not why.
In the heavens are parents single?
No; the thought makes reason stare!
Truth is reason, truth eternal
Tells me I've a MOTHER there.
When I leave this frail existence,
When I lay this mortal by,
Father, MOTHER, may I meet you
In your royal courts on high?
Then, at length, when I've completed
All you sent me forth to do,
With your mutual approbation
Let me come and dwell with you.[12]

The reality of our having a Heavenly Mother was affirmed in 1909 by the First Presidency of the Church (Joseph F. Smith, John R. Winder, and Anthon H. Lund) in a statement entitled "On the Origin of Man." In speaking of our pre-mortal existence with our Heavenly Father, they declared, "Man, as a spirit, was *begotten* and *born* of Heavenly Parents, and reared to maturity in the eternal man-sions of the Father". Man is the "offspring of celestial parentage" and "all men and women are in the similitude of the universal Father and *Mother*, and are *literally* the sons and daughters of Deity."[13]

When we begin to understand our origins with our Father and Mother in Heaven, we begin to understand who we are and what we can become. Women can become like their Mother in Heaven, and men can become like their Father in Heaven. The great plan of happiness provides a way whereby we can be like our Heavenly Parents—inheriting eternal youth, power, glory, and joy.

THE COUNCIL IN HEAVEN

While we were spirits living with our Heavenly Parents in the premortal world, our Heavenly Father called a special family council to present the plan whereby we could descend to this earth, partake of mortal life with physical bod-ies, pass through a probation in mortality, and continue our progress toward immortality and eternal life. In other words, it was discussed as to how, and upon what principles, our salvation, exaltation, and eternal glory would be brought about.

One of the of the items on the agenda was for the Father to make a selection of a Savior who would implement the Plan of Salvation by taking upon himself the sins of the world. Our Father knew that by coming to this earth we would all become subject to imperfections, disease, spiritual darkness and death because of the fallen condition of earth life, and become unclean because of personal sin. Since no unclean thing can be in the presence of God, it was necessary that a Savior be provided for us who could and would atone for Adam's transgression and thereby provide a means for the remission of our personal sins.

In that premortal council, when our Father in Heaven asked for a volunteer to become our Savior, both Jesus and Satan stepped forward. Jesus, the Firstborn of God spoke first and said, "Here am I, send me" (Abraham 3:27).

Lucifer, who was also a son of the Father, came forward with a counterpro-posal, saying: "Behold, send me, I will be thy Son, and I will redeem all mankind, that not one soul shall be lost, and surely I will do it; wherefore, give me thine honor" (Moses 4:1). Already of high status, Lucifer sought to aggrandize himself further without regard to the rights and agency of others, seeking to destroy the agency of man.[14] The Father said, "I will send the first" (Abraham 3:27).

And so it was that Jesus, the Firstborn, the premortal Jehovah, was selected by the Father to come into mortality and become the Savior of mankind. As our Savior, Jesus' calling was to redeem us from the stains of sin and set the example for us to follow. He said, "Come . . . follow me!" (Mark 10:21). Jesus is "the captain of [our] salvation" Hebrews 2:10); he is our file leader; he is our Savior; he is God's Almighty Son, and he is our advocate with the Father. Jesus is the "Lamb slain from the foundation of the world" (Revelation 13:8). Through him we can come to the Father and find eternal life.

THERE WAS WAR IN HEAVEN

When Satan's alternate plan was not accepted by the Father, he became "angry, and kept not his first estate; and at that day, many followed after him" (Abraham 3:28). When we say that Satan and his followers did not keep their *first estate* (Abraham 3:26) we mean that they rebelled against God and sought to destroy our agency. As a result they would never be permitted to come to this world and obtain a physical body. Accordingly, they could never be *added upon.* "They were denied the privilege of being born into this world and receiving mortal bodies.... The Lord cast them out into the earth, where they became the tempters of mankind".[15]

One of the reasons Lucifer's (or Satan's) alternate plan was rejected was because it would disallow our agency, our right to choose good over evil—or evil over good. Satan wanted to initiate a plan of salvation that would *force* people to comply with the laws of the gospel—so that not one soul would be lost. This unprecedented plan, the idea of a probation without threat of falling from eternal blessings, appealed to one third of our brothers and sisters. (see D&C 29:36)

In consequence of the rejection of his alternate plan, Lucifer became enraged and rebelled against the Father. From that time forth he, with unprecedented anger and malice, has sought to obstruct, impede, destroy and thwart the Father's plan of happiness. Satan and his followers were cast out into the earth and they, unseen by us, continue to seek our destruction in any way they can.

The apostle John, the author of the book of Revelation, gives us the following account of their expulsion from the presence of God: "And there was war in heaven: Michael and his angels fought against the dragon; and the dragon fought and his angels, And prevailed not; neither was their place found any more in heaven. And the great dragon was cast out, that old serpent, called the Devil, and Satan, which deceiveth the whole world: he was cast out into the earth, and his angels were cast out with him" (Revelation 12:7-9). And his tail drew the *third part* of the stars of heaven [children of God], and did cast them to the earth." (Revelation 12:4; emphasis added).

Isaiah described Lucifer's expulsion from heaven because of his rebellion:

> How art thou fallen from heaven, O Lucifer, son of the morning! how art thou cut down to the ground, which didst weaken the nations! For thou hast said in thine heart, I will ascend into heaven, I will exalt my throne above the stars of God: I will sit also upon the mount of the congregation, in the sides of the north: I will ascend above the heights of the clouds; I will be like the most High. Yet thou shalt be brought down to hell, to the sides of the pit (Isaiah 14:12-15; see also Moses 4:1-4).

Lehi added, "And because he had fallen from heaven, and had become miserable forever, he sought also the misery of all mankind" (2 Nephi 2:18). It may not have been the fact that Lucifer offered an alternate plan that got him banished from heaven. It is more likely that it was his anger and rebellion and seeking to destroy the salvation of his brother and sister spirits that brought about his fall.

Where do you think you stood in that premortal war in heaven? Did it ever occur to you that you might have been a missionary there, that you earnestly tried to reclaim some of your brothers and sisters who were inclined to follow Satan? Could it be that in heaven you anxiously tried to persuade some of your brother and sister spirits, who were wavering between the two positions, to follow Jesus and support the plan of agency before it was everlastingly too late?

The idea that in the premortal world the spirit children of God were all equally valiant on the side of the Savior or equally rebellious on the side of the Satan is not doctrinally sound. We know that there was great variety and diversity among our brothers and sisters.

GREAT DIVERSITY AMONG THE CHILDREN OF GOD

Among the children of God in the premortal life there were two general groups who were loyal to either Satan or the Savior. Within the group that followed Jesus, there were many different degrees of spirituality, righteousness and devotion (see end of chapter Figure 1-A, The Doctrine of Election). Some spirits were very valiant in the cause of truth and righteousness—others were less so. The valiant ones were known as the "noble and great ones" and were closely associated with the Savior. Abraham writes:

> Now the Lord had shown unto me, Abraham, the intelligences [spirit children] that were organized before the world was; and among all these there were many of the noble and great ones;
> And God saw these souls that they were good, and he stood in the midst

of them, and he said: These I will make my rulers; for he stood among those that were spirits, and he saw that they were good; and he said unto me: Abraham, thou art one of them; thou wast chosen before thou wast born (Abraham 3:22-23).

These *noble and great* spirits were foreordained or fore-appointed to be leaders in mortality. They were nominated, called, and elected to receive specific blessings in this world and in the eternities. Basically, their two callings were: 1) to be born through the lineage of Abraham, Isaac and Jacob in this world (see D&C 84:99; Abraham 2:8-11), and 2) to become gods in the eternities. Does this help you to begin to understand who you really are and what our Father has in store for you—what you are capable of becoming?

The idea that the noble and great ones were assigned to be born through the lineage of Abraham and called and elected to become gods in the eternities provides the foundation for *the doctrine of election* that Joseph Smith said ought to be taught?[16]

THE DOCTRINE OF ELECTION AND FOREORDINATION

Elder Bruce R. McConkie succinctly describes this doctrine of election or foreordination in the following terms:

This election of grace is a very fundamental, logical, and important part of God's dealings with men through the ages. To bring to pass the salvation of the greatest possible number of his spirit children, *the Lord, in general sends the most righteous and worthy spirits to earth through the lineage of Abraham and Jacob*. This course is a manifestation of his grace or in other words his love, mercy, and condescension toward his children.

This election to a chosen lineage is based on *pre-existent worthiness* and is thus made "according to the foreknowledge of God." (1 Pet. 1:2.) Those so grouped together during their mortal probation have more abundant opportunities to make and keep the covenants of salvation, a right which they earned by preexistent devotion to the cause of righteousness.[17]

President Harold B. Lee explained that premortal worthiness qualified people to receive greater blessings in this life. He said:

Those born to the lineage of Jacob, who was later to be called Israel, and his posterity, who were known as the children of Israel, were born into the most illustrious lineage of any of those who came upon the earth as mortal beings.

All these rewards were seemingly promised, or foreordained, before the world was. Surely these matters must have been determined by the kind of lives we had lived in that premortal spirit world. Some may question these assumptions, but at the same time they will accept without any question the belief that each one of us will be judged when we leave this earth according to his or her deeds during our lives here in mortality. Isn't it just as reasonable to believe that what we have received here in this earth [life] was given to each of us according to the merits of our conduct before we came here?"[18]

From these explanations, then, we learn that certain spirit children of God were identified, nominated, called and elected—foreordained—to be born through the lineage of Abraham and Israel because of their prior faithfulness. Paul understood this doctrine when he identified the children of Abraham and Israel as those, "to whom pertained the adoption, and the glory and the covenants, and the giving of the law, and the service of God, and the promises" (Romans 9:4).

Faithful children of Israel in this life are inheritors of eternal life—godhood (D&C 132:20, 37). This principle still continues in this world today. It is a manifestation of God's grace, because it explains that God is not capricious—inconsistent or erratic—in his blessings. "There is a law . . . upon which all blessings are predicated" (D&C 130:20). When you obey God's laws, you are blessed with knowledge and opportunities for greater growth—all of which lead to greater happiness.

The Book of Mormon prophet Alma clearly explains the doctrine of foreordination. He explains that priesthood holders were foreordained in the premortal worlds because of *their faith and good works*—not because of an arbitrary decision made by God as the idea of predestination would have us believe. We read:

And this is the manner after which they were ordained—being called and prepared from the foundation of the world according to the foreknowledge of God, on account of *their exceeding faith and good works;* in the first place being left to choose good or evil; therefore *they having chosen good, and exercising exceedingly great faith*, are called with a holy calling, yea, with that holy calling which was prepared with, and according to, a preparatory redemption for such.

And thus they have been called to this holy calling on account of *their faith*, while others would reject the Spirit of God on account of the hardness of their hearts and blindness of their minds, while, if it had not been for this they might have had as great privilege as their brethren. (Alma 13:3-4; emphasis added).

Father Abraham himself stands as a wonderful example of one of these righteous and worthy spirits, one of the noble and great ones (see Abraham 3:22-23) who was chosen and foreordained before the world was. Because of his premortal devotion and his mortal righteousness, the Lord promised Abraham and his seed:

> I will make of thee a great nation, and I will bless thee above measure, and make thy name great among all nations, and thou shalt be a blessing unto thy seed after thee, that in their hands they shall bear this *ministry* and *Priesthood* unto all nations;
>
> And I will bless them through thy name; *for as many as receive this Gospel shall be called after thy name*, and shall be accounted thy seed, and shall rise up and bless thee, as their father;
>
> And I will bless them that bless thee, and curse them that curse thee; and in thee (that is, in thy Priesthood), and in thy seed (that is, thy Priesthood), for I give unto thee a promise that this fight shall continue in thee, and in thy seed after thee (that is to say, the literal seed, or the seed of the body) shall all the families of the earth be blessed, even with the blessings of the Gospel, which are the blessings of salvation, *even of life eternal* (Abraham 2:9-11; emphasis added).

In this passage the Lord clearly explains that all who enter the Gospel covenants become children of Abraham and thus become heirs to all the blessings of the priesthood. This means exaltation in the highest degree of the Celestial Kingdom—even godhood. In connection with this idea is the notion that we as members of The Church of Jesus Christ of Latter-day Saints are also known as latter-day Israel.

As the children of Abraham and Israel we are natural heirs to the blessings of the Gospel, and we have the responsibility of proclaiming the good news, the great plan of happiness, throughout the world.

The Prophet Joseph Smith frequently made mention of the doctrine of the election of Israel. One such reference is found in his commentary of Romans 9.

> The election there spoken of [in Romans 9] was pertaining to the flesh, and had reference to the seed of Abraham, according to the promise God made to Abraham.... To them belonged the adoption and the covenants.... The election of the promised seed still continues, and in the last day, they shall have the Priesthood restored unto them, and they shall be the "saviors on Mount Zion," the ministers of our God.... The whole of the chapter had reference to the Priesthood and the house of Israel; and unconditional election of individuals to eternal life was not taught by the Apostles. God did elect...that all those who would be saved, should be saved in Christ Jesus, and through obedience to the Gospel; but He passes over no man's sins, but visits them with correction, and if His children will not repent of their sins He will discard them.[19]

In the above passage, Joseph Smith warns that even though we may be called to be born through the lineage of Abraham, we still must be faithful in mortality in order to receive the promised blessings—we still must make our calling and election sure by proving ourselves true and faithful to the end."[20]

Without doubt there were some spirits who were valiant in the premortal life but who failed here in mortality. King David[21] and Samson could probably be cited as examples. Even though they were nominated, called and elected in that premortal world, they did not remain true and faithful here, and because of this they never made their "calling and election sure" (2 Peter 1:10).

In connection with this doctrine of foreordination Joseph Smith explained: "Every man who has a calling to minister to the inhabitants of the world was ordained to that very purpose in the Grand Council of heaven before this world was. I suppose I was ordained to this very office in that Grand Council."[22]

Characteristics of the spirit, which were developed through experiences in the premortal life, play an important part in our progression here by influencing our dispositions and desires in this life.[23]

President Joseph F. Smith affirmed the doctrine that premortal life choices and experiences effect our temperaments in this life. In a vision of the early prophets of this dispensation in the after life, he observed that "Even before they were born, they, with many others, *received their first lessons in the world of spirits* and were prepared to come forth in the due time of the Lord to labor in his vineyard for the salvation of the souls of men" (D&C 138:56; emphasis added).

THE FALSE DOCTRINE OF PREDESTINATION

The key difference between foreordination and predestination is that with foreordination agency is preserved and with predestination it is not. Just as Lucifer "sought to destroy the agency of man" in the premortal life (Moses 4:3), so through false teachers here, he has foisted upon many people the doctrine of predestination which stands in opposition to the true doctrine of election and foreordination.

Predestination is contrived through distortions of the scriptures relative to salvation and damnation. Such teachings hold that we are not and cannot be responsible in any way for our salvation—God predestines or predetermines that for all of us. Accordingly, some souls are irrevocably chosen for salvation, others for damnation; and nothing anyone can do personally has any effect on God's predetermination. Of course, we Latter-day Saints do not believe in this doctrine. If it were true, you and I would have no agency. Salvation and damnation would be assigned simply because God wills it that way.[24] Satan wanted to destroy our agency in the premortal world but failed. Now he tries to make us think that we have no agency by promoting doctrines such as predestination. He never seems to give up on trying to destroy us and the blessings of the gospel.

The following passage from the writings of Paul is cited sometimes to prove that predestination is a Biblical teaching: "[God] having *predestinated* us unto the adoption of children by Jesus Christ... In whom also we have obtained an inheritance, being *predestinated* according to the purpose of him who worketh all things after the counsel of his own will (Ephesians 1:5, 11; emphasis added).

Rather than affirming the doctrine of predestination, Paul is speaking here of the law of obedience stating that when we obey God's laws it is *predetermined* or *predestined* that related blessings will flow. We have a latter-day revelation that states the same principle: "There is a law, *irrevocably* decreed in heaven before the foundation of this world, upon which all blessings are predicated—and when we obtain any blessing from God, it is by obedience to that law upon which it is predicated" (D&C 130:20-21; emphasis added). Accordingly, the *laws* upon which blessings are granted are irrevocably decreed, predicated or predetermined—but *people* are not.

Predestination, then, is a false and terribly misleading doctrine. You do not want to believe in that! Those who believe in it resign themselves to either a false view of salvation without effort or damnation without hope. The freedom to choose our destiny is a wonderful blessing. Lehi taught his son, Jacob, that because we are redeemed from the fall we have become free forever. We are "free to choose liberty and eternal life, through the great Mediator of all men, or to choose captivity and death, according to the captivity and power of the devil" (2 Nephi 2:27). There is no predestination taught here!

One of the reasons I love being a Latter-day Saint is that both my thoughts and feelings are stimulated by the truths found in the gospel teachings. It just makes sense to me that a loving Father in Heaven would provide a plan for our happiness that involves our own decision making. How could we grow and for what purposes would we even exist if predestination were a true doctrine. Thank the Lord for the great restoration of the true Gospel through the Prophet Joseph Smith and the knowledge that we have that we are free to choose life and liberty or death and bondage.

THE GREAT PLAN OF HAPPINESS IN REVIEW

As we have discussed throughout this chapter, our Heavenly Father's great plan of happiness consists of our being *added upon* in various ways (Abraham 3:26).

We first spoke about how our earthly families, when they are built upon the principles of the gospel, can be a reflection of our heavenly home and can provide a taste of heaven. We pointed out that we have always existed as intelligences and that we became the spirit children of heavenly parents as we were literally born and begotten by them. We were loved and tenderly cared for by them, and we grew in righteousness and devotion to truth. We learned that God, our Heavenly Father is called Man of Holiness. He is an exalted, resurrected, glorified man. We also know that we have a loving Mother in Heaven who is an exalted, glorified, woman of perfected loveliness, beauty and holiness.

In our premortal life a grand council was called in which a plan was presented whereby we could descend to this earth, receive a physical body and experience opposition the overcoming of which would qualify us to become gods like our heavenly parents. We rejoiced at these prospects.

Knowing that we would all sin in this mortal world, our Father asked for a volunteer who would become our Savior. Jehovah (Jesus) was the first to step forward. Lucifer (Satan) also volunteered, but wanted the honor and glory that belonged to the Father.

Satan, who lusted after the glory of the Father, and one third of the children of God rebelled against the Father and in consequence were cast out into the earth. Here, they continue to seek to destroy the great plan of happiness by promoting contention and competition, war and destruction, death and disease—taking apart those things that God wants kept together—and putting together things that God wants kept apart.

We discussed the idea that there was great spiritual diversity in heaven. Some were so valiant and true to the Savior that they were identified as the noble and great ones. These favored spirits were nominated, called and elected—foreordained—to be born through the lineage of Abraham and Israel and to become gods in the eternities if they would embrace the fulness of the gospel and remain true and faithful to their covenants. We suggested that you were among those noble and great spirits—you were selected to be born through the lineage of Abraham and are an heir to all the promises of the gospel, including exaltation in the highest degree of the Celestial Kingdom.

So, standing in contrast to the true doctrine of foreordination, the false doctrine of predestination holds that God determines in a capricious way who goes to heaven or hell. The true plan of happiness involves our free will—our right to choose life and liberty or death and damnation.

All that we have discussed to this point has focused on the events, themes and doctrines associated with our premortal life. The premortal life with our heavenly family is a central doctrine of our Church and provides a clear understanding of our journey toward eternal life and everlasting happiness. Elder Boyd K. Packer has compared our eternal journey to a three act play. The first act is like our premortal life; the second is like our present life in this world; and the final act is like eternal life in the world to come. Many people do not believe in a first act nor in a final act, and they are left without the happiness that comes in knowing who we are and where We are going. Having a knowledge of all three acts helps set the stage for understanding other elements of the Lord's eternal plan which we will discuss in detail in future chapters.

A beautiful summary of our Father's great plan for our happiness has been provided by President John Taylor who wrote an inspiring word portrait of the eternal plan of happiness called "The Origin and Destiny of Woman". In this wonderful essay he described a faithful sister's origin and destiny by answering for her three questions: "Where did I come from? .... Why am I here?" and "Where am I going after this life?"[25]

The doctrinal details in President Taylor's response may be relevant in some degree to all of you who may read his beautiful prose. The spirit will whisper to you those parts that are most applicable to you.

Here are portions of President Taylor's essay:

> Lady, whence comest thou? Thine origin? What art thou doing here? Whither art thou going, and what is thy destiny? Declare unto me if thou hast understanding. Knowest thou not that thou art a spark of Deity, struck from the fire of His eternal blaze, and brought forth in the midst of eternal burning?
>
> Knowest thou not that eternities ago thy spirit, pure and holy, dwelt in thy Heavenly Father's bosom, and in His presence, and with thy mother, one of the queens of heaven, surrounded by thy brother and sister spirits in the spirit world, among the Gods? . . .
>
> Thou longed, thou sighed and thou prayed to thy Father in heaven for the time to arrive when thou couldst come to this earth, which had fled and fallen from where it was first organized, near the planet Kolob. Leaving thy father and mother's bosom and all thy kindred spirits thou camest to earth, took a tabernacle, and imitated the deeds of those who had been exalted before you. . . .
>
> Thou heard the voice of the Father saying, go daughter to yonder lower world, and take upon thee a tabernacle, and work out thy probation with fear and trembling and rise to exaltation. But daughter, remember, you go on this condition, that is, you are to forget all things you ever saw, or knew to be transacted in the spirit world; you are not to know or remember anything concerning the same that you have beheld transpire here; but you must go and become one of the most helpless of all things that I have created, while in your infancy, subject to sickness, pain, tears, mourning, sorrow and death. But when truth shall touch the cords of your heart they will vibrate; then intelligence shall illuminate your mind, and shed its lustre in your soul, and

you shall begin to understand the things you once knew, but which had gone from you; you shall begin to understand and know the object of your creation. . . .

Crowns, thrones, exaltations and dominions are in reserve for thee in the eternal worlds, and the way is opened for thee to return back into the presence of thy Heavenly Father, if thou wilt only abide by and walk in a celestial law, fulfill the designs of thy Creator and hold out to the end that when mortality is laid in the tomb, you may go down to your grave in peace, arise in glory, and receive your everlasting reward in the resurrection of the just, along with thy head and husband. Thou wilt be permitted to pass by the Gods and angels who guard the gates, and onward, upward to thy exaltation in a Celestial world among the Gods. To be a priestess queen upon thy Heavenly Father's throne, and a glory to thy husband and offspring, to bear the souls of men, to people other worlds (as thou didst bear their tabernacles in mortality) while eternity goes and eternity comes; and if you will receive it, lady, this is eternal life.[26]

As you read these lines, perhaps you experience the same kinds of feelings that President Taylor mentioned in this text. Maybe they touch the cords of your heart, and you remember things you had known before but have forgotten. You, too, are a precious child of our heavenly Father. You are his offspring in the most literal sense. You have within you the immortal seeds of Deity. Through your faithfulness, you have in store for you blessings that are incomprehensible and unimaginable! You have capacity beyond your grandest imaginations—you have within you the genes of the gods!

REFERENCES:

1 Elder Vaughn J. Featherstone, BYU Devotional, Tuesday, September 12, 1995.
2 In an address delivered on 2 June 1839 Joseph Smith taught, "The Spirit [intelligence] of man is not a created being; it existed from eternity, and will exist to eternity. Anything created cannot be eternal" (JD 6:238) Later in the King Follett address delivered Sunday, 7 April 1844, Joseph Smith said, "The mind of man—the intelligent part—is as immortal as, and is co-equal with, God himself"... "Intelligence is eternal and exists upon a self existent principle. It is a spirit from age to age and there is no creation about it. The first principles of man are self existent with God" While he tried to teach this doctrine plainly, the record that survived the Prophet Joseph does not make it entirely clear whether this "intelligence" he spoke of is something individual or collective in nature.
Because so little has been revealed about the precise nature of intelligence, two basic theological positions have developed in the Church. Several of the twelve have believed that intelligence is individual and that we were self existent entities before we entered our spirit bodies. Others in the presiding quorums of the Church, taking a more cautious approach, have concluded that intelligence or spirit matter

is a collection of primal element from which spirit offspring were created and organized.

President Joseph Fielding Smith summarizes all that is really known about the subject in the following statement, "We know, however, that there is something called intelligence which has always existed. It is the real eternal part of man, which was not created or made. This intelligence combined with the spirit constitutes a spiritual identity or individual." (*Answers to Gospel Questions* 4:127)

3 *Teachings of the Prophet Joseph Smith*, 352; emphasis added.

4 *Teachings*, 354-55; emphasis added.

5 Ballard, Melvin J. *Sermons and Missionary Services of Melvin J. Ballard*, comp. Bryant S. Hinckley, 140. Salt Lake City, 1949.

6 *Journal of Discourses*, 6:31; emphasis added.

7 *Conference Report*, October 1983, 22.

8 *Hymns*, The Church of Jesus Christ of Latter-day Saints, 1985, #301

9 See Joseph Fielding Smith Jr., *Doctrines of Salvation*, Vol. 1:145, 184; Abra. 3:21-26; 5:7; Moses 3:5; 6:51; Ether 3:6-16; 1 Ne. 11:18; Rev. 12:7-9; Abra. 3:22-28; Titus 1:1-2.

10 When Joseph Smith set the words of this revelation in rhyme scheme, he used the expression "Whose inhabitant, too, from the first to the last, Are sav'd by the very same Saviour of ours; And, of course, are begotten God's daughters and sons, By the very same truth, and the very same pow'rs" (*Times and Seasons* Vol. 4, No. 6)

11 *Encyclopedia of Mormonism*, Vol. 2, MAN OF HOLINESS

12 *Hymns*, #292 emphasis added.

13 *Messages of the First Presidency of the Church of Jesus Christ of Latter-day Saints*, 4:200-206; emphasis added.

14 See Talmage, *Jesus the Christ*, 7-8.

15 *Doctrines of Salvation*, 1:65; cf. Jude 1:6.

16 *Teachings*, 149.

17 *Mormon Doctrine*, 2d ed., [Salt Lake City: Bookcraft, 1966], 216. Emphasis added).

18 *Conference Report*, October 1973, 7-8.

19 *Teachings*, 189; emphasis added.

20 Paul said, not all who are born through the lineage of Abraham automatically receive the promised blessings, "For they are not all Israel, which are of Israel" (Romans 9:6). This means that not all who were called Jews in the New Testament times were necessarily among the noble and great ones. This fact is made obvious when one considers the idea that certain Jews killed the God of the universe.

21 For information regarding the fact that David did not make his calling election sure, see *Teaching of the Prophet Joseph Smith*, 339.

22 *Teachings*, 365.

23 Cf. *Doctrines of Salvation* 1:60.

24 For a discussion of agency and the foreknowledge of God, see Neal A Maxwell, "A More Determined Discipleship," *Ensign*, Feb. 1979, 69-73.

25 Some of the doctrinal points President Taylor discusses in this document may apply specifically to the sister in question while other points may have general application to all Church members.

26 John Taylor, in *The Vision; or, The Degrees of Glory* comp. by N. B. Lundwall, [Salt Lake City: Bookcraft, 1951] 145-48.

FIGURE 1-A: THE DOCTRINE OF ELECTION

Principles

1. Man as intelligence is a self-existent being with God. Intelligence never was created (D&C 93:29).

2. "Organized intelligences" are spirit children of God. Intelligences were organized as spirits through a process of procreation (Abraham 3:22-23).

3. There was great variety of devotion to truth among the spirit children of God. Some were noble and great; others were less so. One-third were cast out because of rebellion against God (Abraham 3:22; Rev. 12:4).

4. Abraham was shown in vision that he was among the noble and great ones and had been chosen of God before he was born (Abraham 3:22-23).

5. Generally, the noble and great spirits are born through the lineage of Abraham, Isaac, and Jacob (the House of Israel).

6. These noble and great spirits were called and elected to become rulers and gods. They were foreordained to receive the blessings of the priesthood in mortality and eternal life in the world to come (2 Peter 1:10).

7. Those who were called and elected in the premortal world must make their calling and election sure in mortality by proving themselves true and faithful in all things (2 Peter 1:10).

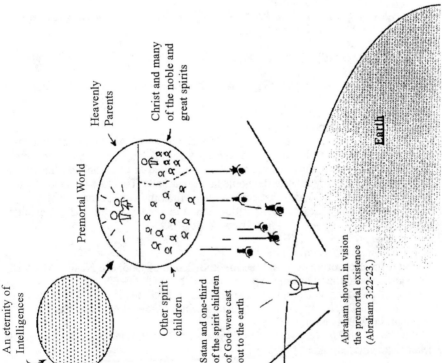

An eternity of Intelligences

Premortal World

Heavenly Parents

Christ and many of the noble and great spirits

Other spirit children

Satan and one-third of the spirit children of God were cast out to the earth

Abraham shown in vision the premortal existence (Abraham 3:22-23.)

Earth

CHAPTER TWO

THE CREATION
OF THE EARTH

The earth rolls upon her wings, and the sun giveth his light by day, and the moon giveth her light by night, and the stars also give their light, as they roll upon their wings in their glory, in the midst of the power of God.

—D&C 88:455

When I was a teenager working for my sister in Canada, I did the spring and fall plowing. I learned quickly that the ground can be too wet for plowing. If it was too wet, the plow shares would stick, and the tractor could not pull through the gooey mess. Sometimes the ground was just slightly wet. Then the soil would turn but would also lump together so that the field looked like waves on the surface of a lake during a wind storm. The clumps made the tractor unmanageable as it meandered to and fro over the hills and valleys.

If the ground was too dry the plowed soil quickly settled into a hard pack not conducive to seed germination. The dust raised by the plow was almost unbearable. Hair, lungs, and skin accumulated layer upon layer of dust and dirt. The oil from the engine of the tractor collected the dust as if it were a magnet, giving the false impression that the thick insulation of dust on moving parts was good for the machinery. The dust collected on me in the same way. When I breathed the dust through my mouth—because my nose was so clogged—my teeth became coated with the dust, making me look like I was toothless.

But when the earth had the right moisture content, it was a delight to plow the ground and sometimes I stopped the tractor and sifted through the spongy soil with my bare hands. To me, the rich, black earth had a peculiar odor like the smell of raw, wet potatoes.

Sometimes I would stop the vibrating tractor to rest my legs and arms from the perpetual shaking. I remember one time I jumped down from the tractor to sift the soil through my fingers, and I wondered just how many particles of dirt make up this earth. I knew there would have to be a finite number of atoms and molecules because this is a finite world. But just how many particles are there? Does such a large number have a name, and how many zeros are there in the number?

Others before me, I am sure, have wondered the same things. Enoch, reflecting upon how the heavens could weep over the wickedness of the people during Noah's time, remarked on the vastness of the cosmos and the extent of God's love for his children. He prayed unto the Lord saying, "How is it that thou canst weep, seeing thou art holy, and from all eternity to all eternity? And were it possible that man could *number* the particles of this earth, yea, millions of earths like this, it would not be a beginning to the *number* of thy creations; and thy curtains are stretched out still; and yet thou art there, and thy bosom is there; and also thou art just; thou art merciful and kind forever" (Moses 7:29-30; emphasis added).

Enoch was awestruck by the loving mercy and the concern of our Heavenly Father for the inhabitants of this small earth which is such an infinitesimal part of the vastness of his creations. I, too, am inspired with the extent of the cosmos of which you and I occupy such a tiny part. I am moved by the vivid imagery used by Enoch, and I wonder with him about the events and processes of the creation. To me every inch of this earth is a miracle and when I ponder the mysteries of how it all came together, I feel overwhelmed—I can't grasp it all.

This desire to merge or become one with in the vastness of beautiful earthly scenery is a constant with me. When I go to the beach across from home, I see, feel, hear, and taste the sea and know that I do not grasp the power and might of what I am witnessing. When the surf pounds against the shore, it sprays in my face, I feel the sand between my toes, I smell and taste the salt in the air and I see the blue-green color of the ocean reflect the brilliance of the kodachrome sky. I am awe struck and feel to look upward and thank Heavenly Father for the beauty of the earth he has created for you and me. I had the same feelings when I went to the Grand Canyon—I knew that I was not taking it all in—I wanted to be one with it, and I couldn't figure out how to do that.

The vastness of our earth is awe-inspiring, yet it *is only one of the creations* which were formed by the power of God's Only Begotten Son (D&C 76:24). Actually, we know so very little regarding *how* the world was made, but we have considerable scriptural information about its *purposes* and some information about the *personalities* involved.

There is so much to learn. Gaining knowledge of our Heavenly Father's great plan for our happiness is such a wonderful treasure hunt. Now let's search further and try to enlarge our understandings of the processes, purposes, and personalities associated with the Creation by reflecting further upon the events of the premortal Council in Heaven.

THE PREMORTAL COUNCIL

From time to time our Heavenly Father has shown his prophets and they have shared with us, some of the extensive preparations that were made in the heavenly Council before the foundations of the earth were ever laid. As children loved by Heavenly Father, we were participants in the grand Council in heaven that was called to plan our descent to this earth. We must have realized more then than we do now the marvelous advantages that earth life would provide us. When the decision to create the earth was presented we are told that we all shouted for joy (Job 38:4-7). A wonderful opportunity was being made available for us. We were being offered experiences that would prepare us to become like our heavenly parents.

As we discussed in the previous chapter, we had observed countless numbers of our spirit brothers and sisters entering mortality on other worlds, gaining their resurrection and exaltation. With yearning anticipation we longed for the time to come when we could imitate them by going to an earth, receiving physical bodies, learning good from evil, and thus advancing on the pathway to exaltation. In order to accomplish these wonderfully exciting objectives this physical earth that we now call our home was created.

Do you know that it is probable that you were a participant in that grand Council, that planning meeting? Do you know that in that premortal state you likely possessed creative powers that are presently beyond your imagination? In this life, with the veil drawn across your mind, you have forgotten who you really were and what role you performed in that great premortal world.

Only through the information learned from latter-day scriptures, the teachings of latter-day prophets, and promptings of the Spirit do the strings of your heart vibrate in holy recognition that you may were among those certain noble and great spirits—the favorites of heaven—who helped to create this beautiful earth.

The scriptural accounts of the Creation with the Prophet Joseph Smith's commentary provide us with a flood of light regarding these events of long ago.

From the book of Genesis we read the simple statement that, "In the beginning God created the heaven and the earth" (Genesis 1:1). However, Joseph Smith explained that before men corrupted the Bible, the first verse read, "'The head one of the Gods brought forth the Gods.' That is the true meaning of the words.... *Thus the head God brought forth the Gods in the grand council.*[1] The Prophet explained further: "In the beginning, the head of the Gods called a council of the Gods; and they came together and concocted a plan to create the world and people it. When we begin to learn this way, we begin to learn the only true God, and what kind of a being we have got to worship."[2]

Who was the *head God* who brought forth the *Gods* in the grand council and who were the *Gods*? What role, if any, did you and I play in that great family meeting? Let's now discuss some possible answers to these questions.

CHRIST AND THE NOBLE AND GREAT ONES

All things relative to our immortality and eternal life are performed by or under the direction of our Heavenly Father—our great and Eternal Heavenly Father, our God who stands at the head of the human family. But our Heavenly Father does not do all the work by himself. Jehovah, Michael, the Holy Ghost, and other faithful spirits had specialized roles and responsibilities and performed important functions under our Heavenly Father's direction.

The Prophet Joseph Smith explained how the roles of the various members of the Godhead are interrelated. He said that an "everlasting covenant was made between three personages before the organization of this earth, and relates to their dispensation of things to men on the earth; these personages, according to Abraham's record, are called God the first, the *Creator*; God the second, the *Redeemer*; and God the third, the *witness* or Testator."³ These three are respectively the Father, the Son, and the Holy Ghost. Heavenly Father is the Creator of our spirit bodies and of Adam's and Eve's physical bodies. Jesus is our Redeemer, and the Holy Ghost is the Witness of the Father and the Son and of the great principles of truth and righteousness that are inherent within the gospel of Jesus Christ.

Even though our Heavenly Father stands supreme in his patriarchal authority as our Creator, it is through Jesus Christ, the Son, that he performs many of his mighty works in the creation of worlds without number. "Worlds without number have I created," declared our Heavenly Father to Moses, "*And by the Son I created them, which is mine Only Begotten*" (Moses 1:33; emphasis added; see also Hebrews 1:2).

In addition to our own earth, many other worlds have been created by Jesus—or Jehovah—as he was known in the premortal world. Furthermore, the inhabitants of these other worlds are also redeemed by Jesus Christ. We learn this from the Doctrine and Covenants which states:

> And now, after the many testimonies which have been given of him, this is the testimony, last of all, which we give of him: That he lives!
>
> For we saw him, even on the right hand of God; and we heard the voice bearing record that he is the Only Begotten of the Father—
>
> That by him and through him and of him, *the worlds are and were created, and the inhabitants thereof are begotten sons and daughters unto God* (D&C 76:22-24; emphasis added).

Jesus, then, was the central figure involved in the actual creation of this and other worlds. From the Book of Abraham we learn other spirits also participated in the Creation. From this sacred text we learn that besides Jesus (who was known as Jehovah) and Adam (who was know as Michael) there were many other spirits—certain noble and great ones—who sat in the grand planning Council and who later assisted in the formation of this earth.

Our Heavenly Father, the head God, commissioned Jesus to call together those noble and great spirits who stood with him, and they—that is Jesus and the noble and great ones—decided to go down and form this earth. We read the book of Abraham: "And there stood *one among them that was like unto God* [Jesus], and he said unto *those who were with him* [the noble and great ones]: We will go down, for there is space there, and we will take of these materials, and we will make an earth whereon these may dwell" (Abraham 3:24; emphasis added).

Do you realize what you have just read? You have just read that as spirits, Jesus along with the noble and great ones, performed the Creation. As we have explained in the previous chapter, the noble and great ones are those spirits who were called and elected to be born through the lineage of Abraham and Israel, and you, my dear reader, are of the house of Israel. Could it be that you not only shouted for joy at the prospects of coming to this earth, but also that you actually performed a role in helping to create this earth?

I have heard some LDS educators suggest that we need to study the sciences—zoology and botany, geography and astronomy and such—so that we will be prepared to create our own worlds in future times. Could it be that we already have this kind of knowledge stored somewhere in our intelligence, knowledge that will be retrieved in the proper time but which for the present is gone from us?

This is not to suggest that gaining scientific and worldly knowledge in this life is not valuable. Serious searching after earthly knowledge helps us appreciate the beauty and exquisite workmanship manifest everywhere we look: in the heavens above and in the earth below. Our eyes are opened more fully, however, when we couple our knowledge of the physical world with revealed truths given us through the prophets by a loving Father in Heaven. The Lord explained the need for this balance when he said, "To be learned is good if they hearken unto the counsels of God" (2 Nephi 9:29).

We do not realize who we really are as members of The Church of Jesus Christ of Latter-day Saints—latter-day Israel! We have a hard time thinking that we may have been among the noble and great ones associated with Jesus in the Creation of the earth. We think too often that that select group included only the prophets and maybe their wives. And yet, this is one of the important the messages of father Abraham's writings.

Because you were actively involved in the planning and creation of this earth, you now thrill when seeing a beautiful sunset, when observing a

magnificent animal, when seeing the magical metamorphosis of a caterpillar turning into a beautifully winged flying creature, or when smelling the fragrance of a
beautiful, breathtaking flower. Could it be that you had a part in the premortal
design of some of these earthly wonders? Could it be that you might have been a
participant in their placement upon the earth? Think about it! Do you really
understand who you are? Do you really understand all that has been done in times
past so that you might experience earth life now and eternal life in the world to
come?

The whisperings of the spirit give us a glimpse from time to time regarding
these thrilling and sacred ideas.

While we consider and admire the beauty of the earth, it is important to realize that the intricate and wonderful organization of plants, animals, earth, sky and
seas did not come about by chance. Happily, the knowledge of your role in the
Creation will be restored in proper time. You will then remember that Jesus Christ
and you along with many other noble and great spirits were actively and joyfully
involved in the creation of this earth. Intelligent design is clearly manifest in all
we observe, and you played a wonderful and important role in this glorious work.

THE CREATION BY INTELLIGENT DESIGN

The earth's complexity and beauty did not come about through random
forces. Unless an intelligent influence is exercised on matter it tends to move
toward the less complex, toward chaos, toward *entropy*— which is the degrada-
tion of matter and energy in the universe to an ultimate state of inert uniformity—
toward death. Mountains wear down, temperatures cool, cars rust, toys break, our
bodies wear out and are subject to disease and death.

As I watch some of the nature and science programs on television I am frequently taken back by how vicious our world is—animals are killing and eating
each other, wars, floods, hurricanes are running rampant—there is death and
destruction all around us. These terrible conditions have not always existed nor
will they exist forever. The Fall of Adam introduced death, this entropy, but
through the Atonement of Christ all that is now broken will be mended. Death
will be overcome, tears will be wiped away and all who are broken will be made
whole. Joseph Smith promised that "all your losses will be made up to you in the
resurrection, provided you continue faithful. By the vision of the Almighty I have
seen it."[4] This promise of the Lord can sustain in the face of losses of things we
hold dear—such as family, friends, possessions, and health—due to the influences of this fallen world. There is growth potential in adversity. As bad as some
things appear in this world now, remember that there is purpose and design
behind all things.

Think of what would happen if your wristwatch were left on an ocean beach. Do you think that over time your watch would become more complex and acquire a second hand or some other sophisticated function? If you were to leave it there for hundreds of years would it become more complex? For sure it would not! Instead, by the action of wind and water, sand particles and salt will work their way into the watch until finally it becomes so clogged with sand that it can function no longer, and the metal parts will deteriorate because of the corrosive agents. The leather strap will rot and fall to pieces. Creating a complex watch and keeping it in proper working order requires the intelligence of both a watchmaker and a repairman.

Similarly, the intelligent design needed to create the earth is also needed to maintain it, and here is an overall plan behind all that happens or is allowed to happen. Jesus Christ is the Creator and the preserver of all the intricately balanced details associated with the earth and the abundant life that resides upon it. He is "The light which is in all things, which giveth life to all things, which is the law by which all things are governed, even the power of God who sitteth upon his throne, who is in the bosom of eternity, who is in the midst of all things" (D&C 88:13). Jesus is truly the Light and Life of the world. By his power all of our Father's creations were formed and are maintained.

A. Cressy Morrison, a scientist and Past President of the New York Academy of Sciences, has observed and celebrated the delicate interplay of complex factors necessary to maintain life on the earth. He has written:

> The earth rotates on its axis in twenty-four hours or at the rate of about one thousand miles an hour. Suppose it turned at the rate of a hundred miles an hour. Why not? Our days and nights would then be ten times as long as now. The hot sun of summer would then burn up our vegetation each long day and every sprout would freeze in such a night.
>
> The sun, the source of all life, has a surface temperature of 12,000 degrees Fahrenheit, and our earth is just far enough away so that this 'eternal fire' warms us just enough and not too much. It is marvelously stable, and during millions of years has varied so little that life as we know it has survived. If the temperature on earth had changed so much as fifty degrees on the average for a single year, all vegetation would be dead and man with it, roasted or frozen.
>
> The earth travels around the sun at the rate of eighteen miles each second. If the rate of revolution had been, say, six miles or forty miles each second, we would be too far from or too close to the sun for our form of life to exist....
>
> The earth is tilted at an angle of twenty-three degrees. This gives us our seasons. If it had not been tilted, the poles would be in eternal twilight. The water vapor from the ocean would move north and south, piling up

continents of ice and leaving possibly a desert between the equator and the ice. Glacial rivers would erode and roar through canyons into the salt-covered bed of the ocean to form temporary pools of brine. The weight of the unbelievably vast mass of ice would depress the poles, causing our equator to bulge or erupt or at least show the need of a new waistline belt. The lowering of the ocean would expose vast new land areas and diminish the rainfall in all parts of the world, with fearful results....

The moon is 240,000 miles away, and the tides twice a day are usually a gentle reminder of its presence. Tides of the ocean run as high as sixty feet in some places, and even the crust of the earth is twice a day bent outward several inches by the moon's attraction. All seems so regular that we do not grasp to any degree the vast power that lifts the whole area of the ocean several feet and bends the crust of the earth, seemingly so solid.

Mars has a moon—a little one—only six thousand miles away from it. If our moon were, say, fifty thousand miles away instead of its present respectable distance, our tides would be so enormous that twice a day all the lowland of all the continents would be submerged by a rush of water so enormous that even the mountains would soon be eroded away, and probably no continent could have risen from the depths fast enough to exist today. The earth would crack with the turmoil and the tides in the air would create daily hurricanes.[5]

All of these intricately balanced laws are manifestations of our Father's love for you and me. Everything the Lord does he does for the overall happiness of all his creations—so that they might fulfill the design of their creation and have joy. There are many other critically balanced conditions that are necessary in order to maintain and sustain life on our marvelous floating sphere. The intricacies of nature detected directly through observation or indirectly through mathematics are indeed wonderful to behold.

Speaking at a BYU Devotional assembly, Dr. Paul Cox suggested that appreciating earth's beauty includes recognizing God's role as creator. Knowledge of the physical mechanisms of the universe is no excuse for rejecting God from a person's life. Instead, understanding scientific principles should actually heighten an appreciation for the creation and the creator. "My understanding of a few scientific details...does not reduce my admiration for the artist," he said. "Instead, each new thing I learn serves only to increase my awe and my appreciation for his work and my desire to protect it."[6]

We are just beginning to fathom the relationships between the theory of relativity and quantum mechanics. The more we learn, the more impressed we are that intelligent design exists behind the Creation of this earth and that this intelligent design centers in Jesus Christ. Our Savior is in and through all things. Through his power the worlds are and were created and are maintained. It is through him that all things have their being. He is the Light and the Life of the world. He is God's Almighty Son—the Creator of the earth and Savior of all mankind. And all things were organized and created for you and me as sons and daughters of God as a part of his great plan for our happiness.

THE PLACE OF THE CREATION—NEARER KOLOB

As we read the scriptures and the words of latter-day prophets, we learn that the earth was created nearer the place where God resides and that when Adam fell, the earth fell through space to where it is now located.

Our separation from God and his other creations may in effect place us in a state of quarantine out in the far limits of the Universe. This idea is plausible when we consider that this is the most wicked of all the worlds (Moses 7:36) and that the Lord may want our world separated from others until it is purified and worthy to be brought back nearer his presence. Because of our quarantine state and other effects of the Fall, this may be the only period in our entire existence in which we live under the illusion that we are not surrounded by love.[7] But this is a temporary state of alienation. That which was lost will be regained.

We have statements in the scriptures and by Presidents of the Church to the effect that this earth was initially formed nearer the star known as *Kolob* which the Lord said was "near unto me" (Abraham 3:2-3). The Prophet Joseph Smith taught his friend, Charles L. Walker, that this earth will be restored to its former place and it will again "revolve in an orbit near to Kolob."[8] Although the information in Brother Walker's diary comes to us secondhand, there were other people close to the Prophet to whom he taught the same idea. President John Taylor, for instance, wrote that the earth "was organized near the planet Kolob."[9] From an 1842 article in the *Times and Seasons*, the Church's newspaper in Nauvoo, we read that sometime after the Fall, the earth was hurled into the immensity of space.[10]

Elder Orson Pratt taught that the earth has occupied its present orbit around the sun "for six thousand years".[11] Although he did not explain where the earth was first created, he dated the earth in its present orbit sometime after the initial creation of the earth and after life had been placed on it. Brigham Young concurred:

> This earth is our home, it was framed expressly for the habitation of those who are faithful to God, and who prove themselves worthy to inherit the earth when the Lord shall have sanctified, purified, and glorified it and brought it back into his presence, from which *it fell far into space*.... When the earth was framed and brought into existence and man was placed upon

it, it was near the throne of our Father in heaven...*but when man fell, the earth fell into space*, and took up its abode in this planetary system, and the sun became our light.... This is the glory the earth came from, and when it is glorified it will return again unto the presence of the Father, and it will dwell there....[12]

In another address President Young stated: "This earthly ball, this little opake substance thrown off into space, is only a speck in the great universe; and when it is celestialized *it will go back into the presence of God*, where it was first framed. All belongs to God, and those who keep his celestial law will return to him."[13]

From these readings we get a glimpse of tremendous cosmic forces used by our Heavenly Father to bring into existence our mortal world—and he will yet bring about other vast cosmic changes all of which are designed for our eternal happiness and glory.

And thus we see that at the time of Creation our *place* in the universe was different from the where it is now. We also learn from the prophets that the measurement of *time* was different at the time of the Creation.

THE CREATION ACCORDING TO GOD'S TIME

The Prophet Joseph Smith gave an affirmative answer to the question "Is not the reckoning of God's time, angel's time, prophet's time, and man's time, according to the planet on which they reside?" (D&C 130:4).

The apostle Peter also taught that time was variable. He compared the Lord's time with our time and said, "Be not ignorant of this one thing, that one day is with the Lord as a thousand years, and a thousand years as one day" (2 Peter 3:8). This statement is probably meant to be taken literally—one day with the Lord is literally a thousand years with man. This is a novel idea when we consider that many Jews and Christians believe that the earth was created in six 24 hour periods, according to our present way of measuring time. However, we as Latter-day Saints understand the six-day time frame to be metaphoric and may represent thousand year periods—or even longer. We know this to be true because in the Book of Abraham the creative periods are not called d "days" but are referred to as "the first time, the second time, etc." (Abraham 4, 5).

The Book of Abraham reports that before the Fall, Adam's measurement of time was after the time of Kolob. The Lord warned Adam when he placed him in the garden of Eden, "For in the *time* that thou eatest thereof, thou shalt surely die. Now I, Abraham, saw that *it was after the Lord's time, which was after the time of Kolob*; for as yet the Gods had not appointed unto Adam his reckoning" (Abraham 5:13; emphasis added).

The fact that the Gods did not "appoint unto Adam his reckoning" when he was first placed in the Garden of Eden means that time as we know it now came as a result of the Fall. The measuring time from the Fall until the end of the Millennium will constitute a temporal existence of seven thousand years (see D&C 77:6, 12).

Now that we have discussed some of the space and time considerations associated with the Creation, let's look at some of the *processes* involved in Creation—in other words what the Lord and those who were with him did and did not do in connection with Creation.

NOTHING COMES FROM NOTHING

Did your ever consider that nothing is the only thing that can ever come from nothing? Yet there are many people who believe that the Lord created the earth out of nothing. During the Nineteenth Century many Christians held the belief, called *Creationism*, that God created the earth *ex nihlio* (out of nothing); and that he created all things in six twenty-four hour days.[14]

Latter-day Saints are the only Bible-oriented people who have always taught that things were happening long, long before Adam appeared on the scene. We have never appreciated just how revolutionary that idea is. This does away with the *creatio ex nihilo*. Mormons understand that when the world was created it was organized out of *existing* material. Forms of matter and energy can be exchanged, but neither can be created nor destroyed. The Prophet Joseph Smith explained,

> You ask the learned doctors why they say the world was made out of nothing; and they will answer, 'Doesn't the Bible say He *created* the world?' And they infer, from the word create, that it must have been made out of nothing. Now, the word create came from the word *baurau* which does not mean to create out of nothing; it means to organize; the same as a man would organize materials and build a ship. Hence, we infer that God had materials to organize the world out of chaos—chaotic matter, which is element, and in which dwells all the glory. Element had an existence from the time he had. The pure principles of element are principles which can never be destroyed; they may be organized and re-organized, but not destroyed. They had no beginning, and can have no end."[15]

So, from this we learn that nothing is the only thing that ever comes from nothing! Everything comes from something else. Just as your mind or intelligence has existed forever, so the matter from which the earth was organized has always existed.

Elder Orson Pratt also taught that the earth was organized from eternally existing materials. He said that when we speak of a *beginning* of the earth, we mean its organization in its *present* form, not that the elements from which it was organized had a beginning.[16] Elder Pratt also suggested that the elements of this earth may have been used many times over, and that they may have gone through many recycling processes.[17]

Had you ever considered before the idea that the Lord may have used and reused the material from which this earth was organized many times over—much like a potter will use and reuse clay in forming beautiful pottery? In addressing the question of how many times this earth's materials may have been used as parts of other systems, Elder Pratt explained:

> How many transformations this earth passed through before the one spoken of by Moses, I do not know, neither do I particularly care. If it had gone through millions on millions of transformations, it is nothing to us. We are willing, for the sake of argument, to admit that the materials themselves are as old as geologists dare to say they are; but then, that does not destroy the idea of a God, that does not destroy the idea of a great Creator, who, according to certain fixed and unalterable laws, brought these materials, from time to time, into a certain organization, and then by his power completed the worlds that were thus made, by placing thereon intelligent and animated beings, capable of thinking and having an existence.[18]

The Prophet Joseph Smith declared that life has been going on in this system for many millions of years. In a letter written by William W. Phelps to William Smith, the Prophet's brother, he stated that Joseph had told him, "that eternity, agreeably to the records found in the catacombs of Egypt, has been going on in this system almost *two thousand five hundred and fifty five millions of years.*"[19] This number when written out looks like this: 2,555,000,000 and that is a lot of years during which eternity has been going on. Since eternity has been going on in this system—which would at least include this earth—for some 2,555 million years, then the materials from which the earth was created or organized should show evidence of an even greater degree of antiquity than has been suggested by science.

This newly revealed information about the creation of the earth from self-existing materials strengthens our faith because it is consistent with what we know scientifically about matter and energy. Matter can be changed back and forth from energy into matter and from matter into energy, but neither energy nor matter can be created nor can they be destroyed—they can only be changed back and forth, shaped, organized and reorganized.

We know that the earth was formed from matter that has eternally existed, but still we know very little regarding the kinds, types, or forms of the elements that were organized. Even though we know that the Lord brought existing materials together, we do not know very much about the *processes* involved in the Creation.

Have you ever wondered how he did it? How long it *really* took to create everything? Were the particles that were brought together small atoms, molecules, cosmic dust, or were they the size of boulders and mountains? Is it possible that there may have even been fossils already existing in these fragments when they were brought together? How are you and I to understand the various scriptural accounts regarding the sequence of days of Creation—especially when they seem to be contradictory within themselves and between each another?

There are many unanswered questions regarding the Creation, but we have the promise that a day will come when our Heavenly Father will reveal all things to us (see D&C 121:26-32). I can hardly wait to learn about dinosaurs, non-historic people, and how true science and religion fit together. In the meantime, while we are patiently waiting for a fuller understanding, let's take a look at what our scriptures say about the Creation.

THE BOOKS OF GENESIS AND MOSES

In addition to the biblical account of the Creation found in Genesis, we Latter-day Saints have two modern restorations of ancient scriptural accounts of the Creation found in the books of Moses and Abraham. In addition we have related authoritative information in the Book of Mormon, the Doctrine and Covenants, and the LDS temple ceremony.

Creation has an important doctrinal role in the Book of Mormon. The Book of Mormon prophets used the Creation as a example of our Heavenly Father's goodness and kindness to his children. Nephi explained, "The Lord hath created the earth that it should be inhabited; and he hath created his children that they should possess it" (1 Nephi 17:36). The events surrounding the Creation are connected with the fall of Lucifer (2 Nephi 2:17; 9:8). His fall led to the Fall of Adam; opposition as a feature of mortal existence; and, ultimately, the need for a divine redemption of mankind (2 Nephi 2:18-27). The Genesis account of the Creation only hints at these doctrines that the Book of Mormon describes in clearer detail.

The Genesis account of the Creation is the one with which most people are familiar. The word *genesis* means literally, "the beginning"—in this case, Genesis means the beginning of events associated with this earth. Accordingly, we read that "In the beginning God created the heaven and the earth" (Genesis 1:1).

Genesis was written by Moses sometime between the time of the burning bush and the exodus from Egypt (Moses 1:17, 24). In his account, Moses describes events associated with the Creation, the Fall, Noah and the Flood, and happenings surrounding the lives of the Patriarchs (Abraham, Isaac, Jacob, and Joseph). God showed Moses, in open vision, all these introductory events and then commanded him to write them down for future generations.

As Bible loving people, we are grateful for Moses' writings regarding the beginning of the earth. However, we are saddened that much of what he wrote originally has been lost. The book of Genesis was a much larger book at one time. We know that translators have made many errors unintentionally, but we also know that they have left out many important truths deliberately. Accordingly, our Eighth Article of Faith states that, "We believe the Bible to be the word of God as far as it is translated correctly."

Happily, the Lord promised Moses that even though important parts of his writing would be lost, they would be restored at a latter day. Through a man like Moses, whom we know to be the Prophet Joseph Smith, they would be had again. Here are the words of the Lord's promise:

> And now, Moses, my son, I will speak unto thee concerning this earth upon which thou standest; and thou shalt write the things which I shall speak. And in a day when the children of men shall esteem my words as naught *and take many of them from the book which thou shalt write*, behold, I will raise up another like unto thee; and *they shall be had again* among the children of men—among as many as shall believe (Moses 1:40-41; emphasis added).

From this scripture we see that the Lord loved us so much that he initially revealed the Creation story to Moses, and then when much of that was lost, he loved us enough to restore these truths through the Prophet Joseph Smith. The Book of Moses, then, is a restoration of many of the lost words from the book of Genesis. In order to restore this material, the Lord showed the Prophet Joseph Smith the *same vision of the Creation* that he had given to Moses originally. This vision made it possible for the Prophet to write the account of the Creation again, just as Moses had seen and had written it originally—hence, our Book of Moses contained in the Pearl of Great Price.[20] Also within that volume, we find another sacred book that contains a wonderful account of the Creation, the Book of Abraham.

THE BOOK OF ABRAHAM

Have you ever noticed that when you talk to a child and describe an event you use different words and examples than you do when you speak to an adult? For example, if a five-year-old asks you where he came from, you might say "Tallahassee" or say the name of the city where the child was born. If the child were older and were to ask the same question, you might be more inclined say "you came from inside Mommy's tummy", or if he or she were much older your might give an in-depth description of human reproduction with illustrations and charts. The maturity level of the child determines the depth of the explanation.

This same principle is true in relationship to the story of the Creation. The Genesis and Moses accounts are much more simplistic than is the account found in the Book of Abraham. The Mosaic accounts found in Genesis and Moses are for the spiritually immature. On the other hand, Abraham's account is for the more mature. The children of Israel received their knowledge of the Creation while they were living under the law of carnal commandments, the Aaronic Priesthood order. The Mosaic accounts are designed to meet their under developed spiritual needs as they came out from Egyptian bondage. They were a people so spiritually immature that they could receive neither the blessings, powers, ordinances, nor the deep spiritual doctrinal understandings associated with the Melchizedek Priesthood (see D&C 84:23-24)—including a full understanding of the Creation. So Moses' account of the creation is a very simplistic, elementary description of complex and sacred events.

By comparison, our great ancestral father, Abraham, and his worthy children enjoyed the greater blessings and doctrinal understandings associated with the highest orders of the priesthood—including a greater knowledge of the Creation. They enjoyed a fulness of the Melchizedek Priesthood blessings. Accordingly, the account of the Creation found in the Book of Abraham[21] reflects a much greater magnitude of light, a more detailed description of what was involved. Abraham's writings are unique among the accounts because they describe, among many other doctrinal principles, the participation of "the Gods" in the Creation, the sequence of "days" as periods of preparation for the placement of life upon the earth, the structure of the cosmos with many stars, one above another, all with their different time periods and orders of government (see Abraham 3:1-10).

As we read and compare Moses' and Abraham's accounts of the Creation, then, it will be helpful to consider Abraham's writings as reflecting the higher or Melchizedek Priesthood point of view and Moses' accounts a lower, or an Aaronic Priesthood point of view. By comparing the contributions of these wonderful books you will find significant differences—none of which are of greater interest than those associated with the events of the seventh day. As you review the comments presented below, you might want to have your Standard Works with you for comparison purposes.

EVENTS OF THE FIRST DAY

Genesis Chapter 1:1-5
1. This is a very terse account.
2. Joseph Smith said that the expression "'Without form and void'... should be read, empty and desolate" (*Teachings*, 181).
3. God speaks here in the third person singular.
4. Light is provided on this day but not from our present sun.
5. Day and night are divided.
6. The measurement of one day begins in the evening and ends in the evening. Jewish customs reflect this belief even today. Their Sabbath day begins at sundown Friday evening and ends Saturday evening.

Moses Chapter 2:1-5
1. God explains that all things were created by "mine Only Begotten."
2. "I, God," is spoken in first person. This is an authoritative style.
3. God *caused* darkness to come upon the face of the deep.
4. This account reflects Joseph's revision of Genesis. Much of the wording, however, is the same as in the Genesis account.
5. It is interesting that light is provided before the sun and the moon as we know them are created.
6. Day and night are divided.

Abraham Chapter 4:1-5
1. Abraham wrote his account in view of the *plans* that were made in the grand council of the Gods.
2. Gods are identified in the third person plural.
3. Light is provided.
4. Day and night are divided.
5. Beginning of the *first time* that they called day and night.

EVENTS OF THE SECOND DAY

Genesis Chapter 1:6-8
1. The waters are separated, those above from those beneath.

2. The firmament appears to consist of the atmosphere, the skies, or the heavens.
3. The heavens are prepared so that rain may fall later.

Moses Chapter 2:6-8
1. Few changes made by Joseph Smith regarding the second day's activities.
2. God continues to speak in first person.
3. The waters are separated, those above from those beneath.

Abraham Chapter 4:6-8
1. Abraham's account uses the term *expanse* in place of *firmament*.
2. Events are completed as ordered on this day.
3. The waters are separated, those above from those beneath.

EVENTS OF THE THIRD DAY

Genesis Chapter 1:9-13
1. The land emerges from the water and becomes dry.
2. The land mass was probably in one piece, not fragmented into continents and islands as we have now (see D&C 133:23-24).
3. God commands the earth to bring forth the vegetation.

Moses Chapter 2:9-13
1. God is still speaking in first person.
2. The land is separated from water, as in the Genesis account.
3. Plant life is brought forth.

Abraham Chapter 4:9-13
1. Land and water are separated, as in Genesis and Moses accounts.
2. A different point of view is introduced in this account. Interestingly, the earth is *prepared* to bring forth plant life, but vegetation is not placed yet on the earth.
3. The earth was organized *to bring forth* vegetation.

EVENTS OF THE FOURTH DAY

Genesis Chapter 1:14-19
1. Two great lights are made, the sun and the moon, and also the stars.
2. This is interesting because on the first day the Lord said, "Let there be light"

and yet the sun, moon, and stars are not created until the fourth day. Where did the light come from that was commanded to appear on the first day?
3. These heavenly bodies—sun, moon, and, stars—are to be for signs, seasons, days, and years.

Moses Chapter 2:14-19
1. No significant changes on this day from the Genesis account.
2. God speaks in first person
3. Some greater detail. The greater light is identified as the sun and the lesser light as the moon. Things were made according to God's word.

Abraham Chapter 4:14-19
1. The Gods organize the lights in the "expanse" of the heavens.
2. The sun, moon, and stars were probably organized away from where the earth was first organized.
3. The earth at this point was in the Lord's time frame. It was near Kolob and was not yet receiving its light from our present sun and moon (see Abraham 5:13).

EVENTS OF THE FIFTH DAY

Genesis Chapter 1:20-23
1. God commands the waters to bring forth life.
2. The fowls are created to fly in the firmament, or skies.
3. All life is commanded to multiply after its own kind.

Moses Chapter 2:20-23
1. God is still speaking in the first person.
2. God creates the fish of the sea and the great whales.
3. Winged fowl are created.
4. All fish and winged fowl are commanded to multiply after their kind.

Abraham 4:20-23
1. The Gods *prepare* the waters for life.
2. They also *prepare* for every winged fowl.
3. The Gods state they *will bless* the fish of the sea and the winged fowls and *will cause* them to multiply (future tense).

Events of The Sixth Day

Genesis Chapter 1:24-31
1. God made the beasts, cattle, and creeping things.
2. God creates man and woman.
3. Man and woman are to have dominion over all other life.
4. They are commanded to multiply.
5. They are given every herb bearing seed and the fruit of trees to be used for meat.
6. Herbs are given as meat for the beasts.
7. Things were pronounced "very good" before the Fall.

Moses Chapter 2:24-31
1. God creates the beasts, cattle, and creeping things.
2. Man and woman are created.
3. They are commanded to multiply, subdue the earth, and have dominion over the animals.
4. They are given plant and tree seeds. Fruits and herbs are to be used for meat.
6. All things pronounced "very good" before the Fall.

Abraham Chapter 4:24-31
1. The Gods *prepare* the earth *to bring forth* the living creatures, cattle, creeping things, and the beasts.
2. The Gods take counsel to go down *to form man* (future time).
3. The Gods go down *to organize* man in their own image.
4. The Gods go down to form man—male and female go down *to form man* and woman (note verse 27).
5. The Gods *will bless* them.
6. The Gods *will give* them seeds of edible plant life.
7. The animals *will be given* life.
8. The Gods say they *will do everything* as they *have planned.*

Events of The Seventh Day

Genesis Chapter 2:1-3
1. God *ended* his work on the seventh day.
2. He *rested* from all his work.
3. God blessed and sanctified the seventh day.

Moses Chapter 3:1-3
1. God *ended* his work on the seventh day.
2. He *rested* from all his work.
3. He blessed and sanctified the seventh day.

Abraham Chapter 5:1-3
1. The Gods will end, or complete, all their work on the seventh day—all that they had counseled to do.
2. They will also *rest* from all their work.
3. These were their *decisions* in the premortal councils.

RECAPITULATION STATEMENTS

This section is a summary or a synopsis of all that has happened.

Genesis 2:4-7
1. The statement "and every plant of the field before it was in the earth, and every herb of the field before it grew" is not clear in this account. The Book of Abraham account for this day provides clarification.
2. All things were prepared, but no man was on the earth.
3. Man is formed of the dust of the earth.

Moses 3:4-7
1. All things were prepared, but man was not yet on the earth.
2. Verse 5 appears to be in interpolation. This verse is inserted here to explain that although the earth was prepared for life, there was none yet placed on it. Reference is made to the fact that all things to be placed on the earth had a spirit body creation in the premortal existence. We have no day-by-day account of this creation, only this statement that it happened.
3. A *mist* from the earth waters the whole face of the ground for the first time.
4. Man is placed on the earth. He is the *first flesh* and the first man.
5. The animals come after Adam is placed on the earth.
6. Life is placed on the earth on the *seventh day.*
7. The seventh day is, therefore, *blessed* and *sanctified* because God rested from all his work.
8. The expression "rest of the Lord" is defined as a "fulness of his glory" (D&C 84:24) and also refers to his "presence" (JST, Exodus 34:1-2).

Abraham Chapter 5:4-7
1. On the seventh day the Gods finally carry out all their plans. They now do as they had said they *would do.*

2. At the beginning of this time, there is neither rain nor man.

3. A mist waters the ground.

4. The Gods finally form man and give him life.

5. "We are to understand that as God made the world in six days, and on the *seventh day he finished his work, and sanctified it, and also formed man out of the dust of the earth*, even so, in the beginning of the seventh thousand years will the Lord God sanctify the earth" (D&C 77:12).

THE SEVENTH DAY—A PERIOD OF REST

When we compare the information presented by Moses and Abraham regarding the Creation, we find important differences with respect to the events of the seventh day. In Moses' account, God finishes his work and rests. In Abraham's account, God is very active and places all life—including man—upon the earth.

A fascinating doctrine, that appears only in our Latter-day Saint scriptures, is the idea that to rest means more than to refrain from physical work. Scripturally speaking, to *rest* means to be in the *presence* of God—the words mean the same. We get this information from the Joseph Smith Translation of Exodus.

In the Joseph Smith translation we find the Lord equating these two terms. He explained to Moses: "I will give unto them the law as at first, but it shall be after the law of a carnal commandment; for I have sworn in my wrath, that they shall not enter into my *presence*, into my *rest*, in the days of their pilgrimage" (JST, Exodus 34:2; emphasis added).

The first set of plates that Moses threw down and broke contained the laws and ordinances that would have prepared Israel to enter into the presence of the Lord. In this scripture the Lord tells Moses that the second set of plates that he would receive would contain only the lesser laws of the gospel—the Aaronic Priesthood portion—and that these laws would not be sufficient to bring the children of Israel into the presence of God, into his rest—as the laws and ordinances on the first set of plates could have.

In the Doctrine and Covenants we find the Lord explaining very clearly the consequences of Israel's provoking the Lord. We read:

Now... Moses plainly taught...the children of Israel in the wilderness, and sought diligently to *sanctify his people that they might behold the face of God*;

But they hardened their hearts and could not endure his presence; therefore, the Lord in his wrath, for his anger was kindled against them, swore that they should not enter into his *rest* while in the wilderness, which *rest is the fulness of his glory* (D&C 84:23-24; emphasis added).

In summary, then, the expression "entering the rest of the Lord" means parting the veil and entering the presence of the Lord. After the Saints in any dispensation are sanctified they are permitted to enter into the presence of the Lord—into his eternal rest (see D&C 93:1; 133:3; Alma 13:12-13). If they do not have the ordinances of the temple, they can not experience this marvelous blessing. This crowning blessing of the gospel will be discussed in greater detail in future chapters.

The example of Enoch and his people gives us insight into the idea that righteous people truly can enter the presence of the Lord in this life, into his eternal rest (see Moses 7:21, 27). After Enoch and his people had been taken into heaven—into the presence and rest of the Lord—he cried unto the Lord wanting to know when the *whole earth* would rest like he and his people; (see Moses 7:48, 54, 58-59, 61-64). He petitioned the Lord in prayer over and over again about when the Lord would honor the remainder of the earth with his presence and usher in a period of *rest*.

In other words, Enoch wanted to know when the Millennium would begin that would be initiated with the Second Coming of the Lord. The Lord answered Enoch's prayer by explaining that the earth will finally rest after a time of two concurrent events: a period of great tribulation among the wicked and a period of great restoration of truth among the righteous—including the building of a New Jerusalem called Zion. "And there shall be mine abode, and it shall be Zion...and for a thousand years the earth shall rest" (Moses 7:64).

This discussion about *rest* being equated with the *presence* of the Lord provides a strong foundation for understanding what really happened during the seventh period of Creation, the day of rest.

THE SEVENTH DAY—A PERIOD OF SACRED ACTIVITY

To rest on the Sabbath does not mean that we should be inactive and sleep away our Sundays. The Lord expects us to *rest* on the Sabbath in the sense that we should involve our thoughts, feelings, and actions in ways that allow us to enjoy the *presence* of the Holy Ghost—a member of the Godhead. Indeed, to rest on the Sabbath means that we participate in activities that allow us to have communion with the Lord by enjoying the presence of his Holy Spirit.

The seventh day is to be a period for righteous labors. Jesus set the example. He performed many works of righteousness on the Sabbath all of which were designed to build up his Father's kingdom. He healed the weak man at the pool of Bethesda on the Sabbath, commanding him to take up his bed and walk (see John 5:2-16). He also healed the man with a withered hand on the Sabbath (see Matthew 12:10-13). The resurrection was accomplished on Sunday (see John 20:1). In commemoration of that sacred work, the Sabbath was changed from Saturday to Sunday.

In explaining the purpose of the Sabbath day, Jesus taught that the Sabbath does not take precedence over the welfare of mankind. When his disciples plucked, husked, and ate ears of corn on the Sabbath, Jesus defended their action with the instruction: "The Sabbath was made for man, and not man for the Sabbath" (Mark 2:27). "Wherefore the Sabbath was given unto man for a day of *rest*; and also that man should glorify God, and not that man should not eat" (JST, Mark 2:26-27; emphasis added).

The Millennium, the seventh thousand years of rest, is frequently spoken of as the Sabbath of the earth's existence. When the Lord comes to usher in his Millennial reign he will initiate a time when there will be an abundance of sacred *activity*, a time of great *rest* in the Lord. Elder Orson Pratt explained that even as God was very active on the seventh day of Creation, so again he and his Saints will be very busy during the Millennium:

> You will find that there is a very great work to be performed, after the seventh thousand years, called the Millennium, has commenced...just as the Lord performed a work on the seventh day of creation, when he planted the Garden of Eden and placed the man Adam therein. He performed quite a temporal work in the process of creation on the morning of the seventh day; and so he will perform a work at the beginning of the seventh thousand years, after the seventh millennium shall open; and the nature of the work, which will then be performed, was typified by that which God performed in the beginning.[22]

The earth rested on the seventh day of Creation in the same way and sense it will rest during the Millennium—the glory and presence of God will be upon it (see D&C 84:24).

When we say that the earth was sanctified and that God rested on the seventh period of Creation, we mean that our Heavenly Father was *present* on the earth during this time.

His presence on the earth was necessary for several activities including the crowning act of creation—the sacred activity of creating and placing Adam and Eve in the garden of Eden.

From sacred scriptures we learn that during the seventh day of Creation, while he was upon the earth, our Father in Heaven performed three important acts: he finished his work, sanctified the earth, and formed man. As a commentary on the 8th chapter of the book of Revelation, Joseph Smith explained these three activities:

Q. What are we to understand by the book which John saw, which was sealed on the back with seven seals?

A. We are to understand that it contains the revealed will, mysteries, and the works of God; the hidden things of his economy concerning this earth *during the seven thousand years* of its continuance, or its temporal existence.

Q. What are we to understand by the sounding of the trumpets, mentioned in the 8th chapter of Revelation?

A. We are to understand that as God made the world in six days, and on the seventh day he *finished* his work, and *sanctified* it, and also *formed* man out of the dust of the earth, even so, in the beginning of the seventh thousand years will the Lord God *sanctify* the earth, and *complete* the salvation of man, and *judge* all things, and shall redeem all things... (D&C 77:6, 12; emphasis added).

The expression "finished his work" means that on the seventh day God actively put the finishing touches on his work of Creation. This glorious act of completion included the placement of all life upon the earth—plants, animals, and Adam and Eve. As you read above in the scriptural comparisons the placement of life on the earth during the seventh day brought to fruition all the preparations as described in the 4th chapter of Abraham. In the 5th chapter of Abraham we read, "We will *finish* the heavens and the earth, and all the hosts of them... On the seventh time *we will end our work*, which we have counseled; and we will *rest* on the seventh time from all our work which we have counseled" (Abraham 5:1-2; emphasis added).

Even in Moses' record we read of sacred activities on the seventh day: "Thus the heaven and the earth were *finished*, and all the host of them. And on the seventh day I, God, *ended my work*, and all things which I had made; and I *rested* on the seventh day from all my work, and all things which I had made *were finished*, and I, God, saw that they were good" (Moses 1:1-2; emphasis added).

Here, in Moses' account, we also learn that the seventh period was a time of action—the placement of life occurred on this final day—in that they actively *finished* or completed their work. In both the Abrahamic and Mosaic accounts of the seventh day of Creation we find that important acts of completion were performed on the seventh day.

The Abrahamic account of the Creation most clearly describes the activities of the seventh period. "And the Gods took counsel among themselves and said: Let us go down and form man in our image, after our likeness.... So the Gods went down to organize man in their own image, in the image of the Gods to form they him, *male and female* to form they them" (Abraham 4:26-27).

In summary then, the meaning of the earth being sanctified and resting on the seventh day is that our Heavenly Parents were present upon the earth to accomplish the crowning acts of creation—the creation and placement of Adam and Eve, the children of God and our first parents on our newly formed earth.

CELESTIAL GLORY—THE ULTIMATE DESTINY OF THE EARTH

This earth has had a most interesting past and yet will go through a fascinating future. President Joseph Fielding Smith explained that when the earth was first created and Adam and Eve were placed thereon, the earth was in a *terrestrial* state. By comparison now we are in a *telestial* state.[23] When the earth was first created and life was placed thereon, God pronounced everything *good*. But now, since the Fall—with all the weeds, thistles, cockroaches, death, disease and war that we know—earthly conditions are not good like they were when everything was first created.

However, when the Lord comes again and ushers in his Millennium of rest, the earth will be refreshed, renewed, and "receive its paradisiacal glory" (10th Article of Faith).

After the seventh thousand years are ended, the earth will be changed again and become a celestial kingdom.[24]

The Doctrine and Covenants provides very explicit information about the destiny of this earth upon which we live. We read, "Therefore, it [the earth] must needs be sanctified from all unrighteousness, that it may be prepared for the celestial glory; For after it hath filled the measure of its creation, it shall be crowned with glory, even with the presence of God the Father; That bodies who are of the celestial kingdom may possess it forever and ever; for, for this intent was it made and created, and for this intent are they sanctified" (D&C 88:18-20).

The idea that the earth will eventually be sanctified and become a celestial kingdom was taught by the Prophet Joseph Smith when he responded to the question, "What is the sea of glass spoken of by John, 4th chapter, and 6th verse of the Revelation? It is the earth, in its sanctified, immortal, and eternal state" (D&C 77:1).

Regarding this earth eventually becoming a celestial sphere, the Lord has given us the following:

> The angels do not reside on a planet like this earth; But they reside in the presence of God, on a globe like a sea of glass and fire, where all things for their glory are manifest, past, present, and future, and are continually before the Lord. The place where God resides is a great Urim and Thummim. This earth, in its sanctified and immortal state, will be made like

unto crystal and will be a Urim and Thummim to the inhabitants who dwell thereon, whereby all things pertaining to an inferior kingdom, or all kingdoms of a lower order, will be manifest to those who dwell on it; and this earth will be Christ's (D&C 130:6-9).

Finally, we have this joyful statement made by Brigham Young who explained that:

> When sin and iniquity are driven from the earth, and the [evil] spirits that now float in this atmosphere are driven into the place prepared for them; and when the earth is sanctified from the effects of the fall, and baptized, cleansed, and purified by fire, and returns to its paradisiacal state, and has become like a sea of glass, a urim and thummim; when all this is done, and the Savior has presented the earth to his Father, and it is placed in the cluster of the celestial kingdoms, [then] the Son and all his faithful brethren and sisters [will receive] the welcome plaudit— "Enter ye into the joy of your Lord."[25]

When we read what the prophets and apostles have said about this earth which, in its sanctified state will be our eternal home, we are led to exclaim, "what a marvelous creation this earth is!" Who presently can contemplate the power and intelligence that brought it into existence? Sanctified and holy men and women in former times have been shown in vision the Creation of the earth— and the time is near at hand when all the faithful Saints will know and understand these marvelous events.

In the meantime, as we sift with our fingers through the sands of our earth and stand in awe at a beautiful sunset, and contemplate the majesty of the sun, moon and stars, let us ponder with gratitude the part that loving heavenly parents played in organizing this beautiful sphere we call our home. Let us rejoice in the marvelous blessing of mortality—for a physical creation of things. Let us remember the promise of the Lord, "Blessed are the meek, for they shall inherit the earth" in its glorified, celestialized state (see Matthew 5:5).

In the next chapter we will discuss the procreation of Adam and Eve, creative acts that are even more sacred and holy than those associated with the Creation of the earth.

REFERENCES:

1 *Teachings of the Prophet Joseph Smith*, 348. Joseph Smith also explained in this sermon that the German Bible is the most correct: "I have an old edition of the New Testament in the Latin, Hebrew, German and Greek languages. I have been reading

the German, and find it to be the most [nearly] correct translation, and to correspond nearest to the revelations which God has given to me for the last fourteen
years" (Teachings, 349). Though Joseph did not say exactly what contributions the
German Bible makes, he did explain that the major source of his information was
not the German or any other Bible: "I thank God that I have got this old book [the
German Bible]; but I thank him more for the gift of the Holy Ghost. I have got the
oldest book in the world; but I [also] have the oldest book in my heart, even the gift
of the Holy Ghost" (Teachings, 349).

2 Teachings, 349-50.
3 Teachings, 190; emphasis added.
4 Teachings, 296.
5 Man Does Not Stand Alone, 16-18.
6 Dr. Paul Cox, BYU Devotional assembly, October 10, 1995.
7 Dr. Paul Cox, October 10, 1995.
8 Journal of Charles L. Walker, 18 Oct. 1880.
9 "The Mormon", 29 Aug. 1857.
10 Times and Seasons, 1 Feb. 1842, 3:672.
11 Journal of Discourses, 15:238.
12 Journal of Discourses, 17:143; emphasis added.
13 Journal of Discourses; 9:317; emphasis added.
14 This idea, held by Creationists will be discussed in greater detail in the next
  chapter.
15 Teachings, 350-52.
16 Journal of Discourses, 21:322; emphasis added.
17 "The Formation of the Earth," The Seer, Apr. 1854, 248.
18 Journal of Discourses, 18:294
19 Times and Seasons, 1 January 1845, 5:758.
20 Through revelation from the Lord, Joseph initially made visions of Genesis in
  1830. He made additional alterations thereafter, and evidence indicates that he
  intended to make further changes. He did not consider the text of the Creation as it
  is now published in the book of Moses to be without some deficiencies. For example, in reviewing Moses 2:2 Joseph Smith said, "In the translation 'without form
  and void' it should be read empty and desolate." The present account in the book
  of Moses was not published until 1851, several years after the Prophet's death.
21 The Book of Abraham's was published in the spring of 1842. It was presented to
  the Church as the Prophet Joseph Smith's translation of a revelation given anciently to the patriarch Abraham. Abraham states that this revelation was given to him
  through the Urim and Thummim. Therefore, he no doubt saw the Creation and the
  associated events as they happened. Besides seeing the events associated with the
  Creation, Abraham explained that he had in his possession records extending back
  to the time of Adam, giving "a knowledge of the beginning of the creation, and also
  of the planets, and of the stars, as they were made known unto the fathers"
  (Abraham 1:28-31).

22 Journal of Discourses, 16:325.
23 Joseph Fielding Smith Jr., Doctrines of Salvation, Vol. 1, 82
24 Ibid
25 Journal of Discourses, 17:117.

CHAPTER THREE

ADAM AND EVE: CHILDREN OF GOD

Where was there ever a son without a father?
And where was there ever a father without first being a son?
Whenever did a tree or anything spring into existence without a progenitor?
And everything comes in this way.

—Joseph Smith

Have you ever witnessed the birth of babies—animal or human? In my youth I was present for the birth of many farm animals, and during those times I sensed that I was witnessing remarkable events. Even more amazing and very sacred to me was being present at the delivery of two of my own children. Even now, as I write these words, I marvel at the wonderful complexity and intricate interplay of physiological processes involved in the birth of a child. It is amazing to me that people actually come from inside other people!

People who have not witnessed the birthing processes may have a tendency to forget that earthly elements of water, blood, and spirit are very much involved in this miracle of birth. We live in societies where these mundane realities of life are concealed from us and we are led to casually believe that our milk simply comes from cartons in refrigerated sections of the local supermarket—not from cows—and that little human babies come pre-wrapped in soft fluffy blankets. Of course mothers who have carried and delivered babies are very much aware of, the physical realities of birthing—the pain, labor, water, and blood that is involved in bringing life into this world.

But, how did the birthing of babies all get started on this earth in the first place? How did Adam and Eve really come into being? Did God first make a model of a man out of clay and then blow the breath of life into his nostrils before Adam began to live, breathe, and walk around? Did Eve really come from a rib of Adam. These are the mental pictures many people get from reading the biblical accounts of the creation of Adam and Eve. Fortunately, as a part of the great restoration of the gospel, God has revealed important and sacred truths about Adam and Eve's beginnings. What before may have been a mystery to us, now becomes wonderfully clear.

In the previous chapter, we discussed the creation of the world and living things. Now in this chapter we will focus on the origins of Adam and Eve—as literal children of God. To begin this discussion let's define two words: *creation* and *procreation*. For our purposes in this chapter we will use the word *creation* to refer to the organization of all non-organic, non-living entities—such as the sun, moon, stars, mountains, rocks, rivers, and streams. However, we will use the word *procreation* to refer to the organization of living entities—such as horses, bears, elephants, giraffes, and *Adam and Eve*.

Non-living things are organized in ways very different from living things. Living things are born and begotten through the reproductive processes involving both mothers and fathers. Reproduction of living things involves a complex interaction of amino acids, DNA, computer-like genes and chromosomes, tissues, and organs—in order that each can "bring forth after his kind".

However, with the reproduction of human beings, we are not confined to the seasonal, hormonal, and chemical triggers to which animals seem to be limited. For us, our minds, spirits, hearts, and physical bodies—the whole of our humanity —seem to be involved in this God-given power of procreation that is so strongly planted in us. Indeed, when we pause to ponder, we see that the influences surrounding romantic love and procreation are deeply spiritual and are at the very heart of our Heavenly Father's great plan of happiness.

I believe that when we look through the eyes of the spirit, everything looks different. For example, the more we view human reproduction through spiritual eyes the more joy we find in romantic love. Indeed, the greatest of all the gifts of God is the gift of "continuation of the seeds forever and ever," or "eternal lives" (D&C 132:19, 24)—the power to bring forth new life throughout the eternities.

ORIGINS OF LIFE: POPULAR VIEWS

As we look into secular and sacred information dealing with the origins of human life, we begin to see that this material can be grouped according into three general categories: 1) Creationism, 2) Organic Evolution, and 3) Theistic Evolution. In the following sections I will briefly describe each of these positions.

Creationism

In the previous chapter we discussed the position of Bible believing people, most of whom take the Genesis version of the Creation to be the *literal* account of how God created the heavens and the earth. According to this view, God created everything out of *nothing* in *six* 24-hour days. This is the position of the Creationists. Coupled with this belief is the notion that God formed Adam and Eve from the dust of the earth—much like we would form clay models—and then God breathed life into them, and they became living beings.

Organic Evolution

Standing in contrast to—and in conflict with—the Creationist's point of view is the position of most secular scientists who believe that organic evolution is the correct explanation for the beginnings of all life, plant and animal, on the earth. Organic evolution is the theory, idea, or working assumption popularized by Charles Darwin that complex living things have evolved from simpler forms of life. Through a process of natural selection—including the survival of the fittest—life has evolved to higher orders, including man, over vast amounts of time.[1]

The biblical view of the Creation has found itself under increasing attack from the evolutionists in the secular world ever since Copernicus overturned the church-sanctioned view of the earth as the center of the universe, and Charles Darwin proposed random mutation and natural selection as the real creators of human life.

Scientists as far back as Galileo (A.D. 1564-1642) struggled privately with conflicts between their religious beliefs and their scientific observations and theories. Eventually, by the 18th century, Enlightenment thinkers were arguing that human reason and scientific methods, rather than religious belief, were best equipped to explain human existence. A century later, Charles Darwin, a lifelong member of the Church of England, published his book, *Origin of Species*, detailing his theory of evolution. However, it was Thomas Huxley, an associate of Darwin's, who expounded on the theological implications of evolution—that man was not a unique creation of God, and that man had evolved from animal ancestors. (See end of chapter Figure 3-A The Evolutionary View of Man's Origin & Destiny.)

The story of the Creation and the origins of life has generated much discussion because it is so intimately connected with who and what we are. It is a narrative over which religious groups and scientific circles have been fighting for centuries. The argument was, "How could one who believes in evolution also believe in God?" The Creationists object to evolution because it leaves God out of the process. The evolutionists reject Creationism because the Bible account does not fit with what they observe in the earth's geological, biological, and paleontological records. For many evolutionists reconciling Creationism and evolution is not an issue. Many evolutionists are either agnostics (who doubt) or atheists (who deny) the existence of God and consider the biblical account of the Creation to be simply myth.

In many respects Latter-day Saints have stood apart from the debate between the Creationists and the evolutionists, but some fallout from the dispute continues at Latter-day Saint colleges and universities where biology and religion are taught in separate departments.

Theistic Evolutionists

There are Bible believing people of integrity who try to reconcile their religious and scientific beliefs by adopting a position that has been called "theistic evolution". This position asserts that evolutionary processes were the means whereby God brought about all living things—plants, animals, and human beings.

A Latter-day Saint Response

1) *Creationism*: In contrast to the position of the Creationists, Latter-day Saints take the Genesis account of the six days of creation to be figurative. We also believe the biblical account of Adam and Eve's creation to be metaphorical. In presenting the creation of Adam and Eve in allegorical terms, the Lord has hidden from the ungodly and from those who would treat holy things too lightly the sacred processes involved in the bringing forth of Adam and Eve.

2) *Organic evolution*: One of the concerns many Latter-day Saints have with the evolutionary explanation of the creation is that it is most often presented independent of God's involvement. As are all scientific approaches, the evolutionary model is a secular model. Science does not propose to deal with the sacred. Scientists form their theories and draw their conclusions strictly from observable data independent of spiritual sources of information such as revelation, intuition, or scripture.

While certain aspects of evolution are not contrary to gospel truths—for example, we can see and accept evolutionary changes since the Fall for there are generational changes that can be observed among plants and animals today—there are other aspects that are opposed to church doctrine. Particularly contrary to Church theology would be any position that held that 1) Adam evolved from lower animal forms, or that 2) there were births and deaths before Adam introduced death into the world by partaking of the forbidden fruit. According to evolutionary theory, a chain of births and deaths would be necessary to account for the vast variety of species that we see today. On the other hand, the scriptures affirm that Adam was indeed d "the son of God"—not a product of millions of years of animal evolution (Luke 3:38; Moses 6:22), and that Adam did indeed introduce birth and death into this world when he partook of the fruit of the Tree of Knowledge of Good and Evil (see 2 Nephi 2:22-25, 1 Corinthians 15:22).

To more fully understand this important doctrine, some background information may be helpful. When Adam and Eve were physically created (more correctly procreated) by God and placed in the garden of Eden, they were not subject to death. Their bodies were physical, but they were also immortal in the sense that they could not die. However, after eating the forbidden fruit, Adam and Eve's physical bodies became mortal—their physical *immortal* bodies became physical *mortal* bodies, meaning they could die.

3) *Theistic evolution*: Of this position, Elder Boyd K. Packer has explained, "I am sorry to say, the so-called theistic evolution, the theory that God used an evolutionary process to prepare a physical body for the spirit of man, is...false. I say I am sorry because I know it is a view commonly held by good and thoughtful people who search for an acceptable resolution to an apparent conflict between the theory of evolution and the doctrines of the gospel."[2]

In the same address Elder Packer explained that an important reason why the theistic view of evolution is false is because the *sealing authority* with its binding of the generations into eternal families "*cannot admit beasts to ancestral blood lines.*" As has been stated above, Adam was a son of God, not of animal-like creatures.

Observing the heated conflicts between creationists and evolutionists, Brother Hugh Nibley suggested that too often the debate that rages between them involves "an apostate religion squaring off against an always inadequate science. The issue is never the merits of the evidence but always the jealous rivalry of the contestants to see which would be the official light unto the world."[3] Thinking that you have to choose creationism, evolution, or even theistic evolution for your own position about the origin of human life is a false dilemma. In reality, the truth lies beyond the rhetoric and sophistry of these positions.

Refreshingly, many of the cobwebs of confusion and controversy regarding the origins of human life have been wiped away through latter-day revelation. Although God has not revealed through the *scriptures* precise details regarding how man was placed on the earth, modern prophets have elaborated sufficiently for us to know that—insofar as the origin of Adam and Eve is concerned—Latter-day Saints need be neither "creationists" nor "evolutionists".

SEARCHING DEEPLY

Learning for yourself the truth about where you came from is vital for your spiritual advancement. Study, prayer, humility and yielding to the guidance of the Spirit are the only ways for you to know for yourself the truth about Adam's origins, and thus your own. By following this pathway you can gain inspiration and revelation from the Spirit to teach and guide you in your life.

The words of Jacob remind us that we must learn by revelation, "Behold, great and marvelous are the works of the Lord. How unsearchable are the depths of the mysteries of him; and it is impossible that man should find out all his ways. And no man knoweth of his ways save it be revealed unto him; wherefore, brethren, despise not the revelations of God" (Jacob 4:8; emphasis added). Isaiah proclaimed the same truth when he said, "For my thoughts are not your thoughts, neither are your ways my ways, saith the Lord. For as the heavens are higher than the earth, so are my ways higher than your ways, and my thoughts than your thoughts" (Isaiah 55:8-9).

I frequently hear people, who are fearful of stretching themselves beyond shallow faith, objecting to gospel discussions of any depth by protesting, "that topic does not pertain to our salvation!" What a sad position to take! What an abrupt stop to honest inquiry and searching! How untrue! Gospel study involves more than tithing and the Word of Wisdom, as important as these are. We must grow in our quest for knowledge. We are promised that if we ask, we shall receive—but if we do not ask, we will not receive.

At a General Conference of the Church which was held on April 7, 1852, President Brigham Young stated that "Every Elder should become a profound theologian.⁴ In keeping with this same thought the Prophet Joseph Smith advised all the Saints to "go on to perfection, and search deeper and deeper in the mysteries of Godliness."⁵

Joseph Smith also exhorted us to search deeply when he said: "The things of God are of deep import; and time, and experience, and careful and ponderous and solemn thoughts can only find them out. Thy mind, O man! if thou wilt lead a soul unto salvation, must stretch as high as the utmost heavens, and search into and contemplate the darkest abyss, and the broad expanse of eternity—thou must commune with God."⁶

Only by stretching our minds instead of limiting ourselves to the view of things as they seem to be in the world around us can we receive revelation and know the mysteries of Godliness, including the great mystery of our own origins as children of God. Now we will discuss one of the great mysteries that our Father has revealed through his prophets—regarding the true origin of Adam and Eve and us.

THE FATHER ELOHIM, NOT JEHOVAH, BROUGHT FORTH ADAM

You may remember that in the previous chapter you read that Jesus and "the noble and great ones" were actively involved in the creation of the earth and the preparing of the world for the placement of life (see Abraham 3:22-24; 4:1) and that he and the noble and great spirits performed the creative acts associated with the preparation of the earth for life.

However, when it came time for Adam and Eve to be placed on the earth, our Father in Heaven became personally involved.

Elder Bruce R. McConkie explained our Heavenly Father's involvement in the placement of Adam and Eve when he said that,

> From...sacred sources we know that Jehovah—Christ, assisted by "many of the noble and great ones" (Abr. 3:22), of whom Michael is but the illustration, did in fact create the earth and all forms of plant and animal life on the face thereof. But when it came to placing man on earth, there was a change in Creators. That is, the Father himself became personally involved. All things were created by the Son, using the power delegated by the Father, except man. *In the spirit and again in the flesh, man was created by the Father.* There was no delegation of authority where the crowning creature of creation was concerned.[7]

From this quotation we learn that Adam is a son of God both spiritually and then physically (see end of chapter Figure 3-B, The Revealed View of Man's Origin & Destiny). This fact is affirmed by Luke in the New Testament. In tracing the genealogy of Joseph, the step-father of Jesus, Luke concluded his list of patriarchs by stating, "Seth, which was the son of Adam, which was the *son of God*" (Luke 3:38; emphasis added). Regarding this passage, Elder McConkie explained, "This statement, found also in Moses 6:22, has a deep and profound significance and also *means what it says.* Father Adam came, as indicated, to this sphere, gaining an immortal body, because death had not yet entered the world. (2 Nephi. 2:22). Jesus, on the other hand, was the Only Begotten in the flesh, meaning into a world of mortality where death already reigned."[8]

The Prophet Joseph Smith also endorsed Luke's statement when he stated emphatically, "Where was there ever a son without a father? And where was there ever a father without first being a son? Whenever did a tree or anything spring into existence without a progenitor? And *everything comes in this way.*"[9] In other words, Joseph Smith is saying that all living things are begotten or procreated by mothers and fathers—including Adam and Eve.

This newly revealed truth about Adam's beginning enlightens our minds and lifts our spirits, for in learning of our origins through Adam we can anticipate our outcomes in the eternities. In other words, by understanding our true premortal *and* earthly beginnings as literal children of God we can predict our own destiny. Because Heavenly Father begat us spiritually and physically (through Adam and Eve), we have the seeds within us to eventually become like him (see D&C 132:19)—if we follow the steps outlined in the great plan of happiness.

In this, the Dispensation of the Fulness of Times, we have been blessed with such an abundance of light and truth regarding our family connectedness with God. And yet, there is much knowledge that lies in futurity that will provide further light and truth about our origins. In the meantime, while waiting with eager expectation to know more about the mysteries of godliness, we rejoice in the abundance of what has been revealed.

CELESTIAL BEINGS HAVE POWER TO CREATE BOTH SPIRIT AND BODY

The power of our heavenly parents to procreate both spirit and body is a characteristic power of all exalted beings. President Heber C. Kimball clearly taught that Celestial Parents can procreate both *spirit* bodies (as we were in the premortal life) and *physical* bodies (as Adam's and Eve's were in Eden). He explained:

> Now,...you have got a spirit in you, and that spirit was created and organized—was *born* and *begotten* by our Father and our God before we ever took these bodies; and these bodies were formed by him, and through him, and of him, just as much as the spirit was; for I will tell you, he commenced and brought forth spirits; and then, when he completed that work he commenced and brought forth tabernacles for those spirits to dwell in. I came through him, both *spirit* and *body*.[10]

President Brigham Young also taught that all those who obtain exaltation in the celestial kingdom will have power to procreate—like the Gods have done before them—both spirit children and physical children. He taught:

> We have not the power in the flesh to create and bring forth or produce a spirit; but we have the power to produce a temporal body. The germ of this, God has placed within us. And when our spirits receive our bodies, and through our faithfulness we are worthy to be crowned, *we will then receive authority to produce both spirit and body*. But these keys we cannot receive in the flesh. Herein, brethren, you can perceive that we have not finished, and cannot finish our work, while we live here, no more than Jesus did while he was in the flesh.[11]

The *crowning* about which President Young spoke in the above quotation has reference to true and faithful Saints—those who will inherit the highest degree of the celestial kingdom—being empowered to procreate life forever throughout the eternities. Thus, they will *rule* and *reign* under their Heavenly Father over an ever increasing posterity whom they will bathe in their eternal love even as our Father loves us now.

ADAM WAS CREATED AS WE CREATE OUR CHILDREN

Through the Prophet Joseph Smith and his successors in this last dispensation we have received a wonderful flood of knowledge regarding our Father's great plan for our happiness. He is so intimately connected to us as his literal children, and he is eager to bless us and envelope us in his eternal love. Sometimes, while I am teaching Old Testament religion classes which focus on Creation and the bringing forth of Adam and Eve, students will ask questions like: "Were Adam and Eve real people or are they simply mythological figures?" "Were Adam and Eve primitive beings who descended from lower animals on the evolutionary scale?" "If they were real historical characters, were they the product of organic evolution?" In other words, "Did God experiment in creating bi-peds and decide at one point on the evolutionary scale that bi-peds were advanced enough to be called humans and be given the names of Adam and Eve?" Answers to these and similar questions can be found in statements by Latter-day prophets and in official proclamations of the First Presidency and Council of Twelve Apostles—the highest authority in the Church.

President Joseph Fielding Smith and the First Presidency declared that Adam was the first man upon this earth, and that the original human being was *not* a development from lower orders of the animal creation. They stated,

> It is held by some that Adam was not the first man upon this earth, and that the original human being was a development from lower orders of the animal creation. These, however, are the theories of men. The word of the Lord declares that Adam was "the first man of all men" (Moses 1:34), and we are therefore in duty bound to regard him as the primal parent of our race. It was shown to the brother of Jared that all men were created in the *beginning* after the image of God; and whether we take this to mean the spirit or the body, or both, it commits us to the same conclusion: Man began life as a human being, in the likeness of our heavenly Father.
>
> True it is that the body of man enters upon its career as a tiny germ or embryo, which becomes an infant, quickened at a certain stage by the spirit whose tabernacle it is, and the child, after being born, develops into a man. There is nothing in this, however, to indicate that the original man, the first of our race, began life as anything less than a man, or less than the human germ or embryo that becomes a man."[12]

Many other General Authorities of the Church have verified the heavenly origins of the physical bodies of Adam and Eve. Elder Parley P. Pratt, for example, taught that Adam was not made by God scooping up a handful of clay from a ditch bank, molding it into the form of a man, and then blowing into this model the breath of life. Elder Pratt refuted such an idea when he affirmed that Adam and Eve were born and begotten by Deity and that a correct understanding of man's origins had to be concealed because of unbelief:

> When Paradise was lost by sin; when man was driven from the face of his Heavenly Father...; when heaven was veiled from view; and when, with few exceptions, man was no longer counted worthy to retain the knowledge of his heavenly origin, then darkness veiled the past... man. neither knew himself, from whence he came, nor whither he was bound. At length a Moses came, who knew his God, and would fain have led mankind to know him too, and see him face to face. But they could not receive his heavenly laws or (a)bide his presence. Thus the holy man was forced again to veil the past in mystery and, in the beginning of his history, assign to man an earthly origin.
> Man, molded from the earth, as a brick!
> Woman, manufactured from a rib!
> Thus, parents still would fain conceal from budding manhood the mysteries of procreation, or the sources of life's ever-flowing river, by relating some childish tale of new-born life.... O man! When wilt thou cease to be a child in knowledge?
> Man, as we have said, is the *offspring* of Deity.[13]

Latter-day Saint doctrine states that Adam and Eve were indeed the offspring of heavenly parents—they were *procreated*, not simply created. Learning this truth reveals in a powerful way our own close relationship to our Heavenly Father because we are physically the descendants of Adam and Eve who were born and begotten children of God.

The prophets Joseph Smith, Brigham Young, and Joseph Fielding Smith taught that Adam was created by the same natural means as we were created.[14] President Joseph F. Smith explained that Adam was created as we are created when he said,

> I know that God is a being with body, parts and passions and that his Son is in his own likeness, and that man is created in the image of God. The Son, Jesus Christ, grew and developed into manhood the same as you or I, as likewise did God his Father, grow and develop to the Supreme Being that he now is. Man was born of woman; Christ the Savior, was born of woman, and God, the Father, was born of woman. *Adam, our earthly parent, was also born of woman into this world the same as Jesus and you and I.*[15]

Emphasizing the role of our Heavenly Father in the procreation of Adam and Eve, Brigham Young explained, "The Father actually begat the spirits, and they were brought forth and lived with Him. Then He commenced the work of creating earthly tabernacles, ... by partaking of the [coarse] material that was organized and composed this earth, until His system was charged with it, consequently, the tabernacles of His children [Adam and Eve] were organized from the coarse materials of this earth."[16] (See end of chapter Figure 3-C, First Spirit Bodies, Then Physical Bodies.) Do you realize what you just read? If not, go back and reread this paragraph. This is a powerful description by a President of the Church—a prophet, seer, and revelator—regarding the true origins of Adam and Eve!

Sometimes my students wonder how we reconcile the idea that Adam was a son of God with passages that say he was created from the "dust of the ground" (Genesis 2:7). Actually, when we stop and think about it, all life on this planet was created *from the dust of the earth*. The elements that compose our bodies can be traced back to the elements of the earth. After we are conceived in our mother's womb, our bodies were nourished and fed through complex biological processes within the womb. But where did the substances of nutrition come from? Our mothers ate a diet of breads, fruits, vegetables, dairy products, and meats—all of which came directly or indirectly, from the elements or "dust of the ground".

Further light and knowledge was provided about the procreation of Adam and Eve when President Young declared:

> I believe that the declaration made in these two scriptures [Genesis 1:26, 27] is literally true. God has made His children like Himself to stand erect, and has endowed them with intelligence and power and dominion over all His works, and given them the same attributes which He Himself possesses. *He created man [Adam and Eve], as we create our children*; for there is no other process of creation in heaven, on the earth, in the earth, or under the earth, or in all the eternities, that is, that were, or that ever will be.... There exist fixed laws and regulations by which the elements are fashioned to fulfill their destiny in all the varied kingdoms and orders of creation, and *this process of creation* is from everlasting to everlasting.[17]

The sanctity of the process of procreation was affirmed by the First Presidency when in a recent proclamation they stated, "We declare the means by which mortal life is created to be divinely appointed."[18] Satan would have us believe the contrary. He has prostituted and contaminated the minds of people regarding these sacred procreative processes. Indeed, the most sacred things are the most easily defiled, so our Heavenly Father withholds them from the world at large. But he delights in revealing to his truth-loving children the wonders of the eternities. He joyfully proclaimed:

I, the Lord, am merciful and gracious unto those who fear me, and delight to honor those who serve me in righteousness and in truth unto the end....

And to them will I reveal all mysteries, yea, all the hidden mysteries of my kingdom from days of old, and for ages to come, will I make known unto them the good pleasure of my will concerning all things pertaining to my kingdom.

Yea, even the wonders of eternity shall they know, and things to come will I show them, even the things of many generations.

And their wisdom shall be great, and their understanding reach to heaven; and before them the wisdom of the wise shall perish, and the understanding of the prudent shall come to naught.

For by my Spirit will I enlighten them, and by my power will I make known unto them the secrets of my will—yea, even those things which eye has not seen, nor ear heard, nor yet entered into the heart of mann" (D&C 76:5, 7-10).

The Lord is telling us here that if we will love him and serve him in righteousness, he will happily reveal to us the wonders of the eternities. President Young exhorted the Saints to teach the truth about what God has revealed. He charged the Saints to "teach the people the faith of the Gospel. Teach them what God is, and what His work is, and that there never was a time such as many of our philosophers speak of, who drift back and back, and come to this theory and that theory, and go back, and back to the time when [our ancestors] were all reptiles."[19]

In addition to the statements of the Apostles just quoted, we find a clear statement in the priesthood course of study, prepared for use in 1910, "Man is, in the most *literal* sense, a child of God. This is not only true of the *spirit* of man, but of his *body* also. There never was a time, probably, in all the eternities of the past, when there was not men or children of God. This world is only one of many worlds which have been created by the Father through His Only Begotten."[20]

The critical principle for you to remember from this material is the idea that we are literal children of Heavenly Father through Adam and Eve. Adam was a son of God, and we are sons and daughters of Adam. You and I are closer to our Heavenly Father than we could ever dream!

STATEMENTS BY THE FIRST PRESIDENCY

Our closeness to our heavenly parents has been affirmed in official proclamations of the Church. The highest *authority* in The Church of Jesus Christ of Latter-day Saints is the First Presidency (see D&C 124:45-46). What they declare as a presidency is official doctrine for the Church—overriding even the ancient and modern scriptures at times. The position of the Church on the origin of Adam was published by the First Presidency in 1909. It was stated again by a different First Presidency in 1925. In their statement they declared, "The Church of Jesus Christ of Latter-day Saints, basing its belief on divine revelation, ancient and modern, declares man to be the *direct* and *lineal* offspring of Deity.... Man is the child of God, formed in the divine image and endowed with divine attributes."[21]

Special attention should be given to the words *direct, lineal,* and *offspring* in the above statement. These words clearly indicate that the body of Adam was neither evolved from lower forms of life, nor was it created like a brick. As we have explained previously, Adam was *procreated* both spirit and body as a son of God!

Another statement by the First Presidency entitled, "Mormon View of Evolution" was signed by Heber J. Grant, Anthony W. Ivins, and Charles W. Nibley. It was published in 1929, and in it they stated, "Man, by searching, cannot find out God. *Never,* unaided, will he discover the truth about the beginning of human life. The Lord must reveal Himself, or remain unrevealed; and the same is true of the facts relating to the origin of Adam's race—God alone can reveal them. Some of these facts, however, are already known, and what has been made known it is our duty to receive and retain."[22]

That Adam is the primal parent of our race, born and begotten into this world by heavenly parents, is a fundamental doctrine of the Church. In 1931, when there was intense discussion on the issue of organic evolution, the First Presidency of the Church, then consisting of Presidents Heber J. Grant, Anthony W. Ivins, and Charles W. Nibley, addressed all of the General Authorities of the Church on the matter, and concluded,

> Upon the fundamental doctrines of the Church we are all agreed. Our mission is to bear the message of the restored gospel to the world. Leave geology, biology, archaeology, and anthropology, no one of which has to do with the salvation of the souls of mankind, to scientific research, while we magnify our calling in the realm of the Church....
>
> Upon one thing we should all be able to agree, namely, that Presidents Joseph F. Smith, John R. Winder, and Anthon H. Lund were right when they said: "Adam is the primal parent of our race."[23]

In response to a student inquiry, "Are the General Authorities of the Church in one accord on the subject of evolution?" Elder Marion G. Romney replied: "I don't suppose that any two minds in the world understand exactly alike any statement on any subject. The General Authorities of the Church are, of course, like all other men, different in their personalities. However, one point on which they are in accord is that *Adam is a son of God, that neither his spirit nor his body is a product of biological evolution* which went on for millions of years on this earth."[24]

We are truly blessed to have an understanding of the origins of our first parents, Adam and Eve, and we rejoice in being trusted with these sacred truths. And yet the Lord has promised that he "will yet reveal many great and important things pertaining to the Kingdom of God" (Ninth Article of Faith).

PREPARE YOURSELF TO RECEIVE NEW TRUTHS

Maybe some of the ideas you have encountered in this chapter are new to you. It is important that you test the truthfulness of new ideas through the standards that have been given by the Lord: the holy scriptures, teachings of the living prophets, and the promptings of the Holy Ghost. New ideas should be compatible with these three standards. When the Lord reveals new truths, it is important that you test them and that you be open and sensitive to the new light.

The challenge to take seriously newly revealed truths is ever before us. We have to overcome our reluctance to embrace new truth in order to receive the promises of the Lord. Our reluctance to accept new revelation keeps us from learning the mysteries of Godliness. Moroni promised that when we rend that veil of unbelief we will receive many marvelous truths. He said, "Behold, when ye shall rend that veil of unbelief which doth cause you to remain in your awful state of wickedness, and hardness of heart, and blindness of mind, then shall the great and marvelous things which have been hid up from the foundation of the world from you...then shall my revelations...be unfolded in the eyes of all the people" (Ether 4:15-16).

Neglecting to search after new truth is a form of rejection. Many people prefer their traditional comfort states to the unsettling restructuring of their mind sets that always comes with startling new insights. The Lord has explained that people do not learn about the wonders of the eternities, "Because their hearts are set so much upon the things of this world, and aspire to honors of men" (D&C 121:35). In other words, when we are preoccupied with the things of the world we don't take time to search and seek after the mysteries of Godliness. We remain spiritually unprepared and then we flinch at new revelations. Joseph Smith declared that newly revealed truths will almost always be rejected. Heber C. Kimball recalled Joseph Smith saying:

> Many men will say, "I will never forsake you, but will stand by you at all times." But the moment you teach them some of the mysteries of the kingdom of God that are retained in the heavens, and are to be revealed to the children of men when they are prepared for them, they will be *the first to stone you and put you to death.*
>
> It was this *same principle* that crucified the Lord Jesus Christ, and will cause the people to kill the prophets in this generation.
>
> Would to God, brethren, I could tell you who I am! Would to God I

could tell you what I know! But *you would call it blasphemy*, and there are men upon this stand who would want to take my life.

If the Church knew all the commandments, one-half they would reject through *prejudice and ignorance*.

When God offers a blessing, or knowledge to a man, and he *refuses to receive it*, he will be damned.[25]

In keeping with the theme of Joseph's statement, President Heber C. Kimball observed that "Revelation is ever the iconoclast of tradition, and such is the bigotry of man, his natural hatred of the new and strange, as opposed to his personal interests or private views, that the very lives of those whose mission is to introduce and establish new doctrines, though designed as a blessing to humanity, are ever in danger from those whose traditions would thus be uprooted and destroyed.[26]

To be sure, the revealed truth that we are literally sons and daughters of God is a new and strange doctrine to many people. It is important that we receive revealed knowledge when it is presented to us. To do otherwise is to reject sacred gifts and our rejection places us under condemnation. Joseph Smith warned, "The moment we revolt at anything which comes from God, the devil takes power."[27] He also said, "I have tried for a number of years to get the minds of the Saints prepared to receive the things of God; but we frequently see some of them, after suffering all they have for the work of God, will fly to pieces like glass as soon as anything comes that is contrary to their traditions: They cannot stand the fire at all.[28] Within this same context, Brigham Young recalled Joseph Smith saying: "The people cannot bear the revelations that the Lord has for them. There were a great many revelations if the people could bear them".[29]

When we reject new doctrines, then, it is as if it had never been revealed in the first place. If we don't believe, then new truths can have no influence on us. When you believe what the Lord has done for you then it opens up your vision and allows you to view in greater detail the great plan of happiness. The more truths you learn, the more you have available to you to focus your faith. If you are humble and teachable, and exercise faith you will receive knowledge and wisdom and understanding. If you are humble you will want to know more, you will want to seek the mind and will of Father. When you hear the truth it will find a place in a pure heart.

Brigham Young said, "A declamatory statement is sufficient for those who are prepared to receive the spirit of revelation for themselves, but with the most of the human family, we have to reason and explain. A really pure person is very scarce; but when the heart is truly pure, the Lord can write upon it, and the truth is received without argument, or doubt, or disputation."[30] When you prepare your mind and heart to receive knowledge from above, you will come to know and understand vital truths about yourself—your origin and your destiny.

ALL THINGS TO BE REVEALED

From the Book of Mormon we learn that specific information regarding the creation of the earth will come forth when the other two-thirds of the Book of Mormon are revealed. Moroni explained the marvelous content of these sealed records when he explained: "The words which are sealed [Joseph Smith] shall not deliver, neither shall he deliver the book. For the book shall be sealed by the power of God, and the revelation which was sealed shall be kept in the book until the own due time of the Lord, that they may come forth; for behold, *they reveal all things from the foundation of the world unto the end thereof*" (2 Nephi 27:10; emphasis added).

When the Lord comes he will "reveal all things" (D&C 101:32-33). The Lord's promise is that a time will come when

> nothing shall be withheld, whether there be one God or many gods, they shall be manifest. All thrones and dominions, principalities and powers, shall be revealed and set forth upon all who have endured valiantly for the gospel of Jesus Christ. And also, if there be bounds set to the heavens or to the seas, or to the dry land, or to the sun, moon, or stars—All the times of their revolutions, all the appointed days, months, and years, and all the days of their days, months, and years, and all their glories, laws, and set times, shall be revealed in the days of the dispensation of the fulness of times (D&C 121:28-31).

Till the Lord comes, we must recognize our vast limitations. Of course we have not discovered all truth either in science or religion. For the present time we seek further light and understanding in both areas, and we are grateful for what has been discovered through science and revealed through living prophets. Both scientists and religionists can afford to speak in subdued and humble tones. But at the same time we should courageously accept and defend what God has restored in this, the Dispensation of the Fullness of Times.

Among the important revelations that have been given in our time through the Prophet Joseph Smith and his successors is the knowledge that Adam and Eve are the literal children of God in both their spirits and bodies. We are the offspring of Adam and Eve. We then are the offspring of God, too, in both spirit and body! What a marvelous flood of meaning these expressions carry.

Now that you know the origin of Adam and Eve, let's discuss why their partaking of the fruit of the Tree of Knowledge of Good and Evil—though a transgression—was pleasing to our Heavenly Father. This is the subject of the next chapter.

REFERENCES:

1 Evolutionists do not assert that man sprang from apes, but they typically do contend that apes and humans have common ancestors.

2 "The Law and the Light," Given at the Book of Mormon Symposium, Brigham Young University, 30 October 1988; emphasis added.

3 Hugh Nibley, "Before Adam," *Collected Works of Hugh Nibley*, Vol. 1, *Old Testament and Related Studies*, 49-50.

4 *Journal of Discourses*, 6:317.

5 *Teachings of the Prophet Joseph Smith*, 364.

6 *Teachings*, 137; emphasis added.

7 Bruce R. McConkie, *The Promised Messiah*, 62.

8 Bruce R. McConkie, *Doctrinal New Testament Commentary*, 1:95; emphasis added. Elder Mark E. Petersen also affirmed the truth of Luke's passage in his book, *Adam: Who Is He?* 5, 13, 16.

9 *Teachings*, 373; emphasis added.

10 *Journal of Discourses*, 6:31; emphasis added.

11 *Journal of Discourses*, 15:137, Aug., 1872; emphasis added.

12 *Messages of the First Presidency*, compiled by James R. Clark, 4:205.

13 Parley P. Pratt, *Key to the Science of Theology*, 30.

14 See *History of the Church*, 6:476; *Journal of Discourses*, 7:285-86; 11:122; *Man: His Origin and Destiny*, 276-77; *Doctrines of Salvation*, 1:139-40.

15 *Deseret Evening News*, 27 Dec. 1913, sec. 3, 7; emphasis added.

16 *Journal of Discourses*, 4:218.

17 *Journal of Discourses*, 11:122; emphasis added.

18 The Family: A Proclamation to the World; Official Proclamation of the First Presidency and Council of Twelve Apostles, September 23, 1995.

19 *Journal of Discourses*, 19:49.

20 Cited in *Church News*, 19 Sept. 1936, 8; emphasis added.

21 Quoted in *Encyclopedia of Mormonism* (New York: Macmillan Publishing Company, 1992), Vol. 2, 478.

22 Joseph F. Smith, John R. Winder, and Anthon H. Lund, "The Origin of Man," In Messages of the First Presidency, 4:205-6; emphasis added.

23 First Presidency Minutes, April, 1931.

24 Personal letter written by Elder Romney to Keith Meservy. Published in "Evolution and the Origin of Adam," 225.

25 *Life of Heber C. Kimball*, 322-23; emphasis added.

26 *Kimball*, 323.

27 *Teachings*, 181.

28 *Teachings*, 331.

29 *Discourses of Brigham Young*, 471.

30 *Deseret News*, 7 June 1873.

FIGURE 3-A
THE EVOLUTIONARY VIEW OF
MAN'S ORIGIN AND DESTINY

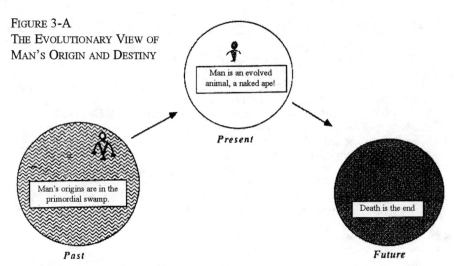

Principles

1. According to this false view, man has evolved from lower forms of life.
2. Man has risen to his present state through a process of natural selection. He is a highly evolved animal.
3. Death is the end of the individual although his children continue.
4. There is no premortal life (protology).
5. There is no postmortal life (eschatology).
6. There is no plan to man's existence.

FIGURE 3-B
THE REVEALED VIEW OF
MAN'S ORIGIN AND DESTINY

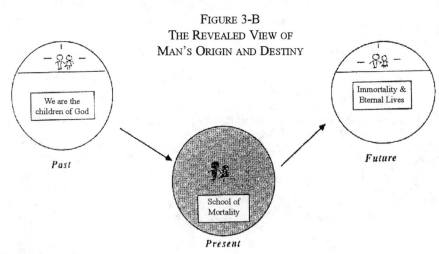

Principles

1. Man is a spirit child of God.
2. Adam, the first man, was a child of God, first in the spirit, then in the flesh.
3. We are in this life as part of a schooling process.
4. At the death of the body, the spirit of man continues to exist.
5. Man's destiny is to return, after a resurrection, to heavenly spheres from whence he came.

FIGURE 3-C
FIRST SPIRIT BODIES, THEN PHYSICAL BODIES

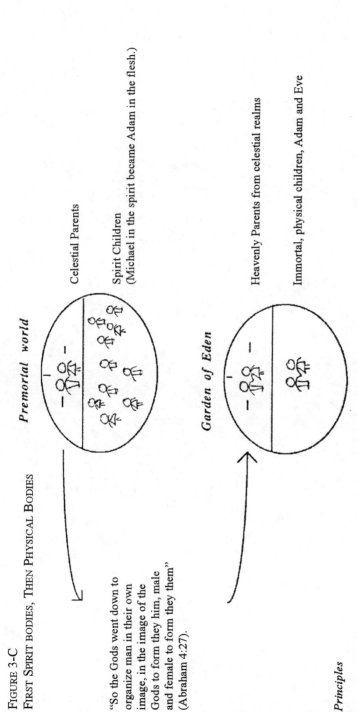

Premortal world

Celestial Parents

Spirit Children
(Michael in the spirit became Adam in the flesh.)

"So the Gods went down to organize man in their own image, in the image of the Gods to form they him, male and female to form they them" (Abraham 4:27).

Garden of Eden

Heavenly Parents from celestial realms

Immortal, physical children, Adam and Eve

Principles

1. "The Father actually begat the spirits, and they were brought forth and lived with Him. Then he commenced the work of creating earthly tabernacles" (Brigham Young, *Journal of Discourses* 4:218).

2. "Adam, our earthly parent, was also born of woman the same as you and I." (Joseph F. Smith, cited in Family Home Evening Manual, 1972, pp. 125-126).

3. "Man is the offspring of God.... We are as much the children of this great being as we are the children of our mortal progenitors. We are flesh of his flesh, bone of his bone.... As the seeds of grains, vegetables and fruits produce their kind, so man is in the image of God" (Brigham Young, *Journal of Discourses* 9:283).

CHAPTER FOUR

THE FALL OF
ADAM AND EVE

For it must needs be that there is an opposition in all things.
—2 Nephi 2:11

Early morning patches of fog floating phantom-like across dew-drenched pastures. Pearls of cool water clinging to green blades of grass, soaking through old leather shoes, creating a sloshing sound with each step. Five a.m. daybreaks. The morning sun beginning to crest over the Alberta prairie, struggling to break over the horizon. Shafts of golden light bursting through warrior-like clouds, radiating outward, striking the earth-orchestrating a drama of multi-colored lights, thunderhead clouds, and kodachrome skies, the beauty of which I associated with the Second Coming. Noonday heat waves rising heavenward from tar-blackened roofs. Cool evenings, long shadows, freshly milked cows grazing in the west pasture, calves playfully kicking up their heels like happy children at recess. Summer evenings—a time to rest, a time for relaxation. Peace.

Southern Alberta during those warm summer months was truly beautiful. In the early mornings there would often be a patchwork of heavy fog or mist that gave the country a fairy-land appearance. Intermittent patches of sunlight would create enchanted silhouettes of cattle, pasture, trees, and far distant houses—all against the backdrop of the blue Canadian Rockies.

On early morning rides to the west pasture to get the cows, I could see Old Chief Mountain, a prominent landmark on the southern horizon which seemed to me to serve as a sort of sentinel, a hallmark of God's approval of the beauty of the country. These are some of the images I recall when reflecting on the months I spent working for my sister and brother-in-law, who owned a farm in Hillspring, Alberta, Canada where they milked about fifteen head of cows and raised their own hay and grain to feed their cows and several hundred pigs.

The scenery of southern Alberta was so beautiful—but farm work was so demanding. During my time on the farm my brother-in-law would wake me at 4:30 a.m. I was dog tired! I couldn't believe that anyone would get up at such an hour. I often thought I would be willing to work twice as hard during the day if I could only sleep until a little more reasonable hour like 7:00 a.m.

My brother-in-law would throw me an orange, and I would climb into well-worn overalls and leave the house just as the morning skies were beginning to glow with a faint light. Wearily I would mount a sometimes reluctant brown Shetland pony—having no saddle and only a rope bridle—and ride to the west pasture to bring in the cows to be milked. After bringing them in, my job was to milk the fifteen Holstein cows, all bearing such descriptive names as Black Spot, White Spot, Blacky, and Whitey, all christened by six and eight-year-old nephews.

I would check for signs of mastitis by squirting milk onto a gray circular disc. If there were yellow flecks or threads in the milk, the milk from that cow would have to be fed to the pigs and the cow then treated with antibiotics. Before milking the sometimes very dirty cows, I would have to clean them with pungent-smelling Purex. It was a trick to get the electric milkers on the cows properly and even trickier to tell when the cows were thoroughly milked.

After the milking, I would have to straw down the shed, feed the pigs, clean their pens, spray for flies, feed the calves—and then get ready for breakfast. Whew! The morning chores seemed like a day's work by themselves. Getting up so early and doing so many chores before breakfast was hard for a city boy from Provo. It took considerable time at the basement sink to clean up from the chores—the smell from the pigs lingered even after Lava soap and hard scrubbing. Finally, it was time for breakfast!

Breakfast consisted of cooked cereal (Sunny Boy Porridge, which we called "mush"), scrambled eggs and cheese with a little ketchup, homemade bread and butter, and Roger's Syrup. But all too soon, breakfast was over, and it was time to start the real work of the day.

One morning after breakfast, as I was walking across the barnyard in my hot rubber boots on my way to get a tractor, I couldn't resist an impulse to lie down in the shade of an old haystack. That temporary rest was quite exquisite. It was such a delight to take off my boots and just flop into the cool, sweet-smelling hay. I thought about burrowing into the hay to hide from my brother-in-law and catch up my sleep—even ten minutes would be wonderful. The rest was fleeting, however, because I would feel guilty; in my mind I could hear him saying, "We sleep at night, not during the day!" I would then drag myself back to labor in the heat of the sun.

The first summer I was in Canada, I was relieved to learn that my brother-in-law had decided not to haul baled hay that year. Instead he was going to try a new technique in which the hay was cut standing in the field and then blown into covered wagons. The wagons would then be pulled by an old car or by a grain truck back to the barn area, and the chopped hay would be drawn out with a winch onto a conveyor belt, which carried it to a blower. This machine would blow the sweet smelling hay into a silo to ferment and become silage, the smell of which the cows loved, and I quickly learned to hate.

This whole new process was supposed to save labor. In fact, it turned out to have its hardships, too. The blower often got so clogged with hay that I would have to dismantle it, clean the insides out with a long-handled rake, and then put the whole thing back together again. This job had to be done quickly because, as my brother-in-law would remind me, newly filled wagons were coming soon and "you have to hurry when sixteen men are waiting on you"—I hated it!

As I would frantically try to unclog the blower, my brother-in-law's hay and my own sweat would combine into an itchy mixture that would either stick to my neck and back or fall into my burning eyes. The red bandanna over my nose and mouth wasn't much protection either because I would still inhale tiny bits of the chopped hay. Somehow, I would manage to keep up with the endless cycle of wagons. I thought more than once that I truly was earning my bread "by the sweat of my brow"—and my neck, back, arms, and legs.

One of the highlights of the hay-hauling day, was the noon dinner. My sister would leave the house and come across the prairie in an old, gray Chevy. I would eagerly watch as her car bounced toward us across the fields, leaving small cyclones of dust billowing behind. I knew what she had on the back seat of the car—huge bologna and lettuce sandwiches and quarts of homemade root beer with chunks of ice floating and clinking in the glass Mason jars. We each got a quart. The coolness and flavor of the drink was delicious in contrast to the heat of the day, and we all would lie on the sweet smelling ground in the shade of the hay wagons to sip the icy refreshment and almost inhale the tasty sandwiches.

And so went the summer months in Canada during my teenage years—I experienced joy in rest because I had experienced hard labor. The harder the labor, the more joy I felt in rest. And so it is with all of us.

Ever since the fall of Adam and Eve, all mankind has had to learn by having experience with opposites and contrasts. We appreciate refreshing coolness in the aftermath of oppressive heat. Comforting warmth is welcomed after the bitter cold. We savor delicious food after the fast, and we recognize that rest is most pleasant after work.

We can only know sweetness after knowing bitterness, light after witnessing darkness, and pleasure after enduring pain.

Without experiencing the hardships of this life, Adam and Eve could not understand or comprehend peace and rest. To experience a fulness of joy they had to fall from paradise and enter a world where they could experience adversity, sorrow, and death—there was no other way.

THE NEED FOR OPPOSITION IN ALL THINGS

While Adam and Eve were in the garden of Eden, they didn't have to haul hay in order to earn their daily bread. They were surrounded by what we would consider heavenly conditions. The various fruits of the trees were there for the plucking. There was no pain, sorrow, disease, nor death. A wonderful harmony existed among the beasts of the forests and the fowls of the air. Elohim (Heavenly Father) and Jehovah (Jesus Christ) made frequent visits to Adam and Eve, and peace, tranquillity, and beauty enveloped all that existed in Eden.

Elder Parley P. Pratt, in his wonderfully descriptive style, provides us with pleasant insights into Edenic life before the Fall. He wrote,

> The beasts of the earth were all in perfect harmony with each other; the lion ate straw like the ox, the wolf dwelt with the lamb, the leopard lay down with the kid, the cow and bear fed together in the same pasture, while their young ones reposed in perfect security, under the shade of the same trees. All was peace and harmony, and nothing to hurt nor disturb in all the holy mountains.
>
> And to crown the whole, we behold man created in the image of God and exalted in dignity and power, having dominion over all the vast creation of animated beings which swarmed through the earth, while at the same time he inhabited a beautiful and well-watered garden in the midst of which stood the tree of life, to which he had free access; while he stood in the presence of his Maker, conversed with him face to face, and gazed upon his glory, without a dimming veil between.
>
> O reader, contemplate for a moment this beautiful creation, with peace and plenty: the earth teeming with harmless animals, rejoicing over all the plain; the air swarming with delightful birds whose never-ceasing notes filled the air with varied melody; and all in subjection to their rightful sovereign, who rejoiced over them; while in a delightful garden, the capital of creation, man was seated on the throne of this vast empire, swaying his scepter over all the earth with undisputed right, while legions of angels encamped round about him and joined their glad voices in grateful songs of praise and shouts of joy. Neither sigh nor groan was heard through the vast expanse; neither were there sorrow, fear, pain, weeping, sickness, nor death; neither contentions, wars, nor bloodshed; but peace crowned the seasons as they rolled, and life, joy, and love reigned over all God's works.[1]

From the Latter-day scriptures we learn that in order to fully appreciate the paradisiacal conditions, Adam and Eve would have to experience a different environment, one that would allow them to gain knowledge by encountering opposition, pain, sorrow, death—including alienation from God. We, too, must experience opposites to recognize differences. In harmony with this principle, the Prophet Joseph Smith taught that "truth is manifest by proving contraries".[2]

This observation is consistent with an important doctrinal point established by Lehi when he explained: "For it must needs be, that there is an opposition in all things. If not so,...righteousness could not be brought to pass, neither wickedness, neither holiness nor misery, neither good nor bad. Wherefore, all things must needs be a compound in one" (2 Nephi 2:11).

Can you imagine an oil painting or a picture of any kind without shades of light and darkness? A photograph that is composed simply of light without any shade of darkness is a picture of nothing. Only by contrasts of light and shadow can we experience any kind of visual perception. Without bitterness neither Adam nor we could prize the sweet. We could not appreciate pleasure, having never experienced pain. We could have no joy, because we had known no sorrow. Furthermore, without opposites offering us choice, we could have no agency. This may be the reason why there were two trees mentioned by name in the garden of Eden.

The two trees represented the idea of opposites. They were identified as the *Tree of Life*, representing life in the presence of God; and the *Tree of Knowledge of Good and Evil*, representing the knowledge that will come through experiencing adversity. Our Heavenly Father explained to Adam and Eve that they could eat freely of all the trees including the Tree of Life, however, they were warned that if they ate of the fruit of the Tree of Knowledge of Good and Evil, the forbidden fruit, they would die—but they were free to choose.

This would seem like an easy choice, but it wasn't because there were both positive and negative consequences associated with each tree. By choosing to eat of the forbidden fruit Adam and Eve would gain knowledge and receive the capacity to bear children—but they would experience pain and sorrow and spiritual and physical death. If they had chosen to eat of the Tree of Life they would have lived forever—but they would have had no children nor would they have known good from evil (see end of chapter Figure 4-A, The Tree of Life and the Tree of Knowledge of Good and Evil). These ideas will be developed in more detail as we continue in this chapter.

Now let's look at the nature of the two commandments that were given to Adam and Eve—to multiply and replenish the earth and to not eat of the forbidden fruit—and see how these two commandments *worked together* to accomplish the purposes of God in bringing joy to his children.

THE FIRST COMMANDMENT—
TO MULTIPLY AND REPLENISH THE EARTH

When plant and animal life were first placed on this earth, the Lord blessed them and gave them the command to, "be fruitful, and multiply, and fill the waters in the sea; and let fowl multiply in the earth" (Moses 2:22). Our Heavenly Father also commanded Adam and Eve to "multiply and replenish the earth" that they might have joy and rejoicing in their posterity (Abraham 4:28; Moses 2:28). However, at the time our Father gave the commandment to multiply, neither plants, nor animals, nor Adam and Eve could have offspring—there were no cycles of births and deaths. Lehi explained this fact when he said:

> And now, behold, if Adam had not transgressed he would not have fallen, but he would have remained in the garden of Eden. And *all things* which were created must have remained in the same state in which they were after they were created; and they must have remained forever, and had no end.
>
> And they *would have had no children*; wherefore they would have remained in a state of innocence, having no joy, for they knew no misery; doing no good, for they knew no sin.
>
> But behold, all things have been done in the wisdom of him who knoweth all things.
>
> *Adam fell that men might be; and men are, that they might have joy* (2 Nephi 2:22-25; emphasis added).

From this scripture we learn that our first parents partook of the forbidden fruit so that they could fulfill the command to multiply and replenish the earth. This commandment has never been rescinded. In fact all couples, when they marry in holy places, receive the same commandment—to multiply and replenish the earth that they might have joy and rejoicing in their posterity.

THE SECOND COMMANDMENT—
THE FORBIDDEN FRUIT

After Adam and Eve were placed in Eden and commanded to multiply, they were given the charge to take care of the garden, to subdue the earth, and to have dominion over it. They were told they could eat the fruit of all the trees in the garden except the Tree of Knowledge of Good and Evil—the forbidden fruit. The second commandment was that the Lord forbade the eating of the fruit of this tree—but they were free to choose. Here is how this charge was worded by the Lord:

And I, the Lord God, commanded the man, saying: Of every tree of the garden thou mayest freely eat,

But of the tree of the knowledge of good and evil, thou shalt not eat of it, *nevertheless, thou mayest choose for thyself, for it is given unto thee*; but, remember that I forbid it, for in the day thou eatest thereof thou shalt surely die (Moses 3:16-17; emphasis added).

In other words, God seems to be saying to Adam: "I am going to tell you what will happen to you if you eat the fruit of that tree. You will die in the same day you eat it. But you decide for yourselves what you want to do. You can stay here in this garden of peace and harmony, not really appreciating it, or you can choose to eat of that tree and thereby experience death and gain knowledge from the adversities that are part of a mortal world. Remember now, if you eat of that tree, you will die, but you choose for yourselves what you really want to do." ·

Sometimes my students point out what seems at first glance to be a conflict, a double bind, for Adam and Eve. The problem they see is that Adam and Eve were commanded to multiply and replenish the earth, but they couldn't have children unless they ate of the fruit—and they were told not to eat of the fruit. The two commandments seem to be contradictory. But could it be that they were not really irreconcilable at all? Could it be that God did not really *want* nor *expect* them to keep the second commandment? The answer to this question is the key to this apparent conflict.

No Conflict Between
The Two Commandments?

There was no real conflict between the two commandments because our Father in Heaven *wanted* Adam and Eve to eat the forbidden fruit so that his great plan of happiness could be put into operation—so that Adam and Eve could have children and experience opposition. Adam and Eve were *not* given a choice concerning the first commandment regarding having children. That was a commandment that God intended they keep. But they *were* given a choice relative to the eating of the fruit. Accordingly, what God had stated regarding the forbidden fruit was more of an *explanation* of consequences than it was an expression of his divine will. The fruit was forbidden only in the sense that if they ate of it they would die. They were to decide what to do, and then they would be responsible for the consequences of their choice.

President Joseph Fielding Smith clarified how the second commandment was structured in such a way as to allow Adam and Eve a choice, and how their disobedience constituted a transgression but not a sin.

I never speak of the part Eve took in this fall as a sin, nor do I accuse Adam of a sin. One may say, "Well did they not break a commandment?" Yes. But let us examine the nature of that commandment and the results which came out of it.

In no other commandment the Lord ever gave to man, did he say: "But of the tree of the knowledge of good and evil, thou shalt not eat of it, *nevertheless, thou mayest choose for thyself.*"

It is true, the Lord warned Adam and Eve that to partake of the fruit they would transgress a law, and this happened. But it is not always a sin to transgress a law....

Before partaking of the fruit Adam could have lived forever; therefore, his status was one of immortality. When he ate, he became subject to death, and therefore he became mortal. This was a transgression of the law, but not a sin in the strict sense, for it was something that Adam and Eve had to do![3]

In other words, what President Smith seems to be saying is that "sins" are actions that offend God (like murder or adultery) because they violate laws established for our eternal progression. On the other hand, "transgressions" are infractions of physical laws (like Adam eating the fruit), the consequences of which may result in suffering, but they do not offend God because good will come from these transgressions.

So again, in the first command, God was expressing his intention that Adam and Eve have children. In the second, he was simply describing the natural consequences of eating the fruit: they would experience opposition, hardships, and death—all of which, they discovered later, would be to their benefit and learning (see Moses 5:10-11).

When God explained that death would be the result of eating the fruit, he was describing the natural consequences of a physical law. These laws stand independent of God's anger or pleasure. For example, if you put your hand on a hot stove, you will be burned—a natural consequence—but God will not be angry with you for doing so. Adam and Eve ate of the fruit and introduced death—also a natural consequence—but God was not angry with them for making this choice. In fact, as we mentioned earlier, our Father in Heaven was was *pleased* with their choice. Even though he knew that the consequences would be suffering, sorrow and death, he also knew that this knowledge was a prerequisite for our first parents to become as the Gods, knowing good and evil.

The idea that God was not angry with Adam and Eve for eating the fruit stands in opposition to almost all other Christian creeds. It is the tradition of the Judeo-Christian world to believe that because of God's hot displeasure he cast our first parents out of Eden and out of his presence. Most Christians also believe that if Adam and Eve had not eaten of the fruit they would still be in paradise today. They do not understand the necessity of the Fall in order to facilitate God's eternal plan for his children. Consequently, while others *condemn* Adam and Eve because of their eating the forbidden fruit, we *rejoice* in their choice.

Free agency, or the ability to choose between alternatives, is a fundamental part of our eternal existence (see 2 Nephi 2:13). God, a perfect being, would not create Adam and Eve in an imperfect, fallen condition. They had to choose to bring upon themselves corruption and death, disease and darkness. So, the predicament in which Adam and Eve found themselves, in connection with the two commandments, was not so much a conflict as it was a need for them to make a hard choice.

It is a blessing for us that they courageously and wisely chose to bring about the Fall. All of us in the pre-earth life rejoiced because Adam and Eve made the hard choice to set in motion our Father's great plan of happiness.

ADAM AND EVE REJOICED IN THE FALL

After partaking of the fruit, Adam and Eve, with their eyes opened, also rejoiced over the results of the Fall. Even though they recognized that they now would be vulnerable to death and disease, pain and sorrow, they regarded their descent into mortality as part of the grand plan of God to provide physical bodies and mortal experiences for his spirit children—their brothers and sisters in the pre-earth life—who were eagerly waiting for their chance to come to earth. Therefore, they rejoiced when they learned the consequences of their eating the fruit. As President Joseph Fielding Smith explained:

> I am sure that neither Adam nor Eve looked upon it as a sin, when they learned the consequences, and this is discovered in their words after they learned the consequences.
>
> Adam said: "Blessed be the name of God, for because of my transgression my eyes are opened, and in this life I shall have joy, and again in the flesh I shall see God."
>
> Eve said: "Were it not for our transgression we never should have had seed, and never should have known good and evil, and the joy of our redemption, and the eternal life which God giveth unto all the obedient." [Moses 5:10-11.]
>
> We can hardly look upon anything resulting in such benefits as being a sin, in the sense in which we consider sin.[4]

With such wonderful blessings resulting from the Fall, you may wonder why would Satan encourage Adam and Eve to partake of the forbidden fruit if the Fall was part of God's plan for our happiness. Let's discuss this interesting idea.

WHY SATAN ENCOURAGED THE FALL

Considering the fact that he is motivated entirely by selfish reasons, why would Satan do something that would further the work of God? There are several points you might keep in mind in this regard. First, Satan had been cast out of heaven when he appeared to Adam and Eve in the garden of Eden. He knew at that point that he would never have further access to the spirit children of God unless they were given mortal birth.

In addition, Satan's eternal punishment was that he would never receive a physical body of his own. Consequently, he desires to unlawfully possess the bodies of Adam and Eve and their children. Possessing the bodies of others would never be available to him if the process of procreation were not begun, and that could only happen by encouraging Adam and Eve to fall.

Finally, the Lord explained to Moses that Satan did not know "the mind of God" (Moses 4:6). Apparently he did not fully comprehend how the Fall would benefit the children of God, nor how it would play a part in their eternal happiness. By telling half truths Satan with guile and malice aforethought willingly encouraged Adam and Eve to partake of the fruit so that he might have access to us and thereby further his own evil designs to seek the misery of all mankind, that we might be miserable like unto himself (see 2 Nephi 2:18).

SATAN'S HALF TRUTHS

While Adam and Eve were in the garden of Eden, Satan first approached Adam and offered the forbidden fruit to him. Adam rejected it. Satan then approached Eve and offered her the fruit. He enticed her by blatantly *lying*, promising her that she would not die. Then he explained *truthfully* that by partaking of the fruit Eve would become as the Gods, knowing good from evil. The narrative of the holy scriptures informs us that Eve was beguiled by Satan, and she partook of the fruit. This example introduces us to a pattern that we see repeatedly throughout the scriptures and in our own lives of how Satan will tell half truths in order to persuade us to follow him. Can you think of examples in your own life where this has been the case?

After she had partaken of the fruit, Eve then sought out Adam and offered the fruit to him. Now Adam was in a dilemma. He had been warned that the consequences of eating the fruit would be physical death and spiritual banishment—but Eve had eaten and was to be driven from the garden of Eden. Adam had to make a choice: either he could stay with Eve and be driven from the garden or he could remain in Eden and thus be separated from her. Adam wisely and lovingly chose to eat of the fruit so that he could remain with Eve and children could be born.

Though in partaking of the forbidden fruit Adam and Eve transgressed a law, they did not enter the fallen world without a reassurance and a promise of a Savior. Through the Atonement and obedience to the principles and ordinances of the gospel of Jesus Christ, the Father would make it possible for them and us to be redeemed and eventually return to his presence. In the meantime, to protect them from the powers of the adversary, our first parents were given coats of skin to replace the ineffective fig-leaf aprons suggested by Satan.

FIG LEAVES AND COATS OF SKINS

From the book of Moses, we learn that after eating of the forbidden fruit, "the eyes of them both were opened, and they knew that they had been naked. And they sewed fig leaves together and made themselves aprons" (Moses 4:13). These aprons are sacred symbols or types representing the frailty of our condition in mortality.

Regarding this idea, in an earlier work I wrote that,

> Satan had them sew fig leaves together to cover their nakedness. Here, the reference of *nakedness* is no doubt a metaphoric allusion to the couples' feelings of self consciousness and unworthiness before the Lord. The figure can be extended to describe how we all feel after we sin. Using ineffective fig leaves—carnal comforters—we try to ease our loneliness, and make the pain go away. They provide only an illusion of relief. [In the end] these false comforters only escalate our stress; the harder we try to ease our pain using them, the worse things get!
>
> In contrast, our Heavenly Father provided Adam and Eve much better covers for their nakedness than fig leaves. They were given coats of skins— which symbolize light and truth. These garments, when honored, cover, heal, and protect. Through obedience and faith, they cover our nakedness (our vulnerability, our low self esteem, our depression, and our feelings of unworthiness) before God.[5]

Satan's meager ways of obtaining security and protection are always deficient. Fig leaves provide poor cover and give little protection on windy days. Though we don't wear literal fig leaves on a regular basis today, sometimes we do select figurative fig leaves, other Satan-inspired defense mechanisms—carnal comforters—such as anger, greed, lust, passion, and materialism, to name just a few, in an effort "to cover our nakedness" and protect ourselves from the fallen world around us.

While we are discussing the nakedness of Adam and Eve it would be well to point out that their transgression did *not* involve any kind of sexual sin as some have falsely believed.[6] The eating of the fruit was not a metaphor for the *original sin* which some believe was sexual lust or concupiscence. Adam and Eve were married by the Lord (see Genesis 2:22-24) while they were yet immortal beings in the garden of Eden—before they partook of the fruit and death entered the world.

THE CONSEQUENCES OF EATING THE FRUIT

As we mentioned earlier, there were both wonderful and painful consequences that came as a result of the Fall. We read that after being taught the plan of salvation, "Adam blessed God and was filled, and began to prophesy concerning all the families of the earth, saying: Blessed be the name of God, for because of my transgression my eyes are opened, and in this life I shall have joy, and again in the flesh I shall see God" (Moses 5:10).

Eve also found reason to rejoice because of the Fall. She exclaimed, "Were it not for our transgression we never should have had seed, and never should have known good and evil, and the joy of our redemption, and the eternal life which God giveth unto all the obedient" (Moses 5:11; also 2 Nephi 2:23-24). Though Adam and Eve rejoiced in these positive consequences, they were also very aware of the negative results of their choice—consequences for the serpent, Adam and Eve, mankind in general, and the earth (see end of chapter Figure 4-B, The Fall of Adam, Eve, and the Earth).

Consequences for the Serpent

Regarding God's curse upon the serpent, we read, "And I, the Lord God, said unto the serpent: Because thou hast done this thou shalt be cursed above all cattle, and above every beast of the field; upon thy belly shalt thou go, and dust shalt thou eat all the days of thy life; And I will put enmity between thee and the woman, between thy seed and her seed; and he shall bruise thy head, and thou shalt bruise his heel" (Moses 4:20-21).

In this passage we find two important doctrinal points. The first is the punishment of the serpent for participating in the Fall. The second is the promise of a Savior. In connection with the first point, from the Prophet Joseph Smith we learn the reality of this curse. While living in Kirtland, Ohio, this latter-day Seer gained access to some ancient Egyptian documents showing a large snake walking about on two legs much as a chicken does.[7] When someone asked him what the figure represented, Joseph Smith explained that before the Fall serpents did indeed walk about upon two legs.[8]

The second point is the promise of a Savior, a Redeemer for mankind. When we understand the referents behind the metaphor, the meaning becomes clear. In symbolic language, the Lord is explaining that even though Satan and his seed (his followers) will have power to bruise our heel (to tempt us), the seed of woman (Christ) will have power to bruise the head of the serpent (overcome the power of Satan). In other words, in this passage we have the first indication that a Savior would eventually overcome Satan's power by providing an Atonement for Adam's transgression and our own sins (see Moses 4:21).

Consequences for the Woman

To mother Eve, the Lord declared: "I will greatly multiply thy sorrow and thy conception. In sorrow thou shalt bring forth children, and thy desire shall be to thy husband, and he shall rule over thee" (Moses 4:22). This declaration was not a vindictive indictment flung out by an angry, vengeful God. It was simply our Heavenly Father verifying one of the natural consequences that would come as a result of eating the fruit. Brother Hugh W. Nibley provided fresh insight into this declaration when he explained:

> Now a curse was placed on Eve, and it looked as if she would have to pay a high price for taking the initiative in the search for knowledge. To our surprise the *identical* curse was placed on Adam also. For Eve, God "will greatly multiply thy sorrow and thy conception. In sorrow shall thou bring forth children." The key is the word for sorrow, *tsavadh* (or atsav), meaning to labor, to toil, to sweat, to do something very hard. To *multiply* does not mean to add or increase but to repeat over and over again; the word in the Septuagint is *plethynomai*, as in the multiplying of words in the repetitious prayers of the ancients. Both the conception and the labor of Eve will be multiple; she will have many children.[9]

In other words, the so-called *curse* pronounced upon Eve was really an announcement that she would labor hard in bringing forth many children. I believe that the Lord looks with great favor upon women who happily choose to go through the pain associated with child bearing. They can be viewed as Christlike figures in the sense that out of their personal pain and suffering life is brought forth. Not to leave men out, they can be Christlike figures if they care for, protect and love their families even as Christ loved and gave his life for the Church. Sadly, the scriptures warn us that almost all men "exercise unrighteous dominion" and do not lead in a Christlike way through gentleness, kindness, and love unfeigned (D&C 121:39-42). This observation has a great bearing on how we sometimes look at the second part of the Lord's pronouncement to Eve.

The other part of God's pronouncement to Eve was that Adam, her husband, would rule over her. This establishes for the first time in our scriptures that there was to be a patriarchal head in the marriage. Apparently this patriarchal order of priesthood leadership will be greatly expanded in the days to come, for as we read, "Now this same Priesthood, which was in the beginning, shall be in the end of the world also" (Moses 6:7).

In a time when many people throughout the world seek to promote egalitarianism as the ideal in all their relationships, we Latter-day Saints, influenced by the spirit of worldliness, sometimes find it hard to accept the fact that the Lord has designated husbands to preside over the wife and that she is to obey him in righteousness. The New Testament teachings of Paul and of our latter-day prophets are consistent with this law of God. Paul explained, "For the husband is the head of the wife, even as Christ is the head of the Church" (Ephesians 5:23).

President Spencer W. Kimball has explained how the husband presides in marriage when he said,

> The wife follows the husband only as he follows Christ. No woman has ever been asked by the Church authorities to follow her husband into an evil pit. She is to follow him as he follows and obeys the Savior of the world, but in deciding this, she should always be sure she is fair.
>
> The husband is head of the family only insofar as he sacrifices for them. One of the most provocative and profound statements in holy writ is that of Paul wherein he directs husbands and wives in their duty to each other and to family. First, he commands the women:
>
> "Wives, submit yourselves unto your own husbands, as unto the Lord.
>
> "For the husband is the head of the wife, even as Christ is the head of the church: and he is the saviour of the body.
>
> "Therefore as the church is subject unto Christ, so let the wives be to their own husbands in every thing." (Ephesians 5:22-24.)
>
> This is no idle jest, no facetious matter. Much is said in those few words. Paul says, "as unto the Lord."
>
> A woman would have no fears of being imposed upon nor of any dictatorial measures nor of any improper demands if the husband is self-sacrificing and worthy. Certainly no sane woman would hesitate to give submission to her own really righteous husband in everything. We are sometimes shocked to see the wife take over the leadership, naming the one to pray, the place to be, the things to do.
>
> Husbands are commanded: "Love your wives, even as Christ also loved the church, and gave himself for it." (Ephesians 5:25.)
>
> Here is the answer: Christ loved the Church and its people so much that he voluntarily endured persecution for them, stoically withstood pain and physical abuse for them, and finally gave his precious life for them.
>
> When the husband is ready to treat his household in that manner, not only the wife, but also all the family will respond to his leadership.[10]

More recently, in 1995, the First Presidency and Council of the Twelve apostles reaffirmed the Lord's law that husbands and fathers are to take the lead in the home, when they unitedly declared: "By divine design, fathers are to preside over their families in love and righteousness and are responsible to provide the necessities of life and protection for their families. Mothers are primarily responsible for the nurture of the children. In these sacred responsibilities, fathers and mothers are obligated to help one another as equal partners".[11]

As Latter-day Saints we are greatly influenced by the worldliness around us where there is great confusion regarding the roles of men and women. The Lord has made it clear that the husband is to take the lead. When two people ride the same horse, one has to sit behind. So it is with marriages, one of the partners has to take the lead, and the Lord has declared that the husband has this responsibility.

I believe that one of the great needs in the Church—and surely in the world— is for good models of good patriarchs in the home by leading in righteousness and women following their husbands in righteousness. By learning correct principles of marriage relationships from the promptings of the Holy Spirit, from the scriptures, from the teachings of the prophets, and from other inspired sources, we can make progress in this vital area. Indeed, the establishment of Zion is conditioned on the Saints becoming pure in heart, particularly in this respect.[12]

Consequences for Adam

In the strict sense of the word, Adam is not cursed here either. The ground was cursed for his sake—meaning that good would come from Adam having to work the ground. Through this experience he would gain knowledge by encountering opposites. He would endure fatigue to appreciate rest, pain in order to sense pleasure, etc.

To the man Adam, the Lord said:

> Because thou hast hearkened unto the voice of thy wife, and hast eaten of the fruit of the tree of which I commanded thee, saying—Thou shalt not eat of it, cursed shall be the ground *for thy sake*; in sorrow shalt thou eat of it all the days of thy life.
>
> Thorns also, and thistles shall it bring forth to thee, and thou shalt eat the herb of the field.
>
> By the sweat of thy face shalt thou eat bread, until thou shalt return unto the ground—for thou shalt surely die—for out of it wast thou taken: for dust thou wast, and unto dust shalt thou return (Moses 4:23-25; emphasis added).

From this we learn that the consequence of Adam eating the fruit would be hard, sweaty labor if he were to have food to eat. Regarding this, Brother Hugh Nibley has said:

The Lord says to Adam, "In *sorrow* shalt thou eat of it all the days of thy life" (i.e., the bread which his labor must bring forth from the earth). The identical word is used in both cases [of the woman and of the man], the root meaning is to work hard at cutting or digging; both the man and the woman must sorrow and both must labor. (The Septuagint word is *lype*, meaning bodily or mental strain, discomfort, or affliction.) It means not to be sorry, but to have a hard time. If Eve must labor to bring forth, so too must Adam labor (Genesis 3:17; Moses 4:23) to quicken the earth so it shall bring forth. Both of them bring forth life with sweat and tears, and Adam is not the favored party. If his labor is not as severe as hers, it is more protracted. For Eve's life will be spared long after her childbearing— "nevertheless thy life shall be spared"—while Adam's toil must go on to the end of his days: "In sorrow shalt thou eat of it *all* the days of thy life!" Even retirement is no escape from that sorrow. The thing to notice is that Adam is not let off lightly as a privileged character; he is as bound to Mother Earth as she is to the law of her husband. And why not? If he was willing to follow her, he was also willing to suffer with her, for this affliction was imposed on Adam expressly "because thou hast hearkened unto thy wife and hast partaken of the fruit."[13]

In other words, Brother Nibley is pointing out that while Eve's labor would be sharp and painful, it would not be extended throughout her life. On the other hand, though, Adam's labor would be less physically acute, but it would stretch out over a longer period of time. While the nature and duration of their labors were to be different there were some consequences of the Fall which came equally upon Adam and Eve.

For example, by eating the fruit both Adam and Eve were to experience both physical and spiritual death. I have often wondered if after leaving Eden our first parents were more anxious about their impending physical death or their present spiritual death—their being driven out of the presence of the Father.

In reference to Adam's impending physical death, it is interesting to note that, as was mentioned in the previous chapter, when the commandments were given to him and Eve in Eden, the earth was nearer Kolob and time was measured by the Lord's time (i.e., a day with the Lord is a thousand years with man; see 2Peter 3:8; also Abra 4:13 and Facsimile 2, figure 1). The warning regarding the consequences of partaking of the fruit was given according to the Lord's time and it was fulfilled according to his time. Adam was 930 years of age when he died. Had he lived longer than one thousand years, he would not have experienced physical death in the same *day*.

Consequences for All Mankind

In addition to those effects of the Fall that we have already mentioned which

Adam and Eve experienced and also passed on to us, the scriptures and the writings of the prophets explain many other consequences which have come upon all of us as children of Adam and Eve. The following are a few examples.[14]

1) *All mankind is lost and fallen.* Have you ever felt that you were a lost child? Have you ever felt that you wanted to go back to your heavenly home? I suspect that many people have these feelings from time to time. Abinadi was quoting Isaiah when he said, "All we, like sheep, have gone astray; we have turned every one to his own way" (Mosiah 14: compare Isaiah 53:6). Alma explained that after partaking of the forbidden fruit, our first parents were cut off from the tree of life, became lost forever, and were cut off both temporally and spiritually from the presence of the Lord. Because of the Fall we are lost and fallen, subject to spiritual death—the separation from God and the separation from things of righteousness (see Alma 12:16, 32; 40:26; 42:7, 9)..

This being the case, "it was expedient that mankind should be reclaimed from this spiritual death. Therefore, as they had become carnal, sensual, and devilish, by nature, this probationary state became a state for them to prepare; it became a preparatory state" (Alma 42:6-10). The scriptures teach us that we would be lost and fallen forever— separated from our heavenly home—were it not for the coming of our Redeemer, Jesus Christ (1 Nephi 10:4-6; compare Alma 42:67). I am grateful that through the spirit of inspiration we are assured from time to time that we are not lost and fallen nor cast off forever and that through our Savior we can find our way back home. These impressions give us encouragement to continue on—to fulfill the measure of our creation—until the time comes for us to be called back home.

2) *In our natural state, all of us are enemies to all righteousness.* King Benjamin, in his final address to his people declared: "For the natural man is an enemy to God, and has been from the fall of Adam, and will be, unless he yields to the enticings of the Holy Spirit, and putteth off the natural man" (Mosiah 3:19). If we refuse to follow the enticings of the Holy Spirit and choose to remain in our carnal state, we will remain in spiritual darkness and will continue to be an enemy to God. The apostle Paul wrote that "the natural man receiveth not the things of the Spirit of God: for they are foolishness unto him: neither can he know them, because they are spiritually discerned" (1 Corinthians 2:14).

Similarly, President Brigham Young explained that "The natural man (or as we now use the language, the fallen or sinful man) receiveth not the things of the Spirit of God.... In no other way can the things of God be understood. Men who are destitute of the influence of the Holy Ghost, or the Spirit of God, cannot understand the things of God; they may read them, but to them they are shrouded in darkness."[15]

Affirming the same idea, Elder Bruce R. McConkie has written that, "There is a natural birth, and there is a spiritual birth. The natural birth is to die as pertaining to premortal life, to leave the heavenly realms where all spirits dwell in the Divine Presence, and to begin a new life, a mortal life, a life here on earth. The natural birth creates a natural man, and the natural man is an enemy to God. In his fallen state he is carnal, sensual, and devilish by nature. Appetites and passions govern his life, and he is alive—acutely so—to all that is evil and wicked in the world."[16]

This is a gloomy picture—but it is so awfully true that the natural man is an enemy to God. We will have to struggle, no doubt, with the temptations of the natural man and the trials of the flesh as long as we are in this fallen world. The only way out is to learn of Christ and of his saving grace. By focusing our faith on him and his teachings, we can partake of his infinite sacrifice and make progress in overcoming the natural man. Like Nephi and Alma, even the fleeting thought that we can really overcome our evil inclinations gives us hope and makes our hearts sing with joy (2 Nephi 4:18; Alma 36:18). As this hope grows within us we find ourselves almost bursting, wanting to shout praises to him who has the loving power to grasp us from the awful clutches of our own natural selves, of Satan, and a fallen world.

3) *All of us inherit a fallen nature through conception.* The Lord clearly explained to Adam that: "Inasmuch as thy children are conceived in sin, even so when they begin to grow up, sin conceiveth in their hearts, and they taste the bitter, that they may know to prize the good" (Moses 6:55). In one sense this passage can mean that at conception and birth we are brought forth into a world where sin and evil are rampant. In another sense it can mean that from conception we inherit all the negative effects resulting from the Fall. Both of these concepts are true but they stand in stark contrast to those held by many Christians who believe that the original sin was sexual in nature. This idea will be discussed in greater detail in a later chapter.

4) *Little children who do wrong because of the Fall are still innocent by virtue of the Atonement.* Even though little children are born innocent, they still do things that are wrong because of the inherent selfishness of the natural man and because they don't have perfect models, they imitate the inappropriate behavior of others. We don't have to observe little children very long before we see that they sometimes can be very mean, hateful and selfish. Anyone who has had extended contact with children has most likely at one time or another seen the truthfulness of this idea in action.

For example, one of the really mean places on the earth is an elementary school ground at recess time. Children bully one another, they pull hair, they steal, and they beat up on one another. At home children sometimes terrorize their younger siblings and vice versa. Even though they sometimes do things that are very wrong—they are not *accountable* for their actions until they reach the age of eight. Little children are innocent, not because they do no wrong, but because Christ has chosen to take upon himself the consequences of their actions.

Regarding the status of little children, Elder Bruce R. McConkie has reminded us:

> Children and others who have not arrived at the years of accountability are automatically saved in the celestial kingdom by virtue of the atonement. "Little children are whole, for they are not capable of committing sin," the Lord says, "wherefore the curse of Adam is taken from them in me, that it hath no power over them." (Moro. 8:8; D&C 29:46-50; Mosiah 15:25; *Teachings*, 107.) The curse of Adam includes both temporal and spiritual death, and accordingly neither of these is binding upon children and those who have "no understanding" (D&C 29:50), that is, those who are not accountable. All such will be raised in immortality and unto eternal life.[17]

This promise is especially comforting to those who have lost little ones in death. If they prove faithful, they will one day be with their departed children in the celestial kingdom.

5) *One may be faithful and pure-hearted and yet still be buffeted by the pulls of a fallen world.* Have you ever wondered why bad things happen to good people? Why have good people—including Jesus and his holy prophets—had to experience opposition and temptations? The answer to these questions is because we have inherited the effects of the Fall through our conception, we are vulnerable to the tugs and pulls of a fallen world. Concerning this idea Brigham Young declared: "There are no persons without evil passions to embitter their lives. Mankind are revengeful, passionate, hateful, and devilish in their dispositions. This we inherit through the fall, and the grace of God is designed to enable us to overcome it."[18]

Nephi also recognized the importance of God's grace in helping us overcome this quandary when he reflected on his desire to rejoice in the Lord and yet was critically conscious of his mortal imperfections. In a time of anguish, he cried out,

> My soul delighteth in the things of the Lord and my heart pondereth continually upon the things which I have seen and heard. Nevertheless, notwithstanding the great goodness of the Lord; in showing me his great and marvelous works, my heart exclaimeth: O wretched man that I am! Yea, my heart sorroweth because of my flesh; my soul grieveth because of mine iniquities. I am encompassed about, because of the temptations and the sins

which do so easily beset me. And when I desire to rejoice, my heart groaneth because of my sins; nevertheless, I know in whom I have trusted (2 Nephi 4:16-19).

Likewise the people of King Benjamin were described as "a diligent people in keeping the commandments of the Lord" (Mosiah 1:11), yet after Benjamin's powerful sermon, he "cast his eyes round about on the multitude, and behold they had fallen to the earth, for the fear of the Lord had come upon them. And they had viewed themselves in their own carnal state, even less than the dust of the earth" (Mosiah 4:1-2). But when they cried unto the Lord in faith for a redemption from their sins, "the spirit of the Lord came upon them, and they were filled with joy, having received a remission of their sins" (Mosiah 4:3).

The great patriarchs and matriarchs of past dispensations, as faithful as they were, suffered by the pulls of this fallen world, and they confessed that they were strangers and pilgrims here. They yearned for a city whose builder and maker was God. They longed to go home! (see Hebrews 11:15-16)

Consequences for the Earth

As we discussed extensively in Chapter 2 on the creation of the earth, the place of the creation was nearer Kolob and the residence of God. As a result of the Fall, one of the consequences for the earth was that the earth fell from where it was first organized to where it is now located in space.

Another consequence for the earth was that because Adam chose to eat of the forbidden fruit, the earth was cursed for his sake. As we mentioned earlier, the phrase *for thy sake* explains the beneficial nature of the fallen world for Adam and all of us: the earth became a place where death, disease, and pain run rampant, thus the opportunity for growth was provided. Through the opposition that came as a result of the Fall, Adam and Eve were blessed. They experienced—and we as their children continue to experience—the opposition and the confrontation with evil that eventually qualified them and that can eventually prepare us to know good from evil even as the Gods.

THE LDS VIEW OF THE FALL IS REMARKABLY OPTIMISTIC

Our Latter-day Saint view of the Fall is remarkably optimistic. We believe that Adam and Eve were placed in the garden of Eden with the express purpose of bringing about the Fall, that what they did had the approval of the Gods and that is why "the partaking of the fruit is termed a *transgression* and not a *sin*." In addition, we believe that "their Fall was as much a part of the foreordained plan of the Father as was the very Atonement".[19]

We also believe in the words of the Prophet Joseph Smith, when he stated that "Adam was made to open the way of the world."[20] Even though the Fall was a move downward it was also a move forward in God's eternal plan for our happiness. It "brought man into the world and set his feet upon progression's highway."[21]

By contrast, as Robert Millet has pointed out, "we do not believe, like John Calvin, that men and women are, by virtue of the Fall, depraved creatures. We do not believe, like Martin Luther, that men and women are so inclined to evil that they do not even have the capacity to choose good on their own. We do not believe, with much of the Christian world, that because of the Fall little children are subject to an *original sin*".

On the other hand, we *do* believe that the Fall of Adam opened the way for us, as literal children of God, to gain the necessary experience to advance toward exaltation. We also believe that, though the Fall took a considerable toll upon all of us, in the end, through Christ's atonement and our own faithfulness, the time will come when we will see the Fall and it's consequences from an eternal perspective. Then we will rejoice in the love of our Heavenly Father in preparing such a wonderful opportunity for us. We will recognize then, perhaps more than we do now, that truly all of the challenges and hardships which have come into our lives here in mortality as a result of the Fall have been for our good and our experience and with shouts of hosanna, we will be led to exclaim, "Blessed be the name of God."

ALL THESE THINGS SHALL GIVE THEE EXPERIENCE

Modern revelation has affirmed that opposition is necessary for our growth and experience. Bitter and sweet, pain and joy, death and life—all these and more are a necessary part of our Father's great plan for our happiness. Even though we are often saddened because of the adversities we face in this life, the Lord has promised that there will come a time of perfect rejoicing.

However, in the meantime, as we seek to patiently endure our times of trial and suffering, and when we may feel very much alone and in need of reassurance regarding the Lord's love for us and his awareness of our present situation, it may comfort us to remember the following experience from the life of Joseph Smith. The Prophet Joseph, while in Liberty Jail, sought the Lord in mighty prayer struggling to understand the purpose of his own sorrow and the suffering of other faithful ones. At one point, after learning of more of the cruelties that the Saints had suffered at the hands of their enemies, he cried out mightily to the Father in these pleading words:

> O God, where art thou? And where is the pavilion that covereth thy hiding place?
>
> How long shall thy hand be stayed, and thine eye, yea thy pure eye, behold from the eternal heavens the wrongs of thy people and of thy servants, and thine ear be penetrated with their cries?
>
> Yea, O Lord, how long shall they suffer these wrongs and unlawful oppressions, before thine heart shall be softened toward them, and thy bowels be moved with compassion toward them?
>
> O Lord God Almighty, maker of heaven, earth, and seas, and of all things that in them are, and who controllest and subjectest the devil, and the dark and benighted dominion of Sheol—stretch forth thy hand; let thine eye pierce; let thy pavilion be taken up; let thy hiding place no longer be covered; let thine ear be inclined; let thine heart be softened, and thy bowels moved with compassion toward us.
>
> Let thine anger be kindled against our enemies; and, in the fury of thine heart, with thy sword avenge us of our wrongs.
>
> Remember thy suffering saints, O our God; and thy servants will rejoice in thy name forever (D&C 121:1-6).

And then by way of sweet reassurance and enlightenment, the Lord gently pointed out to the Prophet Joseph the silver lining that always surrounds our clouds of suffering: "My son, peace be unto thy soul; thine adversity and thine afflictions shall be but a small moment; And then, if thou endure it well, God shall exalt thee on high; thou shall triumph over all thy foes. Thy friends do stand by thee, and they shall hail thee again with warm hearts and friendly hands. Thou art not yet as Job" (D&C 121:7-10).

It is my belief that regardless of the suffering we are called upon to bear in this life, good can come out of it—there truly *is* growth potential in adversity. The Lord explained this important principle to Joseph when he said:

> ...if thou shouldst be cast into the pit, or into the hands of murderers, and the sentence of death passed upon thee; if thou be cast into the deep; if the billowing surge conspire against thee; if fierce winds become thine enemy; if the heavens gather blackness, and all the elements combine to hedge up the way; and above all, if the very jaws of hell shall gape open the mouth wide after thee, *know thou, my son, that all these things shall give thee experience, and shall be for thy good.*
>
> The Son of Man hath descended below them all. Art thou greater than he? (D&C 122:7-8; emphasis added).

I have used these wonderfully comforting passages from time to time to help console friends who have experienced various forms of pain and suffering, sorrow and remorse. One such acquaintance was a student of mine who had been driving a car when a terrible accident occurred in which three of her friends were killed. Later, in my office she lamented, "Why did this happen? Why did Heavenly Father allow this to happen to me?"

At best these questions are difficult to answer, but the Lord has given us the assurance that our times of sorrow and adversity are for but a *"small moment"* compared to the vast eternities of peace and rest that we will have with him if we prove faithful in the furnace of affliction. He has also promised us that these things shall give us experience *and will be for our good*! As we remember these truths and focus our faith on his promises, we can find peace in spite of the adversity that is so much a part of this fallen world.

It is my faith and my trust that our loving and kind Heavenly Father is very much aware of all the conditions that affect each of our individual lives. He is aware of you and your needs and the desires of your heart for peace and happiness. He knows you by name and loves you more than you can comprehend. You are his child and he wants you to rest assured that you are not alone.

The intricacies of God's involvement in our lives are probably much more complex than we can understand with our finite minds. While I don't know to what extent he actually *causes* things to happen, I do know that a natural order, a cause and effect process, operates on the earth. I also know that the Lord allows adversity in our lives so we can become as the Gods, knowing good from evil. I also know that to seek for adversity beyond that which we encounter in our day-to-day lives is not wise.

Though the Lord may allow us to experience adversity so that we can progress, and though it often seems that the greater the pain we experience, the greater the chance for learning, the Lord does not want us to suffer more than is needful for our spiritual development. When we deliberately seek for adversity, we step out of the bounds of his protecting power and leave ourselves vulnerable to overwhelming waves of affliction which are not good for us.

The Lord is the Master Refiner. He controls the heat of the fiery furnace of afflictions that we are called upon to pass through for our good. These challenges come to us on a regular basis without our seeking or asking for them. For this reason the Lord has said "sufficient unto the day is the evil thereof" (Matthew 6:34).

Adversity often comes when we least expect it and when we feel the least prepared to deal with it. However, through the grace, love, power and mercy of the Savior, we can cope with these challenges and realize the growth potential found in adversity. During our times of trial and suffering as we focus our thoughts on the Savior and exercise faith in his promises, we can receive the blessings of spiritual growth that come as we face our challenges with faith.

Joseph Smith stands as a marvelous example of this principle. He experienced tremendous hardships in the three decades of his life. He learned as much in his short time in mortality as most of us will in a much longer time.

Our great Exemplar in all things, Jesus, our Redeemer learned, as we must also, through the things that "he suffered" (Hebrew 5:8). In his greatest hour of agony, he pled with his Father to allow the bitter cup to pass from him. But the Father could not do so and still accomplish the purposes that required an Atonement. He could not grant us the blessings of an Atonement without the sufferings and the sacrifices associated with the Atonement. There was no other way for us to be redeemed except through the suffering of Jesus in Gethsemane and on the cross. Therefore, knowing this, he who is our greatest example of the growth that comes through experience with adversity, submitted to our Father with the words, "Nevertheless, not as I will, but as thou wilt" (Matthew 26:39). As a consequence of Jesus' suffering, the heavens wept and the earth groaned. But because of his suffering and his great love for us he drank of the bitter cup, and we thereby are healed.

It is true that all of us experience less adversity than did Jesus, but all those who enter mortality will have experience with hardships and will come to recognize sweetness by tasting bitterness, light by experiencing darkness, joy because of having felt sorrow. I have learned to enjoy rest after spending a day on the tractor. I have learned to rejoice in the resurrection after experiencing the death of my sister, my mother and father.

Every mother who has labored to give birth to a child and every man who has labored and sweat for his daily bread has gained knowledge, even as the Gods. The earth was indeed cursed for man's sake—but it will not always be so. There will come a time when we will "go no more out" (Alma 29:17). In other words, we will not have to go out into a fallen world to haul hay in the heat of the day nor undergo the pain and labor of earthly childbearing. Our missions will have been completed, and we will be able to rest in the glorious presence of God, our Heavenly Father.

The words of the hymn, "O My Father" find a responsive chord in my heart as we finish this chapter:

When I leave this frail existence,
When I lay this mortal by,
Father, Mother, may I meet you
In your royal courts on high.
Then, at length, when I've completed
All you sent me forth to do,
With your mutual approbation
Let me come and dwell with you. "[22]

The ability to return to our Father and Mother in heaven, as reflected upon in this hymn, is only made possible because them was a Fall of Adam and an Atonement of Jesus Christ. The Fall and the Atonement are intricately connected. We cannot really appreciate one without understanding the other. These two doctrines constitute fundamental doctrines of the gospel.

In addition to introducing birth into the world by partaking of the forbidden fruit, Adam also introduced death and hell. Christ came into the world to reverse these negative consequences of the Fall. Of this truth we mad, "For as in Adam all die, even so in Christ shall all be made alive" (1 Corinthians 15:22). If there had been no Fall, there would have been no need for the Atonement of Jesus Christ.

In the next chapter we will discuss how Jesus Christ was chosen and prepared from before the foundations of the world to be our Savior and Redeemer. Jesus, as we will see, showed us the way and provided the means by which we could become sanctified and purified and prepared to joyously return home again—after fulfilling our missions in this fallen world.

REFERENCES:

1 Parley P. Pratt, *Voice of Warning*, 85.
2 *History of the Church*, 6 vols. (Salt Lake City: Deseret Book Co., 1973), 6:428.
3 Joseph Fielding Smith Jr., *Doctrines of Salvation*, 1:114-115; emphasis added.
4 *Doctrines of Salvation*, 1:115
5 *Unlocking the Powers of Faith*, (American Fork: Covenant, 1993) 112.
6 *Doctrines of Salvation*, 1:114-15
7 See Josiah Quincy, *Figures of the Past* (1883), 386-87.
8 Hugh Nibley has included a picture of a serpent with legs in his book, *The Message of the Joseph Smith Papyri, An Egyptian Endowment*, (Salt Lake City: Deseret Book Company, 1975) 181.
9 "Patriarchy and Matriarchy," in *Blueprints for Living: Perspectives for Latter-day Saint Women*, 1:45-46; also, *The Collected Works of Hugh Nibley:* Vol. 1 "Old Testament and Related Studies", 89.
10 *The Teachings of Spencer W. Kimball*, 316-17.
11 "The Family: A Proclamation to the World", 23 September 1995.
12 I have written extensively on the necessity for cooperative relationships in marriages, families, and all other relationships in *Unlocking the Powers of Faith* (American Fork: Covenant, 1994), chapters 6-11.
13 "Patriarchy and Matriarchy," 46; also, *The Collected Works of Hugh Nibley:* Vol. 1 "Old Testament and Related Studies", 89.
14 Some of these ideas are drawn from Robert Millet, "The Regeneration of Fallen Man", given at the 1995 Sperry Symposium presentation.
15 *Journal of Discourses*, 9:330
16 Bruce R. McConkie, *A New Witness for the Articles of Faith*, 282.
17 Bruce R. McConkie, ATONEMENT OF CHRIST *Mormon Doctrine*, 63-64
18 *Journal of Discourses*, 8:160.

19 Millet, "The Regeneration of Fallen Man", Sidney B. Sperry Symposium, October 7, 1995.
20 *Teachings of the Prophet Joseph Smith,* 12.
21 *Cowley and Whitney on Doctrine,* 217.
22 *Hymns,* The Church of Jesus Christ of Latter-day Saints, 1985, #292.

FIGURE 4-A
THE TREE OF LIFE AND THE TREE OF KNOWLEDGE OF GOOD AND EVIL

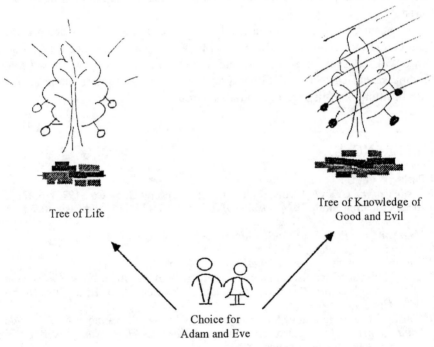

Tree of Life

Tree of Knowledge of
Good and Evil

Choice for
Adam and Eve

Eat not of the Tree of Knowledge of Good and Evil	*Eat of the Tree of knowledge of Good and Evil*
Good News Remain in the Garden of Eden in the presence of God.	*Good News* May become as the gods, knowing good and evil. Eternal plan put into operation.
Bad News Will not know good and evil and will remain in a static state, having no children. The eternal plan for the children of God not operationalized.	*Bad News* Must leave the presence of God and go into a world of death, disease and pain.

FIGURE 4-B
THE FALL OF ADAM, EVE, AND THE EARTH

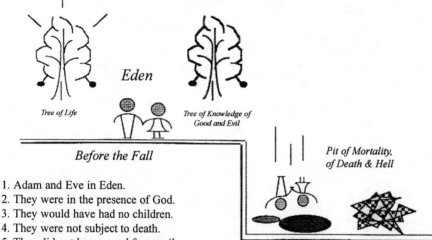

Tree of Life   Eden   *Tree of Knowledge of Good and Evil*

Pit of Mortality, of Death & Hell

Before the Fall

1. Adam and Eve in Eden.
2. They were in the presence of God.
3. They would have had no children.
4. They were not subject to death.
5. They did not know good from evil.
6. They had no blood in their veins.
7. They could have chosen to stay in Eden.
8. To become as the Gods they would need to know good and evil.
9. The fruit of the Tree of Knowledge of Good and Evil could bring the necessary opposition, but it also would bring death.
10. Adam and Eve were free to choose. God would not impose the choice on them.

Adam and Eve After the Fall

1. Adam and Eve were cast out of Eden.
2. They no longer were in the presence of God (Hell).
3. They were now subject to death (Grave).
4. They could now have children.
5. They now have blood in their veins.
6. They now may have experience with good and evil.
7. Men are to earn their bread by the sweat of their brow.
8. Women are to labor in having children.
9. Satan has great power over mankind.
10. The earth has moved away from Kolob where it was first organized.
11. The measurement of time is different. A thousand years with man is now a single day with God.

CHAPTER FIVE

THE PROMISED
REDEEMER

Father, behold the suffering and death of him who did no sin, in whom thou
was well pleased, 'behold the blood of thy Son which was shed, the blood of him
whom thou gavest that thyself might be glorified,'
Wherefore, Father, spare these my brethren that believe on my name, that
they may come unto me and have everlasting life.

—*D&C 45:4-5*

As I approach writing this chapter on Jesus Christ, the promised Redeemer, I feel the same kind of hesitancy I sense each time I begin teaching the New Testament religion class "Life and Teachings of Jesus". Even when I was at the Jerusalem Center for Near Eastern Studies with the sights, sounds, and smells of the Holy City immediately at hand—all of which served as awe-inspiring audio and visual aids—I felt so inadequate teaching about his ministry, the extent of his suffering in Gethsemane and on the cross, and the eternal consequences of his loving sacrifice. The glorious meaning of the Atonement is so vast that I feel that I never am able to adequately teach and testify of his exquisite love for you and me—nor of the depths of his suffering so that we might have immortality and eternal life.

Though difficult to comprehend—and even harder to express—the doctrine of the Atonement is fundamental to our Heavenly Father's plan for our eternal happiness. Because the doctrines of the Fall and the Atonement are so closely associated, we cannot discuss one outside the context of the other. In Chapter 4, we discussed the results of transgression and sin as being *death* and *hell*. In this chapter we will explain how Jesus provided the means of escape from these terrible consequences.

Let's begin our discussion with Paul's concise explanation of the connection between the Fall and the Atonement. He said, "For since by man came death, by man came also the resurrection of the dead. For as in Adam all die, even so in Christ shall all be made alive" (1 Corinthians 15:22). (See end of chapter Figure 5-A, Adam Brought Death, Christ Brought Life). This doctrine is made clear as we read our Third Article of Faith which states, "We believe that through the Atonement of Christ, all mankind may be saved, by obedience to the laws and ordinances of the Gospel."

The word *atonement* literally means the condition of being "at one" with God and the universe. That we might be one was the plea Jesus made in his great High Priestly prayer just before his crucifixion. He prayed that his disciples and those would believe on their words would be one, even as he and his father were one (see John 17:20-21)

In the gospel setting the word *atonement* has reference to what Jesus did for us—his suffering and bleeding from every pore in Gethsemane and his terrible agony on the cross—so that we could escape the pains of death and hell and be united again with our Heavenly Father. In providing the Atonement, Jesus took upon himself the particular sins of everyone who has ever lived, who does now live, or who will ever live upon this earth. He literally took upon himself the sins of *all the world*. In doing so, he opened the door for the resurrection of all living things and provided the way for exaltation of the faithful Saints. Understanding the personal benefits that come to us through the Atonement helps us appreciate why Jesus is called our *Savior, Redeemer*, and *Deliverer*. Because he willingly and lovingly laid down his life for us, his sheep, he also is affectionately known as *The Good Shepherd*.

TYPES, SHADOWS, AND SACRIFICES

Not only is Jesus known figuratively as the Good Shepherd, to reflect his tender caring for us, but he is also known as the Lamb of God which expression reflects his great sacrifice for all mankind. These descriptive names help us to comprehend some of the characteristics and roles of the Savior.

Likewise, our Heavenly Father also has given us many other wonderful symbols, types, shadows, rites, ordinances, and ceremonies that function as learning aids to help us understand, through the use of metaphor, the enormous price that was paid by Jesus Christ for our redemption. Jacob, the brother of Nephi, explained that he delighted in "proving unto my people the truth of the coming of Christ; for, for this end hath the law of Moses been given; and *all things* which have been given of God from the *beginning* of the world, unto man, *are the typifying of him*" (2 Nephi 11:4; emphasis added; also see Moses 6:63). The sacrifice offered by Adam serves as a prime example.

After he was driven from the garden of Eden, Adam was instructed to offer the firstborn of his animals as a sacrifice. Initially he did not know the reason, but after many days an angel appeared to him and asked: "Why dost thou offer sacrifices unto the Lord? And Adam said unto him: I know not, save the Lord commanded me. And then the angel spake, saying: This thing is a similitude of the sacrifice of the Only Begotten of the Father, which is full of grace and truth. Wherefore, thou shalt do all that thou doest in the name of the Son, and thou shalt repent and call upon God in the name of the Son forevermore" (Moses 5:6-8).

Because Jesus was the Firstborn of the Father, our ancient forefathers were commanded to offer as sacrifices their firstborn animals and the first fruits of their fields. Adam and his righteous posterity continued their offerings until the crucifixion of Jesus—the final sacrifice, the sacrifice of the Lamb of God. All of these sacrificial ceremonies were designed to focus attention on the future coming of Jesus Christ.

In the sacrifices of animals, the blood of oxen, sheep, and goats was shed and then all or various parts of their carcasses were burned upon altars. The shedding of the blood of animals was a type or a model of how the Lamb of God would offer himself as a sacrifice for the sins of the world. In doing so, he would sweat great drops of blood from every pore during his anguish in the garden of Gethsemane—this in payment for our sins. At Calvary his precious blood would gush forth as Roman nails were pounded into his holy hands and feet. After the sword pierced his side, blood and water—symbols of new birth—poured out onto the ground.

I believe that our Heavenly Father understands our human reaction to death and therefore he instituted the sacrifice of animals as a way of helping the ancients appreciate, to some extent, the atoning sacrifice of Jesus Christ. His sacrifice was indeed a bloody sacrifice.

From our point of view so distant in time, we often passively visualize the Atonement simply as being painful for Christ but purifying for us. It is difficult for us to comprehend the depth of the physical and spiritual suffering involved. We tend to psychologically block out the blood, the anguish, the agony of Gethsemane, the gore. and the gravity of the cross. We tend to prefer more aseptic and sterile frameworks for our conceptual world. We therefore only selectively attend to the accounts of the Atonement; we pick and choose that which is not too discomforting, and we assimilate what we can.

We are far from capable of grasping the intense suffering, the tremendous price paid by the Lamb of God. We are told that "God so loved the world, that he gave his only begotten Son" (John 3:16), but we do not comprehend the terrible price that was paid. I think the ancients who were asked to sacrifice their animals in anticipation of the promised Redeemer's atoning sacrifice understood better than we the physical realities involved.

Today we do not offer blood sacrifices, so our minds do not connect the harsh realities involved in animal sacrifice with Christ's Atonement. If you were to witness them today, you would probably feel some shock as you saw the killing and bleeding of the animals.

The nearest thing to animal sacrifice that I have witnessed was the killing of "Old Butte", one of our family's dairy cows. This action was certainly not a sacrifice in the biblical sense, but the slaughtering of our milk cow made me think of the stories of sacrifice of Cain and Abel, Enoch, Noah, Abraham, and Moses— stories that I had read about and seen beautifully illustrated in our family's big picture Bible.

Watching the killing of our family cow had a forceful effect on me, and I learned some things about dying. For example, my little boy mind learned that when things die it looks like they go to sleep, but you can't wake them up again. I credit one of my Primary teachers in the Hillspring Ward with helping me to make the connection between animal sacrifices and Christ's suffering.

The first glimmer of the meaning of sacrifice stirred when my father explained that our cow had to die so we would have some meat to eat. Later, my Primary teacher helped me to understand that similarly, Jesus, the Lamb of God, had to sacrifice his life so that we might have eternal life. As a child I didn't understand why this had to be so. I still don't understand it fully, but to our ancient fathers the sacrificing of firstborn animals was an especially powerful learning device which helped them to comprehend the great and last sacrifice that Jesus would make for all of us.

Sacrifice Must be Offered with Faith in Christ

As was mentioned earlier, the ancient Saints were commanded to sacrifice both the firstlings of their flocks *and* the first fruits of their fields—grains, fruits, and vegetables—in anticipation of the coming of the Lamb of God who would take away the sins of the world. Both animal and fruit offerings were acceptable to God as long as they were offered with an eye of faith focused on the infinite and eternal sacrifice of Jesus Christ, the Firstborn of God (Moses 5:19). Apparently, Cain's fruit offering was rejected, not because it involved produce from the field, but because he did not present his sacrifice with an eye of faith in Christ who was to come.[1]

In the Church today we partake of the sacrament in remembrance that he has come and has performed all that the Father commanded him. As with the ancient Saints, we too can appreciate the purpose of sacrifice and the sacrament only if we look at the symbols through the eyes of faith and are able to make the connection between the ritual and the life and mission of the Savior.

As we consider the sacrifices made by the ancient Saints, there is an important point that we should keep in mind. The ceremonies of sacrifice taught the ancient Saints to set priorities. Through their sacrifices, faithful Saints of former times showed that their trust and faith in God was more important to them than their animals. Likewise, in our day, the *new sacrifice* involves a setting of priorities. We show our love for God and our fellow men by willingly sacrificing our pride and our hard-heartedness in favor of a much more peaceful attitude. I sometimes wonder which would require more effort—the offering of our animals or our pride.

The New Sacrifice—A Broken Heart and a Contrite Spirit

Under the law of Moses, the ancient Saints made various kinds of sacrifices.[2] When three particular sacrifices were offered together, the *sin* offering always preceded the *burnt* offering, and the burnt the *peace* offering. Thus the order of the sacrifices symbolized the sequence of atonement, sanctification, and fellowship with the Lord?[3] The whole law of Moses was an elaborate system of such symbolism.[4]

The requirements of the Law of Moses—which included the shedding of blood as a part of animal sacrifices—were fulfilled with the great and eternal sacrifice of the Lamb of God (see 3 Nephi 15:3-8). Now, in our day, the Lord has commanded us, saying, "And ye shall offer for a sacrifice unto me a *broken heart and a contrite spirit.* And whoso cometh unto me with a broken heart and a contrite spirit, him will I baptize with fire and with the Holy Ghost" (3 Nephi 9:20). In other words, we are expected to sacrifice our pride and our vain ambitions and give to him and our fellow men a soft heart which means that we will truly love and serve him and one another.

When we truly participate in the new sacrifice of a broken heart and a contrite spirit, we willingly consecrate everything we possess: our time, our talents, and all of our resources to the blessing of the lives of others. Regarding the necessity of such commitment, the Prophet Joseph Smith declared:

> Let us here observe, that a religion that does not require the *sacrifice of all things* never has power sufficient to produce the faith necessary unto life and salvation; for, from the first existence of man, the faith necessary unto the enjoyment of life and salvation never could be obtained without the sacrifice of all earthly things. It was through this sacrifice, and this only, that God has ordained that men should enjoy eternal life.... When a man has offered in sacrifice all that he has for the truth's sake, not even withholding his life, and believing before God that he has been called to make this sacrifice because he seeks to do his will... he can obtain the faith necessary for him to lay hold on eternal life.
>
> It is vain for persons to fancy to themselves that they are heirs with those...who have offered their all in sacrifice... unless they, in like manner, offer unto him the same sacrifice.[5]

Though none of us will ever be required to offer the kind of sacrifice that Jesus did, he set the example of what we should be willing to do—to be humble and devoted enough to give our very lives, if necessary, for righteousness sake. He laid down his life—the world's greatest act of love—to rescue us from death and hell, the effects of Adam's transgression and our own sins.

THE ATONEMENT—
THE GREATEST ACT OF LOVE

We need to always remember that Jesus did not have to suffer as he did. It was his infinite love for you and me that led him to pay the price so that the Law of Justice might be satisfied. It is my faith that his love is so infinite, extensive, pure, and expansive that, if you alone were to benefit from his agony, he still would be willing to do as he did! He has that much love for you personally.

The power and the love involved in the Atonement is beautifully described in Lehi and Nephi's vision of the tree of life (see Nephi 11). My experience has been that, even after reading the angel's explanation, most readers don't make the connections between the beautiful, white tree and fruit and the *condescension* of God. Let's review the vision and see if we can see how the tree of life with its beautiful, white fruit is a wonderful representation of God's love.

After seeing in vision the same tree that his father had seen, the angel asked Nephi if he understood "the condescension of God"—or if he understood that God would come down among men (see John 1:1, 14). Nephi replied that he knew that God loved his children, but he did not know the meaning of all things.

To guide him in his understanding about God's condescension, the angel showed Nephi a vision of a young woman of Nazareth. He explained that this young woman was the mother of the son of God "after the manner of the flesh" (1 Nephi 11:18). In other words, Mary was to be the mother of Jesus' physical body.

Nephi then beheld Mary carried away in the Spirit. This was something he understood because he had experienced something similar when the Spirit "transported" him to the top of the mountain (see Nephi 4:25) from which he was witnessing this panoramic vision.[6] After Mary had been carried away for the space of a time, Nephi was commanded to look again. This time he saw Mary holding a child in her arms whom the angel identified as the "Lamb of God, yea, even the Son of the Eternal Father!" (1 Nephi 11:21).

Then Nephi was asked if he understood the meaning of the tree which his father had seen, to which Nephi readily replied, "Yea, it is the love of God, which sheddeth itself abroad in the hearts of the children of men; wherefore, it is the most desirable above all things." The angel, who could not contain his own joy added, "Yea, and the most joyous to the soul." (See 1 Nephi 1:22-23).

The tree of life, then, represents the condescension of God—Jesus, the literal Son of God, being born of Mary, coming down to the earth, teaching, healing, and working out the wondrous Atonement so that all mankind could be freed from death and hell and enjoy immortality and eternal life.

Every time I bite into a Japanese pear (one of the kinds that we can buy here in Hawaii) and the sweet juices run down the corners of my mouth, I think of the fruit on the tree that Nephi saw in vision. What a beautiful image the Lord has chosen to represent his abundant love for you and me!

Only Jesus could Provide the Atonement

In the tree of life vision we learn that Jesus is the literal Son of God. Because of his unique dual nature—having received life from his eternal Father and blood from his mortal mother—and having lived a sinless life, Jesus alone was qualified to be our Savior and Redeemer.

Jesus' unique qualifications did not require or determine that he perform the Atonement. He chose to die for us. In order to satisfy the demands of eternal justice, Jesus Christ, the sinless one, "the Good Shepherd" lovingly chose to, "lay down [his] life for [his] sheep" (John 10:14-16) He told his disciples, "No man taketh [my life] from me, but I lay it down of myself. I have power to lay it down, and I have power to take it again. This commandment have I received of my Father" (John 10:18).

The Eternal Father gave "all power" to his Son, including the power of resurrection (D&C 93:17). This power enabled Jesus to glorify his Father by working out the infinite Atonement in our behalf.

Since Jesus is the Only Begotten of the Father in the flesh, his sacrifice was not a human sacrifice. As Amulek declared, "For it is expedient that there should be a great and last sacrifice; yea, not a sacrifice of man, neither of beast, neither of any manner of fowl; for it shall not be a human sacrifice, but it must be an infinite and eternal sacrifice" (Alma 34:10).

Jesus truly was born of mortal Mary and eternal Elohim. He was and is the Son of the Highest. Of his Divine Sonship, Elder Bruce R. McConkie bore witness and provided sacred clarification:

> Some words scarcely need definition. They are on every tongue and are spoken by every voice. The very existence of intelligent beings presupposes and requires their constant use. Two such words are *father* and *son*. Their meaning is known to all, and to define them is but to repeat them. Thus: A son is a son is a son, and a father is a father is a father. I am the son of my father and the father of my sons. They are my sons because they were

begotten by me, were conceived by their mother, and came forth from her womb to breathe the breath of mortal life, to dwell for a time and a season among other mortal men.

And so it is with the Eternal Father and the mortal birth of the Eternal Son. The Father is a Father is a Father; he is not a spirit essence or nothingness to which the name Father is figuratively applied. And the Son is a Son is a Son; he is not some transient emanation from a divine essence, but a literal, living offspring of an actual Father. God is the Father; Christ is the Son. The one begat the other. Mary provided the womb from which the Spirit Jehovah came forth, tabernacled in clay, as all men are, to dwell among his fellow spirits whose births were brought to pass in like manner. There is no need to spiritualize away the plain meaning of the scriptures. There is nothing figurative or hidden or beyond comprehension in our Lord's coming into mortality. *He is the Son of God in the same sense and way that we are the sons of mortal fathers. It is just that simple.* Christ was born of Mary. He is the Son of God—the Only Begotten of the Father...

And so, in the final analysis it is the faithful saints, those who have testimonies of the truth and divinity of this great latter-day work, who declare our Lord's generation to the world. Their testimony is that Mary's son is God's Son; that *he was conceived and begotten in the normal way; that he took upon himself mortality by the natural birth processes*; that he inherited the power of mortality from his mother and the power of immortality from his Father—in consequence of all of which he was able to work out the infinite and eternal atonement. This is their testimony as to his generation and mission.[7]

As the literal Son of God, Jesus alone was qualified to make the Atonement for us. His great mercy led him to pay the price demanded of eternal Justice. Next time you sing a sacrament hymn, try to get mental pictures of what you are singing. If you can visualize what you are singing, it is likely that you will feel swelling motions in your breast and you will have cause to sing praises to his holy name.

JUSTICE—THE LAW OF FAIRNESS

A latter-day hymn reminds us that "The law was broken; Jesus died that justice might be satisfied."[8] Justice is cold, demanding, and hard—but fair. Mercy is loving, kind, soft, and caring. Justice and mercy are characteristics of our Heavenly Father. These attributes are so indelibly a part of his Divine Nature that without them, he would cease to be God (see 2 Nephi 2:13-14; Alma 42:13, 22-23, 25)

In the *Lectures on Faith*, a compilation of lessons prepared under the direction of the Prophet Joseph Smith during the Kirtland era, we are taught that our faith in God is dependent upon our knowledge of his character and attributes including in their fulness the attributes of knowledge, justice, mercy and love. Our faith is like the trunk of a tree with the roots being our knowledge of him (See end of chapter Figure 5-B, The Tree of Faith). The deeper our roots, the stronger our faith. The stronger our faith, the more hope we will feel and the more joy we will experience in the great plan of our God.

Joseph Smith taught that our Heavenly Father arrived at the station of godhood by complying with eternally existing laws, one of which is the eternal Law of Justice.[9] In order for us to qualify for exaltation in the highest degree of the celestial kingdom, the eternal Law of Justice requires payment be made for sin and that we be cleansed every whit. The Lord has made it clear that he "can not look upon sin with the least degree of allowance" (Alma 45:16; D&C 1:31) and that "no unclean thing can enter into his kingdom; therefore nothing entereth into his rest save it be those who have washed their garments in my blood, because of their *faith*, and the *repentance* of all their sins, and their faithfulness unto the end" (3 Nephi 27:19). So faith, repentance and long term commitment are the conditions we meet in order to enter into his presence, but if we do not comply, we cannot enter in—it would not be just.

Despite the obvious nature of this point, there are people in and out the Church who think they can break the commandments and still qualify for all the blessings of salvation. They think that they can sin and still be acceptable to God. They believe in the old and false adage: "God saves us because *he* is good, not because *we* are good." This is a foolish and dangerous belief. Our Father's mercy cannot "rob justice" (Alma 42:25).

Some would Deny Eternal Justice

I have encountered people, as you probably have too, who do not see the need for the Atonement. They altogether reject the idea that an atonement is needed to satisfy some abstract, cosmic, universal Law of Justice. Many of them believe the idea of "sin" is an antiquated concept. To them there are no absolute God-given moral laws. To them *God* is a cultural myth and each sub-culture has its own way of expressing their view of the Divine and that which is moral.

The relativity of morality is a fundamental principle of the anti-Christ. The Book of Mormon character, Korihor, was a chief proponent of this philosophy. He was a classic naturalist, believing that every man prospers according to his own natural strength and cunning independent of any God, thus denying any eternal Law of Justice.

From this atheistic position, Korihor asked Alma to prove there was a God. Alma gave the perfect response. He challenged Korihor to prove that there was no God, arguing that the complexities of the universe, the scriptures, and the words of all the prophets testify of God and his dealings with mankind (see Alma 30).

There are other people who certainly believe in God—as do the Muslims and many other non-Christians—but who believe that there is no abstract Law of Justice that must be satisfied by a suffering God. To them the Atonement of Jesus Christ is unnecessary because God is all powerful (omnipotent) to the point that he can do anything he chooses, and therefore, he can save us any way he wants to. They believe that to receive the blessings of God, one must simply observe certain rules of piety: prayer, giving to the poor, fasting, etc.

The holding of these beliefs is a rejection of the Atonement of Jesus Christ and the eternal Law of Justice. If God were to ignore this law, he would cease to be God. The Book of Mormon prophets are strong on teaching the necessity of eternal law being honored (see 2 Nephi 2:11-13; Alma 42:13). They teach us that for every law there is a punishment; for every cause, an effect (see Alma 42:17).

The Law of Cause and Effect

Among the most obvious laws of the physical universe is one that states "for every action there is and equal and opposite reaction." Sometimes I call this idea the "if this...then that" principle. In other words, for every cause there is an effect.

To illustrate this law of cause and effect to students in a classroom, I sometimes blow up a balloon and then let it go. Of course the balloon rapidly and randomly shoots through the air in a zig-zaggy fashion until all the air is gone. The balloon takes a circuitous route around the room because the little tip on the end where you blow up the balloon waggles back and forth as the air is forced out. I then ask the students "Why does the balloon shoot through the air? Why does it appear to randomly flip around like it does?"

Sometimes it takes a while for the students to conclude, as Newton did, that for every action (the force of the air being expelled) there is an equal and opposite reaction (the balloon moving in the opposite direction of the air being expelled). You can probably think of other examples of the "if this...then that" law.

A form of this law of cause and effect also operates in the spiritual world. (See end of chapter Figure 5-C, The Scales of Eternal Law.) From latter-day scripture we learn that God himself honors eternal laws of cause and effect, obedience and blessings, sin and punishment. One of the first principles that Heavenly Father explained to Adam and Eve was the cause and effect relationship regarding the consequences of eating the forbidden fruit. Adam knew that if he partook of the fruit the result would be death. After Adam had eaten the fruit, the eternal Law of Justice came into effect. Death and hell were the consequences.

"And thus we see," Alma explained, "That all mankind were fallen, and they were in the grasp of justice; yea, the justice of God, which consigneth them forever to be cut off from his presence" (Alma 42:14). As Abinadi, the Book of Mormon prophet explained, the Lord "cannot deny justice when it has its claim" (Mosiah 15:27) nor can he, "look upon sin with the least degree of allowance" (Alma 45:16; D&C 1:31). For every act of righteousness there is a resulting blessing; for every act of sin there is a punishment (see again 2 Nephi 2:13).

The laws pertaining to blessings and punishments are eternally set and are "irrevocable"—they cannot be altered or changed! (D&C 130:20-21). Regarding this idea, the prophet Alma taught, "There is a law given, and a punishment affixed and... justice claimeth the creature and executeth the law, and the law inflicteth the punishment" (Alma 42:22). And again, in another passage the Lord explained: "I, the Lord, *am bound* if ye do what I say; but when ye do not what I say, ye have no promise" (D&C 82:10; 124:47; emphasis added). So, when we are obedient, we are blessed, and when we disobey we experience the consequence, even spiritual death.

Our Own Sins Bring Spiritual Death

Because we have all "sinned and come short of the glory of God" (Romans 3:23), we search—like Adam and Eve—for fig leaves to cover our nakedness, our ashamedness. The aprons of our first parents seem to be universal symbols of our feelings of embarrassment after sinning—symbols of our unworthiness, shame, and vulnerability before the Lord.

Have you ever done something that you knew was very wrong and afterward you felt really guilty, sort of like you had hot rocks in your chest—burning rocks that weighted you down in anguish of soul? These feelings are a common manifestation of spiritual death—for the Spirit will not dwell in unclean tabernacles. They come as a result of the withdrawal of the Spirit of the Lord which is the *hell* that is characterized as being like a lake of fire and brimstone.

In the spirit world there is no *real* lake of fire and brimstone awaiting the wicked. There is no devil in a red suit with a pitch fork ready to torture the wicked in everlasting sulfur and smoke. Several Book of Mormon prophets have explained that "the torment of the unrighteous is *as* a lake of fire and brimstone" (2 Nephi 9:16; Jacob 3:11; 6:10; Mosiah 3:27; Alma 12:17; 14:14; emphasis added). These metaphoric images are employed to describe the mental and physical anguish we feel after sinning.

The experiences of Alma, and the sons of Mosiah who were with him at the time the angel appeared, clearly teach us about the awfulness, the pain and remorse, associated with spiritual death. It is not likely that you have sinned against the light as much as these sons of prophets, but to some degree we all experience these pains of hell when we break the commandments.

Alma the younger described his experience with hell in these poignant words: "I was racked with eternal torment, for my soul was harrowed up to the greatest degree and racked with all my sins. Yea, I did remember all my sins and iniquities, for which I was tormented with the pains of hell ... Oh, thought I, that I could be banished and become extinct both soul and body, that I might not be brought to stand in the presence of my God, to be judged of my deeds. And now, for three days and for three nights was I racked, even with the pains of a damned soul" (Alma 36:12-13, 15-16).

We all have sinned and are in need, to one degree or another, of the Savior to redeem us from the clutches of death and hell. In our fallen state we cry out along with the father of Lamoni when he said that he would be willing to give up all that he possessed if he could have that "wicked spirit rooted out of my breast, and receive his Spirit, that I may be filled with joy, that I may not be cast off at the last day" (Alma 22:15). If we will repent we have the promise that the atoning blood of Christ will rescue, heal, seal, redeem, and sanctify us, but the unrepentant must suffer for their own sins.

Mercy Cannot Rob Justice

No matter how much God loves us, we could not receive the blessings of the Atonement without Jesus paying the price for our sins. If he had not chosen to offer himself as a sacrifice for our sins, or if we were to refuse to embrace his gospel plan, the great plan of happiness, our salvation could not be secured. In brief, Jesus paid the price demanded by justice, and we qualify for his mercy by being obedient to the principles and ordinances of the gospel.

Speaking to Zeezrom, Amulek confirmed these truths when he said, "And he shall come into the world to redeem his people; and he shall take upon him the transgressions of *those who believe on his name*; and these are they that shall have eternal life, *and salvation cometh to none else*" (Alma 11:40; emphasis added). Father Lehi taught his son Jacob and us today that Jesus "offered himself as a sacrifice for sin...unto all who have a broken heart and a contrite spirit; and *unto none else can the ends of the law be answered*" (2 Nephi 2:7).

The benefits of the Atonement are not extended to the hard-hearted, the meanspirited, or the morally careless—to do so would have mercy robbing justice. Alma went to great lengths to stress this idea to his son, Corianton. In words filled with love and concern for his son, Alma explained the importance of repenting, avoiding sin, and remaining faithful in order to qualify for the blessings of Christ's sacrifice for sin—for, as he explained, *mercy cannot rob justice* (see Alma 42:22-25). One cannot commit grievous sin and still expect salvation simply on the basis of God's mercy and grace.

This doctrine is the central message that Amulek delivered to Zeezrom. "And Zeezrom said again: Shall he save his people in their sins? And Amulek answered and said unto him: I say unto you *he shall not,* for it is impossible for him to deny his word" (Alma 11:34) The idea of being "saved in our sins" is a contradiction of terms, an oxymoron, sort of like saying "we are clean dirt." Not only is it a contradiction, but were such a condition to exist, it would constitute a case of mercy robbing justice. If we should expect salvation without obeying the principles and ordinances of the gospel, we would be making the same mistake that Corianton did and many Christians do who believe that the burden of their salvation rests solely on the mercy and grace of Christ.

Interestingly, in connection with this idea of being justified in our sins, the Catholic tradition holds that the mercy of God saves the sinner *in his sins,* and that justice is satisfied through Christ's suffering. The only requirement is that the people have to receive the sacraments (ordinances) of the Catholic Church—but these sacraments are not intended to either purify or sanctify the individual. By contrast, the Protestant churches (Baptist, Methodists, Presbyterian, etc.) typically believe that God saves the sinner *in his sins* by their simply accepting Jesus as their personal Savior.

In both traditions the principle of *repentance* is not stressed as a requirement to lay claim to the Atonement in their lives. If they consider the Law of Justice at all, they see it being satisfied through Christ's suffering.

Nephi observed that this false idea would be common in the last days. He prophesied that:

> There shall be many which shall say: Eat, drink and be merry, for tomorrow we die; and it shall be well with us.
> There shall ... be many which shall say: Eat, drink, and be merry; nevertheless, fear God—he will justify in committing a little sin; yea, lie a little, take the advantage of one because of his words, dig a pit for thy neighbor; there is no harm in this; and do all these things, for tomorrow we die; and if it so be that we are guilty, God will beat us with a few stripes, and at last we shall be saved in the Kingdom of God" (2 Nephi 28:7-8).

The Book of Mormon has been given to us to clarify the confused doctrines of the last days. Its prophets clearly teach that we are not saved *in* our sins—as proposed by the two traditions we have mentioned—but that we are saved *from* our sins. Through the Atonement of Christ and by obedience to the everlasting gospel covenant, we can become sanctified and cleansed from all our sins.

Our salvation, then, is dependent in part upon what we can do including the good works of the gospel such as repentance, baptism, confirmation, service, and acquiring of the attributes of knowledge, temperance, patience, love, chastity, etc. Truly we are saved by grace *"after all we can do"* (2 Nephi 25:23).

There is another common misconception, or corollary doctrine to the idea that God will save us in our sins. A visualization of a balance scale may help you understand the reasoning. Picture the scales with many good deeds on one side with only a few sins on the other side. The false idea is that because the scale is tipped toward the good side, we will make it safely into heaven. I bear you my testimony that this is not true. It is a false idea that we can get into heaven with any sins. Such an idea creates mischief in our minds, enabling us to rationalize evil instead of repenting. The problem with this reasoning is that we still carry the bad with us and no unclean thing—in any degree—can enter the kingdom of heaven. We must become clean, every whit!

Happily, through repentance and the Atonement we can escape eternally suffering the infinite demands of justice. Although mercy cannot *rob* justice, through Christ and the gifts of the Spirit, mercy can *satisfy* justice.

Our repentance makes it possible for the cleansing gifts of the Spirit to operate in our lives until we become clean and spotless. We can become clean, we can get to the point where we lose every desire for sin. We can become like the Nephites who were sanctified, "by the Holy Ghost, having their garments made white, being pure and spotless before God, could not look upon sin save it were with abhorrence; and there were many exceedingly great many, who are made pure and entered into the rest of the Lord their God" (Alma 13:12).

But, still, to fully repent, we must experience some godly sorrow, some personal pain in order for proper healing to take place, and the size of the bandage must be equal to the size of the sore.

Justice Demands Some Individual Suffering

Repentance of serious sin does not come easily. When serious sins have been committed, priesthood leaders have the responsibility to call disciplinary councils so that the behaviors and attitudes of the Church member can be evaluated and consequences imposed if necessary.

In the case of a serious sin, a priesthood penalty must be imposed—probation, disfellowshipment, or excommunication—before forgiveness can be granted by the Lord (see D&C 42:87-92). Brother Robert Millet cites an example when he was a bishop. A member of his ward came to him and wanted to confess a serious sin. She had the misconception that a two-minute confession between Church meetings was all that was necessary for her to qualify for complete clearance. Bishop Millet had to explain to her that more would be required of her than that kind of quick confession. She would have to demonstrate *over time* that she had *ceased* and would *desist* from her sin before she could be in full fellowship with the Church. She would have to show tree contrition and godly sorrow for her sin in order to receive full forgiveness.

President Kimball affirmed this idea when he explained that godly sorrow—which involves some personal suffering—is necessary before we can be cleansed:

"It is an absolute requirement ... it is a requirement by nature and by the very part of a man. This discipline is especially applicable to adults and married people and more especially to those who have been to the temple. They must understand that they cannot tamper with the holy laws of God."[10]

Those who feel godly sorrow for their sins, and who confess and forsake them have this promise of the Lord: "He who has repented of his sins, the same is forgiven, and I, the Lord, remember them no more" (D&C 58:42). "For godly sorrow worketh repentance unto salvation...but the sorrow of the world worketh death (2 Cor. 7:10).

After sincere repentance—confessing, forsaking, and some personal pain—we are made whole again through Christ's Atonement. As fearful as death and hell are, a way of escape has been prepared when we love the Lord and desire to keep his commandments. He endured *the very depths of hell* so that we could escape eternal, everlasting suffering.

What a wonderful plan our Father has prepared for us! The Resurrection and the Redemption are blessings beyond our comprehension or even our imagination. Our Savior "came into the world, even Jesus, to be crucified for the world, and to bear the sins of the world...and [he] saves all the works of his hand, except those sons of perdition who deny the Son after the Father has revealed him" (D&C 76:41, 43). Christ's loving sacrifice satisfied the demands of the eternal Law of Justice, and we are freed from both physical and spiritual death. We sing praises to his name!

If justice were the only attribute of God, we could never be rescued from the grasp of death and hell, the fruits of sin. We could never, worlds without end, pay for our own sins to satisfy the demands of the law. As Lehi explained "By the law no flesh is justified" (2 Nephi 2:5) and as Abinadi warned "Salvation doth not come by the law alone" (Mosiah 13:28). Without our taking advantage of the Atonement, we get exactly what we deserve.

In order to return to the presence of our Heavenly Father, we need the intervention of some powerful influence that can satisfy the demands of justice. That powerful intervention is *mercy* through the Atonement of Jesus Christ. The word *mercy* suggests an advantage given to us that is greater than we deserve. We do not associate mercy with fairness. Justice is fairness, but mercy is a manifestation of God's love and grace.

Speaking at a CES symposium, Elder Dallin H. Oaks described how mercy and justice operate within the framework of the Atonement. He said,

> If justice is a balance, then mercy is counterbalance. If justice is exactly what one deserves, then mercy is *more* benefit than one deserves. In its relationship to justice and mercy, *the Atonement* is the means by which justice is served and mercy is extended. In combination, justice and mercy and the Atonement constitute the glorious eternal wholeness of the justice and mercy of God.

Mercy has several different manifestations in connection with redemption. *The universal resurrection* from physical death is an unconditional act of mercy made possible by the Atonement. Alma taught Corianton that "mercy cometh because of the atonement; and the atonement bringeth to pass the resurrection of the dead" (Alma 42:23).

A second effect of the Atonement concerns our redemption from spiritual death. We are redeemed from the effects of our personal sins on condition of our obedience to the laws and ordinances of the gospel.

Justice is served and mercy is extended by the suffering and shed blood of Jesus Christ. The Messiah "offereth himself a sacrifice for sin, to answer the ends of the law" (2 Nephi 2:7; see also Romans 5:18-19). In this way "God himself atoneth for the sins of the world, to bring about the plan of mercy, to appease the demands of justice, that God might be a perfect, just God, and a merciful God also" (Alma 42:15).[11]

To illustrate this interplay between justice and mercy, I sometimes use an idea borrowed from Stephen Robinson. I ask my students the question, "How many of you expect Heavenly Father to be completely *just* and fair with you on the day of judgment?" Of course, this is a trick question and most of them raise their hands. They are startled when I assure them that they would really not want strict justice because that would mean they would get exactly what they deserve and the fruits of their sins would be death and hell.

What they really need to pray for with all their mights, minds, and strength is *mercy*—the kind of mercy that is offered to us through the Atonement. As one of Shakespeare's characters declared: "In the course of justice, none of us should see salvation: we do pray for mercy."[12]

MERCY IS OFFERED THROUGH THE PURE LOVE OF CHRIST

At a Brigham Young University Devotional in September 1995, Elder Vaughn Featherstone captured God's sublime love and his marvelous power to save us by reciting the nursery rhyme "Humpty Dumpty". With a voice cracking with emotion, he said, "And all the king's horses and all the king's men couldn't put Humpty Dumpty together again. *But the King could, and the King can, and the King will if we come unto him.*" If our lives have been shattered by sin—either our own or as a consequence of someone else's misdeeds—or if we feel as though we are assailed by adversity, he will calm our heavy hearts and comfort our sorrowing spirits. As we earnestly seek to do all we can, Jesus will indeed heal us and make us whole.

Mercy Comes After All We Can Do

The eternal requirements for salvation involving the Atonement of Christ and "all we can do" have been a part of the gospel of Jesus Christ from the very beginning of scriptural history. At sometime in life you may have met people who quote a passage in the New Testament to discount the necessity of any kind of gospel works in order to be saved. They cite Ephesians 2:8-9 which states, "For by grace are ye saved through faith; and that not of yourselves: it is the gift of God: Not of works, lest any man should boast." Yet, on the other hand, in the book of James we read that "faith without works is dead" (James 2:26).

Discussions regarding grace (faith) and works are easily polarized—some people becoming adamant that nothing is needed beyond saying with your lips that you accept Jesus as your Savior, and others clearly arguing that faith without works is dead. Nephi resolved this debate when he explained that, "it is by grace that we are saved, *after all we can do*" (2 Nephi 25:23; emphasis added)—and it truly is by grace that we are saved.

President Ezra Taft Benson explained the meaning of "after all we can do" when he said,

> What is meant by "after all we can do"? "After all we can do" includes extending our best effort. "After all we can do" includes living His commandments. "After all we can do" includes loving our fellowmen and praying for those who regard us as their adversary. "After all we can do" means clothing the naked, feeding the hungry, visiting the sick and giving "succor [to] those who stand in need of [our] succor" (Mosiah 4:15)—remembering that what we do unto one of the least of God's children, we do unto Him (see Matthew 25:34-40; D&C 42:38). "After all we can do" means leading chaste, clean, pure lives, being scrupulously honest in all our dealings and treating others the way we would want to be treated.[13]

These actions that President Benson mentions are characteristic of those who are seeking to obtain and retain a remission of their sins. When we are infused with these fruits of the Spirit, we are filled with charity and our desire is to be of service to our fellow men, even as Christ served others and was willing to descend below all things and sacrifice his very life for us.

Jesus Descended Below All Things

The prophets bear record that "He that ascended up on high, as also he descended below all things, in that he comprehended all things, that he might be in all and through all things, the light of truth" (D&C 88:6).

In Gethsemane Jesus descended below all things by taking upon himself the sins of all the world. He suffered for all mankind—from the most heinous sinner to the least—and everyone in between! On the cross Jesus endured pain both physically and spiritually to bring about the resurrection of all mankind. His agony was intensified when the Father finally withdrew his spirit from him causing Jesus to cry out, Father, "why hast thou forsaken me?" (Matthew 27:46). In other words, Jesus went down to the bottom of the cesspool of evil and pain that he might succor us in our sorrow.

There isn't a person who has ever lived or who ever will live who will ever transcend the depths of the suffering of our Savior. He descended below even our greatest agony. Jesus understands our pain and he can and will help us if we will let him. He knows the way out, he knows the way back; he knows how to lead us, however darkened our minds may be, however much we may be in despair, however far into hell we may have descended.

Jesus is our Savior. He beckons us to come unto him, to enter into his rest, and thereby escape the terribly real demands of the Law of Justice. If we reject his loving call, we will indeed suffer for our own sins and thus the Son of God hath suffered in vain. He wants us to believe him. He promises us that he *will* save us from death, hell, the devil and endless torment if we will but trust him, love him, and walk in obedience to his commandments. And this is what it means to believe in the Lord Jesus Christ. He is mighty to save! The power that enables the promises of the gospel to be realized is the power of eternal and infinite love— the power in Christ's great sacrifice.

We Rejoice in Christ

Describing the fervent devotion the Nephites had for their Good Shepherd, Nephi exclaimed, "We talk of Christ, we rejoice in Christ, we preach of Christ...that our children may know to what source they may look for a remission of their sins" (2 Nephi 25:26). We should show such devotion, such fervor. Elder Dallin H. Oaks encouraged similar devotion and fervor in the hearts and minds of the Latter-day Saints when he said, "The reality of our total dependence upon Jesus Christ for the attainment of our goals of immortality and eternal life should dominate every teaching and every testimony and every action of every soul touched by the light of the restored gospel. If we teach every other subject and principle with perfection and fall short on this one, we have failed in our most important mission."[14]

Indeed, we are totally dependent upon Christ for eternal salvation. He promises us that he will save us and grant us everlasting joy if we will but come to him in his prescribed way. Our obedience to the principles and ordinances of the Gospel, combined with our love and adoration for him, prepare us to receive the full benefit of his eternal and infinite Atonement. His love is beyond our comprehension.

Because of Christ's great love for us, we can indeed be wrapped in the arms of his tender mercy. In his inspiring hymn, Charles H. Gabriel beautifully expressed our Savior's love for all of us. As you read these words, picture yourself being wrapped in his loving arms.

> *I stand all amazed at the love Jesus offers me,*
> *Confused at the grace that so fully he proffers me;*
> *I tremble to know that for me he was crucified,*
> *That for me, a sinner, he suffered, he bled and died.*
>
> *I marvel that he would descend from his throne divine*
> *To rescue a soul so rebellious and proud as mine;*
> *That he should extend his great love unto such as I,*
> *Sufficient to own, to redeem, and to justify.*
>
> *I think of his hands pierced and bleeding to pay the debt!*
> *Such mercy, such love, and devotion can I forget?*
> *No, no, I will praise and adore at the mercy seat,*
> *Until at the glorified throne I kneel at his feet.*
>
> *Chorus:*
> *Oh, it is wonderful that he should care for me,*
> *Enough to die for me!*
> *Oh, it is wonderful wonderful to me!*[15]

I, too, marvel at the love Jesus offers me. Because of his loving Atonement, we may be born again and thus escape the terrible grasps of death, hell, the devil and endless torment (see 2 Nephi 9). It is wonderful to me that according to our Father in Heaven's wisdom, mercy and grace, he has provided a way through his Beloved Son whereby we can be born again and return to his holy presence.

ALL MUST BE BORN AGAIN

In his inspiring discourse on the plan of salvation, Jacob reminds us that "redemption cometh in and through the Holy Messiah for he is full of grace and truth" (2 Nephi 2:6). Filled with the joy of his own redemption, Jacob exclaimed, "O the wisdom of God, his mercy and grace! For behold, if the flesh should rise no more our spirits must become subject to that angel who fell from before the presence of the Eternal God, and became the devil, to rise no more. And our spirits must have become like unto him, and we become devils, angels to a devil, to be shut out from the presence of our God, and to remain with the father of lies, in misery, like unto himself" (2 Nephi 9:8-9). Through the rebirth of water and spirit we can escape these horrific evils and become sanctified, purified and freed from all sin. Thus, we can be made fit candidates to return to our heavenly home.

The Lord taught Adam and Eve, and they were to instruct their children, "That by reason of transgression cometh the fail, which fall bringeth death, and inasmuch as ye were born into the world by water, and blood, and the spirit, which I have made, and so became of dust a living soul, even so ye must be born again into the kingdom of heaven, of water, and of the Spirit, and be cleansed by blood, even the blood of mine Only Begotten; that ye might be sanctified from all sin, and enjoy the *words of eternal life* in this world, and *eternal life* in the world to come, even immortal glory" (Moses 6:58-59).

This passage is a beautiful, succinct description of the gospel requirement of baptism of water and the Spirit and of the promises of sanctification, immortality and eternal life. Baptism and receiving the gift of the Holy Ghost are the first of many steps which prepare us for this glorious state of perfection. But this state is not all to be attained in this life.

Ultimate Perfection Not Required in this Life

We are totally dependent on Christ for our salvation and eternal happiness. Therefore, we can only fully rejoice in the great plan of happiness *when we believe Jesus*—when we believe in his promises that he can make us whole again, even glorified with him as he is glorified in his Father. Of course it is true that in order to receive celestial glory we must become perfect like the Father and the Son—but their perfection is different from the earthly perfection that is expected of us here and now. What is required is that we be as perfect as we know how to be.

The scriptures affirm a certain kind of perfection that has been reached by mortal men. We read that "Noah was a just man and perfect in his generations" (Genesis 6:9), and that "Asa's heart was perfect with the Lord all his days" (1 Kings 15:14; 2 Chronicles 15:17). These men were perfect in a mortal, finite way. I am sure that they had received the gospel ordinances, and their hearts were soft and pliable. They sought to render service and to be faithful throughout their lives. They had become perfect in Christ.

You and I also can attain this kind perfection in this life. We can commit ourselves to tenderness and righteousness that will qualify us for the eternal life spoken of by the Lord. Even though our thoughts, feelings, and actions may not be always perfect, we can move forward, praying for the gift of charity and purity and the Holy Ghost will lead us carefully along. In this regard, President James E. Faust has given us these reassuring words:

We need not claim perfection even for the Prophet Joseph Smith the way we do for the Savior. Joseph's humanity was part of his strength and credibility. He never professed to be perfect; so we should not try to claim something he did not claim for himself. He knew he was only a mortal man with human feelings and imperfections, trying honestly to fulfill his divine mission. In counsel given to some members of the Church who had just arrived in Nauvoo on 29 October 1842, the Prophet so described himself: "I told them I was but a man, and they must not expect me to be perfect; if they expected perfection from me, I should expect it from them; but if they would bear with my infirmities and the infirmities of the brethren, I would likewise bear with their infirmities."[16]

We need to look for opportunities to bear one another's infirmities. In my own life I try to remember what Jesus said about "inasmuch as ye have done it unto one of the least of these my brethren, you have done it unto me" (Matthew 25:40). Such selfless attention to suffering souls does not go unnoticed by the Lord. He recognizes his friends who reach out to others as he did. Such service always demands a price, an inconvenience, but so did his.

We need to get a believing picture in our minds and hearts that Jesus has the power to save us if we will but believe him and love one another. We need to trust in what he has promised us. He knows the pathway. He has walked it himself. He has gained the power to heal and sanctify all things.

Jesus Will Eventually Heal and Sanctify All Things

When the angels sang at the birth of Jesus in Bethlehem of Judea, the shepherds were told that because of the birth of this child, there would be "on earth peace, good will toward men" (Luke 2:14). Jesus did establish peace on earth among the Nephites when he visited them after his resurrection. Among them there were no contentions nor disputations and every man did deal justly with his brother. They were filled with the love of God, and there could never have been a happier people. (see 4 Nephi). They had a mini-Millennium among them.

This wonderful experience of the Nephites is a shadow of what earthly conditions will be like when he comes again to establish his Zion on earth and usher in the Millennial kingdom. Jesus will eventually fix all things that are now broken. His course of redemption will eventually heal, sanctify, and redeem all things that are a part of this fallen world. This is the promise that has been given to us (see D&C 77:12).

As he did during his earthly ministry he will yet heal the sick, raise the dead, give sight to the blind, and make young again those who are now bowed down with age (see 3 Nephi 17:6-10). However, there are still many things to be done to prepare for his coming. Considerable time and effort will yet be required by our Savior and the Lord's people in order to complete the sanctification and the salvation of man. The Lord and the Latter-day Saints are making good progress toward our eventual goals, but a Millennium will be required before all things are completed (see D&C 77:12).

In the meantime, we are still subject to physical and spiritual death and to the stresses and various diseases of mortality—mental and spiritual "dis-ease" such as guilt, anxiety, loneliness, depression, and addictions of various and sundry shades. We are also troubled by birth defects, aging, deafness, blindness, lameness, and sicknesses ranging from mild headaches to vicious cancers and incurable viruses. On the world scene we witness fires, earthquakes, tornadoes, pollutions, worldwide wars, and rumors of war.

Even though we have been instructed by the Lord that all these things "shall give thee experience, and shall be for thy good" (D&C 122:7), we are anxious to pass through this vale of tears and put these pains and problems behind us. We yearn for the great cleansing of the earth and that day when "the branch of the Lord [will] be beautiful and glorious; and the fruit of the earth excellent and comely to them that are escaped of Israel...and the Lord will create upon every dwelling place of mount Zion, and upon her assemblies, a cloud and smoke by day and the shining of a flaming fire by night" (2 Nephi 14:2, 5). Anciently, these were symbols of the Lord's presence among the children of Israel while they were in the wilderness. When the fulness of the Dispensation of the Fulness of Times comes in, we will enjoy these and many other marvelous gifts and blessings which have been foretold to us by prophets both ancient and modern.

Joseph Smith taught that all the ancient prophets looked forward with great anticipation to this, our day, the Dispensation of the Fulness of Times when the great plan of happiness will be fulfilled. In words saturated joy the Prophet exclaimed:

> The building up of Zion is a cause that has interested the people of God in every age; it is a theme upon which prophets, priests and kings have dwelt with peculiar delight; they have looked forward with joyful anticipation to the day in which we live; and fired with heavenly and joyful anticipations they have sung and written and prophesied of this our day; but they died without the sight; we are the favored people that God has made choice of to bring about the Latter-day glory;...
>
> The blessings of the Most High will rest upon our tabernacles, and our name will be handed down to future ages; our children will rise up and call us blessed; and generations yet unborn will dwell with peculiar delight upon the scenes that we have passed through.... a work that God and angels have contemplated with delight for generations past; that fired the souls of the ancient patriarchs and prophets; a work that is destined to bring about the destruction of the powers of darkness, the renovation of the earth, the glory of God, and the salvation of the human family.[17]

The ancients truly did look to and rejoice in our day, a day when Satan and all the corruptions of the earth will be done away, and finally he will reign whose right is to reign, even Jesus Christ (see D&C 58:22). In preparation for that day, we need to come unto him and prepare our hearts for that which is to come (see D&C 58:6). We need to study his word and trust the Savior when he declares that he has power to heal our broken hearts and lives.

We Must Receive the Gift in our Personal Lives

Brother Stephen Robinson writes, "Not only must we believe that he is who he says he is, we must also believe that he can do what he says he can do. We must not only believe in Christ, we must also believe Christ when he says he can clean us up and make us celestial. He says that through his atoning blood, all mankind may be saved (see A of F 3) —and 'all mankind' must logically include you and me. So until we accept the real possibility of our own exaltation in the kingdom of God, we do not yet have faith in Christ; we do not yet believe."[18]

We unlock the powers of faith in our lives when we learn of him and of his teachings—principles of truth, light, and life. We enjoy sweet healing peace and happiness when we come to know that:

> Our Savior, Jesus Christ, is in and through all things. It is through his power that the worlds are and were created and all things are maintained. It is through him that all things have their being. He is the Light and the Life of the world. He is God's Almighty Son. He has descended below all things so that he might comprehend all things. He is the vine; we are the branches. Even as a branch is able to bear fruit because it is connected to and receives nourishment through the vine, even so you can be healed of your loneliness, pain, sorrow, or crippled body through the power of Jesus Christ, the true vine of our Heavenly Father.[19]

The good news of the gospel is that you and I and everyone else (with the exception of the sons of Perdition) will be saved in one of the degrees of glory, the least of which, the telestial, far surpasses anything we can imagine (D&C 76:89). Jesus "glorifies the Father, and saves all the works of his hands, except those sons of perdition who deny the Son after the Father has revealed him" (D&C 76:43). The challenge for us then is to *receive* the good news by believing that salvation, even exaltation, can happen to us—not because we are perfect in this life, but because of the power of the Atonement to save us.

While most of the world refuses to believe Christ, I testify that there are truly wonderful healing and comforting powers to be had in relying on him. He has performed a majestic service in our behalf, now it is up to us to receive his love through the principles and ordinances of the gospel and believe that through them we can unlock the powers of faith and salvation.

As we mentioned earlier, sometimes we think that we are unworthy creatures and that we have made too many mistakes to ever qualify for the blessings of Christ's mercy. We forget that Jesus is the master at separating the deeds from the doer—our sins from our souls. He does not love our unworthiness, but he does love us in ways that are hard for us to imagine or understand.

Perhaps you believe that you have fallen too far to be reached by the Savior's encircling arms of love. You may believe that the gap between sinful you and perfect Jesus is too wide and can never be bridged. As Stephen Robinson has suggested, perhaps you even feel like Peter when he was approached by the Savior and he cried out, "Depart from me; for I am a sinful man, O Lord" (Luke 5:8). Out of the depths of our discouragement we want to say, "Don't look at me. Please pass me by! Your holiness is too bright for unworthy me!"[20]

Until we believe the good news of Jesus' ability to love us and redeem us, we tend to draw back from the very power that can help and heal us. Until we believe and accept the promises of Jesus, we feel like we are outcasts.

In this regard, Brother Robinson tells the story about a time when he sent his son to his room for some act of disobedience. The boy was to stay there until he was told he could come out. Unfortunately, Brother Robinson forgot about his son until hours later when the little boy came to the doorway of his room and interrupted his father who was watching a TV football game and said, "Daddy, isn't there any way we can ever be friends again?" Of course Brother Robinson was crushed for his forgetfulness, and rushed to his son assuring him that "no little boy had ever been loved by a father more than he was loved."[21]

As we discussed previously, because of our sins we feel like hell—literally! We feel like we have been sent to our rooms, and it feels like we will have to stay there forever. Spiritually we feel the same remorse that the little boy felt. We look up to heaven and cry out like Brother Robinson's little boy, "Father in Heaven, isn't there any way we can be friends again?" We plead to be reconciled—to come out of our rooms and be hugged by him again. Jesus will rescue us, but unless we believe that he can we cannot rejoice in the good news of the gospel.

Our Savior, Jesus Christ, has not forgotten us. Through the mouth of Isaiah he promised: "Can a woman forget her sucking child, that she should not have compassion on the son of her womb? yea, they may forget, *yet will I not forget thee*. Behold, I have graven thee upon the palms of my hands; thy walls are continually before me" (Isaiah 49:15-16). Of course the reference to the palms of his hands has reference to his crucifixion.

The tokens in his hand are constant reminders of his love for you and me in providing the Atonement. In return we can show our love for him by keeping his commandments, serving one another and hearkening to the words of our modern prophet and apostles.

CHARTING OUR PRESENT COURSE

President James E. Faust has suggested five beginning, essential measures which will greatly clear the channel for a daily flow of "living water" from the very source of the spring even the Redeemer Himself.

First: A daily communion involving prayer.
Second: A daily selfless service to another.
Third: A daily striving for an increased obedience and perfection in our lives.
Fourth: A daily acknowledgment of His divinity:
Fifth: A daily study of the Scriptures.[22]

I have great faith in the principles that President Faust has outlined here for gaining a personal relationship with the Savior. He knows whereof he speaks. In 1992 I was a tour guide for the members of the Tabernacle Choir who were in Israel performing and preparing a video presentation. At a special meeting in one of the hotels on the shore of the Sea of Galilee, President Faust bore his witness of the resurrected Savior and made this declaration: "My testimony is the same as the brother of Jared's! I know, nothing doubting!" (see Ether 3:19). He had given a similar testimony in General Conference in 1978.[23] Each time as he bore witness of the resurrected Lord and of the Savior's love for us, I was given a witness of the Spirit that he did indeed know that of which he spoke. I knew that he knew (see D&C 46:13-14).

Some of the measures listed by President Faust are easier for me to follow than others. Sometimes I forget to acknowledge the Lord's divinity as much as I should. I often feel that my striving for increased obedience and perfection needs improvement. This is perhaps true for you also. You probably can identify the areas in which you need to be more diligent too. But once again, you and I need to take everything in stride. It is not required that we run faster than we have strength (see Mosiah 4:27).

Our challenge and our joy is to awaken, to listen to the living prophet, to get out of past states of lethargy. Let us remember to "cheerfully do all things that lie in our power; and then may we stand still, with the utmost assurance, to see the salvation of God, and for his arm to be revealed" (D&C 123:17). We don't have to work our souls into hell in order to get to heaven. We need to get past the mentality of salvation by works alone. We need not be perfect in this life, but we do need to chart our course that will lead us to the promised blessings. As Elder Bruce R. McConkie has taught,

As members of the Church, if we chart a course leading to eternal life; if we begin the processes of spiritual rebirth, and are going in the right direction; if we chart a course of sanctifying our souls, and degree by degree are going in that direction; and if we chart a course of becoming perfect, and, step by step and phase by phase, our perfecting our souls by overcoming the world, then it is absolutely guaranteed—there is no question whatever about it—we shall gain eternal life. Even though we have spiritual rebirth ahead of us, perfection ahead of us, the full degree of sanctification ahead of us, if we chart a course and follow it to the best of our ability in this life, then when we go out of this life we will continue in exactly that same course. We'll no longer be subject to the passions and the appetites of the flesh. We will have passed successfully the tests of this mortal probation and in due course we' 11 get the fulness of our Father's kingdom—and that means eternal life in his everlasting presence.[24]

So, according to Elder McConkie, the most important thing for us to do in this life is to chart a course that will lead us to eternal life. You do this as you give your life to Christ, as you subordinate your will to him, living outside your life in the service of others, having the Spirit of the Lord to guide you.

Finding the balance between taking righteous initiative for our lives and turning them over to Christ for his guidance is a struggle for all of us. I worry about my brothers and sisters in the gospel who wear themselves out trying to stockpile good works so they can get into heaven. I also am concerned about others who turn everything over to the Lord and don't take any personal initiative in gaining control of their lives. The pendulum can swing to either extreme. Only by searching the scriptures, the words of the prophets, and sincerely seeking the promptings of Spirit can we find the desired balance.

Please remember that there are times and there are seasons for the various kinds of work of the gospel. (see Ecclesiastes 3:1-8). It is not required that you do everything at once. You can drive yourself and others crazy if you try to do that. You just make sure that you know by the Spirit of the Lord that you are doing all that you should do, and then keep in mind that we grow line upon line and precept upon precept. Through his loving grace, as manifest in the Atonement of Jesus Christ, our promised Messiah, we can receive exaltation and eternal life as we step forward to live the laws and keep the ordinances of the Gospel.

If you are standing on the great celestial escalator and you hang on and you do the things that are required, eventually it will elevate you to the celestial kingdom. Live in peace and don't get so frenzied thinking that you have to keep all the balls in the air juggling at the same time. They are all important but make sure that you give your life to Christ. Make sure that you can feel the power of his Spirit in your life. Then make sure that you live and walk and make every decision that you make with the sanction of the holy Spirit and its direction. In this way you will comply with the requirements of salvation.

Once again, I can not fully comprehend the processes and the powers growing out of the Atonement, but there are times—especially as I try to picture mentally the words of the sacrament hymns—when I have great swellings of emotions, deep feelings of personal gratitude for his voluntary sacrifice for my sins. I am thankful for these peak experiences. They are available to all of us.

I also am grateful for the mental and intellectual understanding that I have received thus far. I pray always that you and I and all the sons and daughters of God might reach out and receive further light and truth as they are presented to us. I pray that our peace and joy might increase, that we might be empowered to strengthen our families, our wards and stakes, and even the whole world as we seek to establish Zion.

Now let us turn our attention to the laws, principles, and ordinances of the gospel—the new and everlasting covenant—that constitute the pathway to peace and protection in this life and eternal life in the world to come.

REFERENCES:

1 *Teachings of the Prophet Joseph Smith,* 58; also LDS temple presentation.
2 For an excellent listing of the various sacrifices offered under the Law of Moses, see *Old Testament Student Manual*—Genesis—2 Samuel, Published by the Church Educational System, The Church of Jesus Christ of Latter-day Saints, 162-63.
3 See "Sacrifices", Bible Dictionary, 767.
4 An interesting discussion about the cleansing of the leper ceremony and the cleansing of a sinner, is found in "Old Testament Types and Symbols", *A Symposium on the Old Testament,* The Church Educational System, 1979, 82-38
5 *Lectures on Faith,* 6:7-8; emphasis added.
6 Philip was carried by the Spirit to Azotus after he had baptized the eunoch as recorded in Acts 8:39-40.
7 Bruce R. McConkie, *The Promised Messiah,* 468-69, 473; emphasis added.
8 *Hymns,* The Church of Jesus Christ of Latter-day Saints, 1985, #173
9 *Teachings,* 346-347.
10 *The Teachings of Spencer W. Kimball,* 491.
11 "Sins, Crimes, and Atonement," An address given to CES religious educators 7 February 1992, Temple Square Assembly Hall, Salt Lake City, Utah; emphasis in original.
12 "The Merchant of Venice", act 4, sc. 1, lines 199-200.
13 "After All We Can Do," Christmas Devotional, Salt Lake City, Utah, 9 December 1982.
14 "Sins, Crimes, and Atonement," 3.
15 *Hymns,* #193.
16 *Ensign,* January 1996, 5.
17 *Teachings,* 231.
18 Stephen Robinson, *Believing Christ,* 10.
19 Garth L. Allred, *Unlocking the Powers of Faith,* 2.
20 *Believing Christ,* 3-4.
21 *Believing Christ,* 4-5.

22 *Ensign,* November 1976, 58-59.
23 *Ensign,* November 1978, 96.
24 "Jesus Christ and Him Crucified," *1976 Devotional Speeches of the Year,* 400-401.

FIGURE 5-A

ADAM BROUGHT DEATH, CHRIST BROUGHT LIFE

Return to the Presence of the Lord

The Fall Made the Atonement Necessary

1. All the sons and daughters of Adam inherit the seeds of death (grave).
2. All of us are subject to hell (spiritual separation from our Heavenly Father because of our own sins).
3. Death is a part of the merciful plan of God because we are permitted to leave this fallen world after we have had experience with opposition.
4. In this world, all are exposed to Satan and his angels. they have power over us because of the Fall and through our own ignorance and sin.
5. Were it not for the Atonement, after death, in the spirit world we would all be subject to Satan. We would become devils ourselves (see 2 Nephi 9:8-9)

The Plan of Salvation

1. An infinite atonement is required.
2. Adam should pay, but he had no power.
3. Justice demanded death–the natural consequence of eating of the fruit of the Tree of Knowledge of Good and Evil.
4. The mercy of God offered a Savior, and a chance to repent and overcome.
5. Our Father in Heaven sent Jesus to satisfy justice–to pay the consequences of Adam's eating the fruit.
6. Jesus' atonement was an act of great love and mercy.
7. Upon repentance, the faithful are restored to the presence of god.
8. All will be resurrected to a degree of glory, except Sons of Perdition.
9. thus Jesus saves all to a kingdom of glory except Sons of Perdition.

Results of the Atonement

1. Death [the grave] is overcome through the Atonement since a resurrection is provided for every living thing.
2. there will be various qualities or kinds of bodies brought forth in the resurrection (see chapter 11).
   a. Some will receive exalted celestial bodies having the power of eternal increase–eternal lives, the power of eternal procreation.
   b. Some will receive celestial bodies without the power of eternal increase (see D&C 131).
   c. Some will receive terrestrial bodies.
   d. Some will receive telestial bodies.
   e. Sons of Perdition will receive a resurrection but to their added misery and suffering.
3. Hell (alienation from God) is overcome through the Atonement since everyone will be restored to God's presence to be judged-–our personal sins are overcome through the Atonement by making it possible for us to repent and be forgiven, by our receiving the Holy Ghost, and by our eventual sanctification and return to the presence of God.

Jesus, Only, Qualifies as Our Redeemer

1. Jesus had a mortal mother and an immortal father.
2. He inherited blood and the capacity to die from Mary.
3. He inherited power over death from his father, God.
4. No man took Jesus' life. He had power to lay his body down in death, and he had power to take it up again.
5. Sin brings death. Since Jesus was sinless the demands of justice had no claim against him.

FIGURE 5-B
THE TREE OF FAITH

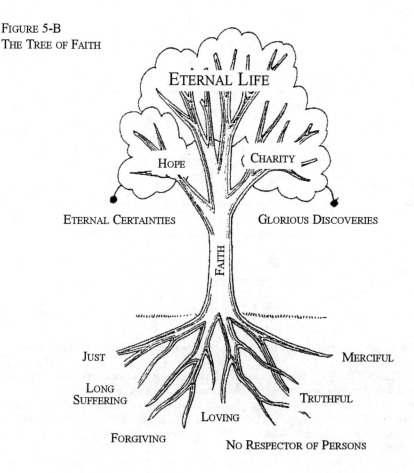

Principles

1. Our faith in God is like the trunk of a tree with the roots being our knowledge of his character and attributes.
2. Our faith is dependent upon our knowledge of God's character and attributes–that he is just, merciful, slow to anger, full of truth, forgiving, etc. (Lectures on Faith, 4:41)
3. The deeper our roots go, the stronger our faith can be.
4. Strong faith, based on a correct knowledge of God, yields a harvest of hope, charity, and eternal life–the greatest of all the gifts of God.
5. Joseph Smith taught "that after any portion of the human family are made acquainted with the important fact that there is a God, who has created and does uphold all things, the extent of their knowledge respecting his character and glory will depend upon their diligence and faithfulness in seeking after him, until, like Enoch, the brother of Jared, and Moses, they shall obtain faith in God, and power with him to behold him face to face.... The inquiry frequently terminated, indeed always terminated when rightly pursued, in the most glorious discoveries and eternal certainty" (Lectures on Faith, 2:23).

FIGURE 5-C
THE SCALES OF ETERNAL LAW

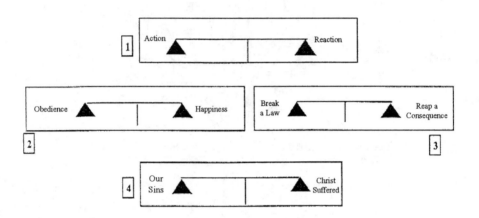

Principles

1. There is an eternal law that for every action there is an equal and opposite reaction–for every effect, a cause.
2. Accordingly, "There is a law...upon which all blessings are predicated–and when we obtain any blessing from God, it is by obedience to that law upon which it is predicated" (D&C 130 :20-21). and again, "I, the Lord, am bound when ye do what I say; but when ye do not what I say, ye have no promise" (D&C 82:10). So, through obedience to eternal law, we are blessed, but only Christ was obedient to the whole law. All of us have come short (see 2 nephi 2:5; D&C 88:34-35).
3. Because all of us have sinned, we are subject to the consequences, death (grave) and hell (alienation from God).
4. Because of his great love, our Father in Heaven sent Christ to pay the price for our sins and Adam's transgression. We are redeemed through his suffering. Death is overcome through the resurrection, and hell is overcome as we are brought back into the presence of God to be judged. Our personal sins are reconciled through our repentance and the cleansing power of Christ's atonement. Justice is satisfied and mercy is granted to those who have a broken heart and a contrite spirit—and to none else (see 2 Nephi 2:7; D&C 19:15-18).

CHAPTER SIX

THE NEW AND EVERLASTING COVENANT

Behold, I say unto you that all old covenants have I caused to be done away in this thing; and this is a new and an everlasting covenant, even that which was from the beginning.

—D&C 22:11

We did not have baptismal fonts in our church meeting houses when I was a child—and the winter months in Canada were so harsh and cold we didn't want to break the ice on the lakes for outdoor baptisms—so baptisms for the living as well as for the dead were performed in the Cardston Temple. For some reason related to his work, my father was not able to baptize me when I turned eight during the wintry month of January. Consequently a cousin agreed to take me and a friend the twenty miles from Hillspring to Cardston for our baptisms.

This was the first time I had entered the temple, though I had driven past it many times with my family. As we entered the temple, an elderly man dressed in white asked us to take off our shoes, "Because," he said, "you are on sacred ground". This expression reminded me of the story of Moses and the burning bush. Moses was told to take off his sandals for the same reason.

Most of the older men in the temple wore white goatees or fuller beards. In the temple all of the workers wore white clothing. Newly painted lockers and private dressing stalls were provided for us so we could put on the heavy, one-piece white jump suits everyone wore who was being baptized. The baptismal font was a large circular basin resting on the backs of twelve oxen. One of the white-bearded workers explained that the oxen represented the twelve tribes of Israel—but I didn't know what that meant.

The water in the font was warm, and a comforting feeling came to me as I stepped into the font and remembered the promise that through baptism my sins may be "washed away." I remember thinking that I would have to be careful not to do anything bad anymore. The white clothing, the dignity of the temple workers, and the solemnity of the surroundings all led me to conclude that baptisms were very sacred ceremonies.

Years later, after I had children of my own, our bishop called me into his office and said that he would like to schedule an interview with our daughter for baptism. The appointment was made with the bishop, then I scheduled my own interview with my daughter. I like to visit with my children before they have their bishop's interview so they understand the purpose of baptism and are prepared for the interview. I remember asking my daughter why she thought people were baptized. She gave a little-girl answer, a true and innocent answer: "Because Heavenly Father asked us to be baptized," she said.

I explained to her that baptism is a promise. At baptism we promise Heavenly Father that we will always try to choose the right, that we will always be on his team and "carry the ball" for him. We promise that we will not make "touchdowns" for the devil. I told her that by being baptized she was promising Heavenly Father that she would always remember his son, Jesus Christ, and try to stand up for what is good and right. If she would always do that, then Heavenly Father promises her something in return—membership in his Church and the Gift of the Holy Ghost.

I also explained to her that after baptism she would be confirmed a member of the Church and receive the Gift of the Holy Ghost to lead her, guide her, walk beside her, and help her find her way back to her heavenly home. Through continued obedience she would always have his Spirit to be with her to help and comfort her—like a fluffy, warm, snuggy quilt on a cold winter's night. When we make promises with the Lord and in return he makes promises with us, these mutual agreements are called *covenants*.

I asked her if she was sure she wanted to make the baptismal promise. She smiled and said that she really wanted to, and she placed her hand over her heart as a sign that she really meant it. I felt great love for her as she expressed her child-like willingness to be baptized. I also sensed, to some extent, what our Heavenly Father must feel when his children make promises with him by entering covenants according to his great plan of happiness.

WE ARE A COVENANT MAKING PEOPLE

God loves us with a perfect love and so does his Son, Jesus Christ. Their desire is to make it possible for all of us to reach our greatest potential, which is to be like them. Through the Atonement that Jesus lovingly provided for us, we can reach that goal.

In the previous chapter we discussed the idea that our Savior fully carried out his perfect Atonement. In order for us to take advantage of the Atonement and thereby qualify for the rich blessing of exaltation in the celestial kingdom, we must walk the pathway of righteousness which includes the making of covenants. Through covenants, God gives us the opportunity to commit ourselves to follow him. With each covenant we make, we more closely bind ourselves to him and commit ourselves to order our lives by his teachings and to keep his commandments.

As a bishop serving in a Polynesian ward in Hauula, Hawaii, I asked a little Polynesian gift what she promised the Lord by being baptized. She answered correctly, "that I will try to keep all his commandments." When I asked her what the Lord promises her in return, she responded with the wisdom, clarity and innocence of a child: "He will bless me happy!"

And so it is! As we receive all the principles, ordinances, and promises of the new and everlasting covenant, our Heavenly Father blesses us with happiness, peace, protection, and eternal life (see D&C 59:23).

THE NEW AND EVERLASTING COVENANT

From the beginning, the Lord has made covenants with his children. The gospel itself is made up of many covenants and commandments which the Lord calls his "new and everlasting covenant" (D&C 22:1).

In a revelation to Joseph Smith on October 25, 1831, the Lord said, "Verily I say unto you, blessed are you for receiving mine everlasting covenant, even the fulness of my gospel, sent forth unto the children of men, that they might have life and be made partakers of the glories which are to be revealed in the last days, as it was written by the prophets and apostles in days of old" (D&C 66:2).

"The new and everlasting covenant is the fulness of the gospel and embraces within its terms and conditions every other covenant that Deity ever has made or ever will make with men (D&C 132:5-7; 133:57). The provisions of this covenant are that if men will believe, repent, be baptized, receive the Holy Ghost, and endure in righteousness to the end, they shall have an inheritance in the celestial world".[1]

Participation in the gospel is like walking a pathway to perfection (see end of chapter Figure 6-A, The Pathway to Perfection). Heavenly Father wants us to receive the first principles of the gospel—faith and repentance—and then we are to add to our faith: virtue, knowledge, temperance, patience, godliness, brotherly kindness, and charity until we become pure in heart (see 2 Peter 1:1-10).

We are also exhorted to accept the first ordinances of the new and everlasting covenant—baptism and receiving the gift of the Holy Ghost—and then attain to the higher ordinances, including receiving the Melchizedek Priesthood and all of the temple ordinances.

Each of the principles and ordinances of the gospel are a part of the "new and everlasting covenant." For example, celestial marriage is a new and everlasting covenant (D&C 132:19)—but so is baptism. Together in their fulness all of the principles and ordinances constitute *the new and everlasting covenant*. Priesthood covenants are the official channels through which the Lord blesses his children.

Sometimes my students ask why the Lord calls it the *new* and *everlasting* covenant. How can something be new and everlasting at the same time? The answer is that although the fulness of the gospel has been revealed in other dispensations, after the Great Apostasy it had to be *newly* revealed to us through the Prophet Joseph Smith. The gospel is also considered to be *everlasting* in the sense that it is the exact same plan of happiness that Adam, Enoch, Noah, Abraham and Peter received. Furthermore, it is the gospel of the Everlasting Father.

As we keep the commandments and endure faithfully we receive the reward of the righteous, "even *peace* in this world, and *eternal life* in the world to come" (D&C 59:23; emphasis added). The final chapter of this work will focus on the greatest of all God's gifts which is eternal life, but in this chapter we will center our attention on the many dimensions of the promise of peace in this world that grow out of the everlasting covenant.

THE PROMISE OF PEACE IN THIS WORLD

As is emphasized in the above passage, the promise of *peace* is a paramount blessing to be had in the everlasting covenant. The peace of the gospel comes to us in ever increasing degrees as we walk the pathway of perfection. It comes to us when we join the Church and receive the Holy Ghost—when we leave the world of spiritual darkness, embrace the light of the gospel, and enjoy the blessings of the Holy Ghost, the Comforter.

As we walk the pathway of the everlasting covenant, our peace increases as we grow in light, knowledge, power, and rest (see John 14:26).

Wonderful peace will come to your heart when the Lord finally promises you that you will gain eternal life (see D&C 68:12; 88:2-5; 131:5). However, the greatest peace you could ever possibly obtain in this life is the indescribable joy you would experience by parting the veil and communing with the Lord face to face. This crowning blessing of peace, to be admitted into the presence of the Savior, will be experienced by all members of the Church who prove themselves true and faithful, are obedient to the new and everlasting covenant, and become pure in heart (see Matthew 5:8; D&C 93:1; Ether 12:19).

The establishment of Zion—which is the pure in heart—is a principal purpose of the everlasting covenant. When sanctified people are collectively organized together according to celestial laws, including the law of consecration—when they are re "of one heart and one mind, and dwell in righteousness" and have "no poor among them"—they are said to be *Zion* (Moses 7:18). Zion, then, is a people who, through the everlasting covenant, become "pure in heart" (D&C 97:21).

The children of Israel with all their prophets and promises have never yet been a Zion people.[2] Thus far, in the history of the world, only Enoch and his people, who predated Israel, were able to live the everlasting covenant to the point of reaching Zion.

They truly did obtain the peace of Zion, were delivered from all their enemies, and because of their purity were even translated and were caught up into heaven (see Moses 7).

Zion, as a society of sanctified Saints, will be organized again in the very near future. Zion and her stakes will experience joy, beauty, protection, and peace—in spite of great calamities, wars, and fires all around them (see D&C 115:4-6). We will live according to the fulness of the everlasting covenant and will be blessed with power from on high. We will be a people at peace in a world gone mad after blood, power, violence, and immorality (see 1 Nephi 14:13-14). Because of the everlasting covenant, we will be the only people who will "not be at war one with another" (D&C 45:69).

We hope to establish Zion in our own generation. As Joseph Smith explained:

> The building up of Zion is a cause that has interested the people of God in every age; it is a theme upon which prophets, priests and kings have dwelt with peculiar delight; they have looked forward with joyful anticipation to the day in which we live; and fired with heavenly and joyful anticipations they have sung and written and prophesied of this our day; but they died without the sight; we are the favored people that God has made choice of to bring about the Latter-day glory ... a work that God and angels have contemplated with delight for generations past; that fired the souls of the ancient patriarchs and prophets; a work that is destined to bring about the destruction of the powers of darkness, the renovation of the earth, the glory of God, and the salvation of the human family.[3]

To help you understand the course that will lead us to peace in this world and to the establishment of Zion, I will outline six progressive steps—each starting with the letter "p" —that have been, are now and will continue to be the main points of the everlasting covenant. They are:

1. *Proclaiming the gospel.* When we enter the everlasting covenant through baptism we take upon ourselves the blessing and obligation to do missionary work, to declare the message of peace and salvation to our family members, our neighbors, and to the nations of the earth.

2. *Perfecting the Saints.* Once in the Church, we move forward with the help of the various priesthood and auxiliary organizations, increasing in faith and righteousness through fasting and prayer until we are perfected in peace as individuals within eternal family organizations. Priesthood quorums, scriptures, meetings, and manuals are directed to facilitate this end. Our labors of love also involve redeeming the dead by providing them with the peace of the gospel ordinances through vicarious temple work.

3. *The Promise of Eternal Life.* When we have sufficiently proven ourselves to be true and faithful in all things, we may receive that wonderful peace and assurance that comes by receiving "the more sure word of prophecy" (D&C 131:5). That is, we know through the authority of the priesthood that we are sealed to eternal life or to use Peter's expression, we make our "calling and election is made sure" (2 Peter 1:10).

4. *Presence of the Lord.* After we have received the promise of eternal life, we will have the right, in the due time of the Lord, to receive the sublime peace of entering his holy presence. This sacred experience involves parting the veil, having the heavens opened, talking with the Lord face to face, communing with the spirits of just men made perfect, and receiving instruction from them and other holy personages.

5. *Priesthood Power.* Faithful Saints who are taught from within the veil receive awesome and superhuman powers to control the elements of the earth and the powers of heaven. They have the peaceful assurance that these powers are available to them as situations may arise in which the Lord would authorize their use. These powers are granted through a fulness of the priesthood ordinances and through strong faith (see JST, Genesis 14:30-32).

6. *Protection and Deliverance.* Through faith, righteousness, and priesthood, the Saints will be empowered to establish Zion and her stakes as places of peace and refuge (see D&C 115:4-6). They will be delivered in a day of calamity. In spite of wars, fires, destructions, pestilence, and plagues, they will be at peace because, as the Lord has promised, he will deliver his people in a dark and gloomy day.[4]

I have found it helpful to illustrate this progressive six-step process of gospel centered peace and protection by associating each of the steps with the fingers on your hand:

Figure 6-B
Six Steps in Progressive Peace, Enlightenment, and Protection

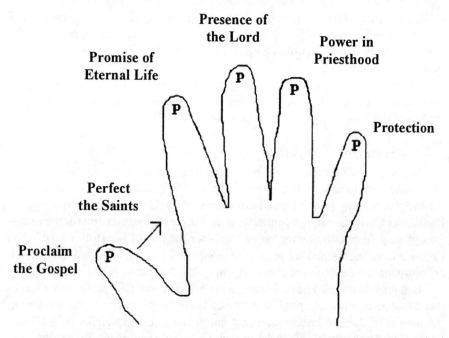

There is great comfort and peace in the promises of the Lord that he will preserve his righteous people: "For the mountains shall depart, and the hills be removed; but my kindness shall not depart from thee, neither shall the covenant of my peace be removed, saith the Lord that hath mercy on thee" (Isaiah 54:10). Now let's discuss in more detail each of these six steps in the everlasting covenant of peace and protection.

1. Proclaiming of The Gospel

Doing missionary work by proclaiming the gospel of Jesus Christ to the nations of the world is a task that is inherent within the everlasting covenant. Members of the Church are expected to proclaim the gospel through missionary work—to invite others to enter the everlasting covenant in order to receive the promised blessings of peace and protection in their own lives. This gathering is necessary because, before people can enjoy the peace that comes through the everlasting covenant, they must be brought to a knowledge of their true Redeemer.

The Church of Jesus Christ of Latter-day Saints, through its great missionary program, is the instrument through which the Lord is gathering his covenant people. The keys authorizing the Church to proclaim the gospel were restored to the earth through the ministering of angels. In 1836 Moses, as a resurrected being, appeared to the Prophet Joseph Smith and Oliver Cowdery and restore "the keys of the *gathering of Israel*" (D&C 110:11). Joseph Smith and all the presidents of the Church who have followed him have been commissioned to proclaim the gospel to every nation, kindred, tongue and people. This is the mighty work that is presently in progress.

After we hear the glorious message of the gospel and join the Church, we must then be perfected in the principles and ordinances of the gospel. This perfecting of the Saints requires much time, love, and effort.

2. Perfecting The Saints

We begin our journey toward perfection when we comply with the first principles and ordinances of the gospel. The fourth Article of Faith states: "We believe that the first principles and ordinances of the Gospel are: first, faith in the Lord Jesus Christ; second, repentance; third, baptism by immersion for the remission of sins; fourth, the laying on of hands for the gift of the Holy Ghost." The first two ideas mentioned are principles—*faith* and *repentance*—and the last two are ordinances—*baptism* and *the laying on of hands for the gift of the Holy Ghost*.

In a previous work I have discussed the principles of faith and repentance. In this chapter, because of space limitations, I will focus primarily on the saving ordinances of the everlasting covenant and mention the principles only briefly. For an in-depth study of these principles, you may want to explore the material found in *Unlocking the Powers of Faith*, published by Covenant Communications, Inc.

Being Baptized

As we have discussed above, baptism is the first of the ordinances we obey to walk the pathway to perfection. From the very beginning, Adam knew and understood the importance and the symbolism of baptism. The Lord instructed Adam to,

> Teach these things freely unto your children, saying: That by reason of transgression cometh the fall, which fall bringeth death, and inasmuch as ye were born into the world by water, and blood, and the spirit, which I have made, and so became of dust a living soul, even so ye must be born again

into the kingdom of heaven, of water, and of the Spirit, and be cleansed by blood, even the blood of mine Only Begotten; that ye might be sanctified from all sin, and enjoy the words of eternal life in this world, and eternal life in the world to come, even immortal glory (Moses 6:58-59).

We all have to be baptized for a remission of sins before we can return to our heavenly home, because no unclean thing can enter the presence of the Lord.

I remember an incident, when I was growing up in Canada, that helped me understand the importance of being clean before the Lord. In the spring, when everything was thawing with the warm Chinook winds, the barnyard would be really mucky. As we would walk around, the manure and stuff from the barnyard would creep up the sides of and into our boots. One time I tried to sneak into the kitchen to get one of my mother's freshly baked cinnamon rolls. She caught me in the act and said I could not come in the house with dirty boots.

Similarly, Heavenly Father can't let us back into his presence when our souls are soiled by sin. For this reason, because of his love for us, Jesus has taken upon himself the consequences of our sins—and that "though [our] sins be [red] as scarlet", through the Atonement, they may become as white "as wool" (Isaiah 1:18). Through his suffering in Gethsemane and on the cross and through our own repentance we can obtain a remission of our sins and thereby be made clean before the Lord.

Receiving the Gift of the Holy Ghost

After we are baptized we are confirmed members of the Church and are charged to "receive the Holy Ghost". The Prophet Joseph Smith identified the Holy Ghost as "the first Comforter". As was mentioned before, I sometimes think of the comforting influence of the Holy Ghost as being like a warm quilt to wrap myself in on cold nights in front of a wood-burning stove. Having a good book to read and a full stomach also adds to my picture of comfort.

As an example related to this idea, I remember a particularly cold and blizzardy winter evening, when my brother and I had to get the cows from the farm that was about one mile from our house. Our horse, whose name was "Midnight", safely brought us home. Our mother, knowing how cold and hungry we were, helped us brush off the snow and ice from our heavy clothes, wrapped us in warm quilts, and fed us hot soup and her cinnamon rolls. Oh what comfort we felt!

Similarly, as a comforter, the Holy Ghost gives us wonderful peace in times of stress and pain and helps us find our way back home, comforting us during our journey through this often lone, cold, frustrating, and fallen world.

The Holy Ghost leads us, guides us, and directs us into all truth—including into the presence of the Lord. When President Harold B. Lee would confirm newly baptized people, he would often say, "Receive the Holy Ghost which shall be a guide to your feet, a light to your path, shall bring all things to your remembrance, and shall even reveal the Lord Jesus Christ to you". This expression clearly describes why we need the Holy Spirit in our lives.

The Holy Ghost guides us in our minds and our hearts. Before his death, Joseph Smith taught that when God reveals things to us, he reveals them "to our spirits precisely as though we had no bodies at all; and those revelations which will save our spirits will save our bodies".[5] In other words, information from the Spirit of the Lord does not come through our five senses. It comes into our minds and hearts, as a modern revelation explains, "Yea, behold, I will tell you in your *mind* and in your *heart*, by the Holy Ghost, which shall come upon you and which shall dwell in your heart. Now, behold, this is the spirit of revelation; behold, this is the spirit by which Moses brought the children of Israel through the Red Sea on dry ground" (D&C 8:2-3; emphasis added).

Through the Holy Spirit we are enabled to receive what Joseph Smith described as "pure intelligence flowing into you" ... "sudden strokes of ideas"—solutions to our problems—that come to us in times of need.[6] This spirit impresses us with feelings of what is right and what is wrong. The Holy Ghost can also fashion, shape and mold our spirits and bodies for eternal purposes.

Parley P. Pratt wrote a beautiful description of how the Holy Ghost can influence us. He said:

> The gift of the Holy Ghost adapts itself to all [our bodily] organs or attributes. It quickens all the intellectual faculties, increases, enlarges, expands and purifies all the natural passions and affections, and adapts them, by the gift of wisdom, to their lawful use. It inspires, develops, cultivates and matures all the fine toned sympathies, joys, tastes, kindred feelings and affections of our nature. It inspires virtue, kindness, goodness, tenderness, gentleness and charity. It develops beauty of person, form and features. It tends to health, vigor, animation and social feelings. It invigorates all the faculties of the physical and intellectual man. It strengthens and gives tone to the nerves. In short, it is, as it were, marrow to the bone, joy to the heart, light to the eyes, music to the ears, and life to the whole being.[7]

What a wonderful, comforting gift the Holy Ghost is in our lives! Through the sanctifying power of the Holy Ghost, we can become clean and spotless—Christlike—and fit to dwell with gods and angels.

Adding to Faith

Peter admonished the members of the Church in his day to draw upon the powers of the Holy Ghost, to press forward and develop all the principles of the gospel by adding to their faith: virtue, knowledge, temperance, patience, godliness, brotherly kindness, and charity (see 2 Peter 1:1-10). These additional principles are developed as gifts of the Spirit after we earnestly seek them. Peter said that by acquiring and improving upon them, we partake of the "divine nature" (2 Peter 1:4), or, to use Alma's words, we receive the image of Christ in our "countenances" (Alma 5:14).

As we grow in these principles and attributes, we begin to think as Christ thinks, feel as he feels, and act as he would act—we begin to be filled with charity, which Moroni identified as the "pure love of Christ" (Moroni 7:47). He assured us that "whoso is found possessed of it at the last day, it shall be well with him". He then admonished us to "pray unto the Father with all the energy of heart, that ye may be filled with this love, which he hath bestowed upon all who are true followers of his Son, Jesus Christ" (Moroni 7:47-48).

As we grow in knowledge, faith and charity we gain power over Satan and progress toward sanctification. The Prophet Joseph Smith taught that sanctification is not obtained in a moment—it is not a static thing but involves dynamic growth, receiving "line upon line, precept upon precept" (D&C 98:12). He declared:

> The nearer man approaches perfection, the clearer are his views, and the greater his enjoyments, till he has overcome the evils of his life and lost every desire for sin and like the ancients, arrives at that point of faith where he is wrapped in the power and glory of his Maker and *is caught up* to dwell with Him. But we consider that *this is a station to which no man ever arrived in a moment: he must have been instructed in the government and laws of that kingdom by proper degrees until his mind is capable in some measure of comprehending the propriety, justice, equality, and consistency of the same....* it is necessary for men to receive an understanding concerning the laws of the heavenly kingdom, before they are permitted to enter it: we mean the celestial glory. So dissimilar are the governments of men, and so divers are their laws, from the government and laws of heaven,... that all who are made partakers of that glory, are under the necessity of learning something respecting it previous to their entering into it."[8]

When we are instructed in the government and laws of that kingdom we learn that progress is made as we express our charity through service to our fellowmen.

Receiving the Melchizedek Priesthood
The Melchizedek priesthood offers men in the Church a wonderful opportunity to develop the gift of charity by rendering service in their families, quorums and communities.

Similarly, the Relief Society, whose motto is "Charity Never Faileth" provides women with a channel through which they may render compassionate service. Here it should be pointed out that in the Church women are not ordained to hold priesthood office, but they do receive all the blessings of the priesthood. There is no blessing of the priesthood that a man may receive that a woman may not also receive—from baptism through sealings.

When men receive the Melchizedek priesthood, they covenant that they will magnify their callings—or in other words, they will enlarge, increase, amplify, or take seriously their priesthood responsibilities. Accordingly, with an oath, the Lord promises that those who do so ultimately will receive *all that he has*. This covenant is known as "the oath and covenant of the Melchizedek priesthood" (D&C 84:33-38). Every prospective elder should know and understand this sacred covenant before he is ordained to the Melchizedek Priesthood.

The oath and covenant of the Melchizedek priesthood is the promise of eventual godhood! It is the promise that in the resurrection our bodies will be filled with glory, health, vigor, vitality, intelligence, joy, and beauty. It is the promise of exaltation which entails the power of creation and procreation. In describing those who will receive their exaltation, the Lord says they will be "gods, because they have no end; therefore shall they be from everlasting to everlasting, because they continue; then shall they be above all, because all things are subject unto them. Then shall they be gods, because they have all power, and the angels are subject unto them" (D&C 132:20).

Receiving the Initiatory Ordinances

Receiving the Melchizedek Priesthood is a prerequisite to men entering the temple and receiving higher ordinances. In the temples we receive sacred ordinances and teachings regarding the Plan of Salvation and our journey back into the presence of God.

The Prophet Joseph Smith explained that the purpose of the gathering of Israel in any age of the earth is "to build unto the Lord a house whereby He could reveal unto His people the ordinances of His house and the glories of His kingdom, and teach the people the way of salvation."[9]

Both men and women must qualify for a temple recommend by bringing their lives into harmony with such basic requirements as believing in our Heavenly Father and Jesus Christ, sustaining the President of the Church and other leaders, paying tithing, living the Word of Wisdom and the law of chastity, and attending Church meetings.

Usually men and women receive their temple blessings immediately before their missions, before marriage, or when their priesthood leaders determine they are spiritually mature enough for these ordinances. In the temple we receive sacred initiatory ordinances that prepare us—or make us candidates—for marvelous eternal blessings having to do with becoming kings and priests unto the Lord (see Revelation 1:6). Because of their sacred nature it is not appropriate to say more about these ordinances outside the temple, but generally speaking they raise us to much higher levels of spirituality in our journey toward exaltation. They are very sacred and contain wonderful promises.

Being Endowed

After receiving the initiatory ordinances described above, we are ready to receive our *temple endowment*. The endowment presents the story of our journey through mortality and how we can, through the blessings and ordinances of the everlasting covenant, return back into the presence of God.

The endowment is one of *knowledge*. Brigham Young described the endowment in these words: "Your endowment is, to receive all those ordinances in the House of the Lord, which are necessary for you, after you have departed this life, to enable you to walk back to the presence of the Father, passing the angels who stand as sentinels, being enabled to give them the key words, the signs and tokens, pertaining to the Holy Priesthood, and gain your eternal exaltation in spite of earth and hell."[10]

The endowment is filled with beautiful symbolism that teaches us about the role of our Savior in making eternal life possible. It also teaches us about the blessings and privileges associated with eternal life. Because much of the endowment is presented symbolically, it is important that we prayerfully seek to understand the meanings of the symbols and "make connections" between them and the wonderful realities for which they stand. We are promised that if we will ask, we will receive. If we will knock, it shall be opened unto us. By contrast, however, if we don't ask, we won't receive. If we don't knock, it will not be opened unto us.

The scriptures and Church leaders publicly teach us important gospel principles, but the most sacred doctrines are withheld from public view because ungodly people would treat them lightly or with contempt. Therefore, much of our understanding of the symbolism used in the sacred endowment will come by personal revelation as we seek to understand and as we honor our temple covenants.

Receiving the Blessings of Eternal Marriage

After the endowment, the next covenant we make with the Lord is *eternal marriage*—the sealing of the wife to the husband. This blessing is made available through the keys to "the dispensation of the gospel of Abraham" that were restored to the Prophet Joseph Smith by the prophet Elias (D&C 110:12).

Temple marriage enables us to make covenants as husband and wife that will continue throughout all eternity. The eternal nature of the marriage covenant, with its promise of eternal posterity, is most clearly described in scriptures that deal with Abraham, our forefather. Regarding the promises made to Abraham, we read:

Abraham received promises concerning his seed, and of the fruit of his loins—from whose loins ye are, namely, my servant Joseph—which were to continue so long as they were in the world; and as touching Abraham and his seed, out of the world they should continue; *both in the world and out of the world* should they continue as innumerable as the stars; or, if ye were to count the sand upon the seashore ye could not number them (D&C 132:30).

Because Abraham, Isaac, and Jacob received the law of celestial marriage and "did none other things than that which they were commanded, they have entered into their exaltation, according to the promises, and sit upon thrones, and are not angels but are gods" (D&C 132:37).

The promises of eternal offspring which the Lord made to Abraham are applicable to all of us who receive temple marriage and endure faithfully to the end. This is tree because we, like Joseph Smith, are children of Abraham—children of the covenant. Of our ability to receive these blessings, the Lord explained:

This promise is yours also, because ye are of Abraham, and the promise was made unto Abraham; and by this law [of celestial marriage] is the continuation of the works of my Father, wherein he glorifeth himself.

Go ye, therefore, and do the works of Abraham; enter ye into my law and ye shall be saved (D&C 132:31-32; emphasis added; see also Galatians 3:29).

Elder Russell M. Nelson adds further insight into our lineal rights when he taught,

The new and everlasting covenant of the gospel allows us to qualify for marriage in the temple and be blessed to "come forth in the first resurrection: and "inherit thrones, kingdoms, principalities, and powers, dominions...to [our] exaltation and glory in all things" (D&C 132:19). Children born to parents thus married are natural heirs to the blessings of the priesthood. They are born in the covenant. Hence, "They require no rite of adoption or sealing to insure their place in the posterity of promise." (James E. Talmage, *The Articles of Faith,* Salt Lake City; The Church of Jesus Christ of Latter-day Saints, 1977, p. 446.)

Rewards for obedience to the commandments are almost beyond mortal comprehension. Here, *children of the covenant become a strain of sin-resistant souls.*[11]

It is important to point out that even though we may have received the blessings of the temple, we must not labor under the misconception that we unconditionally and automatically will receive the promised blessings. Temple blessings are conditioned upon our being true and faithful to the end of our earthly probation.

This, however, is not meant to be a discouraging point. We must believe that we can make it—we can endure faithfully to the end. Of course we are not perfect, but if we desire these blessings with all our heart and seek to live our lives in such a way as to be worthy of them, we will obtain.

As Robert L. Millet explains, "we can be perfect in the sense that we do the best we can and then rely wholly upon the merits and mercy of our Redeemer. That is, we can be perfect in Christ."[12] So, the important thing is that we chart our course to eternal life and exaltation and move forward in faith in our Savior, believing that through the great plan of happiness we shall overcome and obtain these wonderful blessings.

Enduring to the End—Receiving Grace for Grace

As we chart our course toward eternal life, we should focus on *service* to one another as the principle that will enable us to draw upon the powers of heaven and reach our home port.

In the eyes of the Lord, service in the kingdom of God is more important than days and weeks of fasting and praying in the desert. Service is the propellant, the wind in the sails, that moves us steadily toward our goal of exaltation. Jesus demonstrated this principle as he washed the feet of his disciples (John 13:5) and service was the main thrust of King Benjamin's address when he stated that, "when ye are in the service of your fellow beings ye are only in the service of your God" (Mosiah 2:17).

What would you say if someone were to ask you the question: "How can you tell if a person is really converted to the gospel of Jesus Christ?" One answer you could give would be that you can tell how converted a person is by the way he treats his fellow men—by how much love and compassion (or grace) he shows to others. As Jesus declared, "By this shall all men know that ye are my disciples, if ye have love one to another" (John 13:35).

Our worship and our spiritual growth, our enduring to the end, and our ability to receive power through the Atonement are closely tied to our willingness to serve others. Through your willingness to serve others, the Lord promises to bless you: you receive grace for grace. As you seek to build and add to the comfort and joy of others, the Lord will shower upon you those righteous desires for which you yearn and strive. Your willingness to serve, however, must be matched by your sincere asking for the desired blessings. "And all things, whatsoever ye shall ask in prayer, believing, ye shall receive" (Matthew 21:22).

As you show compassion to others, you receive compassion from our Father; as you render service to others, you receive service from him; as you impart knowledge to others, you receive knowledge; as you bless others, the Lord blesses you—you receive grace for grace. By receiving the doctrine of grace for grace into our lives and complying with the principles and ordinances of the gospel we become sanctified by the power of the Holy Ghost like the Nephites of old, who "did fast and pray oft, and did wax stronger and stronger in their humility, and firmer and firmer in the faith of Christ, unto the filling their souls with joy and consolation, yea, even to the purifying and the sanctification of their hearts, *which sanctification cometh because of their yielding their hearts unto God*" (Helaman 3:35; emphasis added). Thus, you develop step by step, drawing upon the powers of the Atonement, becoming sanctified, and receiving a fulness of the Father's power, even as Moses, Enoch, and Noah.

Through his life of love and service, Jesus marked for us the pathway to power and perfection; by following his marvelous example we too may receive grace for grace until we receive a fulness, even as he did (see D&C 93:12-20). Then we shall be able to sit with him, as "joint-heirs with Christ" of all that the Father possesses (Romans 8:17; D&C 84:37), and cry with him "Abba, Father" (Mark 14:36; Romans 8:15).

Being Justified and Sanctified

To become joint-heirs with Jesus requires that we be both *justified* and *sanctified*. Justification is a legal term that means that we are vindicated, acquitted or absolved from guilt. In a gospel context it means that through the Atonement of Christ and obedience to the first principles of the gospel we can become freed from sin. Sanctification, on the other hand, has reference to our becoming pure and holy before the Lord, becoming Christlike, having received the gifts of the Spirit to the point that we are able to receive all the promises of the gospel.

An analogy may further explain the meaning of these terms. When we lived in St. George we had what we called "grow boxes". It is too hot in St. George, and the soil too poor in the part of town where we lived, to grow good crops of vegetables. So, we made our grow boxes—which were supposed to reduce the number of weed seeds that would get into the garden—and added artificial soil made of a mixture of sawdust and sand. Seeds were carefully spaced and planted and specially prepared fertilizers were added weekly. Weeds, however, still grew and had to be pulled regularly as in any other garden. The grow boxes did not fulfill one of the designs of their creation!

In our own lives we must fulfill the designs of our creation by ridding ourselves of the weeds of sin and ignorance which makes us justified, and then by planting and nurturing the seeds of virtue and knowledge we become sanctified. (See end of chapter Figure 6-C, The Doctrines of Justification and Sanctification.)

Of this purification process the Lord explains, "And we know that *justification* through the grace of our Lord and Savior Jesus Christ is just and true; And we know also, that *sanctification* through the grace of our Lord and Savior Jesus Christ is just and true, to all those who love and serve God with all their mights, minds, and strength" (D&C 20:30-31; emphasis added).

Continuing, the Lord has warned: "There is a possibility that man may fall from grace and depart from the living God; Therefore let the church [the members of which are justified through baptism] take heed and pray always, lest they fall into temptation; Yea, and even let those who are *sanctified* take heed also" (D&C 20:32-34; emphasis added). You and I must ever be on guard against Satan's seeds of sin.

We can protect ourselves from Satan's subtle seductions as we increase in our knowledge of and obedience to the principles and ordinances of the gospel, are true to our covenants and are "watchful unto prayer continually" (Alma 34:39). As we follow this course we open ourselves to guidance from the Holy Spirit. Then, as was mentioned earlier, by following the promptings of the Spirit we will be guided into all truth. Thus, as we progress in light and truth, we will gain power over the adversary and grow in the gifts of the spirit which will prepare us to see his face and know that he is.

The Three Veils of Progressive Spiritual Enlightenment

Our Heavenly Father expects us to increase in the light and truth of the gospel until we are prepared to return to his presence. Much of what we are taught by the prophets, living and dead, by the scriptures, and within holy walls is directed toward this culminating reality. Our growth toward this crowning revelation will be gradual, but it can be steady as we continue to walk the pathway toward perfection.

An analogy using three veils may help you to understand how we progress in receiving light and knowledge. These three veils separate us from ever-increasing degrees of spiritual enlightenment until we are prepared to pass sequentially through each one. The first veil separates us from the *words* of truth, the second from the *spirit* of truth, and the third from *personages* of truth (see end of chapter Figure 6-D, The Three Veils of Enlightenment).

The Words of Truth

The first veil through which we must pass separates us from the *words* of truth. Words of truth can come from many sources including: missionaries, scriptures, prophets, seers and revelators, parents and friends. Words are wonderful. They have an almost magical quality about them. They stimulate ideas, which in turn evoke emotions, which in turn can propel us into action. The more pure the word, the more pure the effect it will have in the lives of those who hear it.

As a young missionary and throughout my adult years I have noticed that people are not equally receptive to the truths regarding the resurrection of Jesus, the First Vision, or the miraculous circumstances surrounding the coming forth of the Book of Mormon. Some people are spiritually attuned to the messages of the gospel and receive the information with gladness—they pass through this first veil quickly and easily. Others struggle to have the faith to believe, while others outrightly reject the testimonies borne.

The parables of Jesus were presented in a veiled form to protect those who were spiritually immature and not able to live by the truths they conveyed. Those, however, who had ears to hear—heard. Those who had eyes to see—saw.

People like Laman and Lemuel repeatedly passed back and forth through the first veil. Sometimes they hearkened to the words of Lehi and Nephi, but at other times they would rebel and not remain steadfast in the light, the words of truth they received from Lehi, Nephi and even the angel who appeared to them. They could not respond to the light found in the words of truth and were therefore not able to pass permanently through this first veil.

Obedience to the words of the Lord is vital if we expect to approach a fulness of knowledge and enter back into his presence. To be enlightened by the words of truth is good, but our exaltation requires that we continue to grow by receiving more light and knowledge. The living prophets teach us to search and ponder, test and try, learn and obey, so that we can gain light and understanding through the powers of the Spirit.

The Spirit of Truth

Though it is vital that we build our testimonies on the words of truth it will not always be possible to find all our answers through the written or spoken word. Neither the Lord nor his appointed servants have seen fit to provide in a book all the guidance we need in order to navigate our way through life in this fallen world. Even if it were possible, such a book would be damaging for us because we would not learn to seek direction from the Holy Spirit. It is through the power of the Holy Ghost that we "may know the truth of all things" (Moroni 10:5). Our leaders' source of light—through which they give us the words of truth—must become our source of light. We, too, must learn to walk by faith in the Lord and in his ability to guide us in our individual stewardships as we are taught by the power of the Holy Spirit through personal revelation.

The Prophet was emphatic about the Saints' learning by revelation. He said that "the best way to obtain truth and wisdom is not to ask it from books, but to go to God in prayer, and obtain divine teaching".[13] Furthermore, he explained that, "A person may profit by noticing the first intimation of the spirit of revelation; for instance, when you feel pure intelligence flowing into you, it may give you sudden strokes of ideas, so that by noticing it, you may find it fulfilled the same day or soon; (i.e.) those things that were presented unto your minds by the Spirit of God, will come to pass; and thus by learning the Spirit of God and understanding it, you may grow into the principle of revelation, until you become perfect in Christ Jesus."[14]

Several months after Joseph Smith was martyred, he appeared as a spirit being to Brigham Young at Winter Quarters. President Young asked him to speak to the brethren one more time. The Prophet explained that his mission in mortality was over and that President Young must now do the speaking. Brigham Young then asked for a message to deliver to the brethren. The Prophet replied:

> Tell the people to get the Spirit of the Lord and it will lead them right....They can tell the Spirit of the Lord from all other spirits; it will whisper peace and joy to their souls; it will take malice, hatred, strife and all evil from their hearts and their whole desire will be to do good, bring forth righteousness and build up the kingdom of God. Tell the brethren if they will follow the Spirit of the Lord, they will go right. Be sure to tell the people to keep the Spirit of the Lord.[15]

Elder Boyd K. Packer explained that the influence of the Holy Ghost can help us find answers to our problems:

> If we lose the spirit and power of individual revelation, we have lost much in this Church. You have great and powerful resources. You, through prayer, can solve your problems without endlessly going to those who are trying so hard to help others....
>
> If you become so dependent and insecure about prayer and the answer to prayer that you are hesitant on them, then you are weak....
>
> This Church relies on individual testimony. Each must earn his own testimony. It is then that you can stand and say, as I can say, that I know that God lives, that He is our Father, that we have a child-parent relationship with Him. I know that He is close, that we can go to Him and appeal, and then, if we will be obedient and listen and use every resource, we will have an answer to our prayers.[16]

Elder Packer has spoken frequently about the Holy Ghost and how we can develop our spiritual sensitivities. One such talk, entitled "The Candle of the Lord," appears in the January 1983 *Ensign*. This article is comprehensive, warm, and enlightening. It is filled with the words and the spirit of truth.

The Personages of Truth

As we learn to hearken to the spirit of truth we become pure in heart and are prepared to pass through the third veil. This final veil, that the pure in heart finally pass through, separates the unprepared from personages of truth— the presence of the Lord and other holy beings. For most of us, the privilege of having holy beings teach us face to face will probably be reserved for the after-life. However, it is comforting to know that as we approach the Millennium more and more faithful Saints will be sealed to eternal life and receive all the attendant blessings. As Elder Bruce R. McConkie explained,

> For our day, the Prophet Joseph Smith is the classical example of one who was sealed up unto eternal life.... And can there be any question that the same was true among the Nephites? And Jaredites? That it included all of the City of Zion and those who were thereafter caught up to heaven to dwell with Enoch and his translated brethren? And if this glorious principle has always operated in days past, is it beyond reason that it is still sealing bless-ings upon the heads of the Latter-day Saints? Verily, such is the case now— *a situation which we anticipate shall be increasingly so as the Millennium approaches*, during which period the sealing power and *all its attendant blessings* will abound on every side.[17]

In explaining the fact that one does not have to be an apostle to see the Lord, Elder McConkie said the following,

> Apostles and prophets simply serve as patterns and examples to show all men what they may receive if they are true and faithful. There is nothing an apostle can receive that is not available to every elder in the kingdom. As we have heretofore quoted, from the Prophet's sermon on the Second Comforter: "God hath not revealed anything to Joseph, but what he will make known unto the Twelve, and even the least saint may know all things as fast as he is able to bear them." (*Teachings*, p. 149.) It follows that every-thing stated by Elder Oliver Cowdery in his charge to the apostles could also be given as a charge to all elders. Every elder is *entitled* and *expected* to seek and obtain all the spiritual blessings of the gospel, including the crowning blessing of seeing the Lord face to face.[18]

Prophets and seers are people of great spiritual maturity who have, while in mortality, traversed the pathway of the gospel back through the veil into the pres-ence of God.

Once while attending the Hill Cumorah Pageant in Palmyra, New York, President Harold B. Lee, who was then a member of the quorum of the Twelve Apostles, bore his testimony to a group of missionaries in the Sacred Grove. He bore a powerful witness to us about the reality of the resurrected Lord. He testi-fied, "Because of experiences too sacred for me to talk about, even in this sacred setting, I want you to know that I know that Jesus Christ is a glorified, resurrected being with the most beautiful body of flesh and bones and my hands know, and my eyes know that he lives today." As he spoke, the Spirit bore witness to me that he did indeed know of the reality of which he spoke. I knew that he knew!

From the *Lectures on Faith* we learn that from the time of Adam all testimonies of God have been *dependent* upon the witness of seers—like President Lee—who have an *independent* witness of God and his ways. (See end of chapter Figure 6-E—Dependent and Independent Witnesses.) The promise of the everlasting covenant is that if we will hearken to the testimonies of independent witnesses, we too will reach a point where we will be independent witnesses—seeing and knowing for ourselves the things we had known before "with an eye of faith" (Ether 12:19).

We have other sacred testimonies of apostles and prophets in our own day who stand as independent witnesses. During Elder Bruce R. McConkie's last General Conference address, he testified that he was an independent witness of the Lord, Jesus Christ. He said:

> And as pertaining to Jesus Christ, I testify that he is the son of the Living God who was crucified for the sins of the world. He is our Lord and our God and our King. This I know of myself, *independent of any other person*. I am one of his witnesses, and in the coming day I shall feel the nail marks in his hands and his feet and shall wet his feet with my tears. But I shall not know any better then, than I know now that he is God's Almighty Son, that he is our Savior and our Redeemer, and that salvation comes in and through his atoning blood and in no other way. God grant that all of us may walk in the light as God our Father is in the light. So that according to the promises, the blood of Jesus Christ, his Son, will cleanse us from all sin.[19]

From the *Lectures on Faith*, we read about the process by which we, too, can become independent witnesses. The Prophet explained: How do men obtain a knowledge of the glory of God, his perfections and attributes? By devoting themselves to his service, through *prayer* and *supplication incessantly* strengthening their faith in him, "until, like Enoch the brother of Jared, and Moses," they obtain a manifestation of God for themselves.[20] "Is the knowledge of the existence of God a matter of mere tradition, founded upon human testimony alone, until persons receive a manifestation of God to themselves? It is."[21]

So, those who prove themselves to be true and faithful through prayer and incessant supplication receive further enlightenment. Through obedience they qualify for the privilege of having the heavens opened unto them and of communing with the Lord and are taught many things of a personal and private nature.

Elder Bruce R. McConkie explained that there are many in the Church who do not know about this crowning blessing of seeing the Lord as a part of his plan for our happiness and are thus not motivated to seek it. He wrote, "There are, of course, those whose callings and election have been made sure who have never exercised the [additional] faith nor exhibited the [extra] righteousness which would enable them to commune with the Lord on the promised basis. There are even those who neither believe nor know that it is possible to see the Lord in this day, and they therefore are without the personal incentive that would urge them onward in the pursuit of this consummation so devoutly desired by those with spiritual insight."[22] For those who do pursue the proper course however, their knowledge empowers them. Thus, they receive from beyond this third veil priesthood power to do many wonderful works.

Before one can receive the blessings of passing through this third veil, however, the Lord has provided an authorized channel, a capping ordinance of the priesthood, that serves as a prerequisite to the marvelous blessings of seeing the face of the Lord. This final ordinance is the ordinance of being sealed to eternal life or receiving the promise of eternal life.

3. Promise of Eternal Life

The understanding that we can live our lives in such a way as to receive the promise of eternal life is one of the most glorious and inspiring doctrines ever revealed to mankind. Not only is it an integral part of the gospel of Jesus Christ, but it is also the crowning ordinance in the everlasting covenant, bringing hope to those who *understand* the doctrine and sublime peace to those who actually *receive* the ordinance. It was administered anciently to Adam and Eve and their righteous posterity, and it has been granted to true and faithful Saints in every dispensation of the gospel.

In the October 1977 General Conference, Elder Bruce R. McConkie said, "We have the power to make our calling and election sure, so that while we yet dwell in mortality, having overcome the world and been true and faithful in all things, we shall be sealed up unto eternal life and have the unconditional promise of eternal life in the presence of Him whose we are." Here, Elder McConkie is explaining that members of the Church can be sanctified by the power of the Holy Ghost to the point that they receive a divine witness (through one holding authority) that they will gain their exaltation in the Celestial Kingdom.

Nephi reminds us that it is within our grasp to press forward—feasting upon the word of Christ—until we become sanctified and eventually receive the sacred promise. He explained,

> And now, my beloved brethren, after ye have gotten into this strait and narrow path, I would ask if all is done? Behold, I say unto you, Nay; for ye have not come thus far save it were by the word of Christ with unshaken faith in him, relying wholly upon the merits of him who is mighty to save. Wherefore, you must press forward with a steadfastness in Christ, having a

perfect brightness of hope, and a love of God and of all men. Wherefore, if ye shall *press forward*, feasting upon the word of Christ, and endure to the end, behold, thus saith the Father: *Ye shall have eternal life* (2 Nephi 31:19-20; emphasis added).

Many other ancient scriptures deal with this marvelous blessing. Latter-day prophets have also dwelt upon this glorious subject. During the latter years of his ministry, the Prophet Joseph Smith pleaded fervently with the Saints to press forward in righteousness until they heard the voice of authority proclaim: "Son, thou shalt be exalted.[23] His words were: "I would exhort you to go on and continue to call upon God until you make your calling and election sure for yourselves, by obtaining this more sure word of prophecy..."[24] And again he declared: "Oh! I beseech you to go forward, go forward and make your calling and your election sure; and if any man preach any other Gospel than that which I have preached, he shall be cursed".[25]

In one of the greatest sermons he ever delivered, the latter-day seer clearly explained the process by which we may receive the promise of eternal life or make our calling and election sure:

> After a person has faith in Christ, repents of his sins, and is baptized for the remission of his sins and receives the Holy Ghost, (by the laying on of hands), which is the first Comforter, then let him continue to humble himself before God, hungering and thirsting after righteousness, and living by every word of God, and the Lord will soon say unto him, *Son, thou shalt be exalted.* When the Lord has thoroughly proved him, and finds that the man is determined to serve Him at all hazards, then the man will find *his calling and his election made sure.*[26]

Receiving the promise of eternal life is, in effect, having the day of judgment moved up into mortality. It is the authoritative promise that you have passed the test of this earth's probation and that you will have all the blessings of exaltation in the world to come.

This most desirable of all promises can come directly from the Lord himself, as was the case with the Prophet Joseph Smith (see D&C 132:49), the brother of Jared (see Ether 3:13-28), and Alma (see Mosiah 26:20); or the promise can come to you from the prophets of God who hold the apostolic keys and sealing powers of their dispensation. For as we read in the Doctrine 'and Covenants: "And of as many as the Father shall bear record, to you shall be given power to seal them up unto eternal life" (D&C 68:12). To be sealed in this context is to receive the promise of eternal life. So, the efficacy of the promise is the same, "whether by mine own voice or by the voice of my servants" (D&C 1:38).

Elijah restored the keys of the sealing power to the Prophet Joseph Smith and Oliver Cowdery (see D&C 110:13-16). These keys are held by apostles who, by virtue of their sacred office, are entrusted with all of the keys of the kingdom. They are the legal administrators of the power and authority by which true and faithful saints can be sealed to eternal life.

The Saints who are thus sealed to eternal life receive a "fulness of the priesthood" (D&C 124:28). They are made kings and priests unto God and his father (Revelation 1:6). They become members of the "Church of the Firstborn" (Hebrews 12:23) and, according to latter-day revelation, will be given power to establish "all things pertaining to Zion" (D&C 105:37).

Regarding this wonderful, crowning ordinance of the gospel and the crowning blessing of seeing the face of the Lord which grows out of it (as discussed under the next heading) there are three points that you ought to understand: 1) to get a broader understanding of making your calling and election sure and of receiving that most sacred of all blessings of seeing the face of the Lord, you would benefit by reading all that Elder Bruce R. McConkie has written on these subjects,[27] 2) it would be inappropriate for you to ask any other person if they have received these blessings, and 3) if you don't happen to receive these blessings in this life, don't worry about it. If you have received the blessings of the temple and are living worthily by honoring your covenants, you will not lose anything in the next life.

At this point in our discussion of the promise of eternal life it will be well for us to reflect back on the doctrine of *election* as it was discussed in Chapter One of this book. You may recall that the noble and great spirits were *called* and *elected* to be born through the lineage of Abraham and Jacob in this world and to become gods in the eternities. These pre-earth nominations were given on condition of worthiness in mortality. Those who were called and elected, foreordained in heaven, to be born through the lineage of Abraham would still have to be chosen in this life by making their calling and election *sure*. The phrase "many are called but few are chosen" (D&C 121:34; Matt. 22:14) has important meaning in view of this explanation. It is one thing to be *called* and quite another thing to be *chosen*.

Elder Bruce R. McConkie explained the difference between being *called* and being *chosen* through a series of questions and answers. He asked, "Called to what? Chosen for what?" He answered, "Called into the Church, called to the holy priesthood, called to receive all of the blessings of the gospel, including the crowning blessing of eternal life. Chosen to inherit the blessings offered through the gospel and the priesthood; chosen for eternal life and exaltation. *Called to the Church, but chosen to be sealed up unto eternal life and to have one's calling and election made sure.*[28]

To be chosen, then, is to receive the promise of eternal life, to become sanctified, to have one's calling and election made sure, to receive the more sure word of prophecy, to be sealed to eternal life through the authority of the holy priesthood (see D&C 131:5). All of these expressions mean essentially the same thing.

In explaining the process by which we may be chosen and given this most desirable blessing, the Lord declared, "There has been a day of calling, but the time has come for a day of choosing; and let those be chosen that are worthy. And *it shall be manifest unto my servant*, by the voice of the Spirit, those that are chosen; and they shall be sanctified; And inasmuch as they follow the counsel which they receive, *they* shall have power after many days to accomplish all things pertaining to Zion" (D&C 105:35-37; 68:12 emphasis added).

As we read this passage we learn that when faithful Saints receive the promise of eternal life, they are said to be *sanctified* (see D&C 20:34; 105:36; and Topical Guide, Sanctification). As you continue to learn more about the doctrine of sanctification, your faith will be increased, your soul enlarged, your understanding of the gospel enlightened, and other truths associated with this glorious doctrine will become delicious to you (see Alma 32:28). Your hope will be more firmly grounded in your Savior, and many passages of scripture that were obscure to you in the past will take on a newer, clearer, and more vibrant meaning. For example, all of the following expressions are closely related to the sanctification of the Saints and the promise of eternal life:

1. "A crown of righteousness" (2 Timothy 4:8)
2. "Chosen" (D&C 105:35-36; see also D&C 121:34-40)
3. "Clean from the blood of this generation" (D&C 88:138)
4. "Enter into [the Lord's] rest" (D&C 84:24)
5. "Fulness of the priesthood" (D&C 124:28)
6. "Joint-heirs with Christ" (Romans 8:17)
7. "Kings and priests unto God" (Revelation 1:6)
8. "Ordained after this order and calling" (JST, Genesis 14:30)
9. "Power to seal them to up unto eternal life" (D&C 68:12)
10. "Pure in heart" and "shall see God" (Matthew 5:8)
11. "Purified and cleansed from all sin" (D&C 50:28; see also vv. 27, 29-30)
12. "The more sure word of prophecy" (D&C 131:5)
13. True and faithful (*Teachings*, 150)
14. "Washed white through the blood of the Lamb" (Alma 13:11)
15. Becoming a Zion people— "Zion [is] the pure in heart" (D&C 97:21)
16. Fruit laid up "against the season" (Jacob 5:18; see also vv. 29, 31, 76)
17. Having one's name "written in the Lamb's Book of Life" (D&C 132:19)
18. Making one's "calling and election sure" (2 Peter 1:10)
19. Membership in the "church of the Firstborn" (D&C 76:54)

20. Overcoming by faith (D&C 76:53; see also Revelation 2:26)
21. Being sealed by the Holy Spirit of Promise (see D&C 132:19)
22. "The holy order" (Alma 13:6)
23. The promise of eternal lives (see D&C 132:22)
24. The promise of the first resurrection (see D&C 132:19)
25. The spirit and power of Elijah (*Teachings*, 338).

These expressions, and many others that could be listed, are descriptive phrases that can amplify and enlarge your knowledge regarding the promise of eternal life.[29] The deeper meanings of these expressions will come to you as you ponder them, call upon the Lord, and live in accordance with what you know to be true. They will be more clearly understood as you continue your study of the ancient and latter-day scriptures and the words of the living prophets, receive the blessings of the temple and are guided by promptings of the Holy Ghost.

Father Abraham serves as a magnificent example of a worthy man who sought for and obtained the promise of eternal life and "a fulness of the priesthood" (D&C 124:28). In the Book of Abraham we read:

> And, finding there was greater *happiness* and *peace* and *rest* for me, I sought for *the blessings of the fathers*, and the right whereunto I should be ordained to administer the same; having been myself a follower of righteousness, desiring also to be one who possessed great knowledge, and to be a greater follower of righteousness, and to possess a greater knowledge, and to be a father of many nations, a prince of peace, and desiring to receive instructions, and to keep the commandments of God, *I became a rightful heir, a High Priest, holding the right belonging to the fathers* (Abraham 1:2; emphasis added).

Abraham's desire was granted unto him. He was sealed to eternal life, received a fulness of the priesthood, and became a king and a priest thereby receiving all of the blessings of his fathers Adam, Enoch, Noah, and Melchizedek.[30] These patriarchs provide a pattern for all of us to follow. They received grace for grace until they received a fulness of the Father's blessings (see D&C 132:37).

If we are spiritually in tune our hearts will vibrate with joyful anticipation as we reflect upon these promised blessings. Our Father in heaven has truly prepared a great plan for our happiness.

Growing out of the crowning *ordinance* of the priesthood comes the crowning blessing, that of having the heavens opened, the third and final veil parted, and seeing the face of God.

4. Presence of the Lord

The relationship between receiving the promise of eternal life and seeing the face of the God is made clear in a revelation given through the Prophet Joseph Smith in which the Lord explained that without the ordinances of the Melchizedek priesthood—meaning specifically the promise of eternal life— "no man can see the face of God, even the Father, and live" (D&C 84:19-22).

It is the established order of the everlasting covenant that Saints, who become pure in heart and who are sealed to eternal life, are permitted by their strong faith to part the veil and have communion with heavenly beings.

We have many scriptural examples of the appearance of God to mortals.[31] The Lord appeared to Abraham (Genesis 12:7; 17:1; 18:1; Abraham 2:6-11). Jacob saw God face to face (Genesis 32:30). Moses, Aaron, Nadab, and Abihu and seventy of the elders of Israel saw the God of Israel: "and there was under his feet as it were a paved work of a sapphire stone, and as it were the body of heaven in his clearness" (Exodus 24:9-10). Isaiah saw the Lord "high and lifted up" (Isaiah 6:1; also 2 Nephi 16:1). Amos said he saw the Lord standing on the altar (Amos 9:1). Nephi reported that Isaiah saw his Redeemer, even as he and Jacob had seen him (2 Nephi 11:2).

Can you imagine the peace and happiness that would come to your soul to have this greatest of all experiences? Elder Melvin J. Ballard described his own joy in this regard. In a dream or a vision he was escorted into a sacred room. He reported that he saw seated on a raised platform, "the most glorious being my eyes have ever beheld or that I ever conceived existed in all the eternal worlds." Continuing, he said:

> As I approached to be introduced, he arose and stepped towards me with extended arms and he smiled as he softly spoke my name. If I shall live to be a million years old, I shall never forget that smile. He took me into his arms and kissed me, pressed me to his bosom, and blessed me, until the marrow of my bones seemed to melt! When he had finished, I fell at his feet and, as I bathed them with my tears and kisses, I saw the prints of the nails in the feet of the Redeemer of the world. The feeling that I had in the presence of Him who hath all things in his hands, to have His love, His affection, and His blessings was such that if I ever can receive that of which I had but a foretaste, I would give all that I am, all that I ever hope to be, to feel what I then felt.[32]

In the early days of the Church, the Prophet Joseph Smith spoke with clarity and power regarding this sacred experience. In an address given toward the end of his life, a funeral sermon for a Latter-day Saint by the name of King Follett, Joseph Smith taught that after we receive the Gift of the Holy Ghost, which he called the *First Comforter*, we can press forward in righteousness, proving that we are determined to serve the Lord at all hazards, until we find our calling and election made sure, *then* it will be our privilege to receive the *other* or *Second Comforter* which he identified as being a personal revelation of Jesus Christ himself. The Prophet explained:

> Now what is this other Comforter? It is no more nor less than *the Lord Jesus Christ Himself*, and this is the sum and substance of the whole matter; that when any man obtains this last Comforter, he will have *the personage of Jesus Christ* to attend him, or appear unto him from time to time, and even He will manifest the Father unto him, and they will take up their abode with him, and *the visions of the heavens will be opened unto him*, and the Lord will teach him face to face, and he may have a perfect knowledge of the mysteries of the Kingdom of God; and this is the state and place the ancient Saints arrived at when they had such glorious visions—Isaiah, Ezekiel, John upon the Isle of Patmos, St. Paul in the three heavens, and all the Saints who held communion with the general assembly and Church of the Firstborn.³³

Joseph further explained that it is by having the heavens opened and by communion with holy beings that the *sealing power* comes down. He said,

> I assure the Saints that truth, in reference to these matters, and may be known through the revelations of God in the way of His ordinances, and in answer to prayer. The Hebrew Church "*came unto the spirits of just men made perfect*, and unto an innumerable company of angels, unto God the Father of all, and to Jesus Christ the Mediator of the new covenant." [See Hebrews 12:22-24] What did they learn by coming to the spirits of just men made perfect? Is it written? No. What they learned has not been and could not have been written. What object was gained by this communication with the spirits of the just? *It was the established order of the kingdom of God*: The keys of power and knowledge were with them to communicate to the Saints.... *The spirits of just men are made ministering servants to those who are sealed unto life eternal, and it is through them that the sealing power comes down.*³⁴

The prophet is explaining here that sanctified Saints can receive instruction and direction from just men in the spirit world. They become tutors to those who are sealed to eternal life. At two separate funeral services held for Judge Higbee and James Adams— whom the Prophet Joseph Smith identified as being "just men made perfect"—Joseph Smith explained that by communing through the veil with these brethren, and the spirits of other just men made perfect, we would be enabled to come up to their standard of knowledge and power.

Moses is one who was so tutored by heavenly messengers. He was taken on a heavenly journey during which he saw all the inhabitants of the earth, past, present and future (see Moses 1:8, 28). He even was shown every particle of the earth and was able to comprehend them through the power of the Spirit (see Moses 1:27-28).

Of his own experience in communicating with righteous spirits, the Prophet Joseph Smith said, "Why be so certain that you comprehend the things of God when all things with you are so uncertain." In other words, until we have received light and truth from personages behind the veil, as Joseph had, all things with us remain very tentative.

Paul, the apostle, speaks of a time when he was "caught up into paradise, and heard unspeakable words, which it is not lawful for a man to utter" (2 Corinthians 12:2-4). People like Paul, who are privileged to have this sacred revelation, are given a strict commandment not to speak about what they have seen and heard except as the Spirit shall direct. Alma taught the importance of restricted sharing of sacred information. He said, "It is given unto many to know the mysteries of God; nevertheless they are laid under a strict command that *they shall not impart* only according to the *portion* of his word which he doth grant unto the children of men, according to the heed and diligence which they give unto him" (Alma 12:9; emphasis added).

After viewing the extensive and exquisite vision of the Lord (D&C 76:22-24) and of the three degrees of glory, the Prophet Joseph Smith said he could not write down all that they had seen and heard. He declared, "I could explain a hundred fold more than I ever have of the glories of the kingdoms manifested to me in the vision, were I permitted, and were the people prepared to receive them."[35]

He explained that "they are only to be seen and understood by the power of the Holy Spirit, which God bestows on those who love him, and purify themselves before him; to whom he grants this privilege of seeing and knowing for themselves; That through the power and manifestation of the Spirit, *while in the flesh*, they may be able to bear his presence in the world of glory" (D&C 76:116-118; emphasis added).

The account of the brother of Jared's seeing the finger and then the entire spirit body of Jesus provides the most descriptive scriptural example we have of one who grew spiritually, became sanctified, and, through his great faith, received power to stand in the presence of the Lord. After presenting the 16 stones to the Lord for his sacred touch to fill them with light, the brother of Jared was enlightened himself as he saw the finger of the Lord. Then the great Jehovah, the premortal Jesus, the God of Abraham, Isaac and Jacob said unto him:

> Because of thy faith thou hast seen that I shall take upon me flesh and blood; and never has man come before me with such exceeding faith as thou

hast; for were it not so ye could not have seen my finger. Sawest thou more than this? And he answered: Nay; Lord, show thyself unto me.

And the Lord said unto him: Believest thou the words which I shall speak?

And he answered: Yea, Lord, I know that thou speakest the truth, for thou art a God of truth, and canst not lie.

And when he had said these words, behold, the Lord showed himself unto him, and said: Because thou knowest these things ye are redeemed from the fall; therefore ye are brought back into my presence; therefore I show myself unto you (Ether 3:9-13).

The brother of Jared was only one of many who had passed through the veil and had seen the Lord, for "there were *many* whose faith was so exceedingly strong, even before Christ came, who could not be kept from within the veil, but truly saw with their eyes the things which they had beheld with an eye of faith, *and they were glad*" (Ether 12:19; emphasis added).

This wonderful blessing of seeing the face of the Lord is clearly promised in our latter-day scriptures, "Verily, thus saith the Lord: It shall come to pass that every soul who forsaketh his sin and cometh unto me, and calleth upon my name, and obeyeth my voice, and keepeth my commandments, shall see my face and know that I am" (D&C 93:1).

This glorious revelation, which is available to all who become true and faithful, is the same as when Moses was permitted to speak with the Lord "face to face, as a man speaketh unto his friend" (Exodus 33:11; see also John 14:23; D&C 130:3).

Each of us "have the power—and it is our privilege so to live—that becoming pure in heart we shall see the face of God while we yet dwell as mortals in a world of sin and sorrow."[36] This is in fulfillment of the Lord's promise "Blessed are the pure in heart: for they shall see God" (Matthew 5:8).

At the 1995 BYU Sidney B. Sperry Symposium Elder Jeffrey R. Holland emphasized that ordinary men and women can rend the veil of unbelief and enter the realms of eternity. Referring to the experience of the brother of Jared, he said, "A brother-of-Jared-like appeal is given by God to both Gentiles and Israelites— to both of whom this record is sent—asking the latter-day reader to pierce the limits of shallow faith." Continuing Elder Holland commented,

The Book of Mormon is predicated—and certainly this experience from the brother of Jared is predicated—on the willingness of men and women to rend the veil of unbelief in order to behold the revelations and *the Revelation* of God. It would seem from the brother of Jared's humbling experience—in his failure to pray and his slight embarrassment over the 16 stones—that he is so very much in that sense like the men and women we know. He's like us. His belief in himself and his view of himself may not have been great. It seems to have been quite limited, much like our view of ourselves. But his belief in God was unprecedented. It was without doubt or limit.

Elder Holland concluded with the assuring promise: "And Christ, who was prepared from the foundation of the world to redeem his people, would be, was, and still is standing at the edge of that veil to usher the believer through to the wonders of eternity."[37]

5. Priesthood Power

Those who receive the promise of eternal life who further qualify to have the heavens opened are taught by holy beings and are granted, through their faith, godlike powers that enable them to control the elements of the earth and the powers of heaven. We have many passages of scripture that teach this important principle.[38]

During Jesus' mortal ministry he promised his disciples that they would do even greater works than he because he would go to the Father (see John 14:12). The same promise is given to his disciples in our day (see Mormon 9:22-25).

We have many other examples of the faithful Saints in other dispensations receiving great priesthood power. The ancient Nephites also received great priesthood power through their faith. Jacob, the younger brother of Nephi wrote, "Wherefore, we search the prophets, and we have many revelations and the spirit of prophecy; and having all these witnesses we obtain a hope, and our faith becometh unshaken, insomuch that we truly can command in the name of Jesus and the very *trees* obey us, or the *mountains*, or the *waves* of the *sea*" (Jacob 4:6). This description is not metaphor. This passage provides an example of how "the rights of the priesthood are inseparably connected with the powers of heaven" (D&C 121:36).

Moses also received sacred priesthood powers by which he could control the elements of the earth in order to deliver the children of Israel from Egyptian bondage. In the Book of Moses we read, "And calling upon the name of God, he beheld his glory again, for it was upon him; and he heard a voice, saying: Blessed art thou, Moses, for I, the Almighty, have *chosen* thee, and thou shalt be made stronger than many waters; for they shall obey thy command *as if thou wert God.* And lo, I am with thee, even unto the end of thy days; for thou shalt deliver my people from bondage, even Israel my chosen" (Moses 1:25-26; emphasis added).

In relation to his mission Enoch was also promised priesthood powers, "Behold my Spirit is upon you, wherefore all thy words will I justify; and the mountains shall flee before you, and the rivers shall turn from their course; and thou shalt abide in me, and I in you; therefore walk with me" (Moses 6:34).

One of the most awe-inspiring accounts is found in Joseph Smith's translation of the Bible. We read the following:

For God having sworn unto Enoch and unto his seed with an oath by himself; that every one being ordained after this order and calling should have power, by faith, to break mountains, to divide the seas, to dry up waters, to turn them out of their course;

To put at defiance the armies of nations, to divide the earth, to break every band, to stand in the presence of God; to do all things according to his will, according to his command, subdue principalities and powers; and this by the will of the Son of God which was from before the foundation of the world (JST, Genesis 14:30-31).

The expression "being ordained after this order and calling" in the above passage has reference to being sealed to eternal life or having had their calling and election made sure. The specified powers of the priesthood that are mentioned in the above paragraph require deep pondering to grasp their significance.

In the thirteenth chapter of Alma, the Book of Mormon prophet uses the expressions: "the holy order" and "this holy calling" to refer to high priests in this priesthood order. Those who are received into this holy order are to teach the Lord's commandments unto the children of men, so that "they also might enter into his rest" or his "presence" (Alma 13:6; JST, Exodus 34:2).

Of these high priests, of whom Nephi the son of Helaman was an example, the Lord declared: "Whatsoever ye shall seal on earth shall be sealed in heaven; and whatsoever ye shall loose on earth shall be loosed in heaven; and thus shall ye have power among this people. And thus, if ye shall say unto this temple it shall be rent in twain, it shall be done. And if ye shall say unto this mountain, Be thou cast down and become smooth, it shall be done. And behold, if ye shall say that God shall smite this people, it shall come to pass." (Helaman 10:7-10).

The priesthood powers of which we have been speaking are, of course, expressed in every dispensation through great faith and through the ordinances of the priesthood. As the Prophet Joseph Smith explained:

The Former-day Saints, viewed the plan of salvation [as] a system of faith—it begins with faith, and continues by faith; and every blessing which is obtained in relation to it is the effect of faith, whether it pertains to this life or that which is to come. To this all the revelations of God bear witness.... And through the whole history of the scheme of life and salvation, it is a matter of faith: every man received according to his faith—according as his faith was, so were his blessings and privileges; and nothing was withheld from him when his faith was sufficient to receive it. He could stop the mouths of lions, quench the violence of fire, escape the edge of the sword, wax valiant in fight, and put to flight the armies of the aliens; women could, by their faith, receive their dead children to life again; in a word, there was nothing impossible with them who had faith. All things were in subjection to the Former-day Saints, according as their faith was. By their faith they could obtain heavenly visions, the ministering of angels, have knowledge of the spirits of just men made perfect, of the general assembly and church of the firstborn, whose names are written in heaven, of God the judge of all, of Jesus the Mediator of the new covenant, and become familiar with the third heavens, see and hear things which were not only unutterable, but were unlawful to utter.[39]

Consistent with these promises to ancient Saints, the Latter-day Saints have also been promised priesthood powers, through holy ordinances and a manifestation of great faith (see D&C 121:34-46).

Although our power with the Lord may not yet be at the same high level as these former-day Saints, we must not be discouraged. Their examples provide hope, vision, and direction for us. They describe what we too may eventually receive when we learn the full power and blessings of faith in the Lord Jesus Christ and in his priesthood ordinances.

Through righteousness, the priesthood powers about which we have been speaking flow unto us like a small streamlet that increases until it is like a mighty surging river. We receive power in ever increasing degrees over time.

Through priesthood power and faith, we will be delivered in a day of calamity. We will be rescued from the wars, destructions, fires and enemies of righteousness who will amass themselves against us in the last days. Deliverance from our enemies and the calamities of the last days is one of the important reasons why the everlasting covenant has been restored in our day.

6. Protection and Deliverance

The Lord's plan of peace in this world reaches a grand crescendo in his promise that he will deliver his covenant people in a day of calamity. In the very first chapter of the Book of Mormon, Nephi explains that his intent in keeping his record is to show how God will deliver his chosen ones. "Behold, I, Nephi, will show unto you that the tender mercies of the Lord are over all those whom he hath chosen, because of their faith, to make them *mighty* even unto the power of *deliverance*" (1 Nephi 1:20; emphasis added).

Nephi continues his record by citing one example after an other to give testimony that he was delivered from his enemies, his rebellious brothers and the sons of Ishmael. Nephi concludes his written account by focusing on how the Savior will deliver latter-day Israel from wars and calamities, and also from our greatest enemies—death and hell. (See 1 Nephi 22; 2 Nephi 2, 9).

There are many other examples in the scriptures that show us how individuals were protected by the power of God: Daniel was delivered from the lion's den and his three friends were delivered from the fiery furnace. The children of Israel were delivered from the bondage of the Egyptians through the miracles performed by Moses. The Lord revealed to us the story of Enoch and his holy city to show us how the Lord blesses and rescues his people.

> And so great was the faith of Enoch that he led the people of God, and their enemies came to battle against them; and he spake the word of the Lord, and the *earth trembled*, and the *mountains fled*, even according to his command; and the *rivers of water were turned out of their course*; and the roar of the lions was heard out of the wilderness; and all *nations feared greatly*, so powerful was the word of Enoch, and so great was the power of the language which God had given him.... and went forth a curse upon all people that fought against God;
> And from that time forth them were wars and bloodshed among them; but the Lord came and dwelt with his people, and they dwelt in righteousness.
> *The fear of the Lord was upon all nations*, so great was the glory of the Lord, which was upon his people. And the Lord blessed the land, and they were blessed upon the mountains, and upon the high places, and did flourish (Moses 7:13, 15-17).

Since God is the same yesterday, today, and forever, we would expect that the Lord would also protect his Saints in the last days.

Even as ancient Israel was promised deliverance through the blood of the Lamb of God, and that the destroying angel would pass over them (Exodus 12), those who walk in obedience to their covenants in the last days have received a similar assurance of protection,

"And I, the Lord, give unto them a promise, that the destroying angel shall pass by them, as the children of Israel, and not slay them" (D&C 89:21).

Like Moses, Joseph Smith was called by God to deliver his people. Of Joseph's divine calling to save latter-day Israel, we read,

> Wherefore, I the Lord, *knowing the calamity* which should come upon the inhabitants of the earth, called upon my servant Joseph Smith, Jun., and spake unto him from heaven, and gave him commandments;...
> For I am no respecter of persons, and will that all men shall know that the day speedily cometh; the hour is not yet, but is nigh at hand, *when peace shall be taken from the earth, and the devil shall have power over his own dominion.*
> And also *the Lord shall have power over his saints*, and shall reign in their midst, and shall come down in judgment upon Idumea, or the world (D&C 1:17, 35-36; emphasis added).

Because the world has forsaken righteousness, Joseph Smith warned that "DESTRUCTION, to the eye of the spiritual beholder, seems to be written by the finger of an invisible hand, in large capitals, upon almost every thing we behold.[40] The Prophet then explained what all must do to enjoy the smiles of our Savior and escape the calamities of the last days.[41]

By way of review, he said that we must first comply with the requirements of the gospel covenant including faith in the Lord Jesus Christ, repentance, baptism, and receiving the Gift of the Holy Ghost by the laying on of hands; next, we must add to our faith, virtue; and to virtue, knowledge, etc., until we make our calling and election sure, "Wherefore the rather, brethren, give diligence to *make your calling and election sure*" (2 Peter 1:5-10; emphasis added). Associated with this sanctification process, we must establish Zion and Jerusalem as places of deliverance.

The scriptures are clear that the Latter-day Saints will need places of protection if they are to survive the wars, geophysical upheavals, and refining fire that will destroy the wicked. In discussing how the Lord will preserve his people, the Prophet Joseph Smith explained that the Jews will return to old Jerusalem, but that the ransomed of the Lord, the faithful Latter-day Saints—latter-day Israel— will find safety in the New Jerusalem. He declared:

> The city of Zion [the New Jerusalem] spoken of by David, in the one hundred and second Psalm, will be built upon the land of America, "And the ransomed of the Lord shall return, and come to Zion with songs and everlasting joy upon their heads." (Isaiah 35:10); and then *they will be delivered from the overflowing scourge that shall pass through the land.* But Judah shall obtain deliverance at Jerusalem. See Joel 2:32; Isaiah 26:20 and 21; Jeremiah 31:12; Psalms 1:5; Ezekiel 34:11, 12 and 13. These are testimonies that the Good Shepherd will put forth His own sheep, and lead them out from all nations where they have been scattered in a cloudy and dark day, to Zion, and to Jerusalem; besides many more testimonies which might be brought.[42]

Joseph observed that the word, "Salem" [name of the city later called Jerusalem] itself denotes peace and righteousness.[43] He warned that we need Zion and Jerusalem in order to escape the woes that are to come, "And now I am prepared to say by the authority of Jesus Christ, that not many years shall pass away before the United States shall present such a scene of bloodshed as has not a parallel in the history of our nation; pestilence, hall, famine, and earthquake will sweep the wicked of this generation from off the face of the land."[44]

Ever since this prophecy was given, there have been ever increasing wars, bloodshed, calamities, earthquakes and political upheavals. They will continue to increase in frequency and intensity as we approach the Millennium. "And thus, with the sword and by bloodshed the inhabitants of the earth shall mourn; and with famine, and plague, and earthquake, and the thunder of heaven, and the fierce and vivid lightning also, shall the inhabitants of the earth be made to feel the wrath, and indignation, and chastening hand of an Almighty God, until the consumption decreed *hath made a full end of all nations*" (D&C 87:6; emphasis added).

As these prophecies of war and calamity are being fulfilled, so will the promises be realized that assure the Saints of deliverance. Those who remain will be those who have taken the Holy Ghost to be their guide.

Zion and her stakes, which will grow out of the Church, have been designated by the Lord as places for deliverance: "For thus shall my church be called in the last days, even The Church of Jesus Christ of Latter-day Saints. Verily I say unto you all: Arise and shine forth, that thy light may be a standard for the nations; And that the gathering together upon the land of *Zion*, and upon her *stakes*, may be for a *defense*, and for a *refuge* from the storm, and from wrath when it shall be poured out without mixture upon the whole earth" (D&C 115:4-6; emphasis added). This peace will be afforded all the people who will embrace the everlasting covenant during the times of great tribulation before the Second Coming of the Lord (see D&C 1:17, 35-36).

The New Jerusalem will provide peace and protection when "The Lord God will send forth flies upon the face of the earth, which shall take hold of the inhabitants thereof, and shall eat their flesh, and shall cause maggots to come in upon them;... and their flesh shall fall from off their bones, and their eyes from their sockets" (D&C 29:18-19). In that day "the heavens shall be darkened, and a veil of darkness shall cover the earth; and the heavens shall shake, and also the earth; and great tribulations shall be among the children of men, but *my people* will I preserve" (Moses 7:61; emphasis added).

The Lord will save his people, the elect of Israel, in a dark and gloomy day. He promised Abraham, Isaac, and Jacob that he would remember their seed always (2 Nephi 29:14). The Good Shepherd will save his flocks as they gather to him for safety according to the plan revealed to his servants, the prophets. As a good Shepherd he will yet cause them to lie down in green pastures and lead them beside still waters (see Psalms 23).[45]

Without question the days to follow will be filled with high adventure. We read, "For, behold, the day cometh, that shall burn as an oven; and all the proud, yea, and all that do wickedly, shall be stubble: and the day that cometh shall burn them up, saith the Lord of hosts, that it shall leave them neither root nor branch. But unto you that fear my name shall the Sun of righteousness arise with healing in his wings; and ye shall go forth, and grow up as calves of the stall" (Malachi 4:1-2). The Lord has promised us that, "if ye are prepared, ye shall not fear" (D&C 38:30).

SANCTIFICATION—FOR US HERE AND NOW

As we read of the marvelous blessings and powers that came to the Saints anciently, we are sometimes prone to think that such things were for them, there, and then; but they are not really for us, here, and now. Sometimes it is hard to believe that the marvelous scriptural accounts of the ancients' faith and priesthood power are given to us as examples for us to follow, but they are. It is not that we doubt the scriptural accounts, but that we may feel somehow lacking in our own spiritual development. When it comes right down to it, it requires considerable faith to believe that such things can be attained by the righteous today— that there are today people who are so pure in heart that they enjoy the blessings and powers that we have discussed.

However, there *are* sanctified Saints in the Church today who know through their own sacred experiences that Jesus is the Christ. Those who have had their calling and election made sure have had these experiences because, in part, the Lord can trust them to keep sacred things to themselves. We too can know for ourselves if we will believe on the words of those who know. As the scriptures attest, "To some it is given by the Holy Ghost to *know* that Jesus Christ is the Son of God, and that he was crucified for the sins of the world. To others it is given to *believe* on their words, *that they also might have eternal life if they continue faithful*" (D&C 46:13-14; emphasis added).

Let us rejoice as we read of ancient Saints and the great spiritual heights they attained. And let us have the faith to move, however gradually, toward the marvelous examples of righteousness and faith they provided for us. Let us lift up our heads and rejoice in the promised and present blessings of the everlasting covenant.

HAPPINESS—THE OBJECT AND DESIGN OF OUR EXISTENCE

Our joy and rejoicing, our peace and happiness, our immortality and eternal life are the work and glory of our Heavenly Father and his son, Jesus Christ. The Prophet Joseph Smith has explained this powerful truth in these words:

> *Happiness is the object and design of our existence*; and will be the end thereof, if we pursue the path that leads to it; and this path is virtue, uprightness, faithfulness, holiness, and keeping all the commandments of God.... In obedience there is joy and peace unspotted, unalloyed; and as God has designed our happiness—and the happiness of all His creatures, he never has—He never will institute an ordinance or give a commandment to His

people that is not calculated in its nature to promote that happiness which He has designed, and which will not end in the greatest amount of good and glory to those who become the recipients of his law and ordinances. Blessings offered, but rejected, are no longer blessings, but become like the talent hid in the earth by the wicked and slothful servant.[46]

These words of the Prophet Joseph stress the idea that happiness is a result of obedience to the commandments. They remind us of the teaching of Jesus, "I am come that they might have life, and that they might have it more abundantly" (John 10:10.)

Lehi, too, was affirming the idea that happiness is central to the plan of salvation when he said, "Adam fell that men might be; and men are, that they might have joy" (2 Nephi 2:25.)

The Lord has given us a beautiful symbol—the rainbow—as a reminder that his great plan is a plan of happiness and joy. Most of us know that the rainbow is the symbol that the Lord will never again destroy the world by water. But, few Latter-day Saints know that it is also a symbol of the Lord's promise that the everlasting covenant will indeed be established in its fulness—that Zion will again be found on the earth with all of its beauty, happiness, glory, and peace. The Lord promised Noah:

> The [rain]bow shall be in the cloud; and I will look upon it, that I may remember the everlasting covenant, which I made unto thy father Enoch; that, when men should keep all my commandments, Zion should again come on the earth, the city of Enoch which I have caught up unto myself.
>
> And this is mine everlasting covenant, that when thy posterity shall embrace the truth, and look upward, then shall Zion look downward, and all the heavens shall shake with gladness, and the earth shall tremble with joy;
>
> And the general assembly of the church of the first-born shall come down out of heaven, and possess the earth, and shall have place until the end come. And this is mine everlasting covenant, which I made with thy father Enoch.
>
> And the bow shall be in the cloud, and I will establish my covenant unto thee, which I have made between me and thee, for every living creature of all flesh that shall be upon the earth.
>
> And God said unto Noah, This is the token of the covenant which I have established between me and thee; for all flesh that shall be upon the earth." (JST, Genesis 9:21-25; see also Moses 7:58-64.)

When we view the beauty of the rainbow, we should rejoice in this promise of the Lord that there will come a time when them will be peace on earth and good will toward men. The rainbow is a beautiful token and reminder of this promise.

BAPTISM IS THE BEGINNING

As children we understood very little of what is involved in the ordinance of baptism. By celestial standards we still understand only a part of all that is involved. As we continue to read and ponder the scriptures and the words of living prophets, we get glimpses of some of the power and blessings that are associated with the pathway of the gospel. Baptism is a first step. It is the beginning of the journey that leads us to blessings unimaginable and powers incomprehensible.

I did not know when I was baptized in the great font in the Cardston Temple that I was beginning a course that will, if I remain true and faithful, lead me back into the presence of my Heavenly Father and his Son Jesus Christ—that I will one day see their faces and know that they are. But as a boy of eight, I felt warm in the assurance that I was on the right track, that I was being baptized as the Lord wanted me to be, and I knew that I was moving closer and closer to things that are right, and good, and true.

REFERENCES:

1 Bruce R. McConkie, *Mormon Doctrine*, 166-167 "Covenants".
2 Joseph Smith explained this fact. See *Teachings of the Prophet Joseph Smith*, 14.
3 *Teachings*, 231-32.
4 *Teachings*, 17.
5 *Teachings*, 355; emphasis added.
6 *Teachings*, 151.
7 Parley P. Pratt, *Key to the Science of Theology*, 10th edition, [SLC: Deseret Book, 1973] 100-101).
8 *Teachings*, 51; emphasis added.
9 *Teachings*, 307-308
10 *Discourses of Brigham Young*, 416.
11 "The Children of the Covenant", *Ensign*, May 1995, emphasis added.
12 *Within Reach* (SLC: Deseret Book, 1995.
13 *Teachings*, 191.
14 *Teachings*, 15.
15 Journal History, 23 Feb. 1847.
16 "Self-Reliance," *Ensign*, Aug. 1975, 89.
17 Bruce R. McConkie, *Doctrinal New Testament Commentary*, 3:348; emphasis added.
18 Bruce R. McConkie, *The Promised Messiah*, 595; emphasis added.
19 Bruce R. McConkie, "The Purifying Power of Gethsemane", General Conference, April 6, 1985.
20 see *Lectures on Faith*, 2:55; emphasis added.
21 *Lectures on Faith*, 32.
22 *The Promised Messiah*, 586.
23 *Teachings*, 150.

24 *Teachings*, 299.

25 *Teachings*, 366.

26 *Teachings*, 150; emphasis added.

27 Regarding making your calling and election sure, see for example *Doctrinal New Testament Commentary*, 3:323-55. Here, Elder McConkie provides excellent commentary on 2 Peter 1:10 in which Peter charges the Saints of his day to make their calling and election sure.

Elder McConkie's October, 1977, Conference address entitled "The Ten Blessings of the Priesthood" discusses both making your calling and election sure and seeing the face of the Lord. Another source of wonderful information is found in his work, *Promised Messiah*, the last two chapters, entitled "Seek the Face of the Lord Always" and "Who Has Seen the Lord?" In addition, his work, *Mormon Doctrine*, also provides insightful information on these topics. See headings "Calling and Election Sure" along with related headings and also "Second Comforter" with related headings.

28 *Doctrinal New Testament Commentary*, 3:349; emphasis added.

29 Scriptures that relate to the promise of eternal life include, but are not limited to, the following: D&C 58:12; John 6:27, 66-71 (CF JST John 6:27); John 14:12-15; John 17:2-3; Acts 13:48; Romans 6:23; 2 Corinthians, 1:20-22; 1 Timothy 6:12; 2 Timothy 4:6-8; Titus 1:1-3; Hebrews 11:2, 4-6, 13, 26-27, 33, 39-40; 2 Peter 1:10-11, 19; I John 1:1-3; 2:25 (20-27); 1 John 3:15; 1 John 5:11-13 (1-20); Revelation 7:1-3; 14:1-7; 2 Nephi 31:20; Enos 5-8, 27; Mosiah 5:15, 26:20; Helaman 10:4-15; 3 Nephi 28:3, 10 (1-15); Mormon 2:19; Ether 12:37 (19-40); Moroni 10:34; D&C 53:1; 59:23; 68:12; 76:50-53, 58, 70 (50-70); 77:8-9, 11; 105:35-37; 107:53; 131:5-6; 132:7, 19-24, 26-27, 46-50, 59-60; Moses 1:25-26; 5:4-11; 6:34 (26-36), 52-68; 7:27, 62-64; Abraham 2:6-11 (CF Genesis 22); JST Genesis 9:21-23; JST Genesis 14:26-35 (CF Alma 13).

30 See Andrew F. Ehat and Lyndon W. Cook, *The Words of Joseph Smith* (Provo, Utah: Religious Studies Center, 1980), 246.

31 See Bible Topical Guide "Jesus Christ, Appearances, Antemortal" and Jesus Christ, Appearances, Postmortal" and "God, Manifestations of" for important references to appearances of Christ before and after his mortal life.

32 Melvin J. Ballard, "Seconded Comforter, Revelation", Lewis J. Harmer, 165-66 as recorded in his diary for May 14, 1917. Also in Hinckley, *Melvin J. Ballard*, 66.

33 *Teachings*, 150-51; emphasis added.

34 *Teachings*, 325; emphasis added.

35 *Teachings*, 305

36 McConkie, "Ten Blessings of the Priesthood", *Ensign*, November 1977, 34.

37 Reported in Church News, week ending October 14, 1995, 5.

38 See these passages which deal with priesthood power: Moses 1:25; Moses 6:34; Jacob 4:6; Mormon 8:24; D&C 121:36; JST, Genesis 14:26, 30-32; *Lectures on Faith* 7:1. See also Bible Topical Guide "Priesthood, Power of".

39 *Lectures on Faith* 7:17; emphasis added.

40 *Teachings*, 16.

41 *Teachings*, 16-17.

42 *Teachings*, 17; emphasis added.

43 *Teachings*, 321; emphasis added.

44 *Teachings*, 17.

45 See also Genesis 12:2; 1 Nephi 17:40; 3 Nephi 20:27; Abraham 2:9. Topical Guide Abrahamic Covenant.

46 *Teachings*, 255-57; emphasis added.

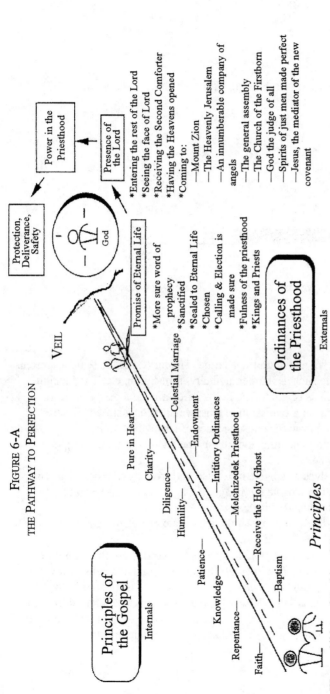

FIGURE 6-A
THE PATHWAY TO PERFECTION

Principles of the Gospel

Internals

Faith—
—Baptism
Repentance—
—Receive the Holy Ghost
Knowledge—
—Melchizedek Priesthood
Patience—
—Initiatory Ordinances
Humility—
—Endowment
Diligence—
—Celestial Marriage
Charity—
Pure in Heart—

VEIL

Protection, Deliverance, Safety

Power in the Priesthood

Presence of the Lord

God

Promise of Eternal Life
*More sure word of prophecy
*Sanctified
*Sealed to Eternal Life
*Chosen
*Calling & Election is made sure
*Fulness of the priesthood
*Kings and Priests

*Entering the rest of the Lord
*Seeing the face of Lord
*Receiving the Second Comforter
*Having the Heavens opened
*Coming to:
—Mount Zion
—The Heavenly Jerusalem
—An innumerable company of angels
—The general assembly
—The Church of the Firstborn
—God the judge of all
—Spirits of just men made perfect
—Jesus, the mediator of the new covenant

Ordinances of the Priesthood

Externals

Principles

1. We are children of God in a fallen world.
2. As such, we are enemies to God (his righteousness) unless we yield to the enticings of the Spirit (see Mosiah 3:19).
3. We can be saved from the effects of our sins by obedience to the laws and ordinances of the gospel of Jesus Christ.
4. We must internalize the attributes of godliness, the divine nature of Christ. These are received as gifts of the Holy Ghost as we earnestly seek them and live righteously.
5. Men must receive the Melchizedek Priesthood and all the ordinances.
6. Women do not receive the priesthood, but they can receive all the blessings of the priesthood including the promise of eternal life, the presence of the Lord, the power of the Lord, and the protection of the Lord.
7. We do not necessarily progress in the principles step by step, as we do with ordinances, but charity and purity of heart are crowning virtues.

FIGURE 6-C
THE DOCTRINES OF JUSTIFICATION AND SANCTIFICATION

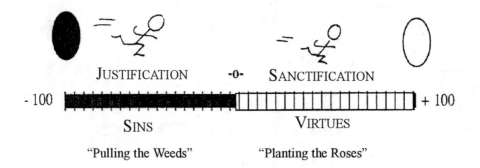

Principles

1. There are degrees of sin and degrees of virtue. The far left of the scale represents sins of moral turpitude such as murder, adultery, fornication, etc. The far right represents virtues such as of godliness, holiness, charity, and purity of heart.
2. When we are baptized for a remission of sins, we are then justified. We are absolved, or vindicated from the consequences of sin. We are to retain our justified state by continually repenting and loving one another as King Benjamin explained (see Mosiah 4).
3. Besides ridding ourselves of sin, we must also go forward and increase in virtuous principles in order to receive the image of Christ in our countenances. We must think his thoughts and do his deeds.
4. As we become more like Christ, we approach a state of sanctification—we become pure in heart.
5. Joseph Smith taught, "the nearer a man approaches perfection, the clearer are his views, and the greater his enjoyments, till he has overcome the evils of his life and lost every desire for sin" (*Teachings*, p. 51). Joseph was describing the process of becoming sanctified. Those who attain this state are referred to in the scriptures as the pure in heart, whose washed in the blood of the Lamb, the true and faithful, those who love the Lord and keep his commandments.

FIGURE 6-D

THE THREE VEILS OF ENLIGHTENMENT

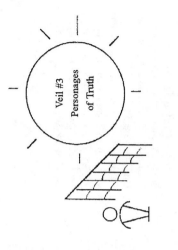

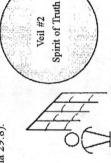

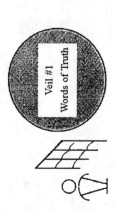

Principles

1. Each veil protects a person from light he is unprepared to receive.
2. The parables of Jesus veiled truth from the spiritually unprepared.
3. The Lord desires us to pass through all three veils, but he will not impose truth upon us in an untimely way (see Alma 29:8).

To advance in truth and light, we must receive the gospel message—the words of truth. Some, for instance, cannot accept the story of the First Vision and cannot, therefore, advance spiritually. "My sheep hear my voice" (John 10:27). It is good to receive words of truth from such external sources as missionaries, prophets, teachers, scriptures, and leaders.

Accepting the words of others is a vital beginning, but we must receive a spiritual witness for ourselves. the prophet's sources of light must become our sources of light. "And by the power of the Holy Ghost ye may know the truth of all things" (Moroni 10:5).

Truths from the Spirit touch our hearts as well as our minds.

Revelation from the Spirit comes to our spirits as though we had no body at all (see *Teachings*, p. 355).

It is good to receive truth from such internal sources.

An important function of the Holy Ghost is to sanctify a person and thus prepare him to commune with the Lord and other holy beings. "Now Moses plainly taught...and sought diligently to sanctify his people that they might behold the face of God" (D&C 84:23).

"When any man obtains this last Comforter, his will have the personage of Jesus Christ to attend him, or appear unto him from time to time, and even He will manifest the Father unto him,... and the visions of the heavens will be opened unto him...and this is the state the ancient Saints arrived at when they had such glorious visions..." (*Teachings*, p. 151).

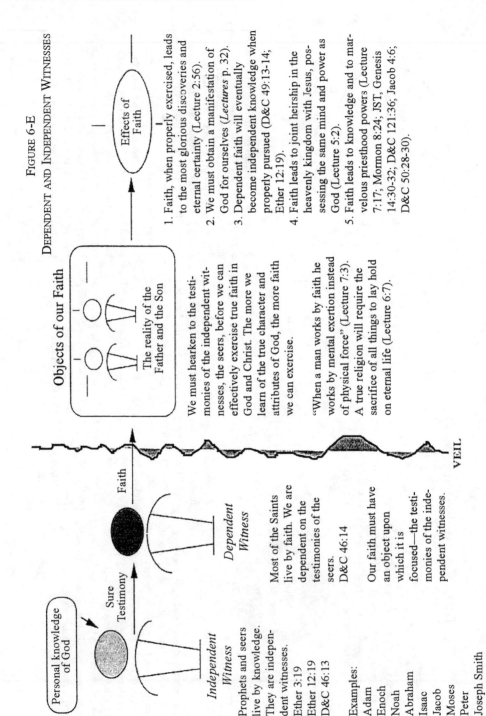

FIGURE 6-E
DEPENDENT AND INDEPENDENT WITNESSES

Objects of our Faith

The reality of the
Father and the Son

Effects of
Faith

1. Faith, when properly exercised, leads to the most glorious discoveries and eternal certainty (Lecture 2:56).

2. We must obtain a manifestation of God for ourselves (*Lectures* p. 32).

3. Dependent faith will eventually become independent knowledge when properly pursued (D&C 49:13-14; Ether 12:19).

4. Faith leads to joint heirship in the heavenly kingdom with Jesus, possessing the same mind and power as God (Lecture 5:2).

5. Faith leads to knowledge and to marvelous priesthood powers (Lecture 7:17; Mormon 8:24; JST, Genesis 14:30-32; D&C 121:36; Jacob 4:6; D&C 50:28-30).

We must hearken to the testimonies of the independent witnesses, the seers, before we can effectively exercise true faith in God and Christ. The more we learn of the true character and attributes of God, the more faith we can exercise.

"When a man works by faith he works by mental exertion instead of physical force" (Lecture 7:3). A true religion will require the sacrifice of all things to lay hold on eternal life (Lecture 6:7).

VEIL

Faith

Dependent Witness

Most of the Saints live by faith. We are dependent on the testimonies of the seers.

D&C 46:14

Our faith must have an object upon which it is focused—the testimonies of the independent witnesses.

Sure
Testimony

Personal knowledge
of God

Independent Witness

Prophets and seers live by knowledge. They are independent witnesses.

Ether 3:19
Ether 12:19
D&C 46:13

Examples:
Adam
Enoch
Noah
Abraham
Isaac
Jacob
Moses
Peter
Joseph Smith

Chapter Seven

The Gospel
Covenant
Through the Ages

God conversed with men, and made known unto them the plan of redemption,
which had been prepared from the foundation of the world; and this he made
known unto them according to their faith and repentance and their holy works.
—Alma 12:30

About ten miles northeast of Hillspring, Alberta, lies the little community of Glenwood, the place where my mother was born and raised. I remember exciting times when my older brother and I were able to visit our grandparents' home there. Sometimes we caught a ride with Dick Law, the local milkman, who transported milk to Glenwood from various surrounding communities. There, the milk was processed into big blocks of wonderful tasting cheddar cheese.

Sometimes we would stay over a weekend and attend our Sunday meetings at the Glenwood ward. When my mother was a young woman her father was the bishop there. He occupied that position for some sixteen years. As I sat with the congregation I tried to visualize my grandfather standing at the carved wooden pulpit conducting his meetings.

During the meetings I had some of the same feelings I had in Hillspring. The faces of the people were different, to be sure, and the building had its own unique smell but there were many similarities. The sacrament prayers were said using the same words, the hymns were the same, and I had the same sense of belonging there that I had in Hillspring—a sense of acceptance, a sense of family.

In some ways these feelings were stronger in Glenwood because my grand-parents, aunts, uncles, and cousins were there—and as my mother assured me, "They are your family." In a way, I felt that the whole ward was part of my fam-ily—they were all so friendly. My father once told me that wherever I went I would feel some of those same kinds of feelings because the whole Church is like a big family.

In my adult years I have had the opportunity to travel extensively, and I have found this to be true. I have felt very comfortable in Latter-day Saint wards and branches wherever I have gone. There is a constancy, a recognizable spirit, in each of the Church units I have visited. I believe that if we were to visit the Saints in former times we would feel some of those same feelings of kinship and love.

The reason I mention the unity I felt in Glenwood, Hillspring, and many other wards is because it represents in a small way the oneness and unity of faith and effort that has been sought by the Lord and his prophets for the Saints throughout the ages. Paul explained that the very purpose for the existence of the Church was "for the perfecting of the saints, for the work of the ministry, for the edifying of the body of Christ: Till we all come in the *unity of the faith*" (Ephesians 4:12-13; emphasis added).

At another time, Paul used the imagery of the various parts of the human body as an example of cooperative effort. He pleaded for the Saints to work together in a similar spirit of unity and oneness (see 1 Corinthians 12:12-31). In our day the Lord has also commanded us to "be one; and if ye are not one ye are not mine" (D&C 38:27). This oneness and unity comes as we participate fully in the plan of peace as was outlined in the last chapter.

In this chapter we will review how the Lord has graciously offered his gospel of peace to his children throughout the ages and how it has been variously received or rejected. These periods of time when the gospel is given out through living prophets are called "gospel dispensations". Throughout the history of the world there have been many gospel dispensations.

MANY GOSPEL DISPENSATIONS

The periods of time when the gospel has been restored to the earth through living prophets are called "gospel dispensations". In consequence of the unsteadi-ness of mankind throughout time in remaining faithful to the gospel, there have been many cycles of apostasy followed by periods of restoration. Speaking of the unsteadiness of men, Mormon observed that the children of men generally are not able to hold constant in the faith, continue in righteousness, and remain in the light.

And thus we can behold how false, and also the unsteadiness of the hearts of the children of men; yea, we can see that the Lord in his great infinite goodness doth bless and prosper those who put their trust in him.

Yea, and we may see at the very time when he doth prosper his people, yea, in the increase of their fields, their flocks and their herds, and in gold, and in silver, and in all manner of precious things of every kind and art; sparing their lives, and delivering them out of the hands of their enemies; softening the hearts of their enemies that they should not declare wars against them; yea, and in fine, doing all things for the welfare and happiness of his people; yea, then is the time that they do harden their hearts, and do forget the Lord their God, and do trample under their feet the Holy One—yea, and this because of their ease, and their exceedingly great prosperity.

And thus we see that except the Lord doth chasten his people with many afflictions, yea, except he doth visit them with death and with terror, and with famine and with all manner of pestilence, they will not remember him. (Helaman 12:1-3).

As we view the history of nations, we can see this familiar cycle of obedience, prosperity, disobedience, and bondage (see end of chapter Figure 7-A, The Cycle of Civilizations). Prosperity leads to pride and other sins. They in turn lead to spiritual and temporal weakness and bondage. Bondage leads to humility and repentance. Once people are repentant and have a change of heart, they are—in the Lord's time—delivered and brought back into the good graces of God.

You may ask the questions, "Has this cycle *always* repeated itself? Haven't there *ever* been a people who have received the gospel and remained righteous?" As we look at some of the major gospel dispensations, we will see that Enoch and his people were the only ones—of whom we have any detailed record—who were able to break out of the cycle and remain righteous and true to their covenants. All other dispensations have fallen into apostasy for various reasons. Now, let's look at how this cycle has repeated itself throughout the ages since the time of Father Adam.

ADAM—THE HEAD OF ALL DISPENSATIONS

To help you track the chronology involved in our search of the dispensations, you will need to refer to end of chapter Figure 7-B, The Gospel through the Ages. As you view this figure you will notice that Adam's name appears at the far left.

From the very beginning the ancient Saints knew and worshipped Jesus Christ and obeyed the same principles and ordinances of the gospel that we do now (see Jacob 4:4-6). When administered in its fulness, as in the cases of Adam,

Enoch, Noah and Abraham, the everlasting covenant has offered the Saints the same principles and ordinances, promises, privileges and powers of protection we discussed in the previous chapter—including receiving baptism, the Holy Ghost, the Melchizedek Priesthood, and all of the temple ordinances.

At one time, however, during Moses' ministry, the Lord modified the rites, ordinances, and requirements of the everlasting covenant with the purpose of spiritually strengthening the people. This modification of the covenant—called the Mosaic Law—was intended to serve as a school master (see Galatians 3:24) to draw people to Christ and his plan of salvation.

The ultimate purpose of the everlasting covenant in every dispensation, no matter what form it takes, is always to draw people to Christ and his teachings. Joseph Smith explained that since there has been no change in the constitution of man since Adam fell, all who are redeemed, must be redeemed by the same plan of salvation that Adam knew and lived. He taught that, "though there were different dispensations, yet all things which God communicated to His people were calculated to draw their minds to the great object [Jesus Christ], and to teach them to rely upon God alone as the author of their salvation, as contained in His law. From what we can draw from the Scriptures relative to the teaching of heaven, we are induced to think that much instruction has been given to man since the beginning which we do not possess now."[1]

It would be difficult to overstate the importance of Adam's role in the affairs of the children of God. In approximately a dozen revelations in the Doctrine and Covenants the Lord has revealed information about Adam's role in the plan of salvation (see entries under ADAM in the index).

Because they had known our Heavenly Father intimately, after the Fall Adam and Eve yearned to return home. They rejoiced therefore in the knowledge they had been given regarding the gospel of Jesus Christ, because it would lead them back into the presence of the Lord from whence they had been driven. Regarding Adam's intimate knowledge of God and of his great plan of happiness, Brigham Young has said:

> God was once known on the earth among his children of mankind, as we know one another. Adam was as conversant with his Father who placed him upon this earth as we are conversant with our earthly parents. The Father frequently came to visit his son Adam, and talked and walked with him; and the children of Adam were more or less acquainted with him, and the things that pertain to God and to heaven were as familiar among mankind in the first ages of their existence on the earth, as these mountains are to our mountain boys, as our gardens are to our wives and children, or as the road to the Western Ocean is to the experienced traveler. From this source mankind have received their religious traditions.[2]

The Lord taught Adam the complete gospel with all the laws, doctrines, and covenants that would enable him and his righteous family to enjoy the blessings of the gospel, "even peace in this life and eternal life in the world to come" (D&C 59:23).

Adam received his patriarchal priesthood from Jehovah and then in due time he bestowed these sacred powers and keys upon his righteous posterity (see Moses 6:7; 8:19; D&C 84:6-16).[3] They honored their father as their patriarchal head, not only because he was the first to receive a gospel dispensation, but also because he had been foreordained to that position and was given authority before the world was.[4] He was to stand at the head of all the human family and all subsequent dispensations.

Regarding Adam's role as the patriarch of the human family, the Prophet Joseph Smith stated: "The Priesthood was first given to Adam; he obtained the First Presidency, and held the keys of it from generation to generation. He obtained it in the Creation, before the world was formed. . . . He had dominion given him over every living creature. He is Michael the Archangel, spoken of in the Scriptures."[5]

Father Adam was assured that "this same Priesthood, which was in the beginning, shall be in the end of the world also" (Moses 6:7; D&C 2:1; 86:8-10). This means that the same patriarchal priesthood that was held by Adam in his time would be put in operation in the last days—with all the attendant blessings associated with the fulness of the priesthood.

Adam was thus given the *first* gospel dispensation.[6] Subsequently, he was commanded to "teach it unto your children, that all men, everywhere, must repent, or they can in nowise inherit the kingdom of God, for no unclean thing can dwell there, or dwell in his presence; for, in the language of Adam, Man of Holiness is his name, and the name of his Only Begotten is the Son of Man, even Jesus Christ, a righteous Judge, who shall come in the meridian of time. Therefore I give unto you a commandment, to teach these things freely unto your children" (Moses 6:57-58).

Those of Adam and Eve's children who believed their parents' teachings were blessed with all the promised gospel blessings. However, not all of Adam and Eve's children believed the teachings of their parents. Of this sad fact we read, "And Satan came among them, saying: I am also a son of God; and he commanded them, saying: Believe it not; and they believed it not, and they loved Satan more than God. And men began from that time forth to be carnal, sensual, and devilish" (Moses 5:13).

Adam and Eve, however, continued faithfully, had many children and continued to exhort them to obey the gospel plan of peace and happiness (see Moses 5:2-3; 16-17). Two of the sons who were eventually born to Adam and Eve were named Cain and Abel. Cain, like others of his brothers and sisters, rejected the ways of righteousness; he had no faith in the promised Redeemer and became a master of evil and corruption (see Moses 5:28-31).

Abel, on the other hand, was obedient to his parents' teachings. He followed in the ways of the Lord by offering to him the firstlings of his flocks. Cain grew angry with his brother, and slew him so that his flocks and herds might fall into his own hands. Abel lost his life, but worse than that, Cain lost his soul to Satan.

Adam and Eve grieved at the loss of their sons but eventually they rejoiced in the birth of another righteous son, whom they named Seth. He grew up to be a "perfect man, and his likeness was the express likeness of his father, insomuch that he seemed to be like unto his father in all things, and *could be distinguished from him only by his age"* (D&C 107:43; emphasis added).

Not only was Seth similar in appearance to Adam, but also he was a replica of his righteous father, spiritually. Through Seth and his posterity the truths of the gospel and the patriarchal priesthood authority were handed down from generation to generation (see D&C 107:42). Seven generations from Adam, we encounter the prophet, Enoch.

ENOCH—AN EXAMPLE FOR ALL

Enoch is generally recognized as the prophet standing at the head of the second gospel dispensation (see again Figure 7-B, The Gospel through the Ages). In the Bible we can find very little information about the Enoch. In the Old Testament we read simply that, "And Enoch walked with God after he begat Methuselah three hundred years, and begat sons and daughters: And all the days of Enoch were three hundred sixty and five years: And Enoch walked with God: and he was not; for God took him" (Genesis 5:22-24). In the New Testament we read simply that: "By faith Enoch was translated that he should not see death; and was not found, because God had translated him; for before his translation he had this testimony, that he pleased God" (Hebrews 11:5).

However, in modern day revelations, we find much more information about Enoch and his righteous people. Such information is truly a pearl of great price. The material that has been revealed about Enoch serves two important purposes. It gives us a glimpse into former times and also provides a pattern for our own day. From the book of Moses we learn that early in the days of Seth "The children of men were numerous upon all the face of the land. And in those days Satan had great dominion among men, and raged in their hearts; and from thenceforth came wars and bloodshed; and a man's hand was against his own brother, in administering death, because of secret works, seeking for power" (Moses 6:15).

Unlike the children of men who were steeped in darkness, Enoch, having come through a righteous line of Adam's descendants, held the priesthood and complied with the terms of the everlasting covenant. He and his righteous followers were known as the "sons of God" (Moses 7:1; see also 6:68). He was called of God to preach the gospel to the "sons of men," the disobedient who either had rejected the gospel or were ignorant of it (Moses 5:52). Enoch's call came in this manner:

> And it came to pass that Enoch journeyed in the land, among the people; and as he journeyed, the Spirit of God descended out of heaven, and abode upon him.
> And he heard a voice from heaven, saying: Enoch, my son, prophesy unto this people, and say unto them—Repent, for thus saith the Lord: I am angry with this people, and my fierce anger is kindled against them; for their hearts have waxed hard, and their ears are dull of hearing, and their eyes cannot see afar off (Moses 6:26-27).

Enoch accepted his call to serve, and he taught the gospel of Jesus Christ to the people (see Moses 6:22-23; 7:1-19). He thoroughly understood and taught the doctrines of the Fall, the Atonement, and the accompanying principles and ordinances of the gospel including the principles of justification and sanctification (see D&C 20:29-34).

Because of his righteousness, Enoch was permitted to speak with the Lord face to face, much as the brother of Jared, Moses and many others would do at a later date (Ether 12:19). Regarding this sacred privilege he recorded, "I saw the Lord; and he stood before my face, and he talked with me, even as a man talketh one with another, face to face" (Moses 7:4).

Enoch was also shown in vision "all the inhabitants of the earth" (Moses 7:21). He beheld nation after nation of men on the earth, and he saw the great power of Satan, who "had a great chain in his hand, and it veiled the whole face of the earth with darkness; and he looked up and laughed, and his angels rejoiced" (Moses 7:26). The Lord told Enoch that "among all the workmanship of mine hands *there has not been so great wickedness as among thy brethren*" (Moses 7:36: emphasis added).[7]

Even though the spiritual condition of the people was extremely degenerate, Enoch was successful in calling out from among the wicked those who would believe. In the process of time a great division took place among the people. Enoch and his people became more righteous and the people of the world became more wicked.

Eventually Enoch and the people of his city who had entered the everlasting covenant became sanctified, entered into the rest of the Lord, and finally were translated and taken from this earth. The Lord called Enoch's people "Zion, because they were of one heart and one mind, and dwelt in righteousness; and there was no poor among them" (Moses 7:18).

From Joseph Smith's translation of the Bible we learn that marvelous priesthood powers were promised to Enoch and his righteous seed insomuch that they could by faith, break mountains, divide the seas, dry up waters, turn them out of their course, put at defiance the armies of nations, divide the earth, break every band, and stand in the presence of God (see JST, Genesis 14:30-32).

These descriptions of Enoch's ministry provide many parallels for our own dispensation. The Prophet Joseph Smith is a man like Enoch. A great division is taking place between the wicked and the righteous even at this time. As the righteous became more righteous in Enoch's time and the wicked more wicked, so it has been in our own time and will continue to be until the Lord comes. Enoch's people were eventually called Zion and were translated, even as the Latter-day Saints will be in days to come. As the righteous became more righteous in Enoch's time and the wicked more wicked, so it has been in our own time and will continue to be until the Lord comes.

In Enoch's day the people who remained upon the earth became so wicked and degenerate that the earth groaned under the weight of sin. From his perspective as a translated being, Enoch "looked upon the earth; and he heard a voice from the bowels thereof, saying: Wo, wo is me, the mother of men; I am pained, I am weary, because of the wickedness of my children. When shall I rest, and be cleansed from the filthiness which is gone forth out of me? When will my Creator sanctify me, that I may rest, and righteousness for a season abide upon my face?" (Moses 7:48).

Enoch yearned and pleaded with the Lord to know the answer to the earth's question—when would the entire earth finally rest from all its wickedness and enjoy the sweetness of Zion as he and his people did?

After much importuning of the Lord, Enoch finally received an answer to his plea. Speaking of the Millennial era, the Lord assured him that the time would come when the entire earth would rest. He explained that, "The day shall come that the earth shall rest, but before that day the heavens shall be darkened, and the veil of darkness shall cover the earth; and the heavens shall shake, and also the earth; and great tribulations shall be among the children of men, *but my people will I preserve*" (Moses 7:61; emphasis added). This is a wonderful explanation and promise.

Even though there would be great darkness and calamity prior to the Millennial period of rest, the Lord promised Enoch that he would provide a way to protect his Saints during a day of calamity. He explained to Enoch:

> And righteousness will I send down out of heaven; and truth will I send forth out of the earth, to bear testimony of mine Only Begotten; his

resurrection from the dead; yea, and also the resurrection of all men; and righteousness and truth will I cause to sweep the earth as with a flood, to gather out mine elect from the four quarters of the earth, unto a place which I shall prepare, an Holy City, that my people may gird up their loins, and be looking forth for the time of my coming; for there shall be my tabernacle, and it shall be called Zion, a New Jerusalem.

And the Lord said unto Enoch: Then shalt thou and all thy city meet them there, and we will receive them into our bosom, and they shall see us; and we will fall upon their necks, and they shall fall upon our necks, and we will kiss each other;

And there shall be mine abode, and it shall be Zion, which shall come forth out of all the creations which I have made; and for the space of a thousand years the earth shall rest (Moses 7:62-64; see also D&C 115:4-6; D&C 84:99-102, esp. vs. 100).

The dispensation of the fulness of times that was ushered in through the Prophet Joseph Smith, and in which we are presently laboring, is the forerunner to that period of rest and peace—the Millennial reign of Christ—that the Lord promised Enoch.

After Enoch and his city were translated and taken from the earth, the inhabitants who remained continued in their wickedness and the Lord called Noah to cry repentance unto them.

NOAH—A NEW BEGINNING

Noah was the great-grandson of Enoch—his father was Lamech, who was the son of Methuselah, who was the son of Enoch. Noah lived at a time when virtually all the righteous people had been translated to Enoch's city and those who remained on the earth were corrupt except Noah, Noah's wife and their three sons (Shem, Ham, and Japeth) and their wives—eight souls in all. They too "hearkened unto the Lord, and gave heed, and they were called the sons of God" (Moses 8:13).

Noah received the same gospel covenant that his forefathers, Enoch and Adam, had received. This we are taught in Joseph Smith's Translation of the Bible. The Lord speaking to Noah said that he would establish the same covenant with him as he had with Enoch, his father, "that of thy posterity shall come all nations" (JST, Genesis 8:22-23; JST, Genesis 9:17).

Having received a fulness of the gospel, Noah went forth teaching. "And it came to pass that Noah prophesied, and taught the things of God, even as it was in the beginning. . . . And the Lord ordained Noah after his own order, and commanded him that he should go forth and declare his Gospel unto the children of men even as it was given unto Enoch. And it came to pass that Noah called upon the children of men that they should repent; but they hearkened not unto his words.

> And God saw that the wickedness of men had become great in the earth; and every man was lifted up in the imagination of the thoughts of his heart, *being only evil continually.*
> And it came to pass that Noah continued his preaching unto the people, saying: Hearken, and give heed unto my words;
> Believe and repent of your sins and be baptized in the name of Jesus Christ, the Son of God, even as our fathers, and ye shall receive the Holy Ghost, that ye may have all things made manifest; and if ye do not this, *the floods will come in upon you;* nevertheless they hearkened not (Moses 8:16, 19-20, 22-24; emphasis added).

Although many did reject his message and were drowned in the flood, through modern revelation we learn that "angels [descended] out of heaven, bearing testimony of the Father and Son; and the Holy Ghost fell on many, and *they were caught up by the powers of heaven into Zion*" (Moses 7:27; emphasis added). No doubt Noah and his sons were instrumental in teaching these souls who were translated.

As more and more of the righteous were translated and taken to Enoch's Zion, the concentration of wickedness on the earth became greater and greater. Finally, "God said unto Noah, The end of all flesh is come before me; for the earth is filled with violence through them; and, behold, *I will destroy them with the earth*" (Genesis 6:13; emphasis added). Because the people would not hearken to the warnings they had been given, God's words were fulfilled and the floods came. But, because of their faithfulness and obedience to the gospel—the everlasting covenant—Noah and his family were preserved. All people living on the earth since that time are children of Noah, and this great patriarch is recognized as a second Adam to the human family.

As has been mentioned in another chapter, the rainbow is the sign of the everlasting gospel covenant. When we view it, we are to remember the promise of the Lord, that he made to Enoch and Noah, that the everlasting gospel covenant would be restored in the latter days (see JST, Genesis 9:21-23; also Moses 7:62-64; D&C 84:100).

As the people of Noah's day were commanded to repent and receive the gospel or be destroyed, so we have been warned. If we do not repent and receive what the Lord has for us, then we will be destroyed when he comes—not by a flood of water, but by the fire of his consuming glory "for they that come shall burn them, saith the Lord of Hosts, that it shall leave them neither root nor branch" (JS-History 1:37).

To be protected from the calamities of the last days we are expected to keep the Lord's commandments as did Noah's family and the people of Enoch's Zion. If we will, the promises and protections of a latter-day Zion will be realized in our time—the dispensation of the fulness of times.

THE TOWER OF BABEL—A TIME OF SCATTERING

At this point it will be helpful to get an orientation to the events that we have been discussing by looking at the Chronology Tables in the Bible Dictionary.[8] They provide us with the following sequence of events:

4000 B.C.   Fall of Adam
            Ministry of Enoch
            Ministry of Noah; the flood
            Tower of Babel (Jaredite migration)
            Ministry of Melchizedek
2000 B.C.   Birth of Abram (Abraham)

After the death of Noah, his descendants erected the great tower of Babel (Babel means *confusion*). This tower, erected to reach heaven, was a manifestation of their apostasy, their loss of faith in the covenants of the Lord. The effort to reach heaven by building a tower—instead of through obedience to the commandments—was displeasing to God, and he confounded their tongues and scattered them abroad upon the earth (see Genesis 11:1, 3-9). All the nations, kindreds, tongues and people we know today have their origins in the events surrounding this great tower.[9]

Regarding the tower of Babel, latter-day scripture records an interesting account of one family who prayed that their language, the Adamic language, might be preserved and that they might be brought to a promised land. Jared and his brother and their families—whose history we read about in the Book of Ether—were directed by the Lord to construct eight barges and depart to a new land, the land we know today as America.[10]

Sometime following the tower of Babel events and the simultaneous departure of the Jaredites to the new world, the Bible records the life and ministry of Abraham, the Head of the next gospel dispensation. Now let's look at the dispensation of Abraham, a period of time that acts as a special touchstone for us because of the amount of information we have regarding this "father of the faithful."

ABRAHAM—THE FATHER OF THE FAITHFUL

The Bible does not contain a great deal of scriptural information about the family of Adam from the time of Noah to the time of Abraham, but there is considerable knowledge about Abraham in both the Old and New Testaments of the Bible. Additionally, as part of the latter-day restoration of the gospel, we have been given important writings of this ancient patriarch while he was in Egypt.

The Book of Abraham in the Pearl of Great Price contains marvelous insights into the life of Abraham. Because he was faithful in hearkening to the Lord, he was blessed, protected and given great knowledge from the Lord.

Of Abraham's valiant quest for righteousness and truth, we read:

> And, finding there was greater *happiness* and *peace* and *rest* for me, I sought for *the blessings of the fathers*, and the right whereunto I should be ordained to administer the same; having been myself a follower of righteousness, desiring also to be one who possessed great knowledge, and to be a greater follower of righteousness, and to possess a greater knowledge, and to be a father of many nations, a prince of peace, and desiring to receive instructions, and to keep the commandments of God, I became a rightful heir, a High Priest, holding the right belonging to the fathers (Abraham 1:2; emphasis added).

Abraham was tutored and taught by Melchizedek, the great high priest.[11] From Latter-day revelation we learn that he also "received the priesthood from Melchizedek, who received it through the lineage of his fathers, even till Noah" (D&C 84:14). Adding further insight into the relationship between these two great prophets, the Prophet Joseph Smith said, "Abraham gave a tenth part of all his spoils and then received a blessing under the hands of Melchizedek *even the last law or a fulness or law of the priesthood* which constituted him *a king and priest* after the order of Melchizedek *or an endless life.*"[12]

Being anointed a king and a priest—or having a fulness of the priesthood— qualified Abraham to see the face of the Lord, as it did the true and faithful Saints before and after him (see JST, Genesis 14:30-31; see also D&C 84:19-24). Being thus blessed, the revelations of the heavens were available to him, and he received extensive knowledge about the relationship of time and space— "celestial time signifies one day to a cubit"—the universe, the planetary bodies, stars, moons, and all their movements (see Abraham 3:12-14 and Facsimile no. 2).

In a remarkable vision, he was also shown the organized intelligences—the spirit children of God—that were begotten before the world was. He viewed the great council in heaven in which the plan of salvation was presented. In that great council, Abraham witnessed the Son of Man being chosen to become the Savior of the world. He saw himself among the noble and great ones, those who were chosen, foreordained, to become rulers in this life and gods in the eternities—based upon their continued faithfulness in their second estate (see Abraham 3). These doctrinal insights add richly to our knowledge of the gospel.

Because of his faithfulness in the pre-earth life and also in mortality, the Lord established his eternal covenant—which also became known as the Abrahamic Covenant—with this faithful father of nations.

The Abrahamic Covenant

Frequently the Abrahamic Covenant is spoken of as though its promises were in some way unique to him. In reality, the promises that Abraham received are the same ones that Adam, Enoch, and Noah received (see JST, Genesis 13:12-13). The uniqueness of the Abrahamic Covenant lies primarily in the degree of *completeness* of the scriptural accounts.

Among the most far-reaching contributions of the records kept by Abraham are the *specific* promises of the everlasting covenant that were given to him, the details of which are spelled out with more clarity in his record than in any other scriptural account that we have to date. From the Book of Abraham we read:

> And I will make of thee a great nation, and I will bless thee above measure, and make thy name great among all nations, and thou shalt be a blessing unto thy seed after thee, that in their hands they shall bear this ministry and Priesthood unto all nations;
>
> And I will bless them through thy name; for as many as receive this Gospel shall be called after thy name, and shall be accounted thy seed, and shall rise up and bless thee, as their father;
>
> And I will bless them that bless thee, and curse them that curse thee; and in thee (that is, in thy Priesthood) and in thy seed (that is, thy Priesthood), for I give unto thee a promise that this right shall continue in thee, and in thy seed after thee (that is to say, the literal seed, or the seed of the body) shall all the families of the earth be blessed, even with the blessings of the Gospel, which are the blessings of salvation, even of life eternal (Abraham 2: 9-11).

We do not yet comprehend the full magnitude and importance of these wonderful blessings which were promised to father Abraham and to us, his children or how they will take effect in reaching all nations. Because of the magnitude of these promises, the Lord changed Abram's name from Abram (exalted father) to Abraham (father of a multitude) to reflect the great blessings of priesthood and posterity that would be his (Genesis 17:5). Abraham became known as the "Father of the Faithful" (Bible Dictionary, ABRAHAM).

In reflecting upon the blessings promised Abraham and his seed, I have found it useful to remember three of the most important promises by using the acronym *"LDS"*.

L stands for a promised *land*

D stands for *deliverance*, protection, redemption, and salvation

S stands for the promise of an everlasting *seed*

Now let's look more closely at each of these covenant blessings.

Land

As listed above, the letter *L* stands for a promised *land*. The first reference we have of the Lord giving land to his children is recorded in Genesis when the Lord placed Adam and Eve in the garden of Eden and told them to care for it (see Genesis 2:8).

Since the days of Cain and Abel people have struggled for possession of lands and properties. Today's newspapers report wars and rumors of wars. The fundamental tensions in these conflicts are over who will possess the land, what the borders will be, and who will control the air, sea, and water. In regards to acquisition of land, a basic principle we need to understand is that "the earth is the Lord's, and the fulness thereof; the world, and they that dwell therein" (Psalm 24:1). Of ourselves we cannot obtain and retain the land. It is a gift of God to those who love him and keep his commandments.

Regarding the conditional nature of this promise, we read of Abraham being promised all the land of Canaan (from Dan to Beersheba) for an everlasting inheritance when his children *would hearken unto the voice of the Lord* (Abraham 2:6). This is an important qualification. No single person nor group of people—whether they be Gentiles, Jews, Polynesians, or Native Americans—have a legitimate claim to any parcel of land upon this earth unless they are obedient to the mind and will of the Lord.

From Abraham this conditional blessing of a promised land was extended to Isaac (Genesis 26:4) and also to Jacob (Genesis 28:13; 35:12; 48:4). When Joshua led the children of Israel into the promised land of Canaan, he divided the land according to tribal units (see Bible Map #5). These were to be an everlasting inheritance based upon faithfulness.

The scriptures state that the posterity of Abraham could not inherit the promised land any earlier than they did because the wickedness of the Amorites—those who possessed the land—was not yet full (see Genesis 15:13-16; see also Alma 37:31; Helaman 13:14; Ether 2:9; D&C 61:31; 101:11). This is an important point because a merciful and just Lord would not destroy one group of people and replace them with another without just cause. However, when the wickedness of the Amorites was full, the Lord raised up Israel's deliverer, Moses, to lead them to the promised land.

Moses sought to bring the children of Israel from Egypt to Canaan. But, because of wickedness, Israel lost the right to enter the promised land at that time (Numbers 14:33). They wandered for forty years in the wilderness—until all who had lived in Egypt had died. Only the children of these wayward Hebrews were allowed, under the direction of Joshua, to enter the promised land.

Before his departure Moses warned Israel that they could only obtain and retain the land through righteousness. They were commanded to honor their righteous parents *so that their days would be long upon the land of promise* (see Exodus 20:12). He warned them that if they were to become disobedient, they would be driven off the land and scattered "among all nations" (Deuteronomy 4:25-27). Scriptural history reveals that they were not obedient and they were scattered as prophesied.

Our present day understanding of the gospel covenant regarding a promised land has been restored through the Prophet Joseph Smith. Through him we learn that Joseph, our forefather, was promised all the land of America (see Genesis 49:22-26) which is a land choice above all other lands (see Jacob 5:43; Ether 1:38; 13:2). This promise, with all the rights of entitlement that were promised to Joseph anciently, is extended to members of the Church today, because they are primarily descendants of Joseph through his sons, Ephraim and Manasseh (see Ether 13:8; Genesis 49:22-26; Deuteronomy 33:24-25).

When Zion is fully established under the law of consecration and steward-ship, each family will have rights to everlasting land inheritances—to our own promised lands—within the promised land of America for Joseph and the Holy Land for other tribes of Israel (see D&C 85:7).

The eternal fulfillment of this "land" blessing is reflected in the Lord's promise "Blessed are the meek for they shall inherit the earth" (Matthew 5:5). The earth in its glorified and sanctified state will become our Celestial king-dom—our eternal promised land (see D&C 130:9; 45:58).

Deliverance

D stands for deliverance. Prospering in the land comes by faith and obedi-ence and it includes not only an abundance of every needful thing, but also deliv-erance from all our enemies. As was mentioned above, Only in recent years have I come to recognize how extensive the promise of deliverance is in the Lord's great plan for our happiness. He has promised that those who come unto him will be delivered from their enemies and will have peace in him (see 2 Thessalonians 1:4-7; D&C 103:12-13; John 16:13; Matthew 11:28-30).

The need for deliverance affects every aspect of our lives. The Book of Mormon indicates that through Christ—he who makes all deliverance possible—we are delivered from death, hell, the devil and endless torment (see 2 Nephi 9). Joseph Smith explained that Christ will "reign until He had put all enemies under

His feet, and the last enemy was death"[13] This last act of deliverance will come through the resurrection.

The scriptures provide many other references—that serve as examples for us—of how the Lord has delivered his people from the bondage of both spiritual and physical enemies. Alma the younger was delivered from hell when he finally called upon the Savior for help (see Mosiah 27:11; Alma 36:6-10). Abraham, with raised arms, was delivered from Pharaoh's lion's couch (Facsimile #1). Moses, with raised arms, defeated the Amalekites (see Exodus 17:11).

Limhi's people were inspired to get the Lamanite guards drunk and were able to escape their bondage (see Mosiah 22:9-12). Alma's people at Helam were delivered after the Lord caused a deep sleep to come upon their Lamanite captors (see Mosiah 24:16-20). Ammon's two thousand young warriors believed their mothers' teachings, and the Lord spared them in mighty battle against seasoned warriors (see Alma 56:54-56). And the more righteous Nephites were delivered from the terrible destructions at the time of Jesus' crucifixion (see 3 Nephi 11:10-13).

A major reason we have been given so many scriptural case studies involving the deliverance of ancient Israel and the Nephites is so that we might have hope regarding our own situation. The Lord has promised that "if ye are prepared, ye shall not fear" (D&C 38:30). The preparation we must make is obedience to the laws and ordinances of the gospel (see D&C 58:6). In one chapter alone in the Book of Mormon, the Lord repeatedly assures us that "the righteous need not fear" (1 Nephi 22:15-31). Through obedience we will be protected.

If, on the other hand, we are not obedient, if we are not prepared by embracing the terms of the covenant, if we trample under our feet the Holy One of Israel, we—as the examples of previous civilizations bear silent witness—will be entirely destroyed, actually "swept off" the earth, when we become fully ripe in iniquity (Ether 2:10).

As we reflect upon the examples of the final destructions of the Nephite people (Mormon 6) and the Jaredite nation (Ether 15) we sense the awful, bone-crunching, bloody reality of this principle. These destructions will most surely come upon our own nations when the wicked become ripened in their iniquity through increased violence, immorality, pride, the lusts of the flesh, and seeking for the vain things of this world (Nephi 16:10-15). The wars and bloodshed we are witnessing among certain nations of the earth may be but a foretaste of the warfare and chaos we will soon see worldwide if people do not repent and embrace the everlasting covenant.

The voice of warning is clear. The wicked will be burned as stubble, leaving neither root nor branch—which means that they will have neither ancestors nor offspring because they will not have received the ordinances of the temple whereby families are sealed for time and eternity (see J.S.—History 1:37).

In spite of the awful picture of the terrible things that will be and are happening among the wicked, we are expected to be of good cheer! We are to be comforted by these words: "Behold, I speak these things unto you for the elect's sake; and you also shall hear of wars, and rumors of wars; see that ye be not troubled, for all I have told you must come to pass" (J.S.—Matthew 1:23).

The Lord expects his people to be filled with hope—and we can be even in these troubled times as we trust in his assurance that he has overcome the world (John 16:33). This means that through his Atonement and his continued care for his people, truth and righteousness will ultimately prevail. One sister has captured in beautiful prose, the essence of coming unto Christ for deliverance. She has written:

> Our deliverance from physical, emotional, and spiritual pain depends upon our trust in Christ—it depends upon how much we truly believe he can and will deliver us.
>
> During our times of trial we must remember to cling to him so that the world won't overcome us in our weakened state. We need to trust in his power of deliverance not just in the sense that we *should* trust in it but also in the sense that trust is really a need that our spirits have. Without that trust, our spirits weary of life here and the burdens of living in a fallen world for what seems like an interminably long time. We need to trust in that power so that we can have the faith and hope that will enable us to keep on being obedient so we can be empowered by him to endure to the end.
>
> We need to, we must believe him when he says he can and will deliver us as we come to him. We must take that leap of faith, come to him and trust his love (which is his delivering power) and as we do he will bless us with the ability to endure and be delivered.
>
> We cannot be redeemed—receive of his mercy—until we recognize our awful state, until we realize that we need deliverance, and cry unto him for mercy. Without recognizing that we are in a lost and fallen world and have need to be delivered we cannot progress in the ways our Father would want us to, the ways that would purify and sanctify us sufficiently to enable us to be prepared to return to him.
>
> But when we do recognize that and feel the weight of it and begin to sense a yearning and a hunger for the things of a better world (the better world of the celestial kingdom) and cry unto him for mercy and deliverance, he will hear and hearken to our cries. That is his promise to us. If we will recognize our state (which takes humility and recognizing that man is nothing which is something we would not have supposed) and cry unto him he *will* hear us and we *will* be delivered. He will not turn away from any who come to him and cry for mercy. His arms are stretched out still to all who will come to him and be embraced by him and be wrapped in the robe of his righteousness.

He is truly gracious to *all* who will trust in his promises, believe in his name and come unto him through faith, repentance and obedience to his laws and ordinances. His Plan is a Plan of happiness because it not only is designed to bring us up to where he is (which is exaltation, which brings great joy) but also it is designed to show us all along the way that he lives and LOVES US. Every part of the Plan is a manifestation of his love for us and the more we understand that and let his love into our lives through faith in him and obedience to his laws, the more joy we will have.[14]

As in the days of Enoch and Noah, the Lord eventually will cause a great division among the people. The two polarized groups are scripturally identified as Zion and Babylon (see 2 Nephi 30:10; Moses 7:62; D&C 133:14). Regarding the state of these two groups in the last days we read, "Great tribulations shall be among the children of men [Babylon], *but my people [Zion] will I preserve*" (Moses 7:61; emphasis added). The Lord will destroy those who remain in the darkness of Babylon, but he will preserve his people who embrace the light and truth of Zion.

Anticipating the calamities that will come upon the wicked in the latter days, the Lord gave revelations through the Prophet Joseph Smith that would provide protection for his righteous children (see D&C 1:17, 35-36). In one of his sermons, the Prophet asked the rhetorical question, "How shall God come to the rescue of this generation?" Joseph then gave the answer: "He will send Elijah the Prophet".[15]

If it were not for the coming of Elijah, the whole world would be "utterly wasted" (D&C 2; Malachi 4:5-6). With the coming of Elijah the keys of the sealing power were restored whereby we, when we are prepared, can be sealed to eternal life and receive the marvelous benefits of such sealing, including great power in the priesthood and the protection from the calamities of the last days.

Thanks be to the Lord that Elijah has returned and has turned the hearts of the children to "the promises made to the fathers"—the promises of the everlasting covenant including deliverance of the faithful (D&C 2). The promise made to Abraham, Isaac, and Jacob regarding their protection are made also to us—because we are their children (see D&C 132:31).

A careful reading of the dedicatory prayer for the Kirtland temple reveals that a major focus of the prayer was the Prophet Joseph Smith's plea for the sealing powers to be revealed so that the Saints could be protected from the awful things that were about to be poured out in the last days (see D&C 109:38-40, 42-46).

This understanding, that the Saints of God will be protected as a result of the sealing powers restored by Elijah, may help you understand passages of scripture that before were difficult to understand (see, for example, Revelation 6 and 7). Building on the vision of the last days witnessed by John the Revelator, Joseph

Smith explained that the four destroying angels mentioned by John will be held in check until the Saints have had time to make their calling and election sure and thereby receive the protective powers associated with these ordinances.[16]

The scriptures are clear that full protection will come to us when we receive a fulness of the temple ordinances (see JST, Genesis 14:30-31). President Howard W. Hunter called for every member of the Church to become temple worthy and President Gordon B. Hinckley has reissued that call. I know that we will be preserved as we hearken to the counsel of the prophets.

I know that the temple is the focus of the righteous life. The temple is a place for revelation and inspiration. Through the temple ordinances and temple worship, coupled with living a Christlike life, we will be enabled to become a sanctified people and through our sanctification the protective powers and blessings of the everlasting covenant will be made available to us.

Seed

The letter *S* stands for *seed*. Our Heavenly Father truly is our father. His work and glory is "to bring to pass the immortality and eternal life of man" (Moses 1:39)—which includes all of us. We are his children, his seed. Every principle of the gospel, every covenant, every commandment from God is designed for our happiness[17] and all of them center in and around establishing the family in time and eternity.

The first steps our Father and Mother in heaven took in this marvelous process of providing for the happiness of their children was giving us spirit bodies and providing a way for our physical birth. In addition, after Adam and Eve left the garden of Eden, our Father revealed to them—and to future prophets—the great plan of redemption whereby we can return as families to his presence and enjoy the same capabilities of eternal offspring as possessed by our heavenly parents.

In the meridian of time, our Father sent his Only Begotten Son, Jesus Christ to reveal again the great plan of happiness. His coming, as foretold by ancient prophets, was a crucial step in the fulfillment of our Father's plan for our happiness. Jesus took upon himself the sins of the world and provided the resurrection of all mankind—both necessary prerequisites to our gaining exaltation and eternal lives. Because of the sealing powers of the everlasting covenant—made possible through the Atonement—we can be together forever as husbands and wives and families.

In the marriage covenant husbands and wives are commanded to multiply and replenish the earth so that they might have joy and rejoicing in their posterity—indeed, they are commanded, as it were, to act like the gods and procreate life! The Lord's words are: "And again, verily I say unto you, if a man marry a wife by my word, which is my law, and by the new and everlasting covenant, and it is sealed unto them by the Holy Spirit of promise...[it] shall be of full force when they are out of the world; and they shall pass by the angels, and the gods, which are set there, to their exaltation and glory in all things, as hath been sealed upon their heads, *which glory shall be a fulness and a continuation of the seeds forever and ever"* (D&C 132:19; emphasis added).

Satan does all in his power to destroy the plan of God that provides for the birth, protection, and advancement of children. Elder Merrill J. Bateman has pointed out that violence to children is the common thread that runs through current evil social trends such as divorce, abortion, abuse, adultery, homosexuality, certain expressions of feminism, and same-sex marriage. While Satan's sole purpose is our misery and destruction, our Heavenly Father, on the other hand, seeks to exalt his children by endowing faithful couples with the power of eternal lives, the divine power to bear children throughout the eternities—to have glory added upon their heads forever. This crowing blessing of the covenant is intended to bring about that joy which our Heavenly Parents have designed for all of their children and which is the ultimate end and aim of our existence (see 2 Nephi 2:25).

Circumcision

At this point it would be well to explain how the rite of circumcision was established as a sign of the Abrahamic Covenant. From the time of Abraham until after the resurrection of Jesus, the rite of circumcision, which was given to Abraham by the Lord, was practiced by him and his descendants. Even today, Jews and Muslims throughout the world, as well as people of other faiths, practice circumcision as a religious rite. It's meaning, however, was not known—at least in modern times—until it was revealed through the Prophet Joseph Smith.

From the Prophet's new translation of the Bible we learn: "But as for thee, behold, I will make my covenant with thee, and thou shalt be a father of many nations. . . . And I will make thee exceedingly fruitful, and I will make nations of thee, and kings shall come of thee, and of thy seed. And I will establish *a covenant of circumcision* with thee, and it shall be my covenant between me and thee, and thy seed after thee, in their generations; that thou mayest know for ever that *children are not accountable before me until they are eight years old"* (JST, Genesis 17:8, 10-11; emphasis added). In other words, circumcision was to remind the early Saints of the eternal covenant, the promise of everlasting seed, and that little children are free from sin until they are eight years of age.

Blessings of Abraham are Offered to All People

From time to time, some have wondered: "Just who are the children of Israel? Why are they a favored people?" Although we do not understand all the details—like why some children are born into certain families—we do know that

God is not capricious nor does he award unearned honor to anyone. As we read of the promises made to Abraham, we need to remember that these same blessing are extended to all people who will embrace the terms of the everlasting gospel covenant. We also need to remember that premortal faithfulness is directly connected with the blessings and opportunities we receive through the gospel in this life.

From the Book of Mormon we read: "Behold, the Lord esteemeth all flesh in one; *he that is righteous is favored of God*" (1 Nephi 17:35; emphasis added). This favor of God for the righteous began in the premortal existence and continues to this day. Alma explained that the selection of priesthood leaders in this life began in the premortal life and was based on the worthiness of each individual (see Alma 13:3-6). From this scripture and others we can begin to understand the important link between the *noble and great ones* in the premortal life and the children or house of Israel in this life.

Throughout the scriptures the house of Israel is known as a chosen and a peculiar people, a royal priesthood. The Lord charged Israel, "Ye shall be a peculiar treasure unto me" (Exodus 19:5). We are to be a peculiar people in the sense that we are to be a godly people, set apart from the rest of the world. In exhorting Israel to keep the commandments, Moses reminded them (and us) that the Lord hath "chosen thee to be a special people unto himself" (Deuteronomy 7:6). "For thou art an holy people unto the Lord thy God, and the Lord hath chosen thee to be a peculiar people unto himself" (Deuteronomy 14:2).

In the New Testament, Peter reaffirmed the chosen status of the children of Abraham and Jacob when he reminded members of the Church in his day that "ye are a chosen generation, a royal priesthood, an holy nation, a peculiar people; that ye should shew forth the praises of him who hath called you out of darkness into his marvelous light" (1 Peter 2:9).

And thus we see that the children of Abraham and Israel were before appointed to be a special treasure to the Lord, rulers in mortality and in the eternities. They are to be a light to the nations of the earth. They were to be the bearers of the holy priesthood and the messengers of salvation to the entire world.

Latter-day prophets have explained that, generally speaking, the children of Israel in this life were the noble and great ones in heaven. In a General Conference held in 1945, Elder Harold B. Lee explained that, "In the spirit world there were some who were valiant—more valiant than others—in choosing to do good, and thus they became the noble and great ones of whom the Lord said, 'These I will make my rulers' (Abraham 3:23), and so in this earth, coming through *a chosen lineage,* those noble and great ones are expected, as members of the Church and kingdom of God in every age, to be rulers of the world of sin and wickedness."[18]

Later, in another General Conference, Elder Lee elaborated on this idea when he explained that the rewards we receive in this life are conditioned on the lives we lived in the premortal world. He said, "It would seem very clear, then, that those born to the lineage of Jacob, who was later to be called Israel, and his posterity, who were known as *the children of Israel, were born into the most illustrious lineage of any of those who came upon the earth as mortal beings.*[19]

Even though individuals may have achieved a chosen status in the premortal life, qualifying them to be born of the lineage of Abraham, the Prophet Joseph warned that an "unconditional election of individuals to eternal life was not taught by the Apostles. God did elect or predestinate, that all those who would be saved, should be saved in Christ Jesus, and through obedience to the Gospel; but He passes over no man's sins, but visits them with correction, and if His children will not repent of their sins He will discard them."[20] So, just because one was faithful in the premortal life, there is no guarantee that he or she will be faithful in this world. However, the probability is great that they would be.

Most people who join the Church probably are of the blood of Abraham, Israel, and Joseph (see D&C 64:36). They are the elect of God; they respond to the message and spirit of the gospel; and they have a right to the blessings of the covenant because of their lineage.

For those people, however, who join the Church who are not of the literal seed of Abraham, it is comforting to know that they become heirs of the promised blessings when they are baptized. Paul explained this point. "For as many of you as have been baptized into Christ have put on Christ . . . And *if ye be Christ's, then are ye Abraham's seed, and heirs according to the promise"* (Galatians 3:27, 29; emphasis added).

In a revelation given to the Prophet Joseph Smith in December 1832, the Lord explained that he (Joseph) had a right to the blessings of the covenant because he was of the blood of Israel. The Lord declared: "Therefore, thus saith the Lord unto you, with whom the priesthood hath continued through the lineage of your fathers—*For ye are lawful heirs, according to the flesh,* and have been hid from the world with Christ in God—Therefore your life and the priesthood have remained, and must needs remain through you and your lineage until the restoration of all things spoken by the mouths of all the holy prophets since the world began" (D&C 86:8-10; see also D&C 64:33-36).

During the presidency of Spencer W. Kimball, the Lord revealed that the full blessings of the priesthood were available to all worthy male members of the Church—regardless of their lineage. Such an invitation to all people to receive the blessings of the gospel had not been made since the days of Cain and Abel. These newly revealed priesthood opportunities have affected the lives of hundreds of thousands of people on both sides of the veil.

Understanding the blessings given our fore-fathers is important because it helps us know and understand what we can expect if we live worthily. If we will but pattern our lives after these worthy men and their wives, we too can receive all the blessings of peace, land, deliverance, and eternal lives.

As members of the Church—as children of father Abraham—we need to look more closely to him to find direction for our own lives. In our prayers, we need to ask our Heavenly Father to help us understand how we can reach Abraham's degree of righteousness. He learned how to approach our Heavenly Father and find answers to his prayers—so can we. Abraham trusted in the promise which is ours also that, "If thou shalt ask, thou shalt receive revelation upon revelation, knowledge upon knowledge, that thou mayest know the mysteries and peaceable things—that which bringeth joy, that which bringeth life eternal (D&C 42:61). This promise is ours also.

Joseph of Old—A Pattern for the Latter-day Joseph

As has been described above, the blessings that God promised Abraham were passed on to Isaac, and from Isaac to Jacob (whose name was changed to Israel) and from Israel to his son Joseph who was sold by his brothers into Egyptian slavery (see Genesis 37-50). While in Egypt, Joseph won the favor and admiration of Pharoah who eventually appointed him to be second in command. In spite of great trials and temptations, because of his integrity, Joseph became a mighty leader in Egypt. From him the blessings of the fathers were then passed on to all his righteous descendants in both ancient and modern days (see D&C 132:30-33). Joseph is not considered a head of a gospel dispensation, because the truths of the covenant really continued from Abraham to him, but without doubt he is one of the greatest prophets of all time.

Joseph, the son of Jacob, is a type or a pattern for the latter-day seer and prophet, Joseph Smith. In two related prophecies—one found in the Book of Mormon (2 Nephi 3) and the other in Joseph Smith's translation of the Bible (JST, Genesis 50:24-38)—Joseph (Jacob's son) prophesied that a mighty seer would be raised up in the latter days like unto Moses who would deliver Israel. The Lord promised Joseph of old:

> But a seer will I raise up out of the fruit of thy loins; and unto him will I give power to bring forth my word unto the seed of thy loins—and not to the bringing forth my word only, saith the Lord, but to the convincing them of my word, which shall have already gone forth among them.
>
> Wherefore, the fruit of thy loins shall write; and the fruit of the loins of Judah shall write; and that which shall be written by the fruit of thy loins, and also that which shall be written by the fruit of the loins of Judah, shall grow together, unto the confounding of false doctrines and laying down of contentions, and establishing peace among the fruit of thy loins, and bringing them to the knowledge of their fathers in the latter days, and also to the knowledge of my covenants, saith the Lord (2 Nephi 3:11-12).

Regarding this latter-day seer, the Lord also told Jacob's son that "His name shall be called Joseph, and it shall be after the name of his father; and he shall be like unto you; for the thing which the Lord shall bring forth by his hand shall bring my people unto salvation" (JST, 50:33). Additional parallels between these two Josephs will be discussed in the next chapter.

As we conclude our discussion of Abraham, Isaac, Israel, and Joseph it will be helpful to look at the chronological order of the lives of the ancient prophets from Noah to Moses (see Bible Dictionary, "CHRONOLOGY"):

Death of Noah (see Genesis 9:28)
Birth of Abraham
Birth of Isaac
Birth of Jacob
Birth of Joseph
Joseph sold into Egypt (see Genesis 37:2)
Joseph stands before Pharaoh (see Genesis 41:46)
Jacob and his family go down to Egypt
Death of Jacob
Death of Joseph
Birth of Moses
The Exodus from Egypt when Moses was 80 years old

Joseph and the family of Israel remained in Egypt for some two hundred years—from about 1706 B.C. until 1491 B.C. By the end of this time, Israel had fallen into apostasy. Subsequent Pharoahs did not honor Israel as the former Pharoah did. Because of their apostasy, the Hebrew people, as the people of Israel were known, fell from favor with the Lord and became slaves to the Egyptians. However, as the cycle of apostasy and restoration continued, the people called upon the Lord for deliverance and in answer to their petition, the Lord raised up a new leader to deliver Israel from bondage. Moses was called to be both a deliverer of the people and the head of a new gospel dispensation.

THE DISPENSATION OF MOSES BEGAN WITH HIGH EXPECTATIONS

As the head of a new dispensation, Moses was called and chosen by God to deliver the people of Israel both from physical and spiritual bondage. Through Moses the Lord fulfilled his promises to Jacob that Israel would be brought back into their promised land of Canaan (see Genesis 46:1-4).[21]

Moses' lifetime can be divided into three sets of forty years. The first forty years were spent in the royal Egyptian courts as the adopted son of Pharaoh's daughter. During this period he became educated and socialized in the finest of Egyptian protocol.

The second period began with Moses' killing of the Egyptian who was abusing an Israelite. Following this incident Moses fled to the hills and plains of Midian where he met and served Jethro, the high priest. Jethro was a holder of the Melchizedek Priesthood and was a faithful descendant of Abraham. Moses received the priesthood from him and was taught by him in the principles and ordinances of the gospel of Jesus Christ. It was during this time that the Lord spoke to Moses from the burning bush and called him to lead the children of Israel out of Egypt to the land of Canaan—Israel's land of promise.

The account of Moses' calling is as follows: "And calling upon the name of God, he beheld his glory again, for it was upon him; and he heard a voice, saying: Blessed art thou, Moses, for I, the Almighty, have chosen thee, and thou shalt be made stronger than many waters; for they shall obey thy command as if thou wert God. And lo, I am with thee, even unto the end of thy days; *for thou shalt deliver my people from bondage, even Israel my chosen*" (Moses 1:25-26; emphasis added).

Moses spent the last forty years of his life striving to deliver Israel from bondage. Although he was able to deliver Israel out of Egypt, he was less successful in getting Egypt out of Israel—they continued to hang tenaciously to the apostate beliefs and customs they acquired in Egypt. This spiritual lingering in Egypt provoked the Lord and his anger was kindled against them insomuch that they lost their chance for a fulness of the blessings of the everlasting covenant.

When Moses descended the mountain and saw the Israelites worshipping the golden calf, he could see that the people were not ready to receive the highest laws of the gospel and, inspired by the Lord, he smashed the original plates, thereby denying Israel the opportunity for the richer blessings of Zion. The Doctrine and Covenants explains the sad consequences of Israel's rejection of the higher laws connected with the Melchizedek Priesthood:

> And this greater priesthood administereth the gospel and holdeth the key of the mysteries of the kingdom, even the key of the knowledge of God.
>
> Therefore, in the *ordinances* thereof, the power of godliness is manifest.
>
> And without the ordinances thereof, and the authority of the priesthood, the power of godliness is not manifest unto men in the flesh;
>
> *For without this no man can see the face of God, even the Father, and live.*
>
> Now this Moses plainly taught to the children of Israel in the wilderness, and sought diligently *to sanctify his people that they might behold the face of God;*

But they hardened their hearts and could not endure his presence; therefore, the Lord in his wrath, for his anger was kindled against them, swore that they should not enter into his rest while in the wilderness, *which rest is the fulness of his glory.*

Therefore, he took Moses out of their midst, and the Holy Priesthood also;

And the lesser priesthood continued, which priesthood holdeth the key of the ministering of angels and the preparatory gospel

Which gospel is the gospel of repentance and of baptism, and the remission of sins, and the law of carnal commandments, which the Lord in his wrath cause to continue with the house of Aaron among the children of Israel until John, who God raised up, being filled with the Holy Ghost from his mother's womb (D&C 84:19-27).

From the Bible it is not clear that Moses intended initially to give Israel the fulness of the gospel. In our day, neither the Jews nor the other Christian churches understand this point. It is from the Joseph Smith Translation that we learn that God commanded Moses to *return to the mountain and there receive a second set of plates which would not contain the fulness of the gospel*—like the first set had. Of this commandment we read:

And the Lord said unto Moses, Hew thee two other tables of stone, like unto the first, and I will write upon them also, the words of the law, according as they were written at the first on the tables which thou brakest; *but it shall not be according to the first, for I will take away the priesthood out of their midst; therefore my holy order, and the ordinances thereof, shall not go before them; for my presence shall not go up in their midst, lest I destroy them.*

But I will give unto them the law as at the first, but *it shall be after the law of a carnal commandment; for I have sworn in my wrath, that they shall not enter into my presence, into my rest,* in the days of their pilgrimage (JST, Exodus 34:1-2; emphasis added).

After breaking the first set of plates, Moses returned to the holy mountain where he received the lesser law that we call the Law of Moses, or the Mosaic Law. This law is called the preparatory gospel because of its elaborate dietary laws and sacrificial rituals which were designed to prepare the people to have faith in the Lord Jesus Christ, the Savior who would come in the meridian of time (see Gal 3:24). Anciently, the Law of Moses functioned under the authority of the lesser—the Aaronic or Levitical—priesthood which continued from Aaron until John the Baptist. There were select individuals and groups among the Israelites, however, who held the Melchizedek Priesthood and still obeyed the requirements of the Mosaic Law.

One time while I was preparing to speak to a group of Saints in Live Oak, Florida, I was trying to think of a way that I could help the members understand how the Levitical laws given to Moses are related to the Melchizedek laws enjoyed in the Church today. The branch president at the time was a car dealer, and the thought struck me that the different levels of the priesthood could be compared to the gears in an automobile (see end of chapter Figure 7-D, Getting in Gear with the Lord).

We use first gear to gradually build up speed so we can shift to second gear. Then we build up more speed and shift into third gear—cruising gear. I thought by analogy that first gear could represent the Aaronic Priesthood—the Law of Moses. Second gear could be likened to the Melchizedek Priesthood—the restored gospel as we have it functioning in the Church today. Third gear, or cruising gear, could represent the highest orders of the patriarchal priesthood. This priesthood order will empower us to establish Zion, the kingdom of heaven on earth like that of Enoch and his people (see Moses 7), Melchizedek and his people (see JST, Genesis 14:33-34), and Nephi and his people after the Lord appeared to them (see 4 Nephi).

In the New Testament, when the Lord instructed his disciples to pray using the words, "thy kingdom come," he was commanding them to pray for the establishment of Zion. In his ministry amongst the Nephites this phrase does not appear because Jesus established his Kingdom among them during his ministry, in other words a Zion-like kingdom was set up that lasted almost 200 years.

In our latter-day scriptures we read, "Wherefore, may the kingdom of God go forth [the Church], that the kingdom of Heaven may come [Zion], that thou, O God, mayest be glorified in heaven so on earth" (D&C 65:5-6). If we will receive and be faithful to the everlasting covenant, we—like the city of Enoch and the Nephites during their zenith period—will be sanctified and privileged to enjoy the Kingdom of Heaven on earth with all its attendant blessings.

The Prophet Joseph Smith explained that Moses and all the prophets in the Old Testament held this higher priesthood and experienced many of the attendant blessings.[22] In addition to the prophets, there were seventy faithful elders mentioned in the Old Testament who held the higher priesthood of Melchizedek. They apparently had received the highest ordinances of this priesthood, because they were empowered to enter into the presence of the Lord. Of them we read, "Then went up Moses, and Aaron, Nadab, and Abihu, and seventy of the elders of Israel: *And they saw the God of Israel:* and there was under his feet as it were a paved work of sapphire stone, and as it were the body of heaven in his clearness" (Exodus 24:9-10; emphasis added).

As a people, the Nephites were another group who both held the Melchizedek priesthood and lived the law of Moses. They recognized that the sole purpose of the Law of Moses was to focus people's faith on Jesus Christ.

Alma explained:

> [The Nephites], did keep the law of Moses; for it was expedient that they should keep the law of Moses as yet, for it was not all fulfilled. But notwithstanding the law of Moses, they did look forward to the coming of Christ, considering that *the law of Moses was a type of his coming,* and believing that they must keep those outward performances until the time that he should be revealed unto them.
>
> Now they did not suppose that salvation came by the law of Moses; but *the law of Moses did serve to strengthen their faith in Christ;* and thus they did retain a hope through faith, unto eternal salvation, relying upon the spirit of prophecy, which spake of those things to come (Alma 25:15-16; emphasis added).

Not only did the Nephites hold the Melchizedek Priesthood, but they also enjoyed—even while living the Law of Moses—the powers of the priesthood that came through great faith. Their faith was so great that the elements of the earth and the powers of the heavens were subject to them (see D&C 121:36-37).

It must be remembered, however, that generally speaking the ancient Israelites were denied the privilege of receiving the Melchizedek Priesthood ordinances and were therefore denied the blessing of entering into the rest or the presence of the Lord.

And thus we see that the affliction that was upon the children of Israel during and after Moses' time was that they were limited to the blessings and powers of the lesser law, the Aaronic priesthood. Without the ordinances of the Melchizedek priesthood, they could not become sanctified in this life, nor could they enter into the rest, or presence, of the Lord. They could not establish Zion, but they continued—with vacillating degrees of righteousness—under the preparatory gospel until the time of John the Baptist.

JOHN THE BAPTIST—PREPARING THE WAY FOR CHRIST

John stood at the crossroads between the Law of Moses and the establishment of the fulness of the everlasting covenant through Jesus Christ. The Baptist was a dynamic preacher of righteousness, and he filled his mission in every respect. He was the son of Zacharias and Elizabeth, being of priestly descent through both parents. This lineage was essential because John was the embodiment of the law of Moses, which was to prepare the way for the Messiah and prepare a people to receive him. As was mentioned earlier, John's forthcoming birth and ministry were announced by the angel Gabriel (see Luke 1:5-25), who the Prophet Joseph Smith identified as being Noah.[23]

Jesus referred to John as a "burning and shining light" (John 5:35), and said that there was no greater prophet born of woman. Joseph Smith said this is true because John: 1) was entrusted with a divine mission of preparing the way before the face of the Lord, 2) was entrusted to baptize the Son of Man, and 3) was the only legal administrator in the affairs of the kingdom on the earth.[24]

Latter-day revelation confirms the biblical account of his life and also makes known additional events in his ministry. In the Doctrine and Covenants we read, "For he was baptized while he was yet in his childhood, and was ordained by the angel of God at the time he was eight days old *unto this power, to overthrow* the kingdom of the Jews, and *to make straight* the way of the Lord before the face of his people, *to prepare* them for the coming of the Lord, in whose hand is given all power" (D&C 84:28). By virtue of this early ordination, John did overthrow the kingdom of the Jews and prepared the way for the Lord's first coming. He was a child of promise whose mission had been prophesied years before by Isaiah, Lehi, and Nephi (see Isa. 40:3; 1 Ne. 10:7-10; 2 Ne. 31:4-8). From the *Encyclopedia of Mormonism,* we read the following regarding John the Baptist's ministry:

> John had begun his preaching and baptizing near the river Jordan probably about a year before Jesus began his public ministry. He had no intention of founding a new sect; his calling was to prepare the way for Jesus; and many of his followers became Jesus' closest and earliest disciples. His intense preaching of repentance had deeply angered those in power. He denounced the marriage of Herod Antipas to his brother's wife, Herodias, which clearly violated Jewish law (Lev. 20:21).[25] Herodias wanted John killed, but Herod Antipas had concern for John's popularity with the people. He had John imprisoned (Mark 6:17), somewhat pacifying the Pharisees, as well as Herodias. During all of this, Jesus went to Galilee. While in prison, John sent two of his disciples to Jesus to confirm their faith in the Savior's identity, and Jesus supported and sustained him (Luke 7:24-28). Through shrewd plotting and the beguiling dance of her daughter Salome, Herodias eventually manipulated Herod into having John beheaded.

As important as John's ministry was during the New Testament times, his work was not restricted to that dispensation. He was also one of the first beings to restore keys during the dispensation of the fulness of times. On May 15, 1829, as a resurrected being John the Baptist appeared to Joseph Smith and Oliver Cowdery on the banks of the Susquehanna River near Harmony, Pennsylvania, and ordained these men to the Priesthood of Aaron (see D&C 13; 27:7-8; also JS-

H 1:68-72; Bible dictionary, s.v. "John the Baptist"), thus John was also instrumental in preparing the way for the final dispensation.

John's ministry was of such importance that Isaiah described him as, "The voice of him that crieth in the wilderness, Prepare ye the way of the Lord, make straight in the desert a highway for our God" (Isaiah 40:3). John did indeed prepare the way of the Lord, our Savior, Jesus Christ.

JESUS CHRIST—THE FULNESS RESTORED

It is impossible to mention here all that Jesus accomplished during his short, three-year ministry. Even the New Testament presents only selected highlights of his life and teachings. According to the Book of Mormon, much that was written by the early disciples of Jesus has been lost (see 1 Nephi 13:20-29). John, the apostle, said that of all that Jesus both said and did even the world itself could not contain the books that should be written (see John 21:25).

From the fragments of information we do have from the New Testament, we know that Jesus called his twelve Apostles and gave them power and authority to preach the gospel and administer in its ordinances. He established his Church with all of its officers and teachers (see Ephesians 4:11-12) and he taught the people the fulness of the gospel, the same gospel that had been taught in the days of Adam, Enoch, Noah, and Abraham.

It is important to understand that Jesus offered the Jews the same laws and principles that had been engraven on the *first* set of plates that Moses brought down from the holy mountain—the *fulness* of the everlasting covenant. He moved those that believed from first gear to second gear—from Aaronic Priesthood levels to Melchizedek. In other words, he replaced the Law of Moses with the higher law of the Melchizedek Priesthood with the intent of eventually moving the Jews into a Zion society—third gear principles and programs—but they would not receive him nor his teachings.

In restoring the Melchizedek dimensions of the everlasting covenant, Jesus taught that outward obedience to the laws of Moses was not sufficient. The heart must be involved. The inner man must respond to the promptings of the Spirit.

As an example, Jesus gave his Sermon on the Mount in which he stressed the importance of rising above the carnal requirements of the Law of Moses. In his sermon he said, "Ye have heard that it hath been said by them of old time [under the Law of Moses] that, Thou shalt not kill; and whosoever shall kill, shall be in danger of the judgment of God. But I say unto you, that whosoever is angry with his brother, shall be in danger of his judgment: and whosoever shall say to his brother, Raca or Rabcha, shall be in danger of the council: but whosoever shall say to his brother, Thou fool, shall be in danger of hell fire" (JST, Matthew 5: 23-24).

In addition to teaching the doctrines and principles of the gospel, Jesus, through his suffering in Gethsemane and on the cross worked out the Atonement for the sins of the world. The Good Shepherd gave his life for his sheep. Furthermore, Jesus taught the saving principles of the gospel to the dead, those in the spirit world (see D&C 138). Then he broke the bands of death through his resurrection and became the "first fruits of them that slept" (1 Corinthians 15:20).

After the resurrection of Christ, Peter, James and John governed the Church, receiving revelation through the Holy Ghost (see Acts 1:2). The apostles of Jesus held the keys and continued to teach the laws and ordinances of the Melchizedek Priesthood (see Acts 2:38, 41, 46-47). Although they did not reach Zion like Enoch's people did, the New Testament records that there were certain faithful Hebrew Saints who did receive many of the highest blessings of the everlasting covenant that are associated with a Zion people (see Hebrew 7:11; 12:22-24).

After Jesus' final ascension into heaven, he appeared to the Nephites. His efforts among them were much more successful than among the Jews. In three days he was able to raise the Nephites to a spiritual level that he was not able to do among the Jews in three years (see 3 Nephi 17:15-25, 19:25; 26:16) and to establish a Zion-like society among them. The Book of Mormon states that after his appearances to the Nephites he went to the lost tribes of Israel to teach them of the same gospel truths (see 3 Nephi 16:1-3) thereby confirming through this visitations that there truly was to be one fold and one Shepherd.

In contrast with the Nephites, the majority of the Jews rejected Jesus. Had they accepted him and his teachings, it is likely they could have established a Zion society like Enoch's or had the peace experienced by the Nephites, when "there were no contentions and disputations among them, and every man did deal justly one with another" (4 Nephi 1:2).

But the Jews would not yield to Jesus' call. He had pleaded for them to gather to him. As he looked out over Jerusalem he cried, "O Jerusalem, Jerusalem, thou that killest the prophets, and stonest them which are sent unto thee, how often would I have gathered thy children together, even as a hen gathereth her chickens under her wings, and ye would not! *Behold, your house is left unto you desolate*" (Matthew 23:37-38; emphasis added).

These fateful words were echoed again as Jesus carried his cross toward Golgotha. When he saw the women weeping for him he said, "Daughters of Jerusalem, weep not for me, but weep for yourselves, and for your children. For, behold, the days are coming, in the which they shall say, Blessed are the barren, and the wombs that never bare, and the paps which never gave suck." (Luke 23:28-29). The terrible plight of these Jews and their posterity ever since then is a matter of ancient and modern history.

In 70 A.D. the city of Jerusalem fell into the hands of the Romans at the end of a siege in which the historian Josephus tells us that 1,100,000 people were killed and tens of thousands were taken captive, later to be sold into slavery or slain by wild beasts or in gladiatorial combat for the amusement of Roman spectators. All of this destruction and dispersion could have been avoided had the Jews accepted the gospel of Jesus Christ and had their hearts changed by it. Instead, they have reaped the consequence of their own desire: "Then answered all the people, and said, His blood be on us, and on our children" (Matthew 27:25). Because the Jews rejected the truth and killed their Messiah, their condemnation was sealed.

Today, we are at the same crossroads that the Jews stood anciently. If we reject the fulness of the gospel that is presented to us, we too will reap terrible destruction (see D&C 45:24:32). A fulness of the gospel cannot be rejected without terrible consequences.

THE GREAT APOSTASY

When the full blessings of the gospel—including the blessings of the priesthood and the Holy Ghost—are present on the earth, great advances are made by the people of the Lord. They receive many revelations; they prosper educationally, politically, socially, and spiritually; they inherit promised lands; they enjoy great priesthood powers; they are delivered from their enemies; they enjoy eternal family ties—they are a happy people (see 4 Nephi 1:1-18).

On the other hand, when an enlightened people reject the messengers of truth, when they kill the prophets and change the Lord's holy ordinances, as they did after the death of Christ and the early apostles, they reap a whirlwind of darkness, error, and superstition (see Isaiah 29:10). When we reject light, we receive darkness.

Of all the apostasies in recorded history, none has been more ruinous, more terrible, more absolute than the one following the death of Christ and his Apostles. For this reason it has become known as the *Great Apostasy*.[26] Paul spoke of this apostasy when he prophesied, "Take heed therefore unto yourselves, and to all the flock, over the which the Holy Ghost hath made you overseers, to feed the church of God, which he hath purchased with his own blood. For I know this, that after my departing shall grievous wolves enter in among you, *not sparing the flock*" (Acts 20:28-29; emphasis added).

Time proved this prophecy to be true. Tradition holds that each of the apostles sealed his testimony with his blood. John alone remained as a translated being to perform his specialized labor (see John 21:20-23). After the death of the apostles, the keys of the priesthood, which are necessary to maintain the organization of the Church, were taken from the earth. When priesthood leaders died—such as bishops and other pastors—there were no apostles holding proper keys of the Priesthood to call and ordain replacements. As a result, unauthorized, uninspired, and unworthy men gradually occupied the sacred offices of the priesthood, and the Church fell into deep corruption and ignorance of the truth. The remnants of the church that continued were in reality only fragments of what existed originally—splinters and slivers of what was formerly a strong and sturdy oak tree.

Because there was not central Church authority to maintain the integrity of the teachings of the gospel, people started worshipping and teaching the wisdom of human understanding. They were like "children, tossed to and fro, and carried about with every wind of doctrine." They were left to the "cunning craftiness [of men] whereby they lie in wait to deceive" (Ephesians 4:14). The heavens were sealed and there was no revelation from heaven through living apostles and prophets as there previously had been (Acts 1:2). Instead, revelation was replaced by the anemic and misleading creeds of men, "having a form of godliness, but denying the power thereof" (2 Timothy 3:5). Over time many false beliefs crept into the church such as vain philosophies and paganistic rituals replaced the simple principles and ordinances that Jesus had taught.

Questions that arose remained unanswered because there were no living apostles to whom church members could appeal. Should infants be baptized? Did Jesus retain his physical body after the resurrection? Were there secret teachings that Jesus gave his disciples during the 40-day ministry (see Acts 1:1-3)? Who held the keys of the Kingdom? How should we act? How do we find answers? Error compounded error, and falsehood was added to falsehood as the heavy curtain of the dark ages rapidly descended upon the people of the world.

It is important that we recognize the Satan-inspired falsehoods that began to grow, cancer-like, as a result of the great apostasy, because they stand in direct opposition to the truths that were later revealed to the Prophet Joseph Smith. Now let's take a look at the history of these beliefs, what some of them are and how they stand in contrast to the truths revealed through the Prophet Joseph Smith.

History of the Creeds

In A.D. 324, Constantine, the Roman emperor, sought to strengthen his kingdom by uniting all the splinter groups of Christianity. He called representatives from the fragmented sects into council meetings that were held at Nicea. There they debated and argued many theological questions—such as the nature of God and his relationship with man—until they arrived at a system of beliefs that would represent the official, creedal, position of the Roman Church. The church that Constantine founded became known as the "universal church", or as we know it today, the Roman Catholic church. Today, most Christians belong to one of the Catholic churches (such as the Roman, the Russian, and the Greek Orthodox) or one of the Protestant churches (such as the Methodist, the Baptist, and the Presbyterian).

Being without revelation these early councils had to resort to Greek rationalism to determine their positions. The Greek philosophers, such as Socrates and Plato, had stressed the value of logic and reason—mental constructs—over that which is perceivable in physical world. Plato reasoned that "reality is conceptual or rational, and consequently the best way to apprehend it is through reason and the analysis of our own mental activities. As our minds are structured, so is the real; through the conceptualizing activities of our own intelligence we gain the best insight into the nature of ultimate reality."[27]

Being very much influenced by Platonic idealism, the council at Nicea fabricated a system of beliefs that emphasized the mind and intellect over anything physical. For example: since God was the supreme being, he could not have a physical body. In their uninspired way of thinking, God is simply the great "mind" or the great "spirit" without body, parts, and passions. This false conclusion is but one example of how human reasoning alone cannot discover eternal truths. If one starts with false premises, all of his conclusions will be in error. The creeds that were formulated at Nice provided the foundation for many other false doctrinal beliefs that followed.

The Creeds are More Greek than Christian.

The apostle Paul warned that the things of God could not be understood by the reasoning of the natural man.

> For what man knoweth the things of a man, save the spirit of man which is in him? even so the things of God knoweth no man, but the Spirit of God. . . .
> But the natural man receiveth not the things of the Spirit of God: for they are foolishness unto him: neither can he know [them], because they are spiritually discerned (1 Corinthians 2:11, 14).

Revelation is essential in knowing truth. Because the creeds were drawn up by scholarly men whose thinking was greatly influenced by the Greeks, they reflect more Greek philosophy than they do New Testament Christian teachings. The creed of Athanasius, for example, was accepted as one of the symbols of orthodox Christian faith. This creedal pronouncement holds that God is incorporeal, that he is an immaterial being without body, parts, and passions. Here is the way it reads:

We worship one God in Trinity, and Trinity in Unity, neither confounding the persons, nor dividing the substance. For there is one person of the Father, another of the Son, and another of the Holy Ghost. But the Godhead of the Father, Son, and Holy Ghost, is all one: the glory equal, the majesty co-eternal. Such as the Father is, such is the Son; and such is the Holy Ghost. The Father uncreate, the Son uncreate, and the Holy Ghost uncreate. The Father incomprehensible, the Son incomprehensible and the Holy Ghost incomprehensible. The Father eternal, the Son eternal, and the Holy Ghost eternal. And yet there are not three eternals; but one eternal. As also there are not three incomprehensibles, nor three uncreated; but one uncreated, and one incomprehensible. So likewise the Father is Almighty, the Son Almighty, and the Holy Ghost Almighty; and yet there are not three Almighties, but one Almighty. So the Father is God, the Son is God, and the Holy Ghost is God, and yet they are not three Gods but one God.[28]

The assorted creeds of the different Christian churches are slight variations of this same incomprehensible Athanasius creed. For example, regarding the nature of God, the Catholic Church teaches, "There is but One God, the creator of heaven and earth, the supreme incorporeal, uncreated being, who exists of Himself and is infinite in all His attributes."[29] Similarly, the Church of England teaches that "There is but one living and true God, everlasting, without body, parts, or passions, of infinite power, wisdom and goodness."[30]

These views—that God is an incorporeal, immaterial, bodiless, partless, passionless being—have been held by most Christians since the days of Constantine. The plain and simple teachings of the New Testament regarding our Heavenly Father and Jesus having glorified bodies of flesh and bones and the Holy Ghost being a personage of spirit (see D&C 130:22) were replaced by the incomprehensible language of the creeds.

As was mentioned earlier, Jesus condemned the creeds as "an abomination in his sight" when he spoke to the Prophet Joseph Smith in the Sacred Grove (J.S.—History, 1:19). One reason why Jesus took such a strong stand against these teachings is probably because they deny that the Father and the Son are separate beings and have bodies of flesh and bones. They also deny the literalness of the family relationship that we have with the Godhead.

In summary, the Latter-day Saints believe that the theological entanglements of the creeds are simply elaborate philosophical constructs reflecting the thinking of unenlightened men. Not only are they untrue, they are hazardous—because they lead the children of God away from the true and living God and his great plan of happiness.

Now let's look at some other specific false doctrines that came about following the death of Christ and the apostles—doctrines which fulfilled Isaiah's prophecy that, "The earth also is defiled under the inhabitants thereof; because *they have transgressed the laws, changed the ordinance, broken the everlasting covenant"* (Isaiah 24:5). (See end of chapter Figure 7-E, Departures from the Doctrines of Christ).

Original Sin

As we have discussed in other chapters, many Christians believe that the original sin of Adam and Eve was sexual in nature. To understand why this would become a common belief it will be helpful to look at the circumstances associated with St. Augustine's youth and education.

Augustine was born in Tagaste (modern Souk Ahras, Algeria) in A.D. 354 and died almost seventy-six years later in Hippo Regius (modern Annaba) on the Mediterranean coast sixty miles away. He was one of the prominent scholars and theologians of his time. He also became one of the primary architects of Catholic doctrine and philosophy. He, among others who were steeped in Greek philosophy, advanced the idea that all of the physical world, including the physical relationship of the sexes, is base and corrupting. In his way of thinking, to be pure, one must rise above the flesh and occupy the world of the mind.

Of Augustine's early youth, Will Durant, the historian, wrote,

> At age twelve Augustine was sent to school at Madaura, and at seventeen to higher studies at Carthage. Salvian would soon describe Africa as "the cesspool of the world," and Carthage as "the cesspool of Africa"; hence Monica's parting advice to her son:
> "She commanded me, and with much earnestness forewarned me, that I should not commit fornication, and especially that I should never defile any man's wife. These seemed to me no better than women's counsels, which it would be a shame for me to follow. . . . I ran headlong with such blindness that I was ashamed among my equals to be guilty of less impudency than they were, whom I heard brag mightily of their naughtiness; yea, and so much the more boasting by how much more they had been beastly; and I took pleasure to do it, not for the pleasure of the act only, but for the praise of it also; . . . and when I lacked opportunity to commit a wickedness that should make me as bad as the lost, I would feign myself to have done what I never did."[31]

When Augustine encountered Catholicism, he believed that he would have to become celibate in order to control his carnal inclinations and become a truly spiritual man. He also wondered why mankind seems to be burdened with such powerful erotic drives. He finally concluded that the original sin of Adam and Eve, the partaking of the forbidden fruit, was a sexual encounter. He believed that because of this act, Adam and Eve and all mankind have become carnal, sensual, and devilish.

In explaining how he developed his ideas about original sin, Durant wrote further,

> Augustine did not invent the doctrine of original sin; . . . but his own experience of sin, and of the "voice" that had converted him, had left in him a somber conviction that the human will is from birth inclined to evil, and can be turned to good only by the gratuitous act of God. He could not explain the evil inclination of the will except as an effect of Eve's sin and Adam's love. Since we are all children of Adam, Augustine argued, we share his guilt, [and] are, indeed, the offspring of his guilt: the original sin was concupiscence [or lust]. *And concupiscence still befouls every act of generation;* by the very connection of sex with parentage mankind is a "mass of perdition," and most of us will be damned. Some of us will be saved, but only through the grace of the suffering Son of God, and through the intercession of the Mother who conceived Him sinlessly. "Through a woman [Eve] we were sent to destruction; through a woman [Mary] salvation was restored to us."[32]

In contrast to this false belief, Latter-day Saints believe that Adam and Eve partook of the forbidden fruit as has been discussed in earlier chapters, but that the fruit was not symbolic of a sexual encounter between Adam and Eve. Our modern prophets have stated emphatically that the forbidden fruit was not a symbol for anything sexual in nature.[33] Because of the sexual connotations associated with the expression "original sin," Latter-day Saints rarely use this phrase. We usually just refer to the partaking of "the forbidden fruit" or "the fruit of the tree of knowledge of good and evil," without any attempt to describe what the fruit was.

Infant baptism

Many Christians have come to believe that since sexual passion is involved in conception, as the fruit of lust, infants need to be baptized—to rid them of original sin. Latter-day scriptures condemn such a belief.

In a letter to his son Moroni, Mormon stressed the idea that little children are innocent and without need of baptism when he said, "Little children are alive in Christ, even from the foundation of the world.... Behold I say unto you, that he that supposeth that little children need baptism is in the gall of bitterness and in the bonds of iniquity; for he hath neither faith, hope, nor charity" (Moroni 8:12, 14).

Sometimes, as support for infant baptism, people cite a passage from the Psalms which says: "Behold, I was shapen in iniquity; and in sin did my mother conceive me" (Psalm 51:5). The true explanation of this passage is that David, who wrote this psalm, recognized that he was born into a world where sin and evil run rampant. He did not mean to say that the act of his conception was evil.

When I have held my babies in my arms to give them a name and a blessing, I have looked fondly upon their sweet countenances and have trusted that someday, through the great plan of redemption, I can be as acceptable to the Lord as they were at that moment.

The Virgin Birth

Another false idea that grew out of the Greek disregard for the physical is the doctrine of the virgin birth which holds that Mary had no connection with a man in order to conceive Jesus. According to this belief, Mary conceived simply "of the Holy Ghost" (Matthew 1:18) so that Jesus would be free from original sin.

By contrast, Latter-day Saints believe that Jesus was born of a virgin in the sense that Mary had no connection with any *mortal* man (see chapter 5, "The Promised Redeemer"). Jesus was and is the Son of the living God.

As was mentioned previously, he was given life by the same process that each of us is begotten by our fathers.[34] Our fathers are mortal; Jesus' father is immortal. Our fathers have bodies of flesh and bone and blood; Jesus' father is a Holy Man, a perfected, celestial, resurrected personage having a body "as tangible as man's"—a "body of flesh and bones" (D&C 130:22). Jesus inherited blood from his mother, Mary, and the power over death from his immortal and eternal Father.

The Immaculate Conception

Many people incorrectly believe that the virgin birth and the immaculate conception are the same doctrine. The virgin birth has to do with Jesus' conception; the immaculate conception has to do with Mary's conception.

Because Latter-day Saints do not believe in the traditional view of original sin nor in the virgin birth, we also do not believe in the doctrine of the immaculate conception. This tradition posits that "The Blessed Virgin Mary was from the moment of her conception in St. Anne's womb kept free from the original sin."[35]

According to this doctrine, Mary was conceived in her mother's womb in an *immaculate* way, i.e., her conception was unspotted and sinless. This idea was invented out of a rational conclusion that suggested that Mary needed to be free from the effects of original sin so she would be a pure vessel to bear the sinless Jesus—otherwise the taint of the original sin within her, her own unregenerated nature, might contaminate him. The implication of this doctrine is that the conception of the rest of us is less than immaculate—sullied by original sin.

Celibacy

Another false belief growing out of the belief in original sin is the idea that celibacy is a more pure lifestyle, that one must forsake the things of the flesh to be truly spiritual. Marriage and marital relationships are approved and even encouraged by God. Paul confirmed the purity of marriage relations when he wrote, "Marriage is honourable in all, and the bed undefiled: but whoremongers and adulterers God will judge" (Hebrews 13:4). On the other hand, celibacy which is an unmarried life-style, is chosen by certain groups of people—like priests, monks, and nuns. By choosing to not marry, devotees believe they can thus be unencumbered with worldly distractions such as marriage, sexual intimacy, and family responsibilities; and thus be free to focus on God and his work.

Believers in celibacy typically hold to the notion that neither Jesus nor the Apostles ever married. This view is completely without scriptural support. To the contrary, we read that one of the miracles of Jesus was the healing of Peter's mother-in-law (see Matthew 8:14-15). Obviously, Peter could not have had a mother-in-law unless he was married.

The apostle Paul warned that celibacy would be one of the false doctrines of the last days. He said, "Now the Spirit speaketh expressly, that in the latter times some shall depart from the faith, giving heed to seducing spirits, and doctrines of devils; . . . Forbidding to marry, and commanding to abstain from meats, which God hath created to be received with thanksgiving of them which believe and know the truth" (1 Timothy 4:1-3). History has proven Paul's prophecy to be true. Today we observe many groups that promote celibate living and other anti-family life-styles.

Latter-day Saints reject celibacy because it nullifies the first commandment given to Adam and Eve—to multiply and replenish the earth that they might have joy and rejoicing in their posterity. This commandment has never been taken away and is a charge given to every couple who enters the new and everlasting covenant of marriage.

On September 23, 1995, The First Presidency and Quorum of the Twelve issued a proclamation to the world in which they solemnly declared "marriage between a man and a woman is ordained of God and that the family is central to the Creator's plan for the eternal destiny of his children".

For Latter-day Saints getting married and rearing families in righteousness is the most important work of God we can ever perform, and it is a vital part of our Heavenly Father's plan for our happiness. Without marriage our eternal progression would be thwarted. None of us can be made perfect without this sacred union. Paul was emphatic about this, declaring that, "Neither is the man without the woman, neither the woman without the man, in the Lord" (1 Corinthians 11:11).

Mary, Forever Virgin and an Object of Worship

In yet another related doctrine, the Roman Catholic Church falsely teaches that throughout her life Mary never had sexual relations and that she was assumed into heaven as a virgin. According to this reasoning, Mary remained forever chaste, pure and holy and never participated in martial acts that are wrongly considered by many to be vulgar and common. This position, of course, would naturally be an outgrowth from previous false premises.

After Jesus' birth, Mary and Joseph lived together as husband and wife and had children of their own (Matthew 13:55-56). These children were half-brothers and sisters to Jesus. When Matthew wrote about Jesus' siblings the context clearly shows that he was talking about family relationships, not brothers and sisters of Jesus' in the Church as some people believe.

Latter-day Saints believe that the Lord's law of chastity is to have no sexual relationships outside of marriage. However, when couples are married they may have sexual intimacy and still be considered chaste.

Another doctrine that has evolved over time, called Mariolatry, is the belief that "the blessed Virgin Mary" is a person worthy of our worship, one to whom we can appeal in prayer, and that she is an intercessor, or a mediator between us and God. In the August 25, 1997 Newsweek magazine, there appeared a special feature article noting a growing movement in the Roman Catholic Church to have the pope proclaim a new, controversial dogma: that Mary is a Co-Redeemer.

Though we honor and respect Mary and hold her in high regard, we do not worship her nor place her on a level with God and Christ. Latter-day prophets and the Bible clearly teach that there is but *"one mediator* between God and men, the man Christ Jesus" (1 Tim. 2:5; emphasis added). We have been taught by the Savior and by the prophets to pray to our Heavenly Father, in the name of Jesus Christ, through the power of the Holy Ghost.

The Depravity of Man

Early reformers, like John Calvin and others, taught—and many still believe—that because of the taint of original sin, mankind is totally depraved, utterly degenerate, and hopelessly evil. Accordingly, they believe that we can be saved only by the goodness of God—not by any good works we can perform.

On the other hand, Latter-day Saints believe that even though we have fallen natures we are not totally depraved. An oft quoted passage in the Book of Mormon sets the record straight. King Benjamin said, "For the natural man is an enemy to God, and has been from the fall of Adam, and will be, forever and ever, unless he yields to the enticings of the Holy Spirit, and putteth off the natural man and becometh a saint through the atonement of Christ the Lord, and becometh as a child, submissive, meek, humble, patient, full of love, willing to submit to all things which the Lord seeth fit to inflict upon him, even as a child doth submit to his father" (Mosiah 3:19).

Through "obedience to the laws and ordinances of the gospel," we believe we can become sanctified and prepared to enter back into the presence of God (Third Article of Faith). The idea that we can become sanctified—made pure and holy—does not appear in either the Protestant or Catholic traditions.

Catholic View of Salvation

Catholic tradition asserts that people access the saving power of Christ through participation in the externally offered sacraments, or ordinances, of the "Holy Mother Church" such as: baptism, confirmation, partaking of communion, marriage and the last rites (see end of chapter Figure 7-F, Sectarian Views of Salvation). The Catholics believe that these sacraments are necessary in order for a person to enter heaven.

Protestant View of Salvation

Martin Luther, like many of the early reformers, objected to the Catholic emphasis on *external* ordinances as a way to salvation. He and many others believed that people access the saving power of Jesus' Atonement by accepting him as their personal Savior.

Protestants get this idea from scriptures such as Ephesians 2:8-9, which says: "For by grace are ye saved through faith; and that not of yourselves: it is the gift of God: not of works, lest any man should boast". Many Christians have misunderstood this point in Paul's writings thinking that no works are necessary to be saved. Here, Paul is not saying we should not obey the works of the gospel of Jesus Christ! (see Matthew 7:21). He was speaking to those who wanted to keep the Jewish traditions alive in the early Church—those who were clinging tenaciously to the works and rituals of the Law of Moses. They thought that any Greek or Gentile who joined the Church should be circumcised and comply with the other laws and customs of the Mosaic law.

Paul was adamant in teaching that the works of the law of Moses could not save the people (see Hebrews 9, 10). The Book of Mormon teaches us that "It is by grace that we are saved, after all we can do" (2 Nephi 25:23). Thus there are certain things that we must do in order to comply with the requirements of the new and everlasting covenant, ultimately, though, it is through the grace, or the love of God in sending his Son to work out the infinite Atonement that we are saved—not through the works of the law of Moses.

Thus we can see how the pendulum of false teachings has swung from the Catholic extreme—emphasis on simply external ordinances—to the Protestant extreme—emphasis on simply internal acceptance of Jesus as the Savior. As was discussed in Chapter Six, through the Restored Gospel of Jesus Christ we get the proper balance between ordinances and principles—works and grace.

Resurrection only Spiritual

By accepting as a starting point the false premise that ultimate reality is of the mind —as the Greek philosophers taught—the conclusion that the resurrection is a non-physical, spiritual phenomenon is a logical conclusion. Accordingly, some Christian churches teach that when people die, their spirits sleep while their bodies lie in the grave and that the resurrection is simply the spirit arising from a long sleep.

The Bible clearly teaches, however, that Jesus' resurrection was a physical reality. His tomb was empty! (see Matthew 28:6.) When Jesus appeared to his disciples, he invited them to come forward and feel the nail prints in his hands and feet. He even ate broiled fish and honeycomb with them after his resurrection (see Luke 24:36-43), demonstrating that he was not a spirit as they had supposed.

Not only was Jesus physically resurrected, but he also opened the door for all us to regain our bodies. Both the Bible and the Book of Mormon witness that many of the bodies of the Saints arose and appeared to many after Jesus' resurrection (see Matthew 27:52-53; Helaman 14:25; 3 Nephi 23:9-11).

The physical nature of the resurrection is one of the most fundamental promises of the everlasting covenant. The promise is made to each of us that in the resurrection we will receive again own physical bodies that will be "fashioned like unto his glorious body, ... whereby he is able even to subdue all things" (Philippians 3:21; see also Alma 40).

What a wonderful promise this true doctrine is—that even though we grow old and die, we will be resurrected with glorified, eternally youthful bodies of flesh and bone, with all the joys and pure sensations experienced in this life magnified many times over. This true principle is one of the most glorious truths restored to mankind as a result of the restoration of the gospel through the Prophet Joseph Smith.

My testimony is that Jesus Christ lives today and has a most beautiful, glorified body of flesh and bones. Because of his love and his atoning sacrifice, the bands of death have been broken for all of us, and we too will be like him if we love him and one another as he has loved us.

REVIEW AND PREVIEW—JOSEPH SMITH'S LETTER TO EDITOR SEATON

As a result of the restoration of the gospel through the Prophet Joseph Smith, the veil of darkness which once covered the earth during the Great Apostasy has been lifted. Yesterday's cobwebs of ignorance and superstition have been swept away with the glorious dawning of a fresh new day of truth, light, knowledge, and beauty. Beginning with his First Vision, the marvelous light of the gospel has begun to burst forth upon the nations of the earth in this the final dispensation, the dispensation of the fulness of times.

In this chapter we have briefly reviewed the various gospel dispensations. We have traced the fulness of the everlasting covenant through the lives of many of the great biblical prophets including Adam, Enoch, Noah, and Abraham. If we had space we could give similar descriptions of the life and ministries of the Book of Mormon prophets.

We have discussed how Moses initially intended to give the children of Israel the fulness of the gospel. But recognizing their spiritual immaturity they were given the Law of Moses as a schoolmaster to bring them lovingly, carefully, gradually to the higher levels of gospel living—including the highest levels of the Melchizedek priesthoods.

We also identified John the Baptist as the forerunner for Jesus and discussed how Jesus, during his earthly ministry, offered the fulness of the everlasting covenants to the Jews which they rejected, thus ushering in a dreadful period of darkness, superstition, ignorance, and error.

Finally we discussed the Great Apostasy—with its many false creedal teachings—that began after the death of the apostles and continued until the time of the Prophet Joseph Smith. These false doctrines were presented to stand in contrast to the wonderful teachings that have been restored through the Prophet Joseph Smith. Through Joseph, the latter-day Seer, we have been given again the fulness of the gospel as it was had by the ancient patriarchs. Through him, God has revealed all the keys, ordinances, powers, doctrines, and authority that can empower us to receive peace in this world and eternal life in the world to come.

In describing the various cycles of restoration and apostasy which have occurred throughout the ages, the Prophet Joseph Smith wrote a very informative letter to one Mr. N.E. Seaton, the editor of a newspaper. In this article the Prophet explained how the everlasting covenant was offered during Christ's mortal ministry—first to the Jews and then to the Gentiles—and how it has been restored again in our dispensation—first to the Gentiles and finally to the Jews. Thus Christ's prophecy was fulfilled that, the "first shall be last; and the last shall be first" (Matthew 19:30; D&C 29:30).

A summary of Joseph's letter can serve as a *review* of the major ideas we have discussed in this chapter and can also provide a *preview* of the remaining chapters in this book. You may want to refer again to Figure 7-B, "The Gospel through the Ages" which can serve as a useful "road map" through this important document.[36]

The following are some of the most important ideas and principles that I have extracted from that letter. I highly recommend that you read the full text of this letter. You will find it a masterpiece of clarity regarding the gospel through the various ages of scriptural history.

Letter to Editor Seaton

1. Because of latter-day wickedness the Lord is progressively withdrawing his Holy Spirit from among the people of the world.
2. As the Spirit is withdrawn, destructions and calamities increase.
3. In every dispensation, God has offered his everlasting covenant which has provided safety for all those who have embraced it.
4. The New Testament Jews did not receive Jesus nor the protection the gospel covenant would have offered them. As a result they were broken off and scattered throughout the world during dark and gloomy days. They were destroyed as a nation.
5. After the time of the Jews, the gospel was taken to the Gentiles nations—the Romans and Greeks. Some of them accepted the gospel but none remained faithful.
6. The modern Gentiles—including the present day Christian Churches—have "changed the ordinances and broken the everlasting covenant" (Isaiah 24:5). They have become high-minded and few of them will embrace the everlasting covenant of Jesus Christ, the fulness of the gospel.
7. Joseph Smith was called by God, and he, as the latter-day Seer, points the way to salvation, safety and deliverance for all mankind in the last days.
8. All of the promises [including land, deliverance, and seed] that God made to Israel will be realized in the dispensation of the fulness of times. Then Israel will be a willing people, and the gospel will be implanted in their hearts and in their thoughts, and their sins will be remembered no more.
9. Deliverance for all people—Israelites and Gentiles alike—is obtained by joining The Church of Jesus Christ of Latter-day Saints, becoming sanctified, and establishing Zion in America and Jerusalem in the Holy Land as places of safety against the wars, destructions, and fires of the last days.
10. All the people in the world are commanded to repent and embrace the everlasting covenant before the overflowing scourge overtakes them.

From this letter we see that the Prophet Joseph Smith plays a central role in the restoration of the everlasting covenant in the last days. Through Joseph, the latter-day Seer, the Lord has launched the final gospel dispensation—the dispensation of the fulness of times thereby opening the door so that all who will may embrace the everlasting covenant. This covenant will restore the children of Israel to their former glory and will also provide for them a way of escape from the destructions of the last days. The divine calling and mission of Joseph Smith, then, becomes the subject of our next chapter.

REFERENCES:

1 *Teachings of the Prophet Joseph Smith*, 61; emphasis added; see also 168-69.

2 *Discourses of Brigham Young*, 104.

3 See also Abraham 1:2-4, 18, 26-27, 31; 2:9, 11; Alma 13:1-9; D&C 76:57; 84:6-17; 86:8.

4 Patriarchal priesthood authority will be discussed in greater detail in Chapter 9.

5 *Teachings*, 157.

6 Adam does not simply preside over the *first* gospel dispensation but over all gospel dispensations. Joseph Smith taught, "Every man holding the Presidency of his dispensation, and one man holding the Presidency of them all, even Adam; and Adam receiving his Presidency and authority from the Lord" (*Teachings*, 169). "The keys [of the Priesthood] have to be brought from heaven whenever the Gospel is sent. When they are revealed from Heaven it is by Adam's authority" (*Words of Joseph Smith*, 52, note #8). Joseph Smith also taught us that Abel held the keys of his dispensation. In discussing the brief reference to Abel made by the apostle Paul in Hebrews 11, the Prophet Joseph stated, "therefore holding still the keys of his dispensation [Abel] was sent down from heaven unto Paul to minister consoling words & to commit unto him a knowledge of the mysteries of Godliness" (*Words of Joseph Smith*, 40).

7 In other words, among all of God's creations, this world is the most corrupt. Similarly, Jacob, the Book of Mormon prophet, was told by an angel that Jesus "should come among the Jews, among those who are the more wicked part of the world; and they shall crucify him—for thus it behooveth our God, and *there is none other nation on earth that would crucify their God*" (2 Nephi 10:3). In describing the wickedness of his own day, the Prophet Joseph Smith said, "*This generation is as corrupt as the generation of the Jews that crucified Christ*; and if He were here to-day, and should preach the same doctrine He did then, they would put Him to death." (TPJS, 328) We live about one-hundred and sixty years since Joseph Smith made this statement. What would he say of the conditions of the world today? They have gotten so much worse since he made this statement.

8 See "Chronology" in the 1979 edition of the Bible.

9 The Jewish historian, Josephus, gives an interesting description of the nations of the world which descended from each of the sons of Noah. See *Josephus, Complete Works*, "Antiquities of the Jews" (Michigan: Kregel Publications, 1969), 30-32.

10 Actually, these people were returning to the land from which Noah had left. From Latter-day revelation we know that the Garden of Eden was on the American Continent (D&C 78: 15; 107:53-57; 116) and that Noah's ark was constructed there. The Genesis account of the flood says it rained for forty days, but "the waters prevailed upon the earth an hundred and fifty days" (Genesis 7:24). The ark was not stationary during that time. After floating for five months it finally settled on Mt. Ararat, in an area we know today as Turkey in the Middle East. So, the Old World is the New World, and the New World is the Old World.

    The Lord has stranger things than this to reveal to us. When he comes "he shall reveal all things—Things which have passed, and hidden things which no man knew, things of the earth, by which it was made, and the purpose and the end thereof—Things most precious, things that are above, and things that are beneath, things that are in the earth, and upon the earth, and in heaven" and the righteous shall "partake of all this glory" (D&C 101:32-35). Those will be exciting times!

11 There is considerable evidence that this Melchizedek was Shem, the righteous son

of Noah, through whom the "Shemetic," or "Semetic," races have descended. From latter-day revelation we learn that Abraham "received the priesthood from Melchizedek, who received it through the lineage of his fathers, even till Noah" (D&C 84:14).

12 Andrew F. Ehat and Lyndon W. Cook, *Words of Joseph Smith,* 246; emphasis added. See also, JST, Genesis 14:25-40.

13 *Teachings of the Prophet Joseph Smith,* 297.

14 Sister Marguerite DeLong.

15 *Teachings,* 323.

16 *Teachings,* 321.

17 *Teachings,* 255-256

18 Conference Report, Oct 1945, 46; emphasis added.

19 Conference Report, Oct, 1973, 7-8; Emphasis added.

20 *Teachings,* 189.

21 It is important to remember that the Holy Land is called *Canaan* in the Old Testament. Presently, it is called *Israel* by the Jews and Palestine by the Arabs.

22 *Teachings,* 181.

23 *Teachings,* 157.

24 *Teachings,* 275-76.

25 Josephus, *Antiquities,* 18.5.1-2.

26 See James E. Talmage's important work, *The Great Apostasy.*

27 Hunter Mead, *Types and Problems of Philosophy,* 58 ff.

28 Quoted in James E. Talmage, *The Great Apostasy Considered in the Light of Scriptural and Secular History,* 104.

29 Bruno, *Catholic Belief,* 1.

30 Church of England Prayer Book.

31 Will Durant, *The Age of Faith,* vol. 4 of *The Story of Civilization,* 65.

32 Augustine, Sermon 289. Durant, *Age of Faith,* 69; emphasis added.

33 Bruce R. McConkie has written, "One thing we do know definitely: The forbidden fruit was not sex sin. The view that immoral indulgence on the part of our first parents constituted the forbidden fruit is one of the most evil and wicked heresies in apostate Christendom. Adam and Eve were married for eternity by the Lord himself before the fall, and the command given them to have children was one directing the begetting of children in legal and lawful wedlock. (Moses 3:20-25)" (*Mormon Doctrine,* p.289 FORBIDDEN FRUIT).

34 Bruce R. McConkie, *The Promised Messiah,* 468-69; *Family Home Evening Manual,* 1972, 125-126.

35 In *Encyclopedia of Religion,* Vergilius Ferm, ed., 1959 [Littlefield, Adams & Co.], 359; see also Durant, *Age of Faith,* 747, 973.

36 This letter can be found in its entirety in the *Teachings of the Prophet Joseph Smith,* 13-18.

FIGURE 7-A
A CYCLE OF CIVILIZATIONS

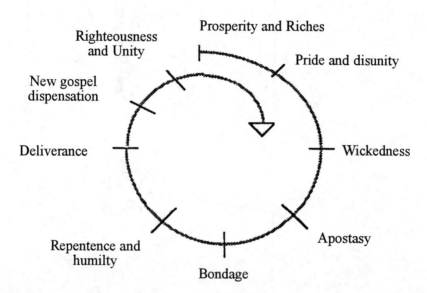

Principles

1. The Lord has promised that he will prosper his people as they keep his commandments and worship Jesus Christ.
2 Often with prosperity comes pride and competition.
3. As the spirit of the Lord withdraws, the people become more wicked in their thoughts and actions.
4. Apostasy, or a falling away from the principles of the gospel, increases as people transgress the laws of God and become more competitive.
5. Without the full armor of Christ, people become vulnerable to their enemies who bring them into captivity.
6. Through suffering people are brought to a state of humility and eventual repentance.
7. In time, after sincere repentance, the Lord brings about deliverance. Righteous men and women are raised up to lead the people out of bondage.
8. Deliverers are usually prophets of God who are given the keys of the priesthood which enable the everlasting covenant to operate again in the lives of the people.
9. Righteousness and cooperation among the Saints leads them to prosperity and riches again.
10. And so the cycle repeats itself... (see Helaman 12:1-13).

FIGURE 7-B

THE GOSPEL THROUGH THE AGES

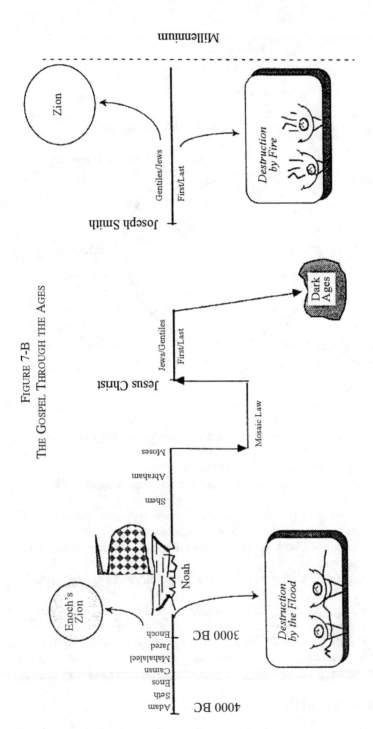

Principles

1. "As it was in the days of Noah, so shall it be at the coming of the Son of Man" (J.S. Matt. 1:41-45).

2. "For the time speedily cometh that the Lord will cause a great division among the people, and the wicked will be destroyed; and he will spare his people, yea, even if it so be that he must destroy the wicked by fire" (2 Nephi 30:10).

FIGURE 7-C
THE EVERLASTING COVENANT AS REVEALED TO ABRAHAM

Abraham covenanted to...	*The Lord promised Abraham that...*
1. Be obedient to the Lord. 2. Offer sacrifices. 3. Seek righteousness and truth all his days. 4. Serve his fellow men. 5. Exercise faith in Christ who was to come. 6. Seek light and knowledge.	1. Abraham would be a father of many nations (see Genesis 12:3). 2. His descendants would be as numerous as the stars of the heavens or as the dust of the earth both is the world and out of the world (see D&C 132:30; Gen. 13:16; 15:5). 3. Kings and nations were to come from him (see Genesis 17:6). 4. Many of his descendants would bear the name of God, even the holy priesthood (see Abra. 2:9; D&C 76:58). 5. Through Abraham and his children all the families of the earth would be blessed (see Gen. 12:3). 6. Circumcision was to be the sign of the covenant until Christ should come (see Gen. 17:1-14; compare JST, Gen. 17:11-12; Acts 17:1-2, 28-29). 7. The covenant was to be everlasting (Genesis 17:7).

FIGURE 7-D
GETTING IN GEAR WITH THE LORD

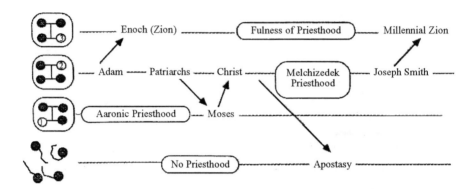

Principles

1. Adam personally held all the keys of the priesthood, but not all his children were faithful; consequently, they could not progress to a Zion society (3rd gear).

2. Enoch's people, however, were true and faithful. They received a fulness of the priesthood and became one in the Lord. They were able to establish Zion (3rd gear).

3. Moses sought diligently to sanctify his people so they could enter the rest of the Lord, but they hardened their hearts, and the Melchizedek Priesthood was taken from them. The people had the benefits of the Aaronic Priesthood only (1st gear).

4. Christ restored the Melchizedek Priesthood to the earth. He sought to gather the Jews as a hen gathereth her chickens, but they would not. Jesus was crucified and the apostles killed. The God of light was rejected, and the priesthood was taken from the earth—the vehicle was completely wrecked.

5. Through Joseph Smith all the keys of the Melchizedek Priesthood have been restored. (We are, as a Church, in 2nd gear—preparing to move into 3rd gear, Zions).

6. "Wherefore, may the Kingdom of God (the Church) go forth, that the Kingdom of Heaven (Zion) may come" (D&C 65:6).

FIGURE 7-E
DEPARTURES FROM THE DOCTRINES OF CHRIST

PROTESTANT VIEW OF SALVATION
People are saved by grace alone.

CATHOLIC VIEW OF SALVATION
People are saved through
the sacraments or ordinances.

THE DEPRAVITY OF MAN
Calvinism holds that mankind is
hopelessly corrupt.

MARIOLATRY
Mary, the mother of Jesus, should be worshipped;
She was forever virgin.

CELIBACY
Neither Jesus nor the apostles married; priests and nuns
live a spiritually higher life.

THE IMMACULATE CONCEPTION
Mary was conceived in an immaculate way to keep her from
original sin.

THE VIRGIN BIRTH
Jesus had no father.

INFANT BAPTISM
Infants must be baptized to remove the taint of original sin.

ORIGINAL SIN
Adam and Eve's sin was concupiscence or lust.

NO PHYSICAL RESURRECTION
The resurrection will be simply a spiritual thing.

ATHANASIAN AND NICEAN CREEDS
God, the ideal, is without body, parts, or passions.

THE ANCIENT GREEK PHILOSOPHERS
Ultimate reality is mental, not physical.

FIGURE 7-F
SECTARIAN VIEWS OF SALVATION

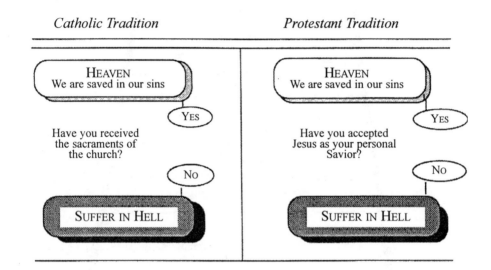

Catholic Tradition   *Protestant Tradition*

Principles

1. Both the Catholic and the Protestant traditions hold that men and women
   are basically depraved—hopelessly corrupt.
2. The Catholic belief holds that people can be saved only as they accept the
   authority of the "Holy Mother Church" and receive the sacraments (ordinances) at her hand.
3. The Protestant tradition holds that people can be saved only as they
   accept and confess Jesus as their personal Savior.
4. In neither tradition is there any belief that people can become pure and
   holy, perfect beings—there is no concept of sanctification. People, according to both views, are saved, not because they are good or can become
   good. They are saved because God alone is good. Both traditions emphasize that it is through the mercy of God that mankind is saved. The idea
   that mercy cannot rob justice—i.e. good works is not emphasized in either
   tradition.

CHAPTER EIGHT

JOSEPH SMITH, PROPHET OF THE RESTORATION

I feel like shouting hallelujah, all the time, when I think that I ever knew
Joseph Smith.

—Brigham Young (*JD* 3:51)

My first recollection of hearing about the Prophet Joseph Smith was during a testimony meeting in the Hillspring Ward. Sister Rae Hurd (who
I think was the Relief Society President and liked listening to opera on Saturday
morning, my mother said) stood up and spoke about the Prophet obtaining the
golden plates from the Hill Cumorah.

I remember her pointing to the hill west of Hillspring and saying that
Cumorah was not much different than that hill. She explained that Joseph went a
place very similar to our hill and looked around for a long stick he could use for
a lever. Finding one, he placed the end of it under the rock that covered the place
where the plates were hidden. Once again Sister Hurd said that that rock probably looked like any of the rocks we could find on the West Hill. (I think she was
trying to impress upon us the reality of the event. It certainly had an impact on
my mind.) Using the stick as a lever he pried up the stone covering the box, and
there for the first time he saw the plates, the Urim and Thummim and other sacred
objects.

Sister Hurd went on to explain that Joseph was not able to take the plates the
first time he saw them. Instead he met with the Angel Moroni every September
for four years to receive information and revelation that would later help him to
translate the Book of Mormon. She also said that during his lifetime, Joseph

225

Smith saw many angels and received keys and authority from them that helped him to bring the true church back to the earth.

As a little boy I didn't realize the magnitude of the Restoration—all that was involved. Even now as an adult, I am sure I still don't grasp the entire significance of this mighty event that is continuing to roll forth until it will one day fill the whole earth. However, what I do know has caused me to be inspired and to be filled with wonderment. There are times when I, like Brigham Young, have felt like shouting, "Hallelujah", that I have been able to learn about Joseph Smith, the man and the Seer of the Lord and of the great work that has come forth through his instrumentality.

In our hymns we frequently sing praise to his name for the marvelous work and wonder that he brought forth. One of these hymns expresses my joy and my deep love for this great prophet and seer of the last dispensation:

Praise to the man who communed with Jehovah!
Jesus anointed that Prophet and Seer.
Blessed to open the last dispensation,
Kings shall extol him, and nations revere.

Hail to the Prophet, ascended to heaven!
Traitors and tyrants now fight him in vain.
Mingling with Gods, he can plan for his brethren;
Death cannot conquer the hero again.[1]

The Prophet truly was an extraordinary man—and the events that took place through him in launching the great Restoration of the everlasting covenant were truly amazing. He communed with the Father and the Son, saw angels, translated the Book of Mormon, brought forth most of the revelations in the Doctrine and Covenants, began a revision of the Bible, translated the papyrus scroll from which we have the Book of Abraham, and was the instrument through whom the Lord restored the Aaronic and Melchizedek Priesthoods. He also viewed the resurrected Moses, Elias and Elijah and received from them the vital keys and glorious doctrines associated with the Priesthood.

These are but a few of the remarkable and marvelous events that transpired during Joseph Smith's lifetime which we will discuss in this chapter. Truly he "lived great, and he died great in the eyes of God and his people" (D&C 135:3). He stands as a mighty colossus, remarkable in his gifts and callings in ushering in the final dispensation of the world—the Dispensation of the Fulness of Times.

THE DISPENSATION OF THE FULNESS OF TIMES

As far as we have any scriptural record, Paul, the New Testament apostle, was the first to use the expression, "the dispensation of the fulness of times." Although other prophets knew of this final era and rejoiced in the anticipation of it, it was Paul who wrote, "that in the dispensation of the fulness of times he [God] might gather together in one all things in Christ, both which are in heaven, and which are on earth; even in him" (Ephesians 1:10). This final dispensation would be marked by a wonderful gathering together of holy scriptures, covenant people, and everlasting truths.

Quoting the prophecy of Zenos, the Book of Mormon prophet Jacob compared the latter-day dispensation to a harvest of olives: "Wherefore, let us go to and labor with our might *this last time,* for behold the end draweth nigh, and *this is for the last time* that I shall prune my vineyard . . . dig about the trees, . . . that all may be nourished once again *for the last time*" (Jacob 5:62-63; emphasis added). This final nourishing began with the opening of this last dispensation and the calling of the Prophet Joseph Smith to bring forth the gospel during this wonderful and exciting period of the earth's temporal history.

Throughout the ages, prophets have looked forward to and spoken with great anticipation of the events relative to this last dispensation. Some of these events include the literal gathering of Israel and the restoration of the Ten Lost Tribes; Zion (the New Jerusalem) being built upon the American continent; Christ reigning personally upon the earth; and the earth being renewed and receiving its paradisiacal glory (see Tenth Article of Faith). This renewing process will accompany the Lord's Second Coming and will greatly change the earth from the way we know it now, as the Lord creates "a new heaven and a new earth" (Revelation 21:1). Prior to this time of awesome changes, however, great destructions will come upon the wicked.

The scriptures testify that: "As it was in the days of Noah, so it shall be also at the coming of the Son of Man" (JST, Matthew 24:44). In the days of Enoch and Noah, Enoch was called by God to cry repentance to the people of his city and to establish the Church among them. In process of time the righteous of Enoch's city were sanctified, established Zion, and were translated—while the wicked were destroyed by the flood. A similar scenario is taking place in the last days.

Joseph Smith was called to restore truths which had been lost to the world as a result of the Apostasy and to establish the Church and the stakes of Zion[2] as places of safety for the Saints of God. These places of refuge will provide protection for the righteous when the global destructions and calamities which have been prophesied of come upon the wicked (see D&C 112:24). These destructions will culminate not in a worldwide *flood* as in the days of Noah, but in an all-consuming *fire* (see D&C 63:34; also D&C 115:6)!

In explaining the Prophet's mission and the consequences that will befall those who will not hearken to his words and the words of his successors, the Lord declared:

> Wherefore, I the Lord, knowing the calamity which should come upon the inhabitants of the earth, called upon my servant Joseph Smith, Jun., and spake unto him from heaven, and gave him commandments. . . .
>
> For I am no respecter of persons, and will that all men shall know that the day speedily cometh; the hour is not yet, but is nigh at hand, when peace shall be taken from the earth, and *the devil shall have power over his own dominion.*
>
> *And also the Lord shall have power over his saints,* and shall reign in their midst, and shall come down in judgment upon Idumea, or the world (D&C 1:17, 35-36; emphasis added).

Wherefore the voice of the Lord is unto the ends of the earth, that all that will hear may hear: Prepare ye, prepare ye for that which is to come, for the Lord is nigh.... And the arm of the Lord shall be revealed; and the day cometh that *they who will not hear the voice of the Lord, neither the voice of his servants, neither give heed to the words of the prophets and apostles, shall be cut off from among the people* (D&C 1:11-12, 14; emphasis added).

By contrast, those who embrace the everlasting covenant and follow the apostles and prophets will not be cut off, but will be spared so that the promise may be fulfilled which the Lord made to Enoch saying, *"My people will I preserve"* (Moses 7:61; emphasis added). They will be preserved in the latter-day Kingdom that Daniel saw in vision.

Daniel prophesied of a Kingdom in the latter days that *"shall stand for ever"* (Daniel 2:44; emphasis added). This latter-day Kingdom is The Church of Jesus Christ of Latter-day Saints and the political kingdom of God—or Zion—that will grow out of her.

Since the latter-day kingdom of God shall stand forever, there will be no other dispensations. This is the dispensation of the fulness of times—all things will be fulfilled in these latter days. To bring about his work in this last dispensation and the gathering together of all things in one, the Lord called a remarkable young man whom he repeatedly and affectionately called "my servant Joseph".

JOSEPH SMITH—THE PREDICTED PROPHET

Joseph Smith's role in the final dispensation was of such marvelous magnitude that the ancient prophets spoke of him with great anticipation. For example,

Joseph who was sold into Egypt, spoke of a latter-day Seer who would not only bear his name, but who would also bear the name of his father, Joseph Smith, Sr.

Regarding this latter-day Seer and the great work God would bring forth through him, the Lord spoke to Joseph in Egypt and promised him:

> A seer will I raise up out of the fruit of thy loins, and unto him will I give power to bring forth my word unto the seed of thy loins; and not to the bringing forth of my word only, saith the Lord, but to the convincing them of my word, which shall have already gone forth among them in the last days;
>
> Wherefore the fruit of thy loins shall write, and the fruit of the loins of Judah shall write; and that which shall be written by the fruit of thy loins, and also that which shall be written by the fruit of the loins of Judah, shall grow together unto the *confounding of false doctrines,* and *laying down of contentions,* and *establishing peace* among the fruit of thy loins, and *bringing them to a knowledge* of their fathers in the latter days; and also *to the knowledge of my covenants,* saith the Lord.
>
> And out of weakness shall he be made strong, in that day when my work shall go forth among all my people, which shall restore them, who are of the house of Israel, in the last days.
>
> And that seer will I bless, and they that seek to destroy him shall be confounded; for this promise I give unto you; for I will remember you from generation to generation; and *his name shall be called Joseph, and it shall be after the name of his father;* and he shall be *like unto you;* for the thing which the Lord shall bring forth by his hand *shall bring my people unto salvation* (JST, Genesis 50:30-33; emphasis added).

Although we do not have this wonderful prophecy in the King James Version of the Bible, it is included in the Joseph Smith translation which appears in the appendix of the 1979 and subsequent editions of our LDS Bible.

This remarkable prophecy was also written upon the Brass Plates that Nephi obtained from Laban. Father Lehi was so impressed with these statements about a latter-day Joseph, he named his last son *Joseph.* He looked forward with great faith to the fulfillment of all of the prophecies regarding the last dispensation—a time when, through a latter-day prophet named Joseph, the Lord would initiate a marvelous work that would bring his seed to salvation (see 2 Nephi 3:3-25).

Brigham Young said that Joseph's whole ancestry were known and watched over by the Lord. He declared:

> It was decreed in the counsels of eternity, long before the foundations of the earth were laid, that he, Joseph Smith, should be the man in the last dispensation of this world, to bring forth the word of God to the people, and

receive the fulness of the keys and power of the Priesthood of the Son of God. The Lord had his eyes upon him, and upon his father, and upon his father's father, and upon their progenitors clear back to Abraham, and from Abraham to the flood, from the flood to Enoch, and from Enoch to Adam. He has watched that family and that blood as it has circulated from its fountain to the birth of that man. He was foreordained in eternity, to preside over this last dispensation.[3]

In a December 1834 blessing, Father Smith confirmed to his son that ancient Joseph in Egypt "looked after his posterity in the last days ... [and] sought diligently to know ... who should bring forth the word of the Lord [to them] and his eyes beheld thee, my son [Joseph Smith, Jr.]: [and] his heart rejoiced and his soul was satisfied."[4]

Others also knew of the Prophet Joseph Smith and the role he would play in the final dispensation. The resurrected Savior to the Nephites (3 Nephi 21:9-11), Moroni (Mormon, 8:14-16, 23-25), and John the Baptist (JST, John 1:20-22), all spoke of a great prophet who was to come.

In an interesting and enlightening book, entitled *His Name Shall Be Joseph,* Brother Joseph Fielding McConkie brings to our attention other ancient prophecies and traditions regarding a latter-day seer who would be raised up by the Lord and whose name would be Joseph. He also points out that the name *Joseph* in Hebrew has an important meaning.

The early Hebrew people had a custom of giving their children names of hope and inspiration. Frequently, people would be named by their parents only to be renamed by the Lord consistent with their special calling or stewardship. Brother McConkie explains, "In like manner Jacob, ('supplanter') was directed to change his name to Israel ('contender with God' or 'soldier of God'). (Gen. 32:28.) Thus those who are truly of Israel are those who march in the army of the Lord. Upon his first meeting with the earthly Messiah, Peter was told that he was to be 'called Cephas, which is, by interpretation, a seer, or a stone.' (JST, John 1:42)".

In tracing some of the traditions of the Jews and the Samaritans, Brother McConkie cites certain legends that point to a great latter-day prophet known by the name of "Messiah ben Joseph"—meaning "the anointed one who is the son of Joseph". He states:

It is in keeping with this tradition that in the legends of the Jews the great prophet of the last days is called Messiah ben Joseph. The name implies that this "anointed" leader will be of the tribe of Joseph and, as the variant title ben Ephraim indicates, he will be of Joseph through Ephraim. Such a tradition takes on additional meaning when it is remembered that both the Book of Mormon and Joseph Smith's Translation of the Bible preserve Joseph of Egypt's prophecy in which he announced that the latter-day seer would bear his name. (JST Gen. 50:33; 2 Ne. 3:15.)

Brother McConkie continues:

> The etymology of the name Joseph is usually given as "the Lord addeth" or "increaser". Though appropriate, such renderings have veiled a richer meaning associated with the name. In Genesis 30:24 where Rachel names her infant son "Joseph" the Hebrew text reads "ASAPH" which means *"he who gathers,"* "he who causes to return," or perhaps most appropriately *"God gathereth".* In the Samaritan tradition, Messiah ben Joseph is given the name "Taheb" meaning "The Restorer". (Bruce, F.F. Biblical Exegesis in the Qumran Texts, London: The Tyndal Press, 1960. Also see Schonfield, 129.) Thus the great prophet of the restoration was given the name that most appropriately points to his divine calling.[5]

In addition to the traditions cited above, the New Testament also contains several passages relative to a latter-day prophet of distinction. One of these is found in the book of John. It reads: "And this is the record of John, when the Jews sent priests and Levites from Jerusalem to ask him, Who art thou? And he confessed, and denied not; but confessed, I am not the Christ. And they asked him, What then? Art thou Elias? And he saith, I am not. *Art thou that prophet?* And he answered, No" (John 1:19-21; emphasis added). Brother McConkie explained this intriguing passage in these words:

But what Prophet did they have reference to? They had already asked if he was the Messiah, and if he was Elijah. Clearly they expected still another, one sufficiently well known that no other introduction was needed than "that prophet." A fourth question followed, "Who art thou?" To which John responded that he was "the voice of one crying in the wilderness" as had been prophesied by Isaiah. Still another question is forthcoming, "Why baptizeth thou then, if thou be not that Christ, nor Elias, *neither that prophet?"*

The questions asked by the Jews show their belief that Elijah, Christ, and a prophet were to come, and that, when they did, they would come baptizing like John. This belief is further illustrated in John 7:40-41, which reads "Many of the people therefore, when they heard this saying, said, Of a truth this is the Prophet. Others said, This is the Christ."

And thus we see that they were looking for both a *prophet*[6] and the *Christ*— both of whom would be called of God, having authority and power given them from him which would enable them to do many marvelous works in his name.

JOSEPH SMITH WAS CALLED OF GOD

Not only did many of the ancient prophets know and testify of Joseph, the latter-day seer, but they also knew that he would be an instrument in the hands of the Lord in restoring much that had been lost, thus laying the foundation for the culminating dispensation in the Lord's great plan of happiness.

Early in this dispensation when Moroni appeared to the young Prophet in his bedroom, he identified himself as, "an angel of God sent to bring the joyful tidings, that the covenant which God made with ancient Israel was at hand to be fulfilled, that the preparatory work for the second coming of the Messiah was speedily to commence; that the time was at hand for the gospel, in all its fulness to be preached in power, unto all nations that a people might be prepared for the Millennial reign. I (Joseph) was informed that I was chosen to be an instrument in the hands of God to bring about some of his purposes in this glorious dispensation."[7]

Because of the special keys, powers, and authority given to Joseph Smith, he was in a position to proclaim, "I step forth into the field to tell you what the Lord is doing, and what you must do, to enjoy the smiles of your Savior in these last days."[8] Joseph had communicated with the Lord and had seen and heard things from behind the veil that qualified him to tell us what we must do to stand approved before the Lord. Regarding his knowledge of eternal truths as compared to that which others of his day possessed, the Prophet exclaimed:

> Why be so certain that you comprehend the things of God, when all things with you are so uncertain. You are welcome to all the knowledge and intelligence I can impart to you. I do not grudge the world all the religion they have got: they are welcome to all the knowledge they possess.
>
> The sound saluted my ears— "Ye are come unto Mount Zion, and unto the city of the living God, the heavenly Jerusalem, and to an innumerable company of angels, to the general assembly and church of the firstborn, which are written in heaven, and to God the Judge of all, and to the spirits of just men made perfect, and to Jesus the Mediator of the new covenant" (Hebrew 12:22, 23, 24). What would it profit us to come unto the spirits of the just men, but to learn and come up to the standard of their knowledge?

Joseph Smith was announcing here that the heavens were opened to him, and, in consequence, he *knew* things that other did not. With other people, the things of God are tentative; with him there was certainty. He knew the mind and will of the Lord and could speak with authority regarding the Father's plan for the happiness of his children. He had been called of God to reveal again the new and everlasting covenant to prepare a generation for the blessings of a promised land, an everlasting seed, and divine protection—the triad blessings of Abraham mentioned in earlier chapters.

The apostles and the prophets who succeeded Joseph Smith have carried on in this work. They have added their own sacrifices and untiring efforts to the work of the dispensation of the fulness of times, for our Heavenly Father "also gave commandments to others, that they should proclaim these things unto the world; and all this that it might be fulfilled, which was written by the prophets... That faith also might increase in the earth; That mine everlasting covenant might be established; That the fulness of my gospel might be proclaimed by the weak and the simple unto the ends of the world, and before kings and rulers" (D&C 1:18, 21-23).

Truly the great work that the Prophet Joseph was instrumental in establishing has gone and will continue to go forth until it has "penetrated every continent, visited every clime, swept every country, and sounded in every ear, till the purposes of God shall be accomplished, and the Great Jehovah shall say the work is done."[10]

PROPHETS ARE GREATER THAN PREACHERS

Through the Prophet Joseph Smith, the *fulness* of the everlasting gospel was restored. This is an important point because had Joseph Smith simply followed the pattern of the preachers of his day—by limiting his preaching to the popular "hell fire and damnation" theme—it is not likely he would have been martyred. But Joseph Smith, the predicted prophet, was much more than a common preacher. He was the prophet appointed by God to restore the everlasting covenant in the final dispensation, and in doing so, he swam against the common religious currents of the day.

Joseph Smith was identified by the Lord as a prophet, seer, revelator and translator (see D&C 21:1). Among the gifts Joseph possessed were the gifts of seership and the gift to translate ancient records.[11] In addition, his prophetic gifts placed him on the level with prophets like Enoch, Abraham and Moses; but, as we will discuss later, no other prophet has brought forth more scriptural and doctrinal truths than has the Prophet Joseph Smith.

At this point you may be wondering what the difference is between a preacher and a prophet. A significant difference is the source of their information about God. Preachers are dependent on the Bible and the writings of the ancient prophets for information about God and his gospel plan—their sources constitute *secondary* sources.

Prophets and seers are spiritually mature, well seasoned men, who have traversed the pathway of the gospel—while in the flesh—back through the veil into the presence of God and other holy beings. They have *seen* and *heard* those things that are often called the "mysteries of God" (Alma 12:9). As a prophet, however, Joseph Smith is a *primary* source—he was not *dependent* on the writings of the ancient prophets. He had firsthand knowledge of the truth of which he spoke; he was a witness in his own right; his witness was *independent* of all others.

With secondary sources there is always the problem of distortion and misinterpretation of the intended message, as the confusion in the Christian world verifies. As a primary source of heavenly truths, Joseph was qualified to be a special witness of the resurrected Lord and of the things of the eternities (see Acts 1:22). This same qualifying knowledge—and the power which accompanies it—rests upon all who have been called as special witnesses of the Lord Jesus Christ.

The apostle Peter serves as yet another example of the power of a primary witness. Peter affirmed that his stewardship involved more than relying on the testimony of others when he proclaimed: "For we have not followed cunningly devised fables, when we made known unto you the power and coming of our Lord Jesus Christ, but were *eyewitnesses* of his majesty" (2 Peter 1:16; emphasis added). This testimony is common to apostles and prophets throughout the ages.

Not only did Peter see for himself, but he also heard the voice of the Father bearing record of the Son. Of this experience he testified: "For he [Jesus] received from God the Father honour and glory, when there came such a voice to him from the excellent glory, This is my beloved Son, in whom I am well pleased. And this voice which came from heaven *we heard,* when we were with him in the holy mount" (2 Peter 1:17-18; emphasis added).[12]

Even as Peter bore witness of the divine Sonship of Jesus, so also did Joseph Smith bear his official witness of the resurrected Lord: "And now, after the many testimonies which have been given of him, this is the testimony, last of all, which we give of him: That he lives! *For we saw him,* even on the right hand of God; and *we heard* the voice bearing record that he is the Only Begotten of the Father—That by him, and through him, and of him, the worlds are and were created, and the inhabitants thereof are begotten sons and daughters unto God" (D&C 76:22-24; emphasis added).

And thus we see that through the gift of seership associated with their callings Peter and Joseph Smith both had firsthand knowledge of the divinity and mission of the Savior. Thus they can be properly called both prophets and seers.

Regarding the marvelous blessing of having seers and prophets among us, the Prophet Joseph Smith declared:

> Wherefore, we again say, search the revelations of God; study the prophecies, and rejoice that God grants unto the world Seers and Prophets. They are they who *saw* the mysteries of godliness; they *saw* the flood before

it came; they *saw* angels ascending and descending upon a ladder that reached from earth to heaven; they *saw* the stone cut out of the mountain ...; they *saw* the Son of God come; ... they *saw* every mountain laid low and every valley exalted; ... they *saw* truth spring out of the earth; ... they *saw* the end of wickedness; ... they *saw* the end of the glorious thousand years; ... they *saw* the heaven and the earth flee away to make room for the city of God.... *And, fellow sojourners upon earth, it is your privilege to purify yourselves and come up to the same glory, and see for yourselves, and know for yourselves. Ask, and it shall be given you; seek and ye shall find; knock, and it shall be opened unto you.*"[13]

The restoration of the ordinances and keys of the Melchizedek priesthood make these marvelous blessings possible for us in our own dispensation. As we reflect upon the profound meaning of these promises, the words of the hymn, "The Spirit of God Like a Fire is Burning" echo in our minds and hearts— "And Ephraim be crowned with his blessing in Zion, As Jesus descends with his chariot of fire! We'll sing and we'll shout with the armies of heaven, Hosanna, hosanna to God and the Lamb! Let glory to them in the highest be given, Henceforth and forever, Amen and amen![14] These crowning spiritual blessings are before us! They are reserved for Latter-day Saints who qualify for the blessing in Zion!

The marvelous light which the Lord brought forth through Joseph Smith, stands as a powerful witness of his divine calling. Indeed he was much more than just a preacher of the gospel—he was a prophet of God in the fullest sense of the word. He was an eyewitness to the mysteries of God and was divinely called by him to usher in the dispensation of the fulness of times. This great restoration began with a humble prayer in a sacred grove of trees in the spring of 1820. In response to that plea, God the Father and his Son, Jesus Christ appeared to Joseph Smith. This glorious experience has become known as the "First Vision".

THE FIRST VISION

An interesting question can be asked at this point. How many times do you think Jesus and our Heavenly Father have *appeared together* on the earth? We know that on several occasions the voice of our Heavenly Father has been heard out of the heavens declaring that Jesus is his Son (Matthew 3:17; 2 Peter 1:17-18)—but there has only been *one time* when both the Father and the Son have appeared *together* to a man on the earth. This was when they appeared to Joseph Smith in the Sacred Grove![15]

The First Vision of the Prophet Joseph Smith is the literal fulfillment of a prophecy of Jeremiah, the Old Testament prophet. Seeing the terrible condition of spiritual ignorance that would exist in the last days he was led to exclaim, "Surely our fathers have inherited lies, vanity, and things wherein there is no profit. Shall a man make gods unto himself, and they are no gods? Therefore, *behold, I will this once cause them to know,* I will cause them to know mine hand and my might; and they shall know that my name is The Lord" (Jeremiah 16:19-21; emphasis added). Only *once* in the history of the world have the Father and the Son appeared together to man on the earth. This once was on a beautiful morning in the spring of 1820.

In Joseph's own words, he describes what happened that spring morning:

> After I had retired to the place where I had previously designed to go, having looked around me, and finding myself alone, I kneeled down and began to offer up the desires of my heart to God. I had scarcely done so, when immediately I was seized upon by some power which entirely overcame me, and had such an astonishing influence over me as to bind my tongue so that I could not speak. Thick darkness gathered around me, and it seemed to me for a time as if I were doomed to sudden destruction.
>
> But, exerting all my powers to call upon God to deliver me out of the power of this enemy which had seized upon me, and at the very moment when I was ready to sink into despair and abandon myself to destruction— not to an imaginary ruin, but to the power of some actual being from the unseen world, who had such marvelous power as I had never before felt in any being—just at this moment of great alarm, I saw a pillar of light exactly over my head, above the brightness of the sun, which descended gradually until it fell upon me.
>
> It no sooner appeared than I found myself delivered from the enemy which held me bound. When the light rested upon me I saw two Personages, whose brightness and glory defy all description, standing above me in the air. One of them spake unto me, calling me by name and said, pointing to the other—*This is My Beloved Son. Hear Him!"* (Joseph Smith—History, 1:15-17).

When he was able to gain his composure, Joseph asked the Lord which of all the churches he should join. He was told that he was to join none of them because none of the existing Christian churches represented the fulness of the gospel of Jesus Christ. Joseph was promised that if he would remain faithful, through him the Lord would restore again many truths that had been lost.

After the vision had closed, young Joseph, with the magnificent light of the First Vision still radiating from him, made his way to his home, where he spoke to his mother. He said, "As I leaned up to the fireplace, mother inquired what the matter was. I replied, 'Never mind, all is well—I am well enough off.' I then said to my mother, 'I have learned for myself that Presbyterianism is not true.'" (J.S.—History 1:20).

With the appearance of the Father and the Son to Joseph Smith in the First Vision, the cobwebs of misinformation about God that had accumulated during the Middle Ages were swept away, and the world would never be the same. With the First Vision and subsequent revelations the answers to mankind's oldest and most puzzling questions: Where did I come from? Why am I here? and Where am I going? were once again restored to the earth. What followed Joseph Smith's prayer in the spring of 1820 has forever illuminated our view of God, ourselves, others, life, and even the universe.

Young Joseph certainly did not go into the Sacred Grove seeking the restoration of the Holy Priesthood, the holy endowment, the sealing power, and other keys of the priesthood. He did not even know of their existence! This information came much later. As he prayed in the Sacred Grove, Joseph merely wanted to know about his own standing with the Lord and which of the several churches to join. His prayer was for personal guidance. The response, however, was of global and eternal significance!

JOSEPH SMITH TRANSLATED
THE BOOK OF MORMON

In the months and years following the First Vision, Joseph Smith experienced bitter resentment and persecution. He wrote, "It seems as though the adversary was aware, at a very early period of my life, that I was destined to prove a disturber and an annoyer of his kingdom; else why should the powers of darkness combine against me? Why the opposition and persecution that arose against me, almost in my infancy?" (J.S.—History 1:20).

Three years after the First Vision, alone in his bedroom, Joseph sought comfort and consolation from the Lord through prayer. On the evening of September 21, 1823, he experienced his next profound vision. Of this experience he relates:

> While I was thus in the act of calling upon God, I discovered a light appearing in my room, which continued to increase until the room was lighter than at noonday, when immediately a personage appeared at my bedside, standing in the air, for his feet did not touch the floor.
>
> He had on a loose robe of most exquisite whiteness. It was a whiteness beyond anything earthly I had ever seen; nor do I believe that any earthly thing could be made to appear so exceedingly white and brilliant. His hands were naked, and his arms also, a little above the wrist; so, also, were his feet naked, as were his legs, a little above the ankles. His head and neck were also bare. I could discover that he had no other clothing on but this robe, as it was open, so that I could see into his bosom.

Not only was his robe exceedingly white, but his whole person was glorious beyond description, and his countenance truly like lightning. The room was exceedingly light, but not so very bright as immediately around his person. When I first looked upon him, I was afraid; but the fear soon left me.

He called me by name, and said unto me that he was a messenger sent from the presence of God to me, and that his name was Moroni; that God had a work for me to do; and that my name should be had for good and evil among all nations, kindreds, and tongues, or that it should be both good and evil spoken of among all people.

He said there was a book deposited, written upon gold plates, giving an account of the former inhabitants of this continent, and the source from whence they sprang. He also said that the fulness of the everlasting Gospel was contained in it, as delivered by the Savior to the ancient inhabitants;

Also, that there were two stones in silver bows—and these stones, fastened to a breastplate, constituted what is called the Urim and Thummim—deposited with the plates; and the possession and use of these stones were what constituted 'seers' in ancient or former times; and that God had prepared them for the purpose of translating the book (J. S.—History 1:30-35).

In vision, Moroni showed Joseph a hill—the Hill Cumorah—which was not far from Joseph Smith Sr.'s farm. The following day Joseph went to the hill, and there he saw the plates for the first time.

After attempting to retrieve the plates and being unable to, he was again visited by Moroni. He explained that Joseph could not take the plates because the time had not come for them to be brought forth. Joseph was to mature physically and spiritually before the Lord would entrust them to him for their safe-keeping and translation. He was told that he should return to the hill each year on the same date (September 21st) until it was time for him to receive them.

When Joseph was 21 years of age he was finally able to receive the golden plates and, through the gift and power of God, was empowered to translate them into what we know today as The Book of Mormon: Another Testament of Jesus Christ.

AN ANCIENT RECORD WRITTEN FOR OUR DAY

The Book of Mormon not only provides a powerful second witness that Jesus is the Christ, but also stands as a testimony that Joseph Smith was indeed a prophet of God. This book, this marvelous work and a wonder, provides streams of vital knowledge, doctrines, powers, and teachings that flow together as a mighty healing river of light and truth.

From Joseph's account of the visitation of the angel Moroni, we learn that the Book of Mormon contains "the *fulness* of the everlasting gospel" (J.S.—History 1:34). Elder Bruce R. McConkie explained that this means that "The Book of Mormon is a record of God's dealings with a people who had the fulness of the gospel, and therefore the laws and principles leading to the highest salvation are found recorded in that book."[16]

The Book of Mormon is a record of several groups of people who came to ancient America—some of whom lived, as we have said, the highest orders of the priesthood at various times in their history. It is a handbook, a voice from the dust, as it were, declaring the conditions upon which we can enjoy peace in this world and eternal life in the world to come. It is the voice of two fallen nations (the Nephites and the Jaredites) that exhorts us not to make the same mistakes they did, but to come unto Christ and enjoy the fruits of righteous living that may be enjoyed in this life as well as in the life to come.

According to the Book of Mormon title page—which is itself "a literal translation, taken from the very last leaf...of the collection or book of plates"[17]—this ancient record "is an abridgment of the record of the people of Nephi, and also of the Lamanites—Written to the Lamanites, who are a remnant of the house of Israel; and also to Jew and Gentile...Which is to show unto the remnant of the House of Israel what great things the Lord hath done for their fathers; and that they may know the covenants of the Lord, that they are not cast off forever—And also to the convincing of the Jew and Gentile that JESUS is the CHRIST, the ETERNAL GOD, manifesting himself unto all nations."

The Book of Mormon was written as a witness of Jesus Christ and of the marvelous blessings that come to those who receive the new and everlasting covenant. It was also written as a warning to us of the destructions that come as a result of being lifted up in pride and rejecting the Lord and our covenants with him.

The Book of Mormon was revealed so that we might know the conditions upon which living upon the promised land of America is based. There are both promises and curses associated with the land "choice above all other land". We are warned that if the time ever comes that the voice of the people chooses evil, then is the time that great destructions will come upon them; the wicked will be swept off when they become sufficiently ripe in iniquity. Such was the case with the ancient inhabitants of this land and so will it be for us in our day if we reject the Holy One of Israel, Jesus Christ.

After viewing the destruction of his people the prophet Mormon exclaimed: "O ye fair ones, how could ye have departed from the ways of the Lord! O ye fair ones, how could ye have rejected that Jesus, who stood with open arms to receive you! Behold, *if ye had not done this, ye would not have fallen.* But behold, ye are fallen, and I mourn your loss" (Mormon 6:17-18; emphasis added). He later records that he has seen our day and that unless we repent we will meet with the same destruction (see Mormon 8:35-41).

On a happier note, we repeatedly are promised in the Book of Mormon that the righteous will be preserved and, not only will they be preserved, but they will be privileged to enter into the presence of the Lord. This profound knowledge gives us hope by providing a picture of what we can obtain if we will remain faithful to our gospel covenants.

In addition, the Book of Mormon is the means by which the Lord has restored many of the plain and precious gospel truths that were lost from the Bible—through ignorance, error and purposeful design—during the Great Apostasy, but that were retained in the records of the Nephite people (see 1 Nephi 13:26).

Plain and Precious Truths Restored in the Book of Mormon

Unlike the Bible, which has been translated many times (often by uninspired and designing men), the Book of Mormon was translated directly into English by a prophet of God. The Lord himself has given his testimony of the truthfulness of the Book of Mormon and of Joseph Smith's divine calling. He testified that Joseph was given "power from on high, by the means which were before prepared, to translate the Book of Mormon:

> Which contains a record of a fallen people, and the fulness of the gospel of Jesus Christ to the Gentiles and to the Jews also; Which was given by inspiration, and is confirmed to others by the ministering of angels, and is declared unto the world by them—Proving to the world that the holy scriptures are true, and that God does inspire men and call them to his holy work in this age and generation, as well as in generations of old; Thereby showing that he is the same God yesterday, today, and forever. Amen.
>
> Therefore, having so great witnesses, by them shall the world be judged, even as many as shall hereafter come to a knowledge of this work" (D&C 20:9-13).

The Lord then promised and warned that "those who receive it [the Book of Mormon] in faith, and work righteousness, shall receive a crown of eternal life; But those who harden their hearts in unbelief, and reject it, it shall turn to their own condemnation" (D&C 20:14-15).

The Book of Mormon was written by the ancient prophets who lived on this continent so that we might know what we need to do to be preserved in peace and safety now and in the eternities. In accomplishing this purpose, the Book of Mormon brings to light many important truths that strengthen our faith in Christ as well as our faith in the prophecies and promises that have been recorded by his chosen servants.

From its pages, we learn that there is a great plan of happiness prepared from before the foundation of the world and that Jesus Christ, the Son of God, is the central figure in that plan and has provided an infinite atonement for all those who would believe on him. We also learn the purpose of our mortal existence—we learn that Adam fell that men might be, and that men are that they might have joy. Through the various examples and illustrations given us we can see that, because our Father loves us he cannot allow mercy to rob justice, but if we will repent, mercy can *satisfy the demands of justice* and set us free to enjoy the gifts and blessings he has for us.

The Book of Mormon also proclaims that the Bible is not a closed canon, and attests to the reality of three great civilizations that once lived upon what we know as ancient America, and to the fact that they kept records of God's dealings with them. It also confirms the idea that there will be many other records that the Lord will yet bring forth as a testimony to the reality of his work.

Because many of the prophecies and promises recorded therein resemble and shed new light on many that are in the Bible, the Book of Mormon serves to confirm and affirm the reality of that holy book of scripture. In other words, it witnesses that the Bible is not a collection of myths and stories, but is a true record of God's dealings with Israel, his ancient covenant people, and that the promises made to Abraham will be literally fulfilled in the latter days.

The Book of Mormon is a reaffirmation of the Lord's loving promise: "Yea, they may forget, yet will I not forget thee, O house of Israel. Behold, I have graven thee upon the palms of my hands; thy walls are continually before me" (1 Nephi 21:15-16).

The Prophet Joseph Smith declared the Book of Mormon to be *"the most correct of any book on earth, and the keystone of our religion, and a man would get nearer to God by abiding by its precepts, than by any other book."*[18]

Drawing Nearer to God

You no doubt would find it very worthwhile to identify in the Book of Mormon those important precepts—or principles of truth—that will draw you to God. The most important principle taught therein is that you have a Heavenly Father who loves you and wants to bless, prosper, and protect you—forever. Righteousness and obedience qualify you for these blessings. On the other hand, the Book of Mormon also warns us that the disobedient will be swept off the land.

Many other magnetic rays of light and truth can draw you to God as you diligently search the Book of Mormon. The following are just a few other principles that I have extracted from 1 Nephi, the first book in the Book of Mormon. These examples are meant to be inspirational and instructive in helping you understand why Joseph Smith would say that by abiding by the precepts of the Book of Mormon you can draw nearer to God than by any other book. These principles

also emphasize the triad blessings of the covenant we have discussed earlier—
Land, Deliverance, and Seed.

1. "The tender mercies of the Lord are over all those whom he hath chosen, because of their faith, to make them mighty even unto the power of deliverance from their enemies" (1 Nephi 1:20) This is one of the major themes throughout the Book of Mormon.
2. Inasmuch as a people keep the Lord's commandments, they shall prosper in the land of promise, which is a land "choice above all other lands" (1 Nephi 2:20).
3. Inasmuch as a people rebel against the Lord, "they shall be cut off from [his] presence" (1 Nephi 2:21).
4. The Lord will never give us a commandment without providing the means for us to keep it. (1 Nephi 3:7).
5. The Spirit of the Lord will lead us step by step so that we can accomplish whatever we are asked to do. In most cases, we will not know at the beginning how we will succeed in the end (1 Nephi 4:6).
6. When others seek our forgiveness, we should frankly forgive them (1 Nephi 7:21).
7. Since Heavenly Father is always the same, we can approach him through repentance and prayer and we will find him. If we diligently seek for them, the Lord will reveal his mysteries unto us by the power of the Holy Ghost just as he did in times of old (1 Nephi 10:18-19).
8. "By small means the Lord can bring about great things" (1 Nephi 16:29).
9. The Lord esteemeth all flesh as one; but he that is righteous is favored of God (1 Nephi 17:35).
10. When a people become fully ripe in iniquity, they will be destroyed (1 Nephi 17:43).
11. Through sin people may reach a point where they are past feeling, a point where they are unable to *feel* the words of the Lord (1 Nephi 17:45; emphasis added).
12. If we will pray frequently, the Lord will show us great things (see 1 Nephi 18:3).
13. We are to liken the scriptures unto ourselves (1 Nephi 19:23).
14. All that fight against Zion shall be destroyed (1 Nephi 22:14).
15. The wicked shall destroy each other (1 Nephi 22:13).
16. "The righteous need not fear" (1 Nephi 22:17).
17. "The righteous shall not perish" (1 Nephi 22:19).

A similar list could be made from each of the books within the Book of Mormon. When you search this ancient, sacred record, you will find great treasures of knowledge and peace.

ADDITIONAL SCRIPTURES

The Book of Mormon is the first wave in a series of many records that have been and will be restored as a result of the great work begun by the Prophet Joseph Smith in the great Restoration of all things. As was mentioned earlier, during the lifetime of the Prophet, we received the Book of Mormon, the Joseph Smith Translation of the Bible, the Pearl of Great Price, and most of the sections found in the Doctrine and Covenants. But this is just a beginning to the revelations that the Lord will give to his people—as we are obedient to what we have and seek for "greater knowledge" even as Abraham of old (Abraham 1:2).

We are promised that, after we hearken to the precepts of the Book of Mormon, the Lord will bring forth many other records. These records will be accounts of other groups of the house of Israel who were led away, and in the Lord's own due time they will be read by all as he has promised,

> For behold, I shall speak unto the Jews and they shall write it; and I shall also speak unto the Nephites and they shall write it; and I shall also speak unto the other tribes of the house of Israel, which I have led away, and they shall write it; and *I shall also speak unto all nations of the earth and they shall write it.*
>
> *And it shall come to pass that the Jews shall have the words of the Nephites, and the Nephites shall have the words of the Jews; and the Nephites and the Jews shall have the words of the lost tribes of Israel; and the lost tribes of Israel shall have the words of the Nephites and the Jews.*
>
> And it shall come to pass that my people, which are of the house of Israel, shall be gathered home unto the lands of their possessions; and my word also shall be gathered in one. And I will show unto them that fight against my word and against my people, who are of the house of Israel, that I am God, and that I covenanted with Abraham that I would remember his seed forever (2 Nephi 29:12-14; emphasis added).

Regarding the Lord's speaking to all nations, and their writing his word, Alma explained: "The Lord doth grant unto all nations, of their own nation and tongue, to teach his word, yea, in wisdom, all that he seeth fit that they should have; therefore we see that the Lord doth counsel in wisdom, according to that which is just and true" (Alma 29:8).

Although the Lord may speak to all nations, it is through the children of Abraham that the *fulness* of the gospel is revealed (see Abraham 2:8-10). The fulness of sacred principles and powers will come to the world through the house of Israel—through the Bible, the Book of Mormon, and other records that will be revealed as part of the restoration of all things "spoken by the mouth of all his holy prophets since the world began" (Acts 3:21).

The simple but important truths given through such religious leaders as Mohammed, Buddha, Confucius, and Zoroaster may have been sufficient for the needs of their people during their time, but what they taught did not, nor does it now, represent the fulness of the everlasting covenant. Though they were without question inspired leaders,[19] they did not have priesthood authority, keys, or power as did the Prophet Joseph Smith and his successors.

What Joseph and his successors have received through the keys and powers of the priesthood has caused a glorious dawning of truth to burst forth upon a darkened world.

This new dawning has prepared the way for an even greater revelation of truth as the other records mentioned earlier are brought home to Zion. The following is a partial list of additional records that will yet be revealed in the due time of the Lord so that the fulness of his purposes and glory might be made manifest. This gathering of scriptures is an important part of the restoration which began through Joseph Smith, the prophet of the dispensation of gathering, the Dispensation of the Fulness of Times.

A More Complete Record of the Nephites

The plates Joseph Smith received from Moroni were an abridgment of all the records of the Nephites. Mormon said that he "made *this* record [the Book of Mormon] out of the plates of Nephi, and hid up in the hill Cumorah *all the records* which had been entrusted to me by the hand of the Lord, *save it were these few plates* which I gave unto my son Moroni" (Mormon 6:6; emphasis added). The Book of Mormon, then, was translated from the *few* plates that Mormon gave to Moroni.

Regarding the bulk of the Nephite records, Mormon explained:

And now there cannot be written in this book even a hundredth part of the things which Jesus did truly teach unto the people;

But behold the plates of Nephi do contain *the more part* of the things which he taught the people.

And *these things* have I written, which are *a lesser part* of the things which he taught the people; and I have written them to the intent that they may be brought again unto this people, from the Gentiles, according to the words which Jesus hath spoken.

And when they shall have received this, which is expedient that they should have first, to *try their faith,* and if it shall so be that they shall believe these things then shall the *greater things* be made manifest unto them.

And if it so be that they will not believe *these things,* then shall the *greater things* be withheld from them, unto their condemnation.

Behold, I was about to write them, all which were engraven upon the plates of Nephi, but the Lord forbade it, saying: *I will try the faith of my people.*

Therefore I, Mormon, do write the things which have been commanded me of the Lord (3 Nephi 26:6-12; emphasis added).

What we have now in the Book of Mormon can have a great impact on our lives for good as we liken it unto ourselves so that it may "be for our profit and learning" (1 Nephi 19:23). As we do so, our hearts will be prepared to receive the greater truths which have been withheld from us for a time.

Concerning the rest of the Nephite records, Brigham Young provides an interesting description of a time when Joseph Smith was permitted to view them in their resting place in the Hill Cumorah. President Young related,

I believe I will take the liberty to tell you of another circumstance that will be as marvelous as anything can be. This is an incident in the life of Oliver Cowdery, but he did not take the liberty of telling such things in meeting as I take. I tell these things to you, and I have a motive for doing so. I want to carry them to the ears of my brethren and sisters, and to the children also, that they may grow to an understanding of some things that seem to be entirely hidden from the human family. Oliver Cowdery went with the Prophet Joseph when he deposited these plates. Joseph did not translate all of the plates; there was a portion of them sealed, which you can learn from the Book of Doctrine and Covenants. When Joseph got the plates, the angel instructed him to carry them back to the hill Cumorah, which he did. Oliver says that when Joseph and Oliver went there, the hill opened, and they walked into a cave, in which there was a large and spacious room. He says he did not think, at the time, whether they had the light of the sun or artificial light; but that it was just as light as day. They laid the plates on a table; it was a large table that stood in the room. Under this table there was a pile of plates as much as two feet high, and there were altogether in this room more plates than probably many wagon loads; they were piled up in the corners and along the walls. The first time they went there the sword of Laban hung upon the wall; but when they went again it had been taken down and laid upon the table across the gold plates; it was unsheathed, and on it was written these words: "This sword will never be sheathed again until the kingdoms of this world become the kingdom of our God and his Christ." I tell you this as coming not only from Oliver Cowdery, but others who were familiar with it, and who understood it just as well as we understand coming to this meeting, enjoying the day, and by and by we separate and go away, forgetting most of what is said, but remembering some things. So is it with other circumstances in life. I relate this to you, and I want you to understand it. I take this liberty of referring to those things so that they will not be forgotten and lost.[20]

At another time, Brigham Young reported that, "It was stated to me by David Whitmer in the year 1877 that Oliver Cowdery told him that the Prophet Joseph and himself had seen this room and that it was filled with treasure, and on a table therein were the breastplate and the sword of Laban, as well as the portion of the gold plates not yet translated, and that these plates were bound by three small gold rings."[21] Orson Pratt said that when the temple is completed in the New Jerusalem, the records from the Hill Cumorah will be transported there.[22]

The Sealed Portion of the Book of Mormon.

Two-thirds of the plates that Joseph Smith received from Moroni were sealed, and Joseph was commanded not to translate them. Concerning this sealed portion, the Lord stated:

> For the book shall be sealed by the power of God, and the revelation which was sealed shall be kept in the book until the own due time of the Lord, that they may come forth; for behold, they reveal all things from the foundation of the world unto the end thereof. And the day cometh that the words of the book which were sealed shall be read upon the house tops; and they shall be read by the power of Christ; and all things shall be revealed unto the children of men which ever have been among the children of men, and which ever will be even unto the end of the earth (2 Nephi 27:10-11).

What a wondrous day it will be when you and I can read of the marvelous truths which deal with information from the foundation of the world to the end thereof! The further light that will come to us through a more complete record of the Nephites can only bring us greater joy and happiness.

The Book of Joseph

As was mentioned earlier, in addition to the Book of Mormon, Joseph Smith was also an instrument in the Lord's hands in bringing forth other ancient records. After receiving and carefully perusing the papyrus scrolls that were a part of the Michael Chandler exhibit,[23] he determined that they were the writings of Abraham and Joseph, the son of Jacob. The Book of Abraham in the Pearl of Great Price was translated from some of the papyri manuscripts of Abraham. To our present knowledge, the papyri of Joseph were never translated and have been lost. However, we can expect that eventually we will have full accounts of Abraham and Joseph's writings (as well as the writings of all the ancient patriarchs) as a part of the Lord's restoration of all things.

The Records of the Ancient Patriarchs

From the book of Abraham, translated by the Prophet Joseph Smith, we learn that Abraham had the records of those who came before him: "But the records of the fathers, even the patriarchs, concerning the right of Priesthood, the Lord my

God preserved in mine own hands; therefore a knowledge of the beginning of the creation, and also of the planets, and of the stars, as they were made known unto the fathers, have I kept even unto this day, and I shall endeavor to write some of these things upon this record, for the benefit of my posterity that shall come after me" (Abraham 1:31; see also Ephesians 1:10).

We expect in days to come to have access to the writings of Adam, Enoch, and Noah which have been lost from our present scriptures. What wondrous words of truth and light will they contain? Undoubtedly our eyes have not seen, nor our ears heard, nor has it even entered into our hearts the marvelous things known by our ancient forefathers, but someday ... we will know.

The Lost Books of the Bible

Under the heading of "lost books", the LDS Bible Dictionary provides a description of books that are not in our Bible. The Lord has not explicitly said that these missing books, will be brought back as a part of the promised "restitution of all things, which God hath spoken by the mouth of all his holy prophets since the world began" (Acts 3:21). However, a restitution of the writings of the holy prophets seems contemplated by this statement. We, therefore, can have hope according to his promise that in the Lord's own time and way these things will be restored to us just as fast as we are able to receive them.

The Record of Enoch

One of the books which is missing from our present Bible is the record of Enoch. We know very little about this record. However, in the Doctrine and Covenants, we find this reference: "And Adam stood up in the midst of the congregation; and, notwithstanding he was bowed down with age, being full of the Holy Ghost, predicted whatsoever should befall his posterity unto the latest generation. *These things were all written in the book of Enoch*, and are to be testified of in due time" (D&C 107: 56-57; emphasis added). I, with you, wait with eager anticipation for the Lord to reveal the writings of this great prophet whom he used as a type for Joseph Smith's work of the latter days (see Moses 7).

The Testimonies of the Twelve Apostles

Not only have many records been lost from the Old Testament but there have been many which have been lost from the New Testament as well. Among the many other records yet to come forth, we expect the lost records of the ancient twelve apostles (see 1 Nephi 13:39-40; Ephesians 1:10).

The New Testament contains the testimonies of only two of Jesus' original apostles—Matthew and John. Mark and Luke were not apostles. The coming forth of the Book of Mormon has helped to restore those plain and precious truths that were lost and to prepare us to receive an even greater fulness of knowledge regarding the Savior and his mission. The Book of Mormon explains to us, however, that each of the twelve apostles wrote his testimony, and in due time we will have their written records. A heavenly messenger explained to Nephi that,

> thou hast beheld that the book [the Bible] proceeded forth from the mouth of a Jew; and when it proceeded forth from the mouth of a Jew it contained the fulness of the gospel of the Lord, of whom the twelve apostles bear record; and they bear record according to the truth which is in the Lamb of God. Wherefore, these things go forth from the Jews in purity unto the Gentiles, according to the truth which is in God. And after they go forth *by the hand of the twelve apostles of the Lamb*, from the Jews unto the Gentiles, thou seest the formation of that great and abominable church, which is most abominable above all other churches; for behold, they have taken away from the gospel of the Lamb many parts which are plain and most precious; and also many covenants of the Lord have they taken away (1 Nephi 13:24-26; emphasis added).

The angel explained that because these plain and precious parts have been taken away, including that which was written by the twelve apostles, "an exceedingly great many do stumble, yea, insomuch that Satan hath great power over them" (2 Nephi 13:29).

The Record of John the Baptist

In the Bible we have partial records of John the apostle. John the Baptist also kept records of his ministry. In the Doctrine and Covenants Joseph records Jesus' promise that we will yet have a full record of John the Baptist who "saw and bore record of the fulness of my glory, and the fulness of John's record is hereafter to be revealed.... And it shall come to pass, that if you are faithful you shall receive the *fulness of the record of John*" (D&C 93:6, 18; emphasis added). What exciting truths must lie within this record, written by he who was identified as "one crying in the wilderness, prepare ye the way of the Lord, make his paths straight" (Matthew 3:3; also Isaiah 40:3).

Records of the Other Tribes of Israel

Since the Lord's people have always been commanded to be a record-keeping people, and it is probable that each of the tribes of Israel has kept records, it is also probable that they will be made known in due time.

Regarding the other colonies of Israel that have no doubt kept sacred records, Nephi said, "There are many who are already lost from the knowledge of those who are at Jerusalem. Yea, the more part of all the tribes have been led away; and they are scattered to and fro upon the isles of the sea; and whither they are none of us knoweth, save that we know that they have been led away" (1 Nephi 22:4). What will the records of the tribes of Reuben, Dan, Gad and Asher and the other tribes of Israel contribute to our knowledge of the great plan of happiness? We will wait with eager anticipation to see what truths these records will reveal!

Important Truths Have Been and Will Yet Be Revealed

In our ninth Articles of Faith we read "We believe all that God has revealed, all that He does now reveal, and we believe that He will yet reveal many great and important things pertaining to the Kingdom of God."

The Restoration of the gospel began with revelation and will continue with revelation as additional keys, powers, and doctrines are given to the Saints.

Regarding the various angels who appeared and revealed keys to the Prophet in the in the early days of the Restoration, we read:

> And again, what do we hear? Glad tidings from Cumorah! Moroni, an angel from heaven, declaring the fulfillment of the prophets—the book to be revealed. A voice of the Lord in the wilderness of Fayette, Seneca county, declaring the three witnesses to bear record of the book! The voice of Michael on the banks of the Susquehanna, detecting the devil when he appeared as an angel of light! The voice of Peter, James, and John in the wilderness between Harmony, Susquehanna county, and Colesville, Broome county, on the Susquehanna river, declaring themselves as possessing the keys of the kingdom, and of the dispensation of the fulness of times!
>
> And again, the voice of God in the chamber of old Father Whitmer, in Fayette, Seneca county, and at sundry times, and in divers places through all the travels and tribulations of this Church of Jesus Christ of Latter-day Saints! And the voice of Michael, the archangel; the voice of Gabriel, and of Raphael, and of divers angels, from Michael or Adam down to the present time, all declaring their dispensation, their rights, their keys, their honors, their majesty and glory and the power of their priesthood; giving line upon line, precept upon precept; here a little, and there a little; giving us consolation by holding forth that which is to come, confirming our hope! (D&C 128:20-21).

Our present dispensation will continue to unfold and roll forward into the Millennium—there will be more angels, more scripture, more truth and light. We have a habit in the Church, however, of thinking that the great era of restoration has passed, that we have received most of what the Lord has to reveal. The truth of the matter is that the Restoration has just begun, as Elder Bruce R. McConkie has pointed out:

> It is our habit in the Church—a habit born of slovenly study and a limited perspective—to think of the restoration of the gospel as a past event and of the gathering of Israel as one that, though still in process, is in large measure accomplished. It is true that we have the fulness of the everlasting gospel in the sense that we have those doctrines, priesthoods, and keys which enable us to gain the fulness of reward in our Father's kingdom. It is also true that a remnant of Israel has been gathered; and a few of Ephraim and Manasseh (and some others) have come into the Church and been restored to the knowledge of their Redeemer.
>
> *But the restoration of the wondrous truths known to Adam, Enoch, Noah, and Abraham has scarcely commenced.* The sealed portion of the Book of Mormon is yet to be translated. All things are not to be revealed anew until the Lord comes. The greatness of the era of restoration is yet ahead. And as to Israel herself, her destiny is millennial; the glorious day when "the kingdom and dominion, and the greatness of the kingdom under the whole heaven, shall be given to the people of the saints of the most High" (Dan. 7:27) is yet ahead. We are now making a beginning, but the transcendent glories and wonders to be revealed are for the future. Much of what Isaiah—prophet of the restoration—has to say is yet to be fulfilled.[24]

It is so important to remember that there is much yet ahead. There is before us "A time to come in which nothing shall be withheld, whether there be one God or many gods, they shall be manifest. All thrones and dominions, principalities and powers, shall be revealed and set forth upon all who have endured valiantly for the gospel of Jesus Christ. And also, if there be bounds set to the heavens or to the seas, or to the dry land, or to the sun, moon, or stars—All the times of their revolutions, all the appointed days, months, and years, ... shall be revealed in the days of the dispensation of the fulness of times" (D&C 121:28-31).

Brigham Young prophesied that we will yet entertain angels in our homes:

> By-and-by Zion will be built up; Temples are going to be reared, and the holy Priesthood is going to take effect and rule, and every law of Christ will be obeyed, and he will govern and reign King of nations as he now does King of Saints.... About the time that the Temples of the Lord will be built and Zion is established—pretty nigh this time, you will see, (those who are faithful enough,) the first you know, there will be strangers in your midst, walking with you, talking with you: they will enter into your houses and eat and drink with you, go to meeting with you, and begin to open your minds,

as the Saviour did the two disciples who walked out in the country in days of old.

About the time the Temples are ready, the strangers will be along and will converse with you, and will inquire of you, probably, if you understand the resurrection of the dead. You might say you have heard and read a great deal about it, but you do not properly understand it; and they will then open your minds and tell you the principles of the resurrection of the dead and how to save your friends: they will point out Scriptures in the Old and New Testament, in the Book of Mormon, and other revelations of God, saying, "Don't you recollect reading so and so, that saviors should come up on Mount Zion?" &c.; and they will expound the Scriptures to you . . . and open your minds, and teach you of the resurrection of the just and the unjust, of the doctrine of salvation: they will use the keys of the holy Priesthood, and unlock the door of knowledge, to let you look into the palace of truth. You will exclaim, That is all plain: why did I not understand it before? and you will begin to feel your hearts burn within you as they walk and talk with you.

. . . Before this work is finished, a great many of the Elders of Israel in Mount Zion will become pillars in the Temple of God, to go no more out: they will eat and drink and sleep there; and they will often have occasion to say— "Somebody came into the Temple last night; we did not know who he was, but he was no doubt a brother, and told us a great many things we did not before understand. He gave us the names of a great many of our forefathers that are not on record, and he gave me my true lineage and the names of my forefathers for hundreds of years back. He said to me, You and I are connected in one family: there are the names of your ancestors; take them and write them down, and be baptized and confirmed, and save such and such ones, and receive of the blessings of the eternal Priesthood for such and such an individual, as you do for yourselves." This is what we are going to do for the inhabitants of the earth. When I look at it, I do not want to rest a great deal, but be industrious all the day long; for when we come to think upon it, we have no time to lose, for it is a pretty laborious work.[25]

No power of evil can stop the work of the Lord and these things from coming to pass. As the Lord declared, "As well might man stretch forth his puny arm to stop the Missouri river in its decreed course, or to turn it up stream, as to hinder the Almighty from pouring down knowledge from heaven upon the heads of the Latter-day Saints" (D&C 121:33). We should feel great gratitude for what the Lord has given us and great anticipation for what yet is to be revealed.

THE RESTORATION OF THE AARONIC PRIESTHOOD

While Joseph Smith was translating the Book of Mormon, he and Oliver Cowdery, who was acting as scribe, encountered many passages that emphasized the necessity for everyone to be baptized. Even though Joseph had seen the Father and the Son in the First Vision, and had received many heavenly manifestations, he recognized that he still needed to be baptized. He knew that none of the churches at that time had the authority. He also recognized that he did not have God's authorization to perform this sacred ordinance for others. Accordingly, as he had done so many times before, Joseph took the matter to the Lord in earnest prayer. He and Oliver retired to the seclusion of the Susquehanna River, which was not far from where they were staying, and there they knelt in humble supplication to the Lord.

In answer to their earnest petition, a heavenly messenger appeared, who explained that he was John, the same who is called John the Baptist in the New Testament. He then laid his hands upon the heads of Joseph and Oliver, and pronounced these words: "Upon you my fellow servants, in the name of Messiah I confer the Priesthood of Aaron, which holds the keys of the ministering of angels, and of the gospel of repentance, and of baptism by immersion for the remission of sins" (D&C 13; J.S—History 1:69). John explained that this Aaronic Priesthood did not have the power to lay on hands for the gift of the Holy Ghost, but that this power would be given them later. They were then commanded to baptize one another, after which they were directed to ordain each other to the Aaronic Priesthood (see J.S.—History 1:70-72).

When John the Baptist appeared to Joseph and Oliver, he explained that he was acting under the direction of Peter, James, and John, the ancient apostles who held the keys of the higher priesthood which is called the Melchizedek Priesthood. John told Joseph and Oliver that in due time, the Priesthood of Melchizedek would be conferred upon them (see Headnote D&C 13; also D&C 1:72).

THE MELCHIZEDEK PRIESTHOOD WAS RESTORED

A short time after the restoration of the Aaronic Priesthood, Peter, James, and John appeared to Joseph and Oliver and conferred upon them the "keys of the kingdom" that are associated with the Melchizedek Priesthood (D&C 128:20).

The power and authority of this higher, Melchizedek Priesthood, is to hold "The keys of all the spiritual blessings of the church—To have the privilege of receiving the mysteries of the kingdom of heaven, to have the heavens opened unto them, to commune with the general assembly and church of the Firstborn, and to enjoy the communion and presence of God the Father, and Jesus the mediator of the new covenant" (D&C 107:18-19).

Accordingly, through the ordinances of the Melchizedek Priesthood, the mysteries of godliness are made manifest. "And without the ordinances thereof, and the authority of the priesthood, the power of godliness is not manifest unto men in the flesh; For without this no man can see the face of God, even the Father, and live" (D&C 84:21-22). In other words, without the authority and ordinances of the Melchizedek Priesthood—including a fulness of the sealing ordinances—we cannot "see the face of God" (D&C 84:19-22; also see *Teachings*, pp. 150-51). As has been mentioned in previous chapters, this crowning ordinance and blessing are bestowed upon members of the Church according to the pattern set forth in the Doctrine and Covenants (see D&C 68:12; 105:35-36; D&C 93:1).

MOSES RESTORED THE KEYS TO GATHER ISRAEL

Before latter-day Israel can receive the blessings and powers of the priesthood described above, they must be gathered in from among the nations of the world—they must become members of the restored Church. Accordingly, after having received the keys of the Aaronic and Melchizedek Priesthoods, the keys to this great missionary activity were restored to Joseph and Oliver by the resurrected Moses—he who led Israel anciently out of the bondage of Egypt.

We learn of the life and mortal ministry of Moses from the biblical books of Exodus, Leviticus, Numbers, and Deuteronomy. His work, however, has extended beyond his mortal ministry.

From the Book of Mormon (see Alma 45:19) we learn that Moses did not die as was reported in Deuteronomy 34, but was taken to heaven without tasting death. Thus when he came during New Testament times, in company with the prophet Elijah, to the Mount of Transfiguration he was a *translated* being. Since the resurrection had not yet taken place, it was necessary that he be translated so he could lay his hands upon the heads of Peter, James, and John and bestow upon them the keys to the gathering of Israel.

As a *resurrected* being, Moses returned again to the earth on April 3, 1836, after the dedication of the Kirtland Temple. There he appeared to the Prophet Joseph Smith and Oliver Cowdery and bestowed upon them "the keys of the gathering of Israel from the four parts of earth, and the leading of the ten tribes from the land of the north" (D&C 110:11). After this bestowal of authoritative keys, the great missionary work was commissioned to go forth with the power and authority of God.

The missionary work of the Church today is unparalleled in the history of the world—a consequence of authoritative keys given to the Prophet Joseph Smith to bring about the gathering together of all things in Christ. This gathering has special meaning as it applies to the restoration of scattered Israel in the last days.

ISRAEL WILL BE GATHERED AND SANCTIFIED

Even as the Lord literally scattered Israel among all nations anciently, so he will literally gather Israel in the last days to the lands of her inheritance and into the everlasting covenant. Moses had to restore keys of the priesthood to the Prophet Joseph Smith so that Israel could be gathered through the power of God and the process of sanctification of latter-day Israel set in motion.

In his teachings Joseph Smith cited many references pertaining to the restoration of Israel in the latter days: Joel 2:32; Isaiah 26:20, 21; Jeremiah 31:12; Psalms 1:5; Ezekiel 34:11-13. Of these verses the Prophet said: "These are testimonies that the Good Shepherd will put forth His own sheep, and lead them out from all nations where they have been scattered in a cloudy and dark day, to Zion [in America], and to Jerusalem [in the Holy Land]; besides many more testimonies which might be brought."[26] This restoration of Israel will result in the realization of all the blessings associated with the new and everlasting covenant—both temporal and spiritual.

As Joseph Smith has explained, much of what Isaiah, Jeremiah, Ezekiel and other prophets have said was couched in their vision of the latter days when Israel would be brought back into the covenant and sanctified in the eyes of the Lord. That Latter-day Saints are latter-day Israel is an important fact to remember. This truth is one of the great keys of knowledge that has been revealed through the Prophet Joseph Smith (see Galatians 3:27-29; D&C 109:60). Latter-day Israel is now being gathered home; and, according to the prophecies, her eventual sanctification will be glorious (see Isaiah 4).

When people join the Church, they become eligible, through continued righteousness, for all the glorious blessings of their fathers: Abraham, Isaac and Israel (see D&C 132:31). Indeed, people generally are moved upon to embrace the gospel because they *are* the blood of Israel and have a lineal right to these blessings (see D&C 64:36; *Teachings*, pp. 149-50). When scattered Israel hears the truths of the gospel, they respond, as it were, to a homing instinct to reach to the intelligence, light and truth that is to be found in the gospel of Jesus Christ.

As we read of the latter-day gathering of Israel, there are few gospel topics which carry more pathos, more hope and more joy. Our Heavenly Father will remember Israel in the last days, and she will be gathered with tender mercies:

"But, behold, Zion hath said: The Lord hath forsaken me, and my Lord hath forgotten me—but he will show that he hath not. For can a woman forget her sucking child, that she should not have compassion on the son of her womb? Yea, they may forget, yet will I not forget thee, O house of Israel. Behold, *I have graven thee in the palms of my hands;* thy walls are continually before me" (1 Nephi 21:14-16; emphasis added). The reference to the palms of his hands is no doubt referring to the symbols of his crucifixion, the prints of the nails.

The power behind the gathering of Israel in the last days lies within the atoning sacrifice of our Lord, Jesus Christ. Because of his atoning sacrifice for us, we, as latter-day Israel, can be washed clean, sanctified, and prepared to enter back into the presence of the Lord God of Abraham, Isaac, and Jacob. Jesus will gather Israel and make all things whole again—that which was broken will be fixed, that which was lost will be found, those who have suffered will be healed!

Nowhere is the need to be healed felt more acutely than among the various known fragments of the house of Israel both ancient and modern. Each of these fragments—the Native Americans (Lamanites), the Jews and the Mormons—have suffered persecutions and oppression at the hands of their enemies. Until Israel is fully gathered into Zion and Jerusalem she will continue to suffer at the hands of her enemies. In her scattered condition among the Gentiles she is described as being like a slave, having chains about her neck.

In regards to the nature of these chains, in a series of questions and answers, the Prophet explained, "What are we to understand by Zion loosing herself from the bands of her neck? We are to understand that the scattered remnants are exhorted to return to the Lord from whence they have fallen; which if they do, the promise of the Lord is that he will speak to them, or give them revelation. . . . *The bands of her neck are the curses of God upon her, or the remnants of Israel in their scattered condition among the Gentiles*" (D&C 113:9-10; emphasis added; see end of chapter Figure 8-B, Wheels Turn).

These chains around the neck of latter-day Israel apply not only to scattered Israel among the Gentiles, but also to members of the Church while we are subject to worldly powers. We too are bound down by man-made political, economic, and religious chains, and will continue to be so until Zion is more fully established, and we are "independent above all other creatures beneath the celestial world" (D&C 78:14).

In the meantime, the Lord has counseled us to be patient and bear the injustices that exist until he comes. He has commanded us, "Wherefore, be subject to the powers that be, until he reigns whose right it is to reign, and subdues all enemies under his feet" (D&C 58:22; see also Articles of Faith 1:12).

Even though we are not now free from troubling times, we, as children of Israel have the promise of an eventual Zion—we will yet lie down in green pastures and beside the still waters (see Psalm 23). In pastoral language, the Lord has promised:

And I will bring them from the people, and gather them from the countries, and will bring them to their own land, and feed them upon the mountains of Israel by the rivers, and in all the inhabited places of the country.

I will feed them in good pasture, and upon the high mountains of Israel shall their fold be: there shall they lie in a good fold, and in a fat pasture shall they feed upon the mountains of Israel.

I will feed my flock, and I will cause them to lie down, saith the Lord God.

I will seek that which was lost, and bring again that which was driven away, and will bind up that which was broken, and will strengthen that which was sick: but I will destroy the fat and the strong; I will feed them with judgment" (Ezekiel 34:13-16).

Besides Ezekiel's prophecy, we can read the prophecies of many other Old Testament prophets who have spoken at length regarding the eventual restoration of Israel. Isaiah, who is frequently called the prophet of the restoration, has spoken extensively on this subject (see Isaiah 2:2-3; 4:2-4; 11:1-16; 29:14; 35:1-10). These passages are well worth reading and marking.

Much more will be said in the next chapter about the blessings that will come to the house of Israel after they are gathered and sanctified in Zion and her stakes—the places of defense and refuge. For now it is important to remember that all the prophets looked forward to the dispensation of the fulness of times as a time when the children of Israel would be gathered in from their long dispersion among the nations of the earth and receive further light and truth about the wonderful, peaceful, glorious blessings of the covenant.

The return of Moses and the restoration of the keys to the gathering of Israel marked a significant milestone in the fulfillment of these blessings.

ELIAS RESTORED THE KEYS TO THE BLESSINGS OF ABRAHAM

After Moses appeared in the Kirtland temple and restored the keys of the gathering of Israel the Doctrine and Covenants records that, "Elias appeared, and committed the dispensation of the gospel of Abraham, saying that in us and our seed all generations after us should be blessed" (D&C 110:12).

The keys restored by Elias are associated with the promises made to couples who marry in the temples of the Lord for time and all eternity. Ordained sealers perform this sacred ordinance in the many temples of The Church of Jesus Christ of Latter-day Saints which increasingly dot the lands and countries of the world.

Worthy couples who are married for time and eternity are given the promises of Abraham, Isaac, and Jacob conditioned upon their faithfulness. If they remain true to their covenants, they are promised all the blessings of a never-ending kingdom including the promise of an everlasting seed—children as numerous as the sands upon the seashore or the stars in the heavens (see Genesis 22; Abraham 2; D&C 132:30-33)—even as Abraham of old.

ELIJAH RESTORED THE KEYS TO THE SEALING POWERS

After the appearance of Moses and Elias, the prophet Elijah appeared and gave Joseph and Oliver the keys of the priesthood whereby "he shall plant in the hearts of the children the promises made to the fathers, and the hearts of the children shall turn to their fathers" (D&C 2:2; D&C 110:13-16).[27]

This return of Elijah marked the fulfillment of the very last prophecy in the Old Testament (Malachi 4:5-6). Malachi prophesied that before the Second Coming, the Lord would send Elijah the Prophet. Much more will be said of the priesthood keys restored by him in the next chapter.

For now, let it be said that the spirit and power of Elijah is the spirit that works to perfect and seal of the Saints—as families—to eternal life. Not only is the spirit of Elijah the driving force behind genealogical research, but it is also the spirit and power that moves upon the Saints motivating them to pursue a path leading to eternal life. As they are touched by the spirit of Elijah they will be prompted to have family prayer, family home evening, receive patriarchal blessings, and be married in the temple. And of course, they will also want to do work for the dead.

Those who yield to the spirit and power of Elijah, will, in proper time, find their calling and election made sure and will be sealed to eternal life by the authoritative keys restored by him.[28] They will be recipients of the fulness of the blessings of the everlasting covenant—the blessings of an everlasting *Land* inheritance, *Deliverance* from all enemies and an everlasting *Seed*—that have been promised to the faithful children of Adam, Enoch, Noah and Abraham in the last days.

Eternal Family Relationships

A discussion of the priesthood keys restored through the Prophet Joseph Smith would be incomplete without a discussion of another important doctrine restored through him—the doctrine of eternal family relationships.

Through the revelations the Prophet Joseph Smith received, we have gained a fulness of light and truth regarding the obligations and blessings associated with the new and everlasting covenant. Among the really astounding doctrines that have come to us through the Prophet is the promise of an everlasting seed. The knowledge that we now have about this sacred promise was revealed to the Prophet in various stages, but it is most clearly explained in D&C 132. In this section, the Lord clarifies the role family relationships play in the everlasting covenant.

Over time, as the Spirit directed him, Joseph Smith revealed this sacred information about eternal family relationships to his close associates, among whom was one of the Twelve Apostles, Parley P. Pratt. To him, Joseph explained the eternal nature of marriages when they are sealed by the priesthood of God. As you read the following account of what Joseph revealed to Elder Pratt, check your own mind and heart for the confirming whisperings of the Spirit. This information will enlighten your mind, enlarge your soul, and will become delicious to you. These words are important seeds of truth that will grow into a "tree springing up unto everlasting life" (Alma 32:28, 41).

Elder Pratt recorded in his journal, "In Philadelphia I had the happiness of once more meeting with President Smith, and of spending several days with him and others, and with the saints in that city and vicinity." He continued by saying,

> During these interviews he taught me many great and glorious principles concerning God and the heavenly order of eternity. It was at this time that I received from him the first idea of eternal family organization, and the eternal union of the sexes in those inexpressibly endearing relationships which none but the highly intellectual, the refined and pure in heart, know how to prize, and which are at the very foundation of everything worthy to be called happiness.
>
> Till then I had learned to esteem kindred affections and sympathies as appertaining solely to this transitory state, as something from which the heart must be entirely weaned, in order to be fitted for its heavenly state.
>
> It was Joseph Smith who taught me how to prize the endearing relationships of father and mother, husband and wife; of brother and sister, son and daughter.
>
> *It was from him that I learned that the wife of my bosom might be secured to me for time and all eternity; and that the refined sympathies and affections which endeared us to each other emanated from the fountains of divine eternal love.* It was from him that I learned that we might cultivate these affections, and grow and increase in the same to all eternity; while the result of our endless union would be an offspring as numerous as the stars of heaven, or the sands of the sea shore.
>
> It was from him that I learned the true dignity and destiny of a son of God, clothed with an eternal priesthood, as the patriarch and sovereign of his countless offspring. It was from him that I learned that the highest dignity of

womanhood was, to stand as a queen and priestess to her husband, and to reign for ever and ever as the queen mother of her numerous and still increasing offspring....

Yet, at that time, my dearly beloved brother, Joseph Smith, had barely touched a single key; had merely lifted a corner of the veil and given me a single glance into eternity."[29]

As an interesting postscript to Elder Pratt's glorious and awe-inspiring journal entry, we should remember that the Latter-day Saints are the only Christian church that formally teaches eternal marriage relationships such as Elder Pratt described. The sectarian Christian world has left out of their heaven the very thing that almost every heart yearns an strives for—to be loving and to be loved, eternally.

The restored gospel of Jesus Christ, the everlasting covenant, promises us that man and woman can be together forever as husband and wife. Joseph Smith, through the revelations given to him by God, placed love and romance at the very center of the gospel, for exaltation in the celestial kingdom cannot be gained except through the organization of eternal marriage and eternal families.

Joseph had the marriage covenant in mind when he explained that, "Happiness is the object and design of our existence; and will be the end thereof, if we pursue the path that leads to it; and this path is virtue, uprightness, faithfulness, holiness, and keeping all the commandments of God."[30]

Truly, the everlasting covenant does provide for sweet and supernal eternal romantic love. In the words of Elder Boyd K. Packer, romantic love "is the very key to the plan of salvation." He said, "No experience can be more beautiful, no power more compelling, more exquisite."[31] "Romantic love," he explained, "is not only a part of life, but literally a dominating influence of it. It is deeply and significantly religious. There is no abundant life without it. Indeed, the highest degree of the Celestial Kingdom is unobtainable in the absence of it."[32]

What we have just considered is an important part of the wonderful theology that the Lord restored through the Prophet Joseph Smith. These and other principles of truth that the Lord revealed to him were so much more lofty than those commonly held that it was difficult for people to comprehend him.

THE PROPHET'S DISTINCTIVE TEACHINGS

Among the significant contributions of the Prophet Joseph Smith are his teachings, divinely revealed doctrines and principles that he delivered fearlessly and authoritatively.

The following are representative of these:

- "I have always declared God to be a distinct personage, Jesus Christ a separate and distinct personage from God the Father, an that the Holy Ghost was a distinct personage and a Spirit: and these three constitute three distinct personages and three Gods."[33]
- "The fundamental principles of our religion are the testimony of the Apostles and Prophets, concerning Jesus Christ, that He died, was buried, and rose again the third day, and ascended into heaven; and all other things which pertain to our religion are only appendages to it. But in connection with these, we believe in the gift of the Holy Ghost, the power of faith, the enjoyment of spiritual gifts according to the will of God, the restoration of the house of Israel, and the final triumph of truth."[34]
- "We consider that God has created man with a mind capable of instruction, and a faculty which may be enlarged in proportion to the heed and diligence given to the light communicated from heaven to the intellect; and that the nearer man approaches perfection, the clearer are his views, and the greater his enjoyments, till he has overcome the evils of his life and lost every desire for sin...."[35]
- "The devil could not compel mankind to do evil; all was voluntary.... God would not exert any compulsory means, and the devil could not."[36]
- "The spirit is a substance;... but...it is more pure, elastic and refined matter than the body;...and will exist separate from the body...."[37]
- "At the first organization in heaven we were all present, and saw the Savior chosen and appointed and the plan of salvation made, and we sanctioned it. We came to this earth that we might have a body and present it pure before God in the celestial kingdom."[38]
- "It is contrary to the economy of God for any member of the Church, or any one, to receive instruction for those in authority, higher than themselves; therefore you will see the impropriety of giving heed to them; but if any person have a vision or visitation from a heavenly messenger, it must be for his own benefit and instruction; for the fundamental principles, government, and doctrine of the Church are vested in the keys of the kingdom."[39]
- The elements are eternal...every principle proceeding from God is eternal... If the soul of man had a beginning, it will surely have and end...."[40]
- "Love is one of the chief characteristics of Deity, and ought to be manifested by those who aspire to be the sons of God. A man filled with the love of God, is not content with blessing his family alone, but ranges through the whole world, anxious to bless the whole human race."[41]
- "The doctrine of baptizing little children, or sprinkling them, or they must welter in hell, is a doctrine not true, not supported in Holy Writ, and is not consistent with the character of God. All children are redeemed by the blood of Jesus Christ...."[42]

One of my favorite teachings of the Prophet Joseph Smith is his desire for the Saints to soberly, solemnly search for truth and righteousness. He taught that "A fanciful and flowery and heated imagination beware of; because the things of God are of deep import; and time, and experience, and careful and ponderous and solemn thoughts can only find them out. Thy mind, O man! if thou wilt lead a soul unto salvation, must stretch as high as the utmost heavens, and search into and contemplate the darkest abyss, and the broad expanse of eternity—thou must commune with God. How much more dignified and noble are the thoughts of God, than the vain imaginations of the human heart! None but fools will trifle with the souls of men."[43]

Joseph Smith was one who followed his own counsel. His mind soared to the highest heavens and he contemplated the darkest abyss. He communed with God in such intimate ways and his knowledge was so expansive, there were none who could comprehend fully what Heavenly Father had revealed to him.

NONE COULD COMPREHEND JOSEPH SMITH

Because of the magnitude and the exalted nature of the truths he received, it was difficult for Joseph Smith to communicate to others what the Lord had given him. Regarding Joseph's knowledge of the things of God, Elder John Taylor said, "No wonder that Joseph Smith should say that he felt himself shut up in a nut-shell, there was no power of expansion, it was difficult for him to reveal and communicate the things of God, because there was no place to receive them. What he had to communicate was so much more comprehensive, enlightened and digni-fied than that which the people generally knew and comprehended, it was diffi-cult for him to speak; he felt fettered and bound, so to speak, in every move he made."[44]

The revelations Joseph received were filled with increasing magnitudes of knowledge, light, and truth. Lorenzo Brown reported that Joseph Smith said: "After I got through translating the Book of Mormon, I took up the Bible to read with the Urim and Thummim. I read the first chapter of Genesis, and *I saw the things as they were done.* I turned over the next and the next, and *the whole passed before me like a grand panorama; and so on chapter after chapter until I read the whole of it. I saw it all!"*[45] What a marvelous thing it must have been for the young prophet to witness in detail such wonderful and sacred events.

Joseph Smith received revelation from the Lord the same way the ancient prophets did—through the voice of inspiration, the Urim and Thummim, the min-istering of angels, and by open vision. Of all these sources of light and truth, Joseph explained, "An open vision will manifest that which is more important"[46]

Besides the visions of the Father and the Son in the Sacred Grove, the visi-tation of Moroni in his bedroom and at the Hill Cumorah, and Moses, Elias and

Elijah in the Kirtland Temple, the Prophet Joseph Smith received communication from many other notable figures of the past. He also knew Nephi, Mormon and Moroni by sight. He described the apostle Paul as being, "about five feet high; very dark hair; dark complexion; dark skin; large Roman nose; sharp face; small black eyes, penetrating as eternity; round shoulders; a whining voice, except when elevated, and then it almost resembled the roaring of a lion. He was a good orator, active and diligent, always employing himself in doing good to his fellow man."[47]

Regarding Joseph Smith's intimate knowledge of the ancient prophets, President John Taylor stated: "The principles [of knowledge] which he had, placed him in communication with the Lord, and not only with the Lord, but with the ancient apostles and prophets; such men, for instance, as Abraham, Isaac, Jacob, Noah, Adam, Seth, Enoch, and Jesus and the Father, and the apostles that lived on this continent as well as those who lived on the Asiatic continent. He seemed to be as familiar with these people as we are with one another."[48]

Not all of Joseph's visions are recorded in our church history documents; some that are written are not well-known in the Church. For example, before he ever received the plates, Moroni showed Joseph in vision, the habits and customs of the Nephites.

As was mentioned previously, each year for four years after his initial view of the plates in Cumorah, Joseph returned to the hill and was met by Moroni. During these visits, the angel showed him in *open vision* many of the things that he would need to know in order to translate the Book of Mormon—some of which he would later share with his family.

Following his regular visits with Moroni, Joseph would meet with his family around the fireplace, and would provide them with the most detailed accounts about the ancient inhabitants of America from the information that he had received from Moroni in open vision. "During our evening conversations," wrote his mother, "Joseph would occasionally give us some of the most amusing recitals that could be imagined. He would describe the ancient inhabitants of this continent, their dress, mode of traveling, and the animals upon which they rode; their cities, their buildings, with every particular; their mode of warfare; and also their religious worship. This he would do with as much ease, seemingly, as if he had spent his whole life among them."[49]

These experiences of Joseph Smith set him apart from all other men then living. Other attributes of Joseph made him extraordinary and made it difficult for others to relate and comprehend him. For example, when he was under the spirit of revelation, several people reported that his physical appearance changed in remarkable ways. Before his martyrdom, in multiple meetings, he transferred priesthood keys, authority, and ordinances to the Twelve Apostles. In one of those meetings, President Wilford Woodruff said that Joseph's, "face was as clear as amber and he was covered with a power [I have] never seen in [an instant] in the flesh before."[50]

Orson Pratt described Joseph's countenance as the spirit of revelation fell upon him: "I had the great privilege, when I was in from my missions, of boarding the most of the time at his house, so that I not only knew him as a public teacher, but as a private citizen, as a husband and father. I witnessed his earnest and humble devotions both morning and evening in his family. I heard the words of eternal life flowing from his mouth, nourishing, soothing, and comforting his family, neighbors, and friends. *I saw his countenance lighted up as the inspiration of the Holy Ghost rested upon him, dictating the great and most precious revelations now printed for our guide.* I saw him translating, by inspiration, the Old and New Testaments, and the inspired Book of Abraham from Egyptian papyrus."[51]

Brigham Young, Joseph's successor to the presidency of the Church, gave a similar account of how Joseph's appearance changed when he was under the spirit of revelation: "Those who were acquainted with him knew when the Spirit of revelation was upon him, for his countenance wore an expression peculiar to himself while under that influence. He preached by the Spirit of revelation, and taught in his council by it, and those who were acquainted with him could discover it at once, for at such times there was a peculiar clearness and transparency in his face."[52]

When I read of the change in Joseph's countenance when he was under the influence of the Holy Spirit, I am reminded of Moses' appearance when he descended the holy mount. The Bible records that "Moses wist not that the skin of his face shone while he talked with [God]." Because the skin of his face shone with the light of the Lord, the people were afraid to come before Moses, so he wore a vail over his face when he talked to them, but when he went before the Lord, he took the vail off his face (Exodus 34:29-34). Joseph Smith was identified by Joseph in Egypt as being a man like Moses (see D&C 28:2; 2 Nephi 3:9). It is fascinating that the same light and spiritual powers that were with Moses when he was receiving revelations from the Lord, were also with Joseph Smith. This similarity is yet another confirming witness that the Prophet Joseph Smith was a man like Moses who communed with the Lord face to face (see 2 Nephi 3:8-9; D&C 103:16).

Joseph's revelations lighted the dark and gloomy world so that we truly now can see "things as they are, and as they were, and as they are to come" (D&C 93:24). Without this latter-day revelation, we would only see hints of truth and glimmers of light in the fragments of the world's religions. As President Joseph F. Smith declared, we find "relics of Christianity" which "date back ... beyond the flood, independent of ... the Bible."[53] Latter-day Saints are therefore unsurprised but instead are enriched whenever discoveries are made which show how the

Lord grants "unto all nations" to teach a portion of "his word" (Alma 29:8).

Regarding the uniqueness of his mission and the extraordinary circumstances surrounding his divine calling, Joseph Smith remarked, "I rejoice in hearing the testimony of my aged friends. You don't know me; you never knew my heart. No man knows my history. I cannot tell it: I shall never undertake it. I don't blame any one for not believing my history. If I had not experienced what I have, I could not have believed it myself."[54]

President George Q. Cannon also expressed his belief that none could fully comprehend the Prophet Joseph Smith when he said, "The Saints could not comprehend Joseph Smith; the Elders could not; the Apostles could not. They did do a little towards the close of his life; but his knowledge was so extensive and his comprehension so great that they could not rise to it. It was so with President Young; and I may say it is so with the leaders of the Church now. It is a continual labor on their part to lift the people up to the comprehension of the will of God and His purposes connected with his work. The people are bound down by their traditions, and because of this it is rarely that you can get even the Elders to see the propriety of certain things."[55]

Of the Prophet's uniqueness, Elder Wilford Woodruff said: "Brother Joseph used a great many methods of testing the integrity of men; and he taught a great many things which, in consequence of tradition, required prayer, faith, and a testimony from the Lord, before they could be believed by many of the Saints. His mind was opened by the visions of the Almighty, and the Lord taught him many things by vision and revelation that were never taught publicly in his days; for the people could not bear the flood of intelligence which God poured into his mind."[56]

Because of Joseph's unique and divine calling, he was shown many things that were unknown to others. His knowledge and intelligence made it difficult for others to really know and relate with him. President Brigham Young affirmed this idea when he exclaimed: "Who can justly say ought against Joseph Smith? I was as well acquainted with him, as any man. I do not believe that his father and mother knew him any better than I did. I do not think that a man lives on the earth that knew him any better than I did; and I am bold to say that, Jesus Christ excepted, no better man ever lived or does live upon this earth" (JD 9:332).

As a seer Joseph became the Revelator of the truths of the eternities. President Young said the Prophet Joseph had the "happy faculty" of communicating things "often in a single sentence throwing...light into the gloom of ages..in one blending flood of heavenly intelligence."[57] His many doctrinal contributions truly qualify him to be called exceptional, remarkable, and extraordinary!

At another time Elder Woodruff stated: "There is not so great a man as Joseph standing in this generation. The Gentiles look upon him and he is like a bed of gold concealed from human view. They know not his principles, his spirit, his wisdom, his virtues, his philanthropy, nor his calling. His mind, like Enoch's expands as eternity, and only God can comprehend his soul." (Journal History, 9 April 1837). As an example of the degree of intelligence that God poured into his mind, Joseph said, *"Could you gaze into heaven five minutes, you would know more than you would by reading all that ever was written on the subject."*[58]

For how long a time did Joseph Smith have the privilege of gazing into the heavens? On how many different occasions? Would the duration of his visionary experiences be measured by minutes or hours? The revelations the Lord gave him were not just momentary flashes of light. According to Philo Dibble, who was present in the room at the time, the vision of the three degrees of glory took more than an hour. Only a fragment of that vision is presently recorded in the Doctrine and Covenants (D&C 76). Together Joseph and Sidney saw that glorious manifestation. Of the circumstances involved Brother Dibble, reported:

> During the time that Joseph and Sidney were in the spirit and saw the heavens open, there were other men in the room, perhaps twelve, among whom I was one during a part of the time—probably two-thirds of the time—I saw the glory and felt the power, but did not see the vision.
>
> The events and conversation, while they were seeing what is written (and many things were seen and related that are not written) I will relate as minutely as is necessary.
>
> Joseph would, at intervals, say: "What do I see?" as one might say while looking out the window and beholding what all in the room could not see. Then he would relate what he had seen or what he was looking at. Then Sidney replied, "I see the same." Presently Sidney would say, "what do I see?" and would repeat what he had seen or was seeing, and Joseph would reply, "I see the same."
>
> This manner of conversation was repeated at short intervals to the end of the vision, and during the whole time not a word was spoken by any other person. Not a sound nor motion made by anyone but Joseph and Sidney, and it seemed to me that they never moved a joint or limb during the time I was there, which I think was over an hour, and to the end of the vision.
>
> Joseph sat firmly and calmly all the time in the midst of a magnificent glory, but Sidney sat limp and pale, apparently as limber as a rag, observing which, Joseph remarked, smilingly, "Sidney is not used to it as I am."[59]

At the conclusion of this vision, Joseph and Sidney were told *not* to write what they had seen while they were yet in the Spirit. In the revelation that was written, they mentioned that they saw things which "surpass all understanding in glory and in might, and in dominion." They then wrote words of great promise and assurance to us, the readers of the revelation.

We, too, may see what they saw, but the vision is "only to be seen and understood by the power of the Holy Spirit, which God bestows on those who *love him, and purify themselves* before him; To whom he grants this privilege of *seeing and knowing for themselves;* That through the power and manifestation of the Spirit, *while in the flesh,* they may be able to bear his presence in the world of glory. And to God and the Lamb be glory, and honor, and dominion forever and ever. Amen (D&C 76:114-119; emphasis added).

How would you like to have been in the room with Brother Dibble when this vision was shown to Joseph and Sidney? You probably would have been very quiet and reverent for the entire hour, too. Perhaps in the near future, we will have the opportunity of witnessing these kinds of dramatic displays of the power of God. From all the promises we have been discussing in previous chapters, we certainly can hope for these kinds of blessings. The frequency and extent of these experiences for which most of us have no basis for comparison truly testify to the Prophet's uniqueness and to the inability of people to comprehend him.

THE PROPHET OPENED THE HEAVENS FOR OTHERS

Not only was Joseph extraordinary in what the Lord revealed to him, but he was also given the remarkable power show others the visions of the eternities. Zebedee Coltrin spoke of one such occasion when he was with the Prophet:

> Once after returning from a mission to Kirtland, I met Brother Joseph, who asked me if I did not wish to go with him to a conference at New Portage, Ohio. The party consisted of Presidents Joseph Smith, Sidney Rigdon, Oliver Cowdery and me. Next morning at New Portage, I noticed that Joseph seemed to have a far off look in his eyes, or was looking at a distance. Presently he stepped between Brother Cowdery and me, and taking us by the arm said, "Let's take a walk."
>
> We went to a place where there was some beautiful grass, and grapevines and swamp birch interlaced. President Joseph Smith then said, "Let us pray."
>
> We all three prayed in turn—Joseph, Oliver and me. Brother Joseph then said, "Now brethren, we will see some visions."
>
> Joseph lay down on the ground on his back and stretched out his arms, and we laid on them. The heavens gradually opened, and we saw a golden throne, on a circular foundation, and on the throne sat a man and a woman, having white hair and clothed in white garments. Their heads were white as snow, and their faces shone with immortal youth. They were the two most beautiful and perfect specimens of mankind I ever saw. Joseph said, "They are our first parents, Adam and Eve."

Adam was a large broad shouldered man, and Eve, as a woman, was as large in proportion.[60]

In connection with the above account, Brother Coltrin also mentioned that, "In the Kirtland Temple I have seen the power of God as it was on the day of Pentecost, and cloven tongues of fire have rested on the brethren, and they have spoken in other tongues as the Spirit gave them utterance. I saw the Lord high and lifted up. The angels of God rested upon the Temple and we heard their voices singing heavenly music."

Because of the keys of presidency he held, Joseph was also authorized to explain to others the meaning of their spiritual experiences. For example, Heber C. Kimball recorded at one time he was in a place in England in which he felt feelings that he had never experienced before. He said,

> But I did not know at the time what it meant. I went through a town called Chadburn, beyond Clithero. Before I went there, some persons told me that there was no use in my going, and asked me what I wanted to go to Chadburn for, saying it was the worst place in the country; for the sectarian priests had preached there faithfully thirty years without making any impression. Notwithstanding that, I went, and preached once, and baptized twenty-five persons, where the priests had not been able to do a thing. I went through the streets of that town feeling as I never before felt in my life. *My hair would rise on my head as I walked through the streets, and I did not then know what was the matter with me. I pulled off my hat, and felt that I wanted to pull off my shoes, and I did not know what to think of it.* When I returned, I mentioned the circumstance to brother Joseph, who said: *"Did you not understand it? That is a place where some of the old Prophets traveled and dedicated that land, and their blessing fell upon you."*[61]

PEOPLE WHO LOVE DARKNESS STRIKE OUT AT BEARERS OF LIGHT

The gospel is the great sifter of people, even as Jesus said (see Matthew 10:34-37). Joseph Smith was a colossal bearer of light and truth which caused people to love him or to hate him. People who were offended by his words of truth struck out at him fulfilling the statement of the Savior when he said, "And this is the condemnation [of the world], that light is come into the world, and men loved darkness rather than light, because their deed were evil (John 3:19; D&C 10:21; D&C 29:45).

When Joseph revealed deep truths to some people who ought to have rejoiced in what he had to say, they would often turn on him—they chose to walk "in darkness at noonday" (D&C 95:6). One of the early apostles, Orson F. Whitney, wrote of this pervasive principle:

> Among those to whom Joseph confided ... was his bosom friend, Heber C. Kimball. Well knowing the integrity of his heart, so many times tested and found true, he felt that he ran no risk in opening to Heber's eyes the treasured mysteries of his mighty soul.
>
> But why careful, among so many friends, to select only a few as the recipients of such a favor? Would not the Saints have died to a man in defense of their Prophet—God's seer and revelator? Alas, none knew so well as Joseph the frailty of man, the inherent weakness and wickedness of the human heart.
>
> *"Many men," said he, "will say, 'I will never forsake you, but will stand by you at all times.' But the moment you teach them some of the mysteries of the kingdom of God that are retained in the heavens, and are to be revealed to the children of men when they are prepared for them, they will be the first to stone you and put you to death. It was this same principle that crucified the Lord Jesus Christ, and will cause the people to kill the prophets in this generation."*
>
> What! would even the Saints have so done? Did not some of those who *were* Saints then, so do?
>
> Had not Joseph said many times—are not men now living who heard him say: *"Would to God, brethren, I could tell you who I am! Would to God I could tell you what I know! But you would call it blasphemy, and there are men upon this stand who would want to take my life."*
>
> *"If the Church," said he, "knew all the commandments, one-half they would reject through prejudice and ignorance."*
>
> No wonder, then, that he should choose his confidants, for their sakes no less than his own. For these also are Joseph's words: *"When God offers a blessing, or knowledge to a man, and he refuses to receive it, he will be damned."*
>
> *Revelation is ever the iconoclast of tradition,* and such is the bigotry of man, his natural hatred of the new and strange, as opposed to his personal interests or private views, that the very lives of those whose mission is to introduce and establish new doctrines, though designed as a blessing to humanity, are ever in danger from those whose traditions would thus be uprooted and destroyed.
>
> Joseph was not a coward. It was he who said that a coward could not be saved in the kingdom of God.[62]

From this powerful quotation we can learn an important principle: when truth is offered to us, even though it may seem strange in view of our present traditions, it is vital that we consider it and cling to it. In the words of Paul, we are expected to "prove all things; [and] hold fast [to] that which is good" (1 Thessalonians 5:21). By recognizing and holding to truth when we hear it, we truly qualify as men and women of faith.

Joseph was unflinching when God revealed to him startling truths. Since we are called as Israel of the latter days, we too must be responsive to truth—especially truths that fly in the face of our worldly traditions. If the world is in a state of spiritual sickness, and we spend our time and energies trying to conform to its values, what does that make us? You can answer this question on your own. As for Joseph, as one called to lead modern Israel out of spiritual Babylon, he did not conform to the world around him—he was willing to stand out. He was not a coward, as the above quotation mentions, and we must not be, either!

Joseph Smith—The Witness

Certainly Joseph Smith was not a coward. He never flinched when it came to revealing new truth. He was called to be the witness of the Father and the Son, and all the truths associated with the Restoration.

Joseph was the Lord's forerunner for the Second Coming. He came before to stand as a witness of he who is to come. As a testimony of his role as witness in the last dispensation, Joseph quoted the Savior who said, "When these tribulations should take place, it [the gospel of the kingdom] should be committed to a man who should be *a witness* over the whole world; the keys of knowledge, power and revelations should be revealed *to a witness* who should hold the testimony to the world."[63]

In the Doctrine and Covenants we read a similar description given by the Lord himself: "I, the Lord, am God, and have given these things unto you, my servant Joseph Smith, Jun., and have commanded you that you should stand as a witness of these things.... But this generation shall have my word through you" (D&C 5:2, 10). Perhaps the most important knowledge we have gained through him is an increased understanding of the life, mission and Atonement of the Savior and how the everlasting covenant blesses our lives in this world and in the world to come.

Elder Neal A. Maxwell reminds us that it is through the Prophet and Seer, Joseph Smith, that we have received the most complete information about the central theme of the gospel of Jesus Christ—our Lord's atoning sacrifice. Elder Maxwell said,

Through Joseph have come translations and revelations which confirmed and described, as never before, the reality of the glorious Atonement, in which, so few really believe today. It is the central act of all human history! Very few words have come directly from Jesus about his specific and personal suffering during that agonizing but emancipating atonement. Almost all of these precious few words come to us through the Prophet Joseph! Jesus truly did bleed at every pore. He trembled because of pain. He suffered both body and spirit. He pled that he might not shrink, or pull back, from performing the Atonement. He finally finished his preparations unto the children of men. Meek Jesus let his will be "swallowed up in the will of the Father"! (Mosiah 15:7). Even in the midst of his astonishing, personal triumph, Jesus, true to his premortal promise, still gave all the glory to the Father. (D&C 19:18-19; Moses 4:2)[64]

Joseph Smith was and is a colossus, a giant standing at the head of this last dispensation—who, like Jesus, directed the honor and glory of his work to the Father of mankind. His position at the head of this final dispensation demanded both in life and in death that he be about his Father's business.

Of Joseph Smith's work in mortality, the Lord declared: "I will give unto him a commandment that *he shall do none other work*, save the work which I shall command him. And I will make him great in mine eyes; for *he shall do my work*. And he shall be great like unto Moses, whom I have said I would raise up unto you, to deliver my people, O house of Israel" (2 Nephi 3:8-9; emphasis added). Though he did not succeed in everything he attempted, Joseph never failed in performing that which he was commanded to do. Shortly before his martyrdom he said, "I never told you that I was perfect; but *there is no error in the revelations which I have taught.*"[65]

Because of his unique calling, Joseph's standing and position is above all other apostles and prophets of our time. President Young explained this strong doctrine:

> Joseph Smith holds the keys of this last dispensation, and is now engaged behind the vail in the great work of the last days. I can tell our beloved brother Christians who have slain the Prophets and butchered and otherwise caused the death of thousands of Latter-day Saints, the priests who have thanked God in their prayers and thanksgiving from the pulpit that we have been plundered, driven, and slain, and the deacons under the pulpit, and their brethren and sisters in their closets, who have thanked God, thinking that the Latter-day Saints were wasted away, something that no doubt will mortify them—something that, to say the least, is a matter of deep regret to them—namely, that no man or woman in this dispensation will ever enter into the celestial kingdom of God without the consent of Joseph Smith. From the day that the Priesthood was taken from the earth to the winding-up scene of all things, every man and woman must have the certificate of

Joseph Smith, junior, as a passport to their entrance into the mansion where God and Christ are—I with you and you with me. I cannot go there without his consent. He holds the keys of that kingdom for the last dispensation—the keys to rule in the spirit-world; and he rules there triumphantly, for he gained full power and a glorious victory over the power of Satan while he was yet in the flesh, and was a martyr to his religion and to the name of Christ, which gives him a most perfect victory in the spirit-world. He reigns there as supreme a being in his sphere, capacity, and calling, as God does in heaven. Many will exclaim,— "Oh, that is very disagreeable! It is preposterous! We cannot bear the thought!" But it is true.[66]

Though there are some who would cast aspersions on the Prophet, Brother Robert Millet reminds us that: "the God of heaven has called and approved Joseph Smith; those who attempt to mar the name and image of the Prophet of the Restoration will eventually answer to God himself for their actions. It was President George Albert Smith who observed: 'Many have belittled Joseph Smith, but those who have will be forgotten in the remains of mother earth, and the odor of their infamy will ever be with them, but honor, majesty, and fidelity to God, exemplified by Joseph Smith and attached to his name, will never die.'"[67]

Joseph's life, mission, and knowledge grew in a "spiritual crescendo."[68] This latter-day prophet saw angels, received visions, and performed miracles in great number. During his ministry he laid the foundation of the great work of the everlasting covenant. He taught the doctrine of Christ, and he gave us what we, who are living during this final era of the earth's history, need to know to find eternal life.

If we are to receive the knowledge of God—the knowledge of truth and the knowledge of the things that we must do to work out our salvation—we must accept the divine calling of Joseph Smith and those presidents of the Church who have followed him. Joseph Smith was the agent of the Lord. He was the representative, the instrumentality through whom the Lord gave the truth about himself and his laws to all men in all the world in our time—the dispensation of the fulness of times.

A dying Brigham Young's last words were, "Joseph! Joseph! Joseph!" He was about to be with his beloved Joseph once again![69] I too love the Prophet Joseph Smith. I love his teachings. I am eternally grateful for the knowledge restored to the earth through him—that we are the children of God, that we can be participants in an everlasting covenant that has been prepared for us whereby we can return joyously to our heavenly home.

I find myself eagerly and anxiously responding to Joseph's call to "go forward and not backward. Courage, brethren; and on, on to the victory! Let your hearts rejoice, and be exceedingly glad. Let the earth break forth into singing. Let the dead speak forth anthems of eternal praise to the King Immanuel, who hath ordained, before the world was, that which would enable us to redeem them out of their prison; for the prisoners shall go free. Let the mountains shout for joy, and all ye valleys cry aloud" (D&C 128:22-23).

May we reach out and receive the blessings of the everlasting covenant restored in this final dispensation through the Prophet Joseph Smith. May we become worthy to some day shake his hand and have him present us to our Savior, the Lord Jesus Christ. May we become worthy to be embraced by Joseph Smith, by our Savior, and by our eternal Heavenly Parents. Joseph Smith, the prophet of the last dispensation, laid the foundation for this, our joyous family reunion!

REFERENCES:

1 *Hymns,* The Church of Jesus Christ of Latter-day Saints, 1985, #27.
2 The places of safety and protection are *Zion* and her *stakes* (D&C 115:4-6).
3 In *Discourses of Brigham Young,* sel. John A. Widtsoe, (Salt Lake City: Deseret Book Company), 1954, 108; emphasis added.
4 *Patriarchal Blessings,* 1:3.
5 Joseph Fielding McConkie, *His Name Shall Be Joseph,* (Salt Lake City: Hawkes Publishing inc, 1980), 157; emphasis added.
6 McConkie, *His Name Shall be Joseph,* 164. Related prophecies record that this latter-day prophet would be killed at the hands of a lawless mob. In fulfillment of this prophecy, Joseph Smith was martyred on June 27, 1844.
7 Dean C. Jesse, Comp., *The Personal Writings of Joseph Smith,* 214.
8 *Teachings of the Prophet Joseph Smith,* 14.
9 *Teachings,* 320.
10 *History of the Church,* 4:540.
11 *History of the Church,* 1:238.
12 See also Matthew 17, which describes Peter, James, and John on the Mountain of Transfiguration when they *saw* Christ's glory and heard the Father's affirmation that he was his Son.
13 *Teachings,* 12-13; emphasis added. See also D&C 76:5-10, 116-119
14 *Hymns,* #2.
15 Some have pointed out that Stephen saw both the Father and the Son at the same time. But his was a vision *into* heaven, not *on* the earth. He said he gazed *into heaven* and saw Jesus standing on the right hand of God; see Acts 7:55-56.
16 Bruce R. McConkie, *Mormon Doctrine,* under the heading, "Gospel", 333
17 *Teachings,* 1.
18 *History of the Church* 4:461; emphasis added; also in *Teachings,* 194.
19 Statement of the First Presidency regarding God's Love For All Mankind, February 15, 1978.
20 *Journal of Discourses,* 19:38.
21 Edward Stevenson, *Reminiscences of the Prophet Joseph,* 14.
22 See *Millennial Star,* 7 July 1866, 417-19.

23 See introduction to the Book of Abraham in the Pearl of Great Price.

24 Bruce R. McConkie, "Ten Keys to Understanding Isaiah," *Ensign*, Oct. 1973, 80-81.

25 *Journal of Discourses*, 6:294-95

26 *Teachings*, 17.

27 Of course the Lord could have restored all of these keys himself to the Prophet Joseph Smith, but it was instructive that he delegate their restoration to prominent figures of the past —such as Moses and Elijah—so that we can make connection between the keys they restored and significant events of the past and present. Elijah was the last prophet in the Old Testament to hold the keys of the sealing power. He restored them to Peter, James, and John and to the Prophet Joseph Smith. Furthermore, Moses—who had led the children of Israel from Egypt to the promised land of Canaan—was the one selected by the Lord to restore the keys of the gathering of latter-day Israel from all parts of the earth, to the latter-day promised land of Zion.

28 *Teachings* 337. In the early days of the Church, the Saints believed that the power of Elijah was just for the sealing of living persons to eternal life. Joseph had to teach them that the sealing power applied to the dead as well. Today, we seem to put the emphasis on the dead and need to be reminded that the spirit and power of Elijah works upon the living also, propelling them to chart a course leading to eternal life.

29 *Autobiography of Parley P. Pratt*, 329-30; emphasis added; see also D&C 131-132, revelations dealing with eternal marriage.

30 *Teachings*, 255-56.

31 Boyd K. Packer, *Eternal Love*, (Salt Lake City: Desert Book Co., 1973), 6.

32 Packer, *Eternal Love*, 4

33 *Teaching of the Prophet Joseph Smith*, 370.

34 *Teachings*, 121.

35 *Teachings*, 51.

36 *Teachings*, 187.

37 *Teachings*, 207.

38 *Teachings*, 181.

39 *Teachings*, 21.

40 *Teachings*, 181.

41 *Teachings*, 174.

42 *Teachings*, 197.

43 *Teachings*, 137.

44 *Journal of Discourses*, 10: 147-48.

45 "Joseph Smith, Jr., Papers," Historical Department, The Church of Jesus Christ of Latter-day Saints, Salt Lake City, Utah; see also Robert J. Mathews, *"A Plainer Translation": Joseph Smith's Translation of the Bible, a History and Commentary*, 25.

46 *Teachings*, 161.

47 *Teachings*, 180.

48 *Journal of Discourses*, 21:94.

49 Lucy Mack Smith, *History of Joseph Smith*, 83.

50 Wilford Woodruff, "Journal History," 12 March 1897.

51 *Journal of Discourses* 7: 176; emphasis added.

52 *Journal of Discourses*, 9:89.

53 *Journal of Discourses,* 15:325.
54 *Teachings,* 361.
55 *Millennial Star,* 5 Oct. 1899, 629.
56 *Journal of Discourses,* 5:83-84.
57 *Journal of Discourses,* 9:310.
58 *Teachings,* 324; emphasis added.
59 *The Juvenile Instructor,* 15 May 1892, 303-304.
60 Hyrum L. and Helen Mae Andrus, *They knew the Prophet,* (Salt Lake City: Bookcraft, 1974) 28-29.
61 *Journal of Discourses,* 5:22; emphasis added.
62 *Life of Heber C Kimball,* 322-323; emphasis added.
63 *Teachings of the Prophet Joseph Smith,* 364; emphasis added.
64 "My Servant, Joseph" *Ensign,* May 1992, 38.
65 *Teachings,* 368; emphasis added.
66 *Journal of Discourses,* 7:289.
67 (Millet 30)
68 *History of the Church,* 6:317.
69 Leonard J. Arrington, *Brigham Young: American Moses,* (New York: Alfred A. Knopt, 1985) 399.

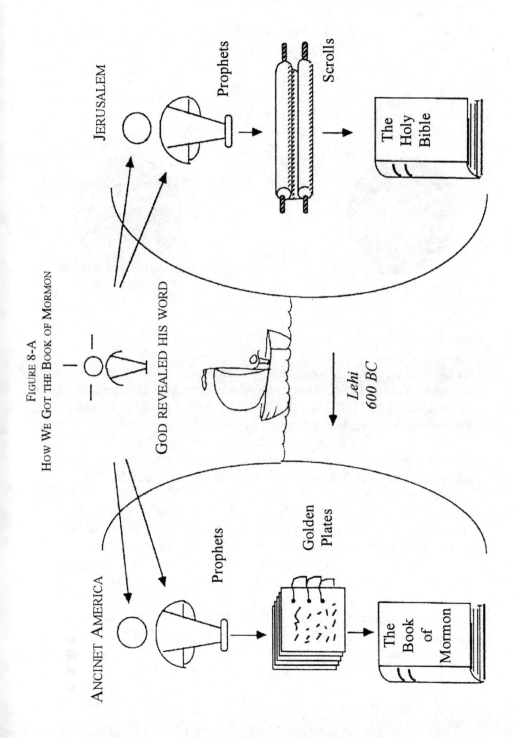

FIGURE 8-A

HOW WE GOT THE BOOK OF MORMON

GOD REVEALED HIS WORD

JERUSALEM

Prophets

Scrolls

The Holy Bible

Lehi 600 BC

ANCINET AMERICA

Prophets

Golden Plates

The Book of Mormon

FIGURE 8-B
WHEELS TURN

Past

Future

Gentiles (Masters)

Israel (Masters)

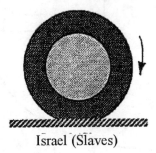

Israel (Slaves)

Gentiles (Slaves)

Principles

1. In the past, the house of Israel has been like slaves— "smitten by the Gentiles". Wicked Gentiles have been like masters who have persecuted, hated, mocked, and killed Israel. This has happened to all the Israelite groups: the Jews, the Lamanites, and latter-day Israel.

2. If, however, the wicked Gentiles do not repent and accept the *fulness* of the gospel, they will be brought down (D&C 87:5; 3 Nephi 16:10-15).

3. The promise to the remnants of Israel, is that if they will embrace the fulness of the gospel, they will be established in the land. "Thus saith the Father, that the sword of my justice shall hang over them (the wicked Gentiles) at that day; and except they repent it shall fall upon them, saith the Father yea, even upon all the nations of the Gentiles. And it shall come to pass that I will establish my people, O house of Israel. And behold, this people will I establish in this land, unto the fulfilling of the covenant which I made with your father Jacob; and it shall be a New Jerusalem. And the powers of heaven shall be in the midst of this people; yea, even I will be in the midst of you" (3 Nephi 20:20-22).

CHAPTER NINE

PREPARING A PEOPLE FOR THE PROTECTION OF ZION

I the Lord, knowing the calamity which should come upon the inhabitants of the earth, called upon my servant Joseph Smith, Jun., and spake unto him from heaven, and gave him commandments.

—D&C 1:17

Many residents of Southern Alberta earn their livings working farmlands where the summers are short and warm and the winters are long and cold. Because my father did not have much farm acreage, he tried raising chickens and shipping eggs. We must have had about two thousand laying hens. I was small and when I tried to gather the eggs in large wicker baskets, those large roosters sometimes attacked me with their strong beaks and leg horns. Since these were days before cleaning solutions for dipping the dirty eggs, my family used to sit in a circle and rub with sandpaper the several dozens of eggs we collected each day. Then we would pack them in cardboard boxes to load them on the railroad train that would pass through our small town of Hillspring.

My family would use this time together to listen to radio programs from station CJOC from Lethbridge. Some of my favorite programs were Superman, the Green Hornet, Fibber Magee and Molly, Edgar Bergen and Charley McCarthy, Pepper Young's Family and the Lux Radio Theater. Those were wonderfully entertaining programs that created vivid mental images of adventure and excitement. But the radio provided more than entertainment—it also provided news and the weather reports that played a vital role in the lives of the Canadian farmers and ranchers.

I remember a time when an early deep freeze hit southern Alberta. Northern Arctic winds caused the thermometer to fall well below zero. My Uncle Archie hadn't heard the weather warning for that day, and some of his sheep were not brought into the protection of barns and sheds. As a result they were caught in the wild, windy, wintry weather that descended on the community so rapidly that the sheep actually froze to death standing in the field. This was such an unusual event that all of my family got into my father's old car and rode across town to Uncle Archie's farm to see the sight.

We found them just as we had heard—standing frozen in the field. I found that by leaning into them I could push them over. Their feet stuck straight up in the air—we could rock them back and forth, stiff as a board. That was one of the most severe freezes I can ever remember. Most of the time, by listening to the weather reports, the livestock farmers and ranchers could avoid such disasters.

In a way, we can compare the radio weathermen to the voice of the Lord's prophets, warning us of forthcoming storms of the last days—wars, destructions, and fires. If we don't hearken to their warnings, we will suffer the consequences of our disobedience. We will not be within the protective shelter of the gospel and will suffer the calamities that will come. However, if we *do* hearken to their warnings, we will be preserved in the midst of the destructions of the last days and will be prepared for the glorious events that will accompany the Lord's Second Coming.

As we hearken to the warning voice of the prophets of the Lord, we will receive the peace and protection that is to be found through obedience. This peace and protection will be realized in a fulness with the establishment of Zion, the New Jerusalem. But Zion can only be built up on the principles of righteousness—those principles which bring us to a unity of heart and mind and which lead us to care for and help one another. These principles stand in contrast to the world's ways and require us to be sanctified in order to receive and live them fully.

As we become sanctified, we will receive great priesthood powers that will enable us to overcome all things and establish Zion (see D&C 105:37). But this power is not to be had all at once. It will require our best efforts and great patience, faith and obedience before we will be ready to receive them, so that we may be protected from the calamities of the last days and Zion may be redeemed (D&C 105:31).

The Lord has promised that "the willing and obedient shall eat the good of the land of Zion" (D&C 64:34). Those who are willing to do his will and to be obedient to the warning voice of the prophets—beginning with the Prophet Joseph Smith and continuing to our present leaders —will be spared from the calamities of the last days and will find peace and rest eventually in Zion.

THE VOICE OF WARNING

In the first section of the Doctrine and Covenants, known as the "Preface", the Lord states explicitly that he called Joseph Smith and gave him commandments in order to provide protection for the righteous in a day of calamity (D&C 1:17, 35. 36, 38). The Lord has also given commandments to succeeding prophets so that the "everlasting covenant might be established; that the fulness of my gospel might be proclaimed by the weak and the simple unto the ends of the world, and before kings and rulers" (D&C 1:22-23).

Through the Prophet Joseph Smith the Lord has given a clear picture of the plan, purposes, and designs of our Heavenly Father in providing safety and protection for his righteous children. The Prophet warned that the Lord is "withdrawing His Spirit from the earth" and as a result "the governments of the earth are thrown into confusion and division; and *Destruction*, to the eye of the spiritual beholder, seems to be written by the finger of an invisible hand, in large capitals, upon almost every thing we behold."[1]

As wickedness increases in the last days, so will the destructions that the prophets have seen. In the Doctrine and Covenants we are warned that, "The day cometh that [all] who will not hear the voice of the Lord, neither the voice of his servants, neither give heed to the words of the prophets and apostles, shall be cut off from among the people; for they have strayed from mine ordinances, and have broken mine everlasting covenant; they seek not the Lord to establish his righteousness, but every man walketh in his own way, and after the image of his own god, whose image is in the likeness of the world, and whose substance is that of an idol, which waxeth old and shall perish in Babylon, even Babylon the great, which shall fall" (D&C 1:14-16).

When the wicked are fully ripe in iniquity, they will fall, and "great shall be the fall of it" (1 Nephi 22:14). Speaking of that day in the scriptures, the Lord gives graphic descriptions of plagues such as flies eating human flesh and maggots coming in upon them and flesh falling from off their bones, and their tongues being stayed so that they can no longer speak blasphemously against the Lord.

In that day "the sun shall be darkened, and the moon shall be turned into blood, and the stars shall fall from heaven, and there shall be greater signs in heaven above and in the earth beneath; and there shall be weeping and wailing among the hosts of men; and there shall be a great hailstorm sent forth to destroy the crops of the earth. And it shall come to pass, because of the wickedness of the world, that I will take vengeance upon the wicked, for they will not repent; for the cup of mine indignation is full; for behold, my blood shall not cleanse them if they hear me not" (D&C 29:14-17).

John the Revelator saw in vision a cataclysmic, worldwide earthquake which will also take place before the Lord comes. With these destructions in view, the all nations, kindreds, tongues, and people of the whole earth are exhorted to: "Prepare ye, prepare ye for that which is to come, for the Lord is nigh" (D&C 1:12).

In the midst of all these calamities the Lord has repeatedly given us the promise that the righteous need not fear. In his love and mercy he has restored the true gospel of Jesus Christ to prepare us for that which is to come, for, in the words of the Lord, "I am no respecter of persons, and will that all men shall know that the day speedily cometh; the hour is not yet, but nigh at hand, when peace shall be taken from the earth, and the devil shall have power over his own dominion." And the Lord shall also *have power over his saints, and shall reign in their midst,* and shall come down in judgment upon Idumea, or the world" (D&C 1:35-36; emphasis added). In other words, an increase in wickedness and righteousness will be concurrent events bringing about the destruction of the wicked and the salvation of the righteous (see 1 Nephi 22:17; 2 Nephi 30:10).

THE LORD HAS PROVIDED A WAY OF DELIVERANCE

The gospel message of hope is that as calamities increase in the world because of wickedness—resulting in the cataclysmic worldwide earthquake we just read about—the Lord have power over his people and will lead them along as calves of the stall or as sheep of his fold and in him they will find pasture—hope, rest, peace and safety (see 1 Nephi 22:16, 19, 22, 24). When the Saints are sanctified and Zion and her stakes are established, they will be preserved from calamities and destructions, while the wicked will be destroyed.

Safety and deliverance will be realized through obedience to the commandments of the Lord—the faithful will be delivered from the overflowing scourge that will surely overtake the wicked. In the preface to the Doctrine and Covenants, the Lord explains the importance of obedience. He declared, "The day cometh that they who will not hear the voice of the Lord, neither the voice of his servants, neither give heed to the words of the prophets and apostles, *shall be cut off from among the people"* (D&C 1:14; emphasis added). We don't have to look to some distant time to see the reality of this passage. Presently, we see individuals who once were members of the Church, but who fell into transgression and were cut off, or excommunicated, from the Church. However, there also seems to be a more far-reaching global meaning to this prophecy.

As the events of the last days unfold, "a great division" will take place among the people (2 Nephi 30:10). Eventually, there will come "an entire separation of the righteous and the wicked" (D&C 63:54). We expect to see wicked becoming more wicked and the righteous becoming more righteous. The Lord revealed this great division to Enoch who saw that there would be "great tribulations...among the children of men, *but my people will I preserve*" (Moses 7:61; emphasis added). These and other scriptures paint a picture showing a great polarization that will shortly take place—a *bright* picture for repentant latter-day Israel, but a *dark* picture for the wicked latter-day Gentiles.

The Lord warned, "And when the times of the Gentiles is come in, a light shall break forth among them that sit in darkness, and it shall be the fulness of my gospel; *But they receive it not;* for they perceive not the light, and they turn their hearts from me because of the precepts of men" (D&C 45:28-29). Pride and high-mindedness continue to prevent the Gentiles from embracing the fulness of the gospel. This rejection will result in the Lord withdrawing his spirit from among the Gentiles—with fearful consequences (see 3 Nephi 16:10, 14; 3 Nephi 20:15-23; 3 Nephi 21:11-21).

The Prophet Joseph Smith was pessimistic regarding the spiritual condition of the latter-day Gentiles. Of them he warned:

> But the Gentiles have not continued in the goodness of God, but have departed from the faith that was once delivered to the Saints, and have broken the covenant in which their fathers were established (see Isaiah 24:5); and have become high-minded, and have not feared; *therefore, but few of them will be gathered with the chosen family. Have not the pride, high-mindedness, and unbelief of the Gentiles, provoked the Holy One of Israel to withdraw His Holy Spirit from them, and send forth His judgments to scourge them for their wickedness?* This is certainly the case."[2]

So, the specific issues that will bring down calamities upon the unrighteous Gentiles in the latter days will be: 1) the precepts of men, 2) pride, 3) high-mindedness, and 4) unbelief. Unfortunately, these evils are not the traits of non-members alone! In his classic address on pride, President Ezra Taft Benson uttered a similar warning to members of the Church He identified "pride is the great stumbling block to Zion." For emphasis, he repeated the same statement: "pride *is* the great stumbling block to Zion. We must cleanse the inner vessel by conquering pride. (See Alma 6:2-4; Matt. 23:25-26.) We must yield 'to the enticings of the Holy Spirit,' put off the prideful 'natural man,' become 'a saint through the atonement of Christ the Lord,' and become 'as a child, submissive, meek, humble.' (Mosiah 3:19; see also Alma 13:28.)."[3]

In stressing the importance of humbly hearkening to the words of the prophets, the Lord said: "What I the Lord have spoken, I have spoken, and I excuse not myself; and though the heavens and the earth pass away, my word shall not pass away, but shall all be fulfilled, *whether by mine own voice or by the*

282 THE ETERNAL PLAN OF HAPPINESS

voice of my servants, it is the same" (D&C 1:38; emphasis added). The Lord considers the voice of his prophets to be the same as his own. Therefore, to repeat the principle of deliverance, it is vital, that we listen to and follow the prophets if we expect to enjoy the blessings of peace and escape the destructions that will come upon the wicked. The options before us are clear: we can hearken to the warning of the latter-day weather men, the apostles and prophets, and be spared—or we can turn a deaf ear to them and die in the storms that will come! The choice is ours to make.

Like the weathermen in the story, the Prophet Joseph Smith, and other servants in the hands of the Lord, have been called to prepare people by bringing them to a knowledge of their Savior, their Redeemer, the Lord Jesus Christ. Those who enter into the waters of baptism and keep the commandments of the Lord, will be called his people. These faithful people will escape the destructions that will accompany "the great and dreadful day of the Lord" (D&C 2, Malachi 4:5-6, Moses 7:61). This promise is found throughout the scriptures and in the teachings of our latter-day prophets.

Deliverance Depends Upon our Obedience

The Lord charted the initial course, the voice of warning, through the Prophet Joseph Smith, but he continues to give living direction through the current prophet. In order to find safety from the calamities that are to come we must hearken to the warnings of the Lord that have come to us through the Prophet Joseph Smith and the successive Presidents of the Church.

Those who will hearken to the warnings of the latter-day weathermen, the apostles and prophets, will escape the scourge—meaning the calamities that are to come. They will have the power and the protection of the everlasting covenant. Others will not "for where I am they cannot come, for they have no power" (D&C 29:29).

In 1980, President Ezra Taft Benson gave an enlightening address at Brigham Young University stressing the importance of following the living prophet in order to secure safety in the last days. In concluding his masterful address, President Benson identified 14 prerogatives of the living prophet. He said:

Let us summarize this grand key, these "Fourteen Fundamentals in Following the Prophet," *for our salvation hangs on them.*

First: The prophet is the only man who speaks for the Lord in everything.
Second: The living prophet is more vital to us than the standard works.
Third: The living prophet is more important to us than a dead prophet.
Fourth: The prophet will never lead the Church astray.
Fifth: The prophet is not required to have any particular earthly training or
credentials to speak on any subject or act on any matter at any time.

Sixth: The prophet does not have to say "Thus saith the Lord" to give us scripture.

Seventh: The prophet tells us what we need to know, not always what we want to know.

Eighth: The prophet is not limited by men's reasoning.

Ninth: The prophet can receive revelation on any matter, temporal or spiritual.

Tenth: The prophet may be involved in civic matters.

Eleventh: The two groups who have the greatest difficulty in following the prophet are the proud who are learned and the proud who are rich.

Twelfth: The prophet will not necessarily be popular with the world or the worldly.

Thirteenth: The prophet and his counselors make up the First Presidency—the highest quorum in the Church.

Fourteenth: The prophet and the presidency—the living prophet and the First Presidency—follow them and be blessed; reject them and suffer.

I testify that these fourteen fundamentals in following the living prophet are true.[4]

From the foregoing list we can see how broad a spectrum the calling of the Prophet truly is. By pondering his divine calling and his authority in so many areas we can truly sing, "We thank thee, O God, for a Prophet, to guide us in these latter days"! By following the Prophet's counsel we are promised blessings—including the blessings of peace, happiness, and safety—both here and hereafter.

THE LORD HAS PROVIDED A TEMPORAL SALVATION FOR HIS SAINTS

Regarding the idea of a temporal salvation, the Orthodox Jews believe in a "this world" salvation—that when Messiah comes he will deliver them from their enemies. The Christian churches, on the other hand, are more focused on a "next world" spiritual salvation—they expect to go to heaven. But in contrast to both of these views, the true gospel of Jesus Christ has power to provide *a temporal salvation* from destructions and calamities in this world as well as *eternal life* in the world to come. Consequently the Latter-day Saints expect deliverance both from temporal enemies in this world—including wars, calamities and destructions in a day of the Lord's wrath—and from death, hell, and the devil in the next world.[5]

Indeed, the Lord has given us the two-fold promise, "He who doeth the works of righteousness shall receive his reward, even *peace in this world,* and *eternal life in the world to come"* (D&C 59:23; emphasis added). On the other hand, it is also true that he who doeth the works of wickedness shall receive his reward, even vulnerability and despair in this world and eternal damnation in the world to come.

The idea that the gospel promises us temporal salvation and protection is a new idea to some, but is clearly taught in the scriptures and by the latter-day prophets. In the "Explanatory Introduction" to the Doctrine and Covenants we read that the book contains "an invitation to all people everywhere to hear the voice of the Lord Jesus Christ, speaking to them for their *temporal well-being* and their everlasting salvation" (emphasis added).

Along this same line, Brigham Young is reported to have said that any religion that does not have power to save its people in this world, certainly would not have power to save them in the eternal worlds. By that statement he no doubt meant that the true gospel of Jesus Christ should be able to save the people from the evils, calamities and destructions of this life as well as from death, damnation, hell and the devil in the world to come. The promise of peace and salvation through living the gospel is an integral part of our hope in Christ and an important theme in the teachings of the prophets both ancient and modern.

Peace on Earth, Good Will Toward Men—Eventually

The promise of eventual "peace on earth and good will toward men" is one of the profound teachings of the scriptures. As a case in point, you may remember Jesus' parable of the two houses—the one built upon the sand and the other upon the rock—*the storms blew upon both,* but the latter withstood the blasts because its rock foundation was the gospel of Jesus Christ (see Matthew 7:24-25).

There are many revelations that connect having safety and peace in this world with receiving a fulness of the blessings of the gospel. For instance, we read in the Doctrine and Covenants, "[One who walks] in the meekness of [His] Spirit, shall have peace in [the Lord]" (D&C 19:23). In addition, the new and everlasting covenant is called "the gospel of peace" (D&C 27:16). In the names of the two latter-day world capitals, Zion (the New Jerusalem) and Jerusalem (in the Holy Land), is the built-in image of peace. The root word *salem* (in Jerusalem) means "shalom" or "peace".

For the Jews, ancient and modern, their greeting and their farewell in Hebrew is SHALOM—a constant reminder of their quest for *peace!* A prophecy of Isaiah proclaims Jesus to be the "Prince of Peace" (Isaiah 90:6) and "of his government and peace there will be no end" (Isaiah 9:7). We read in the Book of Mormon that Melchizedek established peace among his people and "was called the prince of peace" (Alma 13:18). All who hold the Melchizedek Priesthood have the responsibility of establishing peace in the land through their righteousness and the keeping of their covenants (see D&C 98:10-16, 22; 105:38-40).

During the future time of worldwide calamity, the Saints will find peace in Zion and in her stakes—places of refuge and safety. For the Lord has promised, "Verily I say unto you all: Arise and shine forth, that thy light may be a standard for the nations; And that the gathering together upon *the land of Zion, and upon her stakes, may be for a defense, and for a refuge from the storm, and from wrath when it shall be poured out without mixture upon the whole earth"* (D&C 115:5-6; emphasis added).

ZION AND HER STAKES—
PLACES OF SAFETY AND REFUGE

So, an important gospel principle is that those who will not hearken to the voice of warning will be "cut off from among the people" (D&C 1:14; 2 Nephi 30:10). By contrast, the righteous are promised that "if ye are prepared ye shall not fear" (D&C 38:30). The righteous will not fear because they will be prepared—they will have been gathered to places of safety, to Zion in America and her stakes throughout the world, and to Jerusalem in the Holy Land.

The Book of Moses in the Pearl of Great Price provides a *key scripture* that reminds us that safety and protection are to be found in Zion, the New Jerusalem. There we read of a day of wickedness and vengeance that will precede the coming of the Lord, when "the heavens shall be darkened, and a veil of darkness shall cover the earth; and the heavens shall shake, and also the earth; and great tribulations shall be among the children of men, *but my people will I preserve"* (Moses 7:61; emphasis added).

The Lord then explains *how* he will accomplish his task of preserving the righteous. *He will bring about the restoration of the gospel, the everlasting covenant:* he will send righteousness "down out of heaven; and truth will I send forth out of the earth, to bear testimony of mine Only Begotten; his resurrection from the dead; yea, and also the resurrection of all men; and righteousness and truth will I cause to sweep the earth as with a flood, to gather out mine elect from the four quarters of the earth, unto a place which I shall prepare, an Holy City, that my people may gird up their loins, and be looking forth for the time of my coming; for there shall be my tabernacle, and it shall be called Zion, a New Jerusalem" (Moses 7:62).

Zion and her *stakes* are to arise out of the Church as places of defense and refuge. Thus, Joseph Smith's inspired prayer was that the Church might go forth that Zion might be established (see D&C 65:6). This gathering will be in fulfillment of Malachi's prophecy that "unto you that fear my name shall the Sun of righteousness arise with healing in his wings; and ye shall go forth, and *grow up as calves of the stall"* (Malachi 4:2; emphasis added). Because they have listened to a/the prophet's voice and have been obedient to his words, the Saints will be protected in Zion from calamities even as cattle are protected in barns from wild winds and wailing storms—wars, calamities, fires and the great earthquake.

From the Doctrine and Covenants we find an explanation of how the establishment of the New Jerusalem will preserve the people of the Lord:

> And the glory of the Lord shall be there, and the terror of the Lord also shall be there, insomuch that *the wicked will not come unto it,* and it shall be called Zion.
>
> And it shall come to pass among the wicked, that every man that will not take his sword against his neighbor must needs flee unto Zion for safety.
>
> And there shall be gathered unto it out of every nation under heaven; and it shall be the *only people that shall not be at war one with another.*
>
> And it shall be said among the wicked: Let us not go up to battle against Zion, for *the inhabitants of Zion are terrible; wherefore we cannot stand.*
>
> And it shall come to pass that the righteous shall be gathered out from among all nations, and shall come to Zion, singing with songs of everlasting joy (D&C 45:65-71; emphasis added).

Here we read that a latter-day Zion will be established, much like Enoch's Zion, and that the people of God will be delivered from war and the wicked just as they were anciently. And thus we see that the establishment of Zion, the New Jerusalem, in all her glory will bless the Saints with love and beauty, preparing them for the presence of the Lord and Enoch's city. At the same time the glory emanating out of Zion will protect the people from the enemies of righteousness.

ENOCH'S CITY PROVIDES A GOOD EXAMPLE OF ZION

One of the reasons Heavenly Father gave us the record of Enoch and his holy city was to provide us with an example of how the Lord *blesses* and *protects* his people in Zion. As you read the following account, try to make connections in your mind between Enoch's Zion and our anticipated latter-day Zion. There are remarkable parallels between them. In many instances what was said of Enoch and his people can also be said of Joseph Smith and his people Can you see parallels between these two great prophets in these passages about Enoch?

> And so great was the faith of Enoch that he led the people of God, *and their enemies came to battle against them;* and he spake the word of the Lord, and the earth trembled, and the mountains fled, even according to his

command; and the rivers of water were turned out of their course; ... and *all nations feared greatly,* so powerful was the word of Enoch, and so great was the power of the language which God had given him....

And there went forth *a curse upon all people that fought against God;*

And from that time forth there were wars and bloodshed *among them; but the Lord came and dwelt with his people, and they dwelt in righteousness.*

The fear of the Lord was upon all nations, so great was the glory of the Lord, which was upon his people. And the Lord blessed the land, and they were blessed upon the mountains, and upon the high places, and did flourish.

And the Lord called his people Zion, *because they were of one heart and one mind, and dwelt in righteousness; and there was no poor among them.*

And Enoch continued his preaching in righteousness unto the people of God. And it came to pass in his days, that *he built a city* that was called the City of Holiness, even Zion.

And it came to pass that Enoch talked with the Lord; and he said unto the Lord: Surely Zion shall dwell in safety forever. But the Lord said unto Enoch: *Zion have I blessed,* but *the residue of the people have I cursed.*

And it came to pass that the Lord showed unto Enoch all the inhabitants of the earth; and he beheld, and lo, *Zion in process of time, was taken up into heaven.* And the Lord said unto Enoch: Behold mine abode forever (Moses 7:13, 15-21; emphasis added).

Here are some of the parallels or connections I have seen between Enoch's Zion and the latter-day Zion that will grow out of the Church and will provide protection for the Saints in the last days:

1. The enemies of righteousness came against the people of God.
2. Great power in the priesthood was manifest by the righteous over the elements of the earth and the powers of heaven.
3. The nations of the earth feared, so great was the power given the prophet by the Lord.
4. A curse came upon those who fought against God.
5. Wars and bloodshed were among the wicked.
6. The Lord came and dwelt with his people.
7. The fear of the Lord was upon all nations because of the glory of the Lord's people.
8. The Lord blessed the mountains and high places and they did flourish.
9. The Lord called his people Zion because they were of one heart and one mind, and dwelt in righteousness; and there was no poor among them.
10. A great City of Holiness was built called Zion.

Space considerations will not allow further comparison here, but you can find many of these connections between Enoch's Zion and the latter-day Zion.[6]

Now let's look—in some detail—at Enoch's city of Zion so that we can see how we can become compatible with or like them.

The Command to Be One

Anciently, the Zion of Enoch was made up of people who "were of one heart and one mind, and dwelt in righteousness; and there was no poor among them" (Moses 7:18). These features have characterized the Lord's people who have accepted and applied the fulness of the gospel in their lives, such as the people of the city of Enoch (Moses 7:17-18) and the Nephite golden era (4 Nephi 1:2-3, 15-17) and some of the early Christians (Acts 4:32-37).

The single most important distinguishing characteristic of Zion is unity and oneness with the Lord. Have you ever noticed the spiritual strength that comes to a family, a ward, a class of students, or any other group for that matter when everyone is united in their thoughts, feelings, and actions? In holy places we are taught to pray in unison so that our faith may be strengthened. After our public prayers we all say "Amen" to demonstrate our unity of purpose with the utterances of the prayer. We have the Lord's promise that greater power will come to the Saints as we progressively become more unified with the Lord and his prophets in the last days—the days of destruction among the wicked and of peace and protection among the Saints of God. As we become more united, we will be able to establish Zion in all her beauty and glory.

The establishment of Zion will be the fulfillment in part of the Lord's prayer in Jerusalem before his great atoning sacrifice. He prayed that his disciples "all may be one; as thou, Father, art in me, and I in thee, that they also may be one in us: that the world may believe that thou hast sent me" (John 17:21). When the Latter-day Saints reach that kind of unity, they, with Enoch's people, will be called Zion.

The word "atonement" has deep meaning in connections with our striving to be one with the Lord. Jesus suffered, he provided the means—the "at-one-ment" by which we could be one with the Father. In stressing the importance of oneness and unity with the Lord, Elder Orson Pratt taught:

> The Command to 'Be One,' embraces all other commands. There is no law, no statute, ordinance, covenant, nor blessing, but what was instituted to make the Saints one. This is the ultimate end and aim of the great plan of salvation. For this, Jesus suffered and died; for this, his servants have toiled and labored day and night in our fallen world; for this, all the powers of heaven will be exerted, until Satan shall be overcome, and the earth be redeemed, and all the glorified inhabitants thereof become one.... *The grand*

*and ultimate object of the Father, Son, and Holy Ghost, is to take their own
children who have made themselves imperfect, and restore them to perfection, and make them one like themselves.*[7]

The mission of the Church—to proclaim the gospel, perfect the Saints, and
redeem the dead—is an effort toward the kind of atonement about which Elder
Pratt was speaking. Everything we do in the Church should be directed toward
gathering and perfecting the Saints—making them of one mind and one heart as
they dwell together in love and righteousness of the everlasting covenant.

Of One Mind

Even as the inhabitants of Enoch's city were of one mind, so we, too, must
be united in our thoughts. Though we love diversity, we are still to be united in
our thoughts regarding eternal truths and the doctrines of the gospel. The
Nephites attained this remarkable unity. Of them we read: "There were no contentions and disputations among them, and every man did deal justly one with
another" (4 Nephi 1:2). Furthermore, "There was no contention in the land,
because of the love of God which did dwell in the hearts of the people.... Surely
there could not be a happier people among all the people who had been created
by the hand of God" (4 Nephi 1:15-16).

What a blessed state such unity brings! As Latter-day Saints, we need to
pray—ask, seek, and knock—that we may become united in our thinking so that
we, too, may enjoy the remarkable blessings experienced by Enoch's people and
the Nephites.

Of One Heart

In addition to being united in our thoughts, we must also be united in our
hearts. Our ideas and our *feelings* must be harmony with each other if we are to
become a Zion people. As we live the gospel, we will experience many different
kinds of wonderful feelings—love, hope, peace, happiness, joy, optimism, harmony, gratitude, and cheerfulness—but the greatest of these will be love. Moroni
said perfect love is "charity" which he explained is "the pure love of Christ, and
it endureth forever; and whoso is found possessed of it at the last day, it shall be
well with him" (Moroni 7:47).

Because the development of charity is such a vital prerequisite to the revelations and priesthood power we need in order to establish Zion the Lord has
admonished us, "Let thy bowels also be full of charity towards all men, and to the
household of faith, and let virtue garnish thy thoughts unceasingly; then shall thy
confidence wax strong in the presence of God; and the doctrine of the priesthood
shall distil upon thy soul as the dews from heaven. The Holy Ghost shall be thy
constant companion; . . . and without compulsory means it shall flow unto thee

forever and ever" (D&C 121:45-46). As the Holy Ghost flows unto us, we will grow in love for one another and will become spiritually compatible with our brothers and sisters in Zion.

Without these feelings of love we cannot have the Holy Ghost and, therefore, we cannot receive promptings and direction from him. Nephi chided his brothers because of their rebellion and told them they could not receive revelation from the Lord because they were "past *feeling"—they* "*could not feel his words"* (1 Nephi 17:45). Because Laman and Lemuel loved the carnal things of the world more than the truths and righteousness of the Lord, they could not receive direction from the Spirit.

In contrast to the thick spiritual skins of Laman and Lemuel, the Lord wants us to be sensitive to his promptings, to feel his words, and to love one another. If we do not choose to do this, he will allow adverse circumstances to interrupt our comfort states. Sometimes it takes physical adversity to help us overcome human pettiness and experience the kind of feelings involved here. Adversity can act as a propellant that can thrust us forward to greater heights of sensitivity and love.[8]

For example, in LDS Church history we read of many examples of persecution and physical difficulties—the mobbings in Missouri, the persecution in Nauvoo, and the hardships associated with the westward trek to the Salt Lake Valley—that strengthened the Saints and united them in deep bonds of love for one another. Though we may not experience the trials that the pioneers did, our own experiences with adversity will help us—if we are not slow learners—to develop proper feelings of love for one another.

When compared to the magnificent light, beauty, and love that exists in Zion, the world around us lies in deep darkness (see D&C 112: 23). We are commanded to leave the hateful ways of man and live together in the love of God (see D&C 42:45). We are commanded to separate ourselves from the murky and filthy waters of evil so attractively presented to us in base forms of advertisement, entertainment, politics, etc. As the people of the Lord, we have been commanded to heed Isaiah's warning, "Depart ye, depart ye, go ye out from thence, touch no unclean thing; go ye out of the midst of her; be ye clean, that bear the vessels of the Lord" (Isaiah 52:11).

Dwell in Righteousness

Even as Enoch and his people dwelt in righteousness, we must be a pure people. In a well-known Latter-day Saint hymn we sing: "O Babylon, O Babylon, we bid thee farewell; We're going to the mountains of Ephraim to dwell."[9] This hymn affirms the Lord's command to remove ourselves from the sin, corruption, wickedness, violence, materialism, and immorality that are in this world. This vast array of evil is identified in the scriptures as modern day *Babylon* (see D&C 64:24). (See end of chapter Figure 9-A, Zion and Babylon.)

The word "Babylon" has been used as a metaphor for oppression and suffering ever since the Jews were taken captive into Babylon in 587 B.C. Spiritual Babylon is an expression similar in meaning to "the whore of all the earth" (1 Nephi 14:10), the "great and abominable church" (1 Nephi 22:13), and "the great and spacious building" (1 Nephi 11:36).

Concerning the ever-present modern day Babylon, the word of the Lord to his people is, "Go ye out from Babylon. Be ye clean that bear the vessels of the Lord" (D&C 133:5). And again, "Go ye out from among the nations, even from *Babylon*, from the *midst of wickedness, which is spiritual Babylon*" (D&C 133:14; emphasis added). We are to distance ourselves from spiritual Babylon lest we partake of the plagues that will come upon her (see Revelation 18:4)

As we progressively separate ourselves from the wickedness of the world, we are complying in part with James' definition of pure and undefiled religion, which is "to visit the fatherless and widows in their affliction, and to *keep himself unspotted from the world"* (James 1:27; emphasis added). By distancing ourselves from the world and seeking a unity in righteousness, we prepare ourselves for Zion and the wondrous blessings that are associated therewith. These exquisite blessings will come to the Saints only as we obey the principles and ordinances of the gospel of Jesus Christ—including a temporal equality among the Saints.

No Poor Among Them

Besides being of one mind and one heart, and dwelling in righteousness, Enoch's Zion had "no poor among them" (Moses 7:18). They reached this wonderful state of no poverty because the economic laws they lived were revealed to them from heaven. These celestial laws—governing the use and distribution of the wealth of the world—must also be lived by the Saints of the latter days if we are to become a Zion people. Temporal laws are inseparably connected with spiritual laws (see D&C 70:14).

Jesus, recognizing the connection between sharing our material wealth and truly loving one another, charged the rich young ruler to sell all that he had "and come and follow me" (Matthew 19:21). Here, Jesus was inviting the young man to show his love for the Lord and his fellow men consistent with the two greatest commandments—to love the Lord with all our hearts, minds, mights and strength, and our neighbors as ourselves (see D&C 59:5-6; also Matthew 22:37, 39). The young man went away sorrowfully, because he loved his possessions more than he loved the Lord and his fellowmen.

In the New Testament, Jesus taught his disciples, saying, "A new commandment I give unto you, That ye love one another; as I have loved you, that ye also love one another" (John 13:34). He explained that, "by this shall all men know that ye are my disciples, if ye have love one to another" (John 13:35). One of the important ways the ancient Saints showed their love for one another was by liv-ing the Lord's law concerning the distribution of wealth by sharing all that they had—they had "all things common" (Acts 4:32). When Jesus was among the Nephites, he revealed this same celestial law of sharing—they also had "all things common among them" (4 Nephi 1:3).

The Celestial Law of Consecration

The world is in great need of all of the laws of the Lord so that the needs of the poor can be met. Almost every day, television brings into our living rooms a stark view of the unhappy conditions of the ever-growing numbers of hungry and homeless people—our brothers and sisters. Our hearts cry out when we view the poverty, disease, starvation, and ignorance of the poor around us. We yearn to find a way to help those who are lonely and left by themselves without family love and support. The Lord has condemned the world because these conditions are allowed to exist. He said, "It is not given that one man should possess that which is above another, *wherefore the world lieth in sin*" (D&C 49:20). In other words, because of greed, the world lieth in sin.

The distribution of income among the sons and daughters of God is highly unequal, giving rise to the Lord's indictment against a selfish world. I have found some interesting statistics on this issue of greed. For example: The income going to the poorest 20 percent of the population has fallen to 4.1 percent in 1994, while the income going to the wealthiest 20 percent has risen to 47 percent over the same period.[10] The rich earn more than all of the other classes combined. In the ten year period between 1984 and 1994, increases in incomes have accrued almost entirely to those at the top of the income scale. The richest 1/5 have grown 20% and the poorest 1/5 have lost 3%.[11] The highest paid executive in 1995 earned a total of $65.6 million in total compensation. In 1980 the average CEO salary was 42 times an ordinary worker's, but by 1995 it was 141 times as much.[12] More recent statistics show that the rich receive 200 times as much as the laborer. Truly, in the Gentile economic system, the heart of Babylon, the rich are getting richer and the poor are getting...stepped on! And as Hugh Nibley has observed, "Every step in the direction of increasing one's personal holdings is a step away from Zion, which is another way of saying...that one cannot serve two masters".[13]

The reason why loneliness and poverty exist, which cause the world to lie in sin, is because of a lack of knowing and obeying the laws of God. The widespread effects of man's ignorance are on every side. Internationally we are torn apart by what seem to be irreconcilable differences in philosophies concerning land pos-session, economics, politics, justice, progress—even human life. Within our nations, these differences cause suspicion, resentment, and bloody conflict between men and women, employees and employers, masters and slaves (see D&C 87:4)—those who have power and those who do not, those who have possessions and those who do not! How can these problems be resolved, problems that cause so much pain and suffering, hunger and hopelessness—especially among innocent men, women, and children?

Some people have claimed that the reason there is so much suffering in the world is because there are too many people and not enough resources to go around. This is not true! The Lord has declared, "For the earth is full, and there is enough and to spare" (see D&C 104:15-18). The real reason we have so much poverty is because we are so enmeshed in worldly, unjust, economic systems. These systems are both the cause and a result of wide-spread ignorance, and the deeply entrenched greed and pride of power-mad people of influence!

Because the Lord loves all of his children and does not desire that one would have that which would put him above another, the Lord has revealed, through the Prophet Joseph Smith as a part of the final dispensation, the perfect law of economics that will help bring about the greater love, unity, harmony, and spiritual and temporal blessings that are the hallmarks of Zion. Living the Lord's law is important because the abundant gifts of the Spirit —miracles, healings, revelations, and priesthood powers—are to be enjoyed only as we freely share our earthly riches.

The Lord equated temporal equality with abundant spiritual blessings when he commanded us: "Nevertheless, in your temporal things you shall be equal, and this not grudgingly, otherwise the abundance of the manifestations of the Spirit shall be withheld" (D&C 70:14). This passage does not mean that we don't have wonderful spiritual manifestations in the Church today! We do indeed! But there are many other gifts—a greater abundance—to be experienced when we learn to live the celestial laws of Zion, when we live the laws of God in such a way that there are "not rich and poor, bond and free, but [that all are] made free, and partakers of the heavenly gift" (4 Nephi 1:3). This will require that we make a major shift from the false beliefs and values of our fallen earthly systems to the truths and values found within the fulness of the gospel of Jesus Christ.

Consecration—Balancing Freedom and Equality

In every country there exists a tension between two competing values: individual freedom and economic equality or "social justice". These values are often in conflict. Unregulated freedom promotes economic conditions where the rich get richer and the poor get poorer—and the gap between the two increases over time. This happens because powerful and selfish people—having freedom to dominate and control people and resources—often exploit those in weaker positions. On the other hand, where economic equality is forced upon the people by the government, the people have no freedom! Let's examine this apparent dilemma now in greater detail. (See end of chapter Figure 9-B, The Lord's Economic Plan in Perspective.)

Anarchy is a condition where there is a complete breakdown of the government and where confusion and terrorism reigns. Where these conditions exist, the people suffer both a lack of individual freedom and a lack of social justice. There is no governmental authority to control or direct the activities of the people, the streets are not safe, being filled with fear people are not free to go and come as they might please. Furthermore, the needs of the poor are not met, and the law of the jungle—the survival of the fittest—operates, with the big animals eating up the smaller animals.

Under *communistic* rule, the leaders promote economic equality (ideally), but they use force and compulsion to bring it about. The *bait* that attracts many people to communism is the promise of economic equality—but the *hook* is that the equality is gained by sacrificing individual freedom. Under communism the state owns all the capital and all the property. It also tightly controls the lives of the people. People can only come and go under the watchful eye of the bureaucratic government.

Historically, communism has not been able to produce the equality it promised—even under the rule of force. Political leaders eat better, travel in more comfort, and enjoy amenities that the common people just do not have. Of late we have seen communistic countries collapse and fragment with the splinter nations attempting to establish various forms of democracy and capitalism.

In countries where *capitalism* is the governing economic principle, the people have freedom (ideally) from excessive interference by the government, but the needs of the poor are not met. As we have said before, the rich get richer and the poor get poorer. Where capitalism flourishes, so does the spirit of competition—which spirit often crushes human values and morality._

In his well-researched and well-written book, *No contest: The Case Against Competition*, Alfie Kohn makes the bold statement that "healthy competition is actually a contradiction in terms ... competition simply makes no sense." The idea that competition is senseless certainly applies to the field of economics. Continuing Mr. Kohn declared, "If we value sanity, not to mention human life, we must break the grip of a system that predicates one person's success on another's failure and learn some thing entirely different."[14]

We could get much more accomplished through cooperation than we ever could through competition. A major problem that we face, however, is that, like a fish that cannot conceive of life outside of water we are so socially conditioned toward competition as a way of life, that we know little of the advantages of cooperation. We need an example to show us the way but where can we look?

Presently, we just don't have any good examples of cooperative societies! Television does not provide them for us, neither does any other media. Movies, books, and videos are saturated with competition, immorality and violence—and we seem to love it. We are following a pattern that has been followed by previous societies. Because of over-exposure, we have become desensitized to one level of competition and so we demand higher and higher levels in order to satisfy our craving for the violent and the competitive way of life. This is a vicious cycle—it feeds on itself. There must be better ways of interacting with one another, ways that would take us beyond our present worldly systems of competitive economics and which would be in harmony with the mind and will of our Heavenly Father.

The debate between social justice and individual freedom is wonderfully and powerfully resolved through the revelations given by the Lord to the Prophet Joseph Smith. As a important part of the everlasting covenant, the Lord has revealed his law governing the wealth of the world. This law of heaven, known as "the Law of Consecration,"[15] is vastly different from all of the inadequate systems we have just reviewed. The Prophet explained that the Lord's ways are higher than the ways of man. He said, "The government of the Almighty has always been very dissimilar to the governments of men, whether we refer to His religious government, or to the government of nations. The government of God has always tended to promote peace, unity, harmony, strength, and happiness; while that of man has been productive of confusion, disorder, weakness, and misery."[16]

He continued by saying that all man-made attempts to promote universal peace and happiness in the human family "have proved abortive; every effort has failed; every plan and design has fallen to the ground; *it needs the wisdom of God, the intelligence of God, and the power of God to accomplish this. The world has had a fair trial for six thousand years; the Lord will try the seventh thousand Himself.*[17]

The Law of Consecration was introduced through revelations given to the Prophet Joseph Smith. As early as 1829, he was directed by the Lord to "seek to bring forth and establish the cause of Zion" (D&C 6:6; 11:6; 12:2; 14:6). On January 2, 1831, the Lord revealed to the Prophet Joseph Smith in Fayette, New York, that anciently he had taken the Zion of Enoch to himself, and then he commanded the prophet to go to Ohio to receive the law (see D&C 38:4, 32; cf. Moses 7:21). There the revelation was given that established the basic principles of consecration (see D&C 42:32-39). Other scriptural references to consecration are found in D&C 42:29-42; D&C 78:5; D&C 49:20; and D&C 70:10.

The Lord also revealed several purposes of the Law of Consecration: to bring the Church to stand independent of all other institutions (see D&C 78:14); to strengthen Zion, adorning her in beautiful garments, as a bride prepared and worthy of the bridegroom (see D&C 33:17; 58: 11; 65:3; 82:14, 18; etc.); and to prepare the Saints for a place in the Celestial Kingdom (see D&C 78:7).

Orson Pratt, an early apostle under Joseph Smith and Brigham Young, observed that if the Lord's people aspire to the Celestial Kingdom, they must begin to learn the order of life that is there.[18] President John Taylor testified that consecration is a celestial law and, when observed, its adherents become a celestial people.[19] Thus, as we live this law men and women today can become like those of Enoch's day who were, "of one heart and one mind, . . . [with] no poor among them" (Moses 7:18).

The Lord's Law of Consecration is a part of the perfect law of Zion.[20] It reflects the wisdom of God, the intelligence of God and the power of God in its ability to govern those who will accept the Lord's revealed laws of the celestial kingdom and is an integral, fundamental, and indispensable part of the Lord's great plan for our happiness. Joseph was no doubt referring in part to the Law of Consecration, when he declared: "We have the revelation of Jesus, and the knowledge within us is sufficient to organize a righteous government upon the earth, and to give universal peace to all mankind, if they would receive it."[21] Unfortunately, experience has shown that it is not always an easy thing to accept and live truth—even among those who have been called to do so.

The early Saints sought to live this celestial law of Zion in Jackson County, Missouri, in the 1830's, but because of inexperience, ignorance, and not having received a fulness of priesthood ordinances, their attempts were aborted. However, in the wisdom of God, according to his time frame, the redemption of Zion—including living the Law of Consecration—will most assuredly come to pass. This will happen when the Lord has prepared an unselfish people, full of charity, who will be willing to share with one another the temporal blessings they have received from the Lord.

Under the Law of Consecration, individual freedom, liberty, agency and creativity are not only preserved, but are enthusiastically encouraged. At the same time, the needs of the poor are met—not by force, but by sacred *covenants* willingly and lovingly entered into by the Saints of God. Under the Law of Consecration, the problem of poverty is completely solved through a process that brings about a unity and oneness among the people of the Lord. Leonard Arrington has given this succinct description of the law:

> Briefly, the law was a prescription for transforming the highly individualistic economic order of Jacksonian America into a system characterized by economic equality, socialization of surplus incomes, freedom of enterprise, and group economic self-sufficiency. Upon the basic principle that the earth and everything on it belongs to the Lord, every person who was a member of the Church at the time the system was introduced or became a member thereafter was asked to "consecrate" or deed all his property, both real and personal, to the bishop of the church. The bishop would then grant an "inheritance" or "stewardship" to every family out of the properties so received, the amount depending on the wants and needs of the family, as determined jointly by the bishop and the prospective steward. The stewardship might be a farm, building lot, store, workshop, or mill. It was expected

that in some cases the consecrations would considerably exceed the stewardships. Out of the surplus thus made possible the bishop would grant stewardships to the poorer and younger members of the church who had no property to consecrate.[22]

In addition to the examples of Enoch's people and the Nephite Zion mentioned earlier, the scriptures also provide many other ancient echos of the Law of Consecration. In the Old Testament we have acts of consecration covenants with God (see Gen 9:8-17; Numbers 6). The New Testament provides accounts of the Saints having "all things common" (Acts 2, 4, 5).

Essentially, the Law of Consecration and stewardship provides key principles and procedures that are required for celestial living (see end of chapter Figure 9-C, The Law of Consecration and Stewardship).

We must recognize that all that we are and have belongs to the Lord. "The earth is the Lord's, and the fulness thereof" (Psalm 24:1); individuals are the Lord's stewards (see D&C 38:17; 104:11-14). We must esteem others as ourselves (see D&C 38:24-27; 51:3, 9; 70:14; 78:6; 82: 17). Free agency is to be maintained (see D&C 104:17). Men and women are made equal according to their wants, needs, and family situations (see D&C 51:3) There must be accountability for stewardships (see D&C 72:3; 104:13-18).

The Saints who desire to abide by the Lord's temporal law, consecrate all that they have—their time, talents, and possessions—to the Church and its purposes (see D&C 82:19; 64:34; 88:67-68; 987:12-14). Where property is involved, the consecration is done by legal deed through the bishop, the Lord's agent upon the earth. They were to place all their possessions into a common treasury—the rich their wealth, the poor their pittance. Then each member was to receive a sufficient portion—called an "inheritance"—from the common treasury to enable that person to continue in trade, business, or profession as desired. The farmer would receive land and implements; the tradesman, tools and materials; the merchant, necessary capital; the professional person, instruments, books, and the like. Members working for others would receive proportionate interests in the enterprises they served. No one would be without property. All would have an inheritance.[23]

Under the Law of Consecration each individual is expected to magnify his stewardship by being productive. As the basic standard of living is increased throughout the Church—the direct result of cooperative efforts—the Saints become a prosperous people. This cooperative approach to economics has profound ramifications. For example, under the Law of Consecration, where the people are inspired by a cooperative spirit, we will seek to produce the finest possible products at the most reasonable cost to the consumer so that all will benefit. By contrast, all too frequently, under a spirit of competition, companies seek to produce the cheapest commodity possible for the greatest profit. This policy benefits mostly the CEOs and those in the highest positions, and it creates ranks and divisions among the people, which vain things we have been commanded to avoid (see 3 Nephi 6:15-16).

Each individual is expected to give a yearly accounting of his stewardship. Presently, tithing settlement is a rudimentary form of this procedure. Under the Law of Consecration, excesses or "surpluses" go into the bishop's storehouse and are used for other stewardships and for assisting those who are, through no fault of their own, less productive. Here, the strong assist the weak. But the Lord has cautioned, "Thou shalt not be idle; for he that is idle shall not eat the bread nor wear the garments of the laborer" (D&C 42:42). There are two aspects to this commandment. The idle *poor* will not benefit from those who labor diligently, and the idle *rich* shall not eat the bread nor wear the garments of the working laborer! The bishop is the Lord's agent who judges these things. He is the judge in Israel.

The bishop's storehouse corresponds with the storehouse of the Gods. We see the connection between these two storehouses when we consider the promise associated with the oath and covenant of the Melchizedek Priesthood. The Lord promises those who receive the Melchizedek Priesthood and magnify their callings that the time will come when, "all that my Father hath shall be given unto him" (D&C 84:38). This same idea was affirmed by Paul when he explained that we will become "joint-heirs with Christ" in inheriting everything the Father has if we are willing to be obedient to his commandments (Romans 8:17).

Although the implementation of the law of consecration of property as revealed in the early 1830s was temporarily suspended (see History of the Church 4:93), the principles themselves were not discontinued.

Latter-day Saints have been given the law of consecration as an ideal and a challenge and promise for the future (see D&C 42:32-39). Zion can be redeemed only by obedience to this celestial law. At the proper time, the Lord's leaders will implement the program. While it is not clear what procedures will be revealed to implement the details, Latter-day Saints anticipate that the principles of stewardship, equality, agency, and accountability will eventually be subscribed to by all participants and that the goals originally envisioned will be reached (see D&C 78:7, 14; 82:14).

In an important Church welfare publication entitled *Providing in the Lord's Way* (1990) we find outlined current efforts to implement the principles of the Lord's Law of Consecration through the welfare programs of the Church. The booklet is intended for Church Welfare Committees and stresses the importance of individuals working for what they need. Regarding our need to work to obtain the necessities of life, President Marion G. Romney stated, "Let us work for what we need. Let us be self-reliant and independent. Salvation can be obtained on no other principle. Salvation is an individual matter, and we must work out our own salvation, in temporal as well as in spiritual things."[24]

While salvation is an individual matter, it may at times require the assistance of family members and others as well. Of this point we read, "The family . . . seeks first to solve its own problems, seeking assistance, when necessary, through the priesthood quorum, the Relief Society, and the ward. When each of these units has exhausted its ingenuity and resources, the reserves of the stake are utilized."[25] President Thomas S. Monson is also quoted: "The Lord's storehouse includes the time, talents, skills, compassion, consecrated material, and financial means of faithful Church members. These resources are available to the bishop in assisting those in need."[26] This is the way the Lord has revealed for his Saints to care for themselves and the poor and needy.

When we learn to follow the Lord's plan for providing the necessities of life—by learning to take care for ourselves, our families, and Church members in need—we are approximating the Lord's Celestial Law of Consecration, and we are fulfilling in part the Lord's command in which he said: "For Zion must increase in beauty, and in holiness; her borders must be enlarged; her stakes must be strengthened; yea, verily I say unto you, Zion must arise and put on her beautiful garments" (D&C 82:14).

This charge for the Saints of the latter days is in harmony with Isaiah's exhortation to "put on thy strength, O Zion" (Isaiah 52:1). The Prophet Joseph Smith explained that this means that God should call in the last days, those "who should hold the power of priesthood to bring again Zion, and the redemption of Israel; and to put on her strength is to put on the authority of the priesthood, which she, Zion, has a right to by lineage; also to return to that power which she had lost. . . . The bands of her neck are the curses of God upon her, or the remnants of Israel in their scattered condition [outside of Zion] among the Gentiles" (D&C 113:7-10).

Commenting on these and similar revelations, President Spencer W. Kimball said, "Isn't the plan beautiful? Don't you thrill to this part of the gospel that causes Zion to put on her beautiful garments? When viewed in this light, we can see that [welfare] is not a program, but the essence of the gospel. It is the crowning principle of a Christian life."[27]

Living the Law of Consecration and other principles associated with the building up of Zion will bring us the great unity, happiness, joy and that peace that comes from being a true disciple of Christ. On the other hand, if we reject celestial laws we will reap the consequences. We cannot reject truths from heaven without disaster.

We Shall Fail If We Are Not Faithful

The Lord used an interesting and touching parable to teach the true spirit of the Law of Consecration—and the consequences that will follow if we reject it:

> For what man among you having twelve sons, and is no respecter of them, and they serve him obediently, and he saith unto the one: Be thou clothed in robes and sit thou here; and to the other: Be thou clothed in rags and sit thou there—and looketh upon his sons and saith I am just?
>
> Behold, this I have given unto you as a parable, and it is even as I am. I say unto you, be one; *and if ye are not one ye are not mine* (D&C 38:26-27; emphasis added).

It follows that if we are one, we *are* the Lord's and because of the strength this unity brings, the Kingdom of God will roll forward to meet its prophetic destiny. President Hugh B. Brown spoke of these anticipated outcomes when he said, "I want to say to you, brethren, that in the midst of all the troubles, the uncertainties, the tumult and chaos through which the world is passing, almost unnoticed by the majority of the people of the world, there has been set up a kingdom, a kingdom over which God the Father presides, and Jesus Christ is King. That kingdom is rolling forward, as I say partly unnoticed, but it is rolling forward with a power and a force that will stop the enemy in its tracks while some of you live."[28]

The Lord expects us to anxiously anticipate the unfolding of his great plan for our happiness. He wants us to look forward with great hope for the time when we can live all the laws of Zion in their fulness. Then we can truly be the Lord's people—one with each other and with the hosts of heaven.

Although we are not required today to live the Law of Consecration in all of its outward forms, the Lord does expect us to understand his laws, embrace his principles, and willingly consecrate all that we have to the building up of the Church and establishing Zion. If we do not honor our covenants, we will fail not only to receive the promised blessings, but also suffer consequences for breaking our covenants.

The Prophet Joseph Smith reminded us that the Lord "has promised us great things; yea, even a visit from the heavens to honor us with His own presence."[29] However, he also warned us that if we are not faithful in this regard, God will seek another people. We must hearken to the warning voice of God or Zion will yet fail, and we will not be permitted to enter into his rest—his presence.

The scriptures warn us of pending destructions that will come upon the wicked if they do not repent. This warning applies not only to the unrighteous Gentiles *outside* the Church, it also applies to people *within* the Church who do not live up to the standards the Lord has revealed. No doubt it applies to Church members with *greater* force—to those among us who are "walking in darkness at noonday" (D&C 95:6; Job 5:14). Of us the Lord said, "Nevertheless, *Zion shall escape if she observe to do all things whatsoever I have commanded her.* But if she observe not to do whatsoever I have commanded her, I will visit her according to all her works, and with sore affliction, with pestilence, with plague, with sword, with vengeance, with devouring fire" (D&C 97:25-26).

After reading these revelations, I can not help but wonder how we are doing as a people. Will we escape the calamities because of our righteousness, or will we yet have to pass through hardships, pestilence, and calamity before we are a spiritually refined people? Evidently, we are not doing too well. As the Lord has warned us, the calamities of the last days will be first among the members of his own house. Those "who have professed to know" him but have not been true and faithful (see D&C 112:24-26; see also Isaiah 3:16-26; Isaiah 4:1-6).

This warning is related to the condemnation that is presently upon the Church because members have treated too lightly the messages of the Book of Mormon and the revelations that have been given regarding Zion (D&C 84:56-58). President Benson has referred to this condemnation. He exhorted members to repent of not placing the Book of Mormon at the center of their personal study, family teaching and missionary work.

"Because we have treated lightly the Book of Mormon, the Lord has stated in the 84th section of the Doctrine and Covenants that the whole Church is under condemnation...," President Benson said. "Now we not only need to say more about the Book of Mormon, but we need to do more with it."[30]

The principle/primary/main reason that President Benson gives for our remaining under this condemnation is pride. The Prophet Joseph Smith spoke about the effects of pride when he declared that pride is, "the very spirit which is wasting the strength of Zion like a pestilence; and if it is not detected and driven from you, it will ripen Zion for the threatened judgments of God.... All we can say by way of conclusion is, if the fountain of our tears be not dried up, we will still weep for Zion."[31]

While those who reject the laws of God will experience the fulness of his wrath upon them, those who do not take lightly the things of God—but love him and serve him with all their heart, might, mind, and strength—will receive the promised blessings. The Lord has assured us, "And now, behold, if Zion do these things she shall prosper, and spread herself and become very glorious, very great, and very terrible" (D&C 97:18). However, these glorious blessings of Zion are not to be obtained in one big step. Even now, we are building upon the foundation laid by Joseph Smith and his associates so that we might be prepared for the glory that is to come (see D&C 58:2-7).

MAN HAS A NEED FOR PREPARATION

Hugh Nibley, a former professor of Ancient Scriptures at Brigham Young University, once said that if heaven were to be revealed all at once, the culture shock would kill us. In other words, given our present fallen state, we must be brought *gradually* from the darkness of the world into the glorious light of the gospel. The principle of gradual growth relates especially to understanding and receiving the powers and blessings of the celestial kingdom. They are not to be had all at once. In order for us to receive them, there must be a time of preparation first.

The Prophet Joseph Smith taught the need for a preparation before a fulness of these blessings can be realized. He explained, "God has in reserve a time, or period appointed in His own bosom, when He will bring all His subjects, who have obeyed His voice and kept His commandments, into His celestial rest [presence].[32] This rest is of such perfection and glory, that *man has need of a preparation before he can, according to the laws of that kingdom, enter it and enjoy its blessings.* This being the fact, God has given certain laws to the human family, which, if observed, are sufficient to prepare them to inherit this rest."[33] The preparation Joseph spoke of involves being endowed with power, receiving the laws of his kingdom and our duties within the Church, and becoming sanctified before the Lord.

In order to establish Zion, we will need to be endowed with power from on high. This will be brought to pass as we are taught more perfectly, have experience, and know more perfectly concerning our duty and the things which he requires at our hands. Accordingly, the Saints are commanded to "act in the office in which [they are] appointed, in all diligence. He that is slothful shall not be counted worthy to stand, and he that learns not his duty and shows himself not approved shall not be counted worthy to stand" (D&C 107:99-100).

As we learn our appointed duty and stand in the office to which the Lord has called us, the army of the Lord will become very great and will be sanctified before the him, that "it may become fair as the sun, and clear as the moon, and that her banners may be terrible unto all nations; That the kingdoms of this world may be constrained to acknowledge that the kingdom of Zion is in very deed the kingdom of our God and his Christ; therefore, let us become subject unto her laws" (D&C 105:31-32; emphasis added).

We cannot subject ourselves to the laws of Zion however, unless we know them, and we cannot know them unless we are taught what they are and how to live them by those who have been charged with that responsibility. As we discussed in chapter six and elsewhere, the first step in the Lord's plan for the sanctification of his people was the calling of Joseph Smith and other messengers to *proclaim* the truths that constitute our Father's plan of happiness. When truth touches our hearts, we desire to do what the Lord wants us to do by receiving the gospel and being baptized. Through baptism, we leave a spiritually darkened world and come into the wonderful light of the gospel as it is taught within the Church. The gospel principles and ordinances offered within the Church are for the *perfecting of the Saints* to prepare us to receive the *promise of eternal life* and to establish Zion.

The establishment of Zion, the New Jerusalem, and the *power* and *protection* that will be manifest there is a part of her the great Restoration. The restoration of the fulness of the gospel, including the Law of Consecration prepares us for the glorious light and blessings of the Millennium. The Millennium will prepare the sons and daughters of God for the greatest of all his gifts—the incomprehensible blessings of exaltation and eternal life. So, we come from the world of ignorance and error into the light of the restored gospel. The gospel perfects us as families and prepares us to enter into the presence of the Lord and to establish Zion.

At times the way may seem long and the tasks that will lead us to our goal may seem difficult. But by keeping the grand vision of our ultimate destination before us we will not grow weary in well doing, in sacrificing our time and talents to build up the Church throughout the world. Instead we will look forward with eager anticipation for the fulfillment of these promised blessings.

In the Church today, we are laying the foundation for these marvelous blessings—including returning to the presence of our Heavenly Father. Indeed, Elder Howard W. Hunter has stated that, "The whole purpose for the Church . . . is to qualify individuals to return to the presence of God. That can only be done by their receiving the ordinances and making covenants in the temple."[34] As individuals prepare for and receive the ordinances of the temple and return to complete the vicarious work for their kindred dead, they build up/are building up the Church by fulfilling some of the purposes for which it was organized.

The apostle Paul provided us with a concise description of why the Church was organized. He explained that Christ, "gave some, apostles; and some, prophets; and some, evangelists; and some, pastors and teachers; For the *perfecting of the saints*, for the *work of the ministry*, for the *edifying of the body of Christ*; Till we all come in the *unity of the faith*, and of the knowledge of the Son of God, unto a perfect man, unto the measure of the stature of the fulness of Christ" (Ephesians 4:11-13). We will need the organization of the Church until we reach these goals described by Paul—the perfection of the Saints, the completion of missionary work, and a unification of the Saints in Christ—so that Zion may be brought forth out of her, as the woman in travail who brings forth a son (see JST, Revelation 12:7).

From Paul's statement given above, the three-fold mission of the Church may be extracted—1) To *proclaim the gospel* of the Lord Jesus Christ to every nation, kindred, tongue, and people, which involves gathering Israel and as many of the Gentiles who will embrace the everlasting covenant; 2) To *perfect the Saints* by preparing them to receive all the ordinances of the priesthood; and 3) To *redeem the dead* by performing vicarious priesthood ordinances for those who once lived on the earth but had not received them while living.[35]

These efforts stand as three grand pillars that bring people to Christ and perfect them through the new and everlasting covenant—in preparation for the time when Lord will bring his people into the peace, beauty, and joy of Zion, the New Jerusalem—when the Saints will, indeed, return to Jackson County, Missouri (see D&C 105), establish the New Jerusalem (see Ether 13:6), and live the fulness of her celestial laws (see D&C 105:5)—all of which is spoken of in the scriptures as "the redemption of Zion" (see D&C 100:3; D&C 103:15; D&C 105:1-16, 34).

THE REDEMPTION OF ZION

The Lord revealed on 20 July 1831, that the center place where the Zion of the latter days—the New Jerusalem that would live by God's celestial laws—would be located in the land of Missouri. "Behold, the place which is now called Independence is the center place; and a spot for the temple is lying westward, upon a lot which is not far from the courthouse. Wherefore, it is wisdom that the land should be purchased by the saints, and also every tract lying westward" (D&C 57:3-4).

Some have supposed that the Lord has changed his mind about the location of the center place of Zion—that Salt Lake City is to be the Zion of the latter days. We have a revelation that refutes this idea. The Lord said, *"Zion shall not be moved out of her place,* notwithstanding her children are scattered. They that remain, and are pure in heart, shall return, and come to their inheritances, they and their children, with songs of everlasting joy, to build up the waste places of Zion"* (D&C 101:17-18; emphasis added).

Subsequent to the 1831 revelation, selected individuals and families were sent to Missouri by the Prophet Joseph Smith to begin laying the foundations of Zion. But, as we have discussed above, these Saints were unsuccessful because they were without spiritual power. They were immature and greedy. In addition, they then had not received the fulness of the temple ordinances.

The New Jerusalem, the Zion of the latter days, can only be redeemed through increased powers of the priesthood—of which we have only seen a beginning—as they are systematically unfolded in the latter days (see D&C 121:28-32). Receiving a great spiritual endowment is a prerequisite for the redemption of Zion as the Lord affirmed, "And this [the redemption of Zion] cannot be brought to pass until mine elders are endowed with power from on high. For behold, I have prepared a great endowment and blessing to be poured out upon them, inasmuch as they are faithful and continue in humility before me" (D&C 105:11-12).

President Brigham Young described the endowment by saying: "Your *endowment* is, to receive *all* those ordinances of the House of the Lord, which are necessary for you, after you have departed this life, to enable you to walk back to the presence of the Father, passing the angels who stand as sentinels, being enabled to give them the key words, the signs and tokens, pertaining to the Holy Priesthood, and gain your eternal exaltation in spite of earth and hell."[36]

As latter-day Israel becomes sanctified and receives *all* of the ordinances of the House of the Lord, she will be endowed with great power from on high (see JST, Genesis 14:30-31; D&C 121:36; Helaman 10:4-6; *Teachings*, pp. 150-51). Nephi saw the power of God as it would descend upon the church of the Lamb, "And it came to pass that I, Nephi, beheld the power of the Lamb of God, that it descended upon the saints of the church of the Lamb, and upon the covenant people of the Lord, who were scattered upon all the face of the earth; and *they were armed with righteousness and with the power of God in great glory*" (1 Nephi 14:14; emphasis added).

The Spirit and Power of Elias, Elijah, and Messiah

Presently in the Church we are still laying the foundation for Zion (see D&C 64:33). This foundation work includes the gathering in of the house of Israel from all parts of the earth into The Church of Jesus Christ of Latter-day Saints; building temples throughout the world so that families, living and dead, can be sealed together in eternal, patriarchal family chains. Through this process, the Saints are being prepared to receive further knowledge and light that that will be receive in progressive magnitudes in Zion.

In an important sermon delivered on 19 March 1844, Joseph Smith spoke of three spirits and powers which operate upon the children of God to gather them, perfect them and prepare them to enter the presence of the Lord. Practically speaking, these spirits and powers represent phases we all must pass through in order to realize the full blessings of the everlasting covenant. Each phase builds upon the former, and all are necessary for the attainment of the full powers and blessings of Zion.

The Spirit and Power of Elias

As you may recall from the analogy of the hand used in Chapter 6 to illustrate the six steps in progressive peace, enlightenment, and protection (Figure 6-B), the first step (thumb) in the process of establishing Zion is to proclaim the gospel. This first step has to do with the spirit and power of Elias—which is a forerunner. (See end of chapter Figure 9-D, The Spirit and Power of Elias, Elijah, and Messiah.)

In his sermon on these three spirits and powers—Elias, Elijah and Messiah—the prophet Joseph began by explaining that there is a difference between the spirit of Elias and Elijah, and that he would first like to focus on the spirit of Elias. He said that those who have the spirit and power of Elias are involved in preparatory work. For example, John the Baptist's office and calling was that of an Elias. Missionaries also serve in the spirit and power of Elias. As forerunners, they call people from the darkness of the world into the light of the gospel. Joseph explained the preparatory nature of the mission of Elias:

> The spirit of Elias is to prepare the way for a greater revelation of God, which is the Priesthood of Elias, or the Priesthood that Aaron was ordained unto. And when God sends a man into the world to prepare for a greater work, holding the keys of the power of Elias, it was called the doctrine of Elias, even from the early ages of the world.... Any man that comes, having the spirit and power of Elias, he will not transcend his bounds....[37]

In other words, priesthood blessings come in steps *and the first step in receiving a fulness of the blessings of Zion comes through the spirit and power of Elias.* The spirit of Elias is the forerunner, or preparatory spirit, that prepares us for the next order of blessings associated with the spirit and power of Elijah.

The Spirit and Power of Elijah

The second spirit that moves upon the Saints in this enlightenment process is called the spirit and power of Elijah. Whereas the spirit of Elias brings us to the door of the Church, once in the Church, another spirit—the spirit of Elijah—takes over. Under the influence of the spirit and power of Elijah, we can receive further light and knowledge as we continue to hunger and thirst after righteousness. As we continue in light and truth, the spirit of Elijah prepares and perfects us to the point where we can be sealed to eternal life.

The Spirit of Elijah in fact prepares members of the Church to pass through the second door—making our calling and election sure as *families.* (See again Figure 9-D, The Spirit and Power of Elias, Elijah, and Messiah.) Joseph explained:

> Now for Elijah. The spirit, power, and calling of Elijah is, that ye have power to hold the key of the revelations, ordinances, oracles, powers and endowments of *the fulness of the Melchizedek Priesthood* and of the kingdom of God on the earth; and to receive, obtain, and perform all the

ordinances belonging to the kingdom of God, even unto the turning of the hearts of the fathers unto the children, and the hearts of the children unto the fathers, even those who are in heaven....

Now comes the point. What is the office and work of Elijah? It is one of the greatest and most important subjects that God has revealed. He should send Elijah to seal the children to the fathers, and the fathers to the children....

I wish you to understand this subject, for it is important; and if you receive it, this is the spirit of Elijah, that we redeem our dead, and connect ourselves with our fathers which are in heaven, and seal up our dead to come forth in the first resurrection; and here we want the power of Elijah to seal those who dwell on earth to those who dwell in heaven. This is the power of Elijah and the keys of the kingdom of Jehovah....

What you seal on earth, by the keys of Elijah, is sealed in heaven; and this is the power of Elijah, and this is the difference between the spirit and power of Elias and Elijah; for while the spirit of Elias is a forerunner, the *power of Elijah is sufficient to make our calling and election sure....* Here is the doctrine of election that the world has quarreled so much about.[38]

According to Joseph Smith's explanation, the power of Elijah is sufficient to make our calling and elections sure as families—both the living and the dead. Having our calling and election made sure is, Elder McConkie explained, "to be sealed up unto eternal life; it is to have the unconditional guarantee of exaltation in the highest heaven of the celestial world; it is to receive the assurance of godhood; it is, in effect, to have the day of judgment advanced, so that an inheritance of all the glory and honor of the Father's kingdom is assured prior to the day when the faithful actually enter into the divine presence to sit with Christ in his throne, even as he is 'set down' with his 'Father in his throne' (Rev. 3:21)."[39]

Regarding this crowning priesthood ordinance, Elder Bruce R. McConkie stated, "Those members of the Church who devote themselves wholly to righteousness, living by every word that proceedeth forth from the mouth of God, make their calling and election sure. That is, they receive the more sure word of prophecy, which means that the Lord seals their exaltation upon them while they are yet in this life."[40] Elder McConkie has explained this in more detail:

Among those who have received the gospel, and who are seeking diligently to live its laws and gain eternal life, there is an instinctive and determined desire to make their calling and election sure. Because they have tasted the good things of God and sipped from the fountain of eternal truth, they now seek the divine presence, where they shall know all things, have all power, all might, and all dominion, and in fact be like Him who is the great Prototype of all saved beings—God our Heavenly and Eternal Father (D&C

132:20). This is the end objective, the chief goal of all the faithful, and there is nothing greater in all eternity, "for there is no gift greater than the gift of salvation" (D&C 6:13).

Is it little wonder then that the Prophet Joseph, particularly during the latter and crowning years of his mortal ministry, repeatedly exhorted the saints to press forward with that steadfastness in Christ which would enable them to make their calling and election sure? "I am going on in my progress for eternal life," he said of himself; and then in fervent pleading to all the saints, he exclaimed: "Oh! I beseech you to go forward, go forward and make your calling and your election sure" (*Teachings*, p. 366).[41]

There is another dimension of the priesthood associated with the keys restored by Elijah that helps us understand more about what is involved with the spirit and power of Elijah. The prophets have associated making our calling election sure with being ordained kings and priests, and thus, receiving a "fulness *of the priesthood*" (D&C 124:28). John used the expression "kings and priests" when he said: "Unto him that loved us [Jesus Christ], and washed us from our sins in his own blood, and *hath made us kings and priests* unto God and his Father; to him be glory and dominion forever and ever. Amen" (Revelation 1:5-6; emphasis added).

Brigham Young explained that "*for any person to have the fulness of that priesthood, he must be a king and priest.* A person may have a portion of that priesthood, the same as governors or judges of England have power from the king to transact business; but that does not make them kings of England. A person may be anointed king and priest long before he receives his kingdom."[42] More recently, Elder Bruce R. McConkie has equated a fulness of the priesthood with being ordained kings and priests. He said:

> Holders of the Melchizedek Priesthood have power to press forward in righteousness, living by every word that proceedeth forth from the mouth of God, magnifying their callings, going from grace to grace, until through the fulness of the ordinances of the temple they *receive the fulness of the priesthood* and are ordained *kings and priests*. Those so attaining shall have exaltation and be kings, priests, rulers, and lords in their respective spheres in the eternal kingdoms of the great King who is God our Father.[43]

By way of review, then, the spirit and power of Elias comes first—then comes the spirit and power of Elijah. The power of Elijah is sufficient to make our calling and election sure. The keys that Elijah bestowed upon Joseph Smith and Oliver Cowdery (D&C 110:13-16) have been passed on to the successive apostles and presidents of the Church. As a result, true and faithful members of the Church can be sealed and sanctified. According to the word of the Lord: "And it shall be manifest unto my servant, by the voice of the Spirit, those that are chosen; and they shall be sanctified; And inasmuch as they follow the counsel which they receive, they shall have power after many days to accomplish all things pertaining to Zion" (D&C 105:36-37).

The Spirit and Power of Messiah

After Joseph Smith had finished discussing the spirit and power of Elias and Elijah, he concluded his sermon by focusing on the spirit of Messiah. He said: "The spirit of Elias is first, Elijah second, and Messiah last. Elias is a forerunner to prepare the way, and the spirit and power of Elijah is to come after, holding the keys of power, building the Temple to the capstone, placing the seals of the Melchizedek Priesthood upon the house of Israel, and making all things ready; then Messiah comes to His Temple, which is last of all."

The reference to "Messiah" in this statement is a direct reference to Jesus Christ. His mission is "above the spirit and power of Elijah, for He made the world, and was that spiritual rock unto Moses in the wilderness. Elijah was to come and prepare the way and build up the kingdom before the coming of the great day of the Lord, although the spirit of Elias might begin it.[44]

So, in review of this important sermon, Joseph is teaching us that the spirit and power of Elias acts as a forerunner to bring people from the world to a knowledge of the everlasting covenant. Metaphorically speaking, the Spirit of Elias stands outside the door of the Church calling people to accept the gospel covenant through baptism. (See again Figure 9-D, The Spirit and Power of Elias, Elijah, and Messiah.)

So, again, once in the Church, the Spirit of Elijah moves upon the members perfecting and inspiring them to press forward as families until their calling and election is made sure. When a fulness of the spirit and power of Elijah operates upon the Saints of God, making them faithful and true in the laws and covenants of the gospel, they reach a point at which they are prepared to enter the presence of the Lord. The Prophet Joseph Smith summaries the accomplishments of the three spirits and powers in these words.

> The spirit of Elias is first, Elijah second, and Messiah last. Elias is a forerunner to prepare the way, and the spirit and power of Elijah is to come after, holding the keys of power, building the Temple to the capstone, placing the seals of the Melchizedek Priesthood upon the house of Israel, and making all things ready; then Messiah comes to His Temple, which is last of all.
>
> Messiah is above the spirit and power of Elijah, for He made the world, and was the spiritual rock unto Moses in the wilderness. Elijah was to come and prepare the way and build up the kingdom before the coming of the great day of the Lord, although the spirit of Elias might begin it.[45]

As we can see the spirit and power of Elias and Elijah along with building temples, receiving temple ordinances, and honoring temple covenants all prepare the Saints for the coming of the Messiah, Jesus Christ. Beautifully harmonious and consistent with Joseph Smith's teachings is the charge by President Gordon B. Hinckley to have many temples build in the very near future. Temples, we are told, are necessary as places where the fulness of the priesthood may be granted the faithful (see D&C 124:28).

Now let's focus our attention on how the priesthood is connected with the progressive blessings of peace and enlightenment of which we have been speaking.

The Three Grand Orders of Priesthood

While it is true that *in the Church* there are two priesthoods, the Prophet Joseph Smith explained that there are actually *three* orders of the priesthood described in the scriptures: the Aaronic Order, the Melchizedek Order, and the Patriarchal Order.[46]

Even as the spirit and power of Elias is given to prepare us to receive the higher powers and blessings associated with the spirit and power of Elijah and Messiah, so the Aaronic and Melchizedek priesthoods are given to prepare us to receive the blessings and powers associated with the Patriarchal order of the priesthood.

As has been mentioned in earlier chapters, the keys of the Aaronic priesthood (with the Church offices of deacons, teachers, priests, and bishops) were restored by the resurrected John the Baptist (see D&C 13); the keys of the Melchizedek priesthood (with the Church offices including in part apostles, prophets, evangelists, pastors, elders, etc.) were restored by Peter, James, and John (see D&C 128:20). The eternal patriarchal priesthood or "the priesthood", (with kings and priests and queens and priestesses) were restored by Elijah the prophet (see D&C 2; Revelation 1:6).[47]

In a revelation dated 28 March 1835 the Lord revealed the names of the two priesthoods that operate within the Church namely, the Aaronic and the Melchizedek. He further explained,

> There are, *in the church,* two priesthoods, namely, the Melchizedek and Aaronic, including the Levitical Priesthood.
>
> Why the first is called the Melchizedek Priesthood is because Melchizedek was such a great high priest.
>
> Before his day it was called *the Holy Priesthood after the order of the Son of God.* But out of respect or reverence to the name of the Supreme Being, to avoid the too frequent repetition of his name, they, the church, in ancient days, called that priesthood after Melchizedek, or the Melchizedek Priesthood (D&C 107:3-4).

The reason why the patriarchal order of the priesthood is not listed with the Aaronic and Melchizedek orders of the priesthood mentioned above is because the patriarchal priesthood is not limited to the earthly ecclesiastical organization. Even though it is received through the sealing powers of those who hold these sacred keys, the apostles and prophets, the patriarchal priesthood will exist throughout the eternities after the earthly Church has fulfilled its mission. Patriarchal families will be sealed eternally by those holding the authority of the Melchizedek priesthood in the Church.

The Aaronic and Melchizedek Church priesthoods function like scaffolding around a temple under construction. The scaffolding is in place to build the holy temple. The temple under construction is the eternal family organization.

When families are sufficiently strong and dedicated and the Saints have finally reached "a unity of the faith" there will not be a need for the Aaronic and ecclesiastical Melchizedek orders of the Church any longer, and they will be done away. Or, to complete the analogy, when the perfect building is completed the scaffolding will no longer be needed and will be taken down.

Families who have reached this point will be sealed by the keys restored by Elijah—they will receive the blessings of the Patriarchal Order of the priesthood. Saints thus sealed are considered fruit laid up "against the season" (Jacob 5:27, 71). They will be connected and sealed as families—children to parents, wives to husbands, and fathers to fathers—in a patriarchal chain which will eventually extend all the way back to father Adam and mother Eve (see D&C 128:17-18).

This Patriarchal Priesthood chain of kings and priests, when it is fully established, will constitute the social government in Zion and in the celestial kingdom (see Moses 6:7). Interestingly, Jesus is identified in the scriptures as King of these kings and Lord of these lords (see Revelation 19:16).

The Patriarchal Order of the Priesthood

Various important passages in the scriptures help us understand the Patriarchal Order of the priesthood. Section 107 of the Doctrine and Covenants provides information about the three orders of the priesthood: verses 1-38 deal with the Aaronic and Melchizedek Orders while verses 39-57 deal with the Patriarchal Order.

The blessings associated with the Patriarchal Order of the priesthood are mentioned in several passages of modern scripture. For instance, "In the celestial glory there are three heavens or degrees; and in order to obtain the highest, a man must enter into *this order of the priesthood* [meaning the new and everlasting covenant of marriage]; And if he does not, he cannot obtain it. He may enter into the other, but that is the end of his kingdom; he cannot have an increase" (D&C 131:2-4). In other words, eternal marriage in the new and everlasting covenant is a prerequisite to receiving the fulness of the priesthood. Initially, these blessings are given on a conditional basis—*but* if the couple remains true and faithful these blessings are eventually realized.

It is important to stress, in connection with this discussion of the priesthood, that the *blessings* that come through the ordinances of the priesthood—including baptism, confirmation, and all of the temple blessings—are available to both men and women alike. Indeed, the highest blessings of the priesthood cannot be had singly. Husbands and wives must receive them together (see D&C 131:1-4). Only men, however, *hold the priesthood,* which is defined as being the power and authority of God given to men on the earth to administer the ordinances of salvation.

Understanding that all the priesthood orders are branches of the Melchizedek priesthood is an important consideration. Joseph Smith explained this idea in these words: "*All priesthood is Melchizedek,* but there are different portions or degrees of it. That portion which brought Moses to speak with God face to face [Melchizedek including patriarchal] was taken away; but that which brought the ministry of angels [Aaronic or Levitical] remained. All the prophets had the Melchizedek Priesthood and were ordained by God Himself."[48]

The patriarchal order of the priesthood was restored by Elijah in fulfillment of Malachi's prophecy found in Malachi 4:5-6. This prophecy was affirmed by Moroni when he quoted it, with some important variations, to the boy prophet, Joseph Smith. Moroni quoted Malachi by saying, "Behold, I will reveal unto you *the priesthood,* by the hand of Elijah the prophet, before the coming of the great and dreadful day of the Lord. And he shall plant in the hearts of the children the promises made to the fathers, and the hearts of the children shall turn to their fathers. If it were not so, the whole earth would be utterly wasted at his coming" (D&C 2).

"The priesthood" mentioned by Moroni that was to be restored by Elijah is the Patriarchal Order of the priesthood. In the scriptures, receiving the Patriarchal Priesthood is also known as entering "this order and calling" (JST, Genesis 14:30; also D&C 131:2) and the "fulness of the priesthood" (D&C 124:28). Those who receive the Patriarchal Priesthood are made "kings and priests" (Revelation 1:6) in the *eternal* priesthood which functions everlastingly in the eternities.

For example, Abraham received the fulness of the priesthood under the hands of Melchizedek. Joseph Smith explained: "Abraham gave a tenth part of all his spoils and then received a blessing under the hands of Melchizedek even *the last law or a fulness of the law or priesthood which constituted him a king and priest after the order of Melchizedek or an endless life.*"[49] (See end of chapter Figure 9-F, Sealing Powers, Then and Now.) Again, this priesthood is not confined to the Church on the earth—hence, there are indeed three priesthood orders, but only two of them exist within the Church organization.

Another important expression used in connection with being sealed to eternal life and receiving the Patriarchal Priesthood is the term, "evangelist". In speaking about the blessings associated with making one's calling and election sure, or receiving a fulness of the priesthood, Joseph Smith explained that "an Evangelist is a Patriarch."[50] The Doctrine and Covenants explains that, "It is the duty of the Twelve in all large branches of the Church, to ordain *evangelical ministers,* as they shall be designated unto them by revelation. The *order of this priesthood* was confirmed to be handed down from father to son, and rightly belongs to the literal descendants of the chosen seed, to whom the promises were made" (D&C 107:39-40; emphasis added).

This scripture is usually thought of as referring to the selection and ordination of stake patriarchs. However, the fact that this order of the priesthood was to be passed from father to son seems to indicate that it is referring to something other than that—the calling of a stake patriarch is not passed from father to son. Evangelical ministers are natural patriarchs to their families. They hold the fulness of the priesthood. They are kings and priests![51]

Such righteous souls are chosen and sealed to eternal life—they receive the Patriarchal Order of the priesthood. In connection with this sacred process, we are reminded that, "There has been a day of *calling,* but the time has come for a day of choosing; and let those be *chosen* that are worthy, And it shall be manifest unto my servant, by the voice of the Spirit, those that are chosen; and *they shall be sanctified*; And inasmuch as they follow the counsel which they receive, they shall have power after many days to accomplish all things pertaining to Zion" (D&C 105:35-37). Here, those who are *called* are members of the Church. Those who are *chosen* are the true and faithful Saints who, because they have proven themselves worthy have their calling and election made sure.

However, many are called into the Church, but few are chosen and sealed to eternal life! And why are so few chosen? In the Lord gives the answer: "Because their hearts are set so much upon the things of this world, and aspire to the honors of men" (D&C 121:35). As a consequence, they do not learn the relationship between priesthood righteousness and priesthood power; those who are not chosen "do not learn this one lesson—that the rights of the priesthood are inseparably connected with the powers of heaven, and that the powers of heaven cannot be controlled nor handled only upon the principles of righteousness (D&C 121:35-36).

To state this same principle in the positive, we may say that the chosen ones have learned this one lesson that, "the powers of heaven *can* be controlled and handled upon the principles of righteousness!" This idea is vital for us to understand, and peace of mind during the calamities of the last days will follow, because deliverance of the Saints is associated with their learning the relationship between righteousness and priesthood power (see 1 Nephi 14:13-14).

How God Shall CSome to the Rescue of this Generation

In Joseph's sermon on the three orders of Priesthood, he asked the question: "How shall God come to the rescue of this generation?" He gave this answer: "He will send Elijah the prophet.... The anointing and sealing [through the keys of Elijah] is to be called, elected and made sure.⁵² In other words, as we have mentioned earlier, before the "great and dreadful day of the Lord" Elijah must visit the earth (Malachi 4:5-6). Were it not for the return of Elijah and the keys he restored, the whole earth would be utterly wasted or destroyed at the Second Coming. However, since he *did* come and his keys were restored, the righteous will not be wasted but will be preserved in a day of calamity as foreseen by John the Revelator and other prophets both ancient and modern.

The Mystery of the Sixth Seal—Who Shall be Able to Stand?

John the Revelator was permitted to see events that would happen during the seven thousand years of the earth's continuance (see D&C 77:6, 12). When he viewed the happenings of the sixth thousand year period, he wrote:

> And I beheld when he had opened the sixth seal, and lo, there was a great earthquake; and the sun became black as sackcloth of hair, and the moon became as blood;
> And the stars of heaven fell unto the earth, even as a fig tree casteth her untimely figs, when she is shaken of a mighty wind,
> And the heaven departed as a scroll when it is rolled together; and every mountain and island were moved out of their places.
> And the kings of the earth, and the great men, and the rich men, and the chief captain, and the mighty men, and every bondman, and every free man, hid themselves in the dens and in the rocks of the mountains;
> And said to the mountains and rocks, Fall on us, and hide us from the face of him that sitteth on the throne, and from the wrath of the Lamb:
> For the great day of his wrath is come; and *who shall be able to stand?* (Revelation 6:12-17).

John answered question in all important question stated in the last verse above about "who shall be able to stand"? He saw in vision how the Saints would be sealed in the last days —by having their calling and elections made sure and receiving the fulness of the patriarchal priesthood—and thereby escape the destructions that would come upon the wicked. In describing how this would take place he said:

> I saw four angels standing on the four corners of the earth, holding the four winds of the earth, that the wind should not blow on the earth, nor on the sea, nor on any tree.

And I saw another angel ascending from the east, having the seal of the living God: and he cried with a loud voice to the four angels, to whom it was given to hurt the earth and the sea,

Saying, *Hurt not the earth, neither the sea, nor the trees, till we have sealed the servants of our God in their foreheads* (Rev. 7:1-3; emphasis added).

Joseph Smith explained how God would come to the rescue of this generation by referring to these passages in the Book of Revelation and then teaching:

The world is reserved unto burning in the last days. He shall send Elijah the prophet, and he shall reveal the covenants of the fathers in relation to the children, and the covenants of the children in relation to the fathers.

Four destroying angels holding power over the four quarters of the earth until the servants of God are sealed in their foreheads, which signifies sealing the blessing upon their heads, meaning the everlasting covenant, *thereby making their calling and election sure.*"[53]

Here the Prophet tells us categorically that, "the *anointing and sealing is to be called, elected and made sure.*"[54] In other words, safety for the Saints in the last days is associated with making their calling and election sure—or in the words of John, it has to do with the Saints being "sealed in their foreheads."

In this same vision of the last days, John saw 144,000 men who were sealed to eternal life (D&C 77:11). Then he saw "*a great multitude,* which no man could number, of all nations, and kindreds, and people, and tongues ... [who] came out of great tribulation, and have washed their robes, and made them white in the blood of the Lamb" (Rev. 7:9, 14; emphasis added). In short, John saw many men and women who were chosen, sanctified, and sealed to eternal life—who thus escaped the destructions of the last days.

Joseph Smith made the obtaining of these sealing powers—and thus the protection that would accompany them—the central issue of the dedicatory prayer of the Kirtland temple. He petitioned the Lord:

Let the *anointing of thy ministers be sealed upon them* with power from on high....

Put upon thy servants the testimony of the covenant, that when they go out and proclaim thy word they may seal up the law, and prepare the hearts of thy saints for all those judgments thou art about to send, in thy wrath, upon the inhabitants of the earth, because of their transgressions, that thy people may not faint in the day of trouble....

And *until this be accomplished, let not thy judgments fall upon that city....*

But deliver thou, O Jehovah, we beseech thee, thy servants from their hands, and cleanse them from their blood.

O Lord, we delight not in the destruction of our fellow men; their souls are precious before thee;

But thy word must be fulfilled. Help thy servants to say, with thy grace assisting them: Thy will be done, O Lord, and not ours.

We know that thou hast spoken by the mouth of thy prophets terrible things concerning the wicked, in the last days—that thou wilt pour out thy judgments, without measure;

Therefore, O Lord, *deliver thy people from the calamity* of the wicked; *enable thy servants to seal up the law, and bind up the testimony, that they may be prepared against the day of burning* (D&C 109:35, 38, 40, 42-46; emphasis added).

About one week later, in answer to this prayer, Elijah came and endowed Joseph Smith and Oliver Cowdery with these sealing powers (D&C 110:13-16). In a series of remarks on the priesthood, Joseph explained why it was necessary for Elijah to be sent: "Elijah was the last Prophet that held the keys of the Priesthood.... Why send Elijah? Because he holds the keys of the authority to administer in *all the ordinances of the Priesthood;* and without the authority is given, the ordinances could not be administered in righteousness."[55]

In another sermon, Joseph explained the importance of making our calling and election sure when he said: "The Saints have not too much time to save and redeem their dead, and gather together their living relatives, that they may be saved also, before the earth will be smitten, and the consumption decreed fall upon the world. I would advise all the Saints to go with their might and gather together all their living relatives to this place, *that they may be sealed and saved,* that they may be prepared against that day that the destroying angel goes forth."[56]

The keys and authority to receive these ordinances have been restored to the earth. Now we must follow Joseph's admonition mentioned earlier and go forward and make our calling and election sure. The time is not too far distant when these calamities will be upon us, and we will need the power and protection that these ordinances afford us.

Protection through Priesthood Power

At this point it may be useful for you to again review Figure 6-B in chapter 6—The Six Steps in Progressive Peace, Enlightenment, and Protection. With being sealed and receiving a fulness of the priesthood come marvelous powers from on high—powers which will provide protection from the calamities of the last days. However, both priesthood authority and great faith are required before these kinds of miraculous powers of God can be experienced.

From *Lectures on Faith* we read: "As we receive by faith all temporal blessings that we do receive, so we in like manner receive by faith all spiritual blessings that we do receive. But faith is not only the principle of action, *but of power also,* in all intelligent beings, whether in heaven or on earth." (Lecture 1:13; emphasis added).

Regarding former day Saints and the blessings which flowed from their faith, we read:

> According as his faith was, so were his blessings and privileges; and *nothing was withheld from him when his faith was sufficient to receive it.* He could stop the mouths of lions, quench the violence of fire, escape the edge of the sword, wax valiant in fight, and put to flight the armies of the aliens; women could, by their faith, receive their dead children to life again; in a word, there was nothing impossible with them who had faith. All things were in subjection to the Former-day Saints, according as their faith was. By their faith they could obtain heavenly visions, the ministering of angels, have knowledge of the spirits of just men made perfect, of the general assembly and church of the first born whose names are written in heaven, of God the judge of all, of Jesus the Mediator of the new covenant, and become familiar with the third heavens, see and hear things which were not only unutterable, but were unlawful to utter.[57]

So, faith plays a most important role in receiving peace and protection in every dispensation. But how do we gain such faith as they had? The ancient Saints were able to develop the faith necessary for them to receive great knowledge, power and protection by believing the testimonies of those who knew God. We have this same opportunity today. Again from *Lectures on Faith*, we read:

> God became an object of faith among men after the fall; and what it was that stirred up the faith of multitudes to feel after him—to search after a knowledge of his character, perfections and attributes, until they became extensively acquainted with him, and not only commune with him and behold his glory, but *be partakers of his power* and stand in his presence.
>
> It was the testimony of others who knew God, that stirred up the faith among men after the fall ... to search after a knowledge of his character, perfections and attributes, until they became extensively acquainted with him, and not only commune with him, and behold his glory, *but be partakers of his power* and stand in his presence.... The inquiry [after God] frequently terminated, indeed always terminated when rightly pursued, in *the most glorious discoveries and eternal certainty.*[58]

The Nephite Saints are an example of a people who had faith in the things that were taught them. They pursued a righteous course which led them to glorious discoveries and eternal certainty—through which they received great priesthood power. Of their experience Jacob wrote: "Wherefore, we search the prophets, and we have many revelations and the spirit of prophecy; and having all these witnesses we obtain a hope, and *our faith becometh unshaken, insomuch that we truly can command in the name of Jesus and the very trees obey us, or the mountains, or the waves of the sea"* (Jacob 4:6; emphasis added).

Like the Nephites, the righteous descendants of Enoch were promised these same powers and blessings. We are Enoch's descendants through Noah, and if we seek them properly these powers and blessings can and will be ours. Of this promise we read:

> For God having sworn unto Enoch and unto his seed with an oath by himself; that *everyone being ordained after this order and calling* should have power, by faith, to break mountains, to divide the seas, to dry up waters, to turn them out of their course;
> To put at defiance the armies of nations, to divide the earth, to break every band, to stand in the presence of God; to do all things according to his will, according to his command, subdue principalities and powers; and this by the will of the Son of God which was from before the foundation of the world.[59]

In order to obtain these great powers and blessing, however, we must meet the conditions set forth by our Father for obtaining them for "when we obtain any blessing from God, it is by obedience to that law upon which it is predicated" (D&C 130:21).

It Shall be Given You What You Shall Ask

The Lord has given us the conditions upon which the powers and blessings of which we have been speaking are predicated. Latter-day revelation makes clear that these marvelous powers are to be given only after we are cleansed from *all* sin, and that they are to be used only as the Lord directs. The Lord cautions us by explaining, "No man is possessor of all things except he be purified and cleansed from all sin. And if ye are purified and cleansed from all sin, ye shall ask whatsoever you will in the name of Jesus and it shall be done. But know this, *it shall be given you what you shall ask"* (D&C 50:28-30; emphasis added).

Throughout the scriptures we find many examples of faithful Saints receiving this kind of priesthood power through their faith and righteousness. Nephi, the son of Helaman, was one such person. To him the Lord declared:

Blessed art thou, Nephi, for those things which thou hast done; for I have beheld how that hast with unwearyingness declared the word, which I have given unto thee, unto this people. And thou hast not feared them, and hast not sought thine own life, but hast sought my will, and to keep my commandments.

And now, because thou hast done this with such unwearyingness, behold, *I will bless thee forever;* and I will make thee mighty in word and in deed, in faith and in works; yea, even that *all things shall be done unto thee according to thy word, for thou shalt not ask that which is contrary to my will.*

Behold, thou art Nephi, and I am God. Behold, I declare it unto thee in the presence of mine angels, that *ye shall have power over this people,* and shall smite the earth with famine, and with pestilence, and destruction, according to the wickedness of this people.

Behold, *I give unto you power,* that whatsoever ye shall seal on earth shall be sealed in heaven; and whatsoever ye shall loose on earth shall be loosed in heaven; and thus shall *ye have power among this people.*

And thus, if ye shall say unto this temple it shall be rent in twain, it shall be done.

And if ye shall say unto this mountain, Be thou cast down and become smooth, it shall be done.

And behold, if ye shall say that God shall smite this people, it shall come to pass (Helaman 10:4-10; emphasis added).

Similarly we read of Moses and Enoch who were given, because of their righteousness, the powers of heaven—they were chosen and given the power of God. The Lord explained to Moses, "Blessed art thou, Moses, for I, the Almighty, have *chosen thee*, and thou shalt be made stronger than many waters; for they shall obey thy command *as if thou wert God"* (Moses 1:25 emphasis added). And to Enoch, the Lord promised: "Behold my Spirit is upon you, wherefore *all thy words will I justify;* and the *mountains* shall flee before you, and the *rivers* shall turn from their course; and thou shalt abide in me, and I in you; therefore walk with me (Moses 6:34; emphasis added).

By way of review, before we can experience the kind of faith mentioned above, we must join the Church, become perfected, receive the promise of eternal life, have the heavens opened to us and be taught by heavenly beings. Through the instructions we receive in this experience, we will obtain the sealing powers necessary for our protection in the last days."[60]

Lord's Battle Plan Implemented

The faith and righteousness of the people and the sealing powers revealed from heaven will be instrumental in protecting the Saints in the last days—in days of wars, calamities, and fires. The sealing powers are an integral part of the Lord's battle plan for the last days, of which we have spoken in earlier chapters. President Thomas S. Monson reflected upon the Lord's battle plan when he stated:

> Today, we are encamped against the greatest array of sin, vice, and evil ever assembled before our eyes. Such formidable enemies may cause lesser hearts to shrink or shun the fight. But *the battle plan* whereby we fight to save the souls of men is not our own. It was provided ... by the inspiration and revelations of the Lord.... And as we do battle against him who would thwart the purposes of God and degrade and destroy mankind, I pray that each of us will stand in his or her appointed place, that the battle for the souls of men will indeed be won.[61]

Indeed, we do engage the evil one in battle. The forces of darkness are on every side. But we must always remember that we have the reassuring promise of the Lord that he is mighty—even to "the power of deliverance" for those who place their faith in him (1 Nephi 1:20).

When Jacob Comes of Age

On the last day of Joseph Smith's life, he uttered a remarkable prophecy that is relatively unknown by the members of the Church. As a backdrop for his prophecy, he made a comparison between the boyhood of Jesus and the youth-fulness of the latter-day Church. He said of Jesus, *"When still a boy He had all the intelligence necessary to enable Him to rule and govern the kingdom of the Jews,* and could reason with the wisest and most profound doctors of law and divinity, and make their theories and practice to appear like folly compared with the wisdom He possessed; *but he was a boy only, and lacked the physical strength even to defend His own person;* and was *subject to cold, hunger and to death...."*

The Prophet continued by saying, "So it is with the Church of Jesus Christ of Latter-day Saints; we have the revelation of Jesus, and the knowledge within us is sufficient to organize a righteous government upon the earth, and to give universal peace to all mankind, if they would receive it, but we lack the physical strength, as did our Savior when a child, to defend our principles..."

Then Joseph made this statement by way of prophecy: "And we have of necessity to be afflicted, persecuted and smitten, and to bear it patiently *until Jacob is of age, then he will take care of himself."*[62]

Who is Jacob and When Will he Come of Age?

What did Joseph Smith mean when he said that the Saints, the remnant of Jacob, must bear persecution patiently "until Jacob is of age, then he will take care of himself"? Here Joseph is prophesying that the day will come when latter-day Israel, or Jacob, will be able to take care of himself because he is spiritually mature—sanctified—and is endowed with power and protection from on high (see D&C 105:9-14, 31). The idea of Jacob coming of age is a metaphor for the sanctification of the Saints, and their receiving the full blessings and powers of the priesthood associated with the New Jerusalem, the latter-day Zion.

What geophysical powers and sociopolitical evils would necessitate latter-day Israel being endowed with power from on high? In vision Nephi saw such conditions in the latter days and recorded he saw that, "the great mother of abominations did gather together multitudes upon the face of all the earth, among all the nations of the Gentiles, to fight against the Lamb of God." Within in this context of latter-day oppression of the Saints, Nephi saw the Lord's great battle plan put into operation: "And it came to pass that I, Nephi beheld the power of the Lamb of God, that it descended upon the saints of the Church of the Lamb, and upon the covenant people of the Lord, who were scattered upon all the face of the earth; and they were armed with righteousness and with the power of God in great glory" (1 Nephi 14:13-14).

Nephi's vision is consistent with many revelations that speak of certain forces of darkness that will combine in the last days and seek to destroy the people of God and the work of the Lord. In a revelation to Joseph Smith, the Lord warned, "Behold, the enemy is *combined.* And now I show unto you a mystery, a thing which is had in *secret chambers,* to bring to pass even your destruction in process of time, and ye knew it not ... And again, I say unto you that the *enemy in the secret chambers seeketh your lives* ... I tell you these things because of your prayers; wherefore, *treasure up wisdom in your bosoms,* lest the wickedness of men reveal these things unto you by their wickedness, in a manner which shall speak in your ears with a voice louder than that which shall shake the earth; but *if ye are prepared ye shall not fear* (D&C 38:12-13, 28, 30; emphasis added).

The Remnant of Jacob Like a Lion Among Sheep

In the early paragraphs of this chapter we discussed the idea that if we are prepared by following the counsel of our modern prophets and apostles, we will have no need to fear the calamities and oppressions of the latter days. From the time the Book of Mormon was first published in 1830 we have been counseled by the apostles and the prophets to prepare ourselves by reading and pondering and applying the principles of this ancient record. In recent years this counsel has become more and more urgent.[63] There is much within its pages that provides wonderful insight, counsel, and comfort. For example, in addition to the ones already quoted, there are many other scriptures that deal with this theme of deliverance for the Saints in a time of persecution. Three times the resurrected Lord spoke to the Nephites about the great power and protection that would be given to the remnants of Jacob in the last days. Of this empowerment he said:

And I say unto you, that if the Gentiles do not repent after the blessing which they shall receive, after they have scattered my people—

Then shall *ye, who are a remnant of the house of Jacob,* go forth among them; and ye shall be in the midst of them who shall be many; and ye shall be among them as a lion among the beasts of the forest, and as a young lion among the flocks of sheep, who, if he goeth through both treadeth down and teareth in pieces, and none can deliver.

Thy hand shall be lifted up upon thine adversaries, and all thine enemies shall be cut off.

And I will gather my people together as a man gathereth his sheaves into the floor.

For *I will make my people with whom the Father hath covenanted, yea, I will make thy horn iron, and I will make thy hoofs brass.* And thou shalt beat in pieces many people; and I will consecrate their gain unto the Lord, and their substance unto the Lord of the whole earth. And behold, I am he who doeth it.

And it shall come to pass, saith the Father, that the sword of my justice shall hang over them at that day; and except they repent it shall fall upon them, saith the Father, yea, even upon *all the nations of the Gentiles.*

And it shall come to pass that I will establish my people, O house of Israel.

And behold, this people will I establish in this land, unto the fulfilling of the covenant which I made with your father Jacob; and it shall be a New Jerusalem. And the *powers of heaven shall be in the midst of this people; yea, even I will be in the midst of you"* (3 Nephi 20:15-22; see also 3 Nephi 16:13-15; 21:11-21; D&C 87:5; Mal. 4:3; Psalm 2).

The development of these powers is vital for latter-day Israel's protection against the calamities which will certainly come. Joseph Smith prophecy regarding Jacob coming of age has been predicted by the ancient prophets, and we can see events unfolding in our own day that will necessitate the powers and blessings of protection that will undoubtedly come to those who are prepared. In the meantime, what is our duty and responsibility?

THE ENSIGN OF PEACE

While we eagerly and anxiously await the day of the Lord's power and his presence, our current charge is to raise the ensign of peace to all nations. We are to be a peace loving, peace seeking, and peace teaching people. Though we know that the calamities will come upon the wicked, the Saints still have a solemn charge to do all they can to establish peace in the earth.

The Lord has reminded us of our duty to sue for peace. He has commanded us in these words: *"Talk not of judgments, neither boast of faith nor of mighty works,* but carefully gather together, as much in one region as can be, consistently with the feelings of the people" (D&C 105: 24). Continuing, the Lord said:

> And behold, I will give unto you favor and grace in their eyes, that you may rest in peace and safety, while you are saying unto the people: Execute judgment and justice for us according to law, and redress us of our wrongs.
>
> Now, behold, I say unto you, my friends, in this way you may find favor in the eyes of the people, until the army of Israel becomes very great (D&C 105:25-26).
>
> And again, I say unto you, *sue for peace,* not only to the people that have smitten you, but also to all people;
>
> And *lift up an ensign of peace, and make a proclamation of peace unto the ends of the earth;*
>
> And make *proposals for peace* unto those who have smitten you, according to the voice of the Spirit which is in you, and all things shall work together for your good.
>
> Therefore, be faithful; and behold, and lo, I am with you even unto the end. Even so. Amen (D&C 105:38-41; emphasis added).

PATIENCE AND PERSEVERANCE

Though it will one day come, the peace for which we are seeking will not come all at once. It will be established according to the righteousness of the people and the timetable of the Lord. In addition, the miracles and marvelous priesthood powers about which we have been reading can only be realized according to the revelations of our Heavenly Father. Righteousness, great faith, and priesthood ordinances are prerequisites to these awesome and superhuman powers (see D&C 121:36). These too, take time to be realized. In the meantime we must be patient and persevering as we assist in the establishment of Zion.

Elder Bruce R. McConkie has counseled us about the need for patience in our progress. He gave wise counsel when he said, "As we read some of the inspired statements of Joseph Smith, we ... discover that repetitiously the Prophet also equates faith with power. He uses the terms interchangeably. Indeed, the possession of power constitutes the test whereby we can measure and determine the quality and the degree of faith we possess. Our faith consists of the degree of power and influence we have with God our Father whereby we do works of righteousness and do many miraculous things.[64]

In this same address Elder McConkie pointed out that the power to perform miracles is not to be had all at once in the Church or individually. We must increase gradually in faith and in righteousness in order to obtain these mighty works. He continued:

We grow in faith; we go step by step from a lower degree to a higher degree. We add grace to grace until eventually we get to a state where we have perfected our faith.... *Don't go out now and try to cast sycamine trees into the sea. Don't go out and try to move mountains,* but go out and start in a small degree to do the thing you need to do in your life to get what you ought to have temporally and spiritually.... Work on the projects ahead, and when you have taken one step in the acquiring of faith, it will give you the assurance in your soul that you can go forward and take the next step, and by degrees your power or influence will increase until eventually, in this world or in the next, you will say to the Mt. Zerins in your life, "Be thou removed." You will say to whatever encumbers your course of eternal progress, "Depart," and it will be so.⁶⁵

As our faith increases so will our ability to move the work of the Lord forward in an unprecedented way. In 1979, President Spencer W. Kimball stated that the Church was on the verge of major growth—both in numbers and in spiritual strength. He then offered this challenge:

It seems clear to me, indeed, this impression weighs upon me—that the Church is at a point in its growth and maturity when we are at last ready to move forward in a major way.... But the basic decisions needed for us to move forward, as a people, must be made by the individual members of the Church.... Let us not shrink from the next steps in our spiritual growth...by holding back, or side stepping our fresh opportunities for service to our families and our fellowmen. Let us trust the Lord and take the next steps in our individual lives. He has promised us that he will be our tender tutor, measuring what we are ready for: "And ye cannot bear all things now; nevertheless, be of good cheer, for I will lead you along." (D&C 78:18.) He will not ask us to bear more than we can bear nor thrust upon us that for which we are not yet ready. But likewise, we must not tarry too long when we are ready to move on.⁶⁶

The Lord will sustain as we seek to build his kingdom and to bring forth and establish Zion. As we continue to press forward, we have many blessings and promises to look forward to. President Marion G. Romney has spoken of the wonderful blessings that will be realized when the survivors of our present generation are finally sanctified and are thus prepared for Zion. At a gathering of Relief Society sisters, he repeated the Lord's promise:

You know, sisters, if mothers and fathers would under the direction of the Holy Spirit, strictly follow the commandments of the Lord and the counsels of his prophets to train up their children in the way they would walk, the inhabitants of the earth would soon reach that glorious state enjoyed by the Nephites when "there were no contentions and disputations among them, and every man did deal justly one with another," ... Although such a blessed state seems beyond our present hope, *let us not forget that the Lord has given us the assurance that the survivors of our present generation will enjoy a like society.* This assurance should, and I believe it does, give us a determination to train up our children in the way they should go that they with us may be participants in the fulfillment of that glorious promise.[67]

In the days that lie ahead we will see some of the most magnificent developments come to pass among the membership of the Church—and, on the other hand, we will witness some of the most awful developments among the wicked. We must remember that "if [we] are prepared, [we] shall not fear!" (D&C 38:30) The great plan of happiness, prepared by our loving Heavenly Father, does indeed prepare us for every need.

President Joseph F. Smith, one of the great spiritual weather men of our dispensation, has given us a clear call to be obedient to the principles and ordinances of the gospel so we will be eligible for the blessings of power and protection in the last days.

Now, so long as the Latter-day Saints are content to obey the commandments of God, to appreciate the privileges and blessings which they enjoy in the Church, and will use their time, their talents, their substance, in honor to the name of God, to build up Zion, and to establish truth and righteousness in the earth, so long our heavenly Father is bound by His oath and covenant *to protect them* from every opposing foe, and *to help them to overcome every obstacle* that can possibly be arrayed against them or thrown in their pathway.

But the moment a community begin to be wraped up in themselves, become selfish, become engrossed in the temporalities of life, and put their faith in riches, that moment the power of God begins to withdraw from them, and if they repent not the Holy Spirit will depart from them entirely, and *they will be left to themselves.* That which was given them will be taken away, they will lose that which they had, for they will not be worthy of it. God is just as well merciful, and we need not expect favors at the hand of the Almighty except as we merit them, at least in the honest desires of our hearts, and the desire and intent will not always avail unless our acts correspond.[68]

Truly, the words of the prophets are like latter-day weather men who are raising the urgent call for us to get prepared for that which is to come. I am convinced that if we hearken to the warnings of our apostles and prophets, we will be prepared for the storm that is to come—not a cold front like froze Uncle Archie's sheep, but a burning heat front that will leave neither root nor branch of the wicked. If we are obedient and further the work of the Lord and establish Zion and her stakes, we shall not fear, but will enjoy the peace, beauty, joy, and protection of the Lord.

Not let's consider in the next chapter the Second Coming of Jesus Christ, our Savior and Redeemer, and great Millennium that will be ushered in by his spectacular return as King of kings and Lord of lords.

REFERENCES:

1 *Teachings of the Prophet Joseph Smith,* 16; emphasis added.
2 *Teachings,* 15; emphasis added.
3 "Beware of Pride", *Conference Report,* April 1989.
4 "Fourteen Fundamentals in Following the Prophet," in *Speeches of the Year,* 1980, 27; emphasis added.
5 When Nephi's brothers questioned him about the justice of God, they asked him if the results of sin were just spiritual or were they temporal too. Nephi answered that they are both (1 Nephi 15:32).
   The dual consequences for sin may be a new idea for some. Perhaps you have noticed that over time sin has increased in the world so have physical upheavals such as earthquakes, hurricanes, tornadoes, floods and droughts.
   I really believe, too, that as righteousness increases among the Saints, there will be corresponding blessings shed forth among them—nothing can prevent he Lord from pouring down knowledge from heaven upon the heads of the Latter-day Saints (D&C 121:33).
6 The information found in Doctrine and Covenants 45:65-75 is a good example of latter-day parallels with Enoch and his people.
7 *The Seer,* 289; emphasis added.
8 President James E. Faust has written an excellent article on the blessings of adversity which appears in the January, 1998, *Ensign.*
9 *Hymns,* The Church of Jesus Christ of Latter-day Saints, 1985, #319.
10 William A. McEachern, *Economics: A Contemporary Introduction,* South Western College Publishing, 1997, 4th Ed., 723.
11 "Rich Earn More Than All of Middle Class", *USA Today,* June 20, 1996, A1.
12 "Last Year" *USA Today,* April 12, 1996, 2B.
13 *Collected Works of Hugh Nibley,* Vol.9, Ch.2, p.37
14 Alfie Kohn, *No Contest: The Case Against Competition,* (Boston: Houghton Miffiin, 1986).
15 This law is also known as the "United Order" and the "Order of Enoch".
16 *Teachings,* 248.
17 *Teachings,* 252; emphasis added.
18 *Journal of Discourses* 2: 102-103.
19 *Journal of Discourses* 17: 177-81; see also D&C 105:3.
20 In an excellent article by William O. Nelson, entitled, "To Prepare a People", he

addresses three issues relative to the economic law of Zion: first, the Law of Consecration and its operation within the United Order; second, why the 1831-34 effort to implement this order failed; and third, how the Lord is now preparing a people for Zion's eventual redemption. This eloquently brief article is recommended to the reader for further information on the Law of Consecration. (See *Ensign*, January 1979, 18-22)

Also see *The Doctrine and Covenants Student Manual* (Religion 324-325) 421-430, prepared by the Church Educational System and published by the Church. Here, you will find valuable material on the Law of Consecration

Another wonderful source which describes the importance of living the Lord's law and the blessings that flow therefrom, is "The Equality and Oneness of the Saints," *Masterful Discourses and Writings of Orson Pratt*. Compiled by N.B. Lundwall, (Salt Lake City: Bookcraft, 1962) 624 ft.

21 *Teachings*, 392.

22 Leonard Arrington, *Building the City of God*, (Salt Lake City: Deseret Book Co., 1976), 15.

23 Widtsoe, John A. *Evidences and Reconciliations*. Salt Lake City, 1943.

24 Marion G. Romney, in *Conference Report*, Oct. 1976, 167.

25 Quoted from Henry D. Moyle, *Improvement Era*, Dec. 1937, 787.

26 Thomas S. Monson, *Ensign*, Sept. 1986, 5.

27 President Spencer W. Kimball, *Conference Report*, Oct. 1977, 123-24.

28 Hugh B. Brown, "The Kingdom is Rolling Forth", *Improvement Era*, December, 1967, 93.

29 *Teachings*, 19.

30 *Church News*, April 13, 1986, 7

31 *Teachings*, 19.

32 The expression "rest" here is equated with the "presence" of the Lord. See D&C 84:24; JST, Exodus 34:2.

33 *Teachings*, 54.

34 "The Vital Role of Correlation", *General Conference*, 3 April 1987.

35 In *Conference Report*, Apr. 1981, 3; or *Ensign*, May 1981, 5; emphasis added.

36 *Journal of Discourses*, 2:31; emphasis added.

37 *Teachings*, 335-36.

38 *Teachings*, 337-38; emphasis added.

39 *Doctrinal New Testament Commentary*, 3:330-31 .

40 *Mormon Doctrine*, "Calling and Election Sure" (Salt Lake City: Bookcraft, 1958) 102.

41 Bruce R. McConkie, *Doctrinal New Testament Commentary*, .3:326

42 *History of the Church*, 5:527; emphasis added.

43 *Mormon Doctrine*, 425.

44 *Teachings*, 340.

45 *Teachings*, 340

46 *Teachings*, 322.

47 As you read through this section, you will want to refer to end of chapter Figure 9-E, The Three Grand Orders of Priesthood, to help you differentiate between the three priesthood ordinances.

48 *Teachings*, 180-81; emphasis added.

49 *Words of Joseph Smith*, 246.

50 *Teachings*, 151.

51 As has been explained in earlier sections, those whose calling and elections have been made sure are promised, through their faith, great power in the priesthood, but they are also promised, at some future time, that they may see the face of the Lord (D&C 93:1; JST, Genesis 30:30-31; *Teachings,* 149-51). In speaking of the blessings associated with the fulness of the priesthood, and in anticipation of the exploring party going to Oregon and California and selecting a site for a new city for the Saints, Joseph Smith charged, "Send twenty-five men: let them preach the gospel wherever they go. Let that man go that can raise $500, a good horse and mule, a double barrel gun, one barrel rifle, and the other a smooth bore, saddle and bridle, a pair of revolving pistols, bowie-knife, and a good sabre. Appoint a leader, and let them beat up for volunteers. I want every man that goes to be a king and a priest. When he gets on the mountains he may want to talk with his God (*History of the Church,* 6:224; emphasis added).

52 *Teachings,* 323.

53 *Teachings,* 321; emphasis added.

54 *Teachings,* 323; emphasis added.

55 *Teachings,* 172; emphasis added.

56 *Teachings,* 330; emphasis added.

57 *Lectures on Faith,* 7:17; emphasis added.

58 *Lectures on Faith,* 2:34, 56; emphasis added.

59 JST, Genesis 14:30-31; emphasis added.

60 *Teachings,* 325; emphasis added.

61 *Relief Society Magazine,* April 1967, 50; emphasis added.

62 *Teachings,* 392; emphasis added.

63 See President Ezra Taft Benson's address, *Ensign,* May 19899ú

64 Bruce R. McConkie, "Lord, Increase our Faith." *Speeches of the Year,* 1967-1968. Provo, UT: Brigham Young Univ, 1968.

65 McConkie, "Lord Increase our Faith", 11; emphasis added.

66 *Ensign,* May 1979, 82.

67 *Relief Society Magazine,* February 1963, 169; emphasis added.

68 *Journal of Discourses,* 24:176; emphasis added.

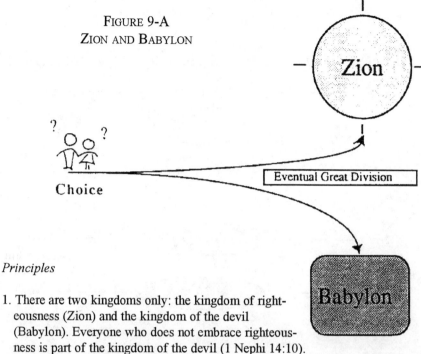

FIGURE 9-A
ZION AND BABYLON

Principles

1. There are two kingdoms only: the kingdom of righteousness (Zion) and the kingdom of the devil
   (Babylon). Everyone who does not embrace righteousness is part of the kingdom of the devil (1 Nephi 14:10).
2. Latter-day Israel is compared to a bride who must prepare herself for the wedding feast. Zions is commanded to put on her beautiful garments and prepare for
   the coming of the bridegroom (Jesus) and the wedding feast, (the Second
   Coming) (D&C 109:73-74).
3. We have been commanded to sanctify ourselves and to gather upon the land of
   Zion—all except those who have been commanded to tarry. We must flee from
   the midst of wickedness, which is spiritual Babylon. (see D&C 133:4-5, 14).
4. We are warned that "the time speedily cometh that the Lord God shall cause a
   great division among the people, and the wicked will he destroy; and he will
   spare his people, yea, even if it so be that he must destroy the wicked by fire"
   (2 Nephi 30:10).
5. We are told that, "The day cometh that they who will not hear the voice of the
   Lord, neither the voice of his servants, neither give heed to the words of the
   prophets and apostles, shall be cut off from among the people. For they have
   strayed from mine ordinances, and have broken mine everlasting covenant; They
   seek not the Lord to establish his righteousness, but every man walketh in his
   own way, and after the image of his own god, whose image is in the likeness of
   the world, and whose substance is that of an idol, which waxeth old and shall
   perish in Babylon, even Babylon the great, which shall fall" (D&C 1:14-15;
   also see verses 35-36).

FIGURE 9-B
THE LORD'S ECONOMIC PLAN IN PERSPECTIVE

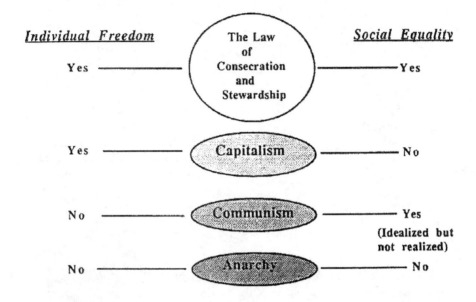

Principles

1. Anarchy exists in places where economic and political confusion are prevalent. In such places individual freedom and social justice are restricted. One is not free to go and come as he pleases, and the needs of the poor are not met.
2. Communism has great appeal to people who are in a state of poverty or who are in political turmoil. Those who promote communism do so with the promise of social justice and an economic equality. However, they seek social justice through force and the loss of individual freedom. Equality is idealized, but not realized. Under communism basic freedoms are denied— such as the right to own private property, freedom of religion, freedom of the press, etc...
3. Capitalistic systems provide individual freedom and stimulate initiative, but the care of the poor is left to individual conscience and thus is often neglected. In most cases, the rich get richer and the poor get poorer.
4. Under Consecration and Stewardship both individual freedom and social justice are preserved. The rich, by covenant willingly give of their substance for the benefit of the poor (see D&C 104:14-18).

FIGURE 9-C

TH LAW OF CONSECRATION AND STEWARDSHIP

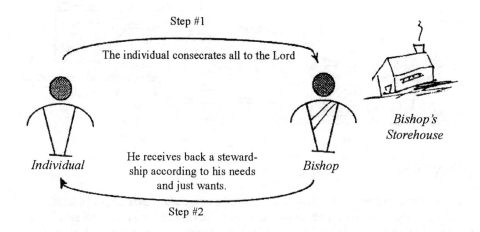

Step #1

The individual consecrates all to the Lord

Individual

He receives back a stewardship according to his needs
and just wants.

Bishop

*Bishop's
Storehouse*

Step #2

Principles

1. To enter the Law of Consecration, one consecrates or dedicates by legal
   deed all that he has to the Lord's agent upon the earth—the Bishop (D&C
   42:29-31).
2. Then, according to an established standard of living, the individual
   receives back his stewardship, or his inheritance (D&C 42:32).
3. Both the consecration and the stewardship transactions are by legal deed.
   The stewardship becomes the private property of the individual (D&C
   42:30).
4. The rich end up consecrating more than they receive back and the poor
   receive more than they consecrate. Thus an equalization among the Saints
   takes place. Excess goods remain in the Bishop's storehouse to provide
   for the poor and for additional stewardships.
5. The Lord has commanded us saying, "Nevertheless, in your temporal
   things you shall be equal, and this not grudgingly, otherwise the abundance of the manifestations of the Spirit shall be withheld" (D&C 70:14).
6. The world lieth in sin because of economic inequality. The Lord said,
   "But it is not given that one man should possess that which is above
   another, wherefore the world lieth in sin" (D&C 49:20).

FIGURE 9-D

THE SPIRIT AND POWER OF ELIAS, ELIJAH, AND MESSIAH

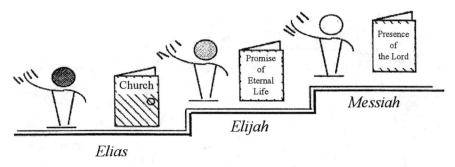

Principles

1. The spirit and power of Elias may be likened to a person standing outside the door of the Church beckoning people to join the Church. Joseph Smith said, "The Spirit of Elias is to prepare the way for a greater revelation of God, which is the Priesthood of Elias, or the Priesthood that Aaron was ordained unto. And when God sends a man into the world to prepare for a greater work, holding the keys of the power of Elias, it was called the doctrine of Elias, even from the early ages of the world" (*Teachings*, pp. 335-36).
2. The spirit and power of Elijah may be likened to a person standing inside the Church, beckoning the members to perfect themselves and their families, living and dead, and receive all the blessings of the priesthood—including making their calling and election sure. Joseph Smith taught that "What you seal on earth, by the keys of Elijah, is sealed in heaven; and this is the power of Elijah, and this is the difference between the spirit and power of Elias and Elijah; for while the spirit of Elias is a forerunner, the power of Elijah is sufficient to make our calling and election sure" (*Teachings*, p. 338).
3. The Spirit and power of Messiah may be likened to a person who has had his calling and election made sure, beckoning the sanctified saints to prepare for the appearance of the Lord. Joseph Smith taught that "The spirit of Elias is first, Elijah second, and Messiah last. Elias is a forerunner to prepare the way, the spirit and power of Elijah is to come after, holding the keys of power, building the Temple to the capstone, placing the seals of the Melchizedek Priesthood upon the house of Israel, and making all things ready; then Messiah comes to His Temple, which is last of all" (*Teachings*, p. 340).
4. The Lord has declared: "Therefore, sanctify yourselves that your minds become single to God, and the days will come that you shall see him; for he will unveil his face unto you and it shall be in his own time, and in his own way, and according to his own will" (D&C 88:68).

FIGURE 9-E
THE THREE GRAND ORDERS OF PRIESTHOOD

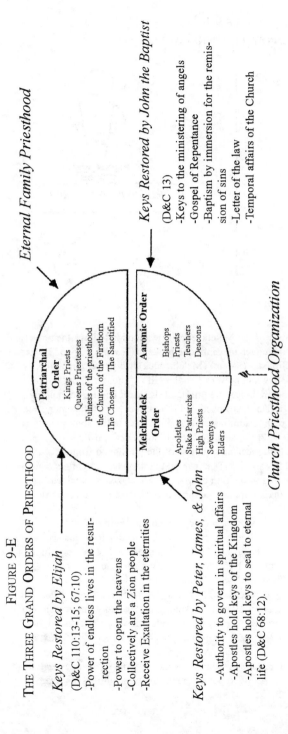

Eternal Family Priesthood

Keys Restored by Elijah

(D&C 110:13-15; 67:10)
-Power of endless lives in the resurrection
-Power to open the heavens
-Collectively a Zion people
-Receive Exaltation in the eternities

Keys Restored by Peter, James, & John

-Authority to govern in spiritual affairs
-Apostles hold keys of the Kingdom
-Apostles hold keys to seal to eternal life (D&C 68:12).

Keys Restored by John the Baptist

(D&C 13)
-Keys to the ministering of angels
-Gospel of Repentance
-Baptism by immersion for the remission of sins
-Letter of the law
-Temporal affairs of the Church

Patriarchal Order

Kings Priests
Queens Priestesses
Fulness of the priesthood
the Church of the Firstborn
The Chosen   The Sanctified

Aaronic Order

Bishops
Priests
Teachers
Deacons

Melchizedek Order

Apostles
Stake Patriarchs
High Priests
Seventys
Elders

Church Priesthood Organization

Principles

1. " All priesthood is Melchizedek, but there are different portions or degrees of it" (*Teachings*, p. 180)
2. "There are, in the Church, two priesthoods, namely, the Melchizedek and Aaronic including the Levitical Priesthood" (D&C 107:1).
3. "There are (in the 7th chapter of Hebrews) three grand orders of the Priesthood referred to here" (*Teachings*, p. 32).
4. "The power of the Melchizedek Priesthood is to have the power of 'endless lives' ... Those holding the fullness of the Melchizedek Priesthood are kings and priests of the Most High God, holding the keys of power and blessings...and stands as God to give laws to the people, administering endless lives to the sons and daughters of Adam.... The anointing and sealing is to be called, elected and made sure" . (*Teachings*, pp. 322-23).

FIGURE 9-F
SEALING POWERS THEN AND NOW

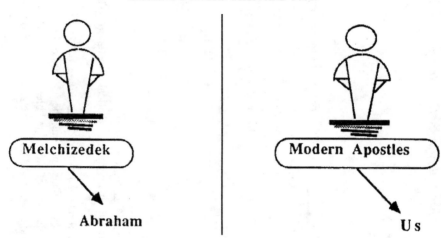

Principles

1. Joseph Smith taught that "The power of the Melchizedek Priesthood is to have the power of 'endless lives'; for the everlasting covenant cannot be broken" (*Teachings*, p. 322). He also explained that "The king of Shiloam (Salem) (Melchizedek) had power and authority over that of Abraham, holding the key and power of endless life... Those holding the fulness of the Melchizedek Priesthood are kings and priests of the Most High God, holding the keys of power and blessings. In fact, that Priesthood is a perfect law of theocracy, and stands as God to give laws to the people administering endless lives to the sons and daughters of Adam. (*Teachings*, p. 322; see also D&C 68:12 and D&C 1:38).

2. Joseph Smith explained that Abraham received a fulness of the priesthood from Melchizedek: "Abraham says to Melchizedek, I believe all that thou has taught me concerning the priesthood and the coming of the Son of Man; so Melchizedek ordained Abraham and sent him away. Abraham rejoiced, saying, Now I have a (fulness of) priest-hood" (*Teachings*, p 322-23).

3. From the words of Joseph Smith, we have this more complete accounting of how Abraham received a fulness of the priesthood: "Abraham gave a tenth part of his spoils and then received a blessing under the hands of Melchizedek even the last law or a fulness of the law or priesthood which constituted him a king and priest after the order of Melchizedek or an endless life" (*Words of Joseph Smith*, p. 246).

4. Abraham's priesthood qualified him to see the face of God. Joseph Smith said: "I ask was there any sealing power attending this priesthood (of Aaron), that would admit a man into the presence of God. Oh no, but Abraham's was a more exalted power or priesthood, he could talk and walk with God..." (*Words of Joseph Smith*, p. 246; see also Abraham 2:6, 19-20

5. In speaking to modern apostles and prophets, the Lord declared, "And of as many as the Father shall bear record, to you shall be given power to seal them up unto eternal life. Amen" (D&C 68:12; see also D&C 131:5-6).

CHAPTER TEN

THE KING OF
KINGS RETURNS

Ye men of Galilee, why stand ye gazing up into heaven? this same Jesus, which is taken up from you into heaven, shall so come in like manner as ye have seen him go into heaven.

—Acts 1:11

I must have been about five years old when a terrible explosion shook our small town of Hillspring in southern Alberta, Canada.

My mother and older sisters were out on the front lawn shelling peas when Young's gasoline station caught fire, causing the terrible blast. The station was about five blocks from our house. We learned that an attendant had been smoking around an open barrel of gasoline when a spark from his cigarette caused the explosion. Before the blast I had been comfortably lying on a quilted blanket, eating fresh peas and casually listening to my mother and sisters as they talked about the last days and signs of the Second Coming.

When the explosion occurred, we first heard the loud blast, then we saw a lot of black, billowy smoke rise into the sky southwest of our house. I was awfully frightened. I could see large fire balls. I thought the heavens were on fire. My sisters wanted to get a closer look. I wanted to go too, so they took me by the hand, and we all ran toward the station. When we got within about two blocks of the station, we had to stop. We could feel the heat and the shaking of the earth as the fire balls and explosive blasts got bigger and louder. The intensity of the heat, the noise, and the roaring balls of fire scared my sisters and me. One explosion followed another as one burning barrel of gasoline ignited the next. After hours of frantic efforts by the men in Hillspring, the fire was finally put out.

My sisters said that the fire in the sky and the loud noises were like what the end of the world and Jesus' Second Coming would be like. I was frightened and confused. What they were saying was different from what I had heard in Sunday

School. The teacher had said that when Jesus came again it would be a happy time. She said that his coming would bring healing and blessings. He would heal the sick, give sight to the blind, and cause the deaf to hear again. He would call the little children to him, hold them in his arms, and bless them. My sisters were talking about death and destruction!

While I was still a child, I worried about whether Jesus' return would be a happy time or a fearful time. Through the experience of Young's garage burning, my young mind had become sensitized to associate the Second Coming of Jesus with loud noises and terrifying balls of fire. If the burning of Young's garage was like the Second Coming, and if Jesus were to come in the midst of fire and smoke like I had seen, I definitely did not want to be around when he came!

As I grew older and became more familiar with the scriptures and the teachings of the prophets, I learned that the Second Coming would be both a terrible time and a great time. For the righteous it would be a wonderful time, but for the wicked it would be a terrible time of great destruction like that I had witnessed with the burning of Young's garage. I decided at a very young age that I did not want to be among the bad people who would be burned at Jesus' coming. As I became older and my knowledge of the Lord's great plan for our happiness grew, I began to focus on the Second Coming of the Lord with great hope—even a joyful anticipation! This hope grew out of my faith in what I had read in the scriptures.

THE PROMISE OF JESUS' RETURN

The Bible promises us that Jesus will come again. In the New Testament we read that after his resurrection, and following his forty-day ministry among the Jewish Saints, Jesus made his final ascension into heaven. Luke explains the circumstances surrounding his ascension from the Mount of Olives in Jerusalem:

> And when he [Jesus] had spoken these things, while they beheld, he was taken up; and a cloud received him out of their sight.
> And while they looked steadfastly toward heaven as he went up, behold, two men stood by them in white apparel;
> Which also said, Ye men of Galilee, why stand ye gazing up into heaven? *this same Jesus, which is taken up from you into heaven, shall so come in like manner as ye have seen him go into heaven* (Acts 1:9-11; emphasis added).

These two men in white apparel were angels—heavenly messengers promising that Jesus would return again to the earth. As the angels promised, Jesus will return to the earth in the same manner that he ascended! Although they did not give the *time* of the Second Coming, their words of promise provide us with comfort and hope for the future as we patiently await their fulfillment.

The time of the Lord's return has been the subject of many prophecies. Paul, the New Testament apostle, prophesied that Jesus would return only after a falling away from the truth. He explained, "Let no man deceive you by any means: for that day shall not come, *except there come a falling away first,* and that man of sin be revealed, the son of perdition" (2 Thess. 2:3; emphasis added). In this verse, Paul is predicting that before Jesus' return, there would be a great falling away—a great apostasy—from the gospel truths. This apostasy was discussed in an earlier chapter.

Even though the early apostles knew that there would be a great apostasy, they also knew that following the apostasy there would come a wonderful time of healing—a time when Jesus would return to the earth in all his magnificent power, and glory and all things would be renewed.

In speaking to the Jews who had participated in Jesus' crucifixion, Peter spoke of this as a time of refreshing when he said, "Repent ye therefore, and be converted, that your sins may be blotted out, *when the times of refreshing shall come from the presence of the Lord;* And he shall send Jesus Christ, which before was preached unto you: Whom the heaven must receive until the time of restitution of all things, which God hath spoken by the mouth of all his holy prophets since the world began" (Acts 3:19-21; emphasis added).

This time of refreshing is the same as is mentioned in the Tenth Article of Faith: "We believe in the literal gathering of Israel and in the restoration of the Ten Tribes; that Zion (the New Jerusalem) will be built upon the American continent; that Christ will reign personally upon the earth; and, that *the earth will be renewed and receive its paradisiacal glory"* (emphasis added).

The refreshing of the earth—when it returns it to his paradisiacal glory—is concurrent with the Second Coming of the Savior and his millennial reign. It will be one of the most remarkable events that this earth will ever pass through. The only other change that will supersede this will be the final transformation of the earth at the end of the Millennium, when it will be changed to a celestial sphere (see D&C 88:18-19).

COMFORTING WORDS OF HOPE

The knowledge that Jesus will return to the earth, a great refreshing of the earth will take place, and the righteous will be resurrected, are truly a comforting doctrines. Paul reassured his readers by explaining: "For the Lord himself shall descend from heaven with a shout, with the voice of the archangel, and with the trump of God; and the dead in Christ shall rise first; Then we which are alive and remain shall be caught up together with them in the clouds, to meet the Lord in the air: and so shall we ever be with the Lord. *Wherefore comfort one another with these words"* (1 Thess. 4:16-18; emphasis added).

The coming of the Lord will usher in a wonderful period of peace on earth that will last for one-thousand years. This time is called *The Millennium*—meaning one thousand years. When he comes, he will come as King of kings and Lord of Lords. He will come as the Prince of Peace, with healing in his wings. During this time Jesus will fix all things that are broken. He will complete the work his father has given him and will make all things right again. All that was sick and diseased will be comforted and healed. The dead will be raised, all disease and deformity will be done away. He will put an end to all contention, war, disease, and even death—as we know it.

Another of the comforting concepts we can draw from the scriptures is that the Second Coming has been anticipated for many centuries. Malachi spoke of one who would prepare the way of the Lord.

HIS MESSENGER SHALL PREPARE THE WAY

The Old Testament prophet, Malachi, is best known, perhaps, for his prophecy regarding the return of "Elijah the prophet before the coming of the great and dreadful day of the Lord" (Malachi 4:4-6). In a less known prophecy of Malachi we read: "Behold, I will send *my messenger*, and he shall prepare the way before me: and the Lord, whom ye seek, shall suddenly come to his temple, even the messenger of the covenant, whom ye delight in: behold, he shall come, saith the Lord of hosts. But who may abide the day of his coming? and who shall stand when he appeareth? for he is like a *refiner's fire*, and like fullers' soap" (Malachi 3:1-2).

Some readers have thought the reference to a messenger in this passage, who would prepare the way for the coming of the Lord's, was John the Baptist. John faithfully prepared the way for the *first coming* of the Lord. But who is the messenger who would prepare the way for the latter-day coming of the Lord which is associated with fire?

An editorial in the Church News describes the Second Coming of the Lord and the need for a special messenger to prepare the way for the latter-day appearance as John prepared the way for the first coming. It states:

> But is there need of a preparatory work in anticipation of such a magnificent event [as the Second Coming]? Or does the world not need it?

Does man-made tradition obscure the truth now as it did when John was but a voice crying in the wilderness?

All must agree that the world is just as divided, just as corrupt, as it was in the days of John. As a forerunner was needed for Christ's first appearance, so one is urgently required for His second coming.

And as the glorious second advent will tremendously transcend His humble first appearance, so the preparatory work must be more extensive than that which John did. This the scriptures foretold:

It will include the gathering of Israel and provide a restitution of all things whatsoever God has spoken from the beginning of the world.

A new volume of scripture is to come forth, called by Isaiah a marvelous work and a wonder. The house of the Lord must be established in the tops of the mountains. And the Gospel of the kingdom shall be preached to all nations and then shall the end come.

But who can direct all this preparatory work?

Only a modern divinely appointed forerunner!

And has he come? He has. And what is his name? Joseph Smith, the Mormon Prophet!

As John the Baptist prepared the way for the Lord's first coming, so Joseph Smith, in a similar role, is the forerunner of latter days. . . .[1]

Jesus is to come again. His Second Coming will stand in remarkable contrast to his first. At first he came as a babe in Bethlehem. When he comes again, he will come in great glory as King of kings and Lord of lords. So spectacular will be this appearance that great signs in the heavens will announce it, the heavenly host will be with Him, and all mankind will see it together.

One of the great contributions that the Prophet Joseph Smith has made, as a part of his role of a forerunner, has been answers to many gospel questions that surround the Second Coming and the great Millennial era that is to accompany his return.

QUESTIONS AND ANSWERS ABOUT THE MILLENNIUM

Have you ever asked yourself any of these questions: Is the Millennium the same thing as heaven? Should the righteous worry? Do we have to be a part of Zion to be saved? Do we have to be in a certain location to be protected? Do we have to be near a temple to be saved from the destructions that will accompany Jesus' return? Will we have our own government at the Second Coming? Will we have jobs out in the world? Will everyone be able to be with Jesus? Will we all speak one language during the Millennium? Will we be surrounded by animals with which we can communicate? What places and people will Jesus be visiting? What is the importance of Israel and the Jews relative to the Second Coming? Will Jesus bring Zion with him or will he come to Zion already on the earth? At what point will Satan be bound?

We do not have the answers to all of these questions, but the Lord has revealed the answers to many of them. The following are some answers to commonly asked questions:

Who Are the Wicked Who will be Burned at His Coming?

The scriptures inform us that the wicked who will be burned at the Lord's coming (see Malachi 4:1-3) are people who are excessively evil—those who remain in spiritual Babylon, those who will be living telestial lives when the Lord comes. Elder Bruce R. McConkie lists among those who are to be burned at the Lord's coming "those who lie and steal and cheat; who take advantage of their neighbor for a word; who set their heart on money and power and worldly applause; who are lewd, lascivious, and immoral; who rob and plunder and murder; who are adulterers, homosexuals, and pornographically oriented; who are vulgar and whose minds dwell on unclean and indecent things."[2]

Elder McConkie has also described the condition of the righteous in this turbulent time:

> The righteous, the God-fearing, the meek—indeed ... all those who are living at least a terrestrial law—these are the ones who shall continue to live on the new earth and breathe the air of the new heavens. They will include faithful members of The Church of Jesus Christ of Latter-day Saints and other upright and decent people who, following the light of Christ, have managed to rise above the world and walk in paths of decency and uprightness. These latter, without much question, will soon join the Church and become inheritors of all the blessings of Israel.[3]

As we have discussed in earlier chapters, we have many promises from the servants of the Lord that the righteous will be protected from the calamities of the last days. One promise that has not been mentioned, though, is that those who are tithed will not be burned at his coming. Of this promise the Lord said, "Behold, now it is called today until the coming of the Son of Man, and verily it is a day of *sacrifice*, and a day for the *tithing* of my people; for *he that is tithed shall not be burned at his coming.* For after today cometh the burning ... for verily I say, tomorrow all the proud and they that do wickedly shall be a stubble; and I will burn them up, for I am the Lord of Hosts; and I will not spare any that remain in Babylon" (D&C 64:23-24).

How Will Jesus Appear When He Comes in Glory?

As we have discussed, Jesus will descend out of the heavens much the same manner as he ascended (see Acts 1:9-11). When he comes, however, he will not be wearing a white robe as some have imagined; *he will be "red in his apparel"* and will be surrounded with great glory and many angels (D&C 133:46-48). Righteous men and women who have died will be resurrected at his coming, and they will make their glorious appearance with Jesus If we are still living on the earth and are righteous at his coming, we will be caught up in the air, in the clouds to meet him and all the angels who accompany him. The earth will be cleansed by fire and then the righteous will dwell with him on this purified earth—a paradise that will be free from sin, sorrow, and disease (see Philippians 3:15-21).

What will People be Doing During the Millennium?

The Millennium will be a period of accelerated temple and missionary activity. Many missionaries will be needed on both sides of the veil during the Millennium since not all will be members of the Church at the beginning of the thousand-year period.

Regarding those individuals who remain in the spirit world at the Second Coming of the Lord to the earth, our latter-day revelations explain that "All who have died without a knowledge of this gospel, who would have received it if they had been permitted to tarry, shall be heirs of the celestial kingdom of God" (D&C 137:7).

In the spirit world, these sons and daughters of God are being and will continue to be taught "faith in God, repentance from sin, vicarious baptism for the remission of sins, the gift of the Holy Ghost by the laying on of hands, And all other principles of the gospel that [are and] were necessary for them to know in order to qualify themselves that they might be judged according to men in the flesh, but live according to God in the spirit" (D&C 138:33-34).

Though these people are being taught the gospel in the spirit world, they will still have to receive the ordinances of the gospel through the vicarious work done in the temples of the Lord. As they accept the Gospel, the Lord will make their names known to those who are directing the temple work, so that their work can be completed.

The gospel will be taught to those who are in the spirit world, as we read, "Thus was the gospel preached to those who had died in their sins, *without a knowledge* of the truth, or in transgression, having *rejected the prophets*" (D&C 138:32; emphasis added). "The dead who repent will be redeemed, through obedience to the ordinances of the house of God" (D&C 138:58).

Because of the wonderful missionary effort by faithful elders in the spirit world and through the convincing power of the Spirit, the time will come when every knee shall bow and every tongue shall acknowledge that Jesus is the Son of God. In the words of Alma the younger, "Every knee shall bow, and every tongue confess before him. Yea, even at the last day, when all men shall stand to be judged of him then shall they confess that he is God" (Mosiah 27:31).

What Does the Phrase "The End of the World" Mean?

The phrase "the end of the world" means the end of wickedness, sin, evil and death as we know it (see Joseph Smith—Matthew 1:4, 55). It means the end of worldliness, not the end of our planet. During the Millennium, the Saints will not know evil, darkness, disease or even death as we know it now (see D&C 101:29-31). Even though the earth at Jesus' coming will be cleansed with fire, it will not cease to exist, but it will be dramatically changed. Our planet will continue on but as a cleansed, paradisiacal garden. Confirming this idea, Elder McConkie said,

> The world is the evil, sensual, devilish way of life that prevails among ungodly men.... *And the end of the world is their destruction, the destruction of the wicked.* Our old world of wickedness shall soon die, and a new heaven and a new earth, whereon righteousness dwells, shall be born. An age shall end, a new era begin. A worldly way of life shall cease and a righteous way of living take its place. In our present probationary estate we are in the world, but we should not be of the world. If we overcome the world and walk thereby in paths of righteousness, we shall abide the day of His coming and be numbered among those who inherit Millennial glory.[4]

Will People be Getting Married and Having Children During the Millennium?

The answer to this question is a resounding YES. In fact, this will be a marvelous time for bearing and rearing children. Because the powers of Satan will be held in check for a thousand years (see D&C 45:55), children born during the Millennium will "grow up without sin unto salvation" (D&C 45:58); they will live until they are one hundred years of age (see Isaiah 65:20), "the age of a tree" (D&C 101:30), and then they will be changed "in the twinkling of an eye" (D&C 63:51), from a translated state to a resurrected body.

What will Day-to-day Life be Like During the Millennium?

The scriptures explain that during the Millennium "the enmity[5] of beasts, yea, the enmity of all flesh, shall cease" (D&C 101:26). All the animals shall mingle together in peace, and the appetites of the carnivorous beasts shall be changed so that, according to Isaiah, the grass of the field will become the common diet of the animal world (see Isaiah 11:6-9; 65:25). These are just a few of the changes that will occur as a part of the great millennial era.

Though the changes incident to life during the millennial era will be great and marvelous, yet mortality as such will continue. Elder McConkie has described day-to-day life during the Millennium. He said, "Children will be born, grow up, marry, advance to old age, and pass through the equivalent of death. Crops will be planted, harvested, and eaten; industries will be expanded, cities built, and education fostered; men will continue to care for their own needs, handle their own affairs, and enjoy the full endowment of free agency. Speaking a pure language (Zeph. 3:9), dwelling in peace, living without disease, and progressing as the Holy Spirit will guide, the advancement and perfection of society during the millennium will exceed anything men have supposed or expected."[6] As we look forward to this great day of the Lord, our Heavenly Father has given us certain signs to watch for that will indicate the nearness of the Second Coming.

SIGNS OF THE TIMES

The scriptures are sprinkled heavily with passages dealing with signs that we are living in the last days before coming of the Lord—the signs of the times.[7] Though the Lord made it clear that only his Father knew the exact time of his coming, he did give many signs by which all could know when the Second Coming is near. For example, during his ministry, Jesus' disciples were anxious to know when he would come again, and he gave them some signs to watch for that would help them to know the time of his coming (see Joseph Smith— Matthew).

Likewise, to the early missionaries of this dispensation, the Lord gave this promise, "And unto you it shall be given to know the signs of the times, and the signs of the coming of the Son of Man" (D&C 68:11).

Elder Bruce R. McConkie listed the following significant events as signs of the times—the signs that we are living in the last days:

1. Spirit to be poured out on all flesh
2. Discovery and use of printing
3. Protestant reformation and age of renaissance
4. Discovery and colonization of America
5. Establishment of the American nation
6. Translation and printing of Bible
7. Establishment of U.S. Constitution
8. Latter-day revelation
9. Coming forth of the Book of Mormon
10. Opposition to the Book of Mormon

11. Restoration of keys and priesthood
12. Restoration of the gospel
13. Messenger to precede Second Coming
14. Church and kingdom set up again
15. Growth of the Church
16. Gathering of Israel
17. Ten Tribes return
18. Times of the Gentiles being fulfilled
19. Return of Judah to Jerusalem
20. Jews to begin to believe in Christ
21. Building of latter-day temples
22. Lord to come suddenly to temple
23. Spirit of Elijah and genealogical research
24. Persecution of the saints
25. Persecution of the Jews
26. True gospel to be preached in all the world
27. Worldly knowledge to increase
28. Scientific and inventive progress
29. Disease, plague, pestilence to sweep earth
30. Elements in commotion
31. Disasters and calamities to abound
32. Strikes, anarchy, violence to increase
33. Latter-day wickedness
34. Spirit ceasing to strive with wicked
35. Peace taken from earth
36. Angels now reaping the earth
37. Wars and rumors of wars
38. Famines, depressions, and economic turmoil
39. Apostate darkness covers earth
40. Many false churches in latter days
41. Refusal of men to believe signs of times
42. Signs on earth and in heavens
43. Lamanites to blossom as the rose
44. The gathering at Adam-ondi-Ahman
45. Final great war to attend Second Coming
46. Sorrow and fear to precede and accompany the Second Coming
47. Fall of the Great and Abominable Church
48. Special mission in Jerusalem of two latter-day prophets
49. Wicked to be burned as stubble
50. Final restitution of all things to be completed
51. Christ to reign personally upon earth[8]

Most of these signs of the last days are not just a one-time event. Most of them are processes that have been going on for some time, but that will build in a wonderful crescendo at the coming of the Lord. The problems of disease, wickedness and turmoil will continue to increase in both frequency and intensity —much like a woman in labor—until the Son is delivered in that "great and terrible day of the Lord".

Though these calamities will increase as the time of his coming approaches, the Lord has done and will yet do many important works to prepare his people for that great and terrible day. These marvelous works began with the calling of Joseph Smith and the instructions that he subsequently received.

THE COMING OF ELIJAH—
A MAJOR SIGN OF THE TIMES

On the night and morning of September 21-22, 1823, the angel Moroni quoted many biblical passages to Joseph Smith that had to do with Joseph's role in the restoration of the gospel and the preparation for the Second Coming. These scriptures included Malachi's prophesy about the day of the Lord's coming. Malachi said, "Behold, I will send you Elijah the prophet before the coming of the great and dreadful day of the Lord: And he shall turn the heart of the fathers to the children, and the heart of the children to their fathers, lest I come and smite the earth with a curse" (Malachi 4:5-6; emphasis added).

When Moroni quoted this passage, however, his wording was different than what we find in our King James Bible. Moroni's words were: "Behold, *I will reveal unto you the Priesthood, by the hand of Elijah the prophet,* before the coming of the great and dreadful day of the Lord.... And he shall plant in the hearts of the children the promises made to the fathers, and the hearts of the children shall turn to their fathers. If it were not so, the whole earth would be *utterly wasted* at his coming" (J.S.—History, 1:38-39; emphasis added).

These differences are remarkable and provide much insight into the purpose of Elijah's return before the Second Coming. As we discussed in the previous chapter, Elijah came to reveal the keys of the sealing powers, the fulness of the priesthood, the Patriarchal Order. Joseph Smith said that "the [spirit and] power of Elijah is sufficient to make our calling and election sure."[9] Were it not for the coming of Elijah and the sealing powers he brought, the whole earth would be utterly wasted—everyone would be destroyed—at the Lord's coming. However, the Lord, anticipating the calamities of the last days, sent Elijah the Prophet to Joseph Smith and gave him the keys that would protect and deliver the Saints in a day of trouble (see D&C 1:17; 35-6).

Because Elijah has returned as Malachi promised, (see Malachi 4:5-6; D&C 110:13-16) we have great reason to rejoice. The sealing powers are presently within the Church, and those holding these keys have the authority—when revealed by the Lord—to seal true and faithful Saints to eternal life (see D&C 68:12; 105:35-41). The recipients of these blessings are not only given the promise of eternal life in the worlds to come but are also promised, through their faith, awesome and superhuman powers in this life—powers that will be necessary for the survival of the righteous during the calamities associated with the Second Coming (see JST, Genesis 14:30-32; D&C 121:36; Helaman 10:7-10; Moses 1:25; 6:34). Through the sealing powers and keys restored by Elijah, the righteous, through their great faith, will be empowered from on high to control the elements of the earth and the powers of heaven (see JST Genesis 14:30-32; 1 Nephi 14:13-14; D&C 45:70).

In addition to quoting the prophecy regarding Elijah's return, Moroni also quoted other passages from Malachi with some variation. For example, "instead of quoting the first verse [of chapter four] as we know it, he quoted it thus: 'For behold, the day cometh that shall burn as an oven, and all the proud, yea, and all that do wickedly shall burn as stubble; *for they that come shall burn them,* saith the Lord of Hosts, that it shall leave them neither *root nor branch*'" (J.S.—History, 1:36-37; emphasis added).

Two points are of particular interest in this prophecy. First, Moroni stated that "they that come shall burn them." In other words, the glory attending Christ and the resurrected beings who come with him will consume the wicked on the earth. This concept is related to a passage in the Doctrine and Covenants which explains, "For he who is not able to abide the law of a celestial kingdom cannot abide a celestial glory. And he who cannot abide the law of a terrestrial kingdom cannot abide a terrestrial glory" (D&C 88:22-23). This means that the unprepared among the earth's inhabitants will not have been empowered through gospel living to endure the intense fire, light, and glory surrounding those heavenly beings who come with Jesus, for, as the Savior explained, "where I am they cannot come, for they have no power" (D&C 29:29).

The second point of specific interest is Malachi's explanation that those who shall be cut off will be left with neither root nor branch. This imagery of roots and branches is common in the scriptures. Roots refer to ancestry, branches to descendants. This particular scripture means that those who will be cut off at Jesus' coming will be left without eternal family relationships—they will have neither ancestors nor descendants. In other words, the wicked will not have taken advantage of the restored priesthood powers by which husbands and wives, children and families can be bound together in eternal chains back to Father Adam. As a result, they will not be prepared for the glory which is to come.

The scriptural evidence regarding the fire attending the coming of the Lord, suggests that the very glory which will consume the ungodly will cause the faithful to rejoice. Nephi mentioned the deliverance of the faithful in these words: "Wherefore, he will preserve the righteous by his power, even if it so be that the fulness of his wrath must come, and the righteous be preserved, even unto the destruction of their enemies by fire. Wherefore, the righteous need not fear; for thus saith the prophet, they shall be saved, even if it so be as by fire" (1 Nephi 22:17; emphasis added).

PRELIMINARY APPEARANCES

Before Jesus comes to the whole world on that great and terrible day, he will make certain preliminary appearances. In an article on the Second Coming by President Charles W. Penrose, one time member of the First Presidency, he pointed out that "we may consider the inhabitants of the earth at the time immediately preceding the coming of Christ under three general divisions." President Penrose identified these as being: 1) the Saints in the New Jerusalem, 2) the Jews at Jerusalem, and 3) "the corrupt nations and the kingdoms of men, who, rejecting the light of the Gospel, are unprepared for the Lord's advent and are almost ripe for destruction."[10]

The appearance of Jesus to the Saints in the New Jerusalem and to the Jews in the Holy Land might be considered *preliminary* appearances to his coming in glory to the whole world. To these two might be added another preliminary appearance—his coming to the Saints in the valley of Adam-ondi-Ahman. Let's discuss each of these important *preliminary* appearances, and then we will discuss Jesus' coming in glory to the whole world—the great and terrible day of the Lord.

Jesus Will Appear in the Valley of Adam-ondi-Ahman

Jesus' first preliminary appearance will be to the Saints gathered at Adam-ondi-Ahman (see D&C 116; Daniel 7:13-22). (See end of chapter Figure 10-A, Adam-ondi-Ahman, Past and Future.) Adam and all the priesthood leaders from all dispensations of the earth will be gathered there for an important meeting that will be held with Christ. At this time, Satan, who now rules with great power in this world, will be bound, and Christ will take the reigns of government. Christ will then begin his rule upon the earth as King of kings and Lord of lords.

The Meaning of "Adam-ondi-Ahman"

The name "Adam-ondi-Ahman," itself is an interesting expression. It comes from the pure language of Adam, or the pure "Adamic" language.[11] The term

"Adam" of course refers to our first father. From latter-day revelation we learn that the name "Ahman" is one of the names of our Heavenly Father.[12] It is not certain what the term "ondi" means but the combined expression "Adam-ondi-Ahman" means the place or land of God where Adam dwelt. This definition "comes down from the early brethren who associated with the Prophet Joseph Smith, who was the first one to use the name in this dispensation."[13]

We first encounter the expression "Adam-ondi-Ahman" in connection with a visit Joseph Smith made to a place in Davies County, Missouri, May 19, 1838. On that date he recorded,

> This morning we struck our tents and formed a line of march, crossing Grand River at the mouth of Honey Creek and Nelson's Ferry.... We pursued our course up the river, mostly through timber, for about eighteen miles, when we arrived at Colonel Lyman Wight's home. He lives at the foot of Tower Hill (a name I gave the place in consequence of the remains of an old Nephite altar or tower that stood there), where we camped for the Sabbath.
>
> In the afternoon I went up the river about half a mile to Wight's Ferry... for the purpose of selecting and laying claim to a city plat near said ferry in Davies County, ... which the brethren called "Spring Hill," but by the mouth of the Lord it was named Adam-ondi-Ahman, because, *said he,* it is the place where Adam shall come to visit his people, or the Ancient of Days shall sit, as spoken of by Daniel the Prophet.[14]

This visitation in the valley of Adam-ondi-Ahman, to which Joseph Smith referred, is the first of the preliminary appearances of Jesus that we mentioned above that will take place at some future time.

Before we can talk about this latter-day meeting, though, it will be well for us to discuss a similar meeting that took place anciently that involved many of the righteous posterity of Adam. (See again Figure 10-A.) As you read about this ancient experience, look for the principles and patterns involved so that you can make connections between this ancient meeting and the one that is to take place in the future. *Many of the events that occurred anciently will be repeated in this future meeting.*

The Ancient Meeting at Adam-ondi-Ahman

From the Doctrine and Covenants we learn that anciently Adam called together his righteous family into the valley of Adam-ondi-Ahman and there he gave them his *last blessing.* Of this experience we read: "Three years previous to the death of Adam, he called Seth, Enos, Cainan, Mahalaleel, Jared, Enoch, and Methuselah, who were all high priests, with *the residue of his posterity who were righteous,* into the valley of Adam-ondi-Ahman, and there bestowed upon them *his last blessing"* (D&C 107:53; emphasis added).

Joseph Smith saw in vision this ancient meeting where Adam blessed his children. He reported, "I saw Adam in the valley of Adam-ondi-Ahman. He called together his children and blessed them with a patriarchal blessing. The Lord appeared in their midst, and he (Adam) blessed them all, and foretold what should befall them to the latest generation."[15]

Joseph Smith explained why Adam blessed his posterity. He said, *"This is why Adam blessed his posterity; he wanted to bring them into the presence of God."*[16] Following this blessing, those who had been thus sealed by their ancient patriarch did in fact see the Lord in the valley of Adam-ondi-Ahman. Of this experience, we read: *"And the Lord appeared, unto them,* and they rose up and blessed Adam, and called him Michael, the prince, the archangel.... And Adam stood up in the midst of the congregation; and, notwithstanding he was bowed down with age, being full of the Holy Ghost, predicted whatsoever should befall his posterity unto the latest generation" (D&C 107: 53-54, 56; emphasis added).

This special blessing given by Adam to his posterity was different from the patriarchal blessing given today by Stake Patriarchs. Adam's last blessing was sealing his righteous children up unto eternal life so they could behold the face of God. When Father Adam gave this blessing he was functioning as the natural patriarch to his children (see D&C 107:39-55, esp. vss. 39-40). He held the fulness of the priesthood and was privileged to seal his righteous children to eternal life.

These priesthood sealing powers, which enabled the children of Adam to see the face of the Lord, have operated in every gospel dispensation since the time of Adam and have been restored in our own day by Elijah to the Prophet Joseph Smith in this, the dispensation of the fulness of times.

This wonderful and vitally important doctrine—of being sealed prior to having the heavens opened, entering the presence of the Lord, and communing with holy beings—was outlined in a sermon on the Priesthood delivered by Joseph Smith. In this talk, he traced the descent of priesthood keys and sealing powers from Adam through the ages. Then he asked the question, "How have we come to the Priesthood [with its sealing powers and attendant blessings] in the last days? It came down, down, in regular succession. Peter, James, and John had it given to them and they gave it to others. Christ is the Great High Priest; Adam next. *Paul speaks of the Church coming to an innumerable company of angels—to God the Judge of all—the spirits of just men made perfect; to Jesus the Mediator of the new covenant"* (Hebrews 12:22-24).[17] The Prophet Joseph Smith clarified this passage when he explained, "Paul...tells us that the Hebrew church had come unto the presence of God and Angels and to the spirits of just men made perfect."[18]

In other words, because the sealing powers of the priesthood with all their attendant blessings came down through authoritative and proper channels, we, like the New Testament Saints, have the keys, authority and ordinances which will empower the Latter-day Saints to entertain angels, commune with the spirits of just men made perfect, and enter the presence of the Father and the Son. This crowning blessing which prepares the pure in heart to see the face of the Lord is the major function of the Melchizedek Priesthood (see D&C 107:18-19; Matthew 5:8; D&C 93:1; D&C 130:3; D&C 67:10-14).

This doctrinal concept is consistent with what has been discussed in previous chapters—that in all dispensations, the crowning ordinance of the priesthood (sealing the Saints up unto eternal life) sanctifies the Saints and prepares them, in due time, to enter the presence of the Lord (see D&C 84:19-23; 93:1). Indeed, we have been commanded in our own day to "seek the face of the Lord always, that in patience ye may possess your souls, and ye shall have eternal life" (D&C 101:38).

The ancient meeting at Adam-ondi-Ahman that we have been discussing is a case study in the blessings that flow from the crowning ordinances of the priesthood. From the record we have regarding that ancient council, we know that Enoch was in attendance. Because of his involvement in this meeting at Adam-ondi-Ahman, he was endowed with power, authority, and knowledge that enabled him to establish Zion. In consequence of this endowment, Enoch and the righteous among his people escaped the forthcoming destruction by water.

Now, as you read of the future latter-day council meeting at Adam-ondi-Ahman, you will notice many similarities between what happened in the past and what will happen in the future. This information can increase your faith and give you great hope and peace of mind. The Lord is not a novice in establishing Zion and in implementing his great plan of happiness (see Moses 7:64). Let's see now how it is that these same blessings will be enjoyed by the righteous posterity of Adam in the latter days.

A Future Meeting at Adam-ondi-Ahman

At a future council meeting in the valley of Adam-ondi-Ahman, the Latter-day Saints who are called to be in attendance, will be endowed with the same powers and blessings that were given the righteous posterity of Adam anciently. At this meeting, many of the Saints will be sealed to eternal life, see the face of the Lord, and be empowered to more fully establish Zion. In addition, this future meeting at Adam-ondi-Ahman will more fully prepare the Saints for divine protection as was foreseen by Daniel the prophet.

In the Old Testament we read that Daniel saw in vision a latter-day meeting in the valley of Adam-ondi-Ahman. Of his vision of the future he said: "I saw in the night visions, and behold, one like the Son of man came with the clouds of heaven, and came to the Ancient of Days, and they brought him near before him"

Daniel continued his description of his latter-day vision:

And there was given him [Christ] dominion, and glory, and a kingdom, that all people, nations, and languages, should serve him: his dominion is an everlasting dominion, which shall not pass away, and his kingdom that which shall not be destroyed....

But the saints of the most High shall take the kingdom, and possess the kingdom forever, even for ever and ever....

I beheld, and the same horn made war with the saints, and prevailed against them;

Until the Ancient of days came, and judgment was given to the saints of the most High; and the time came that the saints possessed the kingdom (Daniel 7:13-14, 18, 21-22).

In referring to this latter-day visit of Christ and Adam to the valley of Adam-ondi-Ahman, President Joseph Fielding Smith explained, "Not many years hence there shall be another gathering of high priests and righteous souls in the same valley of Adam-ondi-Ahman. At this gathering Adam, the Ancient of Days, will again be present. At this time the vision which Daniel saw will be enacted. The Ancient of Days will sit. There will stand before him those who have held the keys of all dispensations, who shall render up their stewardships to the first patriarch of the race, who holds the keys of salvation. This shall be a day of judgment and preparation."[19]

Continuing, President Smith said that at this council,

Christ will take over the reigns of the government, officially on this earth, and the "kingdom and dominion, and the greatness of the kingdom under the whole heaven, shall be given to the people of the Saints of the Most High, whose kingdom is an everlasting kingdom, and all dominions shall serve and obey him," even Jesus Christ....

This council in the Valley of Adam-ondi-Ahman is to be of the greatest importance to this world. At that time there will be a transfer of authority from the usurper and impostor, Lucifer, to the rightful King, Jesus Christ. Judgment will be set and all who have held keys will make their reports, and deliver their stewardships, as they shall be required. Adam will direct this judgment and then will make his report, the one holding the keys for this earth, to his superior officer, Jesus Christ. Our Lord will then assume the reigns of the government; directions will be given to the priesthood, and he, whose right it is to rule, will be installed officially by the voice of the priesthood there assembled. This grand council of priesthood will not only be composed of those who are faithful who *now* dwell on this earth, but also the prophets and apostles of old, who have any directing authority. Others may also be there by appointment, for this is to be an official council called to attend to the most momentous matters concerning the destiny of this earth.

When this gathering is held, the world will not know of it; the members of the Church at large will not know of it, yet it shall be preparatory to the coming in the clouds of glory of our Savior Jesus Christ as the Prophet Joseph Smith said. The world cannot know of it—except those who officially shall be called into this council—for it shall precede the coming of Jesus Christ as a thief in the night, unbeknown to all the world.[20]

As you can see from this statement by President Smith, great spiritual powers will come to the Saints as a result of this marvelous family meeting with Adam and Christ at Adam-ondi-Ahman. Anticipating the necessity of these spiritual powers, during the dedicatory prayer of the Kirtland temple Joseph Smith plead with the Lord that they might be granted the Saints. Joseph's prayer was answered with the coming of Elijah as we have discussed earlier (see D&C 109: 35, 38, 40, 42-43, 45-46; D&C 110).

Through the restoration of these divine powers, the pure in heart will be blessed to have the heavens opened to them. They will have power to communicate with holy personages from behind the veil and thereby receive further instructions relative to more fully establishing Zion and preparing for the Second Coming of the Lord.

Using Jesus' parable of the mustard seed, Joseph Smith explained how Adam's appearance at Adam-ondi-Ahman, along with the visitations of many angels, will help us prepare for the establishment of the Millennial Kingdom of God. He said: "The Kingdom of Heaven is like a grain of mustard seed. The mustard seed is small, but brings forth a large tree, and the fowls lodge in the branches. *The fowls are the angels.* Thus angels come down, combine together to gather their children, and gather them. We cannot be made perfect without them, nor they without us; when these things are done, the Son of Man will descend, the Ancient of Days sit, *we may [then] come to an innumerable company of angels, have communion with and receive instruction from them.*"[21]

It will be necessary for the Saints to receive this kind of heavenly tutoring in order for the powers associated with Zion and the Millennial kingdom to be realized—including the powers for protection of the Saints during days of calamity (D&C 1:17). Joseph Smith illustrated this need for divine tutoring when he explained the powers of the priesthood that descended upon the early Church. He said,

The Hebrew Church "came unto the spirits of just men made perfect, and unto an innumerable company of angels, unto God the Father of all, and to Jesus Christ the Mediator of the new covenant." *What did they learn by coming to the spirits of just men made perfect? Is it written?* No. What they learned has not been and could not have been written. What object was gained by this communication with the spirits of the just? *It was the established order of the kingdom of God*: The keys of power and knowledge were with them to communicate to the Saints.... *The spirits of just men are made ministering servants to those who are sealed unto life eternal,* and it is through them that the sealing *power* comes down.[22]

In the last days, when the Saints are finally sealed and are worthy to have the heavens opened to them, they—like the Hebrew Saints mentioned above—will be tutored and taught by heavenly messengers. Through this instruction the necessary powers of deliverance will come down.

The right to communicate with heavenly beings—including the Lord himself—and receive of their knowledge and power is inherent within the Melchizedek Priesthood (see D&C 107:18-19). Of course we are still in a time of preparation, but we must never lose sight of these vital goals for which we are striving (see D&C 67:10-14).

At the council meeting at Adam-ondi-Ahman, a great number of Saints will receive these crowning blessings. This will mark a time of marvelous spiritual resurgence out of which will grow a fulness of the blessings of the everlasting covenant—including the establishment of Zion (see D&C 45:65-71). Because many of the Saints will be sealed at this time—in the same manner as Saints were sealed anciently at Adam-ondi-Ahman (see D&C 107:53)—the blessings associated with Zion will be realized (see D&C 105:35-37). This will be a day of deliverance for the Saints of the Most High! (see D&C 105:31-32)

In connection with this principle of deliverance through priesthood ordinances, we read that, "The rights of the priesthood are inseparably connected with the powers of the heaven, and that the powers of heaven cannot be controlled nor handled only upon the principles of righteousness" (D&C 121:36). In other words, for any person to have the abundant priesthood powers he must be righteous, he must have received a fulness of the priesthood—the keys of which were restored by Elijah—and he must be tutored by holy beings from behind the veil.

Nephi, for example, met all these qualifications. He was righteous, was sealed to eternal life, was tutored by the Lord and was given power among his people. Of his power, the Lord told him: "If ye shall say unto this temple it shall be rent in twain, it shall be done. And if ye shall say unto this mountain, Be thou cast down and become smooth, it shall be done. And behold, if ye shall say that God shall smite this people, it shall come to pass" (Helaman 10:8-10).

Until these powers are realized among the Latter-day Saints, they will be vulnerable to the persecutions and afflictions imposed upon them by Satan. Concerning these difficulties and eventual deliverance, Joseph Smith referred to the vision of Daniel and said, "The 'Horn' made war with the Saints and overcame them, until the Ancient of Days came; *judgment was [then] given to the Saints* of the Most High from the Ancient of Days; the time came that the Saints possessed the Kingdom."[23] The Prophet Joseph has given us more insight into this remarkable vision of Daniel. He explained:

> Daniel, in his vision, saw convulsion upon convulsion; he "beheld till the thrones were cast down, and the Ancient of Days did sit;" and one was brought before him like unto the Son of Man; and all nations, kindreds, tongues, and peoples, did serve and obey Him. It is for us to be righteous, that we may be wise and understand; for none ... but the wise shall understand.... As a Church and a people it behooves us to be wise, and seek to know the will of God, and then be willing to do it; ... "Watch and pray always," says our Savior, "that ye may be accounted worthy to escape the things that are to come on the earth, and to stand before the Son of Man." If Enoch, Abraham, Moses, and the children of Israel, and all God's people were saved by keeping the commandments of God, we, if saved at all, shall be saved upon the same principle.[24]

From Joseph Smith's explanation we learn that, through faith and righteousness, the Saints of God will be given great priesthood authority which will grant them protection from hostile nations and geophysical upheavals. This great authority will grow out of the council that will be held at Adam-ondi-Ahman. Our eventual deliverance will come as we are empowered and permitted to build Zion.

In order to prepare for safety in the days to come, Joseph Smith explained, "We ought to have the building up of Zion as our greatest object. When wars come, we shall have to flee to Zion. The cry is to make haste. The last revelation says, Ye shall not have time to have gone over the earth, until these things come. It will come [swiftly] as did the cholera,[25] war, fires, and earthquakes; one pestilence after another, until the Ancient of Days comes, then judgment will be given to the Saints."[26]

As we have mentioned before, the ancient meeting at Adam-ondi-Ahman provides us with a pattern whereby we can understand what will take place at some future time in the same location. Under father Adam's direction, priesthood keys will again be exercised to seal his righteous children to eternal life. They will then have the heavens opened unto them and will behold the face of Jesus and the Father, and be tutored and taught by the spirits of just men made perfect. Then the Saints will be endowed with power, authority, and knowledge that will enabled them to more fully establish Zion. In consequence of this endowment, the righteous will escape the destructions that will come upon the wicked— including the final destruction by fire.

Jesus Will Appear to the Saints in the New Jerusalem

As was mentioned earlier, the Lord's first appearance at Adam-ondi-Ahman will pave the way for the building of Zion. After Zion is established and a temple has been built the Savior will make his second preliminary appearance. This one will be to the Saints of God gathered in Zion, the New Jerusalem (see 3 Nephi 21:23-26). This appearance will also be unknown to the rest of mankind. Elder Penrose wrote that Jesus "will come to the Temple prepared for him, and his faithful people will behold his face, hear his voice, and gaze upon his glory. From his own lips they will receive further instructions for the development and beautifying of Zion and for the extension and sure stability of his kingdom."[27]

To prepare for that day, the Saints are commanded, "Hearken, O ye people of my church, saith the Lord your God, and hear the word of the Lord concerning you—*The Lord who shall suddenly come to his temple;* the Lord who shall come down upon the world with a curse to judgment; yea, upon all the nations that forget God, and upon all the ungodly among you (D&C 133:1-2). While those who forget the Lord will be destroyed, those of Israel and of the Gentiles who remember him and are looking forward to his coming will be allowed to assist in building Zion.

The repentant Gentiles will play an important role during this time. The Lord said that they "shall assist my people, the remnant of Jacob, and also as many of the house of Israel as shall come, that they may build a city, which shall be called the New Jerusalem.... And then shall the power of heaven come down among them; and *I also will be in the midst*" (3 Nephi 21:23, 25).

Jesus Will Appear to the Jews at the Mount of Olives

Jesus' final preliminary appearance will be to the Jews who are arrayed in battle because all nations will have gathered to fight against Jerusalem (see Zechariah 12:10; 13:6; 14:1-5). Zechariah foretells that half of the city will go forth into captivity, and then the Lord will go forth and fight against those nations as he had done in former times. "And *his feet shall stand in that day upon the Mount of Olives,* which is before Jerusalem on the east, and the Mount of Olives shall cleave in the midst thereof toward the east and toward the west, and there shall be a very great valley; and half of the mountain shall remove toward the north, and half of it toward the south. And they shall flee to the valley of the mountains" (Zechariah 14:2-5; emphasis added).

Christ will meet them there and as the victorious Jews approach him "one shall say unto him, *What are these wounds in thine hands?* Then he shall answer, Those with which I was wounded in the house of my friends" (Zechariah 13:6; emphasis added). Then will the Lord "pour upon the house of David, and upon the inhabitants of Jerusalem, the spirit of grace and of supplications: and *they shall look upon me whom they have pierced,* and they shall mourn for him, as one mourneth for his only son, and shall be in bitterness for him, as one that is in bitterness for his firstborn (Zechariah 12:10; emphasis added; also D&C 45:51; 133:20).

Of this appearance of Jesus among the Jews, President Penrose has written with particularly descriptive words:

> His next appearance [after appearing to the Saints in the New Jerusalem] will be among the distressed and nearly vanquished sons of Judah. At the crisis of their fate, when the hostile troops of several nations are ravaging the city and all the horrors of war are overwhelming the people of Jerusalem, he will set his feet upon the Mount of Olives, which will cleave and part asunder at his touch. Attended by a host from heaven, he will overthrow and destroy the combined armies of the Gentiles, and appear to the worshipping Jews as the mighty Deliverer and Conqueror so long expected by their race; and while love, gratitude, awe, and admiration swell their bosoms, the Deliverer will show them the tokens of his crucifixion and disclose himself as Jesus of Nazareth, who they had reviled, and whom their fathers put to death. Then will unbelief depart from their souls, and "the blindness in part which has happened unto Israel" be removed. "A fountain for sin and uncleanness will be opened to the house of David and the inhabitants of Jerusalem," and "a nation will be born" unto God "in a day." They will be baptized for the remission of their sins, and will receive the gift of the Holy Ghost, and *the government of God as established in Zion will be set up among them, no more to be thrown down forever.*"[28]

In summary of this wonderful, refreshing, renewing, and life-giving experience for the Jews, these points are made: In the not too distant future, when the Jews are almost overwhelmed by their adversaries, Jesus' feet will touch the Mount of Olives and the earth will shudder in the glory of his presence. The Mount will open and the Jews will find comfort, peace and rest in this cleavage of the earth. There they will find rest and will be delivered from all that has oppressed them for many generations. In this climactic experience, the Jews will look upon him whom their fathers had pierced, and they will be spiritually awakened and given new life. A nation will be born in a day.

What a wonderful thing it will be to have the Jews, who for so long have looked for their Messiah, to finally behold his face and receive the blessings of the everlasting covenant that their fathers Abraham and Moses knew and enjoyed. They will once again know what great things the Lord hath done for their fathers; they will again know the covenants of the Lord and that they are not cast off forever.

The revelations do not indicate how much time there will be between this appearance of Jesus to the Jews and his subsequent appearance to the world at large. Some people have wondered if the Jews, following this appearance of Jesus, will then rebuild their temple in Jerusalem in preparation for the "great and terrible day of the Lord". While this is speculative, it is an interesting idea.

THE FINAL APPEARANCE—THE GREAT AND DREADFUL DAY

The final appearance of Jesus—after these preliminary appearances about which we have been speaking—will be, in the words of Elder Penrose, "to the corrupt nations and the kingdoms of men, who, rejecting the light of the Gospel, are unprepared for the Lord's advent and are almost ripe for destruction."

Continuing, Elder Penrose explained: "The great and crowning advent of the Lord will be subsequent to these [preliminary] appearances; but who can describe it in the language of mortals? The tongue of man falters, and the pen drops from the hand of the writer, as the mind is rapt in contemplation of the sublime and awful majesty of his coming to take vengeance on the ungodly and to reign as King of the whole earth."[29]

In the Doctrine and Covenants we read that at this final appearance people will ask, "Who is this that cometh down from God in heaven with dyed garments; yea, from the regions which are not known, clothed in his glorious apparel, traveling in the greatness of his strength?" and the Lord shall say, "I am he who spake in righteousness, mighty to save."

The revelation continues: "And the Lord shall be red in his apparel, and his garments like him that treadeth in the wine-vat. And so great shall be the glory of his presence that the sun shall hide his face in shame, and the moon shall withhold its light, and the stars shall be hurled from their places" (D&C 133:46-49; see also Topical Guide, *Jesus Christ, Second Coming*). This is the great and dreadful day of the Lord!

THE RIGHTEOUS WILL BE TRANSLATED AT HIS COMING

In connection with this coming of the Lord in his glory from the heavens, the apostle Paul stated, "Then we which are alive and remain shall be caught up together with them in the clouds, to meet the Lord in the air: and so shall we ever be with the Lord" (1 Thess. 4:17). The expression "caught up" in this passage has reference to the Saints being translated at the Lord's coming.

In former dispensations, before the resurrection of Christ, it was an established part of the gospel program that when the Saints were sanctified, they were translated to a terrestrial world. From the Joseph Smith Translation we read: "And men having this faith, coming up unto *this order of God* [the Patriarchal Order of the Priesthood], were translated and taken up into heaven" (JST, Genesis 14:32: emphasis added).

In a very interesting doctrinal pronouncement regarding translation at the time of the Second Coming, President John Taylor affirmed that the Saints who are alive at the coming of Christ will be caught up, or translated, even as Enoch's people were in a day of wickedness. (See end of chapter Figure 10-B, The Doctrine of Translation, Enoch and Us).

President Taylor compared the translation of Enoch's city with the translation of the Saints at the Second Coming. He explained that during Enoch's time, there was a great division among the people, the righteous "assembled themselves together, constituting the city of Zion; and the others became more corrupt". The people, "grew to be so corrupt that 'the imaginations of the thoughts of their hearts were only evil, and that continually; ... But the servants of God went forth preaching the Gospel of life and salvation to this wicked people, and warned them of the destruction that was coming upon the earth. Before this great calamity took place, Enoch and his city were translated."

How is it that they could be translated? In answer to this question President Taylor explained, "The power of translation was a principle that existed in the Church in that dispensation."

The Prophet Joseph taught that translation is a doctrine that belongs to the priesthood. Using Enoch's translation as a background for this point, Joseph Smith said,

> This Enoch God reserved unto Himself, that he should not die at that time, and appointed unto him a ministry unto terrestrial bodies, of whom there has been but little revealed. He is reserved also unto the presidency of a dispensation, and more shall be said of him and terrestrial bodies in another treatise. He is a ministering angel, to minister to those who shall be heirs of salvation, and appeared unto Jude as Abel did unto Paul;...
>
> *Now the doctrine of translation is a power which belongs to this Priesthood.* There are many things which belong to the powers of the Priesthood and the keys thereof, that have been kept hid from before the foundation of the world; they are hid from the wise and prudent to be revealed in the last times.[30]

We are attempting to prepare a people for translation the same as Enoch did. We are trying to perfect a people in a day of wickedness, a people who will be pure in heart, a Zion people. A vital part of our ability to escape the calamities that are to come has to do with establishing Zion.

Regarding the building up of Zion President Taylor stated: "Here we are. We are organized under the direction of the Almighty, and...what are we going to do? We are going to build up Zion. What then? When Zion is built up—and it is not built up yet; but it will be built up; and when that is done Jerusalem that is spoken of shall be built—and we are a long way from that—but when it is built up and the glory of God shall rest upon it, upon every dwelling of Mount Zion as it did in former times—then we will build up our Zion after the pattern that God will show us, and we will be governed by his law and submit to his authority and be governed by the holy priesthood and by the word and will of God."

And then President Taylor explained what will happen to the Saints when the calamities burst forth upon the earth. He said: "*And when the time comes that these calamities we read of, shall overtake the earth, those that are prepared will have the power of translation, as they had in former times, and the city will be translated.*"

President Taylor's statement provides us with a wonderful parallel comparing the translation of Enoch's people with the translation of the righteous in the latter days. In both cases the Saints, by being translated, escape the calamities that accompany the destruction of the wicked. In Enoch's day they escaped the flood—in the latter days they will escape the fire.

Continuing, President Taylor said, "Zion that is on the earth will rise, and the Zion above will descend, as we are told, and we will meet and fall on each other's necks and embrace and kiss each other."

In preparation for this marvelous event, the great missionary work of the Church must go forward. The ensign of the Lord must be clearly visible enabling the righteous of the world to be drawn to it. "By and by", President Taylor declared, "God will work with us in a more powerful manner than he has done yet; and thousands upon thousands will flock to the standard of Zion, and many will come and say, 'we do not know much about your religion, but you are an honorable people and execute justice and we want to be governed by those principles and be under their influence; and if we cannot endorse your religious views, we seek your protection and want to be one with you.'"[31]

From President Taylor's remarks and other sources we can see that in Zion there will be at least three levels of devotion and commitment. These levels could be compared to an archer's target with its concentric rings: the bull's eye represents the sealed and sanctified members of the Church of the Firstborn—those who have the powers of the priesthood to establish Zion (see D&C 76:54, 67, 71, 94, 102; 77:11; 78:21; 88:1-5; Hebrews 12:23; JST, Genesis 14:30-32); the next ring represents the general members of the Church; and the outer ring represents the good and decent non-members who will "flock to the standard of Zion" as President Taylor mentioned in the above statement.

In picture form these levels of commitment look like this:

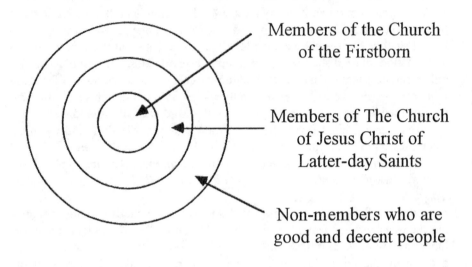

Members of the Church
of the Firstborn

Members of The Church
of Jesus Christ of
Latter-day Saints

Non-members who are
good and decent people

In many respects what has been said about Enoch and his people regarding their translation applies to the Latter-day Saints at the Lord's coming. This information is truly "a pearl of great price"! When the Lord comes, the righteous will be translated as President Taylor explained and will thereby obtain deliverance from death as we know it and the sufferings and tortures of the flesh. As translated beings they will continue to live on this millennial earth until they have fulfilled their life's work.

A Change Equivalent to Death

In an important discourse on the nature of translated beings, Joseph taught, *"Translated bodies cannot enter into rest until they have undergone a change equivalent to death."*[32] This change equivalent to death is and will be necessary for all translated beings—including those who are translated at Jesus' coming. The change from having a translated body to having a resurrected body will be brought about in the "twinkling of an eye" (D&C 63:51). No grave for the physical body will be necessary in this change.

Elder Bruce R. McConkie has written about this change that translated beings must pass through. He said, "This final change from mortality to immortality is, in effect, their death, for all men die, even those who are alive when Christ comes, and those who will live during the Millennium.... It is interesting to note that John, in recording the Lord's promise to him, apparently knew that he should not 'taste' death or 'endure' the pains thereof, yet he knew that he would pass through a change equivalent to death. 'Then went this saying abroad among the brethren, that that disciple should not die,' John says, 'yet Jesus said not unto him, He shall not die; but, If I will that he tarry till I come, what is that to thee?'" (John 21:20-23).

Elder McConkie continued, "All translated beings accordingly receive what amounts to an instantaneous death and resurrection. Those who were translated before the resurrection of our Lord 'were with Christ in his resurrection.' (D&C 133:55.) Those who have been translated since the resurrection of Christ shall continue to live as mortals until the Second Coming when they shall receive their immortal glory. It will be resurrected, not translated beings, who shall return with the city of Enoch."[33]

Enoch, Moses, Elijah, and many others who had been translated before the time of Christ (see JST, Genesis 14:32), were resurrected in this quick manner. Jesus, of course, was the "first fruits" of the resurrection (1 Corinthians 15:20), but these prophets who had been translated were with Jesus in his resurrection (see D&C 133:54-55). They were changed from terrestrial mortal bodies to immortal celestial bodies— "in the twinkling of an eye".

As was mentioned above, this instantaneous resurrection will also be necessary for those people who will be *translated* when Jesus comes. They, too, eventually will have to undergo this change equivalent to death in order for them to become *resurrected* beings.

Mormon explained that the three Nephite apostles of Jesus—who were translated before he left them—will have to pass through this change equivalent to death. Of them Mormon said,

> And now behold, as I spake concerning those whom the Lord hath chosen, yea, even three who were caught up into the heavens, that I knew not whether they were cleansed from mortality to immortality—
>
> But behold, since I wrote, I have inquired of the Lord, and he hath made it manifest unto me that there must needs be a change wrought upon their bodies, or else it needs be that they must taste of death;
>
> Therefore, that they might not taste of death there was a change wrought upon their bodies, that they might not suffer pain nor sorrow save it were for the sins of the world.
>
> *Now this change was not equal to that which shall take place at the last day;* but there was a change wrought upon them insomuch that Satan could have no power over them, that he could not tempt them; and they were sanctified in the flesh, that they were holy, and that the powers of the earth could not hold them.
>
> And in this state they were to remain until the judgment day of Christ; and at that day they were to receive a *greater change* and to be received into the kingdom of the Father to go no more out, but to dwell with God eternally in the heavens (3 Nephi 28:36-40; emphasis added).

In summary, then, when people are translated, their bodies are changed so that they no longer experience pain, disease, sorrow or death—as we know it. But this translation process is not the same as being resurrected. They are still considered mortal beings since they must undergo a change.[34] When the time comes for them to be changed to resurrected beings, their bodies will not be buried in the earth. They will be changed from mortality to immortality in the "twinkling of an eye"—which is a change equivalent to death!

The Good News and the Bad News

Joseph Smith compared terrestrial translated beings to telestial people in this world. In a sense he described the bad news and the good news about each of these conditions.

The bad news for people who are translated is that they have to labor and toil in the ministry *for a prolonged period of time*—sometimes a thousand years or more—before they can enter into their rest.[35] The good news for translated beings, however, is that they are delivered from the sufferings and tortures of the flesh. They do not experience pain, suffering, disease, or death like we do.

Here are Joseph's teachings on this interesting subject:

> Many have supposed that the doctrine of translation was a doctrine whereby men were taken immediately into the presence of God, and into an eternal fulness, but this is a mistaken idea. Their place of habitation is that of the *terrestrial order*, and a place prepared for such characters He held in reserve to be *ministering angels unto many planets*, and who as yet have not entered into so great a fulness as those who are resurrected from the dead. "Others were tortured, not accepting deliverance, that they might obtain a better resurrection." [Hebrews 11:35.]
>
> Now it was evident that there was a better resurrection, or else God would not have revealed it unto Paul. Wherein then, can it be said a better resurrection. This *distinction* is made between the doctrine of the actual resurrection and translation: *translation obtains deliverance from the tortures and sufferings of the body, but their existence will prolong as to the labor and toils of the ministry, before they can enter into so great a rest and glory.*

Regarding our telestial world, in contrast to translated beings, the bad news is that we here are literally tortured and suffer in the flesh. We experience pain, sorrow, disease, heartache, and death. The good news about this world is that our pain and the suffering don't last long. We live here for 70 or 80 years and then the test is all over. We die and go into the spirit world where the righteous rest until the time of their resurrection (Alma 40:11-12). Joseph Smith described us who live in a telestial world as: "those who were tortured, not accepting deliverance, [who receive] an immediate rest from their labors [when they die].... *They rest from their labors for a long time,* and yet their work is held in reserve for them, that they are permitted to do the same work, after they receive a resurrection of their bodies."

"But," said the Prophet in concluding his sermon, "we shall leave this subject and the subject of the terrestrial bodies for another time, in order to treat upon them more fully.³⁶ Joseph never publicly returned to this topic of terrestrial beings before his martyrdom. How wonderful it would have been to have a question and answer session with him regarding this fascinating topic!

Even though we do not have any further information from Joseph Smith regarding translated beings, we do have additional information in the Book of Mormon. In Third Nephi, Chapter 28, we read Mormon's description of the three Nephite apostles. The whole chapter is devoted to the translation of The Three Nephites. These men were translated and were promised that they could remain on the earth, as was their desire, until the Second Coming. Their condition is representative of translated beings in general. What we read of them can be generalized to other translated beings: They were privileged to view the things of eternity. They taught the gospel with great power. Prison walls could not hold them, nor could wild beasts harm them. The powers of the earth could not hold them. They we given permission to appear to those of strong faith. They are as the angels of God "and if they shall pray unto the Father in the name of Jesus they can show themselves unto whatsoever man it seemeth them good" (3 Nephi 28:30).

How wonderful it will be for those who remain on the earth, who have been true and faithful in all things—who will be caught up in the air and translated—to meet the Lord when he comes in his glory as King of kings and Lord of lords.

JESUS WILL RETURN AS KING OF KINGS

One of our beautiful Latter-day Saint hymns vividly contrasts the first coming of Jesus, as a lowly babe in Bethlehem, with his great and glorious Second Coming.

As you read these verses remember this great contrast between Jesus' first coming and his Second Coming. The words of this wonderful hymn explain <u>this</u> great difference:

Jesus, once of humble birth,
Now in glory comes to earth.
Once he suffered grief and pain;

Now he comes on earth to reign;
Now he comes on earth to reign.

Once a meek and lowly Lamb,
Now the Lord, the great I Am;
Once upon the cross he bowed,
Now his chariot is the cloud;
Now his chariot is the cloud.

Once he groaned in blood and tears;
Now in glory he appears;
Once rejected by his own,
Now their King he shall be known;
Now their King he shall be known.

Once forsaken, left alone,
Now exalted to a throne;
Once all things he meekly bore,
But he now will bear no more,
But he now will bear no more.[37]

The righteous will thrill with joy when the Lord comes in his great glory as the great I AM—when he comes whose chariot is the cloud. He who suffered will bear no more—as their King he shall be known. Those who survive the destructions of the last days will dwell with Christ on the newly refreshed, paradisiacal earth, and the earth will remain in that terrestrial condition for a period of one-thousand years.

THE MILLENNIUM—ONE THOUSAND YEARS OF PEACE

Just as the word *century* means a period of 100 years, so the word *millennium* means a period of 1000 years. This earth, according to the divine plan, is passing through a temporal existence of seven millennia or 7000 years (see D&C 77:6, 12). (See end of chapter Figure 10-C, A Day With The Lord Is A Thousand Years With Man.)

During the first six of these millennia—from the Fall of Adam until now—conditions of carnality, corruption, evil, and wickedness of every sort have prevailed upon the earth. Wars, death, destruction and everything incident to the present telestial state of existence have held sway over the earth and all life on its face.

The corrupt governments of men have brought death and misery to many of their subjects. Of these conditions the Prophet Joseph said,

> The government of the Almighty has always been very dissimilar to the governments of men, whether we refer to His religious government, or to the government of nations. The government of God has always tended to promote peace, unity, harmony, strength, and happiness; while that of man has been productive of confusion, disorder, weakness, and misery.... All, all, speak with a voice of thunder, that *man is not able to govern himself,* to legislate for himself, to protect himself, to promote his own good, nor the good of the world.
>
> *It has been the design of Jehovah, from the commencement of the world, and is His purpose now, to regulate the affairs of the world in His own time, to stand as a head of the universe, and take the reins of government in His own hand.* When that is done, judgment will be administered in righteousness; anarchy and confusion will be destroyed, and "nations will learn war no more." It is for want of this great governing principle, that all this confusion has existed; *"for it is not in man that walketh, to direct his steps"* this we have fully shown....

Continuing, the Prophet Joseph explained,

> When Egypt was under the superintendence of Joseph it prospered, because he was taught of God; ... When the children of Israel were chosen with Moses at their head, they were to be a peculiar people, among whom God should place His name; their motto was: *"The Lord is our lawgiver; the Lord is our Judge; the Lord is our King; and He shall reign over us."* While in this state they might truly say, "Happy is that people, whose God is the Lord." *Their government was a theocracy;* they had God to make their laws, and men chosen by Him to administer them; He was their God, and they were His people. Moses received the word of the Lord from God Himself; he was the mouth of God to Aaron, and *Aaron taught the people, in both civil and ecclesiastical affairs; they were both one, there was no distinction; so will it be when the purposes of God shall be accomplished: when 'the Lord shall be King over the whole earth'* and "Jerusalem His throne." "The law shall go forth from Zion, and the word of the Lord from Jerusalem."
>
> This is the only thing that can bring about the "restitution of all things spoken of by all the holy Prophets since the world was"— "the dispensation of the fulness of times, when *God shall gather together all things in one."* Other attempts to promote universal peace and happiness in the human family have proved abortive; every effort has failed; every plan and design has fallen to the ground; *it needs the wisdom of God, the intelligence of God, and the power of God to accomplish this. The world has had a fair trial for six*

thousand years; the Lord will try the seventh thousand Himself; ... To bring about this state of things, there must of necessity be great confusion among the nations of the earth.[38]

As was mentioned earlier, the council at Adam-ondi-Ahman will usher in the political kingdom of God which will be instrumental in promoting the universal peace of which Joseph speaks and which will, in time, find its climax in the millennial reign of Christ.

EVENTS OF THE LAST DAYS— SIGNS OF THE TIMES

Elder Bruce R. McConkie has given an outline of events and conditions as we can expect them during the Millennium. If you will refer to his work, *Mormon Doctrine,* under the title "Millennium," you will find more detailed information regarding each point presented here. For now, let's look at his list of the events and conditions that are associated with the Millennium:

1. The Council at Adam-ondi-Ahman precedes the Millennium.
2. The second coming of Jesus begins the Millennium.
3. The first resurrection ushers in the Millennium.
4. Righteousness will not hasten the Millennium.
5. The wicked will be destroyed at his coming.
6. The day of judgment commences the millennial era.
7. The earth will be renewed to its paradisiacal state.
8. Satan will be bound.
9. Peace on earth will come.
10. There will be changes in the animal kingdom.
11. Mortality continues during Millennium.
12. Death, sorrow, and disease will cease.
13. All things will be revealed.
14. There will be non-members of the Church on the earth.
15. There will be a conversion of all to the truth.
16. The Church is the Kingdom of God on earth.
17. Temple work will be greatly expanded.
18. At the end, the earth will become celestialized.

Each of these conditions evokes images and questions in our minds. As time continues to pass we will see these and many other conditions unfold. There are however, important events yet to take place before the millennial reign of the Lord.

The Prophet Joseph once inquired of the Lord regarding the time of his second coming. In response, he was given specific information about what must yet take place before the Lord will come in his glory. Joseph related,

> I was once praying earnestly upon this subject, and a voice said unto me, "My son, if thou livest until thou art eighty-five years of age, thou shalt see the face of the Son of Man." I was left to draw my own conclusions concerning this; and I took the liberty to conclude that if I did live to that time, He would make His appearance. But I do not say whether He will make His appearance or I shall go where He is. I prophesy in the name of the Lord God, and let it be written—the Son of Man will not come in the clouds of heaven till I am eighty-five years old.... *The coming of the Son of Man never will be—never can be till the judgments spoken of for this hour are poured out: which judgments are commenced.* Paul says, "Ye are the children of the light, and not of the darkness, that that day should overtake you as a thief in the night." *It is not the design of the Almighty to come upon the earth and crush it and grind it to powder but he will reveal it to His servants the prophets.*
>
> *Judah must return, Jerusalem must be rebuilt, and the temple, and water come out from under the temple, and the waters of the Dead Sea be healed.* It will take some time to rebuild the walls of the city and the temple, etc.; *and all this must be done before the Son of Man will make His appearance.* There will be wars and rumors of wars, signs in the heavens above and on the earth beneath, the sun turned to darkness and the moon to blood; earthquakes in divers places, the seas heaving beyond their bounds; then will appear one grand *sign of the Son of Man* in heaven. But what will the world do? They will say it is a planet, a comet, etc. *But the Son of Man will come as the sign of the coming of the Son of Man,* which will be as the light of the morning cometh out of the east.[39]

The Lord has given yet another sign of his coming. In the year the rainbow is *not* seen, the coming of the Messiah is near. Joseph taught this principle in these words: "The Lord deals with this people as a tender parent with a child, communicating light and intelligence and the knowledge of his ways as they can bear it. The inhabitants of the earth are asleep; they know not the day of their visitation. The Lord hath set the bow in the cloud for a sign that while it shall be seen, seed time and harvest, summer and winter shall not fail; *but when it shall disappear, woe to that generation, for behold the end cometh quickly.*"[40]

At another time Joseph Smith taught that the rainbow is a symbol, a token, or a sign of things to come. He explained that "I have asked of the Lord concerning His coming; and while asking the Lord, He gave a sign and said, 'In the days of Noah I set a bow in the heavens as a sign and token that in any year that the bow should be seen the Lord would not come; but there should be seed time and harvest during that year; but *whenever you see the bow withdrawn*, it shall be a token that there shall be famine, pestilence, and great distress among the nations, and that the coming of the Messiah is not far distant.'... Jesus Christ never did reveal to any man the precise time that He would come."[41]

As we have discussed in a previous chapter, the rainbow is also a beautiful reminder of the Lord's covenant with Noah and Enoch that when we keep the commandments Zion from above will come down and join with Zion on earth and there will be great peace and rest. We are living in the time just prior to the fulfillment of that great promise.

What a wonderful time we live in! Even though there are terrible things to happen among the wicked prior to the Millennium, the Lord has promised that if we are prepared, we will not fear.

IF WE ARE PREPARED, WE SHALL NOT FEAR

We must not get discouraged during the trying times we live in. All of the promises of the Lord will come to pass. The more familiar we are with the word of the Lord, the more comfort we will experience. He has assured us that by searching the scriptures we will find peace: "Search these commandments, for they are true and faithful, and the prophecies and promises which are in them shall all be fulfilled. What I the Lord have spoken, I have spoken, and I excuse not myself; and though the heavens and the earth pass away, my words shall not pass away, but shall all be fulfilled, whether by mine own voice or by the voice of my servants, it is the same" (D&C 1:37-38).

Many who do not understand the scriptures, or who are not keeping the commandments become frightened when they hear of and see the signs indicating the nearness of the Lord's coming. However, if we understand the promises of protection and live for them, then the Lord has assured us that "if ye are prepared ye shall not fear" (D&C 38:30).

Elder Joseph Fielding Smith has given us these comforting words regarding the coming of the Lord: "Trouble in the earth will continue; there will be distress, calamity and perplexity among the nations. We need not look for peace in the immediate future because peace will not come. Nevertheless, we may look forward with rejoicing; we need not be downcast, but in the spirit of faith and hope, and in the fear of the Lord, we should look to the future with feelings of joy, of humility, and of worship, with the desire in our hearts, stronger, if possible, than ever of serving the Lord and keeping his commandments."[42]

As we look forward to the future as Elder Smith has admonished us, we can find great peace and comfort in the knowledge that the Lord's timetable is on schedule, and the Church is making rapid progress.

THE CHURCH IS MAKING RAPID PROGRESS

Brigham Young stated that "Twenty-five years of the travel and experience of Enoch with his people had not advanced them so far, in my opinion, as this people have advanced in the same time taking into account the differences of traditions and other advantages." He added, "They had not a diversity of languages, but all spoke one language; they were not trained in the various traditions in which we have been, for they received only one from Adam; they were as intimately associated as we would be in living in this City two hundred years, with the gates shut down upon all egress and ingress, and under such circumstances do you not think our traditions would be all alike?" Continuing, President Young said,

> Yet Enoch had to talk with and teach his people during a period of three hundred and sixty years, before he could get them prepared to enter into their rest, and then he obtained power to translate himself and his people, with the region they inhabited, their houses, gardens, fields, cattle, and all their possessions. *He had learned enough from Adam and his associates to know how to handle the elements,* and those who would not listen to his teachings were so wicked that they were fit to be destroyed, and *he obtained power to take his portion of the earth and move out a little while, where he remains to this day.*[43]

The wicked of our day have been warned to prepare to a day of calamity—even as were the wicked of Enoch's day. The Lord has warned them: "For I, the Almighty, have laid my hands upon the nations, to scourge them for their wickedness. And plagues shall go forth, and they shall not be taken from the earth until I have completed my work, which shall be cut short in righteousness—Until all shall know me, who remain, even from the least unto the greatest, and shall be filled with the knowledge of the Lord, and shall see eye to eye" (D&C 84:96-98).

The preparation for this great time of revelation will be preceded with great signs in the heavens and in the earth. Elder Maxwell has exhorted us to keep balanced the events of the last days. He has written:

> The chiliast, one who believes in a second coming of Christ that will usher in a millennial reign, has special challenges in reading signs. First, he

is urged to notice lest he be caught unawares. Second, he must be aware of how many false readings and alarms there have been in bygone days, even by the faithful. For instance, has any age had more "wonders in the sky" than ours, with satellites and journeys to the moon? Has any generation seen such ominous "vapors of smoke" as ours with its mushroom clouds over the pathetic pyres of Hiroshima and Nagasaki? Yet there is "more to come." *Our task is to react and to notice without overreacting,* to let life go forward without slipping into the heedlessness of those in the days of Noah. It has been asked, and well it might be, how many of us would have jeered, or at least been privately amused, by the sight of Noah building his ark. Presumably, the laughter and the heedlessness continued until it began to rain—and kept raining! How wet some people must have been before Noah's ark suddenly seemed the only sane act in an insane, bewildering situation! To ponder signs without becoming paranoid, to be aware without frantically matching current events with expectations, using energy that should be spent in other ways—these are our tasks.[44]

If we keep balanced in the way Elder Maxwell suggests, then we will be in harmony with the apostles and the prophets. This unity will our leaders will prepare us for that great day when Enoch and his people will return. In that day, because we are in harmony with the Lord's servants here, we will be spiritually compatible with those who will come from above. We "will receive them into our bosom, and they shall see us; and we will fall upon their necks, and they shall fall upon our necks, and we will kiss each other" (Moses 7:63).

The joy of this grand reunion between Enoch's people and the Saints living upon the earth has been set to musical lyrics—when our Zion from below joins with Enoch's Zion from above, the Saints "shall lift up their voice, and with the voice together sing this new song, saying:"

> The Lord hath brought again Zion;
> The Lord hath redeemed his people, Israel,
> According to the election of grace,
> Which was brought to pass by the faith
> And covenant of their fathers.
> The Lord hath redeemed his people;
> And Satan is bound and time is no longer.
> The Lord hath gathered all things in one.
> The Lord hath brought down Zion from above.
> The Lord hath brought up Zion from beneath.
> The earth hath travailed and brought forth her strength;
> And truth is established in her bowels;
> And the heavens have smiled upon her;

And she is clothed with the glory of her God;
For he stands in the midst of his people.
Glory, and honor, and power, and might,
Be ascribed to our God; for he is full of mercy,
Justice, grace and truth, and peace,
Forever and ever, Amen (D&C 84:98-102).

When Young's garage caught fire and those fireballs were raging in the sky and my sisters compared the fire and smoke to the coming of the Lord and the end of the world, my little boy mind did not comprehend much of what was involved.

I am grateful for the scriptures and the words of living prophets that provide a marvelous flood of light regarding the glorious doctrine of the Lord's Second Coming. I am thankful for the assurance that if we are prepared, we shall not fear. And though death may overtake many of us before the Lord comes, we all can rest assured that the Lord has provided a glorious resurrection for his faithful sons and daughters—which is the subject of our next chapter.

REFERENCES:

1 Editorial appearing in the *Church News* section of the *Salt Lake City Deseret News,* December 290, 1969, 16.
2 Bruce R. McConkie, *A New Witness For The Articles of Faith,* (Salt Lake City: Deseret Book Company, 1985) 646.
3 McConkie, *A New Witness for the Articles of Faith,* 646-47.
4 McConkie, *A New Witness for the Articles of Faith,* 646; emphasis added.
5 Enmity means "hatred toward, hostility to, or a state of opposition."
6 McConkie, "Millennium", *Mormon Doctrine,* 2nd Edition, (Salt Lake City: Bookcraft, 1966), 497.
7 Some of our most frequently cited sources are: the writings]and prophecies of Isaiah; Matthew 24, which is clarified in considerable detail in Joseph Smith's Translation; the latter part of the apostle John's Revelation chapters 7-22; and sections 29, 88, and 133 of the Doctrine and Covenants. For additional references see Topical Guide heading, "Jesus Christ, Second Coming."
8 Bruce R. McConkie, "Signs of the Times", *Mormon Doctrine,* (Salt Lake City: Bookcraft, 1958) 646-63
9 *Teachings,* 338.
10 *Millennial Star,* September 10, 1959. Also in *Inspired Prophetic Warnings,* N. B. Lundwall, Comp., Fifth Ed., n.d.
11 Bruce R. McConkie, "Adam-ondi-Ahman", *Mormon Doctrine,* (Salt Lake City: Bookcraft, 1958), 19.
12 See D&C 78:20; Also see Orson Pratt in *Journal of Discourses* 2:342-43.
13 McConkie, *Mormon Doctrine* 19-20.
14 *Teachings,* 122; emphasis added; also D&C 116.

15 *Teachings,* 158.
16 *Teachings,* 158-59; emphasis added. Joseph Smith added to this statement,"Moses [also] sought to bring the children of Israel into the presence of God through the power of the Priesthood, but he could not".
17 *Teachings,* 158.
18 *Words of Joseph Smith,* 255.
19 In these quotations Adam is referred to as the "Ancient of Days" because he was the first man—the most ancient of all men who have ever lived on this earth.
20 Joseph Fielding Smith, *The Way to Perfection,* (Salt Lake City: The Genealogical Society, 1951) 281, 290-291; emphasis added.
21 *Teachings,* 159; emphasis added.
22 *Teachings,* 325; emphasis added.
23 *Teachings,* 159; emphasis added.
24 *Teachings,* 253; emphasis added.
25 This reference to the cholera has to do with the Zion's Camp March during which many of the participants were swiftly struck down by the disease. See *Documentary Church History,* 2:114.
26 *Teachings,* 161; emphasis added.
27 Charles W. Penrose, *Millennial Star,* September 10, 1859. Also in "The Second Advent", *Inspired Prophetic Warnings,* N. B. Lundwall, Comp., Fifth Ed., 72, n.d.
28 Penrose, "The Second Advent", 72-73.
29 Penrose, "The Second Advent", 73.
30 *Teachings,* 170-71; emphasis added.
31 *Journal of Discourses* 21:241 ff; emphasis added.
32 *Teachings,* 191; emphasis added.
33 Bruce R. McConkie, "Translated Beings", *Mormon Doctrine,* 807-808.
34 *Teachings,* 170-71.
35 Those people who were translated before the time of Christ remained in that condition until the time of his resurrection. Enoch and his people had to wait about three thousand years before they were resurrected. However, people who are translated at the time of Christ's Second Coming will remain in that condition until they are one hundred years of age—the age of a tree (Isaiah 65:22).
36 *Teachings,* 170-71; emphasis added.
37 *Hymns,* #196.
38 *Teachings,* 248, 250-252 emphasis added.
39 *Teachings,* 286-87; emphasis added.
40 *Teachings,* 305; emphasis added.
41 *Teachings,* 340-41; emphasis added.
42 Joseph Fielding Smith, "The Reign of Righteousness," *The Deseret News,* Church Section, January 7, 1933, 5.
43 *Journal of Discourses* 3:320 ff; emphasis added.
44 Neal A. Maxwell, *For the Power is in Them,* 20.

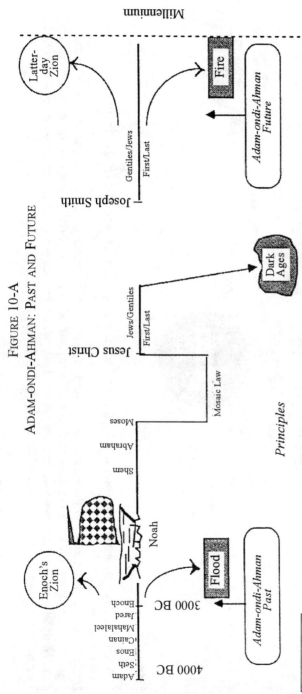

FIGURE 10-A

ADAM-ONDI-AHMAN: PAST AND FUTURE

A-O-A PAST: "Three year previous to the death of Adam, he called Seth, Enos, Cainan, Mahalaleel, Jared, Enoch, and Methuselah, who were all high priests, with the residue of his posterity who were righteous, into the valley of Adam-ondi-Ahman, and there bestowed upon them his last blessing. And the Lord appeared, unto them, and they rose up and blessed Adam, and called him Michael, the prince, the archangel" (D&C 107:53-54). *"This is why Adam blessed his posterity; he wanted to bring them into the presence of God"* (*Teachings*, p. 159; emphasis added).

A-O-A FUTURE: Daniel "saw in the night visions, and behold, one like the Son of Man came with the clouds of heaven, and came to the Ancient of days, and they brought him near before him. And there was given him dominion, and glory, and a kingdom that all people, nations, and languages, should serve him: his dominion is an everlasting dominion, which shall not pass away, and his kingdom that which shall not be destroyed...I beheld, and the same horn made war with the saints, and prevailed against them; Until the Ancient of days came, and judgment was given to the saints of the most High; and the time came that the saints possessed the kingdom" (Daniel 7:13-14, 21-22).

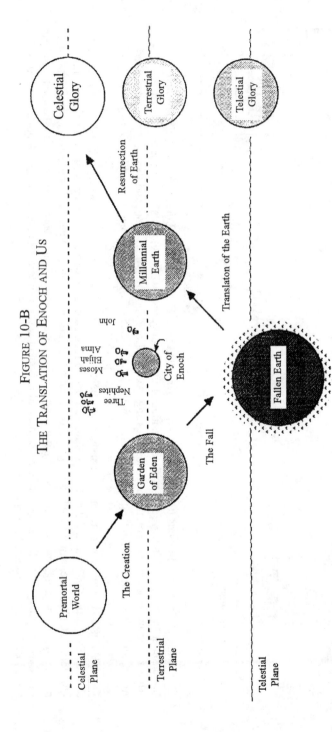

FIGURE 10-B

THE TRANSLATION OF ENOCH AND US

Principles

1. "The Doctrine of translation is a power which belongs to the Priesthood...(It is) to be revealed in the last times" (*Teachings*, p. 170).

2. " And when the time comes that these calamities we read of, shall overtake the earth, those that are prepared will have the power of translation, as they had in former times, and the city will be translated. And Zion that is on the earth will rise, and the Zion above will descend, as we are told, and we will meet and fall on each other's necks and embrace and kiss each other" (John Taylor, *Journal of Discourses*, 21-253; emphasis added).

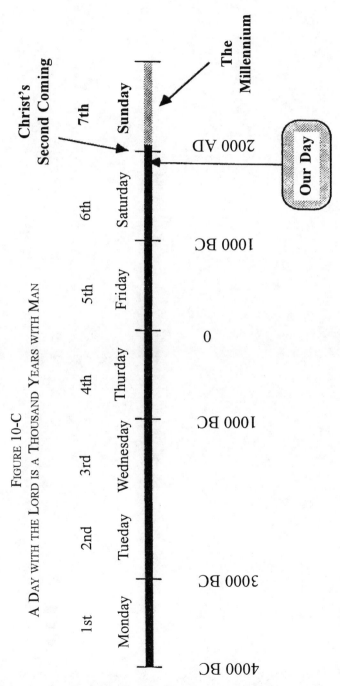

FIGURE 10-C
A DAY WITH THE LORD IS A THOUSAND YEARS WITH MAN

	Monday	Tueday	Wednesday	Thursday	Friday	Saturday	Sunday
	1st	2nd	3rd	4th	5th	6th	7th

4000 BC   3000 BC   1000 BC   0   1000 BC   1000 BC   2000 AD

Christ's Second Coming

The Millennium

Our Day

Principles

1. A day with the Lord is a thousand years with man (see 2 Peter 3:8).
2. We are living in the Saturday night of the earth's existence, the 6th thousand year period.
3. The earth will have a temporal existence, including the Millennium, of seven thousand years (see D&C 77:6, 12).
4. Christ will come in the beginning of the seventh thousand years (see D&C 77:12).
5. "The world has had a fair trial for six thousand years; the Lord will try the seventh Himself" (*Teachings*, p. 252).

CHAPTER ELEVEN

IMMORTALITY— A RESURRECTION FOR ALL

The spirit and the body shall be reunited again in its perfect form; both limb and joint shall be restored to its proper frame, even as we now are at this time.
—Alma 11:43.

Once, when I was a child living in Canada, we had a little puppy named Tippy. One summer he got sick with distemper, and my father said he would have to "put him to sleep." In my tears my father assured me that Tippy would be resurrected, and some day I would play with him again. This was the first time that I ever remember hearing about the Resurrection. I have had many occasions since Tippy's death to reflect upon this wonderful promise—this magnificent hope of a resurrection and a reunion of family and friends—and even pets.

Many years later my aged father required comforting as I once did. He was undergoing surgery for a lower back problem incident to aging. The neurosurgeon performing the delicate operation was a gifted technician with the highest credentials and reputation. The intense pain in my father's lower back and hips, resulting from progressive calcification of the vertebrae in his lower back, necessitated this surgery.

A year earlier he had undergone open heart surgery. Veins had to be stripped from his legs to form new blood vessels for his heart. That surgery involved five by-passes. And then, a year later his body had to be opened up again and repairs made. It was a heart-rending thing to see my father grow old and become vulnerable to the aches, pains, and problems of the elderly. His eyesight and hearing

377

were rapidly waning. Sometimes, not frequently, but sometimes, he would express to me how hard it was to get old. He wanted so bad to go home teaching again and visit with his family and friends. But if one can't see or hear very well at all, how can one communicate with others?

Often, during my father's times of intense pain and discouragement, I would smile and try to cheer him up by reminding him of the bright side of the aging picture. He was a lot closer than I to a glorious resurrection and a perfect body. He would not always be confined to a worn out body—a body that, like machinery, wears out and breaks down and eventually becomes useless. Sometimes he would smiles back. In this manner I often would find myself trying to comfort him as he did me in my childhood.

During his physically failing years my father told me to appreciate my youth. I now sense the aging process in myself. Bifocal glasses for my eyes, crowns for my teeth, diets to control weight, loss of prized hair, and a general waning of stamina are all tell-tale signs of aging. There have been times when I have envied the vigor and vitality of my children who could endlessly, it seems, do handstands and cartwheels.

On the other hand, I am glad to be more than halfway through mortality, and that much closer to a completion of my life's mission. But I have mixed emotions about death as did my father. At times I would remind him that as part of the restored gospel we have been promised that death is not the end. After we die and spend some time in the spirit world, we will come forth as part of the glorious resurrection of all living things.

My father passed away several months after my wife, family and I moved to Laie, Hawaii,. At his passing I experienced a sacred spiritual moment in which I was assured that he had been happily released from the heaviness, the pain, and the confinement of his aged, mortal body. I was given to understand that he could move then with the speed of lightning. He was at last free to go and come, to see and be seen, to hear and be heard. Perhaps, wonder of wonders, he could even go home teaching again clothed in the glorious light, the "flaming fire and glory" of a just man made perfect.[1]

RESURRECTION—ONE OF THE FIRST PRINCIPLES

Through the restoration of the gospel we learn that at death our eternal spirits selves and our physical mortal bodies become separated. Our bodies return to the dust from which they were organized. Out spirit selves enter a realm unseen to us now but which is near to us. After a period of waiting in this spirit world, our spirits and bodies will be reunited—resurrected—never to be separated again.

As wonderful and as merciful as death is in releasing us from the aches and pain of mortality, it is not as wonderful as this reuniting of our spirits and bodies in the resurrection. When we are resurrected, we will enjoy beautiful, perfect, eternally youthful bodies of flesh and bone, and we will be reunited with friends and loved ones whom we will physically embrace with great joy and happiness.

These wonderful blessings associated with the resurrection have been made available to us through the atoning sacrifice of our Savior, Jesus Christ. Our knowledge of his sacrifice on our behalf and the blessings that have been made available because of it provide the foundation for our faith in the reality of a literal resurrection as a part of the great plan of our Heavenly Father. This knowledge can be a source of great comfort and hope in times of sorrow and sadness at the loss of those we love.

The gospel realities associated with the Resurrection and the Judgment are of such importance to our happiness both here and hereafter that the Prophet Joseph Smith was moved to declare, "the Doctrines of the Resurrection of the Dead and the Eternal Judgment are necessary to preach among the first principles of the Gospel of Jesus Christ."[2] These two principles—the Resurrection and the Judgment—are so intertwined it is difficult to talk about them separately. However, let's try to isolate a few principles about the Judgment then we will focus more on various doctrines associated with the Resurrection.

THE ETERNAL JUDGMENT

The Apostle Paul taught that we shall all stand before the judgment seat, "For it is written, As I live, saith the Lord, every knee shall bow to me, and every tongue shall confess to God. So then every one of us shall give account of himself to God" (Romans 14:11-12; see also Mormon 3:17-22; Alma 11:41). Everyone is to answer for the "things done in his body...whether it be good or bad" (2 Cor. 5:10).

President Joseph F. Smith taught that in certain respects, we will judge ourselves. He observed:

> In reality a man cannot forget anything. He may have a lapse of memory; he may not be able to recall at the moment a thing that he knows or words that he has spoken; he may not have the power at his will to call up these events and words; but let God Almighty touch the mainspring of the memory and awaken recollection, and you will find then that you have not forgotten a single idle word that you have spoken! I believe the word of God to be true, and, therefore, I warn the youth of Zion, as well as those who are advanced in years, to beware of saying wicked things, of speaking evil, and

taking in vain the names of sacred things and sacred beings. Guard your words, that you may not offend even man, much less offend God.[3]

As part of the judgment, President John Taylor warned that every word and secret thought will be accounted for. He said, "We may succeed in hiding our affairs from men; but it is written that for every word and every secret thought we shall have to give an account in the day when accounts have to be rendered before God, when hypocrisy and fraud of any kind will not avail us; for by our words and by our works we shall be justified, or by them we shall be condemned.[4] Not only will we be judged on the basis of our thoughts, words and works, but we will also be judged according to the desires of our hearts. From the Doctrine & Covenants CES Student Manual we read:

> The true desire of an individual's heart is the key to his future. For one who has received the laws of God, obedience to these laws demonstrates his true desires. For one who does not have these laws, the desires of his heart determine whether or not he will receive the gospel when given the opportunity, whether in this life or the next. In either case, the desires of one's heart determine how one responds to the gospel, and thus are the just and right basis upon which one will be judged. All whose hearts are right will receive and live the gospel whenever they have the opportunity and will be 'heirs of the celestial kingdom of God' (D&C 137:7).

We are a product, then, of our past desires, thoughts, words, and actions and when we leave this existence will be judged by the sum of these parts. In other words, we will be judged by what we are—by what we have become. President Taylor affirmed this same doctrine when he taught that each one of us has a built-in recording device, "a self-registering machine, his eyes, his ears, his nose, the touch, the taste, and all the various senses of the body, are so many media whereby man lays up for himself a record which perhaps nobody else is acquainted with but himself; and when the time comes for that record to be unfolded all men that have eyes to see, and ears to hear, will be able to read all things as God Himself reads them and comprehends them, and all things, we are told, are naked and open before him with whom we have to do."[5]

The judgment, then, will be a blessing for the righteous and a cursing for the unrighteous—and will largely be a sealing of what we have become as a result of what we have thought, felt and acted upon. In the Book of Mormon King Benjamin affirms this fact. He warned: "And finally, I cannot tell you all the things whereby ye may commit sin; for there are divers ways and means, even so many that I cannot number them. But this much I can tell you, that if ye do not watch yourselves, and your thoughts, and your words, and your deeds, and observe the commandments of God, and continue in the faith of what ye have heard concerning the coming of our Lord, even unto the end of your lives, ye must perish. And now, O man, remember, and perish not (Mosiah 4:29-30; emphasis added).

This scripture is a voice of warning for the wicked and a promise of hope for the righteous. While our negative thoughts, feelings, and actions are being recorded, so also are our noble and righteous thoughts, feelings, and actions. At death, when our spirits enter the spirit world, no information will be lost—all will be retrieved in the day of judgment.

Death is Not the End

Even as birth is not the beginning of our existence, so death is not the end. Through the restoration of the gospel, we have received the comforting assurance that death is simply a doorway that leads us to that other dimension we call the spirit world—a place where our spirits, our minds, the core of our beings continue on and where we continue learning and growing while we await the time for our resurrection (see Alma 40:6). Of all the glorious truths that have been given to us as part of the restored gospel, this knowledge—that we continue on in much the same way as we were in mortality—is perhaps one of the most reassuring doctrines. It is also an important concept to remember as we contemplate our brief but important sojourn in mortality and our eventual judgment.

President Harold B. Lee taught that our spirits continue after death when he spoke at the funeral of a departed brother. He explained:

> Rather than to say he died, I like to say that he has passed from mortality, or he passed on. Thus, as you consider upon his form lying in the casket, I am sure that you realized that what you saw there was not all that you loved about your father, your husband, your brother, your friend: there was something that was vital that was missing. There was that something that looked out through his eyes, that made his lips smile, his intelligence. That something was not there and it isn't in the casket today. That part of him will not be buried in the grave. That something that in the moment of his passing went home to that God who gave him life.[6]

When people die their spirit and intelligence leaves the body, and to us who view them, they seem to be sleeping. Regarding this apparent sleeplike state Henry Ward Beecher wrote: "Is death the last sleep? No, it is the last and final awakening. Death is the golden key that opens the palace of eternity. Living is death; dying is life—on this side of the grave we are exiles, on that citizens, on this side disguised, unknown; on that, disclosed and proclaimed as the sons of God."[7]

In reality, though, we do not have to wait until we die to know that we are the

382 THE ETERNAL PLAN OF HAPPINESS

sons and daughters of God. The everlasting gospel declares our kinship with our Heavenly Father and our interconnectedness to one another.

The knowledge that we are the children of God and that we are connected to one another is yet another of the comforting, inspiring and uplifting truths associated with the gospel. It is especially comforting when we are faced with the death of a loved one because we know that our relationships have always been a part of us, and they will continue in the eternities. Death is only a temporary separation—it does not end the cherished relationships we have cultivated in mortality. This understanding has given peace and hope to many who have lost loved ones—and it can comfort you in your times of need.

This truth was reaffirmed by an experience I had while on my mission. As a young missionary in Elmira, New York, I discovered the burial place of Mark Twain. On his tombstone are inscribed the happy words, "Death is but the starlit strip between the friendships of yesterday and the reunion of tomorrow." These words remind us that our friendships and our other relationships with one another do not have to cease at death. This knowledge will be more indelibly imprinted upon our minds and hearts when we too pass through the veil and fondly embrace our loved ones on the other side.

Many people who have had so called "near-death experiences"—people who have seem to have died and then have been resuscitated—have come to know this truth for themselves.[8] Upon their return many of them have spoken of their eyes being opened to a whole new dimension and of meeting family and friends who had died previously.

While the experience of seeing friends and loved ones brought about great feelings of joy, some who have had these experiences also have spoken of the pain of those they saw in the spirit world whose earthly addictions had persisted with them. These spirits suffered great anguish because, while they could see and hear mortals participating in the carnal and lewd activities they once enjoyed, they could no longer gratify their desires because they lacked a physical body with which to do so.[9]

These life after death accounts do not constitute the foundation for our beliefs, but in many cases they do provide inspiring supportive evidence of the realities already revealed through the Restored Gospel of Jesus Christ. Our relationships with God and with one another do continue beyond the grave, and these interesting reports tend to support many of the truths that the prophets—who are our primary sources for such eternal truths—do declare. The prophets and the scriptures, along with the experiences of many hundreds of people who have died and returned to life, testify not only to the continuance of our existence, but also to the reality that our family and friends and others are very near us in the world of spirits.

THE SPIRIT WORLD IS NEAR US

At death, our spirits leave our physical bodies and immediately our eyes perceive a different world—the world of spirits. The spirit world is all around us in a dimension that our mortal eyes do not generally see. The Prophet Joseph Smith taught that "Hades, Sheol, paradise, spirits in prison, are all one: it is a world of spirits. The righteous and the wicked all go to the same world of spirits until the resurrection.... The spirits of the just ... are not far from us, and know and understand our thoughts, feelings, and motions, and are often pained therewith."[10]

Brigham Young taught the nearness of the world of spirits when he said, "Where is the spirit world? It is right here.... If our eyes could be opened and we could see those who have departed this life, we would see that they are very near. They are not millions of miles away, on some other planet."[11] Though at times we may feel very far away from our loved ones who have gone beyond this veil of tears, the knowledge that the spirit world is very near us is another principle that can serve to comfort us in times of loneliness or sadness. If our eyes were to be opened, and we could see the place where our loved ones and others who have passed on reside, we would see that it is divided into two general places or categories of people.

PARADISE AND SPIRIT PRISON

Though the spirit world is all around us, the scriptures and the teachings of ancient and modern prophets explain that the spirit world is divided into two parts: *paradise*, a place of rest, peace, and happiness which is prepared for the righteous; and *spirit prison*, a place of suffering, sorrow and pain prepared for the unrighteous. This latter place is sometimes called *hell*. Our designation to one or the other of these two places following death, constitutes a partial judgment we undergo as soon as we enter the world of spirits.

In the Book of Mormon, Alma described these two states when he explained the state of the soul between death and the Resurrection. He said:

> Behold, it has been made known unto me by an angel, that the spirits of all men, as soon as they are departed from this mortal body, yea, the spirits of all men, whether they be good or evil, are taken home to that God who gave them life. And then shall it come to pass, that the spirits of those who are righteous are received into a state of happiness, which is called paradise, a state of rest, a state of peace, where they shall rest from all their troubles and from all care, and sorrow (Alma 40:11-12).

And thus we see, that for the righteous, the spirit world of paradise is a place of peace and sweet experiences—the final awakening. For the wicked, on the other hand, the spirit world of spirit prison is a time of pain and sorrow, a time when they reap the results of their unwise and evil choices in mortality. The words of Alma are very clear in describing the place of suffering for the wicked. He warned his son, Corianton, in these words:

> And then shall it come to pass, that the spirits of the wicked, yea, who are evil—for behold, they have no part nor portion of the Spirit of the Lord; for behold, they chose evil works rather than good; therefore the spirit of the devil did enter into them, and take possession of their house—and these shall be cast out into outer darkness; there shall be weeping, and wailing, and gnashing of teeth, and this because of their own iniquity, being led captive by the will of the devil.
>
> Now this is the state of the souls of the wicked, yea, in darkness, and a state of awful, fearful looking for the fiery indignation of the wrath of God upon them; thus they remain in this state, as well as the righteous in paradise, until the time of their resurrection (Alma 40:13-14).

Up until the time of Christ's death and resurrection, these two places in the spirit world were separated by a great gulf which prohibited the intermingling of their respective inhabitants. What the actual "gulf" was that separated the wicked and the righteous is not made clear in the scriptures. We do not know if it is a literal or figurative expression (see Luke 16:26).

The scriptures *do* tell us however, that while his body was in the tomb, Jesus visited the spirit world and his mission there bridged the gulf between righteous and the wicked. Though Jesus did not go among the wicked in spirit prison (see D&C 138:29-37), he arranged the affairs of his kingdom in paradise so that righteous spirits there were able to cross over the gulf and begin teaching the gospel to the spirits held in spirit prison (see 1 Peter 3:18-21; Moses 7:37-39).

Regarding this missionary work established by Jesus while his body lay in the tomb, we read in the Doctrine and Covenants:

> But behold, from among the righteous, he organized his forces and appointed messengers, clothed with power and authority, and commissioned them to go forth and carry the light of the gospel to them that were in darkness, even to all the spirits of men...who would repent of their sins and receive the gospel. Thus was the gospel preached to those who had died in their sins, without a knowledge of the truth, or in transgression, having rejected the prophets....
>
> The dead who repent will be redeemed, through the ordinances of the house of God, And after they have paid the penalty of their transgressions, and are washed clean, shall receive a reward according to their works, for they are heirs of salvation (see D&C 138:30-32, 58-59).

This great missionary activity continues in the spirit world today. However, though many will accept the gospel who had never been exposed to it in this life, it is not likely that people who have been acquainted with it and rejected it here— those who died "in their sins, without a knowledge of the truth, or in their transgression, having rejected the prophets" (D&C 138:32)—will *automatically* accept it in the next life. If, however, as we have read, they do repent and receive the ordinances of the temple, the vicarious work that will have been done for them, "and after they have paid the penalty for their transgressions, and are washed clean, [they] shall receive a reward according to their works, for they are heirs of salvation" (D&C 138:59).

While those who rejected the gospel on earth may still receive it in the spirit world, the truth remains that their attitudes and spiritual receptivity will not change just because they have died. For those who have procrastinated the day of their repentance "even until death, behold, [they] have become subjected to the spirit of the devil, and he doth seal [them] his" (Alma 34:35).

Death Does Not Change Our Basic Attitudes

When people repent and embrace the terms of the new and everlasting covenant their hearts and desires are changed and they become a new creature in Christ. On the other hand, if they have the attitude that it doesn't matter what they do because God will justify them anyway, and therefore do not repent, they will find themselves unable to progress and will be miserable in the world to come.

The Book of Mormon speaks of this false belief or attitude that prevails among some people in our day. In seeking to justify their behavior they say to themselves and others: "Eat, drink, and be merry for tomorrow we die; and it shall be well with us. And there shall also be many which shall say: Eat, drink, and be merry; nevertheless, fear God—he will justify in committing a little sin; yea, lie a little, take the advantage of one because of his words, dig a pit for thy neighbor; there is no harm in this; and do all these things, for tomorrow we die; and if it so be that we are guilty, God will beat us with a few stripes, and at last we shall be saved in the kingdom of God" (2 Nephi 28:7-8).

Elder Neal A. Maxwell calls this belief "spiritual prodigalism" and warns that those who engage in it alienate themselves from the Lord, intending to spend a season rebelling and acting out in Babylon and succumbing to that devilish democratic "everybody does it."[12]

Regarding those who hold this mind-set, Elder Bruce R. McConkie tells of a man who lived in ways that were contrary to the gospel, but who believed that he could continue as he was living and have his wife do the work in the temple for him after his death. He believed that all would then be well for him. Speaking of the state of this man and all who hold this same belief, Elder McConkie taught that,

...there is no such thing as a second chance to gain salvation. This life is the time and day of our probation. After this day of life, which is given us to prepare for eternity, then cometh the night of darkness wherein there can be no labor performed. For those who do not have an opportunity to believe and obey the holy word in this life, the first chance to gain salvation will come in the spirit world. If those who hear the word for the first time in the realms ahead would have accepted the gospel here, had the opportunity been afforded them, they will accept it there. Salvation for the dead is for those whose first chance to gain salvation is in the spirit world. ...Those who reject the gospel in this life and then receive it in the spirit world go not to the celestial, but to the terrestrial kingdom.[13]

In other words, there are some who believe in the "play now, pay later" philosophy of living. They believe that they can "live it up" in this life and then repent either at the end of their lives or once they have passed on and that all will be well with them. This is a dangerous belief to hold. It is dangerous because, as Elder McConkie explained, this life is the time "to prepare to meet God" (Alma 12:24). It is also dangerous because, in addition to being a day of judgment, the resurrection will also be a day of restoration.

Regarding this truth, it could be said that the law of the harvest reigns in the spirit world as well as in mortality. As we plant the seeds of righteousness and seek to cultivate them in our lives, we will receive according to what we have planted—or in other words, what we have sown will be restored to us again in the resurrection. We cannot expect to have sown the seeds of sin in this life and then suddenly find ourselves changed to something that is opposed to the nature we have developed in mortality once we die. As Alma explained to his son Corianton, this idea runs contrary to the plan of our Heavenly Father: "For that which ye do send out shall return unto you again, and be restored; therefore, the word restoration more fully condemneth the sinner, and justifieth him not at all" (Alma 41:15; emphasis added). We will indeed reap what we have sown—whether good or ill.

Quoting the Book of Mormon, Elder Bruce R. McConkie points out that our attitudes, interests, and inclinations continue in the spirit world as they do in this world. He states:

Life and work and activity all continue in the spirit world. Men have the same talents and intelligence there which they had in this life. They possess the same attitudes, inclinations, and feelings there which they had in this life. They believe the same things, as far as eternal truths are concerned; they continue, in effect, to walk in the same path they were following in this life. Amulek said: "That same spirit which possesses your bodies at the time that ye go out of this life, that same spirit will have power to possess your body

in that eternal world" (Alma 34:34). Thus if a man has the spirit of charity
and love of truth in his heart in this life, that same spirit will possess him in
the spirit world. If he has the spirit of unbelief and hate in his heart here, so
will it be with him when he passes through the door into the spirit world.[14]

Likewise, President Lorenzo Snow reminded us that "We are immortal
beings. That [spirit] which dwells in this body of ours is immortal, and will
always exist. Our individuality will always continue. Eternities may begin, eternities may end, and still we shall have our individuality. Our identity is insured.
We will be ourselves, and nobody else. Whatever changes may arise, whatever
worlds may be made or pass away, our identity will always remain the same; and
we will continue on improving, advancing, and increasing in wisdom, intelligence, power and dominion, worlds without end."[15]

Most people when they hear that our natures continue after death, think of the
negative side of the promise of restoration—that if people do not repent and
accept the gospel here, it will be too late or difficult for them in the spirit world.
While this is true (see D&C 76:74), the idea that our basic natures do not change
at death has a positive side to it, too. As we mentioned previously, if we are filled
with faith, hope and charity in this world, these Christlike virtues will continue
on with us in the next. We have the assurance of apostles and prophets that when
we leave this life, if we have charted a course that leads us to eternal life, then we
will continue in that course until we have reached the promised destination of
eternal life.[16] That is as sure and certain as the promise of judgment is for those
who have done wickedly in the days of their probation. This knowledge can fill
us with hope as we strive each day to overcome the natural man and to become
more Christlike by complying with the principles and ordinances of the gospel—
our Father's great plan of happiness.

The eternal plan of happiness involves the interests and efforts of our
Heavenly Father in providing for us the blessings of immortality and eternal life.
When our Heavenly Father said: "For behold, this is my work and my glory—to
bring to pass the immortality and eternal life of man" (Moses 1:39), he was saying in effect: "This is my work and glory—to bring to pass the resurrection and
the godhood of my children." While these two great gifts are different in certain
important ways, they both contribute to the realization of the ultimate and eternal
objective of our Father's great plan of happiness—our everlasting and eternal resurrection, joy, glory, and happiness realized through eternal marriage and family
relationships.

I cannot close this section without making reference to promises made to
faithful latter-day Saint parents who have had children who have strayed from the
gospel. Elder Boyd K. Packer has taught:

It is not uncommon for responsible parents to lose one of their children, for a time, to influences over which they have no control. They agonize over rebellious sons or daughters. They are puzzled over why they are so helpless when they have tried so hard to do what they should.

It is my conviction that those wicked influences one day will be overruled.

The Prophet Joseph Smith declared—and he never taught a more comforting doctrine—that the eternal sealings of faithful parents and the divine promises made to them for valiant service in the Cause of Truth, would save not only themselves, but likewise their posterity. Though some of the sheep may wander, they eye of the Shepherd is upon them, and sooner or later they will feel the tentacles of Divine Providence reaching out after them and drawing them back to the fold. Either in this life or the life to come, they will return. They will have to pay their debt to justice; they will suffer for their sins; and may tread a thorny path; but if it leads them at last, like the penitent Prodigal, to a loving and forgiving father's heart and home, the painful experience will not have been in vain. Pray for your careless and disobedient children; hold on to them with your faith. Hope on, trust on, till you see the salvation of God. (Orson F. Whitney, in *Conference Report*, Apr. 1929, p. 110.)[17]

President James E. Faust gave similar reassurance in the 1997 First Presidency Christmas Devotional. He said he knows some Church members have children who have strayed from the gospel. "To those of you who suffer the pain of an empty chair, be assured that the Savior knows and understands your sorrow. The Good Shepherd is watching over them and they will return, either in this life or in the life to come". Church members feel a particular kind of joy when a child that has been lost, for whatever reason, is found and restored, said President Faust.[18]

So, in this section we have discussed the law of justice as it relates to the resurrection, which is simply stated—as we sow, so shall we reap. But, praise his Holy Name, we have also discussed the tremendous power of the Good Shepherd to feel after and reclaim his sheep through power of his mighty Atonement and by the prayers, the sealing, and the covenants made by anguishing parents who themselves have remained true and faithful to the end.

IMMORTALITY AND ETERNAL LIFE

Frequently I hear the terms immortality and eternal life used interchangeably. Actually they have distinctively different meanings. Gaining an immortality is gaining the resurrection; it is living forever with a glorified body of flesh and bone—one that will never age nor die again. Immortality is the free gift given to all living things that have been upon the earth. It has a *quantitative* meaning in the sense that it deals with an infinity of time—all living things will be resurrected and will live forever.

"The word immortal," writes George F. Richards, "means not mortal; that is, not subject to the power of death. I would define immortality as being that state to which we attain in the progress of life when we have passed through death and the resurrection, the spirit and body being reunited and inseparably connected, constituting the soul of man prepared to receive a fulness of the glory of God. Immortality is a means to an end, the end being the accomplishment of man's eternal salvation and glory."[19] Again, immortality comes by way of the resurrection. While every living thing will gain immortality, not everyone will receive the light, power, glory, and eternal family relationships associated with eternal life. Eternal life is received as a consequence of our obedience to the principles, laws, ordinances and covenants of the gospel of Jesus Christ.

For Latter-day Saints, the expression eternal life has a *qualitative* meaning. Simply stated eternal life means having the same kind of power and glory in the celestial kingdom that our Heavenly Parents enjoy. Eternal life is to be with God, to be like God, and to do the things that Gods do. It is "the greatest of all the gifts of God" (D&C 14:7). We will discuss more fully the many wonderful facets of eternal life in the next chapter. For now let's look more deeply at the Resurrection as it relates to all of our lives.

A RESURRECTION FOR ALL

As was mentioned in the preceding section, immortality—the Resurrection from the dead—will affect all living things. It does not matter if we have done well or ill, whether we have been intelligent or ignorant, or whether we have been members of the Church or not. All men and women will be raised from the dead—but in differing degrees of glory.

In a great sermon on the resurrection preached by the Apostle Paul, he declared this fundamental truth: "For since by man came death, by man came also the resurrection of the dead. For as in Adam all die, even so in Christ shall all be made alive (1 Cor 15:21-22; emphasis added). In other words, because of Adam's fall, we all die; however, through Christ's atonement, all things will be raised from the dead. None, not even the most depraved, will fail to be resurrected. Accordingly, everyone will be saved in the sense that all will receive a degree of glory in the Resurrection—except the sons of perdition.

Sons of perdition will receive a resurrection, but they will not receive a degree of glory. Regarding their state, in the Doctrine and Covenants we read:

> He came into the world, even Jesus, to be crucified for the world, and to bear the sins of the world, and to sanctify the world, and to cleanse it from all unrighteousness; that through him all might be saved whom the Father had put into his power and made by him; Who glorifies the Father, and saves all the works of his hands, except those sons of perdition who deny the Son after the Father has revealed him. Wherefore, he saves all except them— They shall go away into everlasting punishment, which is endless punishment, which is eternal punishment, to reign with the devil and his angels in eternity, where their worm dieth not, and the fire is not quenched, which is their torment" (D&C 76:41-44; emphasis added).

Although knowledge about the final state of the sons of perdition makes us sorrowful, the wonderful thing about the great plan of happiness is that all, except them, eventually will be resurrected and will receive a certain degree of glory— in a telestial heaven, in a terrestrial heaven, or in a celestial heaven. This diversity in the heavens is as Jesus explained to his disciples when he said, "In my fathers house are many mansions: if it were not so, I would have told you.... I will [go and] come again, and receive you unto myself: that where I am, there ye may be also" (John 14:2-3).

Paul, in writing to the Corinthians, also described three different degrees of glory associated with resurrected beings. He explained:

> All flesh is not the same flesh: but there is one kind of flesh of men, another flesh of beasts, another of fishes, and another of birds. There are also celestial bodies, and bodies terrestrial; but the glory of the celestial is one, and the glory of the terrestrial is another. There is one glory of the sun, and another glory of the moon, and another glory of the stars: for one star differeth from another in glory. So also is the resurrection of the dead (1 Corinthians 15:39-42; D&C 76). (See end of chapter Figure 11-A, A Resurrection for All).

In other words, Paul explains that people will be resurrected to various degrees or magnitudes of glory of which the sun, moon and stars are descriptive. This glorious message that comes out of the ministry of Christ has been renewed in our day.

From latter-day revelation we learn that every man, woman, and child— every living thing—that has lived upon this earth shall in due time rise from the grave to everlasting life. From the Doctrine and Covenants we read: "For notwithstanding they die, they also shall rise again, a spiritual body.[20] They who are of a celestial spirit shall receive the same body which was a natural body; even ye shall receive your bodies, and your glory shall be that glory by which your bodies are quickened". (D&C 88:27-28).

Along the same lines, the Prophet Joseph Smith taught that, "God has revealed ... the doctrine of the resurrection also; and we have a knowledge that those we bury here God will bring up again, clothed upon and quickened by the Spirit of the great God; and what mattereth it whether we lay them down, or we [lie] down with them when we can keep them no longer? Let these truths sink down in our hearts, that we may even here begin to enjoy that which shall be in full hereafter."[21] In this quotation, the phrase "in full hereafter" has reference to the idea that if we receive the fulness of the gospel and live in accordance with its requirements, when we are resurrected our bodies will be fashioned like unto Jesus' glorious body, as Paul said, "according to the working whereby he is able even to subdue all things unto himself" (Philippians 3:21).

Jesus, himself, is the pattern of the physical resurrection of all mankind. President Joseph F. Smith explained,

> I believe...that we will come up in the resurrection from death to life again, as literally ourselves as did Christ, the Son of God, rise from the dead.... His body...rose when the spirit returned into it again, with wounds of the nails in His hands and in his feet, and of the spear in His side, so literally, so actually the same identical body that it bore the marks that it received upon the cross. And I believe that He is the first fruits of the resurrection from death to life and that He is the true type of the resurrection; that every man, woman and child will rise from the dead, will come up precisely as He did, because there is no other name given under heaven by which we will be saved, neither is there any other way provided by which man can be raised again from death to life, but by the way instituted by the Son of God.[22]

Even those who did not hear the gospel in this life—but who would have received it if they had had the opportunity to do so while in mortality—will be given the opportunity to embrace the fulness of the gospel and shall receive a glorious resurrection and the assurance of exaltation and eternal life (see D&C 137:7-8).

Just before Jesus died he spoke regarding the state of these people when he said: "Verily, verily, I say unto you, The hour is coming, and now is, when the dead shall hear the voice of the Son of God: and they that hear shall live.... Marvel not at this: for the hour is coming in the which all that are in the graves shall hear his voice, And shall come forth; they that have done good, unto the resurrection of life; and they that have done evil, unto the resurrection of damnation" (John 5:25, 28-29). Thus we see that while all mankind will be resurrected, not everyone will be resurrected to the same glory nor at the same time. In the resurrection there will be two main time periods—the resurrection of the just and the resurrection of the unjust (see Acts 24:15).

THE TWO RESURRECTIONS

The fact that there are different time frames for people to come forth in the resurrection is what Paul meant when he said that everyone will be raised "in his own order" (1 Cor. 15:23). Those people who are raised in the first resurrection will enjoy a greater degree of glory than those who are raised in the second resurrection (see D&C 88:97-101).

Regarding these two general resurrections, Elder James E. Talmage explained that, "These may be specified as first and final, or as the resurrection of the just and the resurrection of the unjust. The first was inaugurated by the resurrection of Jesus Christ; immediately following which many of the saints came forth from their graves. A continuation of this, the resurrection of the just, has been in operation since, and will be greatly extended, or brought to pass in a general way, in connection with the coming of Christ in His glory. The final resurrection will be deferred until the end of the thousand years of peace, and will be associated with the last judgment."[23]

The Doctrine and Covenants also speaks of two resurrections; however, here the two resurrections are broken down into two additional subgroups each of which are introduced by the sounding of four trumpets (See end of chapter Figure 11-B, The Order of the Resurrection). Regarding these four groups, we read from latter-day scripture that at the Second Coming:

> The face of the Lord shall be unveiled;
> And the saints that are upon the earth, who are alive, shall be quickened and be caught up to meet him.
> And they who have slept in their graves shall come forth, for their graves shall be opened; and they also shall be caught up to meet him in the midst of the pillar of heaven—They are Christ's, the first fruits, they who shall descend with him first, and they who are on the earth and in their graves, who are first caught up to meet him; and all this by the voice of the sounding of the trump of the angel of God.
> And after this another angel shall sound, which is the second trump; and then cometh the redemption of those who are Christ's at his coming; who have received their part in that prison which is prepared for them, that they might receive the gospel, and be judged according to men in the flesh.
> And again, another trump shall sound, which is the third trump; and then come the spirits of men who are to be judged, and are found under condemnation;

And these are the rest of the dead; and they live not again until the thousand years are ended, neither again, until the end of the earth.

And another trump shall sound, which is the fourth trump, saying: There are found among those who are to remain until that great and last day, even the end, who shall remain filthy still (D&C 88:95-102; emphasis added).

Elder Bruce R. McConkie has given further enlightenment regarding those people who will come up in the resurrection at the sounding of each of the four trumpets. He explained:

> Two great resurrections await the inhabitants of the earth: one is the first resurrection, the resurrection of life, the resurrection of the just; the other is the second resurrection, the resurrection of damnation, the resurrection of the unjust. (John 5:28-29; Rev. 20; D&C 76.) But even with these two separate resurrections, there is an order in which the dead will come forth. Those being resurrected with celestial bodies, whose destiny is to inherit a celestial kingdom, will come forth in the morning of the first resurrection. Their graves shall be opened and they shall be caught up to meet the Lord at his Second Coming. They are Christ's, the first fruits, and they shall descend with him to reign as kings and priests during the millennial era. (D&C 29:13; 43:18; 76:50-70; 88:97-98; 1 Thess. 4:16-17; Rev. 20:3-7.)
>
> And after this another angel shall sound, which is the second trump; and then cometh the redemption of those who are Christ's at his coming; who have received their part in that prison which is prepared for them, that they might receive the gospel, and be judged according to men in the flesh" (D&C 88:99). This is the afternoon of the first resurrection; it takes place after our Lord has ushered in the millennium. Those coming forth at that time do so with terrestrial bodies and are thus destined to inherit a terrestrial glory in eternity. (D&C 76:71-80.)
>
> At the end of the millennium, the second resurrection begins. In the forepart of this resurrection of the unjust, those destined to come forth will be "the spirits of men who are to be judged, and are found under condemnation; And these are the rest of the dead; and they live not again until the thousand years are ended, neither again, until the end of the earth." (D&C 88:100-101.) These are the ones who have earned telestial bodies, who were wicked and carnal in mortality, and who have suffered the wrath of God in hell "until the last resurrection, until the Lord, even Christ the Lamb, shall have finished his work." (D&C 76:85.) Their final destiny is to inherit a telestial glory. (D&C 76:81-112.)
>
> Finally, in the latter end of the resurrection of damnation, the sons of perdition, those who "remain filthy still"; (D&C 88:102), shall come forth from their graves. (2 Ne. 9:14-16.) "Then is the time when their torments

shall be as a lake of fire and brimstone, whose flame ascendeth up forever and ever; and then is the time that they shall be chained down to an everlasting destruction, according to the power and captivity of Satan, he having subjected them according to his will. Then, I say unto you, they shall be as though there had been no redemption made; for they cannot be redeemed according to God's justice; and they cannot die, seeing there is no more corruption" (Alma 12:17-18).[24]

While Elder McConkie has explained well the four major times of the resurrection, Joseph Smith explained the great variety of beings that will come forth in these four time periods. He taught that, "In the resurrection, some are raised to be angels, others are raised to become gods."[25] Whether we are raised as angels or as gods depends upon the life we have led while in mortality and the degree to which we have received and obeyed the covenants and ordinances of the everlasting gospel.

In order to inherit any degree of glory, one has to become sanctified. Not all who become sanctified, however, will inherit celestial glory and eternal life. There will be some people who are sanctified who will receive terrestrial or telestial glory. These lower degrees of glory are wonderful heavens, and they are inhabited by sanctified beings. Our discussion of sanctification at this point is important because each pathway helps us understand the love and mercy of our Heavenly Father in providing a degree of glory for all his children except sons of perdition. Of them we read, "Wherefore, he saves all except them—they shall go away into everlasting punishment..." (D&C 76:44).

The Doctrine and Covenants describes four ways that people can become sanctified and receive the blessings of the Father: through the law, mercy, justice, and judgment. Of these four methods we read: "And again, verily I say unto you, that which is governed by law is also preserved by law and perfected and sanctified by the same. That which breaketh a law, and abideth not by law, but seeketh to become a law unto itself, and willeth to abide in sin, and altogether abideth in sin [i.e., sons of perdition], cannot be sanctified by *law,* neither by *mercy, justice,* nor *judgment.* Therefore, they must remain filthy still" (D&C 88:34-35; emphasis added). In other words, there is no way that sons of perdition can be sanctified, but there are four ways that all others can be. Let's talk about these four means of sanctification.

The first way mentioned in the above scripture by which a person can be sanctified is through the law—meaning complete and full obedience to the laws of righteousness. Jesus is the only one who ever became sanctified in this manner, through obedience to the law. Only he was completely obedient to the law of his Father. During his mortal life it was he alone who was without sin. He was sanctified by obedience to the *law.* Because of his obedience to law he is now an exalted, glorified, and sanctified resurrection being who dwells in the presence of the Father.

Those who are sanctified by *mercy* are the pure in heart who receive the priesthood ordinances of the everlasting covenant and walk in obedience to the commandments. They are sanctified through the cleansing mercy and power of Jesus' atonement. They *obtain* a remission of their sins through baptism and *retain* a remission of their sins and eventual sanctification through service in the kingdom—they receive grace for grace. Through the infinite atonement and the loving mercy of God they will become sanctified as exalted beings, celestial beings.

Those who receive terrestrial glory are sanctified through the *justice* of God. Terrestrial beings are they "who died without law" (D&C 76:72). The idea here is that where there is no law, there is no transgression of the law and, thus, through the justice of God they will be sanctified and receive "of his glory, but not of his fulness. These are they who receive of the presence of the Son, but not of the fulness of the Father" (D&C 76:76-77). There is a up-side and a down-side to being without the law. While those people who are sanctified through justice are *not punished* for not living the law they never received, neither are they able to receive the *blessings* that would come through living the law. They are sanctified through the justice of the Lord, but inherit a terrestrial glory. The scriptures tell us that the heathen nations will be redeemed and inherit a degree of glory through the *justice* of God (see D&C 45:54; 75:22; 90:10; Alma 29:8).

Telestial people, people who are sanctified through *judgment,* suffer the punishments of God in the spirit world in order to pay the penalty for their own transgressions. "These are they who received not the gospel of Christ, neither the testimony of Jesus" (D&C 76:82). Regarding the suffering of these, the Lord has warned: "For behold, I God, have suffered these things for all, that they might not suffer *if they would repent; But if they would not repent they must suffer even as I;* Which suffering caused myself, even God, the greatest of all, to tremble because of pain, and to bleed at every pore, and to suffer both body and spirit— and would that I might not drink the bitter cup, and shrink—" (D&C 19:16-18; emphasis added; see also Mark 14:36; Alma 11:40; D&C 29:17).

Telestial beings are thus sanctified through their own suffering of the judgments of God upon them. But after they have paid the last penny for their own sins (see Matthew 5:26), they will come out and inherit a telestial glory. And thus, Jesus prepares a mansion for telestial beings and saves all the children of God except sons of perdition (D&C 76:40-44).

But, again, those who receive the full law of the gospel of Jesus Christ and remain true and faithful, shall be sanctified through the mercy of Christ and will escape the sufferings of the disobedient in the spirit world. They will enjoy the *words* of eternal life in this world and the joy and *powers* of eternal life in the world to come.

Of those who are sanctified by mercy, the Lord has said: "And it shall be manifest unto my servant, by the voice of the Spirit, those that are chosen, and *they shall be sanctified*" (D&C 105:36; emphasis added). Those who are sanctified in this manner receive the words of eternal life here in this fallen and darkened world and are promised the eventual incompressible and unimaginable blessings and powers associated with eternal life in the world to come. These crowning truths, along with many others, were revealed to the Prophet as a part of the great restoration of all things.

Not only has the Lord revealed these glorious truths regarding the resurrection to the Prophet Joseph, but he has also shown them to many other righteous people (see D&C 76:114-119), including President Wilford Woodruff. In a vision in which he saw many of the events of the last days, President Woodruff was also given knowledge regarding the first and second resurrections. His record of what he saw provides further insights and understanding regarding the marvelous doctrine of the Resurrection.

A VISION OF THE TWO RESURRECTIONS

After laboring as a missionary in Memphis, Tennessee, for a length of time, Wilford Woodruff, who later became the fourth president of the Church, was privileged to see in vision the signs of the Second Coming and the resurrection of the dead. He described his heavenly vision in these words:

> While I was upon my knees praying, my room was filled with light. I looked and a messenger stood by my side. I arose, and this personage told me he had come to instruct me. He presented before me a panorama. He told me he wanted me to see with my eyes and understand with my mind what was coming to pass in the earth before the coming of the Son of Man. He commenced with what the revelations say about the sun being turned to darkness, the moon to blood, and the stars falling from heaven. Those things were all presented to me one after another, as they will be, I suppose, when they are manifest before the coming of the Son of Man. Then he showed me the resurrection of the dead—what is termed the first and second resurrection.
>
> In the first resurrection I saw no graves nor anyone raised from the grave. I saw legions of celestial beings, men and women who had received the gospel all clothed in white robes. In this form they were presented to me; they had already been raised from the grave.
>
> After this he showed me what is termed the second resurrection. Vast fields of graves were before me, and the Spirit of God rested upon the earth

like a shower of gentle rain, and when that fell upon the graves, they were opened, and an immense host of human beings came forth. They were just as diversified in their dress as we are here, or as they were laid down. This personage taught me with regard to these things....

I refer to this as one of the visitations that was given me in my boyhood, so to speak, in the gospel. I was a priest at the time. Of course, there was a motive in this personage visiting me and teaching me these principles. He knew a great deal better than I did what lay before me in life. It was doubtless sent me for the purpose of strengthening me and giving me encouragement in my labors.[26]

What a blessing it was for President Woodruff to view the resurrection of the dead! Not only would such a vision have been a strength and comfort to him, but it can also strengthen and comfort us as we look forward to that great day of restoration.

The resurrection to eternal life has been made possible through the atoning sacrifice of Jesus Christ and our obedience to the everlasting covenant. From the teachings of our modern prophets, we learn also that the priesthood—which is the authority and power to act in the name of God—plays a very active part in the Resurrection.

PRIESTHOOD KEYS INVOLVED IN THE RESURRECTION

The powers, keys, and authority of the priesthood are specifically designed to assist in bringing about the immortality and the eternal life of man. Through the keys of the Melchizedek Priesthood— "the Holy Priesthood after the Order of the Son of God" (D&C 107:3)—our spirits and our bodies will be reunited. They will be eternally fused, never to be separated again. "For man is spirit. The elements are eternal, and spirit and element, inseparably connected, receive a fulness of joy; And when separated, man cannot receive a fulness of joy" (D&C 93:33-34).

In a discourse regarding the Priesthood, the Prophet Joseph Smith explained that there are certain keys of the priesthood to be revealed in the last times. He taught, "There are many things which belong to the powers of the Priesthood and the keys thereof, that have been kept hid from before the foundation of the world; they are hid from the wise and prudent to be revealed in the last times."[27]

Along the same line Brigham Young taught that there are many different kinds of keys of the priesthood, and that the power to resurrect someone comes as a result of holding specific keys of the priesthood. He said,

It is supposed by this people that we have all the ordinances in our possession for life and salvation, and exaltation, and that we are administering in these ordinances. This is not the case. We are in possession of all the ordinances that can be administered in the flesh; but there are other ordinances and administrations that must be administered beyond this world. I know you would ask what they are. I will mention one. We have not, neither can we receive here, the ordinance and the keys of the resurrection. They will be given to those who have passed off this stage of action and have received their bodies again, as many have already done and many more will. They will be ordained, by *those who hold the keys of the resurrection, to go forth and resurrect the Saints,* just as we receive the ordinance of baptism, then the keys of authority to baptize others for the remission of their sins. This is one of the ordinances we can not receive here, and there are many more.[28]

In providing further information about the keys of the priesthood that are associated with the resurrection, President Young said that after we die, "The spirit within [us] goes back pure and holy to God, dwells in the spirit world pure and holy, and by-and-by, will have the privilege of coming and taking the body again. Some *person holding the keys of the resurrection,* having previously passed through that ordeal, will be delegated to resurrect our bodies, and our spirits will be there and prepared to enter into their bodies.[29] Here we learn that there are certain keys of the Priesthood directly associated with the doctrine of the Resurrection.

President Joseph F. Smith taught that if we keep our covenants, we will gain power of resurrection as Jesus did. He said, "Jesus, the Only Begotten of the Father...had power to lay down His life and take it up again, and if we keep inviolate the covenants of the Gospel, remaining faithful and true to the end, we too, in His name and through His redeeming blood, will have power in due time to resurrect these our bodies after they shall have been committed to the earth."[30]

Thus we encounter the age-old question, "If a man die shall he live again?" (Job 14:14) has been answered with a resounding, "Yes!" But even with this assurance, the reality of the Resurrection is often difficult for us to comprehend. When a loved one dies, their departing seems so final. We of ourselves in the present moment cannot awaken them and cause the ache of their loss to be softened. Though we are incapable of such a magnificent act in the present, the Lord in his infinite goodness and power has promised us that he can and will awaken them in proper time—the time of the glorious resurrection. We can have faith in his promise. Nothing is impossible for him.

IS ANYTHING TOO HARD FOR THE LORD?

I have often wondered how it is that the priesthood power of the Lord can resurrect people. How can people who have died terrible deaths, people who may have been buried at sea and their bodies eaten by fish or who may have been cremated—how can God collect all those bodily fragments and bring about the resurrection? I just don't know, but I trust that the Lord is able to do it.

Though as yet we may not understand how our Father will be able to sort everything out, though we may also wonder at the processes involved in the restoration of our bodies to their perfect form, the teachings of our modern prophets testify that our Father is indeed able to perform this marvelous work.

According to the prophets, we will receive the same fundamental elements of our bodies again in the Resurrection. Speaking of this reality the Prophet Joseph Smith taught, "there is no fundamental principle belonging to a human system that ever goes into another in this world or in the world to come. I care not what the theories of men are. We have the testimony that God will raise us up, and he has the power to do it. If anyone supposes that any part of our bodies, that is, the fundamental parts thereof, ever goes into another body, he is mistaken."[31]

Joseph Smith's teaching that the basic elements of our bodies remain our own was echoed by President Brigham Young. He said, "The question may be asked, do not the particles that compose man's body, when returned to mother earth, go to make or compose other bodies? No, they do not. . . Neither can the particles which have comprised the body of man become parts of the bodies of other men, or of beasts, fowls, fish, insects, or vegetables."

President Young then explained that the particles of our bodies "are governed by divine law and though they may pass from the knowledge of the scientific world, that divine law still holds, governs and controls them. Man's body may be buried in the ocean, it may be eaten by wild beasts, or it may be burned to ashes, they may be scattered to the four winds, yet the particles of which it is composed will not be incorporated into any form of vegetable or animal life, to become a component part of their structure." At the time of the resurrection, he said, "every particle of our physical structures necessary to make our tabernacles perfect will be assembled, to be rejoined with the spirit, every man in his order. Not one particle will be lost."[32]

Brigham Young's successor, John Taylor, also taught that our resurrected bodies will be our own. He said,

> All must come forth from the grave, some time or other, in the selfsame tabernacles that they possessed while living on the earth. It will be just as Ezekiel has described it—bone will come to its bone, and flesh and sinew will cover the skeleton, and at the Lord's bidding breath will enter the body, and we shall appear, many of us, a marvel to ourselves....

I know that some people of very limited comprehension will say that all the parts of the body cannot be brought together, for, say they, the fish probably have eaten them up, or the whole may have been blown to the four winds of heaven, etc. It is true the body, or the organization, may be destroyed in various ways, but it is not true that *the particles out of which it was created can be destroyed. They are eternal; they never were created.* This is not only a principle associated with our religion, or in other words, with the great science of life, but it is in accordance with acknowledged science. You may take, for instance, a handful of fine gold, and scatter it in the street among the dust; again, gather together the materials among which you threw the gold, and you can separate one from the other so thoroughly, that your handful of gold can be returned to you; yes, every grain of it. You may take particles of silver, iron, copper, lead, etc., and mix them together with any other ingredients, and there are certain principles connected with them by which these different materials can be eliminated, every particle cleaving to that of its own element.[33]

As I read these words of promise that every particle will cleave to its own element, I am reminded of the passage, "For intelligence cleaveth unto intelligence; wisdom receiveth wisdom; truth embraceth truth; virtue loveth virtue; light cleaveth unto light..." (D&C 88:40). While we do not understand, as yet, this divine law of spiritual and physical magnetism that draws together, through the keys of the priesthood, all things that belong together, we have the assurance of the prophets that all things that belong together will come together. We are promised that not even one hair of our heads will be lost.

Regarding the complete restoration of our bodies and spirits, Alma declared: "Now, this restoration shall come to all, both old and young, both bond and free, both male and female, both the wicked and the righteous; and even there shall not so much as a hair of their heads be lost; but everything shall be restored to its perfect frame, as it is now, or in the body, and shall be brought and be arranged before the bar of Christ the Son, and God the Father, and the Holy Spirit, which is one Eternal God, to be judged according to their works, whether they be good or whether they be evil" (Alma 11:44).

Our bodies in this life are not perfect, but in the resurrection they will be restored to their perfect frame and upgraded to a far greater degree of beauty and power than we can even comprehend now. They will also be changed so that we will no longer have blood coursing through our veins as we do now. This and other changes will be brought to pass to prepare us to dwell in the midst of the glory that is associated with the various kingdoms.

CHARACTERISTICS OF RESURRECTED BODIES

Much confusion has arisen among many Bible readers because of a statement by Paul. He said, "Now this I say, brethren, that flesh and blood cannot inherit the kingdom of God; neither doth corruption inherit incorruption" (1 Corinthians 15:50). Based on this scripture many Christians have falsely concluded that resurrected beings do not have tangible bodies of flesh and bone. This false belief is corrected when we distinguish between *blood* and *bone*. Although flesh and *blood* cannot enter the kingdom of God—resurrected flesh and *bone* can. Jesus had no blood in his body after the resurrection, but the Bible records that he did have a body of "flesh and bones" (Luke 24:39).

In the resurrection we will not have blood in our bodies. The Prophet Joseph Smith taught that, "God Almighty Himself dwells in eternal fire; flesh and blood cannot go there, for all corruption is devoured by the fire. 'Our God is a consuming fire.' When our flesh is quickened by the Spirit, there will be no blood in this tabernacle."[34]

Brigham Young taught the same doctrine when he explained:

> The blood He spilled upon Mount Calvary he did not receive again into His veins. That was poured out, and when He was resurrected another element took the place of the blood. It will be so with every person who receives a resurrection; the blood will not be resurrected with the body, being designed only to sustain the life of the present organization. When this is dissolved, and we again obtain our bodies by the power of the resurrection, that which we now call the life of the body, which is formed from the food we eat and the water we drink, will be supplanted by another element; for flesh and blood cannot inherit the kingdom of God.[35]

Again, there was no blood present in Jesus' body after he was resurrected. He spilt his blood at Gethsemane and at Calvary. Many scriptures testify, however, that Jesus did have an immortal body of flesh and *bone*. On the third day, Jesus' tomb was empty of his physical body. Jesus, in his resurrected body of flesh and bone, appeared to his apostles, and they felt the nail prints in his hands and feet (see Luke 24:36-39). After his resurrection Jesus also physically ate broiled fish and honeycomb with his beloved disciples (see Luke 24:42).

In the resurrection, those who gain exaltation in the Celestial Kingdom will have beautiful bodies of flesh and bone even as do the Father and the Son. Of their exalted bodies we read: "The Father has a body of flesh and bones as tangible as man's; the Son also" (D&C 130:22). Once again, Jesus is the type for our own resurrection. He was, and we will be, raised with beautiful and perfect physical bodies with power "to subdue all things" (Philippians 3:21).

President Young taught we will have beautiful bodies in the resurrection. He explained:

> I think it has been taught by some that as we lay our bodies down, they will so rise again in the resurrection with all the impediments and imperfections that they had here; and that if a wife does not love her husband in this state she cannot love him in the next. This is not so. Those who attain to the blessing of the first or celestial resurrection will be pure and holy, and perfect in body. Every man and woman that reaches to this unspeakable attainment will be as beautiful as the angels that surround the throne of God. If you can, by faithfulness in this life, obtain the right to come up in the morning of the resurrection, you need entertain no fears that the wife will be dissatisfied with her husband, or the husband with the wife; for those of the first resurrection will be free from sin and from the consequences and power of sin.[36]

At another time, President Lorenzo Snow described the loveliness of resurrected personages when he taught that: "In the next life we will have our bodies glorified and free from sickness and death. Nothing is so beautiful as a person in a resurrected and glorified condition. There is nothing more lovely than to be in this condition, and have our wives and children and friends with us.[37]

In similar language, B. H. Roberts stated: "We shall live, believe me, not in decrepit, worn out or deformed bodies, but in resurrected bodies restored to the full stature of the spirits they are to clothe. We shall inhabit them erect and strong and young and unwrinkled; with every power increasing and developing through all the ages in which we shall live. Christ is the type of the resurrection and he was raised at about 33 years of age in the perfection of his manly beauty and powers, and so ultimately shall it be with men."[38]

Similarly President Spencer W. Kimball has explained that the resurrected body is a regenerated body—renewed and revitalized. He taught: "The resurrected body is regenerated. As Jesus' spirit left his body hanging on the cross and later lying in the tomb, so shall our spirits eventually leave our bodies lying lifeless. As Jesus preached to spirits in the spirit world in his spiritual state, so shall our spirits continue active and expand and develop. As Jesus appeared in the garden a resurrected soul, so shall each of us come forth a perfect immortal with every organ perfect, every limb intact, with every injury or deformity restored and put right; with the infirmities of mortality replaced with strength and vigor and power and beauty of virile maturity."[39]

Not only will bodies be beautiful in the resurrection, but they will also have wonderful powers of motion. Speaking of resurrected persons, Brigham Young taught that, "They move with ease and like lightning.... God has revealed some little things with regard to His movements and power, and the operation and motion of the lightning furnish a fine illustration of the ability and power of the Almighty. If you could stretch a wire from this room around the world until the two ends nearly meet here again, and were to apply a battery to one end, if the electrical condition were perfect, the effect of the touch would pass with such inconceivable velocity that it would be felt at the other end of the wire at the same moment. This is what the faithful Saints are coming to; they will possess this power, and if they wish to visit different planets, they will be there."[40] If Brigham Young were alive today, I am sure he would find even greater delight in using illustrations from modern science and technology—which even now would be seriously lacking—to describe the marvelous powers of resurrected beings.

Elder James E. Talmage has also written about the wondrous powers of the resurrection . He explained: "A resurrected body, though of tangible substance, and possessing all the organs of the mortal tabernacle, is not bound to earth by gravitation, nor can it be hindered in its movements by material barriers. To us who conceive of motion only in the directions incident to the three dimensions of space, the passing of a solid, such as a living body of flesh and bones, through stone walls, is necessarily incomprehensible. But that resurrected beings move in accordance with laws making such passage possible and to them natural, is evidenced not only by the instance of the risen Christ, but by the movements of other resurrected personages."

Continuing, Elder Talmage commented on the amazing ability of the resurrected Moroni to pass through the walls of Joseph Smith's bedroom. He said, "Thus, in September, 1823, Moroni, the Nephite prophet who had died about 400 A.D. appeared to Joseph Smith in his chamber, three times during one night, coming and going without hindrance incident to walls or roof.... That Moroni was a resurrected man is shown by his corporeity manifested in his handling of the metallic plates on which was inscribed the record known to us as the Book of Mormon. So also resurrected beings possess the power of rendering themselves visible or invisible to the physical vision of mortals."[41]

Even more amazing to me, beyond Elder Talmage's observations, is the fact that Moroni, as a space traveler, traveling from the presence of God to this earth, did so without the aid of a space craft or space suit. I stand in awe at the power and majesty of resurrected beings—and yet, at this point of our mortal journey, we still know so very little about them.

The characteristics and powers of resurrected beings are all so much beyond our understanding, that we must continue to rely on the promises of the Lord that these things are real. As we put our trust in his words we remember the words of Paul, who assured us: "But as it is written, Eye hath not seen, nor ear heard, neither have entered into the heart of man, the things which God hath prepared for them that love him" (1 Cor. 2:9).

PROCREATION LIMITED TO EXALTED BEINGS

To those that love him, the Lord has promised that they will dwell with him as husbands and wives and families in the eternities. Of this eternal uniting of husbands and wives in the resurrection, President John Taylor said, "It is the gospel that teaches a woman that she has a claim upon a man, and a man that he has a claim upon a woman in the resurrection; it is the gospel that teaches them that, when they rise from the tombs in the resurrection, they will again clasp hands, be reunited, and again participate in that glory for which God designed them before the world was."[42]

A vital part of that glory, in fact at the very core of it, lies in the great power of eternal increase—being added upon throughout the eternities. This magnificent power is the power of eternal procreation—the ability to have children in the resurrection. President Joseph Fielding Smith taught that only those who obtain the resurrection of exaltation, or in other words, those who reach the highest degree of the celestial kingdom, will have this power of eternal procreation which is called "eternal lives" in the Doctrine and Covenants (D&C 132:24). President Smith explained further that

> Some will gain celestial bodies with all the powers of exaltation and eternal increase. These bodies will shine like the sun as our Savior's does, as described by John. Those who enter the terrestrial kingdom will have terrestrial bodies, and they will not shine like the sun, but they will be more glorious than the bodies of those who receive the telestial glory.
>
> In both of these [lower] kingdoms there will be changes in the bodies and limitations. They will not have the power of increase, neither the power of nature to live as husbands and wives, for this will be denied them and they cannot increase.
>
> Those who receive the exaltation in the celestial kingdom will have the "continuation of the seeds forever." They will live in the family relationship. In the terrestrial and in the telestial kingdoms there will be no marriage. Those who enter there will remain "separately and singly" forever.
>
> Some of the functions in the celestial body will not appear in the terrestrial body, neither in the telestial body, and the power of procreation will be removed. I take it that men and women will, in these kingdoms, be just what the so-called Christian world expects us all to be—neither man nor woman, merely immortal beings having received the resurrection.[43]

This divine power of procreation, reserved for those who gain an exaltation in the celestial kingdom of God, is in part the realization of the everlasting covenant triad blessings that we have discussed in former chapters: land, deliverance and seed—LDS. It is the crowning blessing associated with eternal life which will be discussed more fully in the next chapter. These are the blessings of the Abrahamic covenant, the result of remaining true and faithful after having been sealed in the new and everlasting covenant of marriage.[44]

The Lord explained that the promises he made to Abraham, about having children as numerous as the sands upon the sea shore or the stars in the heavens, are ours also because we are Abraham's descendants—as our patriarchal blessings indicate. According to the Lord's promise if we do the works of Abraham, we will be united as husbands and wives in the resurrection. If we don't, we won't (see D&C 132:31-33).

These important promises of husbands and wives being reunited in the resurrection and having the power of procreation are consistent with Paul's teaching that "Neither is the man without the woman, neither the woman without the man, in the Lord" (1 Corinthians 11:11) and Peter's declaration that the man and the woman are "heirs together of the grace of life" (1 Peter 3:7). These promises, along with many others we have talked about, fill us with great joy and comfort as we reflect upon them. Another reassuring and wonderful truth that has been revealed regarding the eternal nature of families is that those who die as little children are resurrected as celestial beings.

LITTLE CHILDREN RESURRECTED
TO CELESTIAL GLORY

Why does our Heavenly Father allow pure and innocent children to die? Sometimes it seems so unfair that little children die while wicked men and women are allowed to remain on the earth. Perhaps we have our thinking backwards. Maybe we should mourn when a child is born into this fallen and wicked world and rejoice when a righteous old man or woman dies. Why little children are sometimes taken in their infancy was a question pondered by the Prophet Joseph Smith. He said:

> I have meditated upon the subject, and asked the question, why is it that infants, innocent children, are taken away from us, especially those that seem to be the most intelligent and interesting. The strongest reasons that present themselves to my mind are these: This world is a very wicked world.... The Lord takes many away even in infancy, that they may escape the envy of man, and the sorrows and evils of this present world; they were too pure, too lovely, to live on earth; therefore, if rightly considered, instead of mourning we have reason to rejoice as they are delivered from evil, and we shall soon have them again....

All children are redeemed by the blood of Jesus Christ, and the moment that children leave this world, they are taken to the bosom of Abraham. The only difference between the old and young dying is, one lives longer in heaven and eternal light and glory than the other, and is freed a little sooner from this miserable wicked world.[45]

From these teachings we learn that little children who die escape the sufferings and the tortures of this life. They are permitted to return to their heavenly home to rest with their Father until the Resurrection. Regarding the state of these little ones, the Prophet Joseph Smith learned through a glorious vision that "all children who die before they arrive at the years of accountability are saved in the celestial kingdom of heaven" (D&C 137:10).

President Joseph F. Smith explained that in the Resurrection these little children will not be brought forth in the resurrection as adults. Instead they will be resurrected as children, and then as resurrected beings they will grow to adulthood. President Smith explained: "The body will come forth as it is laid to rest, for there is no growth or development in the grave. As it is laid down, so will it arise, and changes to perfection will come by the law of restitution. But the spirit will continue to expand and develop, and the body after the resurrection will develop to the full stature of man.[46]

Continuing, President Smith explained children who die will be resurrected as children—but in the spirit world they are adults.

The spirits of our children are immortal before they come to us, and their spirits, after bodily death, are like they were before they came. They are as they would have appeared if they had lived in the flesh, to grow to maturity or to develop their physical bodies to the full stature of their spirits. If you see one of your children that has passed away it may appear to you in the form in which you would recognize it, the form of childhood; but if it came to you as a messenger bearing some important truth, it would perhaps come ... in the stature of full-grown manhood.... The spirit of Jesus Christ was full grown before He was born into the world; and so our children were full grown and possessed their full stature in the spirit before they entered mortality, the same stature that they will possess after they have passed away from mortality, and as they will also appear after the resurrection, when they shall have completed their mission.[47]

How comforting these principles of truth are to our minds and hearts! We can also take comfort in the knowledge that our little ones who have died before the age of accountability are beyond Satan's power.

BEYOND SATAN'S POWER

In addition to the beautiful truths we have just been discussing, Joseph F. Smith also taught that little children who die before the age of accountability are beyond Satan's power because they are free from sin. Furthermore, when they die, those who are beyond the age of accountability who have been sanctified to a celestial glory through the mercy of Christ and by obedience to the gospel of Jesus Christ, are also beyond the power of Satan.

Concerning these marvelous truths, President Smith explained: "Little children who are taken away in infancy and innocence before they have reached the years of accountability ... are redeemed by the blood of Christ, and they are saved just as surely as death has come into the world through the fall of our first parents. It is further written that Satan has no power over men or women, except that power which he gains over them in this world. In other words, none of the children of the Father who are redeemed through obedience, faith, repentance and baptism for the remission of sins, and who live in that redeemed condition, and die in that condition are subject to Satan. Thereafter he has no power over them. They are absolutely beyond his reach, just as little children are who die without sin."[48]

Even as little children and those who are sanctified are delivered from the power of Satan, so also will the earth—having been baptized in the flood and having been cleansed by fire at his coming—be delivered from his power at the beginning of the Millennium. Then, at the end of the Millennium, the earth will die, be resurrected and receive celestial glory. It will be the celestial kingdom and will be home to those who are prepared to dwell there.

THE RESURRECTION OF THE EARTH

In describing the conditions that will exist during the Millennium, President Joseph Fielding Smith taught, "When the Millennium is ended Satan will be loosed for a little season, there will be a final war between good and evil, Michael and the righteous will be victorious, the last resurrection will take place, and all men will be judged according to their works.

"Then the end shall come and the earth shall pass away in death, but to be raised in the resurrection by which it shall be made a celestial body and the fit abode of celestial beings who shall dwell in the presence of God the Father and his Son Jesus Christ forever as priests and kings unto the Most High"[49] (see also D&C 29:23; 45:58; 56:18; 77:1, 6; 84:101; 88:17-26; 130:9).

From this statement we can see that not only will all mankind be resurrected, but the earth and everything that has ever lived upon it will also enjoy a resurrection. In a sermon regarding certain beasts mentioned in the Book of Revelation, Joseph Smith taught that animals, too, will be resurrected. He explained,

> John saw the actual beast in heaven, showing to John that beasts did actually exist there, and not to represent figures of things on the earth.... John saw curious looking beasts in heaven; he saw every creature that was in heaven—all the beasts, fowls and fish in heaven,—actually there, giving glory to God.... I suppose John saw beings there of a thousand forms, that had been saved from ten thousand times ten thousand earths like this,—strange beasts of which we have no conception: all might be seen in heaven. The grand secret was to show John what there was in heaven. John learned that God glorified Himself by saving all that His hands had made, whether beasts, fowls, fishes or men; and He will glorify Himself with them.[50]

As was mentioned in the previous chapter at the Second Coming of the Lord "every corruptible thing, both of man, or of the beasts of the field, or of the fowls of the heavens, or of the fish of the sea, that dwells upon all the face of the earth, shall be consumed.... And in that day the enmity of man, and the enmity of beasts, yea, the enmity of all flesh, shall cease from before my face" (D&C 101:24, 26). After this cleansing will come the glorious resurrection. Then all life forms, including the animals, will come up "in their destined order or sphere of creation, in the enjoyment of their eternal felicity" (D&C 77:3).

When I stop and think about the resurrection of all the plants and animals that have lived upon this earth—not to mention all the people—I wonder how the earth will ever accommodate or hold everything and everyone. Maybe one answer lies in the fact that not all that is resurrected will reside on this planet.

From latter-day scripture we read, "he who is not able to abide the law of a celestial kingdom cannot abide a celestial glory" (D&C 88:22). By contrast, those who do keep the law of the celestial kingdom will inherit this resurrected earth. "The poor and the meek of the earth will inherit it. Therefore, it must needs be sanctified from all unrighteousness, that it may be prepared for the celestial glory; For after it hath filled the measure of its creation, it shall be crowned with glory, even the presence of God the Father; That bodies who are of the celestial kingdom may possess it forever and ever; for, for this intent was it made and created, and for this intent are they sanctified" (D&C 88:17-20). From these verses we learn that this earth will be reserved for those who have been sanctified and resurrected as celestial beings. This being the case, there have to be other worlds to accommodate resurrected beings other than celestial ones.

Though we do not know a great deal about other worlds nor what people do in the other degrees of glory, what information we do have focuses our minds on the requirements for celestial living. As we comply with the terms and conditions of these requirements, we will be sanctified and will have glory added upon us forever.

The glorified beings that will dwell on this earth after it has received its celestialization will have the privilege, as was mentioned earlier, of being resurrected as families. Their family ties will not have been severed at death, and they will be reunited as families in the Resurrection. As with all other aspects of the gospel, the Resurrection will be a family affair.

JOSEPH SMITH WANTED TO BE BURIED NEAR HIS FAMILY

From the Prophet Joseph Smith, we learn that the Resurrection will provide for a happy reunion with our families and friends. The anticipation of being together with his family and friends in the Resurrection brought joy to the heart of the Prophet Joseph Smith. He said, "More painful to me are the thoughts of annihilation than death. If I have no expectation of seeing my father, mother, brothers, sisters and friends again, my heart would burst in a moment, and I should go down to my grave. The expectation of seeing my friends in the morning of the resurrection cheers my soul and makes me bear up against the evils of life. It is like their taking a long journey, and on their return we meet them with increased joy.... Hosanna, hosanna, hosanna to Almighty God, that rays of light begin to burst forth upon us even now. I cannot find words in which to express my self."[51]

Because of the expectation of embracing his family and friends in the resurrection, Joseph Smith wanted to be buried near them. Regarding burial sites, Joseph the Prophet said,

> There is something good and sacred to me in this thing. The place where a man is buried is sacred to me. . . . Even to the aborigines of this land, the burying places of their fathers are more sacred than anything else.... I believe those who have buried their friends here [in the cities of the Saints] their condition is enviable. Look at Jacob and Joseph in Egypt, how they required their friends to bury them in the tomb of their fathers. See the expense which attended the embalming and the going up of the great company to the burial.... I will tell you what I want. If tomorrow I shall be called to lie in yonder tomb, in the morning of the resurrection let me strike hands with my father and cry, "My father," and he will say, "My son, my son," as soon as the rock rends and before we come out of our graves.

And may we contemplate these things so? Yes, if we learn how to live and how to die. When we lie down we contemplate how we may rise in the morning; and it is pleasing for friends to lie down together, locked in the arms of love, to sleep and wake in each other's embrace and renew their conversation.

Would you think it strange if I relate what I have seen in vision in relation to this interesting theme? Those who have died in Jesus Christ may expect to enter into all that fruition of joy when they come forth, which they possessed or anticipated here.

So plain was the vision, that I actually saw men, before they had ascended from the tomb, as though they were getting up slowly. They took each other by the hand and said to each other, 'My father, my son, my mother, my daughter, my brother, my sister.' And when the voice calls for the dead to arise, suppose I am laid by the side of my father, what would be the first joy of my heart? To meet my father, my mother, my brother, my sister; and when they are by my side, I embrace them and they me.[52]

ALL LOSSES WILL BE MADE UP

Regarding this vision and the many other visions that were before him, the Prophet Joseph Smith said: "It is my meditation all the day, and more than my meat and drink, to know how I shall make the Saints of God comprehend the visions that roll like an overflowing surge before my mind." Among the principles of the gospel that Joseph Smith wanted the Saints to comprehend was the love, mercy and justice of our Father in Heaven.

According to his great plan of happiness, and because he is a God of love, mercy and justice, our Father has promised that he will make up to us in the Resurrection all those injustices—the heartache, pain, sorrow and suffering—we experience here. We also have the happy and comforting promise that in the Resurrection all of our losses will be made up to us if we continue faithfully.

Regarding this comforting and correct principle, the Prophet offers us these inspiring and encouraging words of promise: "All your losses will be made up to you in the resurrection, provided you continue faithful. By the vision of the Almighty I have seen it."[53] In connection with these encouraging words of promise if we continue faithful, we may remember Lehi's promise to his son Jacob, "Nevertheless, Jacob, my firstborn in the wilderness, thou knowest the greatness of God; and he shall consecrate thine afflictions for thy gain" (2 Nephi 2:2).

This promise that Lehi made to his son Jacob is yours and mine also. As we pass through our own trials and witness unfairness and injustice in the lives of those around us, we must bolster our faith, trust in the Lord, and remember the principle purposes behind our descent into mortality are for us to gain experience, to encounter and overcome opposition in all things, and to learn that there is great growth potential in adversity.

The Prophet Joseph Smith had many experiences with opposition and learned much about the growth potential that can be had in the midst of adversity. During a time of great personal suffering, the Prophet Joseph sought the Lord in mighty prayer. In answer to his supplications the Lord reminded him—and us—that even though we experience suffering in this life— "all these things shall give thee experience, and shall be for thy good. The Son of Man hath descended below them all. Art thou greater than he?" (D&C 122:7-8).

As we remember that he has indeed descended below them all so that he might be able to comprehend our pain and trials and know how to succor us, we will feel the comforting assurance of his love and understanding (see Alma 7:11-12). And as we remember his promises and put our trust in him, we will come to know for ourselves the great truth Alma explained to his sons Helaman and Shiblon that "whosoever shall put their trust in God shall be supported in their trials, and their troubles, and their afflictions, and shall be lifted up at the last day" (Alma 36:3; 38:5).

When we allow these truths to take root in our hearts and minds, they truly can bring us that peace to our souls which the Savior has promised—his blessed peace "which passeth all understanding" (Philippians 4:7).

THE RESURRECTION BRINGS PEACE TO OUR SOULS

Remembering the love, mercy, justice and promises of our Heavenly Father brings peace to our souls—especially as we anticipate a glorious resurrection with perfect, beautiful, and eternally youthful bodies in peaceful eternal family relationships.

Jesus, just before leaving his disciples, promised them his priceless peace. He assured his disciples: "In my Father's house are many mansions: if it were not so, I would have told you. I go to prepare a place for you. And if I go and prepare a place for you, I will come again, and receive you unto myself; that where I am, there ye may be also. And whither I go ye know, and the way ye know.... Peace, I leave with you, my peace I give unto you: not as the world giveth, give I unto you. Let not your heart be troubled, neither let it be afraid" (John 14:2-4, 27).

The sure and unchangeable promise of our Lord and Savior, Jesus Christ, is that he "shall change our vile body, that it may be fashioned like unto his glorious body, according to the working whereby he is able even to subdue all things unto himself" (Philippians 3:21).

I trust with all my heart that the day will come when I will see and hug my little dog, Tippy, again—and I will see and embrace my father again in the flesh. I fully expect to be and rejoice with him and many others whom I love dearly among my family and friends. This is according to the glorious and eternal plan of happiness that our loving and kind, merciful and just Heavenly Father has provided for us. Such is the faith and hope of all Latter-day Saints.

Our firm faith and hope in Christ and in his promise of a glorious resurrection are reflected in these beautiful, comforting, and reassuring words of Joseph Austlander which can be applied to both the spirit world and the resurrection:

He is not dead,
Your son, your dear beloved son,
Your golden one,
With his blond tousled head,
The shining and excited words he said!
Oh no! Be comforted.
For him the world will never
Grow flat and tired and dull;
He is part of all swift things forever,
All joyous things that run or fly,
Familiar to the wind and cloud and sky,
Forever beautiful!

As I reflect upon these beautiful words and try to visualize their meaning, my soul is touched deeply. I am so eternally grateful for Jesus' loving sacrifice—the greatest act of love this world has ever known—that made it possible for all of us to overcome the grave and receive a glorious resurrection. Through Jesus Christ and him alone can we escape the tortures and sufferings of this life—like that associated with in the painful aging and death of my father—and gain eternally youthful bodies in the resurrection of the just.

Our worship and praise are directed to our Savior, Jesus Christ, the Good Shepherd, the Son of God, "Who shall change our vile body, that it may be fashioned like unto his glorious body, according to the working whereby he is able even to subdue all things unto himself" (Philippians 3:21).

Not only did Jesus Christ provide for a universal resurrection of all mankind, but he also set the perfect example and provided the infinite power so that true and faithful Saints can be resurrected and inherit eternal life—the subject of our last chapter in this work.

REFERENCES:

1 See *Teachings of the Prophet Joseph Smith*, 325. What is said of Patriarch Adam may be likened to other righteous men.

2 *Teachings*, 149; emphasis added.

3 *Improvement Era*, 6:503-4.

4 *Journal of Discourses*, 24:232.

5 *Journal of Discourses*, 26:31.

6 Recorded in the Congressional Record, January 30, 1973 E 503.

7 Original source unknown.

8 The expression "near death experiences" has been coined by nonbelievers in life after death. Latter-day Saints would have no problem using the expression: "after death experiences".

9 Ritchie, George G. M.D. *Return from Tomorrow* (Grand Rapids, Michigan: Chosen Books), 58-67.

10 Joseph Smith, Jr., *Teachings of the Prophet Joseph Smith*, (Salt Lake City: Deseret Book Co., 1976) cmp. Joseph Fielding Smith, 310, 326.

11 *Journal of Discourses* 3:368-74; emphasis added; also see 4: 133-34.

12 Neal A. Maxwell, "Answer Me", *Ensign*, November 1988, 33.

13 Bruce R. McConkie, "The Seven Deadly Heresies," in *Speeches of the Year*, 1980 [Provo: Brigham Young University Press].

14 Bruce R. McConkie, *Mormon Doctrine*, 762; emphasis added.

15 *Conference Report*, April, 1901, 2; emphasis added.

16 McConkie, Bruce R. in Millett, Robert L. *Within Reach* 10-17, 97-98.

17 Elder Boyd K. Packer, "Our Moral Environment," *Ensign*, May 1992, 68.

18 *Church News*, Week Ending December 13, 1997, 4.

19 In Doxey, Roy W. *The Latter-day Prophets and the Doctrine and Covenants*, (Salt Lake City: Deseret Book Co., 1963-1965) 374.

20 A resurrected body is sometimes called a spiritual body because of its magnificent spiritual powers. This expression is not to be confused with unembodied spirit beings in premortal world the who await mortal birth or with disembodied spirits in the postmortal world who await the resurrection.

21 *Teachings*, 296.

22 *Millennial Star* 74:803.

23 James E. Talmage, *Articles of Faith*, 385.

24 *Mormon Doctrine*, 640-41; emphasis in original.

25 *Teachings*, 312.

26 *The Deseret Weekly*, Vol. 53, No. 21, November 7, 1896, 642.

27 *Teachings*, 170.

28 *Journal of Discourses*, 15:137; emphasis added. At the dedication of the Washington D.C. Temple, which I was privileged to attend, President Spencer W. Kimball mentioned that temples were built so that keys of the priesthood could be revealed to mankind. He made reference to this statement by Brigham Young showing that there were various, other keys of the priesthood. President Kimball then pointed out that as yet we do not have these keys of the resurrection—neither do we have the keys "to give life", nor to "cause things to grow".

29 *Journal of Discourses*, 9: 139; emphasis added.

30 *Journal of Discourses*, 18:277.

31 *History of the Church*, 5:339.

32 Daniel Ludlow, *Latter-day Prophets Speak,* (Salt Lake City: Bookcraft, 1951), 42.
33 *Journal of Discourses,* 18:332-34; emphasis added.
34 *Teachings,* 367.
35 *Journal of Discourses,* 7:163.
36 *Journal of Discourses,* 10:24.
37 *Conference Report,* October 1900. 63.
38 As quoted in Garth L. Allred, *The Eternal Plan for the Children of God,* 1986, 213
39 *The Teachings of Spencer W. Kimball,* 44-45.
40 *Journal of Discourses,* 14:231.
41 James E. Talmage, *Jesus the Christ,* (Salt Lake City, Utah: *Deseret News,* 1915, 698.
42 *Journal of Discourses,* 16:376.
43 Joseph Fielding Smith, *Doctrines of Salvation,* (Salt Lake City, Utah: Bookcraft, 1960-1974, c1954-c1956), 2:287-288; see also D&C 131; 132.
44 Regarding the elements of the Abrahamic covenant see S. Michael Wilcox, "The Abrahamic Covenant", *Ensign,* January 1998, 42-48.
45 *Teachings,* 196-97; emphasis added.
46 *Improvement Era,* June, 1904; emphasis added.
47 *Latter-day Prophets Speak,* 45; emphasis added.
48 *Young Women's Journal,* 6:370; emphasis added; see also Alma 40: 12; *Teachings,* 170.
49 *Doctrines of Salvation,* 3:66; emphasis added
50 *Teachings,* 291.
51 *Teachings,* 296; emphasis added.
52 *Teachings,* 294-96; emphasis added.
53 *Teachings,* 296; emphasis added.

FIGURE 11-A
A RESURRECTION FOR ALL

Principles

1. "In the celestial glory there are three heavens or degrees. And in order to obtain the highest, a man must enter into this order of the priesthood (meaning the new and everlasting covenant of marriage); And if he does not he cannot obtain it... He may enter into the other, but that is the end of his kingdom; he cannot have an increase (D&C 131:1-4).

2. Because of Christ's atonement, all will be resurrected to a degree of glory, except Sons of Perdition, who will be raised, but to a kingdom of no glory. "Wherefore, he saves all except them" (D&C 76:44).

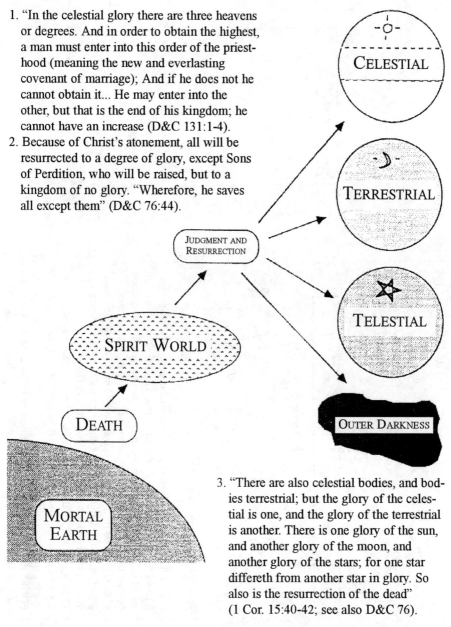

3. "There are also celestial bodies, and bodies terrestrial; but the glory of the celestial is one, and the glory of the terrestrial is another. There is one glory of the sun, and another glory of the moon, and another glory of the stars; for one star differeth from another star in glory. So also is the resurrection of the dead" (1 Cor. 15:40-42; see also D&C 76).

FIGURE 11-B
THE ORDER OF THE RESURRECTION

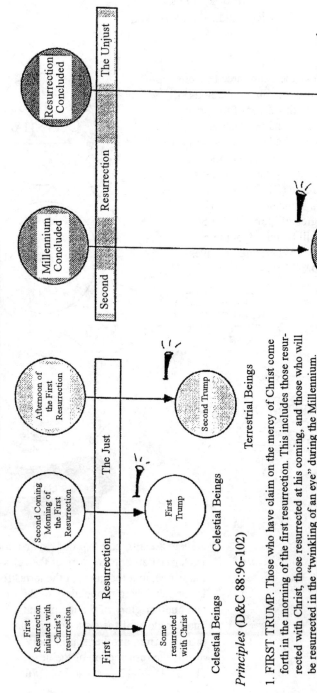

Principles (D&C 88:96-102)

1. FIRST TRUMP. Those who have claim on the mercy of Christ come forth in the morning of the first resurrection. This includes those resurrected at his coming, and those who will be resurrected in the "twinkling of an eye" during the Millennium.
2. SECOND TRUMP. Those who had a chance but did not receive the gospel in the flesh, but afterwards did, come forth in the afternoon of the first resurrection according to the justice of God.
3. THIRD TRUMP. As the Millennium is concluded, the resurrection of the unjust who are sanctified by the judgement of God, commences and telestial beings are resurrected.
4. FOURTH TRUMP. After the Millennium ends, the Sons of Perdition are resurrected. They cannot be sanctified by law, mercy, justice, nor judgment.

CHAPTER TWELVE

ETERNAL LIFE— THE GREATEST OF ALL THE GIFTS OF GOD

And if you keep my commandments and endure to the end you shall have eternal life, which gift is the greatest of all the gifts of God.

—D&C 14:7

When my family lived in St. George, Utah, we lived in a split-level house. When I would come home in the evenings, I would climb the stairs to the living room and invariably I was met by my four-year-old son, Marc. Hearing the car drive up, he would gleefully announce to everyone, "Daddy's home!" Then Michael would come running, and if the little girls were around, they would get in on the action, too. I would pick each of them up, and we would give each other hugs. They would routinely go through my pockets to see if I had brought them anything. Marc would often want me to take him to the video rental store to get a video about the Muppets. Most of the older children were busy with their own various affairs—it was the younger ones for whom my arrival marked a high point of the day.

Some might think these little ones loved their Dad just for what he could get for them. But I know, and they know, that our love for each other has a much greater depth. It is not propped up with mere gifts and entertainment—although when one is small, such things *can* mean a lot. We know there are ties binding us together that defy explanation. These same ties bind me to my wife and to my older sons and daughters. Younger children, however, seem to have a delightful openness and a frankness in the way they express their love.

With the passage of time, the bonds of love I feel for my own family and for my extended family have continued to grow. My ties with my parents, my brothers and sisters, and their children have grown stronger and stronger. Over time I have come to see my family as an ever-increasing network of faces, smiles, personalities, and love and I have come to sense the great power that exists in the unity of my family. The power that comes from this unity has often been manifest in remarkable ways. For example, when one of my sisters was very ill a special family fast was called. There were dramatic results. In her case, the pain and suffering were promptly halted.

Not only do I feel the increasing power of my connectedness to my own family but I feel more connected to my wife's family too. Years ago, my wife's sister had an accident in her home and was killed. I was asked to speak at her funeral. During that funeral I experienced feelings of love, compassion, and bonding with her that I had only faintly recognized while she was alive.

As the years have passed, the love I feel for my family has taken on deeper meaning and richer tones. Several years ago a family reunion for the descendants of my father was scheduled in Canada. My wife, children, and I would have to travel one-thousand miles from St. George, Utah, to Hillspring in Southern Alberta to attend the reunion. My wife and I had the children—along with a multitude of books, tapes, and food supplies—loaded into our VW campmobile. We were heading northward toward Cedar City when disaster struck! Our vehicle kept stalling on us. It repeatedly coughed, sputtered, and finally died. After a few minutes of waiting, I could start it up again, but after a few miles the same things happened again. This was not a new problem. It had happened before, so I was familiar with this routine! I knew the symptoms—the fuel pump was vapor-locking!

So, we returned to St. George for a new *electric* fuel pump that would correct the problem. After about a two-hour wait in the St. George heat, having repacked all the children and stuff back in the van, we started out again. Again we got as far as the steep incline leading up to Cedar City when the van konked out. We coaxed it to a service station where the mechanic found a simple solution—a ground wire to the new fuel pump had not been secured. After this problem was corrected, I had the feeling that all would be well, and that we could proceed without any other incidents.

But now we had a problem of a different sort. During the frustration of getting the van repaired, my family had lost faith in our temperamental vehicle—and in me who kept saying "It will be all right. Everything is okay. We can go now!" They would no longer trust the thing as far as the next town, let alone to carry them across the plains of Montana into Canada.

Finally, using my best possible persuasion—stressing the importance of family reunions—I convinced a few members of the family who still wanted to go, to board our van, and we proceeded all the way to Canada without further problems. However, every time the van coughed or hesitated on a hill, my heart sank, but my sense of determination to attend that family reunion increased.

To me it was very important that my children be with me at that family reunion. It was a worthy goal, and I knew that the Lord would help us get there. I kept picturing over and over in my mind that if I had to, I would push that temperamental van myself all the way to Canada. Nothing was going to stop me. I would be with my family. I was so happy when we finally pulled into the driveway of my brother-in-law's home where the reunion was being held. The whole family was seated and was about to begin the meal just as we arrived. We had made it just in time! My wife later joined us, having taken a plane to Provo and the rest of the way to Hillspring with my brother-in-law in a more reliable truck. It was a sweet experience to be together with my mother and father and my brothers and sisters and their families.

Even as there are physical ties that bind me to my family I really sense that there is a spiritual connectedness that binds us all together too. Through my experiences in my father's home and in my own home, I have come to sense more and more that I am a member of a much larger, everlasting family—the eternal family of God—and that the whole human race is a part of my family. I have come to understand more fully the truth that God, our Heavenly Father, truly is our Father, and we are all his children. As such we are all interconnected and are participants in our Father's great and eternal plan of happiness.

In addition to the idea that the whole human family is a part of my family, another wonderful insight I have gained by being a child in my father's home and by having children of my own is the common but amazing realization that children grow up to be like their parents.

CHILDREN GROW TO BECOME LIKE THEIR PARENTS

One afternoon while I was working on the computer at our home in St. George, four-year-old Marc came running through the house with one of his friends. He suddenly stopped, gave my knee a hug—that was as high as he could reach—and said happily, "Daddy, when I grow up, I want to be just like you!"

Do you think I was offended with his aspirations? On the contrary, what happiness that youthful expression brought to my soul! What an honor! I took what he said to be the supreme compliment. He wanted to be like me! This was the genuine, spontaneous, unaffected expression of the love of a child for his father.

As I have pondered this experience, I have concluded that Marc's expression of love and respect for me was also a reflection of what he thought of himself. He understood, even at the tender age of four years, that he had within himself the power to someday grow up to be a father like his father. As I have reflected more deeply on this incident, I have seen powerful gospel connections as they relate to our heavenly family.

The faith of the Latter-day Saints holds that after the Resurrection we may advance and eventually grow to become like our Heavenly Parents. As I am honored by my son's regard for me, how much more do our Heavenly Parents feel honored that we want to be like them? By contrast, anything less than our most diligent quest for exaltation may be offensive to our Heavenly Father. He was willing to give his Only Begotten Son, that we, through his atoning sacrifice, might have immortality and eternal life. This is why Jesus commanded us to, "Be ye therefore perfect, even as your Father which is in heaven is perfect" (Matthew 5:48). He would not have given us this commandment if he had not made the attainment possible.

Some Christians however, think the idea of becoming like God is blasphemous. To them this hope, this expectation, is too presumptuous—too overly ambitious. And yet, since we are literally the children of God, what is more natural than to expect that by following our Heavenly Father's great plan of happiness, this lofty state of perfection can be realized?

The Lord has given us a glorious promise that by obeying the requirements of the everlasting covenant, we can rise to the same glory and exaltation that he now possesses. In fact, the entire plan of the gospel of Jesus Christ is so designed as to enable the true and faithful sons and daughters of God—those who are willing to serve the Lord with all their heart, might, mind and strength—to receive eternal life. Eternal life is the greatest of all the gifts of God—it is to become like him. When we receive this most glorious gift we will experience a heavenly reunion and be one with our eternal family (see D&C 27:5-14). We will be made joint heirs with Jesus in receiving all that the Father has and will become even as he is.

This marvelous truth, that a little child can become like his parent—and that we mere mortals can become like God our eternal Father—has been suggested to us so simply and beautifully by the happy admiration of a little child for his father!

WE ARE CAPABLE OF ETERNAL DEVELOPMENT

Becoming like our Heavenly Parents involves a process of eternal growth and development. President John Taylor taught that we are capable of such eternal progression and expansion. He said, "If we take man, he is said to have been made in the image of God, for the simple reason that he is a son of God, and being His son, he is, of course, His offspring, an emanation from God, in whose likeness, we are told, he is made. He did not originate from a chaotic mass of matter, moving or inert, but came forth possessing, in an embryonic state, all the faculties and powers of a God. *And when he shall be perfected, and have progressed to maturity, he will be like his Father—a God, being indeed His offspring. As the horse, the ox, the sheep, and every living creature, including man, propagates its own species and perpetuates its own kind, so does God perpetuate His.*"[1]

Since we are the children of eternal beings, the seeds of deity are within us, and we are capable of reaching exaltation if we will but follow that spirit that teaches us all things. The power is within us, "[For] as many as received him, to them gave he power to become the sons of God, even to them that believe on his name" (John 1:12; also see D&C 39:4).

President Lorenzo Snow confirmed the idea that man is a god in embryo and that the power is within us to become like him when he said, *"We are the offspring of God,* born with the same faculties and powers as He possesses, capable of enlargement until his fulness is reached which He has promised—until we shall sit upon thrones, governing and controlling our posterity from eternity to eternity, and increasing eternally."[2]

Similarly, President Joseph F. Smith taught that "man is the child of God, formed in the divine image and endowed with divine attributes, and even as the infant son of our earthly father and mother is capable in due time of becoming a man, so the undeveloped offspring of celestial parentage is capable, by experience through ages of aeons, of evolving into a God."[3]

One of my former students, Marguerite De Long, has written about the connection between gaining experience and gaining eternal life. She writes,

> Experience is the great enlarger. We are added upon through experience. It is given to us as an act of charity from our Heavenly Father. Without it we could not be made perfect because our godlike qualities could not be exercised. All the trials and challenges of this life are designed to provide us with experiences that will help us in our development to become like our Heavenly Parents—who, because of their experiences, know good from evil.
>
> Hardships and adversity are especially interesting when viewed in this light. Why do the scriptures say that all these things would give us *experience* (D&C 122:7-8)? It is because experience is the key to the rest of the promises. Through experience we gain greater trust in the Lord and learn how to become as he is.
>
> We can and should learn as much as we can through revelation through others, but then we must learn to receive it ourselves and even once we have obtained revelation for ourselves we must use it—continue to have experience—so that it can be multiplied.

Adam and Eve could not have been multiplied in any degree without experience. Though they may have had all knowledge and walked with Father they could not be perfected without experience because through experience with using knowledge comes greater faith, and through faith we become purified and can go back to our heavenly home.

Thus, our experiences here in mortality play a vital role in preparing us to return to our Heavenly Father's presence to enjoy the marvelous gift of eternal life.

ETERNAL LIFE—THE GREATEST OF GOD'S GIFTS

As was mentioned in the previous chapter, Latter-day Saints use the expression "eternal life" in a very distinctive way. Elder Bruce R. McConkie explained this distinction when he wrote these words:

As used in the scriptures, eternal life is the name given to the kind of life that our Eternal Father lives. The word *eternal,* as used in the name *eternal life,* is a noun and not an adjective. It is one of the formal names of Deity (Moses 1:3; 7:35; D&C 19:11) and has been chosen by him as the particular name to identify the kind of life that he lives. He being God, the life he lives is God's life; and his name (in the noun sense) being Eternal, the kind of life he lives is eternal life. Thus; *God's life is eternal life; eternal life is God's life*—the expressions are synonymous.

Accordingly, eternal life is not a name that has reference only to the unending duration of a future life; immortality is to live forever in the resurrected state, and by the grace of God all men will gain this unending continuance of life. But only those who obey the fulness of the gospel law will inherit eternal life (D&C 29:43-44). It is "the greatest of all the gifts of God" (D&C 14:7), for it is the kind, status, type, and quality of life that God himself enjoys. Thus those who gain eternal life receive exaltation; they are sons of God, joint heirs with Christ, members of the Church of the Firstborn; they overcome all things, have all power, and receive the fulness of the Father. They are gods.[4]

So, according to this explanation, when Jesus and the prophets speak of eternal life they mean much, much more than just living forever, much more than immortality, much more than a resurrection from the dead. Those who gain eternal life enjoy the quality of life lived by God—they attain Godhood! This understanding of eternal life is important in order to gain an understanding of the deeper, richer meanings taught in the scriptures.

To gain eternal life is to be a king and a priest to God; to be a member of the Church of the Firstborn, to be a joint-heir with Christ in inheriting all that the Father has, to be after the order of Enoch, to be gods, even the sons of God, to overcome all things, to dwell in the presence of God and his Christ forever and ever, to come with Christ when he shall come in the clouds of heaven to reign on the earth over his people, to come forth in the first resurrection, to have their names written in heaven, where God and Christ are the judge of all, to have bodies that are celestial, "whose glory is that of the sun, even the glory of God, the highest of all, whose glory the sun in the firmament is written of as being typical" (D&C 76:70; see also JST, Revelation 1:6; D&C 76:50-70 for characteristics of beings who inherit eternal life).

Succinctly stated, to receive eternal life is to be with God, to be like God, and to do the kinds of things that Gods do. Eternal life is the greatest of all the gifts of our Heavenly Father and is the principal goal of his great plan for our happiness. Eternal life is to receive the Lord's happy salutation, "Well done, thou good and faithful servant: thou hast been faithful over a few things, I will make thee ruler over many things: enter thou into the joy of thy lord" (Matthew 25:21).

The promise is that if we keep commandments of the Lord and continue to receive light and knowledge, we will receive the gift of eternal life (see D&C 93:27-28). Latter-day scriptures attest to the idea that even Jesus, himself, did not receive a fulness at first, but received, we are told, "grace for grace" (D&C 93:12). After explaining this progressive development of Jesus, the Lord are promises us that "if you keep my commandments you shall receive of his fulness, and be gloried in me as I am in the Father; therefore, I say unto you, you shall receive grace for grace" (D&C 93:20).

So we learn that the wonderful, incomprehensible blessings of eternal life are not be gained in one giant step of righteousness. The Prophet Joseph explained, "we consider that [eternal life] is a station to which no man ever arrived in a moment: he must have been instructed in the government and laws of that kingdom by proper degrees, *until his mind is capable in some measure of comprehending the propriety, justice, equality, and consistency of the same.*"[5]

In our quest to comprehend these things, the Lord has promised that he will lead us along. He is our tender tutor and will "teach [us] all that [we] must do to live with him someday."[6] All that he requires is that we seek him with a broken heart and contrite spirit, and that we be willing to stretch ourselves—our minds and hearts—to comprehend and obey the glorious truths he has for us to learn.

STRETCHING OUR MINDS TO COMPREHEND

In order to understand the truths that the Lord is willing to reveal to us when we seek them, we must first be prepared to receive them. This preparation involves stretching our minds beyond the confines and constraints of our fallen world. As was the case with the Saints in the Prophet Joseph Smith's day, so it is with us—the world is still too much with us.

In speaking to the Saints of his day, Joseph stated, "How vain and trifling have been our spirits, our conferences, our councils, our meetings, our private as well as public conversations—too low, too mean, too vulgar, too condescending for the dignified characters of the called and chosen of God, according to the purposes of His will, from before the foundation of the world! We are called to hold the keys of the mysteries of those things that have been kept hid from the foundation of the world until now. Some have tasted a little of these things, many of which are to be poured down from heaven upon the heads of babes; yea, upon the weak, obscure and despised ones of the earth.[7]

Continuing, Joseph charged the Saints to stretch their minds that they might be able to call down and to comprehend what our Father has to reveal to them. He said: "The things of God are of deep import; and time, and experience, and careful and ponderous and solemn thoughts can only find them out. *Thy mind, O man! if thou wilt lead a soul unto salvation, must stretch as high as the utmost heavens, and search into and contemplate the darkest abyss, and the broad expanse of eternity—thou must commune with God."[8]

GOD WAS ONCE AS WE ARE NOW

From the very first accounts of his first vision to his final sermon in the grove near Nauvoo, the Prophet Joseph testified of the nature and character of the God we worship. The knowledge given through our latter-day seer, has swept away (for the believers) in one fell swoop, the cobwebs of the Middle Ages, the dark millennium. Joseph disclosed many important truths about our Heavenly Father—including how he came to be God and how we, as his literal children, may become even as he is. Joseph Smith's knowledge on this subject was ever expanding.

In April of 1844 the Prophet Joseph Smith delivered what is perhaps his most important public sermon regarding our Heavenly Father and our relationship to him. This discourse has become known as the King Follett Discourse—two months after he had given this sermon, Joseph the prophet was martyred.

The occasion of the sermon was the funeral service for Elder King Follett, who was crushed by a tub of falling rocks while he was digging a well in Nauvoo. In this unparalleled speech, Joseph revealed magnificent truths about the nature of God—truths that had been hidden for centuries.

At the beginning of the discourse, Joseph Smith establishes the thesis for his presentation. He declared, *"If men do not comprehend the character of God, they do not comprehend themselves"*[9] Here, Joseph Smith is explaining that if we do not understand the nature of God, we do not understand ourselves because we are the *offspring* of God and he is our *Father*. Unless we understand the character of God, we would neither understand our own origins nor our own destiny.

Joseph Smith expands our minds as he continued: *"God himself was once as we are now, and is an exalted man, and sits enthroned in yonder heavens! That is the great secret"*[10] (see end of chapter Figure 12-A, As Man Now Is, God Once Was).

Continuing, Joseph explained further: "If the veil were rent today, and the great God who holds this world in its orbit, and who upholds all worlds and all things by his power, was to make himself visible—I say, *if you were to see him today, you would see him like a man in form—like yourselves in all the person, image, and very form as a man;* for Adam was created in the very fashion, image and likeness of God, and received instruction from, and walked, talked and conversed with him, as one man talks and communes with another."[11]

The Prophet then declared: *"I am going to tell you how God came to be God.* We have imagined and supposed that God was God from all eternity. I will refute that idea, and take away the veil so that you may see. . . . *He was once a man like us: yea, that God himself, the Father of us all, dwelt on an earth,* . . . and I will show it from the Bible."[12]

Joseph Smith was not dependent on the Bible for his knowledge of these eternal verities, nor was he dependent on any other man's testimony for his knowledge of this sacred information. The heavens had been opened to him, and he knew these truths for himself. He delighted, however, in identifying passages from the Bible that affirmed his teachings.

Joseph then went on to declare "What did Jesus say? ...The Scriptures inform us that Jesus said, As the Father hath power in Himself, even so hath the Son power—to do what? Why, what the Father did. The answer is obvious—in a manner to lay down His body and take it up again. Jesus, what are you going to do? To lay down my life as my Father did, and take it up again."[13]

Elder Joseph Fielding Smith, who compiled the book, *Teachings of the Prophet Joseph Smith,* inserted a footnote at this point that further clarifies the doctrinal point that the Prophet was making.[14] The note has reference to John 5:19 which states that "The Son can do nothing of himself, but what he seeth the Father do; for what things soever he [the Father] doeth, these also doeth the Son likewise." From the statement of the Prophet and this scripture, we can understand that Jesus followed the same steps that he had seen his Father follow. His Father obtained a body of flesh and blood which he later laid down and which finally was resurrected. The tracks of the Father provided the pathway for the Son and all of us to follow. Jesus became—and each of us seeks to become—even as our holy Father who dwells in the celestial heavens.

As God Now is, Man May Become

Joseph Smith not only witnessed that our Heavenly Father was once upon an earth like this, but he also testified that we, the children of God, can advance to the station of godhood ourselves. The Prophet Joseph Smith revealed that we can, indeed, become like our Heavenly Parents. This single doctrine separates us more from the rest of the Christian world as no other that could be mentioned. Many Christians are offended by the notion that we can become like God. They think it blasphemous to entertain such an idea. Metaphorically speaking they ask, How can a pot ever become like the potter?

In reality this doctrinal truth is perhaps the greatest mystery ever revealed to us here on the earth. In pure and simple words the Prophet is proclaiming to the world that, "Here, then, is eternal life—to know the only wise and true God; and *you have got to learn how to be Gods yourselves,* and to be kings and priests to God, *the same as all Gods have done before you;* namely by going from one small degree to another, and from a small capacity to a great one; from grace to grace, from exaltation to exaltation, until you attain to the resurrection of the dead, and are able to dwell in everlasting burnings, and to sit in glory, as do those who sit enthroned in everlasting power"[15] (See end of chapter Figure 12-B, As God Now Is, Man May Become).

What we learn through this marvelous King Follett discourse is that through the principles and ordinances of the gospel of Jesus Christ—the everlasting covenant, the great and eternal plan of happiness—we can advance to a point where we can be like our Heavenly Parents and enjoy a fulness of the glory, joy, power, intelligence, and love that they and all other exalted beings have obtained. But as we have said before this progress, this learning, and this advancement is a gradual process. It began in the premortal life, continues here, and will be greatly accelerated beyond the grave and especially so after the Resurrection—until we reach the position of godhood, the same as all other gods who have attained their exaltation before us.

Continuing his sermon, Joseph Smith explained that the revealed knowledge of the character of God and our relationship to him can console our sorrowful and broken hearts at the time of death of loved ones. He declared:

These are the first principles of consolation. How consoling to the mourners when they are called to part with a husband, wife, father, mother, child, or dear relative [such as those loved ones of Elder King Follett], to know that, although the earthly tabernacle is laid down and dissolved, they shall rise again to dwell in everlasting burnings in immortal glory, not to sorrow, suffer, or die anymore, but they shall be heirs of God and joint heirs with Jesus Christ.... To inherit the same power, the same glory and the same exaltation, *until you arrive at the station of a God,* and ascend the throne of eternal power, the same as those who have gone before. What did Jesus do? Why; I do the things I saw my Father do when worlds came rolling into existence. *My Father worked out his kingdom with fear and trembling,* and I must do the same; and when I get my kingdom, I shall present it to my Father, so that he may obtain kingdom upon kingdom, and it will exalt him in glory. He will then take a higher exaltation, and I will take his place, and thereby become exalted myself. So that Jesus treads in the tracks of his father, and inherits what God did before, and God is thus glorified and exalted in the salvation and exaltation of all his children. It is plain beyond disputation, and you thus learn some of the first principles of the Gospel, about which so much hath been said.

When you climb up a ladder, you must begin at the bottom, and ascend step by step, until you arrive at the top; and so it is with the principles of the Gospel—you must begin with the first, and go on until you learn all the principles of exaltation. But it will a great while after you have passed through the veil before you will have learned them. It is not all to be comprehended in this world; it will a great work to learn our salvation and exaltation even beyond the grave.[16]

Through the scriptures and through magnificent discourses such as this King Follett sermon, members of the Church can know of these soul satisfying, eternal doctrines and principles. As we have discussed in earlier chapters, these truths were also known by righteous men and women who proceeded us in former dispensations. Adam, Enoch, Noah, and Abraham along with many of the Saints in former dispensations understood the principles of the new and everlasting covenant, the true nature of their God and their relationship to him.

Again, it would be difficult to overly emphasize the idea that exaltation involves a gradual process of learning and growing and that it is not all be accomplished in this life. We are assured, however, that persistent diligence and dedication in this life will pay great dividends in the world to come. Accordingly, we read that "Whatever principle of intelligence we attain unto in this life, it will rise with us in the resurrection. And if a person gains more knowledge and intelligence in this life through his diligence and obedience than another, he will have so much the advantage in the world to come" (D&C 130:18-19).

In order to obtain the knowledge that we need to attain our exaltation, the Lord has given members of the Church a precious gift, the gift of the Holy Ghost, whereby we may know the truth of all things. Through the power of the Holy Ghost and the principle of personal revelation, we can come to know for ourselves the truths that the Prophet taught, as others have before us. Lorenzo Snow, for example, had unveiled to him our true nature as children of God. Long before Joseph Smith ever publicly taught it, it was made known to him by the spirit of revelation that he could become like his Heavenly Father.

LORENZO SNOW LEARNED OF HIS ETERNAL POTENTIAL

Lorenzo Snow, who became the fifth President of the Church, had a mind and heart that searched the deep things of God. Early in his life the Lord revealed to him that through Jesus Christ we can advance along the gospel pathway to the point where we become like our Heavenly Parents.

In Kirtland, Ohio, before he was even a member of the Church, Lorenzo met the father of the Prophet Joseph Smith—Joseph Smith, Sr., the first patriarch to the Church—who promised the young Lorenzo, "You will soon be convinced of the truth of the latter-day work, and be baptized, and you will become as great as you can possibly wish—*even as great as God,* and you cannot wish to be greater."[17]

What a remarkable promise! It must have astonished the young man and awakened thoughts in his mind of which he had never before dreamed. Two weeks later, in June, 1836, at the age of twenty-two, he was baptized by Apostle John Boynton. Four years later, in the spring of 1840, just before leaving on his first mission to England, Lorenzo had the following personal revelation that clarified Father Smith's mysterious saying: "The Spirit of the Lord rested mightily upon me—the eyes of my understanding were opened, and I saw as clear as the sun at noonday, with wonder and astonishment, the pathway of God and man. I formed the following couplet which expresses the revelation, as it was shown to me, and explains Father Smith's dark saying to me at a blessing meeting in the Kirtland temple, prior to my baptism, as previously mentioned in my first interview with the Patriarch: *'As Man now is, God once was; and as God is, man may be.'"*[18]

At first, Lorenzo Snow shared this revelation with no one except his sister Eliza. Then he privately related it to Brigham Young, who wisely told him: "Brother Snow that is a new doctrine; if true, it has been revealed to you for your own private information, and will be taught in due time by the Prophet to the

Church; till then I advise you to lay it upon the shelf and say no more about it."[19]

Soon after his return from England, in January, 1843, in a confidential interview in Nauvoo, Lorenzo Snow related to the Prophet Joseph Smith what had been revealed to him. The Prophet's reply was: "Brother Snow, that is true gospel doctrine, and it is a revelation from God to you."[20]

However, even with the prophet's private confirmation, Lorenzo did not discuss his revelation until the Prophet Joseph Smith had delivered the King Follett discourse and taught the same doctrine publicly for the first time. Thereafter, Lorenzo Snow felt free to teach it.

This principle of personal revelation is very much active in the Church today. The Lord is constantly revealing truths to his children who seek after further light and truth. However, they are counseled by the Spirit and the prophets that they must keep these sacred truths to themselves and not reveal them to others (see Alma 12:9). *When* the Lord's mouthpiece, he who stands at the head of the Church, formally announces the doctrine, then others would be free to teach the same principles involved.

It was not until the year 1892, many years after receiving his initial revelation regarding his and our divine destiny, that President Snow wrote these words: "Let this mind be in you, which was also in Christ Jesus, who, being in the form of God, thought it not robbery to be equal with God" (Philippians 2:5, 6). Then, in rhymed couplets he wrote these now famous lines:

Has thou not been unwisely bold,
Man's destiny to thus unfold?
To raise, promote such high desire,
Such vast ambition thus inspire?

Still, 'tis no phantom that we trace
Man's ultimatum in life's race;
This royal path has long been trod
By righteous men, each now a God:

As Abra'm, Isaac, Jacob, too,
First babes, then men—to gods they grew.
As man now is, our God once was;
As now God is, so man may be,—
Which doth unfold man's destiny.

The boy, like to his father grown,
Has but attained unto his own;
To grow to sire from state of son,
Is not 'gainst Nature's course to run.

A son of God, like God to be,
Would not be robbing Deity;
And he who has this hope within,
Will purify himself from sin.

You're right, St. John, supremely right;
Whoe'er essays to climb this height,
Will cleanse himself of sin entire—
Or else 'twere needless to aspire.[21]

I love the words of this poem that so beautifully pinpoint our own destiny as children of God. As God's children we can indeed become like him as we receive gospel covenants and remain true and faithful to the end of our mortal probation. If we prove to faithful not only will become even as our Father is, but also we can inherit all that the Father possesses.

INHERITING ALL THAT THE FATHER HAS

The scriptures are replete with passages explaining that those who gain their exaltation receive all that the Father has. One scripture that addresses this doctrine directly is found in the oath and covenant of the priesthood. Speaking of those who receive and honor the Melchizedek Priesthood, the Lord promises:

> For whoso is faithful unto the obtaining these two priesthoods of which I have spoken, and the magnifying their calling, are sanctified by the Spirit unto the renewing of their bodies.
> They become the sons of Moses and of Aaron and the seed of Abraham, and the church and kingdom, and the elect of God.
> And also all they who receive this priesthood receive me, saith the Lord;
> For he that receiveth my servants receiveth me;
> And he that receiveth me receiveth my Father;
> *And he that receiveth my Father receiveth my Father's kingdom; therefore all that my Father hath shall be given unto him.*
> And this is according to the oath and covenant which belongeth to the priesthood (D&C 84:33-39; emphasis added).

Briefly, this passage is saying that men who are willing to receive the Melchizedek Priesthood and magnify their callings in due time will be sanctified and receive all that the Father has. Just what does our Heavenly Father have— what is it that we can receive if we prove faithful?

On some clear night, when the stars are bright, you go out and look up into the heavens and contemplate the answer to this question. Although our mortal minds cannot even begin to grasp what is involved here, we know from the revelations that inheriting all our Father has has to do with a fulness of power, truth, light, glory, intelligence, knowledge, and love. It also involves receiving from him the eternal power to create worlds and to procreate lives.

As has been stated earlier, Jesus receives, as the natural heir, all that the Father possesses (see Hebrews 1:1-2). We are promised that through our Savior's love and mercy and our own obedience, we may become "joint-heirs with Christ" (Romans 8:17; also Galatians 4:7) and inherit, when we prove faithful, all that the Father has. For example, consider the following:

The Father Possesses the Power of Creation

Biblical passages indicate that all things were created by the Father through Christ. Of this truth Paul testified to the Hebrews, "God . . . hath in these last days spoken unto us by his Son, whom he hath appointed heir of all things, *by whom also he made the worlds*" (Hebrews 1:1-2; emphasis added). Modern scriptures affirm the fact that under the direction of the Father, Jesus was the creator of all things. From latter-day scriptures we read,

> And it came to pass that Moses looked, and beheld the world upon which he was created; and Moses beheld the world and the ends thereof, and all the children of men which are, and which were created; of the same he greatly marveled and wondered.... And behold, the glory of the Lord was upon Moses, so that Moses stood in the presence of God, and talked with him face to face. And the Lord God said unto Moses: For mine own purpose have I made these things. Here is wisdom and it remaineth in me. *And by the word of my power, have I created them, which is mine Only Begotten Son,* who is full of grace and truth.
>
> And worlds without number have I created; and I also created them for mine own purpose; and *by the Son I created them,* which is mine Only Begotten (Moses 1:8, 31-33; emphasis added).

From these passages we learn that the word of God's power of creation is through his "Only Begotten Son, who is full of grace and truth". Referring to the power of creation inherent in the Only Begotten, the Lord revealed to the Prophet Joseph Smith: "This is the light of Christ. As also he is in the sun, and the light of the sun, and the power thereof by which it was made. As also he is in the moon, and is the light of the moon, and the power thereof by which it was made; As also the light of the stars, and the power thereof by which they were made; And the earth also, and the power thereof, even the earth upon which you stand" (D&C 88:7-10).

Since the promise is given that the faithful will inherit all that the Father has, part of the inheritance would include the powers of creation as we have just discussed.

Yet another of the characteristics of our Father, one that the faithful will inherit, is the power of eternal lives—the power of eternal increase.

The Father Possesses the Power of Eternal Increase

As we have established above, our Heavenly Father and Mother are our literal parents. We were begotten of them in the world of spirits through the glorious eternal process of procreation. Again, in the flesh we are the children of Adam and Eve who were the children of God (see Luke 3:38). As Gods our Heavenly Parents will continue to bear children throughout eternities. Such a course is their work and glory. The Prophet Joseph Smith explained their commitment to us in these words:

> The first principles of man are self-existent with God. God himself, finding he was in the midst of spirits and glory, because he was more intelligent, saw proper to institute laws whereby the rest could have a privilege to advance like himself. The relationship we have with God places us in a situation to advance in knowledge. He has power to institute laws to instruct the weaker intelligences, that they may be exalted with himself, so that they might have one glory upon another, and all that knowledge, power, glory, and intelligence, which is requisite in order to save them in the world of spirits.
>
> This is good doctrine. It tastes good. I can taste the principles of eternal life, and so can you. They are given to me by the revelations of Jesus Christ; and I know that when I tell you these words of eternal life as they are given to me, you taste them, and I know that you believe them. You say honey is sweet, and so do I. I can also taste the spirit of eternal life. I know it is good; and when I tell you of these things which were given my by inspiration of the Holy Spirit, you are bound to receive them as sweet, and rejoice more and more.[22]

The doctrine that we can be exalted with God truly is sweet to the pure in heart who receive such truths without argument. The chance to become exalted is promised the faithful as part of the everlasting gospel covenant. Of this power that our Father and Mother possess and that we may one day also receive, Elder Melvin J. Ballard taught:

> Through the righteousness and faithfulness of men and women who keep the commandments of God they will come forth with celestial bodies, fitted and prepared to enter into their great, high and eternal glory in the celestial kingdom of God; and unto them, through their preparation, there will come spirit children. . . .

When the power of endless increase shall come to us, and our offspring grow and multiply through ages that shall come, they will be in due time, as we have been, provided with an earth like this wherein they too may obtain earthly bodies and pass through all the experiences through which we have passed. . . .We shall stand in our relationship to them as God our Eternal Father does to us, and thereby this is the most glorious and wonderful privilege that ever will come to any of the sons and daughters of God.[23]

This "most glorious and wonderful privilege" will be granted to all who qualify themselves for it by complying with the terms of the new and everlasting covenant of marriage. Latter-day revelation makes this clear:

In the celestial glory there are three heavens or degrees; And in order to obtain the *highest*, a man must enter into this order of the priesthood [meaning the new and everlasting covenant of *marriage*]; And if he does not, he cannot obtain it. He may enter into the other, but that is the *end of his kingdom; he cannot have an increase* (D&C 131:1-4; emphasis added).

On the other hand, reflecting the positive side of the doctrine, all those who *do* enter into this covenant and are sealed by the Holy Spirit of Promise, shall inherit all that the Father has, including the power of eternal lives, eternal increase. Power will be given to bear children in the eternities, to people other worlds the same as all the gods before them. Regarding this awesome promise, we read again from the Doctrine and Covenants:

And again, verily I say unto you, if a man marry a wife by my word, which is my law, and by the new and everlasting covenant, *and it is sealed unto them by the Holy Spirit of promise, by him who is anointed,* unto whom I have appointed this power and the keys of this priesthood; *and it shall be said unto them—Ye shall come forth in the first resurrection* ... it shall be done unto them in all things whatsoever my servant hath put upon them, in time and through all eternity; and shall be of full force when they are out of the world; and they shall pass by the angels, and the gods, which are set there, to their exaltation and glory in all things, as hath been sealed upon their heads, which glory shall be a fulness and *a continuation of the seeds forever and ever.*
Then shall they be gods, because they have no end; therefore shall they be from everlasting to everlasting, because they continue; then shall they be above all, because all things are subject unto them. *Then shall they be gods,* because they have all power, and the angels are subject unto them.... This is eternal *lives*—to know the only wise and true God, and Jesus Christ, whom he hath sent. I am he. Receive ye, therefore, my law (D&C 132:19-20, 24; emphasis added).

Not only will those who receive and obey the Lord's law receive the power of eternal lives, but they will also receive the power to dwell in his presence in the midst of everlasting burnings.

The Father Has Power to Dwell In Everlasting Burnings

When I was a child, I thought the bad people would be the ones who would go to everlasting burnings. And I had pictures in my mind of people burning in flames like I saw in the sky when Young's gasoline station caught fire. It wasn't until my later years that I discovered that it is the *righteous* who will dwell in everlasting burnings, or that the magnificent glory of God is like everlasting fire.

In the King Follett funeral sermon, Joseph Smith affirmed: "You have got to learn how to be Gods yourselves ... by going from one small degree to another, and from a small capacity to a great one; from grace to grace, from exaltation to exaltation, *until you attain to the resurrection of the dead, and are able to dwell in everlasting burnings,* and to sit in glory, as do those who sit enthroned in everlasting power."[24]

In the same sermon, Joseph Smith reminded us that at death the bodies of our loved ones are laid down and dissolved, but we are promised that *"they shall rise again to dwell in everlasting burnings in immortal glory,* not to sorrow, suffer, or die any more; but they shall be heirs of God and joint heirs with Jesus Christ."[25]

The gospel prepares us to dwell in such glory—which the prophets tell us has much to do with intense joy and sublime love. In one account of the First Vision, Joseph Smith speaks of the joy he felt as the glory of the Lord fell upon him in the Sacred Grove. He said, "A pillar of fire appeared above my head; which presently rested down upon me, and *filled me with unspeakable joy.* A personage appeared in the midst of this pillar of flame, which was spread all round and yet nothing consumed. Another personage soon appeared like unto the first: he said unto me thy sins are forgiven thee. He testified also unto me that Jesus Christ is the son of God. I saw many angels in this vision. I was about 14 years old when I received this first communication..."[26]

Accordingly, we see that the faithful will inherit all that the Father has, including, as we have read in this section, the power to dwell in everlasting burnings, the fire of God's love and glory—his unspeakable *joy!*

The powers we have discussed in this section are general descriptions of the blessings of those who gain eternal life. In the book of Revelation however, John the Revelator explains in greater detail the blessings and powers associated with eternal life.

THE WONDROUS POWERS OF
THOSE WHO OVERCOME

After being shown in vision the blessings and powers of those who overcome the world, John the Revelator, described nine gifts that are associated with eternal life. These magnificent blessings and powers are as follows:

1) "To him that overcometh *will I give to eat of the tree of life,* which is in the midst of the paradise of God" (Revelation 2:7; emphasis added). This promise has two possible meanings. It may be a figurative expression describing the joy felt by people such as Lehi and Nephi when they understand the condescension of God—in sending his only Begotten Son to die for the sins of the world (see 1 Nephi 8:10; 11:25; 15:36). It may also relate to a real tree from which we will eat and receive life-giving nourishment much like Adam and Eve did in the garden of Eden (see Genesis 2:9; see footnote 9c).

2) "He that overcometh *shall not be hurt of the second death*" (Revelation 2:11; emphasis added). Satan and his angels and those who become sons of perdition in this estate will experience a second death in the sense that they will be cast out forever from the presence of God. This will take place after the Millennium is over (see Rev. 20:14; Alma 12:16-18; Helaman 14: 16-19; D&C 76:36-37).

3) "To him that overcometh *will I give to eat of the hidden manna, and will give him a white stone, and in the stone a new name written, which no man knoweth saving he that receiveth it*" (Revelation 2:17; emphasis added). Physical manna was given to the children of Israel in the wilderness. It was food for physical bodies. Hidden manna has to do with revelation—light and knowledge about the mysteries of God—given to those who inherit the celestial kingdom. Regarding the light and knowledge they will receive, we read:

> The place where God resides is a great Urim and Thummim.
> This earth, in its sanctified and immortal state, will be made like unto crystal and will be a Urim and Thummim to the inhabitants who dwell thereon, whereby *all things pertaining to an inferior kingdom or all kingdoms of a lower order, will be manifest to those who dwell on it;* and this earth will be Christ's.
> Then the white stone, mentioned in Revelation 2:17, will become a Urim and Thummim to each individual who receives one, whereby things pertaining to a higher order of kingdoms will be made known;
> And a white stone is given to each of those who come into the celestial kingdom, whereon is a new name written, which no man knoweth save he that receiveth it. The new name is the key word (D&C 130:8-11).

4) "And to him that overcometh, and keepeth my commandments unto the end, *will I give power over many kingdoms;* And he shall rule them with the word of God; and they shall be in his hands as the vessels of clay in the hands of a potter; and he shall govern them by faith, with equity and justice, even as I received of my Father." (JST Revelation 2:26-27; emphasis added). The ideas expressed in this statement have to do with the blessings of eternal life and the power exalted beings have over their own posterity. They will preside over, enlarge, and protect an ever expanding posterity that will consist of many nations throughout the eternities. This quotation may also have reference to powers given the Saints when Zion is established and when the Millennium is ushered in. (See Chapter 9, "Preparing a Righteous People;" also JST Genesis 14:30-31; 3 Nephi 16:14-15; 20:16-19; 21:12-19; Moses 1:25; Helaman 10:4-10; Jacob 4:4-6; D&C 45:65-70; D&C 105:29-31; Joel 2; Psalms 2; Mormon 5:22-24).

5) "He that overcometh, *the same shall be clothed in white raiment.*" (Revelation 3:5; emphasis added; see also J.S.—History 1:30-32; D&C 110:1-4). White raiment is symbolic of sanctification and may also have reference to real clothing of light which will be given to those who inherit eternal life. When Moroni appeared to the Prophet Joseph Smith, he was clothed in similar attire. Joseph gave a lengthy description of Moroni and his brilliantly white clothing which is recorded in the Pearl of Great Price, J.S.—History 1:30-32.

6) "*I will not blot out his name out of the book of life,* but I will confess his name before my Father, and before his angels" (Revelation 3:5; emphasis added). Those who have their calling and election made sure are promised they will not have their names blotted out of the Lamb's book of life. This means that those who are sealed and continue faithful will indeed receive their exaltation and eternal life. Once they have overcome, they will not fall (See also 2 Peter 1:10; D&C 132:19).

7) "Him that overcometh will I make a pillar in the temple of my God, and *he shall go no more out*" (Revelation 3:12). This life is the time of our probation. This is the day of our labors in the Lord's vineyard. After the pure in heart gain a celestial resurrection, they will enter into the rest of the Lord and go no more out to labor in a probationary period in a fallen world. Their rest will be eternal and glorious (see 3 Nephi 28:40).

8) "*I will write upon him the name of my God*" (Revelation 3:12; emphasis added). The name of God is God. The faithful will receive the title of God themselves. They will be among the Elohim—the Gods. More will be said of this later when we discuss Joseph's sermon on the plurality of the Gods (see Revelation 1:6; 5:10; 14:1).

9) "To him that overcometh *will I grant to sit with me in my throne,* even as I also overcame, and am set down with my Father in his throne (see Revelation 3:21; emphasis added). As Jesus inherits all that the Father has, so the faithful

will sit down with Christ as joint-heirs and will inherit with our Savior all that the Father has.

These are just a few of the gifts that those who are faithful will receive when they inherit all that our Father in Heaven has prepared for them. The bestowal and receipt of these blessings follows a pattern—one which has been followed by all who have gone before us who have become Gods. This pattern involves learning about, receiving, and living the principles of the eternal plan of happiness. As we follow this pathway, we too will become Gods—even as our Father and all those who have gone before him.

THE PLURALITY OF THE GODS

The powerful King Follett sermon that we discussed earlier was given by the Prophet Joseph Smith about two months before his martyrdom. Just eleven days before his death, he delivered his final public sermon in the Grove east of the temple in Nauvoo. His subject was the plurality of the Gods—a sermon that caused the pure in heart to rejoice exceedingly and caused the impure in heart to call him a fallen prophet and seek his life. In this sermon, Joseph disclosed what he called strong doctrine.

For months he had been verbally attacked by apostates in the Church who ridiculed him for teaching such doctrines as plural marriage and the plurality of the Gods, and for declaring that he had the power to seal people to eternal life. In defense of his prophetic calling, "President Joseph Smith read the 3rd chapter of Revelation, and took for his text 1st chapter, 6th verse— 'And hath made us kings and priests unto God and *His Father:* to Him be glory and dominion forever and ever. Amen.'"[27] Of this passage, the Prophet declared:

> It is altogether correct in the translation.... I will preach on the plurality of Gods.... When I have preached on the subject of the Deity, it has been the plurality of Gods. It has been preached by the Elders for fifteen years.
>
> I have always declared God to be a distinct personage, Jesus Christ a separate and distinct personage from God the Father, and that the Holy Ghost was a distinct personage and a Spirit: and these three constitute three distinct personages and three Gods. If this is in accordance with the New Testament, lo and behold! we have three Gods anyhow, and they are plural; and who can contradict it? Our text says, "And hath made us kings and priests unto God and *His Father.*" *The Apostles have discovered that there were Gods above, for John says God was the Father of our Lord Jesus Christ.* My object was to preach the scriptures, and preach the doctrine they contain, *there being a God above, the Father of our Lord Jesus Christ.* I am

bold to declare I have taught all the strong doctrines publicly, and always teach stronger doctrines in public than in private....

In the very beginning the Bible shows there is a plurality of Gods beyond the power of refutation. It is a great subject I am dwelling on. The world *Eloheim* ought to be in the plural all the way through—Gods. *The heads of the Gods appointed one God for us;* and when you take [that] view of the subject, it sets one free to see all the beauty, holiness and perfection the Gods. All I want is to get the simple, naked truth, and the whole truth.[28]

Space considerations do not allow the whole sermon to be printed here, but for the spiritually motivated reader, it would be well to read the whole sermon in context. At the conclusion of his sermon on the plurality of the Gods, Joseph Smith made reference to Jesus Christ's great High Priest's prayer—in which he prayed that his disciples might be one as he and his father were *one*—Joseph explained that the Hebrew expression "one" should be translated "agreed." Prophet explained that the prayer should read:

"Father, I pray for them which Thou hast given me out of the world, and not for those alone, but for them also which shall believe on me through their word, that they all may be *agreed,* as Thou, Father, are with me, and I with Thee, that they also may be *agreed* with us," and all come to dwell in unity, and in all the glory and everlasting burnings of the Gods; and then we shall see as we are seen, and be as our God and He as His Father. I want to reason a little on this subject. I learned it by translating the papyrus which is now in my house. . . .

If Abraham reasoned thus—If Jesus Christ was the Son of God, and John discovered that *God the Father of Jesus Christ had a Father,* you may suppose that *He had a Father also.* Where was there ever a son without a father? And where was there ever a father without first being a son? Whenever did a tree or anything spring into existence without a progenitor? *And everything comes in this way.* Paul says that which is earthly is in the likeness of that which is heavenly, Hence if Jesus had a Father, can we not believe that He had a Father also? I despise the idea of being scared to death at such a doctrine, for the Bible is full of it....

These Scriptures are a mixture of very strange doctrines to the Christian world, who are blindly led by the blind....

John said he was a king. "And from Jesus Christ, who is the faithful witness, and the first begotten of the dead, and the Prince of the kings of the earth. Unto Him that loved us, and washed us from our sins in His own blood, and *hath made us kings and priests unto God, and His Father*"... [See end of chapter Figure 12-D, Orson Hyde's Explanation of *The Patriarchal Chain of Gods.*][29]

So, from this marvelous sermon we can see that as children of God we belong to an eternal family chain of Gods. This eternal chain which reaches into the far distant past, will extend into the eternal future as we grow, progress and eventually attain to the station of godhood and receive the power of eternal procreation or the power of endless lives—and are bound together patriarchal priesthood organizations. Ever expanding eternal glorious family units—involving a plurality of the Gods—is the very key to our Father's work and glory, which is to bring to pass our immortality and eternal life. Those who keep their second estate, who fulfill the requirement of the everlasting covenant, will "have glory added upon their heads forever and ever" (Abraham 3:26).

THE GREAT PLAN OF HAPPINESS CONSISTS OF BEING ADDED UPON FOREVER

So impressed am I with the wonderful flood of light, knowledge, and truth presented by the Prophet Joseph Smith during his last public sermons regarding the character of God and our potential to become like him, along with the notion of the plurality of the Gods, and our being added upon forever, I have seriously entertained the idea of having written upon the my grave stone, these succinct words: "The Great Plan of Happiness Consists of Being Added Upon Forever."

This expression carries the central message of the gospel of Jesus Christ—families can be forever. Our Lord and our Savior, Jesus Christ provided the perfect *example* for us to follow including the covenants of baptism, receiving the Holy Ghost, receiving the Melchizedek Priesthood, and all of the sacred temple ordinances. Jesus also provided the power by which we, as the sons and daughters of God, can overcome the effects of the Fall and of our own sins by complying with the conditions of the everlasting gospel covenant. Those who receive eternal life will have all the powers, glory, intelligence, and eternal increase as all the gods who have gone before them. How can we even begin to comprehend the vastness of our Father's eternal plan of happiness. Our minds cannot grasp in this finite world the eternal consequences of loving the Lord and keeping his commandments. William W. Phelps sought to describe the wonder of eternal things in an insightful and popular LDS hymn.

IF YOU COULD HIE TO KOLOB

William W. Phelps set to music some of the marvelous and infinite doctrines revealed through the Prophet Joseph Smith as part of the Restoration of all things.

The majesty of these eternal truths are expressed in these thought provoking lyrics:

If you could hie [hurry] to Kolob
In the twinkling of an eye,
And then continue onward
With that same speed to fly,
D'ye think that you could ever,
Through all eternity,
Find out the generation
Where Gods began to be?

Or see the grand beginning,
Where space did not extend?
Or view the last creation,
Where Gods and matter end?
Methinks the Spirit whispers,
"No man has found 'pure space',"
Nor seen the outside curtains,
Where nothing has a place.

The works of God continue,
And worlds and lives abound;
Improvement and progression
Have one eternal round.
There is no end to matter;
There is no end to space;
There is no end to spirit;
There is no end to race.

There is no end to virtue;
There is no end to might;
There is no end to wisdom;
There is no end to light.
There is no end to union;
There is no end to youth;
There is no end to priesthood;
There is no end to truth.

There is no end to glory;
There is no end to love;

There is no end to being;
There is no death above.
There is no end to glory;
There is no end to love;
There is no end to being;
There is no death above.[30]

These phrases express the characteristics and perfections of our Heavenly Father and the environment in which he dwells—and they will be ours if we will receive the gift of eternal life that the Father and the Son have prepared and offered to us out of their great love for us.

MY TESTIMONY OF THESE THINGS

As I conclude this chapter and this book, I wish to express my witness to you of the things that I have written. My testimony is that the great and eternal plan of happiness, as I have tried to present it in this book, constitutes the doctrines of Christ as they have been restored to us through the Prophet Joseph Smith, through the ancient and modern scriptures, through the Holy Spirit, and through latter-day prophets. I trust that I have been accurate—true and faithful—in the content and manner in which I have presented these wonderful truths to you. My wish is that the gospel—the good news of Jesus Christ—will bring you greater happiness, even greater peace in this world and the incomprehensible joy of eternal life in the world to come.

I have come to know that Jesus Christ is the divine Son of our Heavenly Father. He is the Only Begotten of the Father in the flesh. He was the chosen Firstborn in that great premortal life, I have received this witness born of the Holy Spirit. I have heard the voice of the Holy Spirit many times, and it has helped me to know what to think, do, and say in many instances. Indeed, this book could never have been written without that quiet, encouraging spirit.

I know that through Jesus' atoning sacrifice and by way of priesthood ordinances, we can receive into our lives the refining and purifying influence of the Holy Spirit, and, through its direction, we can overcome the evils of this life, lose every desire for sin and eventually become sanctified. I know that the gospel of Jesus Christ is the only plan for us to receive peace in this world and eternal life in the world to come and that only by becoming pure in heart, being true and faithful, and receiving the holy priesthood ordinances can we come to know Christ. I long for a future day to come when I may be embraced by our Savior.

I know that Joseph Smith was divinely appointed to be the Prophet of this last dispensation. I rejoice in my knowledge that through observing the doctrines and principles taught by the Prophet, we can return to our Father in Heaven. I earnestly yearn for a time to come when I can shake hands and embrace "Brother Joseph"! As I continue to study his teachings, my yearnings for a closer relationship with him grow stronger.

I know that The Church of Jesus Christ of Latter-day Saints is the only true and living church upon the face of the earth. Only through the Church can the blessings of the everlasting covenant be administered to us, the children of God. Through the Church, latter-day Israel is gathered, instructed, perfected, and thus prepared to enter his holy presence. I am eternally grateful for my membership in the Church. I love my fellowship with the Saints.

My testimony is that all of the revelations, all of the commandments, all of the efforts of the Father, the Son, and the Holy Ghost are preparatory—they prepare us to receive "eternal lives" (D&C 132:24). Jesus performed his great atoning sacrifice so that man and woman and families could be together forever! I sense more strongly with the passage of time that the family is the central organization of the eternities. Through family relationships we can experience great learning and deep emotions. Through our families we can develop Christlike traits including the crowning traits of *faith, hope* and *charity.* I am grateful for a gospel that strengthens family units in this life and establishes, through priesthood ordinances, eternal family relationships in celestial realms. Is it any wonder that Satan is so active and so powerfully effective in wreaking havoc upon the families of the world? Being miserable himself, without family connections, he desires "the misery of all mankind" (2 Nephi 2:18). Satan does not want us to be together at the eternal family reunion dinner (see D&C 27:5-14). He will do anything possible to break up marriages, families, and the great plan of happiness which is so family centered.

I am grateful for a gospel that is logical and reasonable—one that embraces all truth. I am thankful for living prophets who seek and teach truth and manifest it in their lives.

I am convinced that all of us need to increase in our faith in the Lord Jesus Christ, which in turn will give us a greater hope in the promises of the gospel. Only as we develop a growing hope can we manifest a growing purity of love—true charity—in our relationships with one another. As this charity is manifest in our relationships with one another, we will then be made one in Christ, even as he is one or agreed with his Father, and we will experience great peace in this life and ever increasing happiness in the world to come.

My final testimony to you is best expressed by Mormon in his letter to his son, Moroni, in which he exhorted the followers of Christ regarding faith, hope and charity as was mentioned above. Mormon declared:

And again, my beloved brethren, I would speak unto you concerning hope. How is it that ye can attain unto faith, save ye shall have hope?

And what is it that ye shall hope for? Behold I say unto you that *ye shall have hope through the atonement of Christ and the power of his resurrection, to be raised unto life eternal, and this because of your faith in him according to the promise.*

Wherefore, if a man have faith he must needs have hope; for without faith there cannot be any hope.

And again, behold I say unto you that he cannot have faith and hope, save he shall be meek, and lowly of heart.

If so, his faith and hope is vain, for none is acceptable before God, save the meek and lowly in heart; and if a man be meek and lowly in heart and confesses by the power of the Holy Ghost that Jesus is the Christ, he must needs have charity; for if he have not charity he is nothing; wherefore he must needs have charity.

And charity suffereth long, and is kind, and envieth not, and is not puffed up, seeketh not her own, is not easily provoked, thinketh no evil, and rejoiceth not in iniquity but rejoiceth in the truth, beareth all things, believeth all things, hopeth all things, endureth all things.

Wherefore, my beloved brethren, if ye have not charity, ye are nothing, for charity never faileth. Wherefore, cleave unto charity, which is the greatest of all, for all things must fail—

But charity is the pure love of Christ, and it endureth forever; and whoso is found possessed of it at the last day, it shall be well with him.

Wherefore, my beloved brethren, *pray unto the Father with all the energy of heart, that ye may be filled with his love,* which he hath bestowed upon all who are true followers of his Son, Jesus Christ; that ye may become *the sons of God;* that when he shall appear we shall be like him, for we shall see him as he is; that we may have this hope; that we may be purified even as he is pure. Amen (Moroni 7:40-48; emphasis added).

If we will always retain in our minds and hearts these words of Mormon, we will truly have a hope in Christ, a joyful anticipation that the wonderful blessings associated with the everlasting covenant—LDS—will be realized. These promised blessings—an eternal promised *land* which will be this earth in its sanctified condition as a celestial sphere, *deliverance* from our enemies (death, hell, the devil and endless torment), and everlasting *seed*, which will consist of eternal families in the presence of our Heavenly Father with posterity as numerous as sands upon the sea shores or the stars in the heavens—will be ours as we increase in our knowledge and understanding of the gospel of Jesus Christ—our Father's great plan for our happiness.

The Lord has promised us that if we will be full of charity and if we will let virtue garnish our thoughts unceasingly, then shall "thy confidence wax strong in the presence of God; and the doctrine of the priesthood shall distill upon thy soul as the dews from heaven...and without compulsory means it shall flow unto thee forever and ever" (D&C 121:45-46). I know that when I follow this important counsel, the doctrines of the priesthood do indeed come to me without compulsion as the dews of heaven—and they cause my soul to sing the songs of his redeeming love.

I have come to know, through the spiritual dews of revelation from heaven, that we are the children of kind, loving Heavenly Parents. They are glorious and beautiful; they are perfect, holy, resurrected personages. Before we came into this world, we knew them and they knew us intimately. We are deeply loved by them. We are indeed their offspring; we are truly "sparks struck from the fire of their eternal blaze." I know that their desire is that we become as they are. They want us to experience the same joy and happiness they enjoy. This will come to us as we embrace with all our hearts the great plan of happiness, the everlasting covenant, the gospel of Jesus Christ.

May you and I continue to grow in the light of the gospel of Jesus Christ. May it warm our souls as we increase in our humility, our faith, our hope, and our charity. May we truly be faithful in all things so that we may enjoy eternal life— the fulness of the blessings of our Heavenly Father's great plan for our happiness which promises us *"peace* in this world, and *eternal life* in the world to come" (D&C 59:23).

May these words, and other wonderful gospel principles that are yet to be revealed, find a place in your mind, heart, and actions, so that you may find the answers to your most intimate prayers. The answers will come through the "good news" of the gospel of Jesus Christ—the eternal plan of happiness. Answers will come through the Holy Spirit that testifies of our Heavenly Father and his Almighty son, Jesus Christ, our Lord, our Savior—and our friend.

REFERENCES:

1 *Mediation and Atonement,* 164-165, Published in 1892; emphasis added.
2 *Millennial Star,* 56:772, October 5 1894; emphasis added.
3 *Improvement Era,* 13:81, November 1909; emphasis added.
4 *Mormon Doctrine,* 237; emphasis in the original.
5 *Teachings of the Prophet Joseph Smith,* 51.
6 *Hymns,* The Church of Jesus Christ of Latter-day Saints, 1985, #301.
7 *Teachings,* 137.
8 *Teachings,* 137; emphasis added.
9 *Teachings,* 343; emphasis added.
10 *Teachings,* 345; emphasis added.

11 *Teachings*, 345; emphasis added.
12 *Teachings*, 345-6; emphasis added.
13 *Teachings*, 346.
14 *Teachings*, 346.
15 *Teachings*, 346-47; emphasis added.
16 *Teachings*, 347-48; emphasis added.
17 *Biography and Family Record of Lorenzo Snow*, 10.
18 In Eliza R. Snow, *Biography and Family Record of Lorenzo Snow*, (Salt Lake City: Deseret News Company, printer, 1884) 7-10; emphasis added.
19 *Juvenile Instructor*, Jan. 1900, 4.
20 See LeRoi C. Snow, "Devotion to a Divine Inspiration," *Improvement Era*, Vol. 22, No. 8, June, 1919.
21 *Improvement Era*, 22:660, June, 1919; emphasis added.
22 *Teachings*, 354-355.
23 Elder Melvin J. Ballard, *Melvin J. Ballard, Crusader for Righteousness*, [Salt Lake City, Utah: Bookcraft, 1966] 211-212.
24 *Teachings*, 346-347.
25 *Teachings*, 347; emphasis added.
26 Mitton V. Backman, *Joseph Smith's First Vision*, (Salt Lake City: Bookcraft, 1980) 159.
27 *Teachings*, 369; emphasis added.
28 *Teachings*, 369-370, 372; emphasis added.
29 *Teachings*, 372-375; emphasis added.
30 *Hymns*, #284.

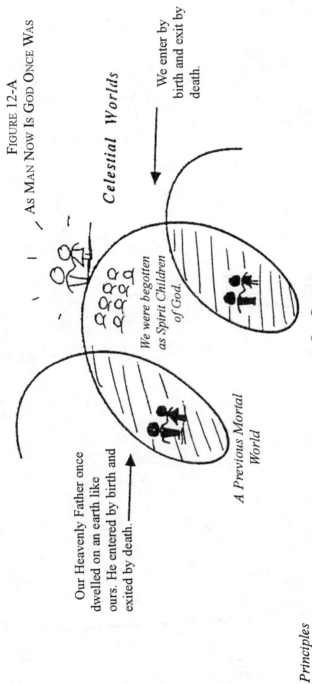

FIGURE 12-A
AS MAN NOW IS GOD ONCE WAS

Celestial Worlds

We enter by birth and exit by death.

We were begotten as Spirit Children of God.

A Previous Mortal World

Our Present Mortal Earth

Our Heavenly Father once dwelled on an earth like ours. He entered by birth and exited by death.

Principles

1. "God himself was once as we are now, and is an exalted man, and sits enthroned in yonder heavens! That is the great secret". *(Teachings, p. 345)*.
2. "I am going to tell you how God came to be God...he was once a man like us; year, that God himself, the Father of us all, dwelt on an earth... *(Teachings* pp. 345-346).

FIGURE 12-B
AS MAN NOW IS, MAN MAY BECOME

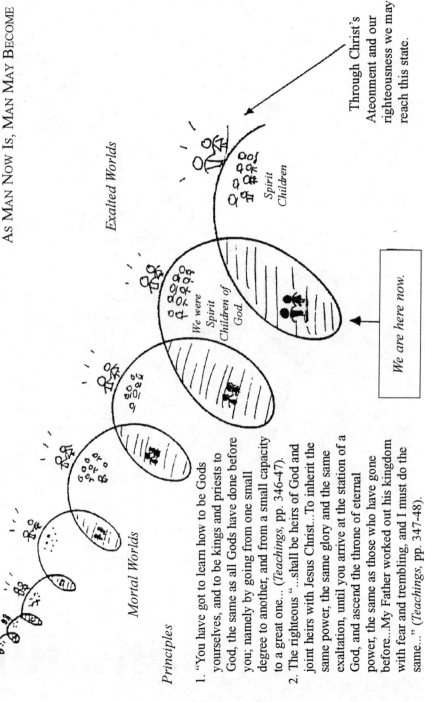

Through Christ's Atonement and our righteousness we may reach this state.

Exalted Worlds

Spirit Children

We were Spirit Children of God

We are here now.

Mortal Worlds

Principles

1. "You have got to learn how to be Gods yourselves, and to be kings and priests to God, the same as all Gods have done before you; namely by going from one small degree to another, and from a small capacity to a great one... (*Teachings*, pp. 346-47).

2. The righteous "...shall be heirs of God and joint heirs with Jesus Christ...To inherit the same power, the same glory and the same exaltation, until you arrive at the station of a God, and ascend the throne of eternal power, the same as those who have gone before...My Father worked out his kingdom with fear and trembling, and I must do the same..." (*Teachings*, pp. 347-48).

FIGURE 12-C
THE ETERNAL FAMILY OF GODS

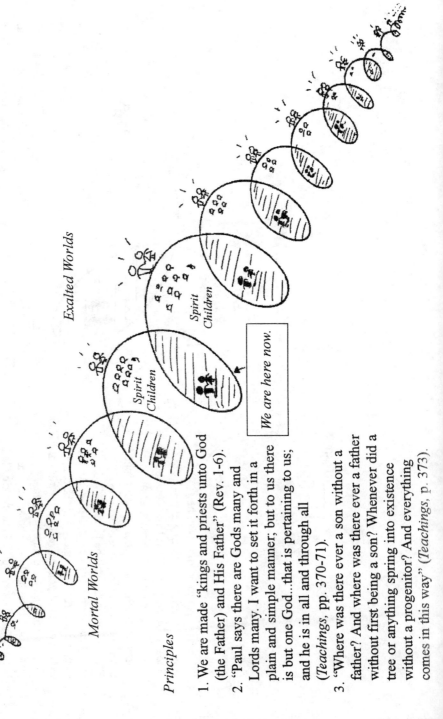

Exalted Worlds

Spirit Children

Spirit Children

We are here now.

Mortal Worlds

Principles

1. We are made "kings and priests unto God (the Father) and His Father" (Rev. 1-6).

2. "Paul says there are Gods many and Lords many. I want to set it forth in a plain and simple manner; but to us there is but one God...that is pertaining to us; and he is in all and through all (*Teachings*, pp. 370-71).

3. "Where was there ever a son without a father? And where was there ever a father without first being a son? Whenever did a tree or anything spring into existence without a progenitor? And everything comes in this way" (*Teachings*, p. 373).

FIGURE 12-D
ORSON HYDE'S EXPLANATION OF THE PATRIARCHAL CHAIN OF GODS

A DIAGRAM OF THE KINGDOM OF GOD

Principles

The above diagram shows the order and unity of the kingdom of God. The Eternal Father sits at the head, crowned King of kings and Lord of lords. Whenever the other lines meet, there sits a king and a priest unto God, bearing rule, authority, and dominion under the Father. He is one with the Father, because his kingdom is joined to his Father's and becomes part of it....

These kingdoms, which are one kingdom, are designed to extend till they not only embrace this world, but every other planet that rolls into the blue vault of heaven. Thus will all things be gathered in one during the dispensation of the fulness of times, and the Saints will not only possess the earth, but all things else, for, says Paul, 'All things are yours, whether Paul, or Apollos, or Cephas, or the world, or life or death, or things present, or things to come; all are yours, and ye are Christ's, and Christ is God's (Orson Hyde, "A Diagram of the Kingdom of God". *Millennial Star,* 9 (15 January 1847):23-24).

INDEX